Haynes

THE BOOK ®

Audi 100 & 200
Service and Repair Manual

John S Mead

(907-304-11X4)

Models covered

All Audi 100 and 200 front-wheel-drive models including Turbo & Avant
1781 cc, 1921 cc, 1994 cc, 2144 cc, 2226 cc & 2309 cc

Does not cover Quattro or Diesel engine versions

© Haynes Publishing 1996

A book in the **Haynes Service and Repair Manual Series**

All rights reserved. No part of this book may be reproduced or transmitted in any form or by any means, electronic or mechanical, including photocopying, recording or by any information storage or retrieval system, without permission in writing from the copyright holder.

ISBN 1 85960 172 3

British Library Cataloguing in Publication Data
A catalogue record for this book is available from the British Library.

ABCDE
FGHIJ
KLMNO
PQRS

2

Printed by **J H Haynes & Co. Ltd,** Sparkford, Nr Yeovil, Somerset BA22 7JJ

Haynes Publishing
Sparkford, Nr Yeovil, Somerset BA22 7JJ, England

Haynes North America, Inc
861 Lawrence Drive, Newbury Park, California 91320, USA

Editions Haynes S.A.
147/149, rue Saint Honoré, 75001 PARIS, France

Contents

LIVING WITH YOUR AUDI

Introduction	Page	0•4
Safety First!	Page	0•5
Dimensions, weights and capacities	Page	0•6

Roadside Repairs

Jacking and towing	Page	0•8
Identifying leaks	Page	0•9
Tyre checks	Page	0•10
Jump starting	Page	0•11
Routine maintenance	Page	0•12
Lubricants and fluids	Page	0•16

Contents

REPAIRS & OVERHAUL

Engine and Associated Systems

Engine *(also see Chapter 13)*	Page 1•1
Four-cylinder engines	Page 1•6
Five-cylinder engines	Page 1•23
Cooling system *(also see Chapter 13)*	Page 2•1
Fuel and exhaust systems *(also see Chapter 13)*	Page 3•1
Carburettor and associated fuel system components	Page 3•4
Fuel injection system	Page 3•23
Igniton system *(also see Chapter 13)*	Page 4•1

Transmission

Clutch *(also see Chapter 13)*	Page 5•1
Manual gearbox and final drive *(also see Chapter 13)*	Page 6•1
Automatic transmission and final drive *(also see Chapter 13)*	Page 7•1
Driveshafts	Page 8•1

Brakes

Braking system	Page 9•1

Electrical

Electrical systems *(also see Chapter 13)*	Page 10•1

Suspension

Suspension and steering *(also see Chapter 13)*	Page 11•1

Body Equipment

Bodywork and fittings *(also see Chapter 13)*	Page 12•1

Additional Information

Supplement: Revisions and information on later models	Page 13•1

Wiring Diagrams

	Page 14•1

REFERENCE

MOT Test Checks	
Checks carried out from the driver's seat	Page REF•1
Checks carried out with the vehicle on the ground	Page REF•2
Checks carried out with the vehicle raised	Page REF•3
Checks carried out on your vehicle's exhaust emission system	Page REF•4
Tools and Working Facilities	Page REF•5
General Repair Procedures	Page REF•8
Fault Finding	Page REF•9
Buying spare parts and vehicle identification numbers	Page REF•12
Conversion factors	Page REF•13
Glossary of Technical Terms	Page REF•14

Index

	Page REF•19

Introduction to the Audi 100, 200 and 5000

The 'new' Audi 100 was announced in October 1982 with the 200 version becoming available in early 1984. The North American version, the Audi 5000, was launched in 1983.

All models feature startling new advances in automotive design and technology, foremost among these being the meticulous attention to aerodynamic shape. With a drag coefficient (Cd) of 0.30 for the Audi 100, these cars are of a design which is amongst the most aerodynamically efficient in their class.

In addition to aerodynamic excellence, all models offer a comprehensive package of standard and optional equipment features.

The model range is extensive and offers a choice of trim, Saloon or Estate (Avant) body styles, four or five-cylinder engines, and four or five-speed gearbox or automatic transmission. Full instrumentation is provided, together with electric windows, central locking, on-board computer, extensive audio system, and power steering, according to model. UK models are available with carburettor, fuel injection or fuel injection with turbocharger engines.

Acknowledgements

Thanks are due to the Champion Sparking Plug Company Limited who supplied the illustrations showing spark plug conditions. Thanks are also due to Mr John Day of JP and S Day, South Lee Garage, South Molten, Devon for the loan of the project car, to Swallowdale Motors, Seaton, Devon for technical assistance, to Sykes-Pickavant Limited who provided some of the workshop tools, and all those people at Sparkford who assisted in the production of this manual.

Audi 100 CD

Audi 100 Avant CD

Safety First! 0•5

Working on your car can be dangerous. This page shows just some of the potential risks and hazards, with the aim of creating a safety-conscious attitude.

General hazards

Scalding
• Don't remove the radiator or expansion tank cap while the engine is hot.
• Engine oil, automatic transmission fluid or power steering fluid may also be dangerously hot if the engine has recently been running.

Burning
• Beware of burns from the exhaust system and from any part of the engine. Brake discs and drums can also be extremely hot immediately after use.

Crushing
• When working under or near a raised vehicle, always supplement the jack with axle stands, or use drive-on ramps. *Never venture under a car which is only supported by a jack.*
• Take care if loosening or tightening high-torque nuts when the vehicle is on stands. Initial loosening and final tightening should be done with the wheels on the ground.

Fire
• Fuel is highly flammable; fuel vapour is explosive.
• Don't let fuel spill onto a hot engine.
• Do not smoke or allow naked lights (including pilot lights) anywhere near a vehicle being worked on. Also beware of creating sparks (electrically or by use of tools).
• Fuel vapour is heavier than air, so don't work on the fuel system with the vehicle over an inspection pit.
• Another cause of fire is an electrical overload or short-circuit. Take care when repairing or modifying the vehicle wiring.
• Keep a fire extinguisher handy, of a type suitable for use on fuel and electrical fires.

Electric shock
• Ignition HT voltage can be dangerous, especially to people with heart problems or a pacemaker. Don't work on or near the ignition system with the engine running or the ignition switched on.
• Mains voltage is also dangerous. Make sure that any mains-operated equipment is correctly earthed. Mains power points should be protected by a residual current device (RCD) circuit breaker.

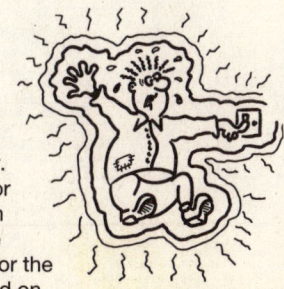

Fume or gas intoxication
• Exhaust fumes are poisonous; they often contain carbon monoxide, which is rapidly fatal if inhaled. Never run the engine in a confined space such as a garage with the doors shut.
• Fuel vapour is also poisonous, as are the vapours from some cleaning solvents and paint thinners.

Poisonous or irritant substances
• Avoid skin contact with battery acid and with any fuel, fluid or lubricant, especially antifreeze, brake hydraulic fluid and Diesel fuel. Don't syphon them by mouth. If such a substance is swallowed or gets into the eyes, seek medical advice.
• Prolonged contact with used engine oil can cause skin cancer. Wear gloves or use a barrier cream if necessary. Change out of oil-soaked clothes and do not keep oily rags in your pocket.
• Air conditioning refrigerant forms a poisonous gas if exposed to a naked flame (including a cigarette). It can also cause skin burns on contact.

Asbestos
• Asbestos dust can cause cancer if inhaled or swallowed. Asbestos may be found in gaskets and in brake and clutch linings. When dealing with such components it is safest to assume that they contain asbestos.

Special hazards

Hydrofluoric acid
• This extremely corrosive acid is formed when certain types of synthetic rubber, found in some O-rings, oil seals, fuel hoses etc, are exposed to temperatures above 400°C. The rubber changes into a charred or sticky substance containing the acid. *Once formed, the acid remains dangerous for years. If it gets onto the skin, it may be necessary to amputate the limb concerned.*
• When dealing with a vehicle which has suffered a fire, or with components salvaged from such a vehicle, wear protective gloves and discard them after use.

The battery
• Batteries contain sulphuric acid, which attacks clothing, eyes and skin. Take care when topping-up or carrying the battery.
• The hydrogen gas given off by the battery is highly explosive. Never cause a spark or allow a naked light nearby. Be careful when connecting and disconnecting battery chargers or jump leads.

Air bags
• Air bags can cause injury if they go off accidentally. Take care when removing the steering wheel and/or facia. Special storage instructions may apply.

Diesel injection equipment
• Diesel injection pumps supply fuel at very high pressure. Take care when working on the fuel injectors and fuel pipes.

⚠ *Warning: Never expose the hands, face or any other part of the body to injector spray; the fuel can penetrate the skin with potentially fatal results.*

Remember...

DO
• Do use eye protection when using power tools, and when working under the vehicle.

• Do wear gloves or use barrier cream to protect your hands when necessary.

• Do get someone to check periodically that all is well when working alone on the vehicle.

• Do keep loose clothing and long hair well out of the way of moving mechanical parts.

• Do remove rings, wristwatch etc, before working on the vehicle – especially the electrical system.

• Do ensure that any lifting or jacking equipment has a safe working load rating adequate for the job.

DON'T
• Don't attempt to lift a heavy component which may be beyond your capability – get assistance.

• Don't rush to finish a job, or take unverified short cuts.

• Don't use ill-fitting tools which may slip and cause injury.

• Don't leave tools or parts lying around where someone can trip over them. Mop up oil and fuel spills at once.

• Don't allow children or pets to play in or near a vehicle being worked on.

Dimensions, Weights & Capacities

Dimensions
Overall length:
　Audi 100 .... 4792 mm (188.8 in)
　Audi 200 .... 4808 mm (189.4 in)
　Audi 5000 .... 4894 mm (192.8 in)
Overall width .... 1814 mm (71.5 in)
Overall height (unladen) .... 1428 mm (56.2 in) approximately
Ground clearance (laden):
　Saloon models .... 133 mm (5.2 in)
　Avant models .... 140 mm (5.5 in)
　Vehicles with self-levelling suspension .... 187 mm (7.3 in)
Wheelbase .... 2687.5 mm (105.8 in)
Front track .... 1468 mm (57.8 in)
Rear track .... 1469 mm (57.8 in)
Turning circle (between walls) .... 11500 mm (453.1 in) approximately

Weights
Kerb weight:
　Saloon models:
　　55 kW engine .... 1090 kg (2403 lb)
　　66 kW engine .... 1090 kg (2403 lb)
　　74 kW engine .... 1145 kg (2524 lb)
　　85 kW engine .... 1250 kg (2756 lb)
　　100 kW engine .... 1210 kg (2668 lb)
　　101 kW engine .... 1250 kg (2756 lb)
　　134 kW engine .... 1300 kg (2866 lb)
　Avant models:
　　55 kW engine .... 1130 kg (2491 lb)
　　66 kW engine .... 1140 kg (2513 lb)
　　85 kW engine .... 1290 kg (2844 lb)
　100 kW engine .... 1260 kg (2778 lb)
　101 kW engine .... 1290 kg (2844 lb)

Add 75 kg (33 lb) for automatic transmission on five-cylinder engines. Add 25 kg (55 lb) for automatic transmission on four-cylinder engines

Gross vehicle weight:
　Saloon models:
　　55 and 66 kW engine .... 1640 kg (361 6 lb)
　　74 kW engine .... 1645 kg (3627 lb)
　　85 kW engine .... 1800 kg (3969 lb)
　　100 kW engine .... 1710 kg (3770 lb)
　　101 kW engine .... 1800 kg (3969 lb)
　　134 kW engine .... 1790 kg (3946 lb)
　Avant models:
　　55 and 66 kW engine .... 1680 kg (3704 lb)
　　85 kW engine .... 1840 kg (4057 lb)
　　100 kW engine .... 1760 kg (3880 lb)
　　101 kW engine .... 1840 kg (4057 lb)
Maximum roof rack load .... 75 kg (165 lb)
Maximum towing weight (12% gradient):
　Saloon models:
　　55 and 66 kW engines .... 1150 kg (2535 lb)
　　74 kW engine:
　　　Manual gearbox .... 1300 kg (2866 lb)
　　　Automatic transmission .... 1400 kg (3087 lb)
　　85 kW engine:
　　　Manual gearbox .... 1200 kg (2646 lb)
　　　Automatic transmission .... 1300 kg (2866 lb)
　　100 kW engine:
　　　Manual gearbox .... 1500 kg (3307 lb)
　　　Automatic transmission .... 1600 kg (3528 lb)
　　101 and 134 kW engines:
　　　Manual gearbox .... 1400 kg (3087 lb)
　　　Automatic transmission .... 1500 kg (3307 lb)
　Avant models:
　　55 and 66 kW engines .... 1100 kg (2425 lb)
　　74 kW engine:
　　　Manual gearbox .... 1200 kg (2646 lb)
　　　Automatic transmission .... 1300 kg (2866 lb)

Dimensions, Weights & Capacities

Weights (continued)

85 kW engine:
    Manual gearbox .... 1150 kg (2535 lb)
    Automatic transmission .... 1250 kg (2756 lb)
100 kW engine:
    Manual gearbox .... 1400 kg (3087 lb)
    Automatic transmission .... 1500 kg (3307 lb)
101 kW engine:
    Manual gearbox .... 1350 kg (2976 lb)
    Automatic transmission .... 1450 kg (3197 lb)

Capacities

Engine oil:
    Four-cylinder engines with filter change .... 3.0 litre; 5.3 Imp pt; 3.2 US qt
    Four-cylinder engines without filter change .... 2.5 litre; 4.4 Imp pt; 2.6 US qt
    Five-cylinder engines with filter change .... 4.5 litre; 7.9 Imp pt; 4.8 US qt
    Five-cylinder engines without filter change .... 4.0 litre; 7.0 Imp pt; 4.2 US qt
    Difference between MIN and MAX marks on dipstick .... 1.0 litre; 1.8 Imp pt; 1.1 US qt
Cooling system (including heater):
    Four-cylinder engines .... 7.0 litre; 12.3 Imp pt; 7.4 US qt
    Five-cylinder engines (Except MC) .... 8.1 litre; 14.2 Imp pt; 8.5 US qt
    MC 121 kW engine .... 8.5 litre; 14.9 Imp pt; 9.0 US qt
Fuel tank:
    All models .... 80 litre; 17.6 Imp gal; 21.1 US gal
Manual gearbox:
    012 .... 2.35 litre; 4.1 Imp pt; 2.5 US qt
    013 .... 2.0 litre; 3.5 Imp pt; 2.1 US qt
    014 .... 1.7 litre; 3.0 Imp pt; 1.8 US qt
    016 .... 2.6 litre; 4.5 Imp pt; 2.7 US qt
    093 .... 2.3 litre; 4.0 Imp pt; 2.4 US qt
Automatic transmission:
    089 gearbox ATF (total) .... 6.0 litre; 10.6 Imp pt; 6.3 US qt
    089 gearbox ATF (service) .... 3.0 litre; 5.3 Imp pt; 3.2 US qt
    089 final drive .... 0.75 litre; 1.3 Imp pt; 0.8 US qt
    087 gearbox ATF (total) .... 6.0 litre; 10.6 Imp pt; 6.3 US qt
    087 gearbox ATF (service) .... 3.0 litre; 5.3 Imp pt; 3.2 US qt
    087 final drive .... 0.7 litre; 1.2 Imp pt; 0.7 US qt
Combined hydraulic system:
    Power-assisted steering and brake servo unit .... 1.6 litre; 2.8 Imp pt 1.7 US qt
    Power-assisted steering, brake servo unit and self-levelling
    suspension .... 2.7 litre; 4.7 Imp pt; 2.8 US qt

Roadside Repairs

Jacking and towing

Jacking

To change a roadwheel, first remove the spare wheel and jack from the left-hand side of the luggage compartment and remove the tool kit from the rear panel. With the car on firm level ground apply the handbrake and chock the wheel diagonally opposite the one to be changed. Using the tools provided, remove the hub cap where necessary, then loosen the wheel bolts half a turn. Locate the lifting arm of the jack beneath the reinforced seam of the side sill panel directly beneath the wedge shaped depression nearest to the wheel to be removed. Turn the jack handle until the base of the jack contacts the ground directly beneath the sill, then continue to turn the handle until the wheel is free of the ground. Unscrew the wheel bolts and remove the wheel. On light alloy wheels prise off the centre trim cap and press it into the spare wheel.

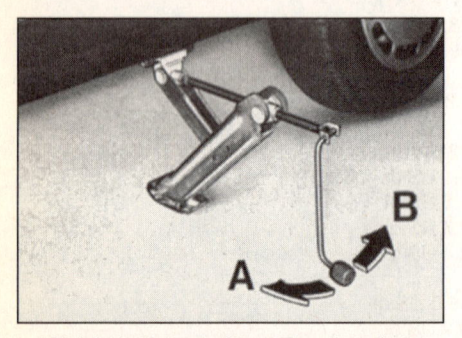

Locate the spare wheel on the hub, then insert and tighten the bolts in diagonal sequence. Lower the jack and fully tighten the bolts. Refit the hub cap where necessary, remove the chock and relocate the tool kit, jack and wheel in the luggage compartment.

Note that certain models are equipped with a space saving temporary spare wheel which is smaller and lighter than an ordinary wheel and is only intended for temporary use over short distances. With this type of wheel in place. do not exceed 50 mph (80 km/h), and avoid full throttle acceleration, heavy braking and fast cornering.

When jacking up the car with a trolley jack, position the jack beneath the reinforced plate behind the front wheel (see illustration) Or beneath the reinforced seam at the rear of the side sill panel. Use the same positions when supporting the car with axle stands. *Never jack up the car beneath the suspension or axle components, the sump, or the gearbox.*

Towing

Towing eyes are fitted to the front and the rear of the vehicle and a tow line should not be attached to any other points. It is preferable to use a slightly elastic tow line, to reduce the strain on both vehicles, either by having a tow line manufactured from synthetic fibre, or one which is fitted with an elastic link.

When towing, the following important precautions must be observed:

(a) Turn the ignition key of the vehicle being towed, so that the steering wheel is free (unlocked)
(b) Remember that when the engine is not running the brake servo will nor operate, so that additional pressure will be required on the brake pedal after the first few applications
(c) On vehicles with automatic transmission, ensure that the gear selector lever is at N. Do not tow faster than 30 mph (50 kph), or further than 30 miles (50 km) unless the front wheels are lifted clear of the ground.

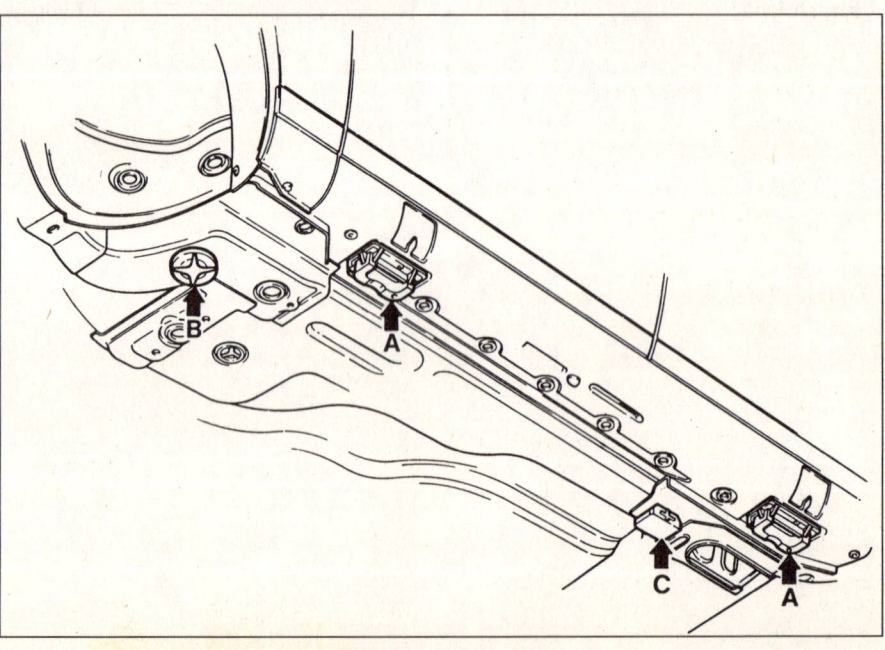

Vehicle jack in position. Turn handle in direction 'A' to raise and 'B' to lower

Spare wheel and tool kit location on saloon models

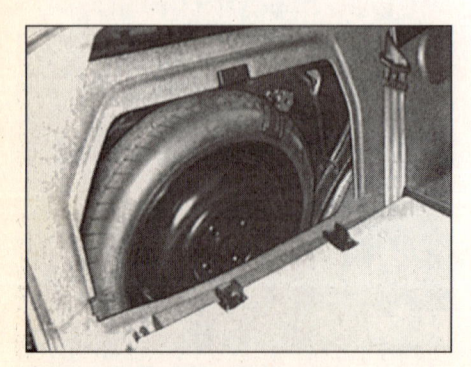

Spare wheel and tool kit location on Avant models

Vehicle jacking points
A Lifting point using vehicle jack only   B and C Lifting points for hydraulic or trolley jack

Roadside Repairs 0•9

Puddles on the garage floor or drive, or obvious wetness under the bonnet or underneath the car, suggest a leak that needs investigating. It can sometimes be difficult to decide where the leak is coming from, especially if the engine bay is very dirty already. Leaking oil or fluid can also be blown rearwards by the passage of air under the car, giving a false impression of where the problem lies.

Warning: Most automotive oils and fluids are poisonous. Wash them off skin, and change out of contaminated clothing, without delay.

Identifying leaks

HAYNES HiNT *The smell of a fluid leaking from the car may provide a clue to what's leaking. Some fluids are distinctively coloured. It may help to clean the car carefully and to park it over some clean paper overnight as an aid to locating the source of the leak.*
Remember that some leaks may only occur while the engine is running.

Sump oil

Engine oil may leak from the drain plug...

Oil from filter

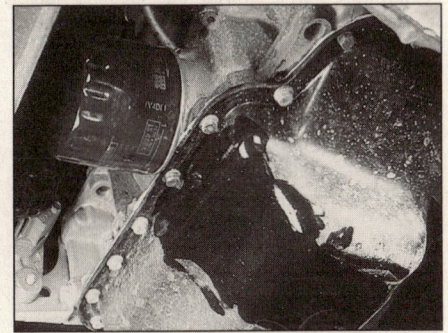

...or from the base of the oil filter.

Gearbox oil

Gearbox oil can leak from the seals at the inboard ends of the driveshafts.

Antifreeze

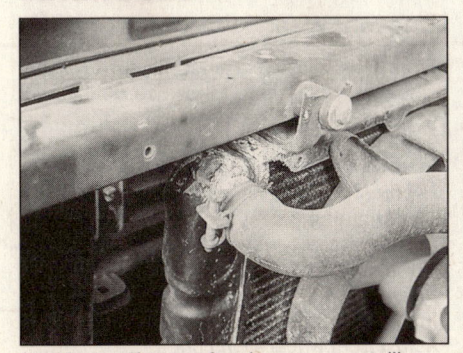

Leaking antifreeze often leaves a crystalline deposit like this.

Brake fluid

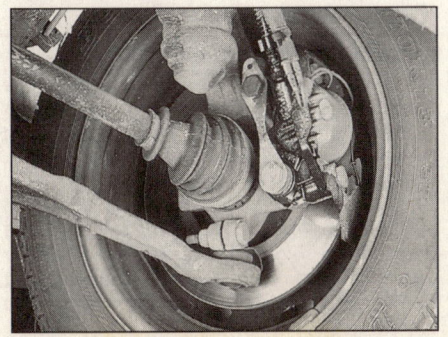

A leak occurring at a wheel is almost certainly brake fluid.

Power steering fluid

Power steering fluid may leak from the pipe connectors on the steering rack.

Roadside Repairs

Tyre condition and pressure

It is very important that tyres are in good condition, and at the correct pressure - having a tyre failure at any speed is highly dangerous. Tyre wear is influenced by driving style - harsh braking and acceleration, or fast cornering, will all produce more rapid tyre wear. As a general rule, the front tyres wear out faster than the rears. Interchanging the tyres from front to rear ("rotating" the tyres) may result in more even wear. However, if this is completely effective, you may have the expense of replacing all four tyres at once!

Remove any nails or stones embedded in the tread before they penetrate the tyre to cause deflation. If removal of a nail does reveal that the tyre has been punctured, refit the nail so that its point of penetration is marked. Then immediately change the wheel, and have the tyre repaired by a tyre dealer.

Regularly check the tyres for damage in the form of cuts or bulges, especially in the sidewalls. Periodically remove the wheels, and clean any dirt or mud from the inside and outside surfaces. Examine the wheel rims for signs of rusting, corrosion or other damage. Light alloy wheels are easily damaged by "kerbing" whilst parking; steel wheels may also become dented or buckled. A new wheel is very often the only way to overcome severe damage.

New tyres should be balanced when they are fitted, but it may become necessary to re-balance them as they wear, or if the balance weights fitted to the wheel rim should fall off. Unbalanced tyres will wear more quickly, as will the steering and suspension components. Wheel imbalance is normally signified by vibration, particularly at a certain speed (typically around 50 mph). If this vibration is felt only through the steering, then it is likely that just the front wheels need balancing. If, however, the vibration is felt through the whole car, the rear wheels could be out of balance. Wheel balancing should be carried out by a tyre dealer or garage.

1 Tread Depth - visual check
The original tyres have tread wear safety bands (B), which will appear when the tread depth reaches approximately 1.6 mm. The band positions are indicated by a triangular mark on the tyre sidewall (A).

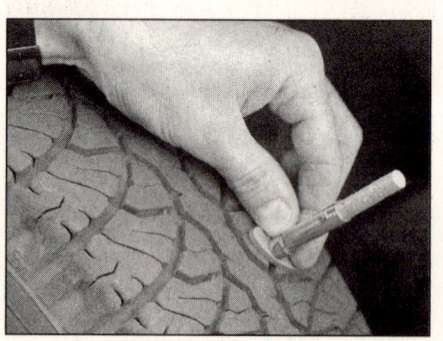

2 Tread Depth - manual check
Alternatively, tread wear can be monitored with a simple, inexpensive device known as a tread depth indicator gauge.

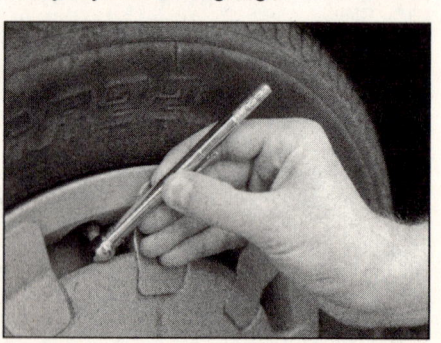

3 Tyre Pressure Check
Check the tyre pressures regularly with the tyres cold. Do not adjust the tyre pressures immediately after the vehicle has been used, or an inaccurate setting will result.

Tyre tread wear patterns

Shoulder Wear

Underinflation (wear on both sides)
Under-inflation will cause overheating of the tyre, because the tyre will flex too much, and the tread will not sit correctly on the road surface. This will cause a loss of grip and excessive wear, not to mention the danger of sudden tyre failure due to heat build-up.
Check and adjust pressures
Incorrect wheel camber (wear on one side)
Repair or renew suspension parts
Hard cornering
Reduce speed!

Centre Wear

Overinflation
Over-inflation will cause rapid wear of the centre part of the tyre tread, coupled with reduced grip, harsher ride, and the danger of shock damage occurring in the tyre casing.
Check and adjust pressures

If you sometimes have to inflate your car's tyres to the higher pressures specified for maximum load or sustained high speed, don't forget to reduce the pressures to normal afterwards.

Uneven Wear

Front tyres may wear unevenly as a result of wheel misalignment. Most tyre dealers and garages can check and adjust the wheel alignment (or "tracking") for a modest charge.
Incorrect camber or castor
Repair or renew suspension parts
Malfunctioning suspension
Repair or renew suspension parts
Unbalanced wheel
Balance tyres
Incorrect toe setting
Adjust front wheel alignment
Note: *The feathered edge of the tread which typifies toe wear is best checked by feel.*

Roadside Repairs 0•11

Jump starting

> **HAYNES HiNT**
>
> Jump starting will get you out of trouble, but you must correct whatever made the battery go flat in the first place. There are three possibilities:
>
> **1** The battery has been drained by repeated attempts to start, or by leaving the lights on.
>
> **2** The charging system is not working properly (alternator drivebelt slack or broken, alternator wiring fault or alternator itself faulty).
>
> **3** The battery itself is at fault (electrolyte low, or battery worn out).

When jump-starting a car using a booster battery, observe the following precautions:

✔ Before connecting the booster battery, make sure that the ignition is switched off.

✔ Ensure that all electrical equipment (lights, heater, wipers, etc) is switched off.

✔ Make sure that the booster battery is the same voltage as the discharged one in the vehicle.

✔ If the battery is being jump-started from the battery in another vehicle, the two vehcles MUST NOT TOUCH each other.

✔ Make sure that the transmission is in neutral (or PARK, in the case of automatic transmission).

1 Connect one end of the red jump lead to the positive (+) terminal of the flat battery

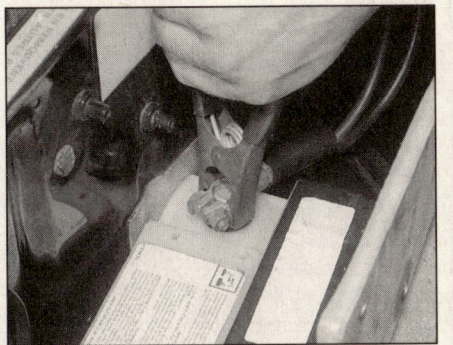

2 Connect the other end of the red lead to the positive (+) terminal of the booster battery.

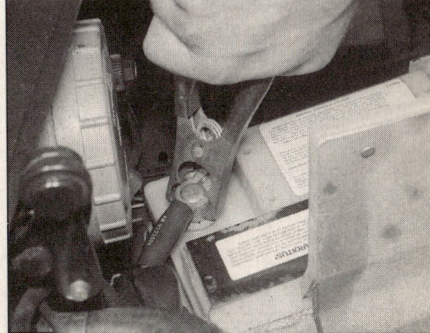

3 Connect one end of the black jump lead to the negative (-) terminal of the booster battery

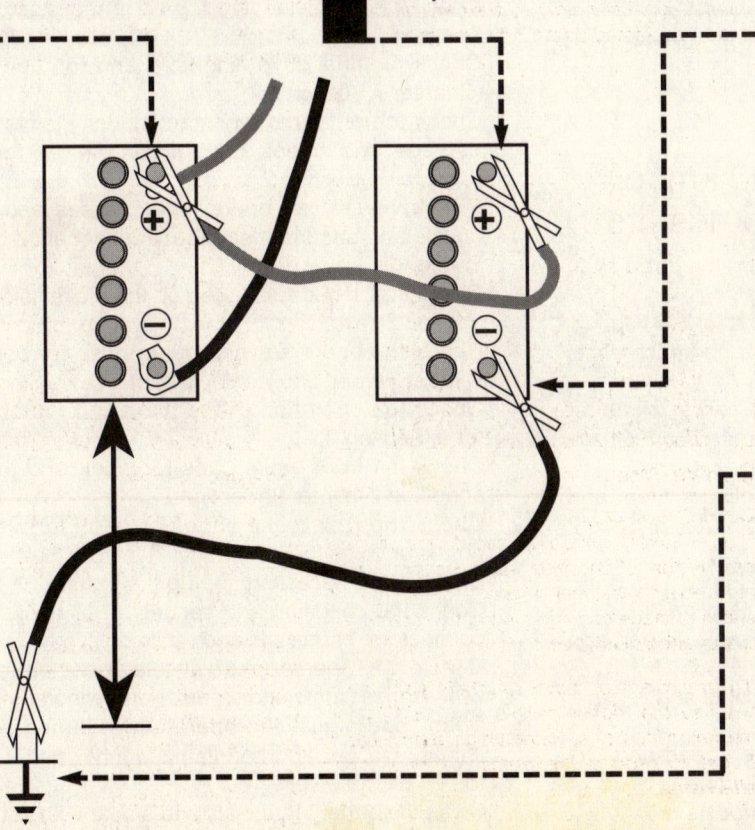

4 Connect the other end of the black jump lead to a bolt or bracket on the engine block, well away from the battery, on the vehicle to be started.

5 Make sure that the jump leads will not come into contact with the fan, drive-belts or other moving parts of the engine.

6 Start the engine using the booster battery, then with the engine running at idle speed, disconnect the jump leads in the reverse order of connection.

Routine Maintenance

Maintenance is essential for ensuring safety and desirable for the purpose of getting the best in terms of performance and economy from your car. Over the years the need for periodic lubrication has been greatly reduced if not totally eliminated. This has unfortunately tended to lead some owners to think that because no such action is required, the items either no longer exist, or will last forever. This is certainly not the case; it is essential to carry out regular visual examination as comprehen-sively as possible in order to spot any possible defects at an early stage before they develop into major expensive repairs.

The following service schedules are a list of the maintenance requirements and the intervals at which they should be carried out, as recommended by the manufacturers. Where applicable these procedures are covered in greater detail throughout this Manual, near the beginning of each Chapter.

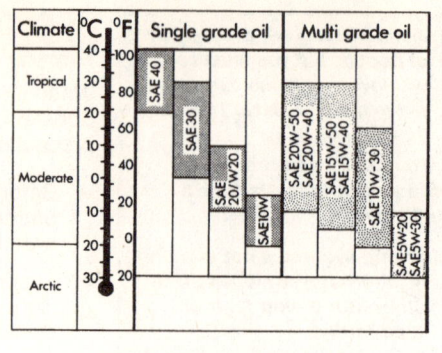

Engine oil viscosity chart

Every 250 miles (400 km) or weekly – whichever comes first

- [ ] Check the engine oil level and top up, if necessary (Chapter 1, Section 2 or 30)
- [ ] Check the coolant level and top up, if necessary (Chapter 2, Section 2)
- [ ] Check the oil level in the power-assisted steering reservoir and top up, if necessary (Chapter 10, Section 2)
- [ ] Check the brake fluid level in the master cylinder reservoir and top up, if necessary (Chapter 9, Section 2)
- [ ] Check the operation of the horn, and all lights, wipers and washers
- [ ] Check and if necessary, top up the washer reservoirs, adding a screen wash
- [ ] Check the tyre pressures (Chapter 10, Section 30)
- [ ] Visually examine the tyres for wear or damage (Chapter 10, Section 30)

Every 10 000 miles (15 000 km) or 12 months – whichever comes first

- [ ] Renew the engine oil and filter – including the turbo filter, if applicable (Chapter 1, Section 2 or 30)
- [ ] Visually check the engine for oil leaks and for the security and condition of all related components and attachments (Chapter 1, Section 2)
- [ ] Check the hoses, hose clips and visible joint gaskets for leaks and any signs of corrosion or deterioration (Chapter 2, Section 2)
- [ ] Check and if necessary top up the cooling system and have the antifreeze strength checked (Chapter 2, Secs 2 and 6)
- [ ] Visually check the fuel pipes and hoses for security, chafing, leaks and corrosion (Chapter 3, Section 2)
- [ ] Check the fuel tank for leaks and any signs of damage and corrosion (Chapter 3, Section 2)
- [ ] Check the operation of the accelerator cable and linkage. (Chapter 3, Section 2)
- [ ] Check and if necessary adjust the idle speed and CO settings (where applicable) (Chapter 3, Section 11)
- [ ] Renew the additional oil filter on Turbo models
- [ ] Check the exhaust system for corrosion, leaks and security (Chapter 3, Section 2)
- [ ] Check and if necessary adjust the ignition timing (where applicable) (Chapter 4, Secs 6 and 7 or 1 5)
- [ ] Clean the distributor cap, HT leads and coil tower (Chapter 4. Secs 5 and 9)
- [ ] Check the operation of the clutch and clutch pedal
- [ ] Check the clutch adjustment on cable operated clutches (Chapter 5, Section 2)
- [ ] Visually check for oil leaks around the joint faces and oil seals (Chapter 6, Section 2)
- [ ] Check and if necessary top up the gearbox oil (Chapter 6, Section 2)
- [ ] Visually check for oil leaks around the joint faces and oil seals (Chapter 7, Section 2)
- [ ] Check the fluid level and top up if necessary (Chapter 7, Section 2)
- [ ] Check the final drive fluid level and top up if necessary (Chapter 7, Section 2)
- [ ] Check the driveshaft constant velocity joints for wear or damage and check the rubber gaiters for condition (Chapter 8, Section 2)
- [ ] Check visually all brake pipes, hoses and unions for corrosion, chafing, leakage and security (Chapter 9, Section 2)
- [ ] Check and, if necessary, top up the brake fluid (Chapter 9, Section 2)
- [ ] Check the brake servo vacuum hose for condition and security (where applicable) (Chapter 9, Section 22)
- [ ] Check the operation of the hand and footbrake (Chapter 9, Section 2)
- [ ] Check the front brake pads for wear, and the discs for condition (Chapter 9, Section 2)
- [ ] Check the rear brake shoes or pads for wear and the drums or discs for condition (Chapter 9, Section 2)
- [ ] Check and if necessary top up the battery
- [ ] Check the condition and security of all accessible wiring connectors, harnesses and retaining clips
- [ ] Check the operation of all electrical equipment and accessories (lights, indicators, horn, wipers, etc)
- [ ] Check and adjust the operation of the screen washer, tailgate washer and headlamp washer and if necessary, top up the reservoirs
- [ ] Clean the battery terminals and smear with petroleum jelly

Routine Maintenance 0•13

- [ ] Have the headlamp alignment checked, and if necessary, adjusted
- [ ] Check and if necessary renew or adjust the alternator drivebelt (Chapter 12, Section 7)
- [ ] Check and if necessary renew or adjust the power-assisted steering pump drivebelt (where applicable) (Chapter 10, Section 27)
- [ ] Check the front and rear suspension struts for fluid leaks (Chapter 10, Section 2)
- [ ] Check the condition and security of the steering gear, steering and suspension joints, and rubber gaiters (Chapter 10, Section 2)
- [ ] Check the front wheel toe setting (Chapter 10, Section 29)
- [ ] Check and adjust the tyre pressures (Chapter 10, Section 30)
- [ ] Check the tyres for damage, tread depth and uneven wear (Chapter 10, Section 30)
- [ ] Inspect the roadwheels for damage (Chapter 10, Section 30)
- [ ] Check the tightness of the wheel bolts
- [ ] Check, and if necessary, top up the power-assisted steering oil (where applicable) (Chapter 10, Section 2)
- [ ] Carefully inspect the paintwork for damage and the bodywork for corrosion (Chapter 11, Section 2)
- [ ] Check the condition of the underseal (Chapter 11, Section 2)
- [ ] Oil all hinges, door locks and the bonnet release mechanism with a few drops of light oil

Every 20 000 miles (30 000 km) or 2 years – whichever comes first

- [ ] Check and if necessary adjust the valve clearances (where applicable) and renew the valve cover gaskets (Chapter 1, Section 17 or 46)
- [ ] Check the timing belt tension (Chapter 1, Section 18 or 47)
- [ ] Drain the system, flush and refill with fresh antifreeze (Chapter 2, Secs 3, 4, 6 and 6)
- [ ] Renew the air cleaner element (Chapter 3, Section 2)
- [ ] Renew the fuel filter, models up to 1985 (Chapter 3, Section 2)
- [ ] Renew the spark plugs (Chapter 4, Section 9)
- [ ] Drain the transmission fluid, clean the oil pan and strainer and renew the gasket. Refill with fresh fluid (Chapter 7, Section 3)
- [ ] Renew the brake fluid (Chapter 9, Section 17)
- [ ] Clean the sunroof guide rails (when applicable) and spray with a silicone lubricant
- [ ] Clean sunroof drain hoses (Chapter 13, Section 10)

Every 40 000 miles (60 000 km) or 4 years – whichever comes first

- [ ] Renew the timing belt (recommended as a precautionary measure) (Chapter 1, Section 18 or 47)

Engine and underbody component locations (2.2 litre Audi 100 with fuel injection)

1. Fusebox
2. Brake master cylinder reservoir
3. Idle stabilisation valve
4. Ignition coil
5. Battery
6. Power-assisted steering hydraulic oil reservoir
7. Suspension strut upper mounting
8. Cooling system expansion tank
9. Radiator cooling fan
10. Power-assisted steering drivebelt adjuster
11. Warm-up valve
12. Engine oil dipstick
13. Distributor
14. Cold start valve
15. Air cleaner
16. Fuel metering distributor
17. Windscreen and headlamp washer reservoir
18. Fuel filter
19. Throttle valve housing
20. Vehicle identification plate

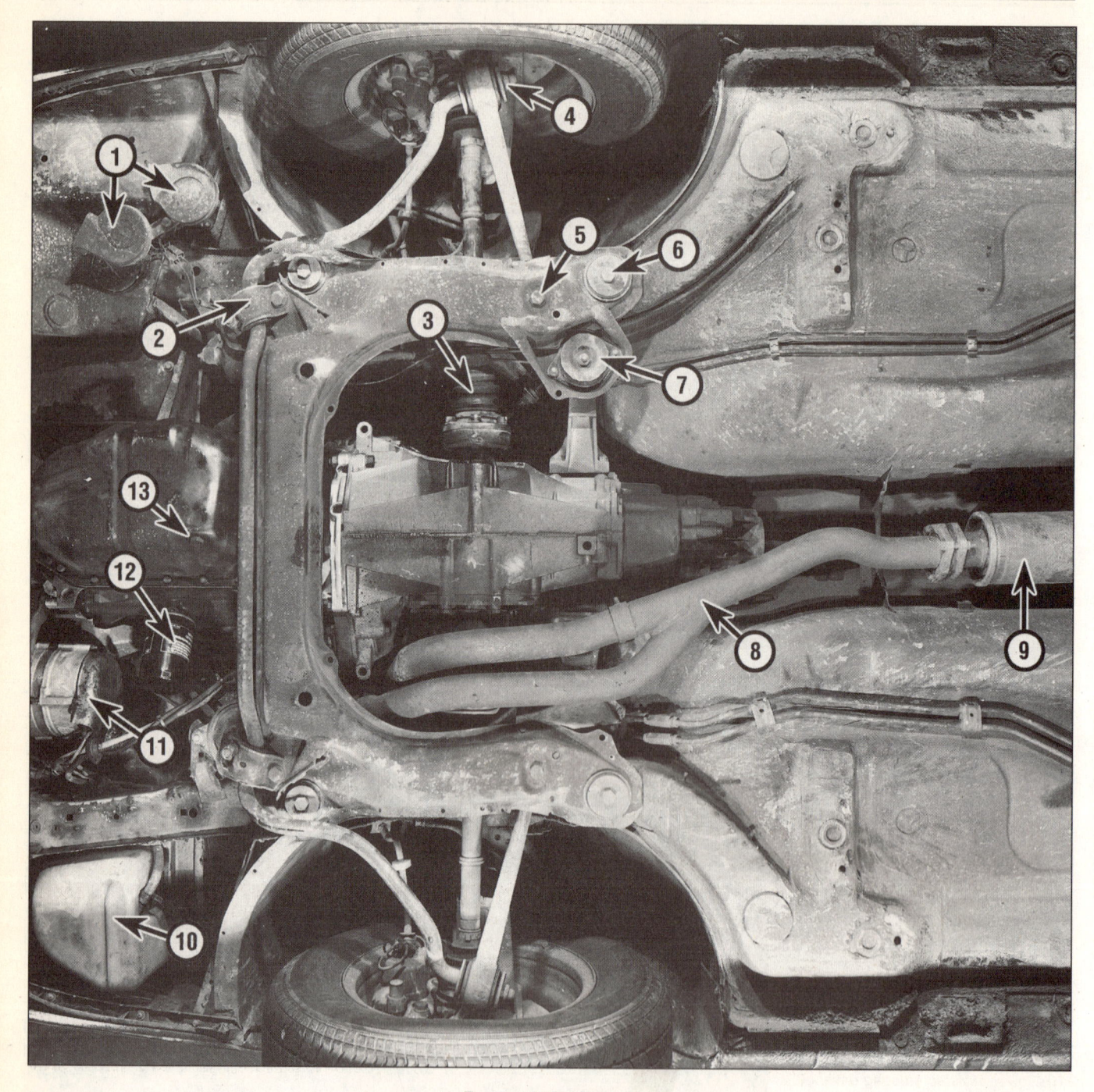

0•14 Routine Maintenance

Front underbody view

1. Horns
2. Anti-roll bar clamp
3. Driveshaft constant velocity joint
4. Anti-roll bar-to-track control arm mounting
5. Track control arm inner mounting
6. Subframe mounting
7. Gearbox mounting
8. Exhaust front pipe
9. Exhaust intermediate silencer
10. Windscreen and headlamp washer reservoir
11. Alternator
12. Oil filter
13. Engine oil drain plug

Routine Maintenance 0•15

Rear underbody view

1 Trailing arm mounting
2 Brake pressure regulator
3 Tailpipe silencer
4 Rear axle beam
5 Panhard rod
6 Rear shock absorber lower mounting
7 Fuel pressure accumulator
8 Fuel tank
9 Main silencer
10 Handbrake cable

Recommended Lubricants and Fluids

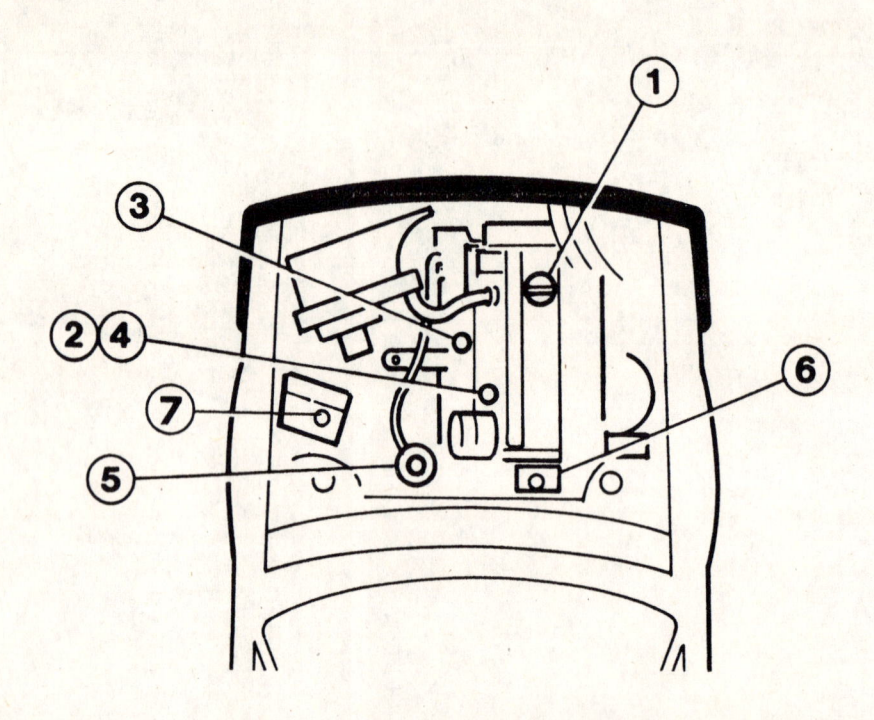

Component or system	Lubricant type/specification
Engine (1)	Multigrade engine oil, viscosity SAE 15W/40 to 20W/50, to API SF or better
Manual gearbox (2)	VW/Audi gear oil G50, viscosity SAE 75W/90
Automatic transmission (3)	Dexron II type ATF

Automatic transmission final drive (4)
  3-speed
  4-speed
	
	Gear oil, viscosity SAE 90, to API GL5
	VW/Audi gear oil G50, viscosity SAE 75W/90

Power steering, hydraulic brake servo and self-levelling suspension (5)	VW/Audi hydraulic oil G 002 000
Brake and clutch hydraulic systems (6)	Hydraulic fluid to FMVSS 116 DOT 4
Cooling system (7)	VW/Audi antifreeze G11, to TL-VW 774

Chapter 1 Engine

For modifications, and information applicable to later models, see Supplement at end of manual

Contents

Part A – Four-cylinder engines

Ancillary components – removal and refitting	8
Camshaft and bearings – examination and renovation	13
Camshaft and tappets – refitting	15
Camshaft and tappets – removal	10
Crankshaft – removal, examination and refitting	27
Crankshaft oil seals – renewal	22
Cylinder head – examination and renovation	12
Cylinder head and camshaft – refitting	16
Cylinder head and camshaft – removal	9
Engine – removal and refitting	6
Engine dismantling – general	7
Engine mountings – removal and refitting	28
Fault finding	See end of Chapter
Flywheel/driveplate – removal and refitting	19
General description	1
Intermediate shaft – removal and refitting	20
Maintenance and inspection	2
Major operations possible with the engine in the car	3
Major operations requiring engine removal	4
Methods of engine removal	5
Oil pump – removal, examination and refitting	23
Pistons and connecting rods – reassembly and refitting	26
Pistons and connecting rods – removal and dismantling	24
Pistons and cylinder bores – examination	25
Sump – removal and refitting	21
Timing belt and gears – removal and refitting	18
Valve clearances – checking and adjustment	7
Valves – refitting	14
Valves – removal and renovation	11

Part B – Five-cylinder engines

Ancillary components – removal and refitting	36
Camshaft and bearings – examination and renovation	42
Camshaft and tappets – refitting	45
Camshaft and tappets – removal	37
Crankshaft – removal, examination and refitting	55
Crankshaft oil seals – renewal	50
Cylinder head – examination and renovation	41
Cylinder head – refitting	44
Cylinder head removal – engine in car	38
Cylinder head removal – engine on bench	39
Engine – removal and refitting	34
Engine dismantling – general	35
Engine mountings – removal and refitting	56
Fault finding	See end of Chapter
Flywheel/driveplate – removal and refitting	48
General description	29
Maintenance and inspection	30
Major operations possible with the engine in the car	31
Major operations requiring engine removal	32
Method of engine removal	33
Oil pump – removal, examination and refining	51
Pistons and connecting rods – reassembly and refitting	54
Pistons and connecting rods – removal and dismantling	52
Pistons and cylinder bores – examination	53
Sump – removal and refitting	49
Timing belt and gears – removal and refitting	47
Valve clearances – checking and adjustment	46
Valves – refitting	43
Valves – removal and renovation	40

Degrees of difficulty

Easy, suitable for novice with little experience	**Fairly easy,** suitable for beginner with some experience	**Fairly difficult,** suitable for competent DIY mechanic	**Difficult,** suitable for experienced DIY mechanic	**Very difficult,** suitable for expert DIY or professional

Specifications

Part A – Four-cylinder engines

General

Code letters	DR, DS
Capacity	1781 cc (108.6 cu in)
Power output:	
Code DR	55 kW (75 bhp)
Code DS	66 kW (90 bhp)
Bore	81.0 mm (3.19 in)
Bore maximum ovality	0.08 mm (0.003 in)
Stroke	86 4 mm (3.40 in)
Compression ratio:	
Code DR	8.75:1
Code DS	10.0 :1

Cylinder compression

Compression pressure (warm engine, throttle open):
   Code DR .... 7.0 bar (102 lbf/in^2)
   Code DS .... 7.5 bar (110 lbf/in^2)
Maximum pressure difference between cylinders .... 3.0 bar (44 lbf/in^2)

Firing order

Firing order .... 1-3-4-2 (No 1 at timing belt end)

Crankshaft

Needle spigot bearing fitted depth .... 1.5 mm (0.059 in)
Endplay:
   New .... 0.07 to 0.17 mm (0.003 to 0.007 in)
   Wear limit .... 0.25 mm (0.010 in)
Maximum main bearing running clearance .... 0.17 mm (0.007 in)
Main bearing journal diameter:
   Standard size .... 53.96 to 53.98 mm (2.1244 to 2.1252 in)
   1st undersize .... 53.71 to 53.73 mm (2.1146 to 2.1154 in)
   2nd undersize .... 53.46 to 53.48 mm (2.1047 to 2.1055 in)
   3rd undersize .... 53.21 to 53.23 mm (2.0949 to 2.0967 in)
Big-end bearing journal diameter:
   Standard size .... 47.76 to 47.79 mm (1.8803 to 1.8815 in)
   1st undersize .... 47.51 to 47.53 mm (1.8705 to 1.8712 in)
   2nd undersize .... 47.26 to 47.29 mm (1.8606 to 1.8618 in)
   3rd undersize .... 47.01 to 47.03 mm (1.8508 to 1.8516 in)
Maximum journal ovality .... 0.03 mm (0.0012 in)

Pistons and rings

Piston-to-bore clearance:
   New .... 0.03 mm (0.0012 in)
   Wear limit .... 0.07 mm (0.0028 in)
Ring-to-groove clearance:
   New .... 0.02 to 0.05 mm (0.0008 to 0.0020 in)
   Wear limit .... 0.15 mm (0.0059 in)
Piston size:

	Piston diameter	**Bore diameter**
Standard size	80.98 mm (3.1882 in)	81.01 mm (3.1894 in)
1st oversize	81.23 mm (3.1980 in)	81.26 mm (3.1992 in)
2nd oversize	81.48 mm (3.2079 in)	81.51 mm (3.2091 in)

Piston ring end gap clearance (ring 15 mm/0.6 in from bottom of bore):
   Compression rings:
     New .... 0.30 to 0.45 mm (0.012 to 0.018 in)
     Wear limit .... 1.0 mm (0.040 in)
   Scraper rings:
     New .... 0.25 to 0.50 mm (0.01 to 0.02 in)
     Wear limit .... 1.0 mm (0.040 in)

Connecting rods

Maximum endplay .... 0.37 mm (0.015 in)
Big-end bearing running clearance:
   New .... 0.015 to 0.062 mm (0.0006 to 0.0024 in)
   Wear limit .... 0.12 mm (0.0047 in)

Camshaft

Maximum endplay .... 0.15 mm (0.006 in)
Maximum run-out .... 0.01 mm (0.0004 in)

Cylinder head

Minimum height (between faces) .... 132.6 mm (5.220 in)
Maximum gasket face distortion .... 0.1 mm (0.004 in)
Valve seat angle .... 45°

Lubrication system

Oil type/specification .... Multigrade engine oil, viscosity SAE 15W/40 to 20W/50, to API SF or better
Oil filter .... Champion C101
Oil pressure (minimum at 2000 rpm – engine hot) .... 2.0 bar (29 lbf/in^2)
Oil pump gear backlash .... 0.05 to 0.20 mm (0.002 to 0.008 in)
Oil pump gear endplay (maximum) .... 0.15 mm (0.006 in)

Intermediate shaft

Endplay .... 0.25 mm (0.010 in)

Valves

Valve clearances:
  Engine warm:
    Inlet .... 0.20 to 0.30 mm (0.008 to 0.012 in)
    Exhaust .... 0.40 to 0.50 mm (0.016 to 0.020 in)
  Engine cold:
    Inlet .... 0.15 to 0.25 mm (0.006 to 0.010 in)
    Exhaust .... 0.35 to 0.45 mm (0.014 to 0.018 in)
Adjusting shim thickness .... 3.00 to 4.25 mm (0.118 to 0.167 in) in increments of 0.05 mm (0.002 in)
Valve stem diameter:
  Inlet .... 7.97 mm (0.3138 in)
  Exhaust .... 7.95 mm (0.3129 in)
Valve head diameter:
  Inlet .... 38.0 mm (1.497 in)
  Exhaust .... 33.0 mm (1.300 in)
Valve length:
  Inlet .... 98.70 mm (3.8858 in)
  Exhaust .... 98.50 mm (3.8779 in)
Valve seat angle .... 45°
Valve guides:
  Maximum valve rock (measured at head):
    Inlet .... 1.0 mm (0.039 in)
    Exhaust .... 1.3 mm (0.051 in)

Valve timing at 1.0 mm lift /0 mm clearance:

	Engine code		
	DR	DS (up to August 85)	DS (from August 85)
Inlet opens BTDC	1°	1°	3°
Inlet closes ABDC	37°	37°	33
Exhaust opens BBDC	42°	42°	41°
Exhaust closes ATDC	2°	2°	5°

Torque wrench settings

	Nm	lbf ft
Cylinder head bolts:		
Stage 1	40	30
Stage 2	60	44
Stage 3	Tighten further by half a turn (180°)	
Engine to transmission	55	41
Engine mounting bracket to cylinder block:		
M8 bolts	25	18
M10 bolts	45	33
Engine mountings to mounting bracket	35	26
Timing belt covers	10	7.4
Timing belt tensioner	45	33
Intermediate shaft gear retaining bolt	80	59
Crankshaft pulley to gear	20	15
Crankshaft gear to crankshaft	200	148
Camshaft gear to camshaft	80	59
Camshaft bearing cap nuts	20	15
Valve cover to cylinder head	10	7.4
Main bearing cap bolts	65	48
Big-end bearing cap nuts:		
Stage 1	30	22
Stage 2	Tighten further by one quarter turn (90°)	
Intermediate shaft sealing flange	25	18
Front oil seal housing	20	15
Rear oil seal housing	10	7.4
Flywheel or driveplate to crankshaft	100	74
Oil filter housing to cylinder block	25	18
Oil pump to crankcase	20	15
Oil pump cover to body	10	7.4
Sump to crankcase	20	15
Oil drain plug	30	22

1•4 Engine

Part B – Five-cylinder engines

General

Code letters:
- 1.9 .... WH
- 2.0 .... KP
- 2.2 .... KG, WC
- 2.3 .... KU

Capacity:
- 1.9 .... 1921 cc (117.2 cu in)
- 2.0 .... 1994 cc (121.6 cu in)
- 2.2 .... 2144 cc (130.7 cu in)
- 2.3 .... 2226 cc (135.7 cu in)

Power output:
- 1.9 .... 74 kW (96.2 bhp)
- 2.0 .... 85 kW (115 bhp)
- 2.2:
  - Code WC .... 100 kW (130 bhp)
  - Code KG .... 134 kW (174.2 bhp)
- 2.3 .... 101 kW (131.3 bhp)

Bore:
- 1.9 and 2.2 .... 79.5 mm (3.13 in)
- 2.0 and 2.3 .... 81.0 mm (3.19 in)

Bore maximum ovality .... 0.08 mm (0.003 in)

Stroke:
- 1.9 and 2.0 .... 77.4 mm (3.05 in)
- 2.2 and 2.3 .... 86.4 mm (3.40 in)

Compression ratio:
- 1.9 .... 10.0 : 1
- 2.0 .... 10.0 : 1
- 2.2:
  - KG .... 8.8 : 1
  - WC .... 9.3 : 1
- 2.3 .... 10.0 : 1

Cylinder compression

Compression pressure (warm engine, throttle open):
- 1.9 and 2.0 .... 10 to 14 bar (145 to 203 lbf/in^2)
- 2.2 .... 10 to 14 bar (145 to 203 lbf/in^2)
- 2.3 .... 8 to 11 bar (116 to 159.5 lbf/in^2)

Minimum pressures:
- 1.9 and 2.0 .... 8.0 bar (116 lbf/in^2)
- 2.2 .... 8.0 bar (116 lbf/in^2)
- 2.3 .... 6.5 bar (94.25 lbf/in^2)

Maximum pressure difference between cylinders:
- 1.9, 2.0 and 2.2 .... 3.0 bar (43.5 lbf/in^2)
- 2.3 .... 2.0 bar (29 lbf/in^2)

Firing order .... 1-2-4-5-3 (No 1 at timing belt end)

Crankshaft

Needle spigot bearing fitted depth .... 5.5 mm (0.217 in)

Endplay:
- New .... 0.07 to 0.18 mm (0.003 to 0.007 in)
- Wear limit .... 0.25 mm (0.010 in)

Maximum main bearing running clearance .... 0.16 mm (0.006 in)

Main bearing journal diameter:
- Standard size .... 57.96 to 57.98 mm (2.2819 to 2.2827 in)
- 1st undersize .... 57.71 to 57.73 mm (2.2720 to 2.2728 in)
- 2nd undersize .... 57.46 to 57.48 mm (2.2622 to 2.2629 in)
- 3rd undersize .... 57.21 to 57.23 mm (2.2524 to 2.2532 in)

Big-end bearing journal diameter:
- Standard size .... 45.96 to 45.98 mm (1.8094 to 1.8102 in)
- 1st undersize .... 45.71 to 45.73 mm (1.7996 to 1.8004 in)
- 2nd undersize .... 45.46 to 45.48 mm (1.7898 to 1.7906 in)
- 3rd undersize .... 45.21 to 45.23 mm (1.7799 to 1.7807 in)

Maximum journal ovality .... 0.03 mm (0.001 2 in)

Pistons and rings

Piston-to-bore clearance:
- New .... 0.03 mm (0.0012 in)
- Wear limit .... 0.07 mm (0.0028 in)

Ring-to-groove clearance:
- New .... 0.02 to 0.08 mm (0.0008 to 0.0032 in)
- Wear limit .... 0.1 mm (0.004 in)

Piston size:

	Piston diameter	Bore diameter
1.9 and 2.2:		
Standard size	79.48 mm (3.1291 in)	79.51 mm (3.1303 in)
1st oversize	79.73 mm (3.1389 in)	79.76 mm (3.1402 in)
2nd oversize	79.98 mm (3.1488 in)	80.01 mm (3.1500 in)
3rd oversize	80.48 mm (3.1685 in)	80.51 mm (3.1697 in)
2.0 and 2.3:		
Standard size	80.98 mm (3.1882 in)	81.01 mm (3.1894 in)
1st oversize	81.23 mm (3.1980 in)	81.26 mm (3.1992 in)
2nd oversize	81.48 mm (3.2079 in)	81.51 mm (3.2091 in)

Piston ring end gap clearance (ring 15 mm/0.6 in from bottom of bore):
- New .... 0.25 to 0.50 mm (0.010 to 0.020 in)
- Wear limit .... 1.0 mm (0.040 in)

Connecting rods

Maximum endplay .... 0.4 mm (0.016 in)
Big-end bearing running clearance:
- New .... 0.015 to 0.062 mm (0.0006 to 0.0024 in)
- Wear limit .... 0.12 mm (0.0047 in)

Camshaft

Maximum endplay .... 0.15 mm (0.006 in)

Valves

Valve clearances .... See 1.8 litre four-cylinder engine
Valve stem diameter:
- Inlet .... 7.97 mm (0.3138 in)
- Exhaust .... 7.95 mm (0.3129 in)

Valve head diameter:
- Inlet .... 38.0 mm (1.4961 in)
- Exhaust .... 33.0 mm (1.2992 in)

Valve length:
- Inlet .... 91.0 mm (3.5827 in)
- Exhaust .... 90.8 mm (3.5748 in)

Valve seat angle .... 45°

Valve guides:
- Maximum valve rock (measured at head):
  - Inlet .... 1.0 mm (0.039 in)
  - Exhaust .... 1.3 mm (0.051 in)

Valve timing at 1.0 mm lift/0 mm clearance:

	Engine code				
	WH	KP	KG	WC	KU
Inlet opens BTDC	10°	1°	4°	0°	0¡
Inlet closes ABDC	36°	37°	36°	51°	41°
Exhaust opens BBDC	45°	37°	42°	40°	40°
Exhaust closes ATDC	3°	1°	6°	10°	1°

Cylinder head

Minimum height (between faces) .... 132.75 mm (5.2264 in)
Maximum gasket face distortion .... 0.1 mm (0.004 in)
Valve seat angle .... 45°

Lubrication system

Oil type/specification and filter .... See Part A
Oil pressure (minimum at 2000 rpm – engine hot) .... 2.0 bar (29 lbf/in^2)

Torque wrench settings

	Nm	lbf ft
Cylinder head bolts:		
Stage 1	40	30
Stage 2	60	44
Stage 3	Tighten further by half a turn (180°)	
Engine to transmission:		
M8 bolts	20	15
M10 bolts	45	33
M12 bolts	60	44
Engine mounting bracket to cylinder block:		
M8 bolts	25	18
M10 bolts	45	33
Engine mountings to mounting bracket	45	33
Timing belt covers	10	7.4
Water pump to engine	20	15
Crankshaft pulley to crankshaft (using tool 2079 – see text)	350	258
Camshaft gear to camshaft	80	59
Camshaft bearing cap nuts	20	15
Valve cover to cylinder head	10	7.4
Main bearing cap bolts	65	48
Big-end bearing cap nuts:		
Flat-sided nuts	50	37
Notched-sided nuts:		
Stage 1	30	22
Stage 2	Tighten further by one quarter turn (90°)	
Rear oil seal housing	10	7.4
Oil pump to block:		
Short bolts and stud	10	7.4
Long bolts	20	15
Oil intake pipe to crankcase	10	7.4
Idler pulley to oil pump	10	7.4
Oil pump backplate	10	7.4
Oil pressure relief valve	40	30
Oil filter housing to block (Turbo models)	70	52
Oil feed and return pipe flanges (Turbo models)	25	18
Oil cooler hose union nuts (Turbo models)	40	30
Sump to crankcase	25	18
Oil drain plug	30	22

Part A – Four-cylinder engines

1 General description

The engine is of four-cylinder, in-line overhead camshaft type mounted conventionally at the front of the car. The crankshaft is of five-bearing type and the centre main bearing shells incorporate flanged or separate thrust washers to control crankshaft endfloat (endplay). The camshaft is driven by a toothed belt from the crankshaft sprocket, and the belt also drives the intermediate shaft which is used to drive the distributor, oil pump and the fuel pump. The valves are operated from the camshaft through bucket type tappets, and valve clearances are adjusted by the use of shims located in the top of the tappets.

The engine has a full-flow lubrication system from a gear type oil pump mounted in the sump, and driven by an extension of the distributor which is itself geared to the intermediate shaft. The oil filter is of the cartridge type, mounted on the left-hand side of the cylinder block.

2 Maintenance and inspection

1 At the intervals given in Routine Maintenance at the beginning of this manual, carry out the following service operations on the engine.
2 Visually inspect the engine joint faces, gaskets and seals for any sign of oil or water leaks. Pay particular attention to the areas around the valve cover, cylinder head and sump joint faces. Rectify any leaks by referring to the appropriate Sections of this Chapter.
3 Place a suitable container beneath the oil drain plug on the left-hand side of the sump. Unscrew the plug using a spanner or socket and allow the oil to drain. Inspect the condition of the drain plug sealing washer and renew it if necessary. Refit and tighten the plug after draining.
4 Move the container rearwards, beneath the oil filter.
5 Using a strap wrench or filter removal tool, slacken the filter and then unscrew it from the engine. Once removed, the filter should be discarded.
6 Wipe the mating face on the oil filter bracket and lubricate the seal of a new filter using clean engine oil.
7 Screw the filter into position and tighten it firmly by hand only. Do not use any tools for tightening.
8 Refill the engine with the specified grade and quantity of oil through the filler on the valve cover (photo), until the level reaches the MAX mark on the oil level dipstick.
9 Start the engine and run it for a few minutes while checking for leaks around the filter.
10 Switch off, and after allowing time for the oil to return to the sump, check the level on

Four-cylinder engines 1•7

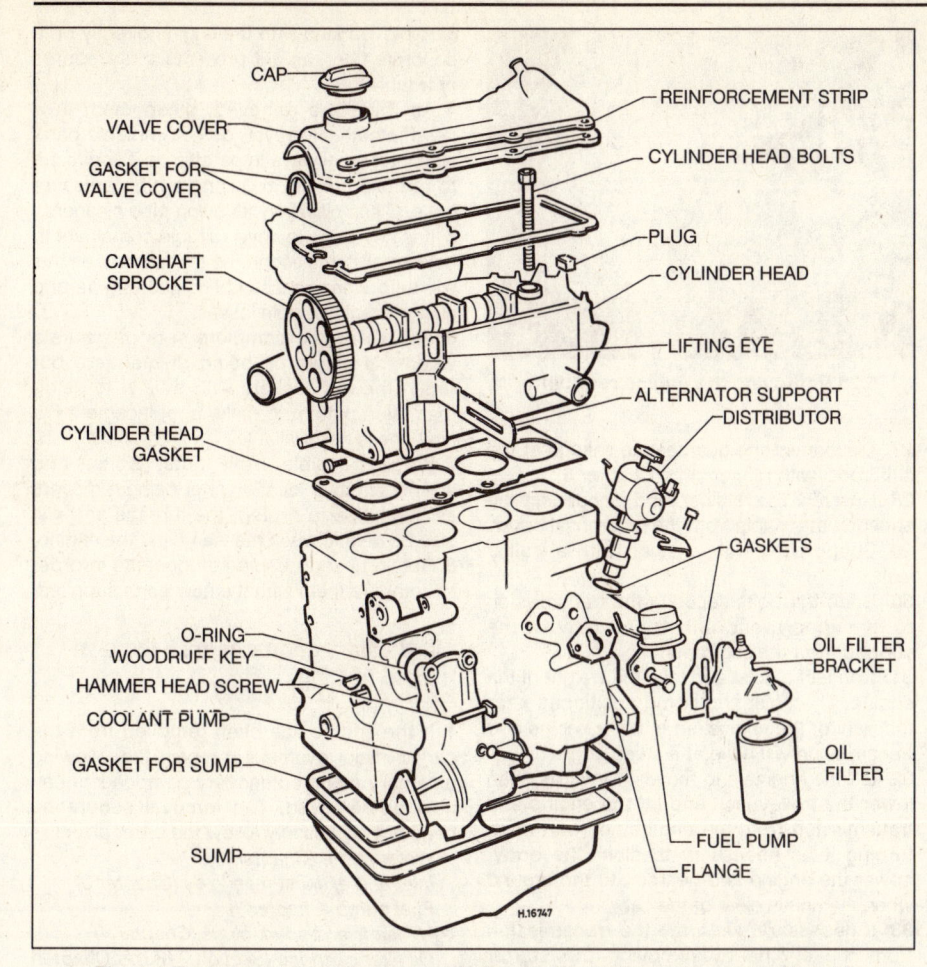

Fig. 1.1 Exploded view of the four-cylinder engine major components (Sec 1)

2.8 Fill the engine with oil through the filler on the valve cover

the dipstick once more. Top up as necessary to bring the level to the MAX mark, noting that the difference between the MIN and MAX marks on the dipstick is approximately 1.0 litre (1.76 Imp pt).
11 Check and if necessary adjust the valve clearances, as described in Section 17, and renew the valve cover gasket.
12 Check the tension of the timing belt and adjust if necessary, as described in Section 18, paragraph 22.

3 Major operations possible with the engine in the car

The following operations can be carried out without having to remove the engine from the car:
(a) Removal and servicing of the cylinder head and camshaft
(b) Removal of the timing belt and gears
(c) Removal of the flywheel or driveplate (after first removing the transmission)
(d) Removal of the sump (after first lowering the subframe)
(e) Removal of the oil pump, pistons and connecting rods

4 Major operations requiring engine removal

The following operations can only be carried out after removal of the engine from the car:
(a) Removal of the intermediate shaft
(b) Removal of the crankshaft and main bearings

5 Methods of engine removal

The engine can be lifted from the car either separately, or together with the manual gearbox. On automatic transmission models, it is recommended that the engine is removed separately because of the extra weight involved.

6 Engine – removal and refitting

1 Remove the bonnet, as described in Chapter 11 and stand it on cardboard or rags in a safe place.
2 Disconnect the battery negative lead.
3 Remove the radiator, as described in Chapter 2.
4 Disconnect the wiring from the rear of the alternator – where a cooling duct is fitted it will be necessary to disconnect the bypass hose from the cylinder head outlet and remove the duct first.
5 Remove the air cleaner, as described in Chapter 3.
6 Identify all fuel and vacuum hoses using masking tape, then disconnect those affecting engine removal. These will include, where applicable:
Fuel hoses to the fuel pump and filter, vacuum hoses to the inlet manifold, carburettor, distributor and emission control equipment
7 Identify all wiring for location using masking tape, then disconnect those affecting engine removal. These will include, where applicable:
Wiring to the oil pressure switch, temperature sender, distributor, coil, inlet manifold preheater, gearchange indicator switch, carburettor bypass and cut-off valve and air channel heating, automatic choke, thermotime valve and overrun control valve
8 On manual gearbox models, disconnect the clutch cable from the release lever and cable bracket.
9 Disconnect the accelerator cable (Chapter 3), throttle and accelerator pedal cables (automatic transmission – Chapters 3 and 7), and choke cable (Chapter 3).
10 Disconnect the hose from the inlet manifold (where applicable) and the heater hoses from the bulkhead. Also disconnect the hose from the cylinder head outlet.
11 On models with air conditioning, remove the compressor as described in Chapter 11, leaving the refrigerant hoses connected. Secure the compressor to one side, without straining the hoses.
12 On models with power-assisted steering, remove the pump, as described in Chapter 10, but leave the hydraulic pipes connected. Secure the pump to one side without straining the hoses.
13 Remove the right-hand engine mounting cover plate, and disconnect the exhaust front

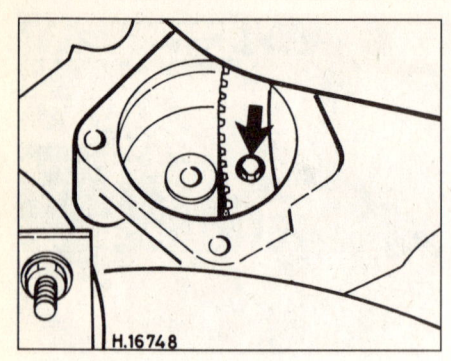

Fig. 1.2 Automatic transmission torque converter-to-driveplate retaining bolt (arrowed) viewed through starter aperture (Sec 6)

6.23 Removing the engine rear plate

pipe at the manifold flange. Also detach the front pipe at the transmission bracket.
14 Slacken the engine left and right-hand mountings. Disconnect the engine earth strap.

Removing engine without transmission

15 Remove the starter motor, as described in Chapter 12.
16 Unbolt the cover plate from the front of the transmission.
17 On automatic transmission models, unscrew the torque converter-to-driveplate bolts, while holding the starter ring gear stationary with a screwdriver. It will be necessary to rotate the engine to position the bolts in the starter aperture using a socket on the crankshaft pulley bolt.
18 Connect a hoist and take the weight of the engine. The hoist should be positioned centrally over the engine.
19 Support the weight of the transmission with a trolley jack.
20 Unscrew the engine-to-transmission bolts, noting the position of any brackets or cable supports.
21 Unscrew the engine mounting bracket-to-engine bolts, and swing the mounting brackets forward, clear of the engine.
22 Lift the engine slightly, and pull it forward off the transmission. On automatic transmission models, make sure that the torque converter remains fully engaged with the transmission splines.
23 Manipulate the engine as necessary, and lift it from the engine compartment. Lower the engine to the floor, and if necessary remove the engine rear plate (photo).

Removing engine with manual transmission attached

24 Disconnect the wiring to the reversing light switch and release the cable clip. Remove the earth strap.
25 Disconnect the exhaust front pipe-to-intermediate pipe joint, and remove the front pipe from the car.
26 Disconnect the driveshafts from the transmission flanges, with reference to Chapter 8.

27 Disconnect the gearchange linkage at the shift rods, with reference to Chapter 6.
28 Unscrew the retainer, and disconnect the speedometer cable from the differential cover.
29 Support the transmission with a trolley jack.
30 Undo the bolts securing the transmission to its support, and unbolt and remove the support from the subframe.
31 Connect a hoist and take the weight of the engine. The hoist should be positioned near the front of the engine, so that the engine and transmission will hang at a steep angle
32 Lift the engine and move it forwards, then lower the trolley jack and lift the engine and transmission from the engine compartment; turning it as necessary to clear the body. Lower the engine and gearbox to the ground when the unit is clear of the car.
33 If necessary, separate the transmission from the engine by removing the starter motor, transmission cover plate, and engine-to-transmission attachment bolts. Remove the engine rear plate after separation.

Refitting

34 Refitting is a reversal of the removal procedure, but smear the manual transmission input shaft and release bearing face with molybdenum disulphide grease before fitting. Ensure that all the engine and transmission mountings are fitted free of tension, and tighten all nuts and bolts to the specified torque. Refit, and where applicable adjust, all engine related components and systems with reference to the Chapters concerned. Ensure that the engine is filled with oil, and that the cooling system is topped up before starting the engine.

7 Engine dismantling – general

1 If possible position the engine on a bench or strong table for the dismantling procedure. Two or three blocks of wood will be necessary to support the engine in an upright position.
2 Cleanliness is most important, and if the engine is dirty, it should be cleaned with paraffin before commencing work.

3 Avoid working with the engine directly on a concrete floor, as grit presents a real source of trouble.
4 As parts are removed, clean them in a paraffin bath. However, do not immerse parts with internal oilways in paraffin as it is difficult to remove, usually requiring a high pressure hose. Clean oilways with nylon pipe cleaners.
5 It is advisable to have suitable containers to hold small items according to their use, as this will help when reassembling the engine and also prevent possible losses.
6 Always obtain complete sets of gaskets when the engine is being dismantled, but retain the old gaskets with a view to using them as a pattern to make a replacement if a new one is not available.
7 When possible, refit nuts, bolts, and washers in their location after being removed, as this helps to protect the threads and will also be helpful when reassembling the engine.
8 Retain unserviceable components in order to compare them with the new parts supplied.

8 Ancillary components – removal and refitting

1 If the engine has been removed from the car for major overhaul or repair, the following externally mounted ancillary components can now be removed. The removal sequence need not necessarily follow the order given:
   Water pump (Chapter 2)
   Inlet and exhaust manifolds (Chapter 3)
   Fuel pump (Chapter 3)
   HT leads and spark plugs (Chapter 4)
   Oil filter cartridge (Section 2 of this Chapter)
   Distributor (Chapter 4)
   Dipstick
   Alternator (Chapter 12)
   Engine mountings (Section 28 of this Chapter)
2 Refitting is essentially a reversal of the removal sequence, with reference to the Sections and Chapters indicated.

9 Cylinder head and camshaft – removal

Note: If the engine is still in the car, first carry out the following operations:
(a) Disconnect the battery negative lead
(b) Drain the cooling system
(c) Remove the alternator
(d) Remove the inlet and exhaust manifolds
(e) Remove the HT leads and spark plugs
(f) Disconnect all wiring, cables and hoses
(g) Disconnect the exhaust downpipe from the exhaust manifold

1 Unscrew the nuts and lift off the upper timing cover, using an Allen key where necessary (photo).
2 Unscrew the nuts and lift off the valve cover, together with the reinforcement strips and gaskets (photos).
3 Unbolt the outlet elbows and remove the gaskets, if necessary (photos).

Four-cylinder engines 1•9

9.2A Removing the reinforcement strips . . .

9.2B . . . and valve cover

9.2C Removing the valve cover front gasket . . .

9.2D . . . and rear plug

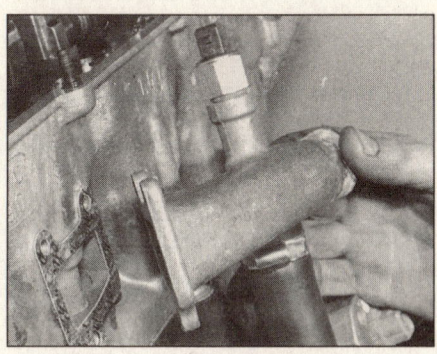

9.3A Removing the cylinder head side outlet . . .

9.3B . . . and rear outlet

9.4 Crankshaft pulley notch aligned with TDC arrow on the lower timing cover

4 Using a socket on the crankshaft pulley bolt, turn the engine so that the piston in No 1 cylinder is at TDC on its compression stroke. The notch in the crankshaft pulley must be in line with the arrow on the lower timing cover (photo), and both No 1 cylinder valves must be closed (ie cam peaks away from the tappets). The notch on the rear of the camshaft gear will also be in line with the top of the timing belt rear cover.

5 Loosen the nut on the timing belt tensioner and, using an open-ended spanner, rotate the eccentric hub anti-clockwise to release the belt tension.

6 Remove the timing belt from the camshaft gear and tensioner and move it to one side while keeping it in firm contact with the

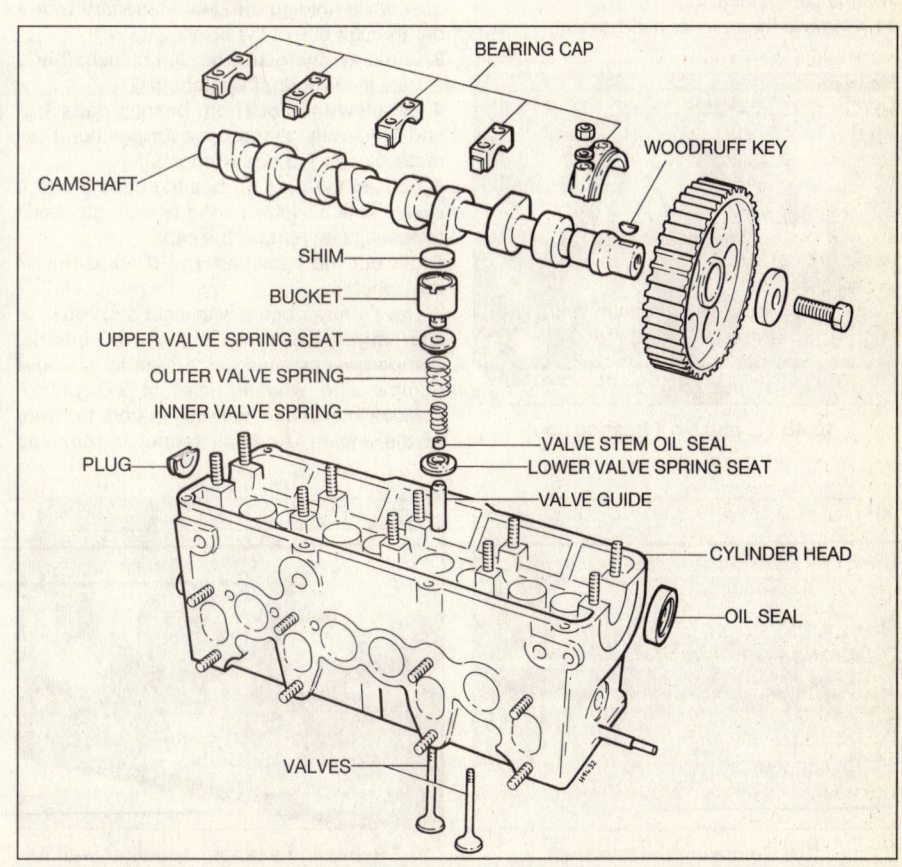

Fig. 1.3 Exploded view of the cylinder head, camshaft and valve gear (Secs 9, 10 and 11)

10.3A Removing the camshaft gear

10.3B Woodruff key location in camshaft

10.4A Removing No 3 camshaft bearing cap . . .

intermediate and crankshaft gears. *The intermediate gear must not be moved, otherwise the ignition timing will be lost and the lower timing cover will have to be removed.*
7 Unscrew the nut and remove the timing belt tensioner.
8 Unscrew the bolt securing the timing belt rear cover to the cylinder head.
9 Using a splined key, unscrew the cylinder head bolts a turn at a time in reverse order to that shown in Fig. 1.7.
10 With all the bolts removed lift the cylinder head from the block. If it is stuck, tap it free with a wooden mallet. *Do not insert a lever into the gasket joint.*
11 Remove the cylinder head gasket.

10.4B . . . and No 1 bearing cap

10 Camshaft and tappets – removal

Note: *If the engine is still in the car, first carry out the following operations:*
(a) Disconnect the battery negative lead
(b) Disconnect the wiring, cables and hoses which cross the engine valve cover – remove the air cleaner
(c) Remove the alternator/water pump drivebelt

1 Follow paragraphs 1 to 6 of Section 9, excluding paragraph 3.
2 Unscrew the centre bolt from the camshaft gear while holding the gear stationary with a bar through one of the holes.
3 Withdraw the gear from the camshaft and extract the Woodruff key (photos).
4 Unscrew the nuts from bearing caps 1, 3 and 5. Identify all the caps for position then remove caps 1, 3 and 5 (photos).
5 Loosen the nuts on bearing caps 2 and 4 evenly until all valve spring tension has been released, then remove the caps.
6 Lift out the camshaft and discard the oil seal (photo).
7 Have ready a board with eight pegs on it, or alternatively use a box with internal compartments, marked to identify cylinder number and whether inlet or exhaust or position in the head, numbering from the front of the engine. As each tappet is removed (photo), place it on the appropriate peg, or mark the actual tappet to indicate its position. *Note that each tappet has a shim (disc) fitted into a recess in its top. This shim must be kept with its particular tappet.*

11 Valves – removal and renovation

1 With the cylinder head removed, as previously described, the valve gear can be dismantled as follows. Because the valves are recessed deeply into the top of the cylinder head, their removal requires a valve spring compressor with long claws or the use of some ingenuity in adapting other types of compressor.
2 Have ready a board with holes in it, into which each valve can be fitted as it is removed, or have a set of labelled containers so that each valve and its associated parts can be identified and kept separate. Inlet valves are Nos 2-4-5-7, Exhaust valves are Nos 1-3-6-8, numbered from the timing belt end of the engine.
3 Compress each valve spring until the collets can be removed (photo). Take out the collets, release the spring compressor and remove it.
4 Remove the valve spring cover, the outer and inner spring and the valve (photos).

10.6 Removing the camshaft

10.7 Removing a tappet, together with its shim

11.3 Compress the valve springs and remove the collets

Four-cylinder engines 1•11

11.4A Removing the valve spring cover . . .

11.4B . . . outer valve spring

11.4C . . . inner valve spring . . .

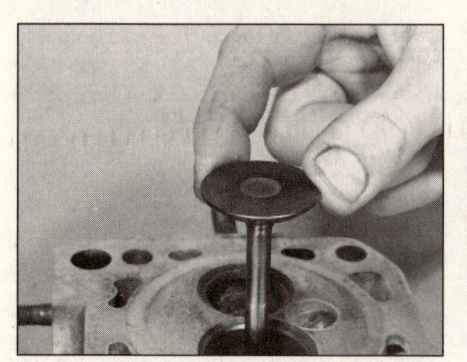

11.4D . . and the valve

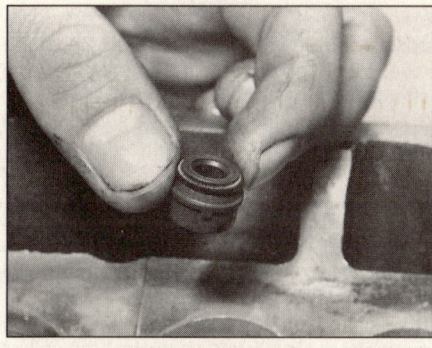

11.5A Removing the valve stem seal . . .

11.5B . . and valve spring seat

5 Prise off the valve stem seals, or pull them off with pliers and discard them, then lift off the valve spring seat and place it with its valve (photos).

6 Examine the heads of the valves for pitting and burning, paying particular attention to the heads of the exhaust valves. The valve seats should be examined at the same time. If the pitting on the valve and seat is only slight, the marks can be removed by grinding the seats and valves together with coarse and then fine grinding paste. Where bad pitting has occurred, it will be necessary to have the valve seat re-cut and either use a new valve, or have the valve re-faced. Exhaust valves must not be refaced, but ground in by hand only.

7 Scrape away all carbon from the valve head and valve stem. Carefully clean away every trace of grinding paste, taking care to leave none in the ports, or in the valve guides. Wipe the valves and valve seats with a paraffin soaked rag and then with a clean dry rag.

12 Cylinder head – examination and renovation

1 Check the cylinder head for distortion, by placing a straight-edge across it at a number of points, lengthwise, crosswise and diagonally and measuring the gap beneath it with feeler gauges If the gap exceeds the limit given in the Specifications, the head must be re-faced by a workshop which is equipped for this work. Re-facing must not reduce the cylinder head height below the minimum dimension given in the Specifications.

2 Examine the cylinder head for cracks. If there are minor cracks of not more than 0.5 mm (0.020 in) width between the valve seats, or at the bottom of the spark plug holes, the head can be re-used, but a cylinder head cannot be repaired or new valve seat inserts fitted.

3 Check the valve guides for wear. First clean out the guide and then insert the stem of a new valve into the guide. Because the stem diameters are different, ensure that only an inlet valve is used to check the inlet valve guides, and an exhaust valve for the exhaust vaive guides. With the end of the valve stem flush with the top of the valve guide, measure the total amount by which the rim of the valve head can be moved sideways. If the movement exceeds the maximum amount given in the Specifications, new guides should be fitted, but this is a job for an Audi dealer or specialist workshop.

13 Camshaft and bearings – examination and renovation

1 Examine the camshaft for signs of damage or excessive wear. If either the cam lobes or any of the journals have wear grooves, a new camshaft must be fitted.

2 With the camshaft fitted in its bearings, but

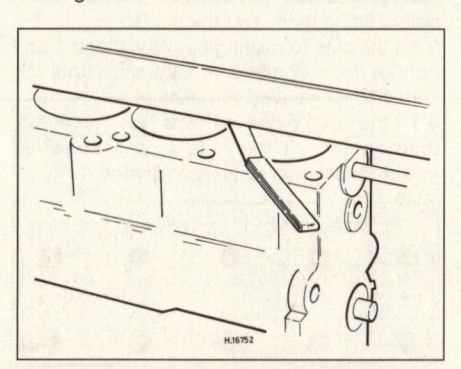

Fig. 1.4 Checking the cylinder head for distortion using a straight-edge and feeler blade (Sec 12)

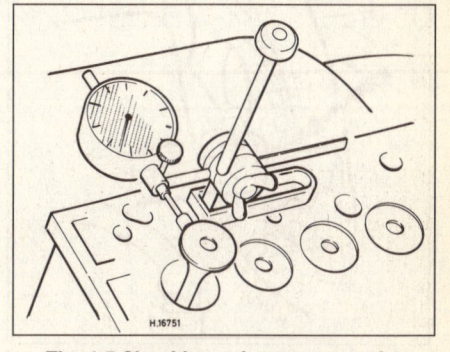

Fig. 1.5 Checking valve gear wear by measuring valve movement using a dial gauge (Sec 12)

1•12 Four-cylinder engines

15.4 Tightening the camshaft bearing cap nuts

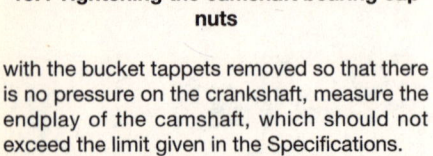

15.5 Installing the camshaft oil seal

15.8 Tightening the camshaft gear centre bolt

with the bucket tappets removed so that there is no pressure on the crankshaft, measure the endplay of the camshaft, which should not exceed the limit given in the Specifications.

3 The camshaft bearings are part of the cylinder head and cannot be renewed. The bearing clearance is very small and the clearances can only be checked with a dial gauge. *If there is excessive looseness in the camshaft bearings, do not attempt to decrease it by grinding or filing the bottoms of the bearing caps.*

14 Valves – refitting

1 Locate the valve spring seats over the guides, then press a new seal on the top of each valve guide. A plastic sleeve should be provided with the valve stem seals, so that the seals are not damaged when the valves are fitted.

2 Apply oil to the valve stem and the stem seal. Fit the plastic sleeve over the top of the valve stem and insert the valve carefully. Remove the sleeve after inserting the valve. If there is no plastic sleeve, wrap a piece of thin adhesive tape around the top of the valve

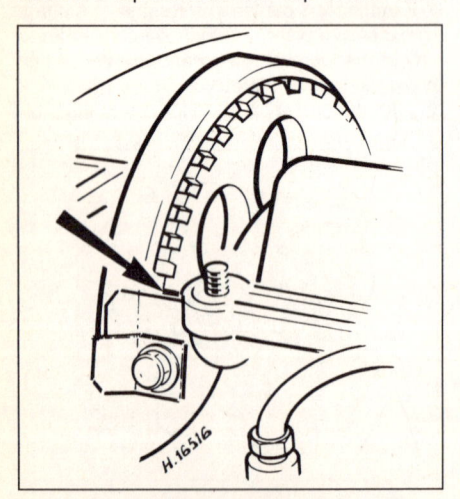

Fig. 1.6 Camshaft gear TDC mark aligned with the top of the timing belt rear cover (Sec 15)

stem, so that it covers the recess for the collets and prevents the sharp edges of the recess damaging the seal. Remove the tape after fitting the valve.

3 Fit the inner and outer valve springs, then the valve spring cover. If renewing springs, they must only be renewed as a pair on any valve.

4 Fit the spring compressor and compress the spring just enough to allow the collets to be fitted. If the spring is pressed right down there is a danger of damaging the stem seal.

5 Fit the collets, release the spring compressor slightly and check that the collets seat properly, then remove the compressor.

6 Tap the top of the valve stem with a soft-headed hammer to ensure that the collets are seated.

7 Repeat the procedure for all the valves.

15 Camshaft and tappets – refitting

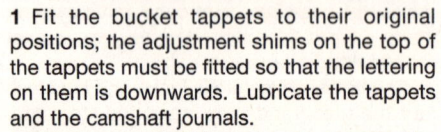

1 Fit the bucket tappets to their original positions; the adjustment shims on the top of the tappets must be fitted so that the lettering on them is downwards. Lubricate the tappets and the camshaft journals.

2 Lay the camshaft into the lower half of its bearings so that the lowest point of the cams of No 1 cylinder are towards the tappets, and fit the bearing caps in their original positions, making sure that they are the right way round before fitting them over the studs.

3 Fit the nuts to bearing cap Nos 2 and 4 and tighten them in diagonal sequence until the camshaft fully enters its bearings.

4 Fit the nuts to bearing caps Nos 1, 3 and 5, then tighten all the nuts to the specified torque in diagonal sequence (photo).

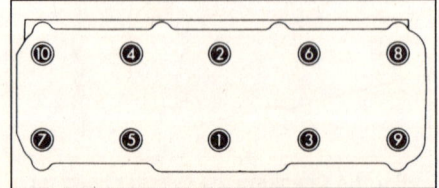

Fig. 1.7 Cylinder head bolt tightening sequence (Sec 16)

5 Smear a little oil onto the sealing lip and outer edge of the camshaft oil seal, then locate it open end first in the cylinder head No 1 camshaft bearing cap (photo).

6 Using a metal tube, drive the seal squarely into the cylinder head until flush with the front of the cylinder head – *if the seal is driven in further, it will block the oil return hole.*

7 Fit the Woodruff key in its groove and locate the gear on the end of the camshaft.

8 Fit the centre bolt and spacer and tighten the bolt to the specified torque while holding the gear stationary with a bar through one of the holes (photo).

9 Turn the camshaft gear and align the rear notch with the top of the timing belt rear cover.

10 Without disturbing the intermediate gear setting, and keeping the timing belt in firm contact with the intermediate gear and crankshaft gear, locate the timing belt on the camshaft gear and tensioner. The crankshaft must be positioned with No 1 cylinder at TDC. If the position of the intermediate gear is in doubt, it must be checked with reference to Section 18.

11 Turn the timing belt tensioner clockwise and tension the timing belt until it can just be twisted 90° with the thumb and index finger midway between the camshaft and intermediate gears. Tighten the nut to secure the tensioner.

12 Check and, if necessary, adjust the valve clearances, as described in Section 17.

13 Refit the valve cover and reinforcement strips, together with new gaskets and seals, and tighten the nuts.

14 Refit the upper timing belt cover and tighten the nuts.

15 If the engine is in the car, reverse the preliminary procedures given in Section 10.

16 Cylinder head and camshaft – refitting

1 Check that the top of the block is perfectly clean, then locate a new gasket on it with the words OBEN – TOP facing upward (photos).

2 Check that the cylinder head face is perfectly clean. Place two long rods or pieces

Four-cylinder engines 1•13

16.1A Locate the new cylinder head gasket on the block . . .

16.1 B . . .with the OBEN – TOP words uppermost

16.2 Lowering the cylinder head into place

of dowel in two cylinder head bolt holes at opposite ends of the block, to position the gasket and give a location for fitting the cylinder head. Lower the head on to the block (photo), remove the guides and insert the bolts and washers. Do not use jointing compound on the cylinder head joint.
3 Tighten the bolts using the sequence shown in Fig. 1.7 in the three stages given in the Specifications to the specified torque (photo).
4 Insert and tighten the bolt securing the timing belt rear cover to the cylinder head.
5 Refit the timing belt tensioner and fit the nut finger tight.
6 Follow paragraphs 9 to 14 inclusive of Section 15.
7 Refit the outlet elbow, together with a new gasket, and tighten the bolts.
8 If the engine is in the car, reverse the preliminary procedures given in Section 9

17 Valve clearances – checking and adjustment

1 Valve clearances are adjusted by inserting the appropriate thickness shim to the top of the tappet. Shims are available in thicknesses from 3.00 to 4.25 mm (0.118 to 0.167 in) in increments of 0.05 mm (0.002 in).
2 Adjust the valve clearances for the initial setting-up after fitting a new camshaft, or grinding in the valves with the engine cold.

16.3 Tightening the cylinder head bolts

The valve clearances should be re-checked after 620 miles (1000 km), with the engine warm, and the coolant over 35°C (95°F).
3 Remove the valve cover after removing the upper timing cover.
4 Fit a spanner to the crankshaft pulley bolt and turn the crankshaft until the highest points of the cams for one cylinder are pointing upwards and outwards at similar angles. Use feeler gauges to check the gap between the cam and the tappet and record the dimension.
5 Repeat the operation for all four cylinders and complete the list of clearances. Valves are numbered from the timing belt end of the engine. Inlet valves are Nos 2-4-5-7, exhaust valves are Nos 1-3-6-8.
6 Where any tolerances exceed those given

17.6A Using a cranked dowel rod to depress the tappets

in the Specifications. remove the existing shim by placing a cranked dowel rod with a suitably shaped end between two tappets with the rod resting on the edge of the tappets (photo). With the piston for the relevant cylinder at TDC compression, lever against the camshaft to depress the tappets sufficiently to remove the shim(s) from the top of the tappet(s). Do not over depress the tappets so that the valves touch the pistons. Note that each tappet incorporates notches in its upper rim so that a small screwdriver or similar tool can be used to remove the shim (photos).
7 Note the thickness of the shim (engraved on its underside), and calculate the shim thickness required to correct the clearance (photo). If the clearance is too large, a thicker

17.6B Removing a shim from a tappet (tappet removed)

17.6C Notches in tappet (arrowed) for shim removal

17.7 The thickness (in mm) engraved on the underside of the tappet shim

1•14 Four-cylinder engines

17.9 Fitting a new valve cover gasket and rear plug

18.2 Removing the water pump pulley

18.5 Removing the crankshaft pulley

shim is required, and a smaller shim is needed when there is insufficient clearance.
8 Provided they are not worn or damaged, shims which have been removed can be re-used in other positions if they are of the correct thickness.
9 Refit the valve cover and upper timing cover, together with new gaskets, after checking and adjusting the valve clearances (photo).

18 Timing belt and gears – removal and refitting

Note: *If the engine is still in the car, first carry out the following operations:*
(a) Disconnect the battery negative lead
(b) Remove the power-assisted steering pump drivebelt on models so equipped, as described in Chapter 10
(c) Remove the alternator, as described in Chapter 12

1 Unscrew the nuts and lift off the upper timing cover, using an Allen key where necessary.
2 Unbolt and remove the pulley from the water pump (photo).
3 Using a socket on the crankshaft pulley bolt, turn the engine so that the piston in No 1 cylinder is at TDC (top dead centre) on its compression stroke. The notch in the crankshaft pulley must be in line with the arrow on the lower timing cover, and both No 1 cylinder valves must be closed (ie cam peaks away from the tappets).

4 If it is required to remove the crankshaft gear, loosen the centre bolt now. Hold the crankshaft stationary with a wide-bladed screwdriver in the starter ring gear (starter motor removed) or engage top gear and apply the handbrake if the engine is still in the car.
5 With the TDC marks aligned, unbolt the crankshaft pulley from the gear (photo).
6 Unbolt and remove the lower timing cover (photo).
7 Loosen the nut on the timing belt tensioner and, using an open-ended spanner, rotate the eccentric hub anti-clockwise to release the belt tension (photo).
8 Remove the timing belt from the crankshaft, camshaft and intermediate gears, and from the tensioner.

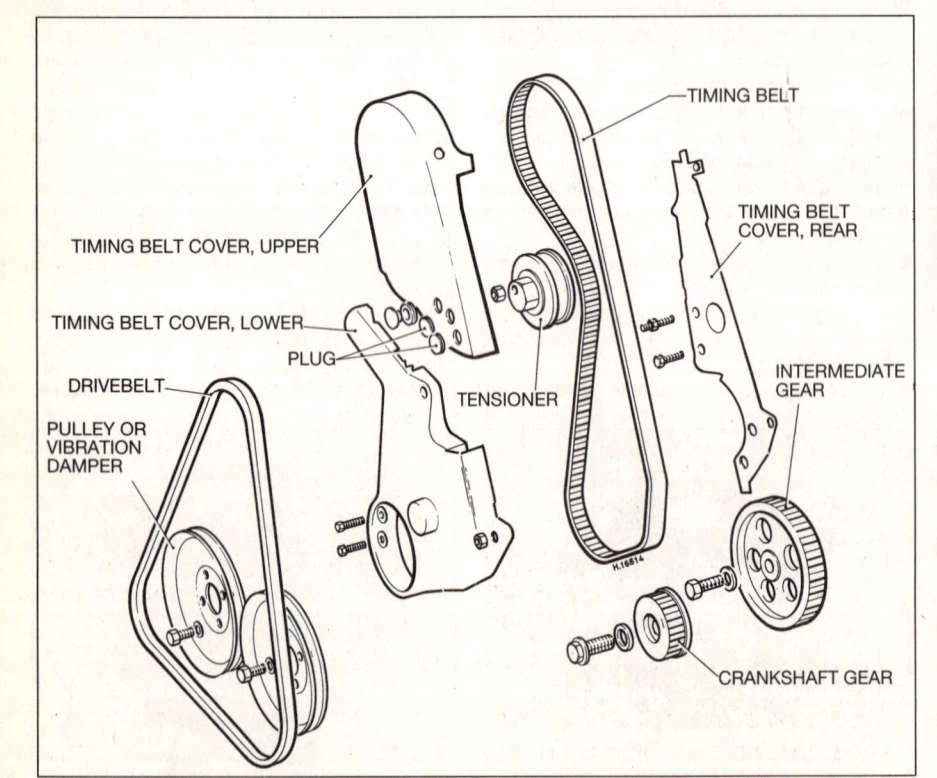

18.6 Removing the lower timing cover

18.7 Turn the tensioner anti-clockwise to release the belt tension

Fig. 1.8 Exploded view of the timing belt and gears (Sec 18)

Four-cylinder engines 1•15

18.9 Removing the timing belt tensioner

18.10 Removing the gear from the intermediate shaft

18.11A Unscrew the centre bolt

9 Unscrew the nut and remove the timing belt tensioner (photo)
10 Unscrew the centre bolt and withdraw the intermediate gear (photo). Remove the Woodruff key. When loosening the centre bolt, hold the gear stationary with a socket and bar on the rear timing cover bolt.
11 Remove the centre bolt and withdraw the crankshaft gear (photos). Remove the Woodruff key.
12 Unscrew the centre bolt from the camshaft gear while holding the gear stationary with a bar through one of the holes. Withdraw the gear and remove the Woodruff key.
13 Unbolt and remove the rear timing cover.
14 Commence refitting by locating the rear timing cover on the engine and tightening the bolts.
15 Locate the Woodruff key and camshaft gear on the camshaft, insert the centre bolt and washer, and tighten the bolt.
16 Locate the Woodruff key and crankshaft gear on the crankshaft, coat the threads of the centre bolt with a liquid locking agent, then insert the bolt with its washer and tighten it while holding the crankshaft stationary (photo).
17 Locate the Woodruff key and intermediate gear on the intermediate shaft, then insert the centre bolt and washer, and tighten the bolt (photo).
18 Refit the timing belt tensioner and fit the nut finger tight.

18.11B . . . and withdraw the crankshaft gear

19 Make sure that the notch on the rear of the camshaft gear is aligned with the top of the timing belt rear cover.
20 Temporarily fit the crankshaft pulley to the gear then, with No 1 piston at TDC, turn the intermediate gear so that the indentation is aligned with the notch in the pulley (photo). If the distributor has not been disturbed the rotor arm will point in the direction of No 1 distributor cap segment.
21 Locate the timing belt on the gears and tensioner, turn the tensioner clockwise to pretension the timing belt, and check that the TDC marks are still correctly aligned.
22 Turn the tensioner clockwise until the timing belt can just be twisted 90° with the thumb and index finger midway between the

18.16 Tightening the crankshaft gear centre bolt

camshaft and intermediate gears. Tighten the nut to secure the tensioner.
23 Remove the crankshaft pulley, fit the lower timing cover, and tighten the bolts.
24 Refit the crankshaft pulley and tighten the bolts.
25 Locate the pulley on the water pump and tighten the bolts.
26 Refit the upper timing cover and tighten the nuts.
27 If the engine is in the car, reverse the preliminary procedures given at the beginning of this Section.

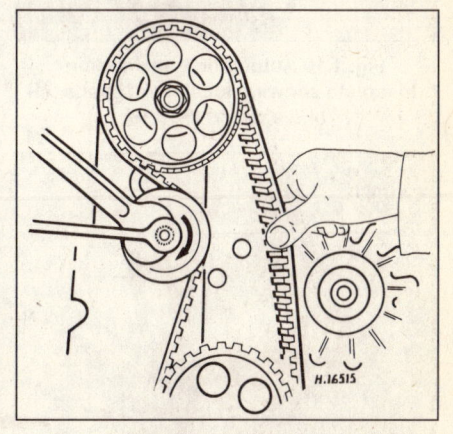

18.17 Tightening the intermediate shaft gear centre bolt

18.20 Crankshaft pulley TDC notch aligned with the indentation in the intermediate gear (arrowed)

Fig. 1.9 Checking timing belt tension (Sec 18)

Turn tensioner clockwise until belt can just be twisted through 90°

19.1A Removing the flywheel bolts

19.1B Using a bar and angle iron to hold the flywheel stationary

19.2 Removing the flywheel

19 Flywheel/driveplate – removal and refitting

Note: *If the engine is still in the car, first carry out the following operations:*
(a) *On manual gearbox models, remove the gearbox (Chapter 6), and clutch (Chapter 5)*
(b) *On automatic transmission models, remove the automatic transmission (Chapter 7)*

1 The flywheel/driveplate bolts are offset to ensure correct refitting. Unscrew the bolts while holding the flywheel/driveplate stationary (photos)

2 Lift the flywheel driveplate from the crankshaft (photo). If removing a driveplate note the location of the shim and spacer.

3 Refitting is a reversal of removal, but coat the threads of the bolts with a liquid locking agent before inserting them and tightening them to the specified torque (photo). If a replacement driveplate is to be fitted, its position must be checked and adjusted if necessary. The distance from the rear face of the block to the torque converter *mounting face* on the driveplate (Fig. 1.11) must be between 30.5 and 32.1 mm (1.20 and 1.26 in). If necessary, remove the driveplate and fit a spacer behind it to achieve the correct dimension.

20 Intermediate shaft – removal and refitting

1 Remove the distributor (Chapter 4), and the fuel pump (Chapter 3).
2 Remove the timing belt and intermediate gear, as described in Section 18.
3 Remove the two bolts from the sealing flange, take off the sealing flange and the O-ring (photos).
4 Withdraw the intermediate shaft from the block (photo).
5 With the flange removed, the oil seal can be removed (photo). Fit a new seal with its open face towards the engine and use a block of

Fig. 1.10 Automatic transmission driveplate showing location of spacer (1) and shim (2) (Sec 19)

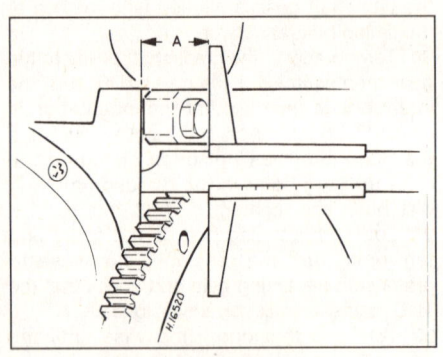

Fig. 1.11 Checking the driveplate-to-block dimension 'A' (Sec 19)

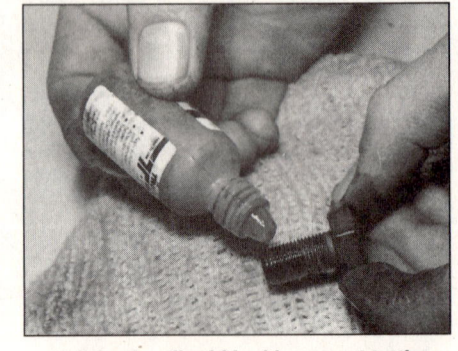

19.3 Apply a liquid locking agent to the flywheel bolts

20.3A Removing the intermediate shaft sealing flange . . .

20.3B . . . and O-ring

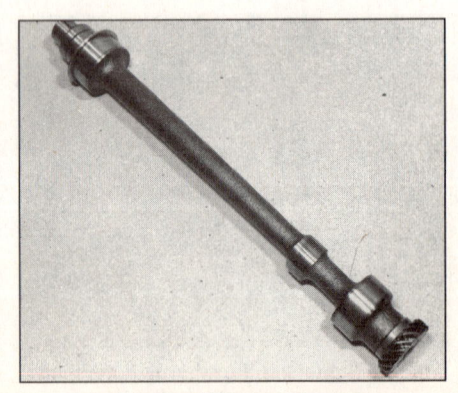

20.4 The intermediate shaft

Four-cylinder engines

20.5 Levering out the intermediate shaft oil seal from the flange

21.3 Locating a new sump gasket on the block

22.2 Removing the crankshaft front oil seal housing

wood to drive the seal in flush. Oil the lips of the seal before fitting the sealing flange.

6 Refitting is a reversal of removal, but fit a new O-ring and check that the shaft endplay does not exceed the amount given in the Specifications. Refer to Section 18 when refitting the timing belt and intermediate gear, and to Chapters 3 and 4 when refitting the fuel pump and distributor.

21 Sump – removal and refitting

Note: *If the engine is still in the car, first carry out the following operations:*
(a) Jack up the front of the car and support it on axle stands
(b) Support the weight of the engine with a hoist
(c) Unbolt and remove the transmission front cover
(d) Drain the engine oil
(e) Unscrew the subframe front bolts and lower the subframe

1 Unbolt and remove the sump, using an Allen key where necessary. Remove the dipstick.
2 Remove the gasket.
3 Refitting is a reversal of removal, but use a new gasket without adhesive (photo), and tighten the bolts evenly to the specified torque.

22 Crankshaft oil seals – renewal

Front oil seal

1 Remove the timing belt and crankshaft gear, as described in Section 18.
2 If an extractor tool is available the seal may be renewed without removing the housing, otherwise unbolt and remove the housing (including the relevant sump bolts) and remove the gasket (photo). If the sump gasket is damaged while removing the housing it will be necessary to remove the sump and fit a new gasket. However, refit the sump *after* fitting the housing.
3 Drive the old seal out of the housing then dip the new seal in engine oil and drive it into the housing with a block of wood or a socket until flush (photo). Make sure that the closed end of the seal is facing outwards.
4 Fit the housing, together with a new gasket, and tighten the bolts evenly in diagonal sequence.
5 Refit the crankshaft gear and timing belt, as described in Section 18.

Rear oil seal

6 Remove the flywheel or driveplate, as described in Section 19.
7 Follow paragraphs 2 to 4 inclusive (photo).
8 Refit the flywheel or driveplate, as described in Section 19.

22.3 Using a socket to fit a new crankshaft front oil seal

23 Oil pump – removal, examination and refitting

1 Remove the sump, as described in Section 21.
2 Using an Allen key, unscrew the socket-headed bolts and withdraw the oil pump and strainer from the cylinder block (photo).
3 Remove the two hexagon-headed bolts from the pump cover and lift off the cover (photo).
4 Bend up the metal rim of the filter plate so that it can be removed and take the filter screen out (photo). Clean the screen thoroughly with paraffin and a brush.
5 Clean the pump casing, cover and gears.

22.7 Removing the crankshaft rear oil seal housing

23.2 Removing the oil pump and strainer

23.3 Removing the oil pump cover

1•18 Four-cylinder engines

23.4 Oil pump filter screen

23.6A Checking the oil pump gear backlash . . .

23.6B . . . and endplay

6 Check the backlash of the gears with a feeler gauge (photo) and, with a straight-edge across the end face of the pump, measure the endplay of the gears (photo). Examine the pump cover grooves worn by the ends of the gears, which will effectively increase the endplay of the gears. If the wear on the pump is beyond the specified limits a new pump should be fitted.

7 Fill the pump housing with engine oil then reassemble and refit it using a reversal of the removal and dismantling procedure. Refer to Section 21 when refitting the sump.

24 Pistons and connecting rods – removal and dismantling

1 Remove the cylinder head (Section 9), timing belt (Section 18) and oil pump (Section 23).

2 Mark each connecting rod and cap in relation to its cylinder and position.
3 Turn the crankshaft so that No 1 piston is at the bottom of its bore, then unscrew the nuts and remove the big-end bearing cap (photo).
4 Using the handle of a hammer, push the piston and connecting rod out of the top of the cylinder. Put the bearing cap with its connecting rod and make sure that they both have the cylinder number marked on them. If any of the bearing shells become detached while removing the connecting rod and bearing cap, ensure that they are placed with their matching cap or rod.
5 Repeat the procedure given in paragraphs 3 and 4 to remove the remaining pistons and connecting rods.
6 Before removing the pistons from the connecting rods, if necessary, mark the connecting rods to show which side of them is towards the front of the engine. The casting marks on the rod and cap face towards the front of the engine (photo).
7 Remove the circlips from the grooves in the gudgeon pin holes and push the pin out enough for the connecting rod to be removed (photo). Do not remove the pins completely unless new ones are to be fitted, to ensure that the pin is not turned end for end when the piston is refitted. If the pin is difficult to push out, heat the piston by immersing it in hot water.
8 New bushes can be fitted to the connecting rods, but as they need to be reamed to size

after fitting, the job is best left to an Audi agent.
9 Using old feeler gauges, or pieces of rigid plastic inserted behind the piston rings, carefully ease each ring in turn off the piston. Lay the rings out so that they are kept the right way up and so that the top ring can be identified. Carefully scrape the rings free of carbon and clean out the ring grooves on the pistons, using a piece of wood or a piece of broken piston ring.

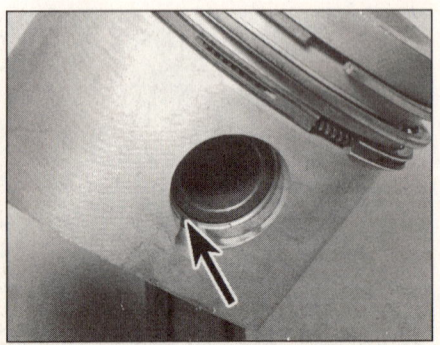

25 Pistons and cylinder bores – examination

1 Examine the pistons and the bores for obvious signs of damage and excessive wear. If they appear to be satisfactory, make the following checks.
2 Measure the piston diameter at a position 15 mm (0.60 in) from the lower edge of the skirt and at 90° to the axis of the piston (Fig. 1.12) and compare this with the information in the Specifications.
3 Push a piston ring into the cylinder bore and use a piston to push the ring down the bore so that it is square in the bore and about 15 mm (0.6 in) from the bottom of the cylinder. Measure the ring cap using a feeler gauge (photo). If the gap is above the top limit, look for obvious signs of bore wear, or if a new piston ring is available, measure the gap when a new piston ring is fitted to the bore.

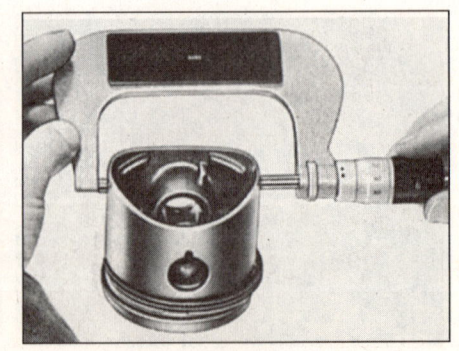

24.3 Removing a big-end cap

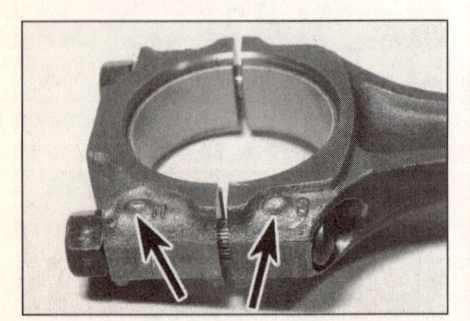

24.6 The casting marks (arrowed) which must face the front of the engine

24.7 Location of a gudgeon pin circlip (arrowed) in the piston

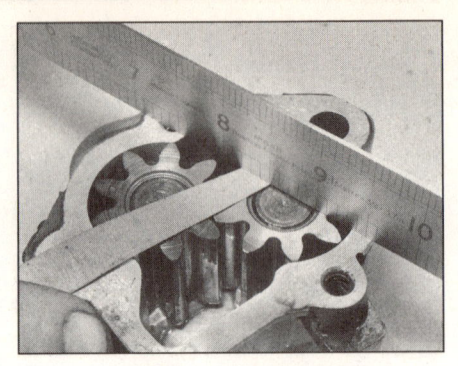

Fig. 1.12 Checking the piston diameter (Sec 25)

Four-cylinder engines 1•19

25.3 Checking the piston ring gap

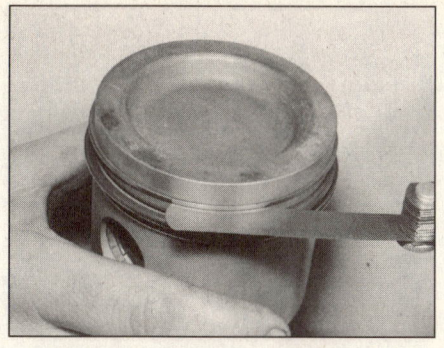

25.6 Checking the piston ring-to-groove clearance

26.1 The arrow on the piston crown (arrowed) must face the front of the engine

4 To measure the bore diameter directly a dial gauge with an internal measuring attachment is required. If one is available, measure each bore in six places and compare the readings with the wear limit given. Bore diameter should be measured 10 mm (0.4 in) from the top of the bore, 10 mm (0.4 in) from the bottom and at the mid-point. At each of the three stations, measure in-line with the crankshaft and at right angles to it. If the bores are worn beyond the limit, they will need to be rebored and new pistons fitted.

5 If one bore is oversize, all four must be rebored and a new set of pistons fitted, otherwise the engine will not be balanced. Connecting rods must only be fitted as complete sets and not be replaced individually.

6 Fit the rings to the pistons and use a feeler gauge to measure the gap between the piston ring and the side of its groove (photo). If the gap is beyond the wear limit, it is more likely that it is the piston groove rather than the ring which has worn, and either a new piston or a proprietary oversize ring will be required. If new piston rings are fitted the wear ridge at the top of the cylinder bore must be removed, or a stepped top ring used..

26 Pistons and connecting rods – reassembly and refitting

1 Heat each piston in hot water, then insert the connecting rod and push in the pin until central. Make sure that the casting marks on the connecting rod and the arrow on the piston crown (photo) are facing the same way, then refit the circlips.

2 Before refitting the piston rings, or fitting new rings, check the gap of each ring in turn in its correct cylinder bore using a piston to push
the ring down the bore, as described in the previous Section. Measure the gap between the ends of the piston ring, using feeler gauges. The gap must be within the limits given in the Specifications.

3 If the piston ring gap is too small, carefully file the piston ring end until the gap is sufficient. Pistons rings are very brittle, so handle them carefully.

4 When fitting piston rings, look for the word TOP etched on one side of the ring and fit this side so that it is towards the piston crown. The outer recessed edge on the centre ring must face the gudgeon pin.

5 Unless the big-end bearing shells are known to be almost new, it is worth fitting a new set when reassembling the engine. Clean the connecting rods and bearing caps thoroughly and fit the bearing shells so that the tang on the bearing engages in the recess in the connecting rod, or cap, and the ends of the bearing are flush with the joint face (photo).

6 To refit the pistons, first space the joints in the piston rings so that they are at 120° intervals. Oil the rings and grooves generously and fit a piston ring compressor over the piston.

7 Oil the cylinder bores and insert the pistons (photo) with the arrow on the piston crown pointing towards the front of the engine. Make sure that the relevant crankpin is at its furthest point from the cylinder.

8 When the piston is pushed in flush with the top of the bore, oil the two bearing halves and the crankshaft journal and guide the connecting rod half-bearing on to the crankpin.

9 Fit the big-end bearing cap, complete with shell, and tighten the nuts to the specified torque wrench setting (photo).

10 Rotate the crankshaft to ensure that everything is free, before fitting the next piston and connecting rod.

11 Using feeler gauges between the machined face of each big-end bearing, and the machined face of the crankshaft web, check the endplay, which should not exceed the maximum amount given in the Specifications.

12 Refit the oil pump (Section 23), timing belt (Section 18), and cylinder head (Section 16).

27 Crankshaft – removal, examination and refitting

1 With the engine removed from the car, remove the pistons and connecting rods, as described in Section 24.

2 Reassemble the big-end bearings to their matching connecting rods to ensure correct refitting.

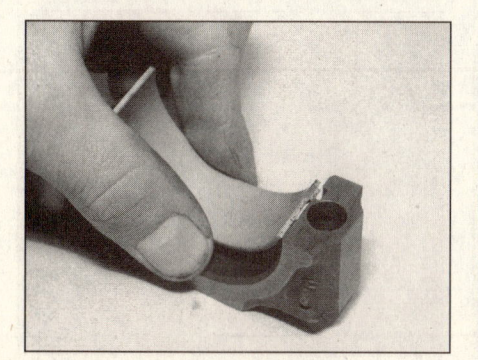

26.5 Fit the bearing shells so that the tang engages the recess in the cap and rod

26.7 Fitting the piston and connecting rods

26.9 Tightening the big-end cap nuts

1•20 Four-cylinder engines

27.5A Removing a crankshaft main bearing cap

27.5B Removing the crankshaft

27.6 Using Plastigage to check the crankshaft journal clearances

3 Remove the crankshaft oil seals complete with housings, as described in Section 22.

4 Check that each main bearing cap is numbered for position.

5 Remove the bolts from each bearing cap in turn, then remove the caps and lift out the crankshaft (photos).

6 If the bearings are not being renewed, ensure that each half-bearing shell is identified so that it is put back in the same place from which it was removed. This also applies to the thrust washers if fitted – see paragraph 7. If the engine has done a high mileage and it is suspected that the crankshaft requires attention, it is best to seek the opinion of an Audi dealer or crankshaft re-finishing specialist for advice on the need for regrinding. Unless the bearing shells (and thrust washers if applicable) are known to be almost new, it is worth fitting a new set when the crankshaft is refitted. If available, Plastigage may be used to check the running clearance of the existing bearings (photo).

7 Clean the crankcase recesses and bearing caps thoroughly and fit the bearing shells so that the tang on the bearing engages in the recess in the crankcase or bearing cap. Make sure that the shells fitted to the crankcase have oil holes, and that these line up with the drillings in the bearing housings. The shells fitted to the bearing caps do not have oil holes, with the exception of No 4 bearing cap which does. Note that the bearing shells of the centre bearing (No 3) may either be flanged to act as thrust washers, or may have separate thrust washers. These should be fitted oil groove outwards as shown. Fit the bearing shells so that the ends of the bearing are flush with the joint face (photos).

8 Oil the bearings and journals, then locate the crankshaft in the crankcase.

9 Fit the main bearing caps (with centre main bearing thrust washers if applicable) in their correct positions.

10 Fit the bolts to the bearing caps and tighten the bolts of the centre cap to the specified torque (photo), then check that the crankshaft rotates freely.

11 Working out from the centre, tighten the

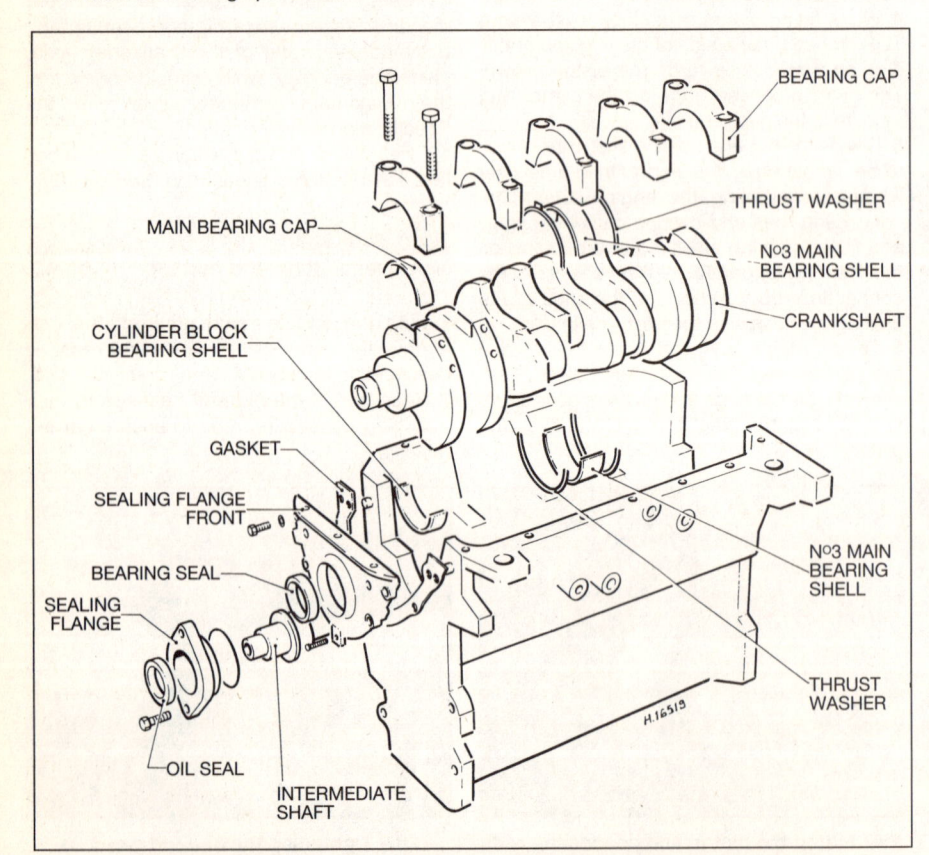

Fig. 1.13 Exploded view of the crankshaft and crankcase (Sec 27)

BEARING CAP
THRUST WASHER
N°3 MAIN BEARING SHELL
MAIN BEARING CAP
CRANKSHAFT
CYLINDER BLOCK BEARING SHELL
GASKET
SEALING FLANGE FRONT
BEARING SEAL
N°3 MAIN BEARING SHELL
SEALING FLANGE
THRUST WASHER
OIL SEAL
INTERMEDIATE SHAFT

27.7A Fitting the flanged type centre main bearing to the cap

27.7B Fitting the flanged type centre main bearing to the crankcase . . .

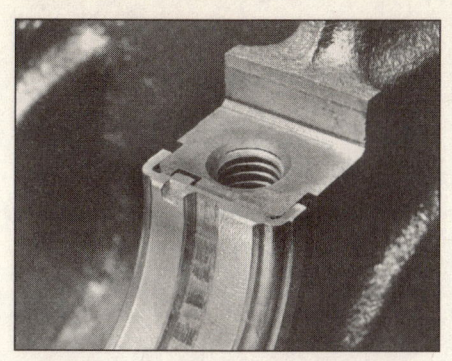

27.7C . . . ensuring that the ends of the bearing are flush with the joint face

27.7D Fitting the alternative type centre main bearing to the crankcase . . .

27.7E . . . together with the thrust washers

27.10 Tightening the main bearing cap bolts

27.12 Checking the crankshaft endplay

27.13A Location of the spigot needle roller bearing in the end of the crankshaft

27.13B Checking the spigot bearing fitted position

remaining bearing caps in turn, checking that the crankshaft rotates freely after each bearing has been tightened.

12 Check that the endplay of the crankshaft is within specification, by inserting feeler gauges between the crankshaft and the centre bearing thrust face/washer while levering the crankshaft first in one direction and then in the other (photo).

13 The rear end of the crankshaft carries a needle roller bearing (photo) which supports the front end of the gearbox input shaft. Inspect the bearing for obvious signs of wear and damage. If the gearbox has been removed and dismantled, fit the input shaft into the bearing to see if there is excessive clearance. If the bearing requires renewing, insert a hook behind the bearing and pull it out of the end of the crankshaft. Install the new bearing with the lettering on the end of the bearing outwards. Press it in until the end of the bearing is 1.5 mm (0.059 in) below the face of the flywheel flange (photo).

14 Fit new crankshaft oil seals (Section 22) then refit the pistons and connecting rods, as described in Section 26.

28 Engine mountings – removal and refitting

1 Jack up the front of the car and support it on stands.
2 Support the engine under the sump using a trolley jack.
3 Undo the bolts securing the mounting to the body, and the through-bolt and nut securing the mounting to the engine support brackets. If working on the right-hand mounting it will be necessary to remove the cover plate to gain access to the mounting.
4 Raise the engine slightly, then remove the mountings from their locations.
5 Refitting is a reversal of removal.

Part B – Five-cylinder engines

29 General description

The engine is of five-cylinder, in-line, overhead camshaft type, mounted conventionally at the front of the car. The crankshaft is of six-bearing type and the No 4 (from front) main bearing shells incorporate flanged thrust washers to control crankshaft endfloat (endplay). The camshaft is driven by a toothed belt from the crankshaft sprocket, and the belt also drives the water pump mounted on the left-hand side of the block. A gear on the rear of the camshaft drives the distributor, and on carburettor models the camshaft also drives the fuel pump.

The valves are operated from the camshaft through bucket type tappets, and valve clearances are adjusted by the use of shims located in the top of the tappets, or self-adjusting with hydraulic tappets.

The engine has a full-flow lubrication system. A gear and crescent type oil pump is mounted on the front of the crankshaft. The oil filter is of the cartridge type, mounted on the right-hand side of the cylinder block.

1•22 Five-cylinder engines

30.1A Engine oil drain plug . . .

30.1B . . . and oil filter location

30 Maintenance and inspection

1 Refer to Section 2 of this Chapter, with the following exceptions:
(a) The oil drain plug is located on the right-hand side of the sump, and the oil filter is located on the right-hand side of the cylinder block (photos)
(b) Valve clearance adjustment is not necessary on engines with hydraulic tappets
(c) The timing belt adjustment procedure is contained in Section 47
(d) On Turbo models there is an additional oil filter for the turbocharger

31 Major operations possible with the engine in the car

The following operations can be carried out without having to remove the engine from the car:
(a) Removal and servicing of the cylinder head and camshaft
(b) Removal of the timing belt and gears
(c) Removal of the flywheel or driveplate (after first removing the transmission)
(d) Removal of the sump (after first lowering the subframe)
(e) Removal of the oil pump
(f) Removal of the pistons and connecting rods

32 Major operations requiring engine removal

The following operation can only be carried out after removal of the engine from the car:
Removal of crankshaft and main bearings

33 Method of engine removal

The engine must be disconnected from the transmission, then lifted from the car.

34 Engine – removal and refitting

All models except Turbo

1 Remove the bonnet, as described in Chapter 11 and stand it on cardboard or rags in a safe place.
2 Disconnect the battery negative lead.
3 Remove the radiator, as described in Chapter 2.
4 Remove the radiator grille and the front bumper upper trim strip, as described in Chapter 11.
5 Remove the distributor cap and plug leads.
6 Refer to Chapter 3, and remove the air cleaner and, where applicable, the air intake hoses at the front of the engine.
7 Refer to Chapter 10 and remove the power-assisted steering pump, but leave the hydraulic pipes connected. Secure the pump to one side without straining the hoses.
8 On models equipped with air conditioning, remove the compressor, as described in Chapter 11, leaving the refrigerant hoses connected. Secure the compressor to one side without straining the hoses.
9 Identify all wiring for location using masking tape, then disconnect those affecting engine removal. These include, where applicable:
Wiring to the oil pressure switches (photo), temperature sender (photo), distributor (photo), coil, gearchange indicator, warm-up valve, thermo-switches, idle stabiliser (photo), thermotime switch, cold start valve (photo), throttle switch (photo), intake temperature

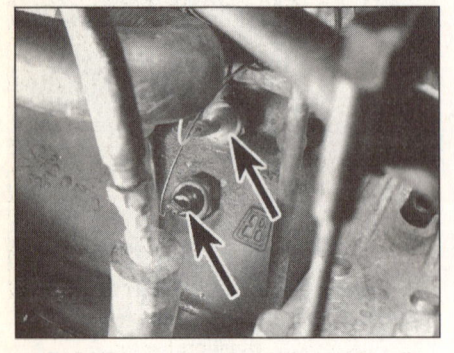

34.9A Disconnect the wiring at the oil pressure switches (arrowed) . . .

34.9B . . . temperature sender . . .

34.9C . . . distributor . . .

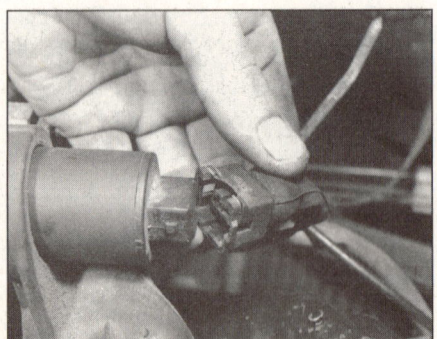

34.9D . . . idle stabiliser . . .

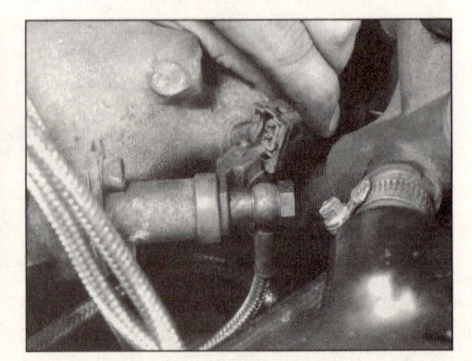

34.9E . . . cold start valve

Five-cylinder engines 1•23

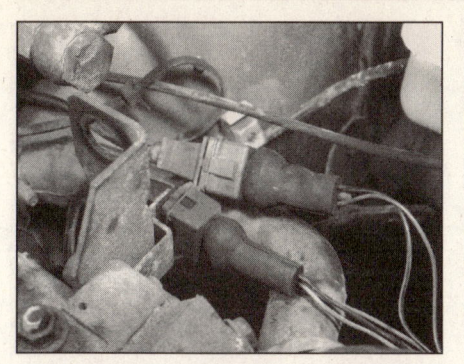

34.9F . . . and throttle switch

34.10A Slacken the hose clips and cable clamp (arrowed) . . .

34.10B . . . and remove the idle stabiliser assembly

sender, ignition timing sender, rpm sender, automatic choke, inlet manifold preheater. and additional emission control components (see Chapter 3)

10 On fuel injection models, slacken the hose clips and lift away the complete idle stabiliser valve and hose assembly (photos).
11 Working clockwise around the engine, disconnect all coolant and heater hoses and pipes which affect engine removal (photo).
12 Refer to Chapter 3, and disconnect the accelerator cable.
13 On automatic transmission models, refer to Chapters 3 and 7, disconnect the throttle and accelerator pedal cables and linkage.
14 On fuel injection models, slacken the clip and withdraw the air duct from the throttle valve housing (photo).
15 Identify all fuel and vacuum hoses using masking tape, then disconnect those affecting engine removal. These will include, where applicable:

Carburettor models: *Fuel line at fuel pump, return line at return valve, vacuum pipes at vacuum reservoir, econometer, and distributor*

Fuel injection models: *Fuel hoses at the metering distributor (photo), cold start valve (photo) and warm-up valve (photo), vacuum hoses at warm – up valve, econometer, throttle valve housing (photo) and distributor (photo), also any additional emission control components (see Chapter 3)*

34.11 Disconnect the coolant and heater hoses and pipes

34.14 Withdraw the air duct from the throttle valve housing

34.15A Disconnect the fuel hoses at the metering distributor . . .

34.15B . . . cold start valve . . .

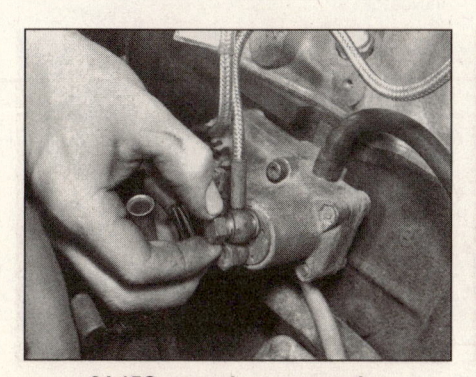

34.15C . . . and warm-up valve

34.15D Disconnect the vacuum hoses at the throttle valve housing . . .

34.15E . . . and distributor

1•24 Five-cylinder engines

34.18 Disconnect the exhaust front pipe at the manifold

34.19 Remove the engine front mounting

34.22 Disconnect the engine earth strap

16 Disconnect the earth braid at the rear of the valve cover.
17 Refer to Chapter 12 and remove the alternator and starter motor.
18 Disconnect the exhaust front pipe at the manifold and transmission bracket (photo).
19 Remove the engine front mounting, and the body-mounted bracket (photo).
20 On automatic transmission models, unscrew the torque converter-to-driveplate bolts, while holding the starter ring gear stationary with a screwdriver. It will be necessary to rotate the engine to position the bolts in the starter aperture, using a socket on the crankshaft pulley bolt.
21 Using an Allen key, unscrew the nuts and lift off the timing belt upper cover. Recover the distance pieces.
22 Disconnect the clutch cable from the release lever and left-hand engine mounting (where applicable) and disconnect the engine earth strap from the mounting (photo).
23 Remove the cover plate over the right-hand engine mounting (photo).
24 Connect a hoist and take the weight of the engine. The hoist should be positioned centrally over the engine.
25 Support the weight of the transmission with a trolley jack.
26 Unscrew the engine-to-transmission bolts, noting the position of any brackets or cable supports.
27 Unscrew the engine mounting bracket-to-mounting through-bolts (photo), then lift the engine slightly and remove the left-hand mounting bracket (photo).
28 Lift the engine and pull it off the transmission. On automatic transmission models, make sure that the torque converter remains fully engaged with the transmission splines.
29 Manipulate the engine as necessary, and lift it from the engine compartment, then lower the unit to the floor (photo).

Turbo models

30 Carry out the operations described in paragraphs 1 to 5.
31 Refer to Chapter 11 and remove the front bumper.
32 Refer to Chapter 10 and remove the power-assisted steering pump, but leave the hydraulic pipes connected. Secure the pump to one side without straining the hoses.
33 Disconnect the wiring at the thermo-switch.
34 Disconnect the wiring at the thermotime switch, oil pressure switches and warm-up valve.
35 Detach the warm-up valve vacuum hose, then undo the two bolts and move the valve to one side.
36 On automatic transmission models, disconnect the transmission pushrod at the bellcrank lever.
37 Disconnect the wiring connectors for the engine speed sender, reference mark sender, and knock sensor at the bulkhead bracket.
38 Disconnect the wiring at the distributor and ignition coil.
39 Remove the injector cooling fan duct over the valve cover.
40 Disconnect the injector cooling fan wiring, then remove the fan assembly.
41 Remove the engine speed and reference mark sender support bracket.
42 Disconnect the engine earth strap at the left-hand engine mounting.
43 Detach the coolant and heater hoses at the coolant pipe, then remove the pipe from the engine.
44 Disconnect the vacuum hose at the cruise control system.
45 Disconnect the wiring connectors at the cold start valve and idle stabiliser switch.
46 Unscrew the earth lead and bracket at the throttle linkage relay.
47 Detach the vacuum hose at the electronic ignition control unit and at the gearchange indicator.

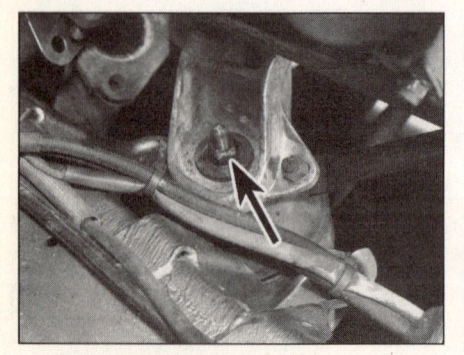

34.23 Remove the engine mounting cover plate

34.27A Unscrew the engine mounting through-bolts (arrowed) . . .

34.27B . . . then remove the left-hand mounting bracket

34.29 Removing the engine

Five-cylinder engines 1•25

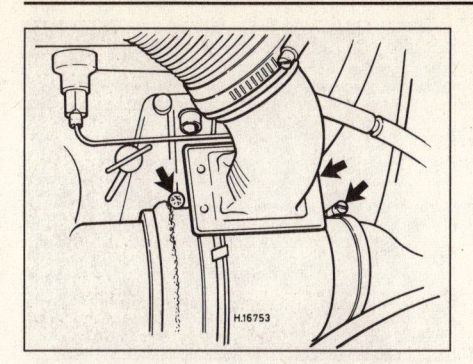

Fig. 1.14 Injector cooling fan attachments – Turbo models (Sec 34)

48 Remove the cold start valve from the manifold, leaving the fuel line connected.
49 Disconnect the cruise control linkage pushrod and accelerator cable at the throttle valve housing. Release the cable from its supports.
50 Disconnect the throttle valve switch wiring connector, and release the wiring from the cable clips.
51 Remove the air temperature sensor from the throttle valve housing. Seal the manifold opening, and cover the sensor with a protective cap.
52 Disconnect the wiring at the injector cooling fan thermo-switch on the waste gate heat deflector plate. Release the wiring from the cable clips.
53 Firmly pull each injector out of the cylinder head, with fuel hose still attached, then move all the fuel lines and injectors clear of the engine.
54 Slacken the clips and remove the air duct from the airflow sensor and intake tube.
55 Unclip the air cleaner cover and remove it, complete with the intake tube.
56 Remove the connecting hose from the intercooler to the throttle body.
57 Disconnect the idle stabilizer hose at the intercooler, remove the hose between intercooler and turbo, then remove the intercooler.
58 Disconnect the exhaust front pipe at the turbo unit flange.
59 Remove the cover plate over the right-hand engine mounting.
60 Disconnect the exhaust corrugated branch pipe at the front pipe flange.
61 Disconnect the exhaust front pipe at the intermediate pipe flange and transmission support, then remove the pipe from the car.
62 From under the car, remove the alternator air duct.
63 Remove the alternator adjustment and mounting bolts, lift the unit away, and support it clear of the engine with the wiring still attached.
64 Undo the starter motor bolts, withdraw the starter, and support it clear of the engine with the wiring still attached.
65 Unscrew the oil cooler hoses at the oil filter housing.
66 On models equipped with air conditioning, remove the compressor, as

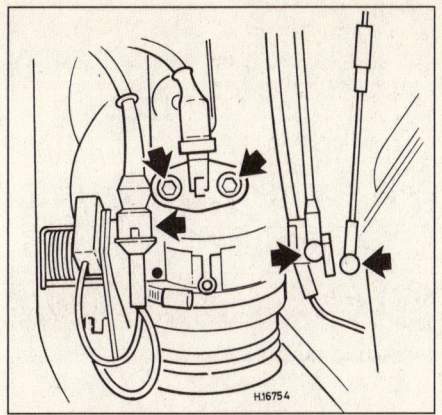

Fig. 1.15 Air temperature sensor, throttle valve switch and cruise control attachments at the throttle valve housing – Turbo models (Sec 34)

described in Chapter 11, leaving the refrigerant hoses connected. Secure the compressor to one side without straining the hoses, then remove the compressor bracket.
67 On automatic transmission models, unscrew the torque converter-to-driveplate bolts while holding the starter ring gear stationary with a screwdriver. It will be necessary to rotate the engine to position the bolts in the starter aperture, using a socket on the crankshaft pulley bolt.
68 Connect a hoist and take the weight of the engine. The hoist should be positioned centrally over the engine.
69 Support the weight of the transmission with a trolley jack.
70 Unscrew the engine-to-transmission bolts noting the position of any brackets or cable supports.
71 Unscrew the engine mounting bracket-to-mounting through-bolts, then remove the left-hand mounting bracket.
72 Lift the engine and pull it off the transmission. On automatic transmission models, make sure that the torque converter remains fully engaged with the transmission splines.
73 Manipulate the engine as necessary and lift it from the engine compartment, then lower the unit to the floor.

Refitting – all models

74 Refitting is a reversal of the removal procedure, but smear the manual transmission input shaft and release bearing face with molybdenum disulphide grease before fitting. Ensure that all the engine and transmission mountings are fitted free of strain, and tighten all nuts and bolts to the specified torque. Refit, and where applicable adjust, all engine related components and systems with reference to the Chapters concerned. Ensure that the engine is filled with oil and that the cooling system is topped up before starting the engine.

35 Engine dismantling – general

Refer to Section 7 of this Chapter.

36 Ancillary components – removal and refitting

Refer to Section 8 of this Chapter, with the following exception:
Oil filter cartridge (Section 30 of this Chapter)

37 Camshaft and tappets – removal

Note: *If the engine is still in the car, first carry out the following operations:*
(a) Disconnect the battery negative lead
(b) On carburettor models remove the air cleaner and fuel pump (Chapter 3)
(c) Remove the distributor (Chapter 4)
(d) Remove the upper radiator cowl
(e) Remove the alternator, air conditioning and power-assisted steering drivebelts as applicable (Chapter 12, 11 and 10 respectively)
(f) Disconnect all relevant wiring, cables and hoses
(g) On Turbo models remove the injector cooling fan duct over the valve cover, the cruise control linkage and the intercooler (Chapter 3)

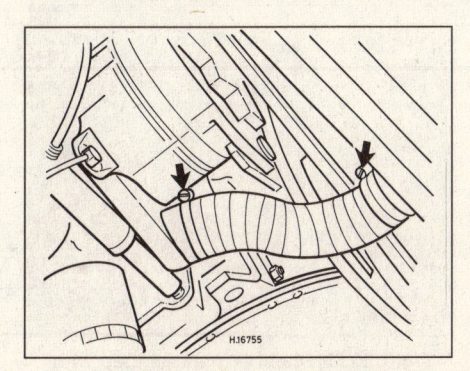

Fig. 1.16 Alternator air duct location and attachments – Turbo models (Sec 34)

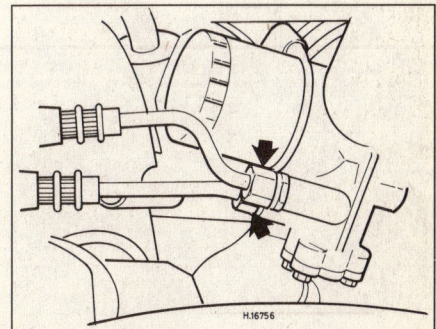

Fig. 1.17 Oil cooler hose connections at the oil filter housing (Sec 34)

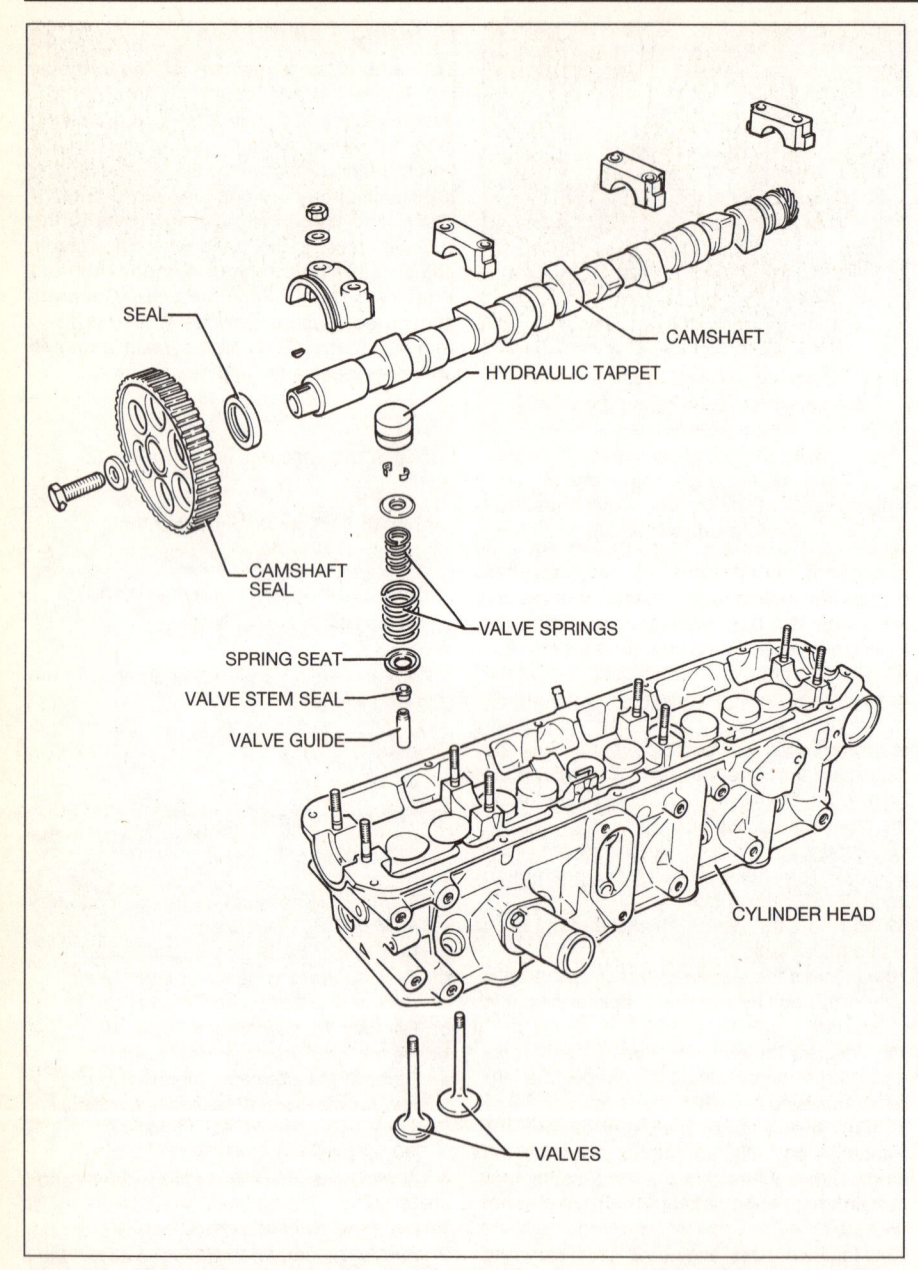

1•26 Five-cylinder engines

Fig. 1.18 Exploded view of the cylinder head and valve gear (Sec 37)

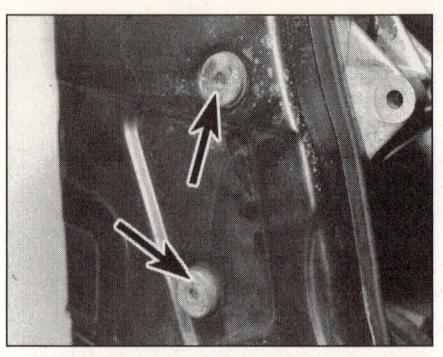

Labels: SEAL, CAMSHAFT, HYDRAULIC TAPPET, CAMSHAFT SEAL, VALVE SPRINGS, SPRING SEAT, VALVE STEM SEAL, VALVE GUIDE, CYLINDER HEAD, VALVES

37.2A Unscrew the timing belt cover nuts (arrowed) and remove the cover . . .

37.2B . . . then remove the distance pieces (arrowed)

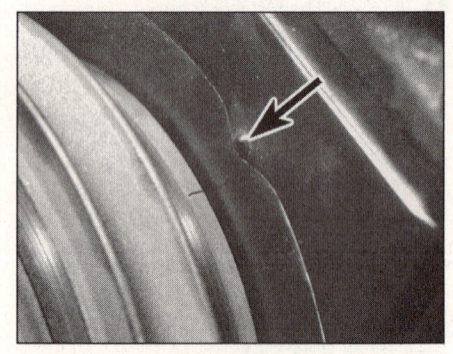

37.3 Notch on crankshaft pulley aligned with pip on timing belt lower cover (arrowed)

Fig. 1.19 Crankshaft pulley notch aligned with pointer on oil pump housing – arrowed (Sec 37)

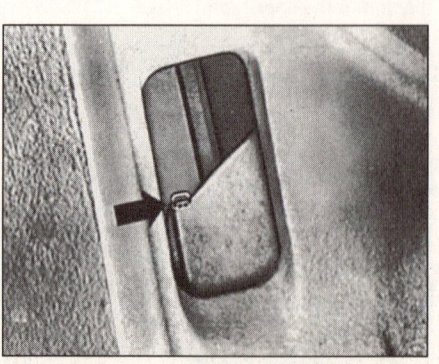

Fig. 1.20 Flywheel O mark aligned with bellhousing pointer (Sec 37)

Fig. 1.21 Camshaft gear indentation (arrowed) aligned with upper surface of valve cover gasket (Sec 37)

Five-cylinder engines 1•27

37.5 Removing the timing belt from the camshaft gear. Belt marked to show fitted running direction

Fig. 1.22 Using a wide-bladed screwdriver to hold the camshaft gear stationary (Sec 37)

37.7 Camshaft gear Woodruff key (arrowed)

1 Unscrew the nuts and lift off the valve cover, together with the reinforcement strips and gaskets. Note the location of the HT lead holder.
2 Using an Allen key, unscrew the nuts and lift off the timing belt upper cover. Recover the distance pieces (photos).
3 Using a socket on the crankshaft pulley bolt, turn the engine so that the piston in No 1 cylinder is at TDC on its compression stroke. The notch in the crankshaft pulley must be in line with the pip on the timing belt lower cover (photo), or the pointer on the oil pump housing – alternatively the O mark (TDC) on the flywheel/driveplate must be aligned with the pointer in the bellhousing aperture. Both No 1 cylinder valves must be closed (ie cam peaks away from the tappets) and the indentation on the rear of the camshaft gear in line with the upper surface of the valve cover gasket (temporarily refit the gasket and valve cover, if necessary)
4 Loosen the water pump mounting and adjustment bolts and rotate the pump clockwise to release the tension on the timing belt.
5 Remove the timing belt from the camshaft gear and move it to one side (photo).
6 Unscrew the centre bolt from the camshaft gear while holding the gear stationary with a bar through one of the holes or using a wide-bladed screwdriver, as shown in Fig. 1.22.

7 Withdraw the gear from the camshaft and extract the Woodruff key (photo).
8 Check that each bearing cap has its number stamped on it; if not, make an identifying mark to ensure that each cap is put back where it was originally. Note that the caps are offset and can only be fitted one way round.
9 *It is important that the camshaft is removed exactly as described so that there is no danger of it becoming distorted.* Loosen one of the nuts on bearing cap No 2 about two turns and then loosen the diagonally opposite nut on bearing cap No 4 about two turns. Repeat the operations on the other nut of bearing cap No 2 and bearing cap No 4. Continue the sequence until the nuts are free, then remove them. Loosen and remove the nuts of bearing caps Nos 1 and 3 using a similar diagonal sequence.
10 Lift the bearing caps off and lift the camshaft out (photo). Discard the oil seal.
11 Withdraw each tappet in turn (photo) and mark its position (1 to 10 numbering from the timing belt end of the engine) using adhesive tape or a box with divisions. Take care to keep the adjustment shims with their respective tappets (where fitted). On engines with hydraulic tappets, store the tappets upside down once they have been removed from the engine.

38 Cylinder head removal – engine in car

All models except Turbo

1 Disconnect the battery negative lead.
2 Drain the cooling system, as described in Chapter 2.
3 Remove the radiator grille (Chapter 11) and the upper radiator cowl.
4 Remove the air cleaner, as described in Chapter 3, and the front intake ducts on fuel injection models.
5 Refer to Chapter 12 and remove the alternator drivebelt.
6 On models equipped with air conditioning, remove the compressor, as described in Chapter 11, leaving the refrigerant hoses connected. Secure the compressor to one side without straining the hoses.
7 Refer to Chapter 10 and remove the power-assisted steering pump, but leave the hydraulic pipes connected. Secure the pump to one side without straining the hoses.
8 Remove the radiator top hose and any heater hose connections or clips likely to impede cylinder head removal.
9 Identify all fuel and vacuum hoses using masking tape and disconnect those affecting

37.10 Removing the camshaft

37.11 Removing a tappet

38.9A Disconnect the fuel lines at the metering distributor . . .

1•28 Five-cylinder engines

389B . . . cold start valve . . .

38.9C . . . and warm-up valve

38.10A Disconnect the wiring at the temperature sender and . . .

cylinder head removal. These will include, where applicable:

Carburettor models: *Fuel lines at fuel pump, return line at return valve, vacuum pipes at vacuum reservoir, econometer and distributor*

Fuel injection models: *Fuel hoses at the metering distributor (photo), cold start valve (photo) and warm-up valve (photo), vacuum hoses at econometer, throttle valve housing and distributor as well as any additional emission control components (see Chapter 3)*

10 Identify all wiring for location using masking tape, then disconnect those affecting cylinder head removal. These will include, where applicable:

Wiring to temperature sender (photo), distributor, coil, gearchange indicator, thermo-switches, idle stabiliser, thermotime switch, cold start valve, throttle switch (photo), intake temperature sender, automatic choke, inlet manifold preheater and additional emission control components (see Chapter 3)

11 Pull off the spark plug HT leads, remove the HT lead holder from the valve cover and remove the leads and distributor cap (photo).

12 On fuel injection models, slacken the hose clips and lift away the complete idle stabiliser valve and hose assembly (photo).

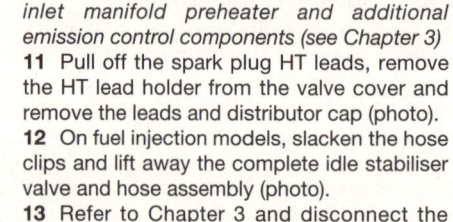

13 Refer to Chapter 3 and disconnect the accelerator cable and, where applicable, the cruise control linkage.

14 On automatic transmission models refer to Chapters 3 and 7 and disconnect the throttle and accelerator pedal cables and linkage.

15 Disconnect the earth braid at the rear of the valve cover.

16 On fuel injection models, slacken the clip and withdraw the air duct from the throttle valve housing.

17 Disconnect the exhaust front pipe at the manifold and transmission bracket.

18 Using an Allen key, unscrew the nuts and lift off the timing belt upper cover. Remove the distance pieces (photo).

19 Unscrew the nuts and lift off the valve cover, together with the reinforcement strips and gaskets (photo).

20 Using a socket on the crankshaft pulley bolt, turn the engine so that the piston in No 1 cylinder is at TDC on its compression stroke. The notch in the crankshaft pulley must be in line with the pip on the timing belt lower cover or the pointer on the oil pump housing – alternatively the O mark (TDC) on the flywheel/driveplate must be aligned with the pointer in the bellhousing aperture. Both No 1 cylinder valves must be closed (ie cam peaks away from the tappets) and the indentation on the rear of the camshaft gear in line with the upper surface of the valve cover gasket (temporarily refit the gasket and valve cover, if necessary). The distributor rotor arm should be pointing to the No 1 cylinder segment in the distributor cap (temporarily refit the cap to check).

21 Loosen the water pump mounting and adjustment bolts, and rotate the pump

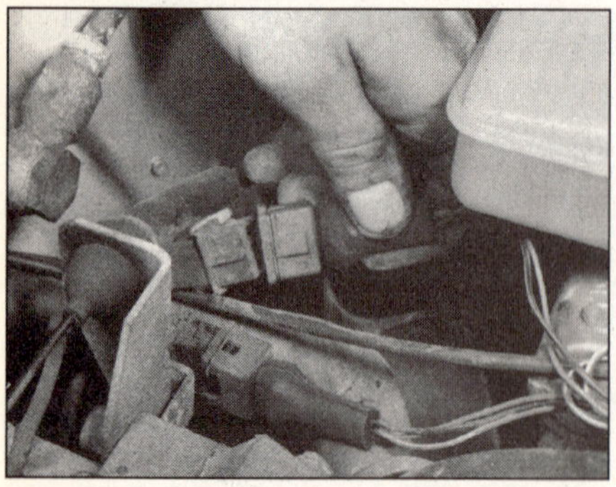

38.10B . . . throttle switch

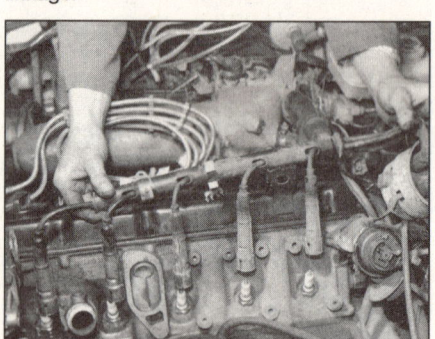

38.11 Removing the distributor cap and leads

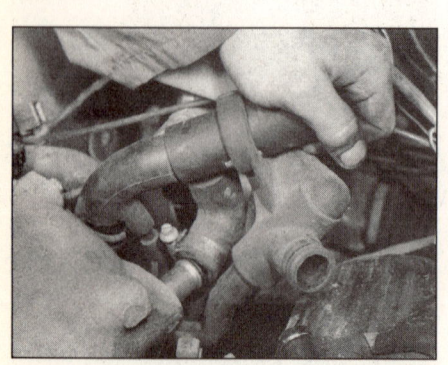

38.12 Removing the idle stabiliser valve assembly

38.18 Removing the timing belt upper cover

38.19 Lift off the valve cover and reinforcement strips

Five-cylinder engines 1•29

clockwise to release the tension on the timing belt.
22 Remove the timing belt from the camshaft gear and move it to one side.
23 Unscrew the centre bolt from the camshaft gear while holding the gear stationary with a bar through one of the holes or using a wide bladed screwdriver, as shown in Fig. 1.22.
24 Withdraw the gear from the camshaft and extract the Woodruff key.
25 Using two nuts locked together, unscrew the timing belt upper cover retaining stud from the cylinder head (photo). Also remove the bolt securing the inner cover to the right-hand side of the head.
26 Using a splined key, unscrew the cylinder head bolts a turn at a time in the reverse order to that shown in Fig. 1.25.
27 With all the bolts removed, ease the timing belt inner cover forwards to clear the camshaft, and lift the cylinder head from the block (photo). If it is stuck, tap it free with a hide or plastic mallet. Remove the gasket.
28 If required, remove the cylinder head ancillary components with reference to the Chapters concerned.

Turbo models

29 Carry out the operations described in paragraphs 1 to 8 with the exception of paragraph 4.
30 Identify all fuel and vacuum hoses using masking tape, and disconnect those affecting cylinder head removal. These will include, where applicable:
Fuel hoses at the metering distributor, cold start valve and warm-up valve, vacuum hoses at cruise control, econometer, throttle valve housing, and distributor, also any additional emission control components (see Chapter 3)
31 Identify all wiring for location using masking tape, and disconnect those affecting cylinder head removal. These will include, where applicable:
Wiring to temperature sender, distributor, coil, gearchange indicator, thermo-switch, idle stabliser, thermotime switch, cold start valve, throttle valve switch and injector cooling fan thermo-switch, also any additional emission control components (see Chapter 3)
32 Refer to Chapter 3 and disconnect the accelerator cable and the cruise control linkage.
33 On automatic transmission models refer to Chapters 3 and 7 and disconnect the throttle and accelerator pedal cables and linkage.
34 Pull off the spark plug HT leads, remove the HT lead holder from the valve cover, and remove the leads and distributor cap.
35 Remove the injector cooling fan duct over the valve cover.
36 Remove the air temperature sensor from the throttle valve housing. Seal the manifold opening, and cover the sensor with a protective cap.

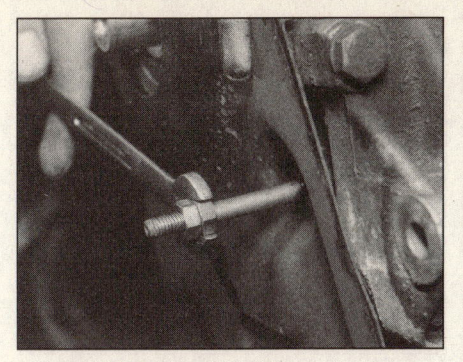

38.25 Unscrew the timing belt cover retaining stud

38.27 Removing the cylinder head

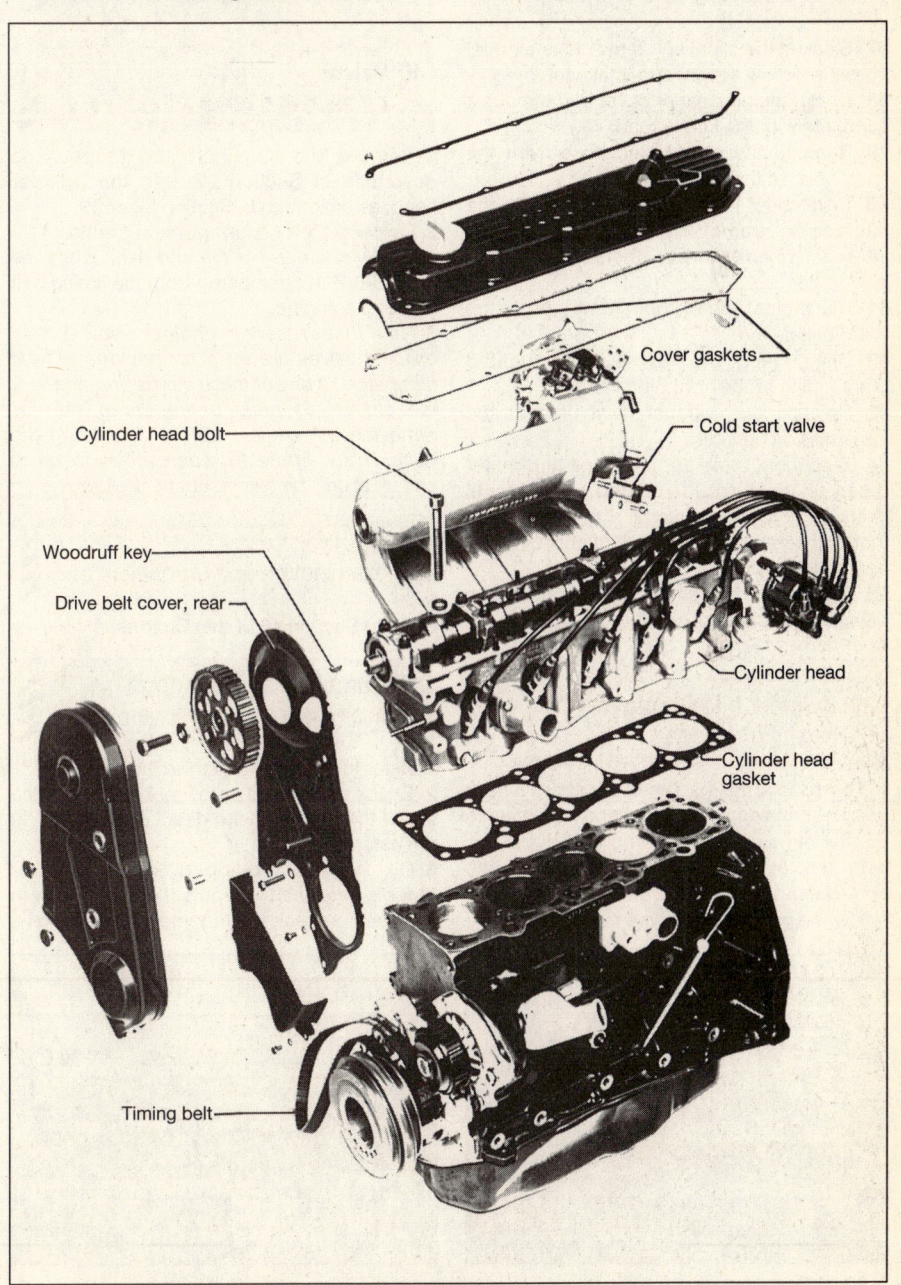

Fig. 1.23 Exploded view of the cylinder head and related components (Sec 38)

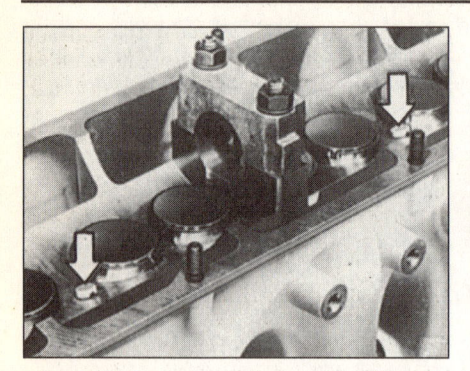

1•30 Five-cylinder engines

Fig. 1.24 Correct position of the oil spray jets (arrowed) in the cylinder head (Sec 42)

44.1A Locate a new gasket on the block . . .

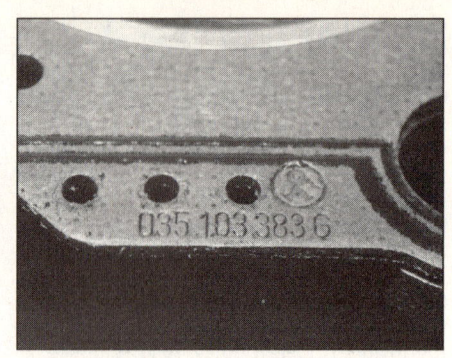

44.1 B . . . with the part number uppermost . . .

37 Slacken the clips, and remove the air duct from the airflow sensor and intake tube.
38 Unclip the air cleaner cover and remove it complete with the intake tube.
39 Remove the connecting hose from the intercooler to the throttle body.
40 Disconnect the idle stabiliser hose at the intercooler, remove the hose between intercooler and turbo, then remove the intercooler.
41 Disconnect the exhaust front pipe at the turbo unit flange.
42 Disconnect the exhaust corrugated branch pipe at the front pipe flange.
43 Release the exhaust front pipe at the transmission bracket.
44 Disconnect any additional oil and water pipes to the turbo or related components likely to impede removal. The turbo and manifolds remain attached to the cylinder head during removal.
45 Carry out the remaining operations as described in paragraphs 18 to 28 inclusive.

39 Cylinder head removal – engine on bench

The procedure for removing the cylinder head with the engine on the bench is similar to that for removal when the engine is in the car, with the exception of disconnecting the controls and services. Refer to Section 38 and follow the procedure given as applicable.

40 Valves – removal and renovation

1 Remove the camshaft and tappets, as described in Section 37, and the cylinder head. as described in Section 38 or 39.
2 Follow the procedure given in Section 11 – inlet valves are 2-4-5-7-9 and exhaust valves are 1-3-6-8-10, numbered from the timing belt end of the engine.
3 *Note that on certain engines sodium filled exhaust valves are used for reasons of heat dissipation. If any of these valves are renewed, the old valves must be rendered safe by removing the sodium before discarding the valve. This is a potentially dangerous operation and must only be carried out by an Audi dealer.*

41 Cylinder head – examination and renovation

Refer to Section 12 of this Chapter.

42 Camshaft and bearings – examination and renovation

1 Refer to Section 13 of this Chapter.
2 Check that the oil spray jets located in the top of the cylinder head direct spray at 90° to the camshaft.
3 On engines equipped with hydraulic tappets, renew any tappets that were noisy in service. To check the tappets with the engine installed, run the engine until the cooling fan operates at least once. Increase the engine speed to 2500 rpm for two minutes, then return it to idling speed. Any tappets which are now still noisy should be renewed.

43 Valves – refitting

Refer to Section 14 of this Chapter.

44 Cylinder head – refitting

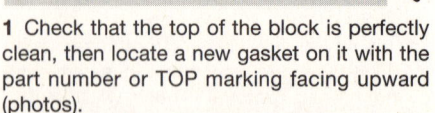

1 Check that the top of the block is perfectly clean, then locate a new gasket on it with the part number or TOP marking facing upward (photos).
2 Check that the cylinder head face is perfectly clean. Insert two long rods, or pieces of dowel into the cylinder head bolt holes at opposite ends of the block, to position the gasket and to give a location for fitting the cylinder head. Lower the head on to the block, remove the guide dowels and insert the bolts and washers. Do not use jointing compound on the cylinder head joint (photo).
3 Tighten the bolts using the sequence shown in Fig. 1.25 in the three stages given in the Specifications to the specified torque.
4 Secure the timing belt inner cover to the cylinder head (where applicable), with the bolt on the right-hand side and the upper cover retaining stud (photo).

44.2 . . . then lower the cylinder head onto the block

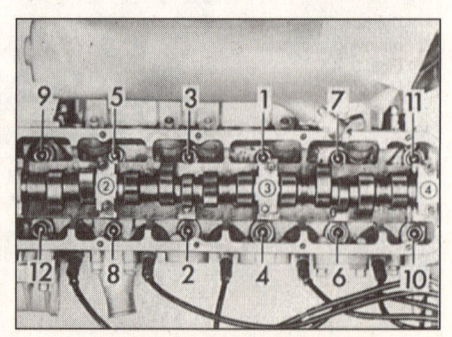

Fig. 1.25 Cylinder head tightening sequence (Sec 44)

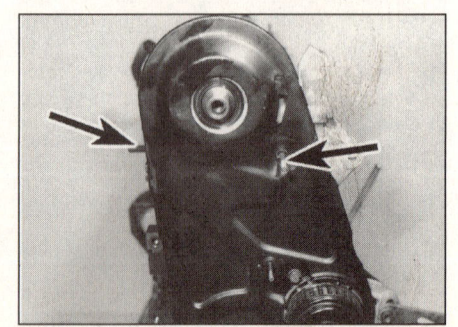

44.4 Timing belt inner cover stud and retaining bolt locations (arrowed)

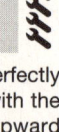

Five-cylinder engines 1•31

44.5 Refit the camshaft gear

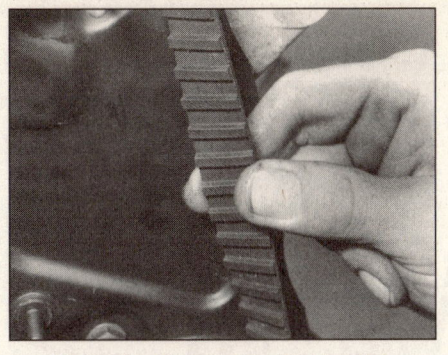

44.10 Checking timing belt tension

5 Fit the Woodruff key in its groove and locate the gear on the end of the camshaft (photo).
6 Fit the centre bolt and spacer and tighten the bolt to the specified torque while holding the gear stationary with a bar through one of the holes, or using a wide-bladed screwdriver as shown in Fig. 1.22.
7 Turn the camshaft gear and align the rear indentation with the upper surface of the valve cover gasket (temporarily locate the gasket on the head).
8 Check that No 1 piston is at TDC with the O mark on the flywheel aligned with the pointer in the bellhousing aperture. The notch in the crankshaft pulley will also be in line with the pointer on the oil pump housing or timing belt lower cover.
9 Locate the timing belt on the crankshaft, camshaft and water pump gears, turn the water pump anti-clockwise to pre-tension the belt, then check that the TDC timing marks are still aligned.
10 With the upper radiator cowl removed (if engine is in the car) use a screwdriver, to turn the water pump anti-clockwise and tension the timing belt until it can just be twisted 90° with the thumb and index finger midway between the camshaft and water pump gears. Tighten the water pump mounting and adjustment bolts when the adjustment is correct (photo).
11 Refit the cylinder head ancillary components with reference to the Chapters concerned.

12 If the engine is in the car, carry out the operations in reverse order described in Section 38, paragraphs 1 to 19 for all models except Turbo and paragraphs 29 to 45 for Turbo models.
13 Adjust the valve clearances, as described in Section 46, on completion, except on engines with hydraulic tappets.

45 Camshaft and tappets – refitting

1 Fit the bucket tappets in their original positions – the adjustment shims on the top of the tappets must be fitted so that the lettering on them is downwards (photos). Lubricate the tappets and the camshaft journals.
2 Lay the camshaft into the lower half of its bearings so that the lowest point of the cams of No 1 cylinder are towards the tappets, then fit the bearing caps in their original positions, making sure that they are the right way round before fitting them over the studs (photo).
3 Fit the nuts to bearing caps Nos 2 and 4 and tighten them in diagonal sequence until the camshaft fully enters its bearings.
4 Fit the nuts to bearing caps 1 and 3, then tighten all the nuts to the specified torque in diagonal sequence.
5 Smear a little oil onto the sealing lip and outer edge of the camshaft oil seal, then locate it open end first in the cylinder head and No 1 camshaft bearing cap.

6 Using a metal tube drive the seal squarely into the cylinder head until flush with the front of the cylinder head – *do not drive it in further otherwise it will block the oil return hole.*
7 Carry out the operations described in paragraphs 5 to 10 inclusive of Section 44.
8 Refit the timing belt upper cover.
9 Check and if necessary adjust the valve clearances, as described in Section 46.
10 Refit the valve cover and reinforcement strips, together with the HT lead holder, new gaskets and seals and tighten the nuts.
11 If the engine is in the car, reverse the preliminary procedures given in Section 37.

46 Valve clearances – checking and adjustment

Refer to Section 17 of this Chapter. The procedure is identical to that for the four-cylinder engine with the following exceptions:
(a) *It is not necessary to remove the timing belt cover*
(b) *From the timing belt end of the engine the inlet valves are numbered 2-4-5-7-9, and the exhaust valves 1-3-6-8-10*
(c) *It is not necessary to adjust the valve clearances on engines with hydraulic tappets*

47 Timing belt and gears – removal and refitting

Note: *If the engine is still in the car, first carry out the following operations:*
(a) *Disconnect the battery negative lead*
(b) *Remove the radiator grille, ventilation grille and upper radiator cowl*
(c) *Remove the alternator, air conditioning and power-assisted steering drivebelts as applicable (Chapters 12, 11 and 10 respectively)*
(d) *On Turbo models remove the intercooler (Chapter 3)*

1 Using Audi tool 2084 lock the vibration damper on the front of the crankshaft stationary, then using Audi tool 2079 loosen the centre bolt. The bolt is tightened to a high torque and it is recommended that these tools are used if at all possible.

45.1A Refit the tappets to their original locations . . .

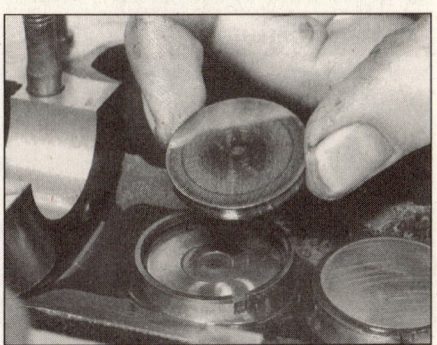

45.1B . . . and fit the shims with their size marking towards the tappet

45.2 Fitting the camshaft bearings

1•32 Five-cylinder engines

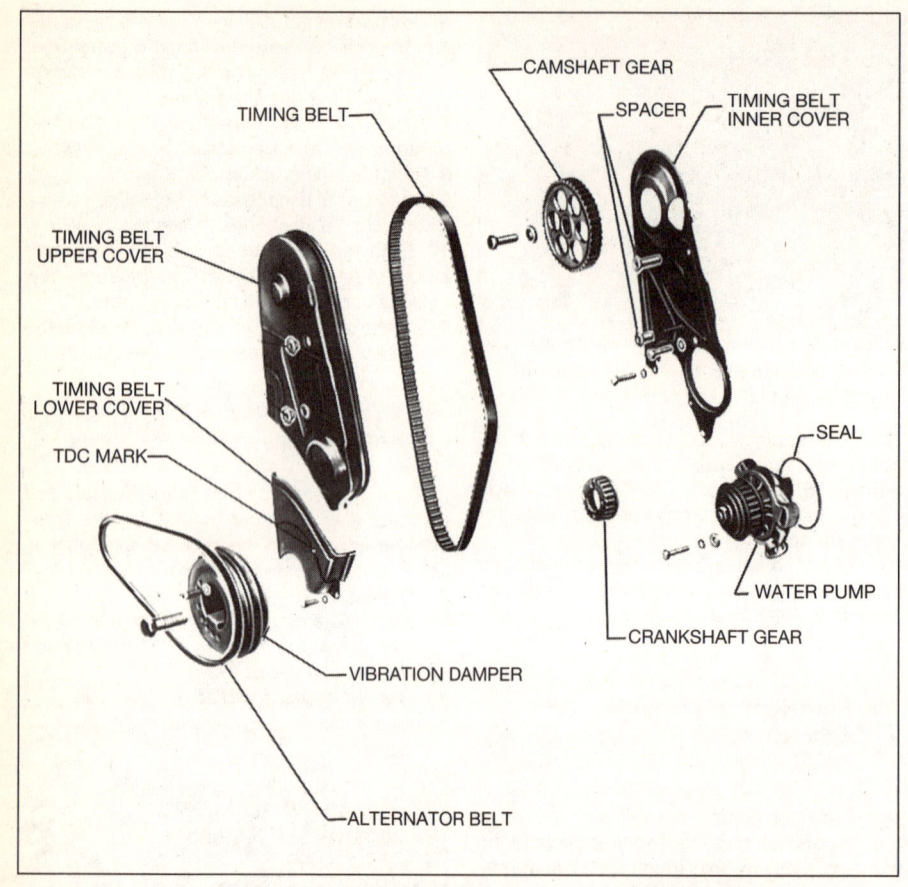

Fig. 1.26 Exploded view of the timing belt and gears (Sec 47)

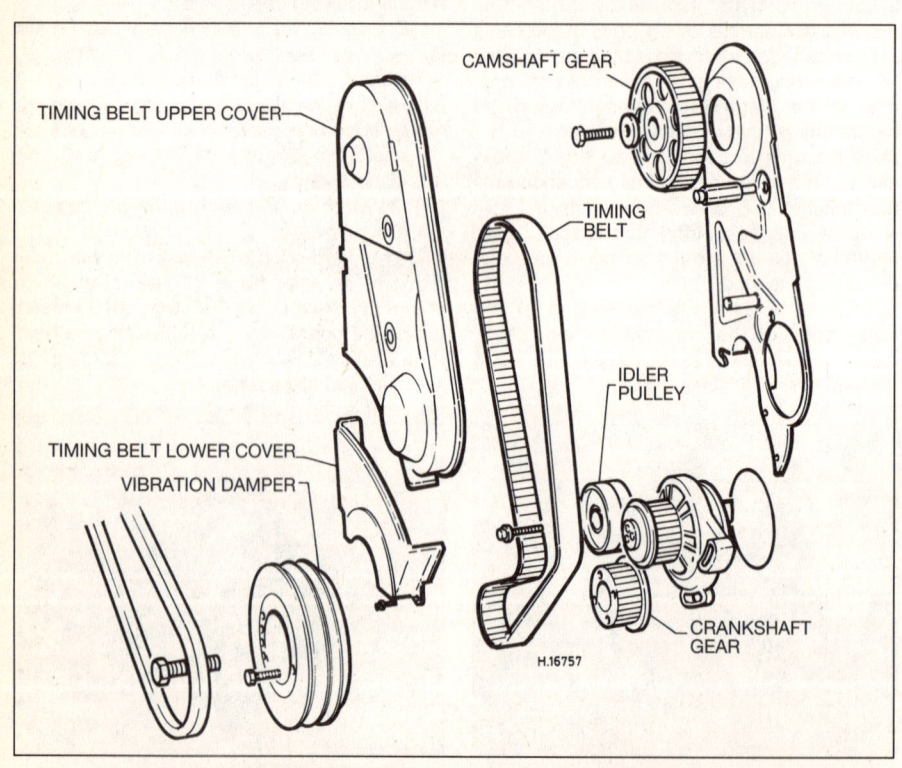

Fig. 1.27 Exploded view of the timing belt, gears and idler pulley fitted to later 1.9 litre engines (Sec 47)

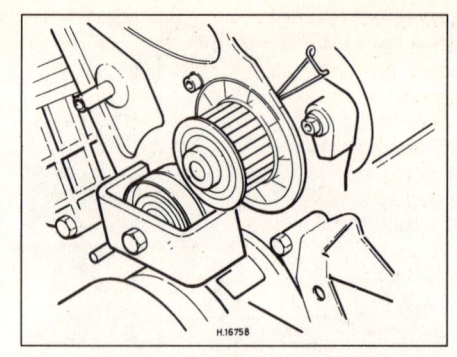

Fig. 1.28 Using a puller to remove the idler pulley – 1.9 litre engines (Sec 47)

47.5 Refitting the crankshaft gear and vibration damper

2 Carry out the operations described in paragraphs 2 to 7 of Section 37, but remove the timing belt upper and lower covers.

3 Unscrew the centre bolt and withdraw the vibration damper, together with the crankshaft gear and timing belt.

4 On later 1.9 litre engines remove the idler pulley by undoing the bolt and withdrawing the pulley using a puller (Figs. 1.27 and 1.28).

5 Locate the timing belt on the crankshaft gear, then refit the gear and vibration damper, followed by the idler pulley (where applicable) (photo)

6 Coat the threads of the centre bolt with a liquid locking agent then insert the bolt and tighten it while holding the crankshaft stationary. *Note that the torque wrench*

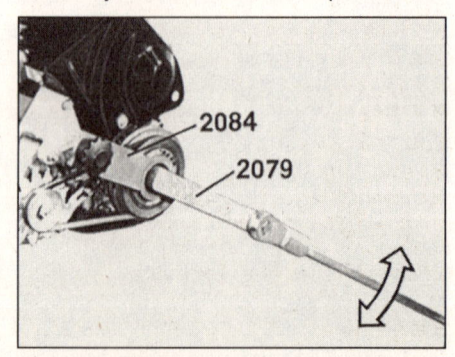

Fig. 1.29 Using tools 2084 and 2079 to unscrew the vibration damper centre bolt (Sec 47)

Five-cylinder engines 1•33

setting given for this bolt is only applicable when using Audi tool 2079. If you are not using this tool tighten the bolt to at least the specified torque, and have an Audi dealer check its tightness. (The special tool increases the leverage of the standard torque wrench).
7 Carry out the operations described in paragraphs 5 to 10 inclusive of Section 44.
8 If the engine is still in the car, reverse the preliminary procedures at the beginning of this Section.

48 Flywheel/driveplate – removal and refitting

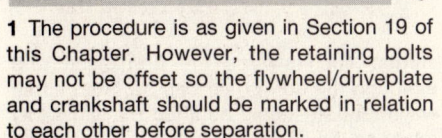

1 The procedure is as given in Section 19 of this Chapter. However, the retaining bolts may not be offset so the flywheel/driveplate and crankshaft should be marked in relation to each other before separation.
2 When refitting a driveplate note that the raised pip must face the torque converter. If a replacement driveplate is to be fitted, its position must be checked and adjusted if necessary. The distance from the rear face of the block to the torque converter mounting face on the driveplate (Fig. 1.30) must be between 17.2 and 18.8 mm (0.667 and 0.740 in). If necessary, remove the driveplate and fit a spacer behind it to achieve the correct dimension.

49 Sump – removal and refitting

Refer to Section 21 of this Chapter.

50 Crankshaft oil seals – renewal

Front oil seal
1 Remove the timing belt and crankshaft gear, as described in Section 47
2 If an extractor tool is available the seal may be renewed without removing the oil pump, otherwise refer to Section 51. It is also recommended that Audi tool 2080. together with a guide sleeve, be used to install the new seal. Dip the seal in engine oil before fitting, and if the old seal has scored the crankshaft, position the new seal on the unworn surface.
3 Refit the crankshaft gear and timing belt, as described in Section 47.

Rear oil seal
4 Remove the flywheel or driveplate, as described in Section 48.
5 If an extractor tool is available the seal may be renewed without removing the housing, otherwise unbolt and remove the housing (including the two sump bolts) and remove the gasket (photo). If the sump gasket is damaged while removing the housing it will be necessary to remove the sump and fit a new gasket. However, refit the sump *after* fitting the housing.

Fig. 1.30 Torque converter-to-cylinder block dimension checking faces – check in two places for average (Sec 48)

50.5 Removing the rear oil seal housing

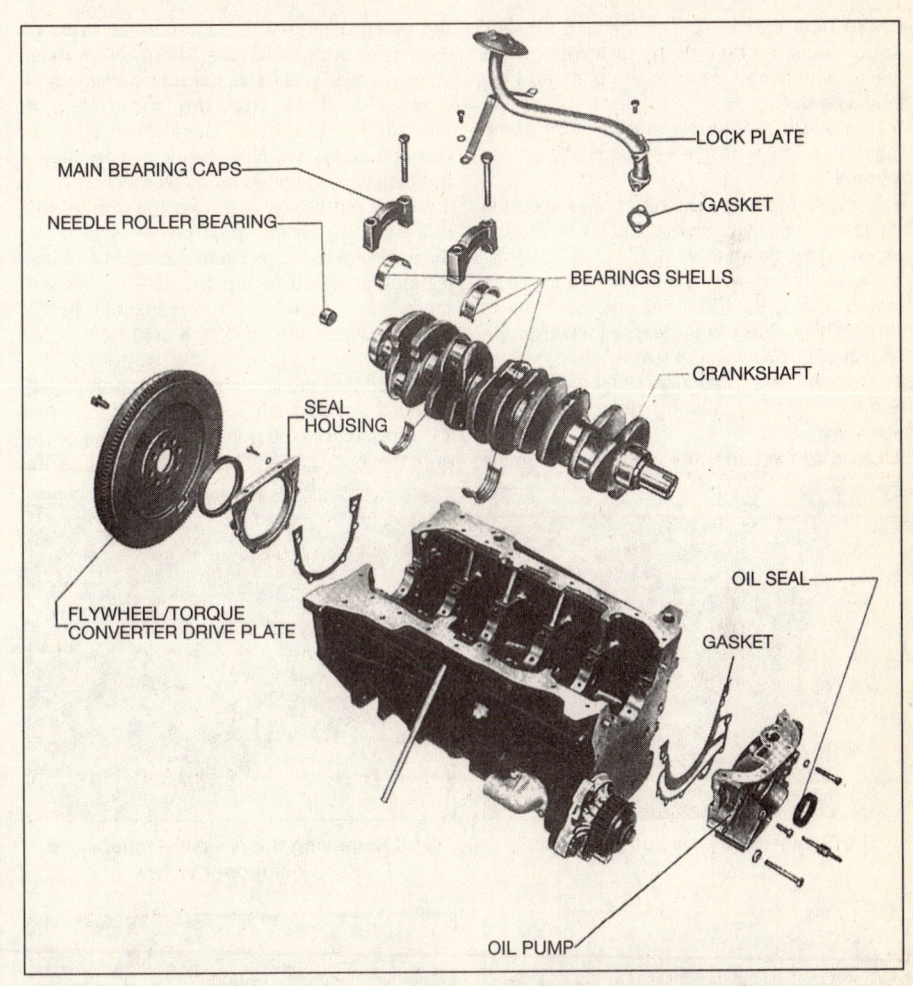

Fig. 1.31 Exploded view of the crankshaft, main bearings and oil pump (Secs 50, 51 and 55)

6 Drive the old seal out of the housing, then dip the new seal in engine oil and drive it into the housing with a block of wood or a socket, until flush. Make sure that the closed end of the seal is facing outwards.
7 Fit the housing, together with a new gasket, and tighten the bolts evenly in diagonal sequence.
8 Refit the flywheel or driveplate, as described in Section 48.

51 Oil pump – removal, examination and refitting

1 Remove the timing belt and crankshaft gear, as described in Section 47.
2 Remove the sump, with reference to Section 49.
3 Remove the timing belt inner cover.
4 Remove the two bolts securing the oil

1•34 Five-cylinder engines

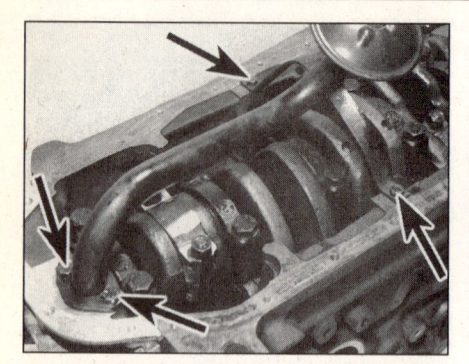

51.4 Oil intake pipe and stay attachments (arrowed)

51.5A Remove the oil pump retaining bolts . . .

51.5B . . . and withdraw the pump

intake pipe stay to the crankcase (photo). Knock back the tabs of the lockplate on the intake pipe flange, remove the bolts and the intake pipe.

5 Remove the bolts securing the oil pump (photo) and take off the oil pump and gasket (photo).

6 Remove the countersunk screws securing the pump backplate and lift the backplate off, exposing the gears (photo).

7 Check that there is a mark on the exposed face of the gears and if not, make a mark to show which side of the gears is towards the engine before removing them.

8 Unscrew the pressure relief valve and remove the plug, sealing ring, spring and plunger (photo).

9 Clean all the parts thoroughly and examine the pump casing and backplate for signs of wear or scoring. Examine the pressure relief valve plunger and its seating for damage and wear and check that the spring is not damaged or distorted. Clean the gears for damage and wear. New gears may be fitted, but they must be fitted as a pair (photo).

10 Prise out the oil seal from the front of the pump (photo). Oil the lip of the new seal, enter the seal with its closed face outwards and use a block of wood to tap the seal in flush. If there is any scoring on the crankshaft in the area on which the lip of the seal bears, the seal may be pushed to the bottom of its recess so that the lip bears on an undamaged part of the crankshaft.

11 Reassemble the pump by fitting the gears and the backplate. The inner gear has its slotted end towards the crankshaft and although the outer gear can be fitted either way round, it should be fitted the same way round as it was before removal. Some gears have a triangle stamped on them and this mark should be towards the pump backplate (photo).

12 Refit the oil pump, together with a new gasket, making sure that the slot on the inner gear engages the dog on the crankshaft.

13 Insert the bolts and tighten them in diagonal sequence to the specified torque.

14 Fit the oil intake pipe, together with a new gasket, tighten the bolts, and bend the lockplate tabs onto the flange bolts (photo).

15 Refit the timing belt inner cover, sump (Section 49), and timing belt and crankshaft gear (Section 47).

51.6 Removing the oil pump backplate

51.8 Removing the pressure relief valve components

51.9 Examine the oil pump parts for wear or damage

51.10 Removing the front oil seal from the pump

51.11 Triangle mark (arrowed) on pump gear must face the backplate

51.14 Bend up the locktabs to secure the intake pipe bolts

52 Pistons and connecting rods – removal and dismantling

Refer to Section 24 of this Chapter. Removal of the cylinder head is described in Section 38, and the timing belt in Section 47. Instead of removing the oil pump, remove the sump, as described in Section 49, then unbolt the oil intake pipe, as described in Section 51.

53 Pistons and cylinder bores – examination

Refer to Section 25 of this Chapter.

54 Pistons and connecting rods – reassembly and refitting

Refer to Section 26 of this Chapter. With the pistons fitted, refit the oil intake pipe, together with a new gasket, tighten the bolts, and bend the lockplate tabs onto the flange bolts. Refitting of the sump is described in Section 49, the timing belt in Section 47 and the cylinder head in Section 44.

55 Crankshaft – removal, examination and refitting

1 With the engine removed from the car, remove the pistons and connecting rods, as described in Section 52. Keep the big-end bearings with their matching connecting rods to ensure correct refitting.
2 Remove the oil pump (Section 51) and rear oil seal complete with housing (Section 50).
3 Follow the procedure in Section 27 of this Chapter, paragraphs 4 to 13 inclusive (photos) but note the following exceptions
(a) The flanged main bearing shells or thrust washers are fitted to main bearing No 4 (from the front of the engine)
(b) The needle roller bearing in the rear of the crankshaft must be pressed in to a depth of 5.5 mm (0.217 in) below the face of the flange
4 Fit the oil pump and rear oil seal housing complete with new seals, as described in Sections 51 and 50 respectively.
5 Refit the pistons and connecting rods, as described in Section 54.

56 Engine mountings – removal and refitting

1 Refer to Section 28 of this Chapter, but note that an additional snubber type front mounting is used on the five-cylinder engine. To remove the front mountings, first remove the alternator (Chapter 12), then undo the bolts and lift the mounting away. The mounting support, or snubber cup, is attached with bolts through the front body panel. Access to the nuts behind entails removal of the front bumper assembly (Chapter 11)

55.3A Crankshaft main bearing cap showing flanged thrust washers

55.3B Checking crankshaft endplay at No 4 main bearing

Fault Finding commences overleaf

Fault finding – all engines

Engine fails to start
- [ ] Discharged battery
- [ ] Loose battery connection
- [ ] Loose or broken ignition leads
- [ ] Moisture on spark plugs, distributor cap, or HT leads
- [ ] Incorrect spark plug gap
- [ ] Cracked distributor cap or rotor arm
- [ ] Dirt or water in carburettor (where applicable)
- [ ] Empty fuel tank
- [ ] Faulty fuel pump
- [ ] Faulty starter motor
- [ ] Low cylinder compression
- [ ] Other fuel or ignition system fault (see Chapters 3 and 4)

Engine misfires
- [ ] Spark plug gap incorrect
- [ ] Faulty coil, condenser or transistorised ignition component (as applicable)
- [ ] Dirt or water in carburettor (where applicable)
- [ ] Burn out valve
- [ ] Leaking cylinder head gasket
- [ ] Distributor cap cracked
- [ ] Incorrect valve clearances
- [ ] Uneven cylinder compressions
- [ ] Idling adjustments incorrect
- [ ] Other fuel or ignition system fault (see Chapters 3 and 4)

Engine stalls
- [ ] Idling adjustments incorrect
- [ ] Intake manifoid air leak
- [ ] Ignition timing incorrect

Engine idles erratically
- [ ] Intake manifold air leak
- [ ] Leaking cylinder head gasket
- [ ] Worn camshaft lobes
- [ ] Faulty fuel pump
- [ ] Incorrect valve clearances
- [ ] Loose crankcase ventilation hoses
- [ ] Idling adjustments incorrect
- [ ] Uneven cylinder compressions
- [ ] Other fuel or ignition system fault (see Chapters 3 and 4)

Excessive oil consumption
- [ ] Worn pistons and cylinder bores
- [ ] Valve guides and valve stem seals worn
- [ ] Oil leaking from crankshaft oil seals, valve cover gasket, etc

Engine backfires
- [ ] Idling adjustments incorrect
- [ ] Ignition timing incorrect
- [ ] Incorrect valve clearances
- [ ] Intake manifold air leak
- [ ] Sticking valve
- [ ] Other fuel or ignition system fault (see Chapters 3 and 4)

Engine lacks power
- [ ] Incorrect ignition timing
- [ ] Incorrect spark plug gap
- [ ] Low cylinder compression
- [ ] Excessive carbon build up in engine
- [ ] Air filter choked
- [ ] Other fuel or ignition system fault (see Chapters 3 and 4)

Chapter 2 Cooling system

For modifications, and information applicable to later models, see Supplement at end of manual

Contents

Antifreeze mixture 6
Coolant temperature sender unit – removal and refitting 11
Cooling fan thermo-switch – testing, removal and refitting 10
Cooling system – draining 3
Cooling system – filling 5
Cooling system – flushing 4
Fault finding – cooling system .... See end of Chapter
General description 1
Maintenance and inspection 2
Radiator – removal, inspection, cleaning and refitting 7
Thermostat – removal, testing and refitting 8
Water pump – removal and refitting 9

Degrees of difficulty

| Easy, suitable for novice with little experience | Fairly easy, suitable for beginner with some experience | Fairly difficult, suitable for competent DIY mechanic | Difficult, suitable for experienced DIY mechanic | Very difficult, suitable for expert DIY or professional |

Specifications

System type .... Pressurized radiator and expansion tank, belt driven water pump, thermostatically controlled electric cooling fan

Filler cap opening pressure .... 1.2 to 1.35 bar (17 to 19 lbf/in^2)

Thermostat
Start-to-open temperature:
　Four-cylinder engines .... 85°C (185°F)
　Five-cylinder engines .... 87°C (188°F)
Fully open temperature:
　Four-cylinder engines .... 106°C (221°F)
　Five-cylinder engines .... 102°C (216°F)
Stroke (minimum) .... 7.0 mm (0.27 in)

Electric cooling fan thermoswitch operating temperatures
Switches on .... 93° to 98°C (199° to 208°F)
Switches off .... 88° to 93C (190° to 199°F)

Antifreeze
Type/specification .... VW/Audi antifreeze G11, to TL-VW 774 A
Concentration for protection down to: **Percent antifreeze by volume**
　−25°C (−14°F) 40
　−30°C (−22°F) 45
　−35°C (−31°F) 50

Torque wrench settings   Nm   lbf ft
Radiator mountings (except five-cylinder upper support) 20   14
Radiator mountings (five-cylinder upper support) 10   7
Electric cooling fan and shroud 10   7
Air deflector shrouds 10   7
Thermo-switch (on cylinder head) 25   18
Water pump to engine 20   14
Water pump to housing (four-cylinder) 10   7
Water pump pulley (four-cylinder) 20   14
Thermostat cover 10   7
Cylinder head rear outlet (four-cylinder) 10   7

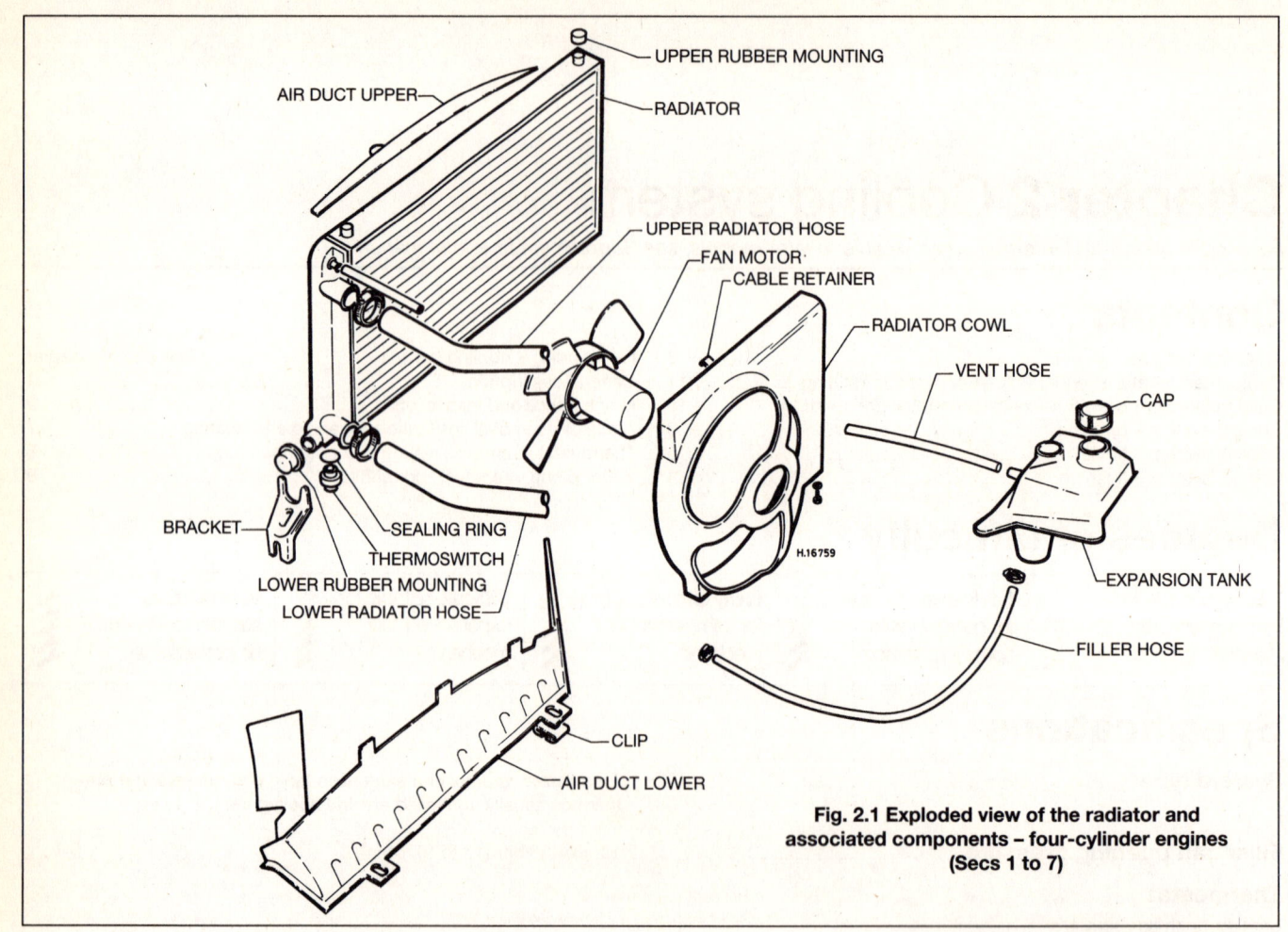

2•2 Cooling system

Fig. 2.1 Exploded view of the radiator and associated components – four-cylinder engines (Secs 1 to 7)

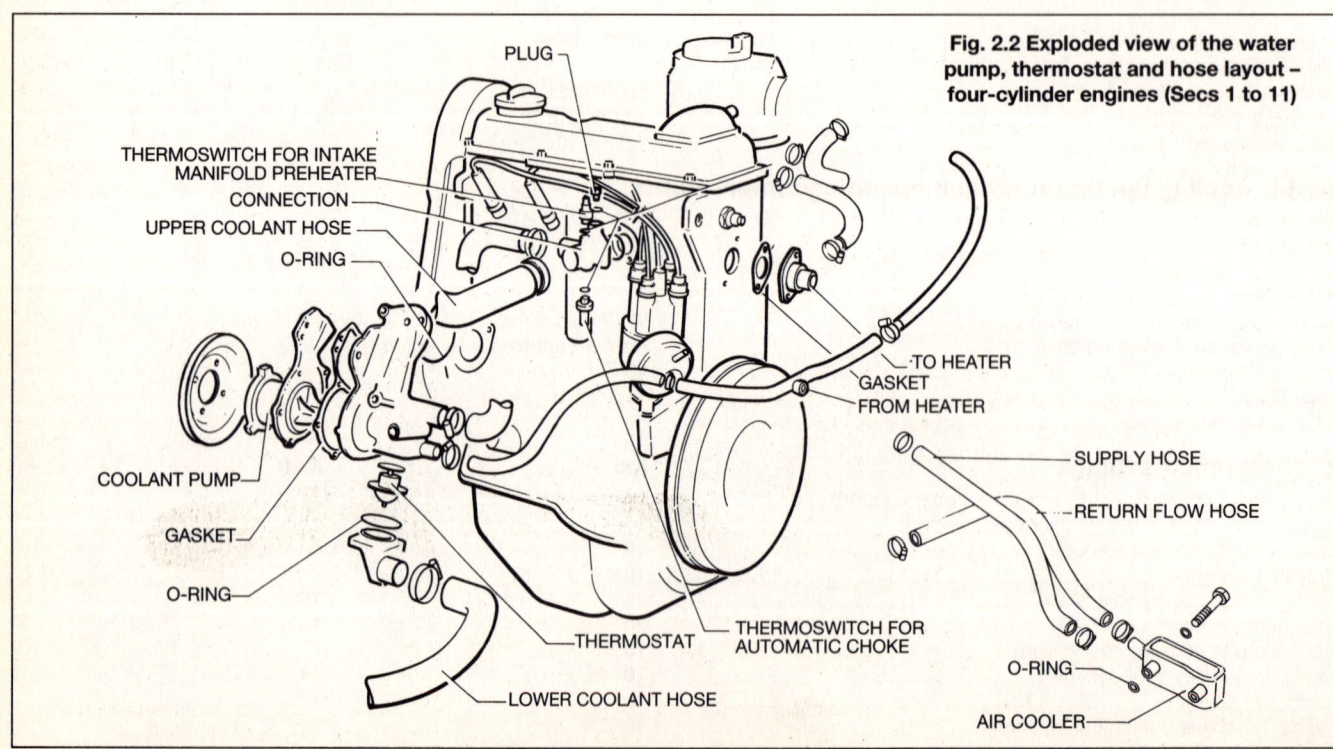

Fig. 2.2 Exploded view of the water pump, thermostat and hose layout – four-cylinder engines (Secs 1 to 11)

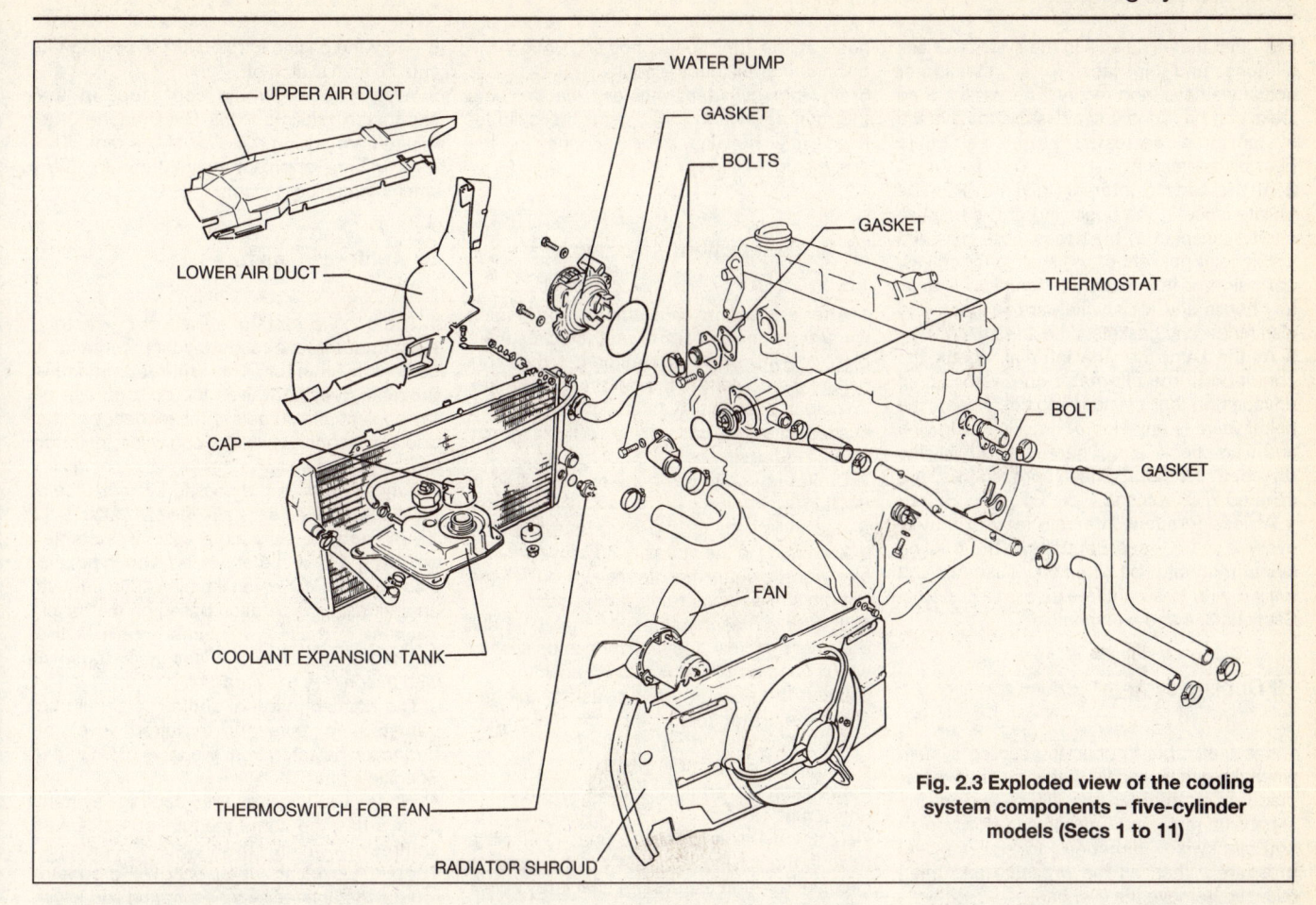

Cooling system 2•3

Fig. 2.3 Exploded view of the cooling system components – five-cylinder models (Secs 1 to 11)

1 General description

The cooling system is of the pressurized, pump assisted, thermo-syphon type, and includes a front mounted (four-cylinder), or side mounted (five-cylinder) radiator, a water pump driven by an external V-belt on four-cylinder engines, or by the timing belt on five-cylinder engines, an electric cooling fan, and a remote expansion tank. The cooling system thermostat is located in the water pump housing on four-cylinder engines, and in the inlet on the left-hand side of the cylinder block on five-cylinder engines.

The system functions as follows. With the engine cold, the thermostat is shut and the water pump forces the water through the internal passages then via the bypass hose (and heater circuit if turned on) over the thermostat capsule and to the water pump inlet again.

This circulation of water cools the cylinder bores, combustion surfaces and valve seats. However, when the coolant reaches the predetermined temperature, the thermostat begins to open. The coolant now circulates through the top hose to the top of the radiator. As it passes through the radiator matrix it is cooled by the inrush of air when the car is in forward motion, supplemented by the action of the electric cooling fan when necessary. Finally the coolant is returned to the water pump via the bottom hose and through the open thermostat.

The electric cooling fan is controlled by a thermo-switch located in the bottom of the radiator. Water temperature is monitored by a sender unit in the cylinder head.

Note: *The electric cooling fan will operate when the temperature of the coolant in the radiator reaches a predetermined level even if the engine is not running. Therefore extreme caution should be exercised when working in the vicinity of the fan blades.*

2 Maintenance and inspection

1 Check the coolant level in the system weekly and, if necessary, top up with a water and antifreeze mixture until the level is up to the minimum mark indicated on the expansion tank (photos). Check the level with the engine switched off, and only top up when the engine is cold. (If the engine is warm the level may be slightly higher). With a sealed type cooling system, topping-up should only be necessary at very infrequent intervals. If this is not the case and frequent topping-up is required, it is

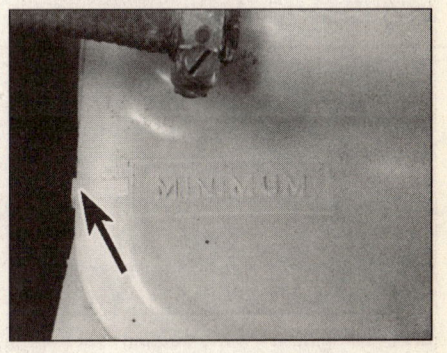

2.1A Top up the expansion tank . . .

2.1B . . . until the level reaches the minimum mark (arrowed)

2•4 Cooling system

likely that there is a leak in the system. Check all hoses and joint faces for any staining or actual wetness, and rectify if necessary. If no leaks can be found it is advisable to have the system pressure tested, as the leak could possibly be internal.

2 At the service intervals given in Routine Maintenance at the beginning of this manual, carefully inspect all the hoses, hose clips and visible joint gaskets of the system for cracks, corrosion, deterioration or leakage. Renew any hoses and clips which are suspect, and also renew any gaskets, if necessary.

3 At the same service interval, check the condition of the alternator and water pump drivebelt on four-cylinder engines. Renew the belt if there is any sign of cracking or fraying and also check, and if necessary adjust, the drivebelt tension. These procedures are covered in Chapter 12.

4 At less frequent intervals (approximately every 2 years – see Section 6). The cooling system should be drained, flushed, and refilled with fresh antifreeze, as described in Sections 3, 4 and 5 respectively.

3 Cooling system – draining

1 It is preferable to drain the cooling system when the engine is cold. If this is not possible, place a cloth over the filler cap on the expansion tank, and turn the cap slowly in an anti-clockwise direction to relieve the pressure. When all the pressure has been released, remove the filler cap.
2 Set the heater controls on the facia to warm.
3 On four-cylinder engines, place a suitable container beneath the water pump, then disconnect the bottom hose and heater/inlet manifold return hoses from the water pump housing. Allow the coolant to drain into the container.
4 On five-cylinder engines, place a suitable container beneath the hose connections on the left-hand side of the engine. Unscrew the bolt securing the heater return pipe to the cylinder block, then disconnect the pipe from the hose. Also disconnect the radiator bottom hose at the thermostat housing. Allow the coolant to drain into the container.
5 On four-cylinder engines, slacken the thermotime switch located on the cylinder head outlet housing, after disconnecting the wiring plug.

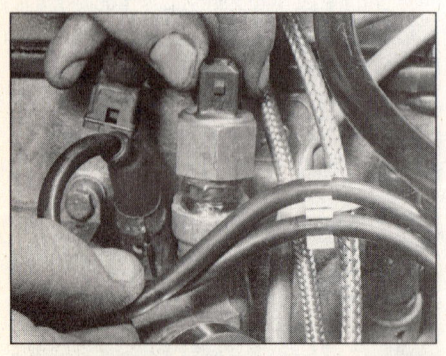

5.3 Purging air from the cooling system by slackening the thermo-time switch (four-cylinder engines)

4 Cooling system – flushing

1 After some time the radiator and engine waterways may become restricted or even blocked with scale or sediment. When this occurs the coolant will appear rusty and dark in colour and the system should then be flushed. In severe cases, reverse flushing may also be required.
2 Drain the cooling system, as described in Section 3.
3 Disconnect the top hose from the radiator, insert a hose in the radiator and allow water to circulate through the matrix and out of the bottom of the radiator until it runs clear.
4 If, after a reasonable period the water still does not run clear, the radiator can be flushed with a good proprietary cleaning agent.
5 Insert the hose in the expansion tank and allow the water to run through the supply hose.
6 In severe cases of contamination remove the radiator, invert it, and flush it with water until it runs clear.
7 To flush the engine and heater, insert a hose in the top hose, and allow the water to circulate through the system until it runs clear from the return hose.

5 Cooling system – filling

1 Reconnect all hoses and check that the heater controls are set to the warm position.
2 Pour a mixture of water and antifreeze (see Section 6) into the expansion tank until full, then proceed as follows according to model.

Four-cylinder engines

3 Continue filling the system until water free from air bubbles emerges from the thermotime switch (photo), then tighten the switch. Refit the switch wiring plug.
4 Top up the expansion tank until the level reaches the minimum mark on the side of the tank.
5 Refit the filler cap and run the engine until the cooling fan cuts in, then switch off.
6 Allow the engine to cool then top up the expansion tank if necessary. When the engine is cold the level should be up to the minimum mark, but will rise approximately 20 mm (0.75 in) when the engine Is warm.

Five-cylinder engines

7 Start the engine and add coolant as necessary until the level remains constant, then refit the expansion tank filler cap.
8 Allow the engine to run until the cooling fan cuts in, then switch off.
9 When the engine is cool, top up the expansion tank until the level reaches the minimum mark on the side of the tank. The level will rise approximately 20 mm (0.75 in) when the engine is warm.

6 Antifreeze mixture

1 The cooling system is filled at the factory with an antifreeze mixture which contains a corrosion inhibitor. The antifreeze mixture prevents freezing, raises the boiling point of the coolant and so delays the tendency of the coolant to boil, while the corrosion inhibitor reduces corrosion and the formation of scale. For these reasons the cooling system should be filled with antifreeze all the year round.
2 Any good quality antifreeze is suitable, providing it is of the ethylene glycol type and also contains corrosion inhibitors. Do not use an antifreeze preparation based on methanol, because these mixtures have the disadvantage of being inflammable, together with a high rate of evaporation.
3 The concentration of antifreeze should be adjusted to give the required level of protection selected from the table given in the Specifications.
4 When topping-up the cooling system always use the same mixture of water and antifreeze which the system contains. Topping-up using water only will gradually reduce the antifreeze concentration and lower the level of protection against both freezing and boiling.
5 At the beginning of the winter season, check the coolant for antifreeze concentration and add pure antifreeze if necessary.
6 Antifreeze mixture should not be left in the system for longer than its manufacturers' recommendation, which does not usually exceed two years. At the end of this time drain the system and refill with fresh mixture. **Note:** *Do not use engine antifreeze in the screen washer system as it will cause damage to the vehicle paintwork. Screen washer antifreeze is available from most accessory shops.*

7 Radiator – removal, inspection, cleaning and refitting

1 Disconnect the battery negative terminal.
2 Drain the cooling system, as described in Section 3.

Four-cylinder engines

3 Slacken the clips and disconnect the top and bottom hoses and expansion tank hoses at the radiator.
4 Disconnect the wiring at the electric cooling fan and at the thermoswitch.
5 Undo the lower mounting bracket retaining bolts and remove the brackets.
6 Disengage the radiator from its upper

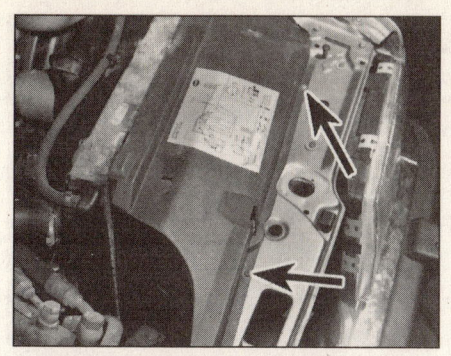

Cooling system 2•5

7.8 Undo the retaining screws (arrowed) and remove the radiator upper cowl (five-cylinder engines)

7.10 Disconnect the wiring plug (arrowed) at the electric cooling fan (five-cylinder engines)

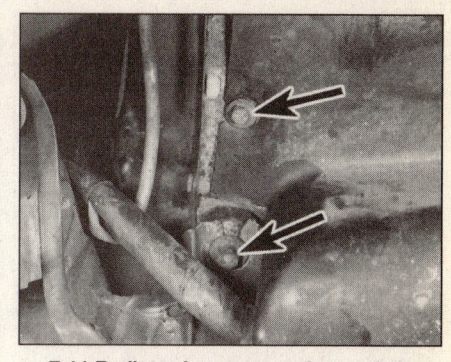

7.11 Radiator lower mounting and air deflector retaining nuts – arrowed (five-cylinder engines)

mountings, then lift the unit, complete with cooling fan and cowl, upwards and out of the engine compartment.

7 If necessary unbolt the cooling fan and cowl from the radiator, then unscrew the nuts and separate the fan and motor from the cowl.

Five-cylinder engines

8 Undo the retaining screws and remove the radiator upper cowl (photo).

9 Slacken the clips and disconnect the top and bottom radiator hoses and the expansion tank hoses.

10 Disconnect the wiring at the electric cooling fan and at the thermoswitch (photo).

11 From under the car, undo the bolts securing the air deflector cowl to the radiator, and the nut securing the lower mountings to their brackets (photo).

12 Undo the upper mounting nuts and lift the radiator, complete with cooling fan and cowl, upwards and out of the engine compartment (photos).

13 If necessary unbolt the cooling fan and cowl from the radiator, then unscrew the nuts and separate the fan and motor from the cowl.

All models

14 Radiator repair is best left to a specialist, although in an emergency minor leaks can be cured by using a radiator sealant with the radiator in situ. The outside matrix of the radiator may be cleared of flies and small leaves by hosing, or a soft brush.

15 Reverse flush the radiator, as described in Section 4 and renew the hoses and clips if they are damaged or have deteriorated.

16 Refitting is a reversal of removal, and fill the cooling system as described in Section 5. If the thermo-switch is removed, fit a new sealing washer when refitting it.

8 Thermostat – removal, testing and refitting

1 On four-cylinder engines the thermostat is located in the bottom of the water pump housing, but on five-cylinder engines it is located behind the water pump on the left-hand side of the cylinder block.

2 To remove the thermostat first drain the cooling system, as described in Section 3.

3 Unbolt and remove the thermostat cover, and remove the sealing ring (photos).

7.12A Radiator upper mounting . . .

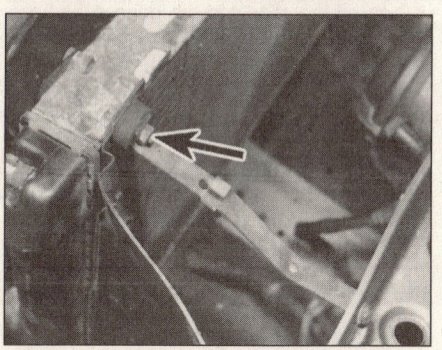

7.12B . . . and upper mounting stay (five-cylinder engines)

7.12C Radiator removal (five-cylinder engines)

8.3A Removing the thermostat cover (four-cylinder engines)

8.3B Thermostat cover and sealing ring (four-cylinder engines)

8.3C Thermostat cover removal (five-cylinder engines)

2•6 Cooling system

8.4 Removing the thermostat (four-cylinder engines)

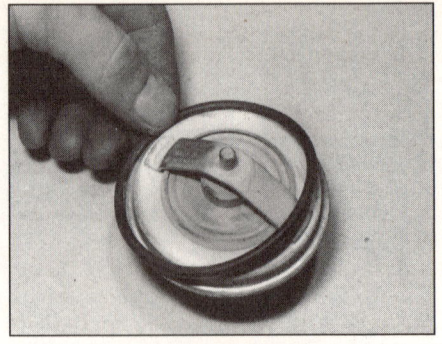

8.6 Fit a new sealing ring to the thermostat (five-cylinder engines)

9.4 Hose connections at the rear of the water pump housing (four-cylinder engines)

4 Prise the thermostat from its housing (photo).
5 To test whether the unit is serviceable, suspend it with a piece of string in a container of water. Gradually heat the water and note the temperatures at which the thermostat starts to open and is fully open. Remove the thermostat from the water and check that it is fully closed when cold. Renew the thermostat if it fails to operate in accordance with the information given in the Specifications.
6 Clean the thermostat housing and cover faces, and locate a new sealing ring on the cover (four-cylinder engines). On five-cylinder engines, fit a new sealing ring to the thermostat and fit the thermostat in its housing (photo).

7 Fit the thermostat cover and tighten the bolts evenly
8 Fill the cooling system, as described in Section 5.

9 Water pump – removal and refitting

1 Drain the cooling system, as described in Section 3.

Four-cylinder engines

2 Remove the alternator and drivebelt, as described in Chapter 12.
3 Unbolt the pulley from the water pump drive flange.
4 Loosen the clips and disconnect the hoses from the rear of the water pump housing (photo).
5 Unscrew the nut and remove the special bolt retaining the lower timing cover to the water pump assembly.
6 Unbolt the water pump assembly from the cylinder block and remove the sealing ring (photos).
7 Unscrew the bolts and remove the water pump from its housing using a mallet to break the seal. Remove the gasket.

Five-cylinder engines

8 Remove the alternator drivebelt, as described in Chapter 12, and where fitted the air conditioning compressor drivebelt, as described in Chapter 11.
9 Remove the power steering pump, leaving the hoses connected, and place it to one side. Refer to Chapter 10 if necessary.
10 Using an Allen key where necessary, unscrew the nuts and lift off the timing belt outer cover.
11 Slacken but do not remove the bolt securing the camshaft gear to the camshaft. Hold the gear stationary during removal using a screwdriver engaged with one of the teeth and resting against the belt cover retaining stud.
12 Set the engine on TDC compression for No 1 cylinder (refer to Chapter 1 if necessary).
13 Slacken the water pump mounting and adjustment bolts, again using an Allen key where necessary, and rotate the pump to release the tension on the timing belt. Slip the timing belt off the water pump and camshaft gears. Do not turn the camshaft or crankshaft with the timing belt removed.
14 Unscrew the camshaft gear retaining bolt and withdraw the gear.
15 Undo the bolts securing the water pump and timing belt inner cover to the engine.
16 Lift off the timing belt inner cover, then withdraw the water pump and remove the sealing ring (photo).

All models

17 If the water pump is faulty, renew it, as individual components are not available.

Fig. 2.4 Using a wide-bladed screwdriver to hold the camshaft gear stationary (Sec 9)

9.6A Water pump assembly removal (four-cylinder engines)

9.6B Water pump housing sealing ring (four-cylinder engines)

9.16 Removing the water pump and sealing ring (five-cylinder engines)

Clean the mating faces of the water pump, cylinder block, and pump housing (four-cylinder engines).
18 Refitting is a reversal of the removal procedure, but use a new sealing ring or gasket as applicable. On five-cylinder engines check that the camshaft and crankshaft are still on TDC compression for No 1 cylinder and correctly tension the timing belt using the procedures described in Chapter 1.
19 Refit the power steering pump, air conditioning compressor, and alternator drivebelts as applicable with reference to Chapter 10, 11 and 1 2 respectively.
20 Fill the cooling system, as described in Section 5, on completion.

10 Cooling fan thermo-switch – testing, removal and refitting

1 If the thermo-switch located in the bottom of the radiator develops a fault, it is most likely to fail open circuit. This will cause the fan motor to remain stationary even though the coolant reaches the operating temperature.
2 To test the thermo-switch for an open circuit fault, disconnect the wiring and connect a length of wire or suitable metal object between the two terminals in the wiring plug. The fan should operate (even without the ignition switched on) in which case the thermo-switch is proved faulty and must be renewed.
3 To remove the thermo-switch first drain the cooling system, as described in Section 3.
4 Disconnect the battery negative terminal.
5 Disconnect the wiring, then unscrew the thermo-switch from the radiator and remove the sealing washer.
6 To check the operating temperature of the thermo-switch, suspend it in a pan of water so that only the screwed end of the switch is immersed and the electrical contacts are clear of the water. Either connect an ohmmeter between the switch terminals, or connect up a battery and bulb in series with the switch. With a thermometer placed in the pan, heat the water and note the temperature at which the switch contacts close, so that the ohmmeter reads zero, or the bulb lights. Allow the water to cool and note the temperature at which the switch contacts open. Discard the switch and fit a new one if the operating temperatures are not within the specified limits.
7 Refitting is a reversal of removal, but always fit a new sealing washer. Fill the cooling system, as described in Section 5.

11 Coolant temperature sender unit – removal and refitting

1 The temperature sender unit is located on the rear of the cylinder head. To remove it, first drain half of the cooling system, with reference to Section 3.
2 Disconnect the wiring and unscrew the sender unit from the connector or cylinder head, as applicable. Remove the sealing washer(s).
3 Refitting is a reversal of removal, but always renew the washer(s). Top up the cooling system, with reference to Section 5.

Fault finding – cooling system

Overheating
☐ Low coolant level
☐ Faulty pressure cap
☐ Thermostat sticking shut
☐ Drivebelt broken (four-cyl)
☐ Open circuit thermo-switch
☐ Faulty cooling fan motor
☐ Clogged radiator matrix
☐ Retarded ignition timing

Slow warm-up
☐ Thermostat sticking open
☐ Short circuit thermo-switch

Coolant loss
☐ Deteriorated hose
☐ Leaking water pump or cooling system joints
☐ Blown cylinder head gasket
☐ Leaking radiator
☐ Leaking core plugs

2•8 Cooling system

Notes

Chapter 3
Fuel, exhaust and emission control systems

For modifications, and information applicable to later models, see Supplement at end of manual

Contents

Part A – 1.8 and 1.9 litre carburettor models
Accelerator cable – removal, refitting and adjustment	8
Air cleaner – removal and refitting	3
Automatic air temperature control – checking	4
Carburettor – adjustments	11
Carburettor – dismantling and reassembly	10
Carburettor – removal and refitting	9
Exhaust system – checking, removal and refitting	13
Fault finding	See end of Chapter
Fuel gauge sender unit – removal and refitting	7
Fuel pump – removal and refitting	5
Fuel tank – removal and refitting	6
General description	1
Inlet and exhaust manifolds – removal and refitting	12
Maintenance and inspection	2

Part B – 2.0, 2.2 and 2.3 litre fuel injection models
Accelerator cable – removal, refitting and adjustment	20
Air cleaner – removal and refitting	16
Airflow meter – removal and refitting	25
Airflow sensor lever and control plunger – checking	30
Automatic air temperature control – checking	17
Cold start valve – checking	28
Electric fuel pump – removal and refitting	31
Emission control systems – general	38
Emission control systems – operating precautions	39
Exhaust manifold – removal and refitting	40
Exhaust system – checking, removal and refitting	41
Fault finding	See end of Chapter
Fuel accumulator – removal and refitting	32
Fuel gauge sender unit – removal and refitting	19
Fuel injection system – general description	21
Fuel injection system – precautions and general repair information	22
Fuel injectors – removal and refitting	33
Fuel metering distributor – removal and refitting	24
Fuel tank – removal and refitting	18
General description	14
Idle speed and idle mixture – adjustment	23
Inlet manifold – removal and refitting	34
Maintenance and inspection	15
Pressure relief valve – removal, servicing and refitting	26
Thermo time switch – checking	27
Turbocharger – description	35
Turbocharger – removal and refitting	36
Turbo intercooler – removal and refitting	37
Warm-up regulator – checking	29

Degrees of difficulty

Easy, suitable for novice with little experience	**Fairly easy**, suitable for beginner with some experience	**Fairly difficult**, suitable for competent DIY mechanic	**Difficult**, suitable for experienced DIY mechanic	**Very difficult**, suitable for expert DIY or professional

Specifications

Part A – 1.8 and 1.9 litre carburettor models

Air cleaner element

Type .... Automatic air temperature control with renewable paper element (Champion W102)

Fuel pump

Type .... Mechanical, diaphragm, operated by eccentric on intermediate shaft or camshaft

Operating pressure:
- 1.8 litre engine .... 0.2 to 0.25 bar (2.9 to 3.6 lbf/in^2)
- 1.9 litre engine .... 0.35 to 0.40 bar (5.1 to 5.8 lbf/in^2)

3•2 Fuel, exhaust and emission control systems

Carburettor 1.8 litre – 1B3
Application .... Engine code DR
Carburettor type .... Single choke downdraught, automatic choke
Jets and settings: **Manual gearbox**   **Automatic transmission**
   Venturi diameter 24   24
   Main jet X112.5   X110
   Air correction jet with emulsion tube 90   90
   Idle fuel/air jet 47.5/130   47.5/130
   Auxiliary fuel/air jet 37.5/130 37.5/130
   Float needle valve diameter .... 1.75 mm   1.75 mm
   Part throttle enrichment valve 0.50   0.50
   Pump injection tube diameter .... 0.40 mm   0.40 mm
   Injection capacity .... 0.75 to 1.05 cc/stroke   0.75 to 1.05 cc/stroke
   Choke valve gap:
      Stage 1 .... 2.15 to 2.45 mm   1.95 to 2.25 mm
      Stage 2 .... 2.85 to 3.15 mm   2.85 to 3.15 mm
   Fast idle speed .... 3400 to 3800 rpm   3400 to 3800 rpm
   Automatic choke identification 251   250
   Idle speed .... 700 to 800 rpm   700 to 800 rpm
   CO content .... 0.5 to 1.5%   0.5 to 1.5%

Carburettor 1.8 litre – 2E2
Application .... Engine code DS
Carburettor type .... Twin choke downdraught, automatic choke
Jets and settings: **Stage 1**   **Stage 2**
   Venturi diameter .... 22 mm   26 mm
   Main jet X105   X120
   Air correction jet with emulsion tube diameter .... 1.0 mm   1.0 mm
   Idle fuel/air jet 40   –
   Full throttle enrichment valve diameter .... –   1.25 mm
   Pump injection tube diameter .... 0.35 mm   –
   Injection capacity .... 0.95 to 1.25 cc/stroke   –
   Choke valve gap .... 2.15 to 2.45 mm   4.55 to 4.85 mm
   Fast idle speed .... 2800 to 3200 rpm
   Automatic choke cover identification 258
   Idle speed .... 700 to 800 rpm
   CO content .... 0.5 to 1.5%

Carburettor 1.9 litre – Keihin
Application .... Engine code WH
Carburettor type .... Twin choke downdraught, automatic choke
                                                          Manual gearbox   **Automatic transmission**
Jets and settings: **Stage 1**   **Stage 2**   **Stage 1**   **Stage 2**
   Venturi diameter .... 22 mm   28 mm   22 mm   28 mm
   Main jet 120   165   120   150
   Idling jet 50   90   50   90
   Air correction jet 80   110   80   110
   Idling air jet 120   1.5   120   1.5
   Float needle valve diameter .... 2.8 mm   –   2.8 mm   –
   Pump injection tube diameter .... 0.35 mm   –   0.35 mm   –
   Enrichment valve diameter .... 50 mm   –   60 mm   –
   Fast idle speed .... 3500 rpm   3500 rpm
   Injection capacity .... 0.7 to 0.94 cc/stroke   0.7 to 0.94 cc/stroke
   Choke valve gap .... 5.45 to 5.75 mm   5.45 to 5.75 mm
   Throttle valve gap:
      Starting gap .... 1.2 to 1.4 mm   1.4 to 1.6 mm
      Idling gap .... 0.53 to 0.67 mm   0.63 to 0.77 mm
   Idle speed .... 700 to 800 rpm   700 to 800 rpm
   CO content .... 0.5 to 1.5%   0.5 to 1.5%

Fuel octane rating .... 98 RON (four-star)

Torque wrench settings

	Nm	lbf ft
Fuel tank mountings	25	18
Fuel pump	20	15
Inlet manifold	25	18
Carburettor	10	7.4
Inlet manifold preheater	10	7.4
Exhaust manifold	25	18
Exhaust pipe flanges and clamps	25	18

Fuel, exhaust and emission control systems 3•3

Part B – 2.0, 2.2 and 2.3 litre fuel injection models
General
System type	Bosch K or KE-Jetronic continuous injection system (CIS), turbocharged on certain 2.2 litre models
System pressure	4.7 to 5.4 bar (68 to 78 lbf/in^2)

Air cleaner element
Air cleaner element	Champion U505

Adjustment data
Idle speed	750 to 850 rpm
CO content	0.5 to 1.5%
Fuel octane rating	98 RON (four-star)

Torque wrench settings
	Nm	lbf ft
Fuel tank mountings	25	18
Thermotime switch	15	11
Fuel metering distributor screws	3.5	2.5
Pressure relief valve	25	18
Airflow meter	3.5	2.5
Cold start valve	3.5	2.5
Turbocharger to manifold	60	44
Waste gate to manifold	25	18
Oil supply and return lines to turbocharger	25	18
Exhaust manifold	30	22
Exhaust front pipe to turbocharger	35	26
Exhaust pipe flanges and clamps	25	18
Inlet manifold	25	18

Part A – 1.8 and 1.9 litre carburettor models

1 General description

Warning: *Many of the procedures in this Chapter entail the removal of fuel pipes and connections which may result in some fuel spillage. Before carrying out any operation on the fuel system refer to the precautions given in Safety First! at the beginning of this Manual and follow them implicitly. Petrol is a highly dangerous and volatile liquid and the precautions necessary when handling it cannot be overstressed*

The fuel system consists of a centrally mounted fuel tank, mechanical fuel pump, and single or twin choke downdraught carburettor.

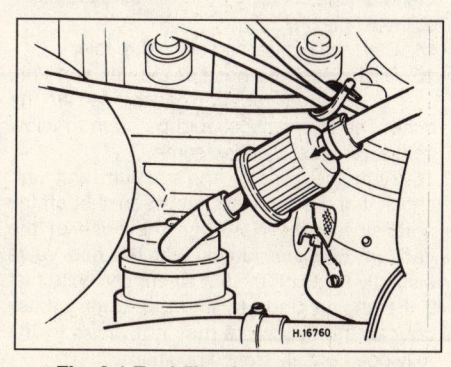

Fig. 3.1 Fuel filter location showing direction of fitting (Sec 2)

The air cleaner is of the automatic air temperature control type. and contains a disposable paper element.

The exhaust system is in four sections, comprising twin front pipes and main and intermediate silencers. The system is bolted to a cast iron manifold at the front, and suspended on flexible rubber mountings throughout its length.

2 Maintenance and inspection

1 At the intervals given in Routine Maintenance at the beginning of this Manual, carry out the following service operations to the fuel system components.
2 With the car raised on a vehicle lift, or securely supported on axle stands carefully inspect the fuel pipes, hoses and unions for chafing, leaks and corrosion. Renew any pipes that are severely pitted with corrosion or in any way damaged. Renew any hoses that show signs of cracking or other deterioration.
3 Examine the fuel tank for leaks, particularly around the fuel gauge sender unit, and for signs of corrosion or damage.
4 Check condition of exhaust system. as described in Section 13.
5 From within the engine compartment, check the security of all fuel hose attachments and inspect the fuel hoses and vacuum hoses for kinks, chafing or deterioration.
6 Renew the air cleaner element and check the operation of the air cleaner automatic temperature control, as described in Section 4.
7 Check the operation of the accelerator linkage and lubricate the linkage, cable and pedal pivot with a few drops of engine oil.
8 Renew the fuel filter by slackening the clips and disconnecting the fuel lines at the filter. Fit the new filter, ensuring that the arrows on the filter body face the direction of fuel flow. Tighten the fuel line clips securely (models up to 1985).
9 Check the carburettor idle speed and CO adjustment, as described in Section 11.

3 Air cleaner – removal and refitting

Element renewal

1 Remove the two screws (where fitted), and spring back the air cleaner cover retaining clips.
2 Lift off the cover, noting its fitted direction, and take out the element. Renew the element if it is dirty or has exceeded its service life.
3 Cover the carburettor intake and wipe out the inside of the air cleaner body.
4 Refit the element and secure the air cleaner cover in place.

Air cleaner assembly

5 Remove the element, as previously described.
6 Slacken the clips and disconnect the intake hoses and breather hoses.

3•4 1.8 and 1.9 litre carburettor models

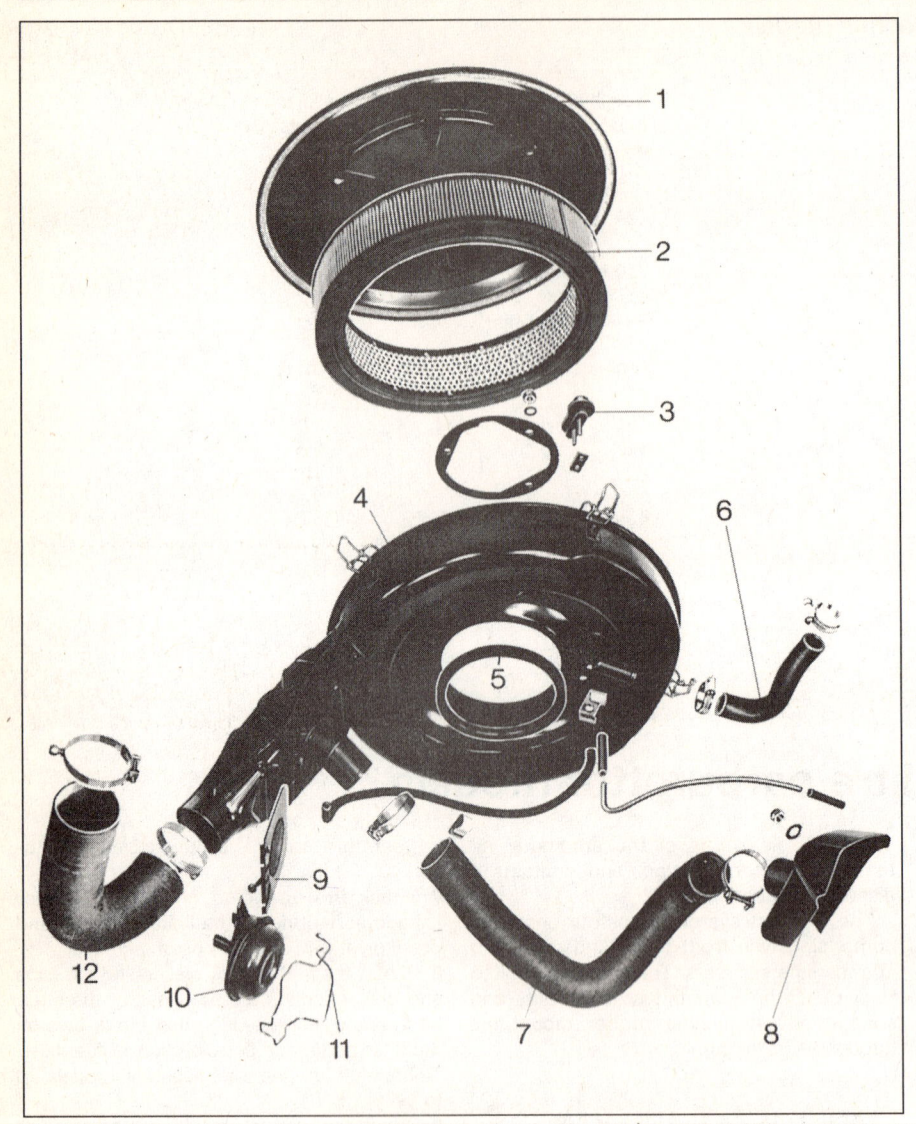

Fig. 3.2 Air cleaner assembly and automatic air temperature components – typical (Secs 3 and 4)

1 Air cleaner cover
2 Filter element
3 Thermostatic control valve
4 Air cleaner housing
5 Seal
6 Crankcase breather hose
7 Preheating hose
8 Warm air duct
9 Regulator flap
10 Vacuum unit
11 Spring clip
12 Cold air duct

7 Undo the retaining nut or bolt and lift up the air cleaner body, noting its fitted position.
8 Disconnect the vacuum hoses, noting their locations, and remove the air cleaner from the car.
9 Refitting is the reverse sequence to removal.

4 Automatic air temperature control – checking

1 The air cleaner is equipped with a temperature and load sensitive intake air preheating device, comprising a temperature regulator, vacuum unit and flap valve. According to air temperature and engine load, the system operates to admit cold air or hot air regulated by the position of the flap valve. The operation of the components can be checked as follows according to model.

1.8 litre engines

2 Remove the air cleaner. as described in Section 3, but leave the vacuum hoses connected at this stage
3 Disconnect the hose from the notched brass connection on the temperature regulator and check that the flap valve can be heard to open and close as suction is applied to the hose. If this is not the case, check the condition and security of the vacuum hoses, and check that the flap valve is not binding. If the flap valve still does not operate under suction, check the temperature regulator as follows.
4 For this check the ambient air temperature must not be above 20°C (68°F) .
5 Lay the air cleaner on a suitable place in the engine compartment and connect the notched brass connection on the temperature regulator to the carburettor, using a long length of vacuum hose.
6 Start the engine and allow it to idle, the flap valve should be in the open position.
7 Disconnect the vacuum hose between the carburettor and regulator at the carburettor end. The flap valve must return to its at rest position after a maximum of 20 seconds.
8 Remake the original connections and refit the air cleaner on completion of the checks.

1.9 litre engines

9 With the engine cold. disconnect the air cleaner cold air intake and observe the position of the flap valve through the intake. Use a mirror if necessary. The flap valve should be open to admit cold air into the air cleaner.
10 Disconnect the vacuum hose from the temperature regulator to the vacuum unit at the temperature regulator. Disconnect the vacuum hose from the temperature regulator to the carburettor at the carburettor, and connect the hose from the vacuum unit to this outlet.
11 Start the engine and allow it to idle. Observe the flap valve which should be positioned to admit hot air into the air cleaner, Pull the hose off the vacuum unit and check that the flap valve now closes off the hot air supply. If the flap valve does not function as described, check the vacuum hose, and if satisfactory the vacuum unit is faulty.
12 Remake the original connections on completion of the checks.
13 To check the temperature regulator, make sure that the vacuum unit is operating correctly, as previously described, and that the engine is cold. Remove the cold air intake at the air cleaner.
14 Start the engine and allow it to idle.
15 Disconnect the hose at the vacuum unit, and check that vacuum can be felt at the hose. The flap valve should be open to allow cold air to enter the air cleaner.
16 Refit the hose to the vacuum unit and check that the flap valve moves to shut off the cold air supply. Now pull the hose of the vacuum unit and check that the flap valve instantly shuts off the hot air supply. Note that if the engine starts to warm up during these checks the flap valve may not move to the fully open or fully closed positions.
17 Remake the original connections on completion of the checks.

1.8 and 1.9 litre carburettor models 3•5

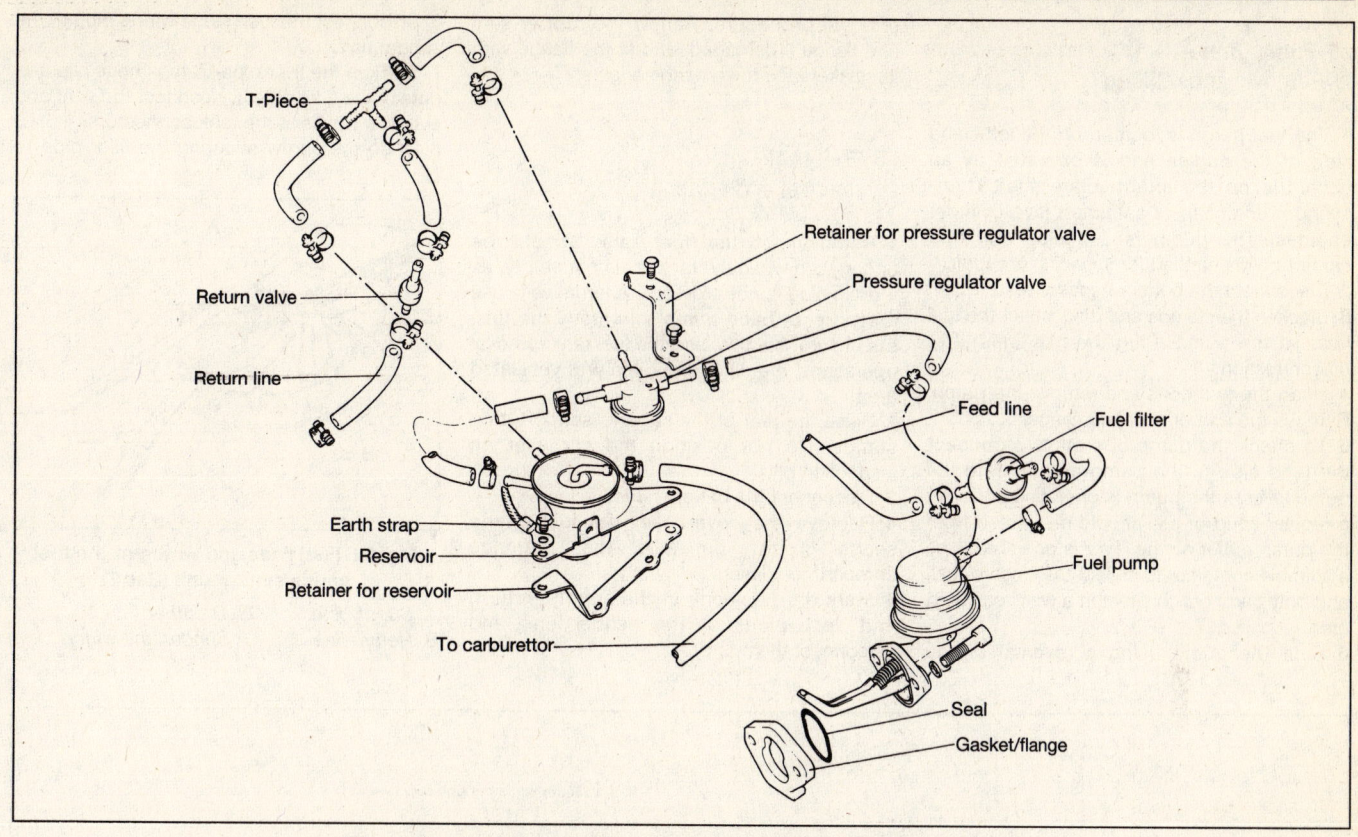

Fig. 3.3 Fuel pump and related components – 1.9 litre engines (Sec 5)

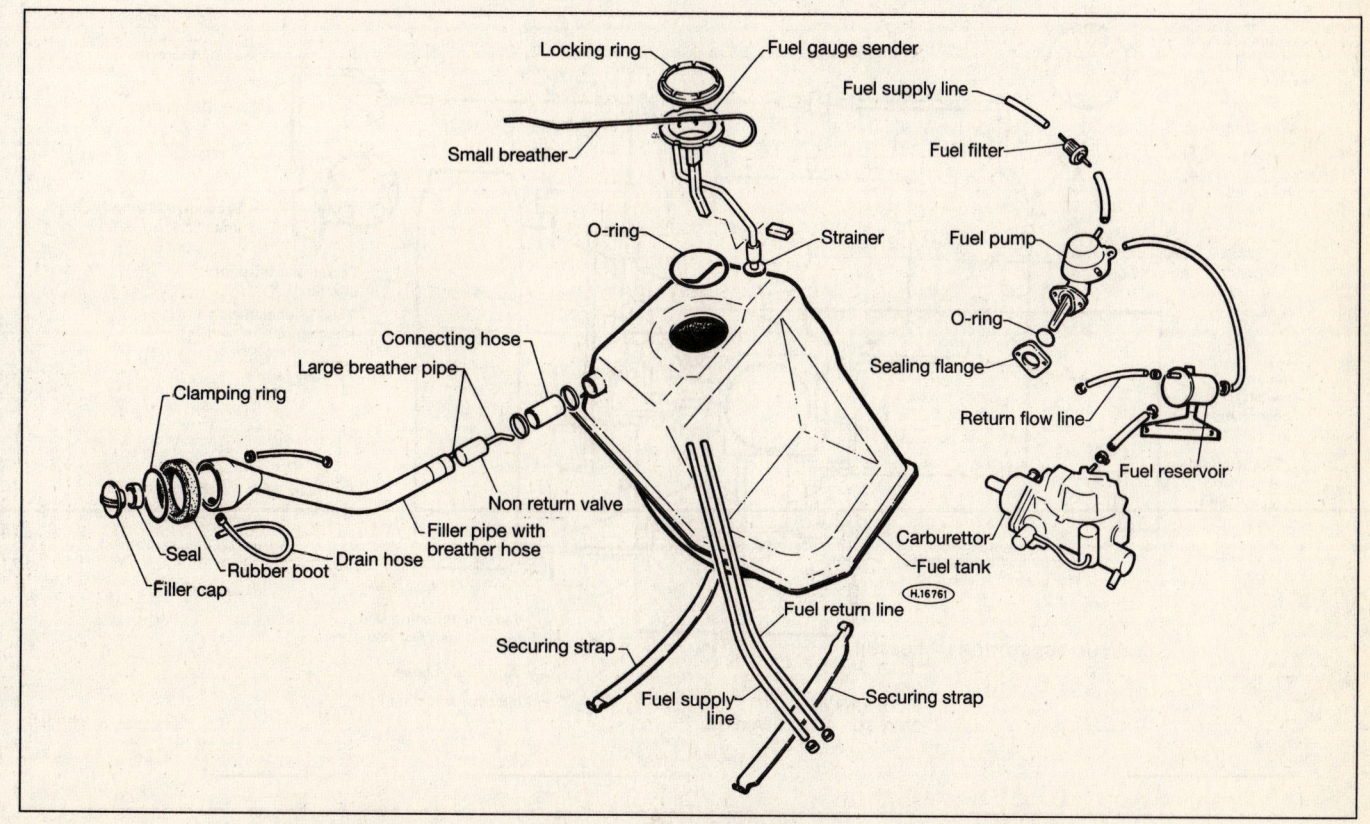

Fig. 3.4 Fuel tank, fuel gauge sender unit and related components – 1.8 litre engines (Secs 6 and 7)

5 Fuel pump – removal and refitting

1 The fuel pump is located on the left-hand side of the engine and is operated by an eccentric on the intermediate shaft (four-cylinder engines), or camshaft (five-cylinder engines) The pump is a sealed unit and cannot be dismantled for servicing or repair.
2 Disconnect the battery negative lead
3 Slacken the clamps and disconnect the fuel lines at the pump. Plug the fuel lines after disconnection.
4 Undo the two bolts and remove the pump. Remove the rubber seal and flange.
5 To check the pump operation. reconnect the feed pipe to the pump and operate the pump lever. If the pump is operating correctly a regular spurt of fuel should be ejected from the pump outlet as the lever is operated. Use a suitable container to collect the ejected fuel, and only carry out this test in a well ventilated area.
6 Refit the pump using a reversal of the removal procedure. Renew the rubber seal and flange if damaged, and fit the flange with its gasket face towards the engine.

6 Fuel tank – removal and refitting

1 Removal of the fuel tank should be undertaken when the tank is almost empty, as a drain plug is not provided. Alternatively, use a syphon or hand pump to remove the fuel, but ensure that this, and the fuel tank removal operations, are carried out in a well ventilated area.
2 Raise the rear of the car and support it on stands. Do not position the car over an inspection pit.
3 Disconnect the battery negative lead.
4 Remove the cover over the fuel gauge sender unit beneath the luggage compartment lining.
5 Mark the positions of the supply, return, and vent pipes at the sender unit and disconnect them.
6 Disconnect the fuel gauge wiring plug at the sender unit.
7 Slacken the filler pipe-to-tank hose clip and detach the filler pipe. Disconnect the vent and overflow hoses at the tank connectors.
8 Undo the screw securing the filler pipe to

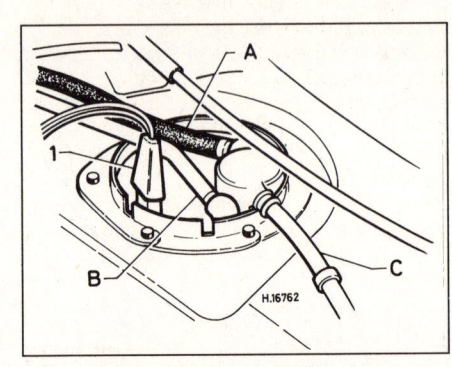

Fig. 3.5 Fuel lines and wiring at the fuel gauge sender unit (Sec 7)

A Supply line C Breather
B Return line 1 Sender unit wiring

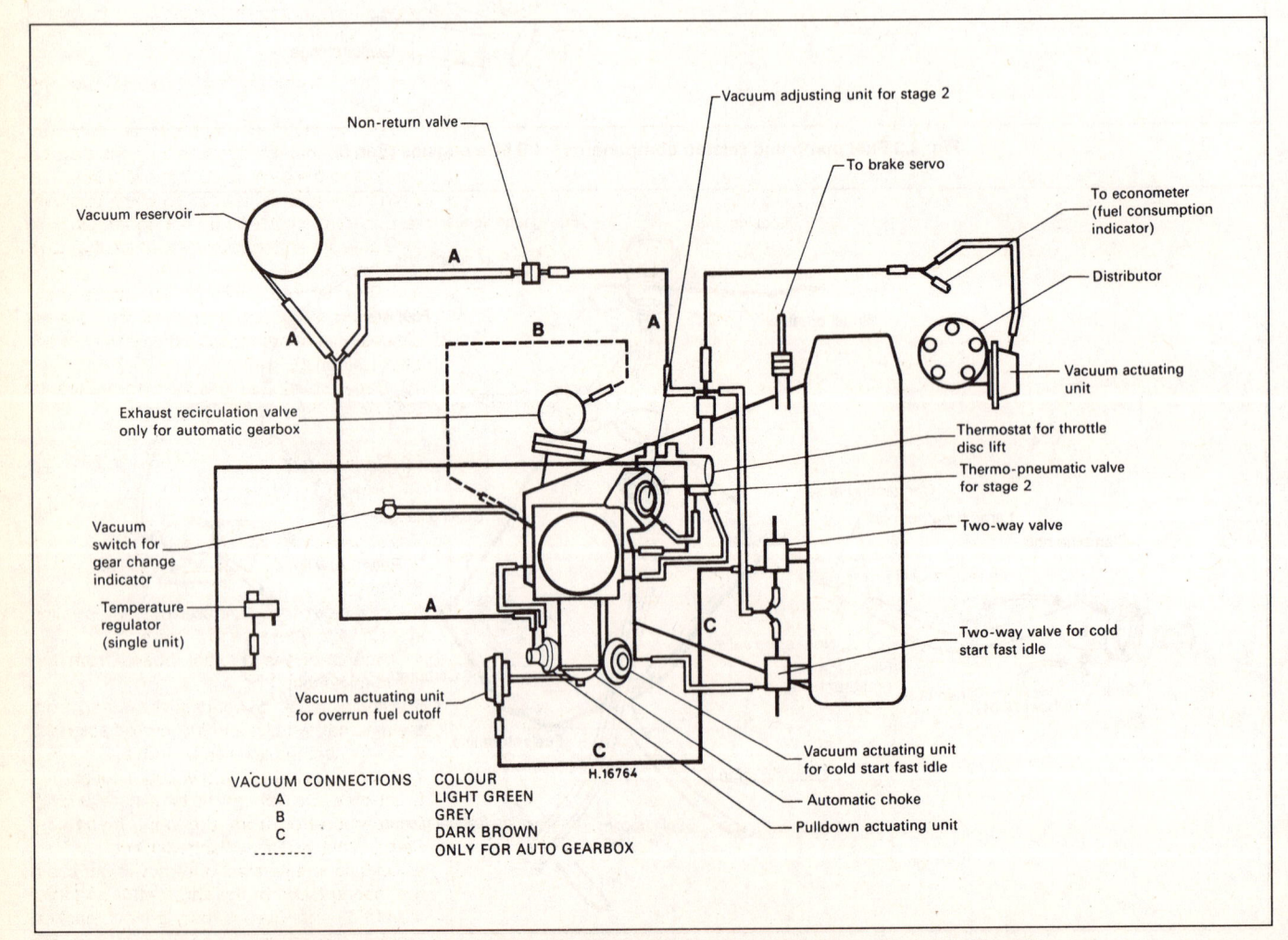

Fig. 3.6 Vacuum connections on the 1.9 litre engines with Keihin carburettor (Sec 9)

VACUUM CONNECTIONS COLOUR
A LIGHT GREEN
B GREY
C DARK BROWN
      ONLY FOR AUTO GEARBOX

1.8 and 1.9 litre carburettor models

the body just inside the filler flap, and withdraw the filler pipe.
9 Support the tank on a trolley jack with interposed block of wood.
10 Remove the tank retaining straps, lower the tank, and remove it from under the car.
11 If the tank is contaminated with sediment or water, remove the gauge sender unit, as described in Section 7, and swill the tank out with clean fuel If the tank is damaged or leaks, it should be repaired by specialists, or alternatively renewed. **Note:** *Do not, under any circumstances. solder or weld a fuel tank, for safety reasons.*
12 Refitting is a reversal of removal, but ensure that the vent pipe at the sender unit is laid on the top of the tank and secured with adhesive tape, and that the fuel lines are retained by their clips.

7 Fuel gauge sender unit – removal and refitting

1 Disconnect the battery negative lead.
2 Remove the cover over the sender unit beneath the luggage compartment lining.
3 Mark the positions of the supply, return and vent pipes at the sender unit and disconnect them. Disconnect the lead at the wiring terminal.
4 Using two crossed screwdrivers, turn the locking ring anti-clockwise, then withdraw the sender unit and float. Remove the sealing ring.
5 Refitting is a reversal of removal, but use a new sealing ring and ensure that the unit is positioned with the wiring terminal facing forwards. Secure the vent pipe with adhesive tape to the top of the tank. and secure the fuel lines with their retaining clips.

8 Accelerator cable – removal, refitting and adjustment

1 On automatic transmission models refer to Chapter 7 where necessary.
2 Refer to Section 3 and remove the air cleaner.
3 Disconnect the cable from the engine.
4 Disconnect the cable from the top of the accelerator pedal or the automatic transmission, as applicable, and withdraw the cable.
5 Refitting is a reversal of removal, but make sure that the cable is not kinked.
6 Adjustment of the cable on automatic transmission models is described in Chapter 7. On manual gearbox models, first disconnect the cable from the throttle lever on the carburettor.
7 Set the accelerator pedal to the idle position so that the distance from the stop on the floor to the pedal is 60.0 mm (2.36 in).
8 With the throttle lever in its idling position, reconnect the cable and take up the slack in the cable. Insert the clip in the nearest groove to the bracket.
9 To check the adjustment, fully depress the accelerator pedal and check that the distance between the throttle lever and stop is no more than 1.0 mm (0.04 in).
10 Refit the air cleaner with reference to Section 3.

9 Carburettor – removal and refitting

1 Disconnect the battery negative lead.
2 Remove the air cleaner, as described in Section 3.
3 Drain half of the coolant from the cooling system, with reference to Chapter 2.
4 Disconnect the coolant hoses from the automatic choke.
5 As applicable, disconnect the wiring from the automatic choke and fuel cut-off solenoid.
6 Disconnect the accelerator cable.
7 Disconnect the fuel and vacuum hoses.
8 Unscrew the through-bolts or nuts, and lift the carburettor from the inlet manifolds. Remove the insulating flange gasket.
9 Refitting is a reversal of removal, but clean the mating faces of the carburettor and inlet manifold, and always use a new gasket. Tighten the mounting bolts evenly to the specified torque.

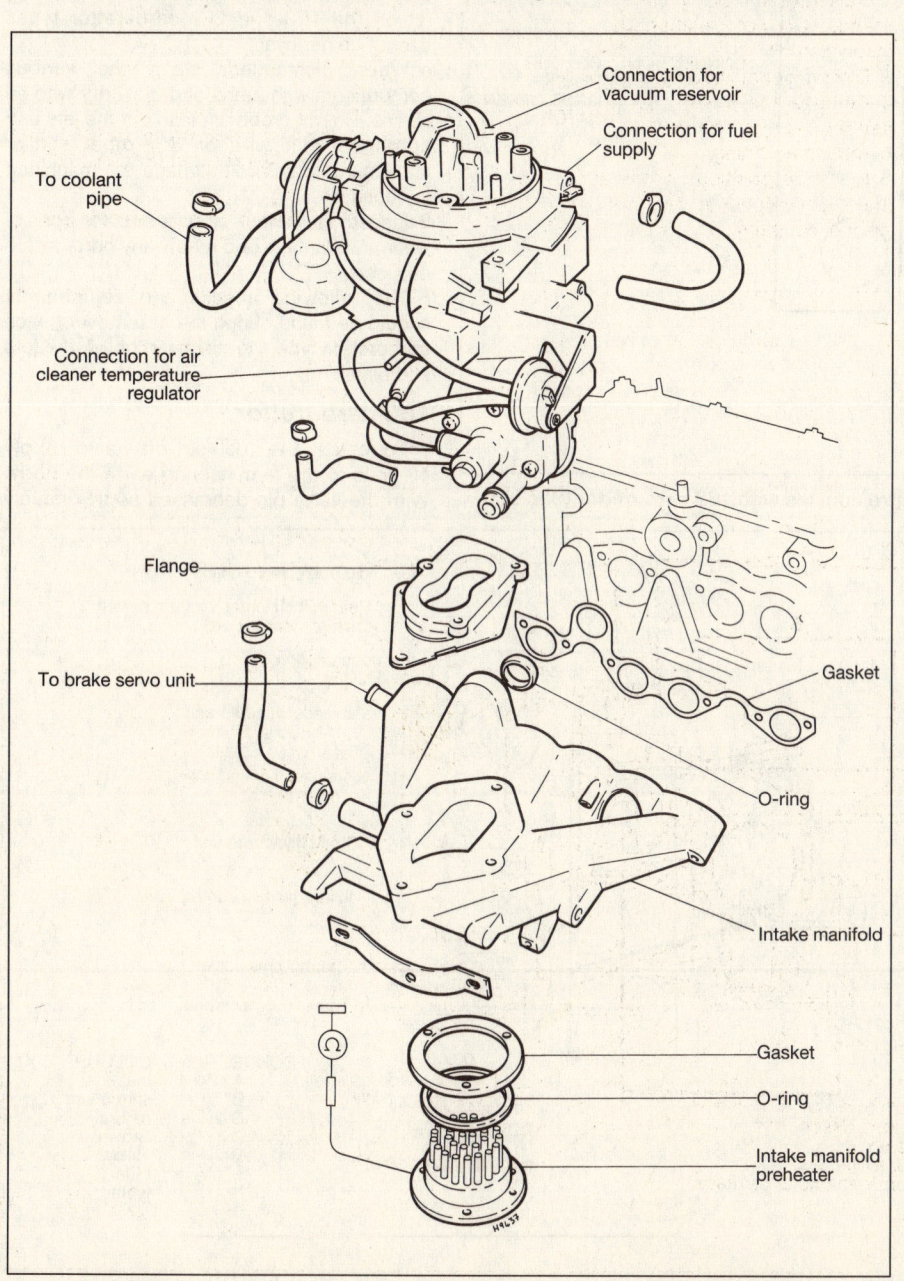

Fig. 3.7 inlet manifold and carburettor components – 1.8 litre engines (Sec 9)

3•8 1.8 and 1.9 litre carburettor models

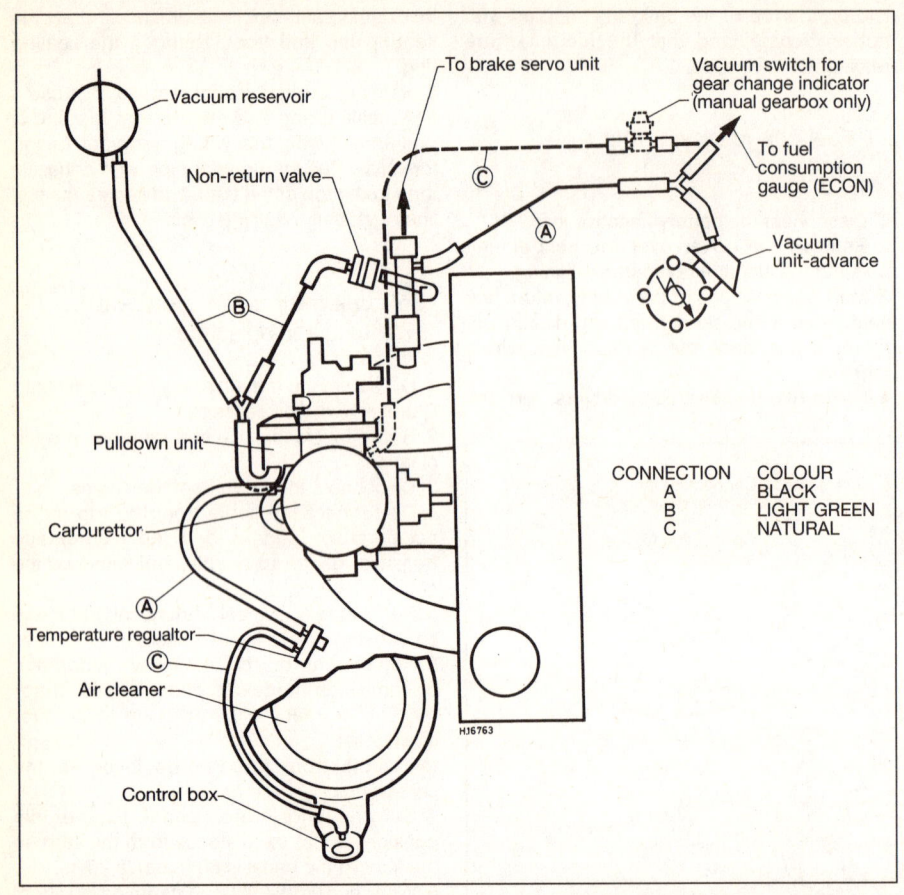

Fig. 3.8 Vacuum connections on the 1.8 litre engines with 1B3 carburettor (Sec 9)

10 Carburettor – dismantling and reassembly

1 With the carburettor removed from the inlet manifold, as described in the previous Section, wash it externally with a suitable solvent and allow to dry.
2 Dismantle and reassemble the carburettor, with reference to Figs. 3.10 to 3.19, having first obtained a repair set of gaskets. Before dismantling the automatic choke, note the position of the cover in relation to the carburettor cover.
3 Before removing the respective jets note their locations and note that the air correction jet on the 1B3 and 2E2 carburettor types cannot be removed.
4 When dismantled, clean the various components with petrol and blow dry with an air line. Do not probe or clean out the jets and apertures with wire or any other similar implement as this will damage the machined surfaces.
5 Inspect the various components for signs of wear and damage and renew any parts where necessary.
6 The following checks and adjustments should be made during the assembly of each carburettor type. Do not overtighten the jets and fastenings.

1B3 carburettor

7 To check the fuel cut-off valve, apply 12 volts to the terminal and earth the body. With the valve pin depressed approximately

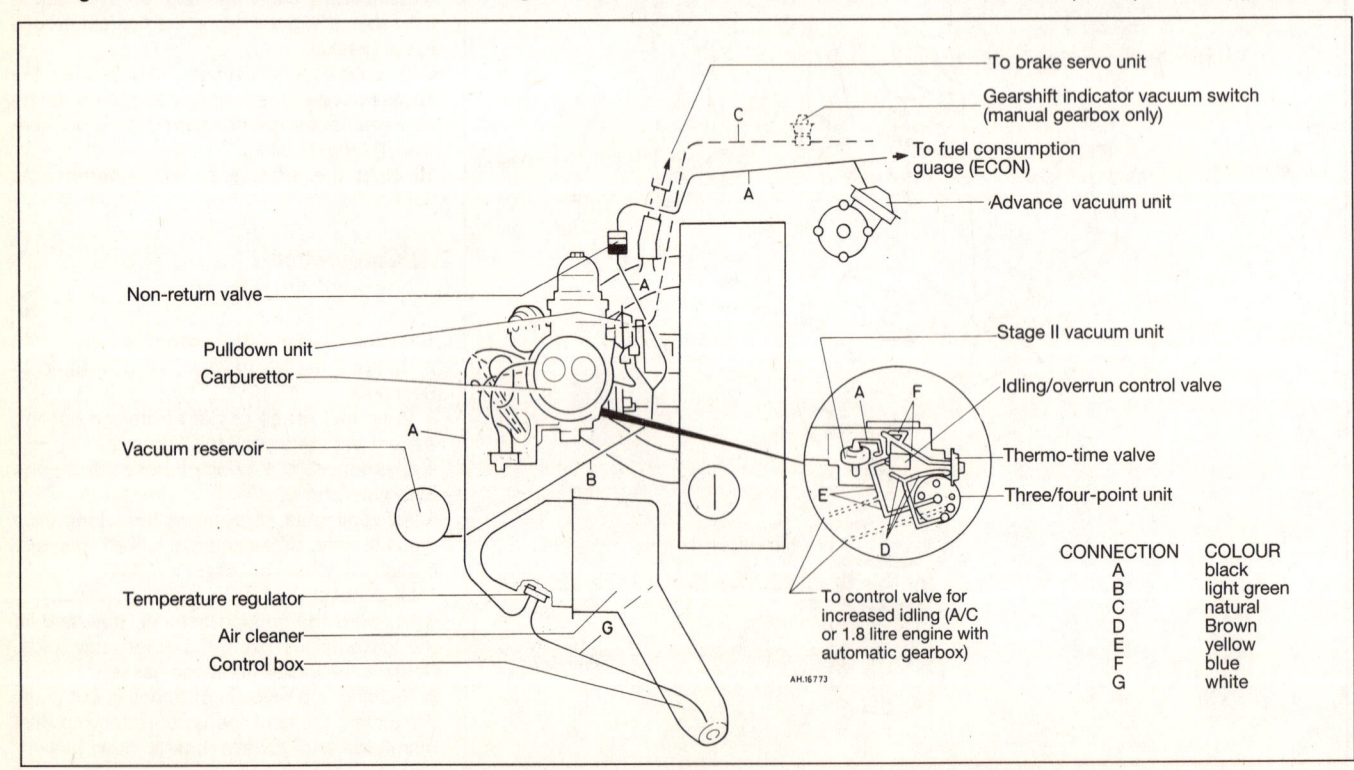

Fig. 3.9 Vacuum connections on the 1.8 litre engines with 2E2 carburettor (Sec 9)

1.8 and 1.9 litre carburettor models 3•9

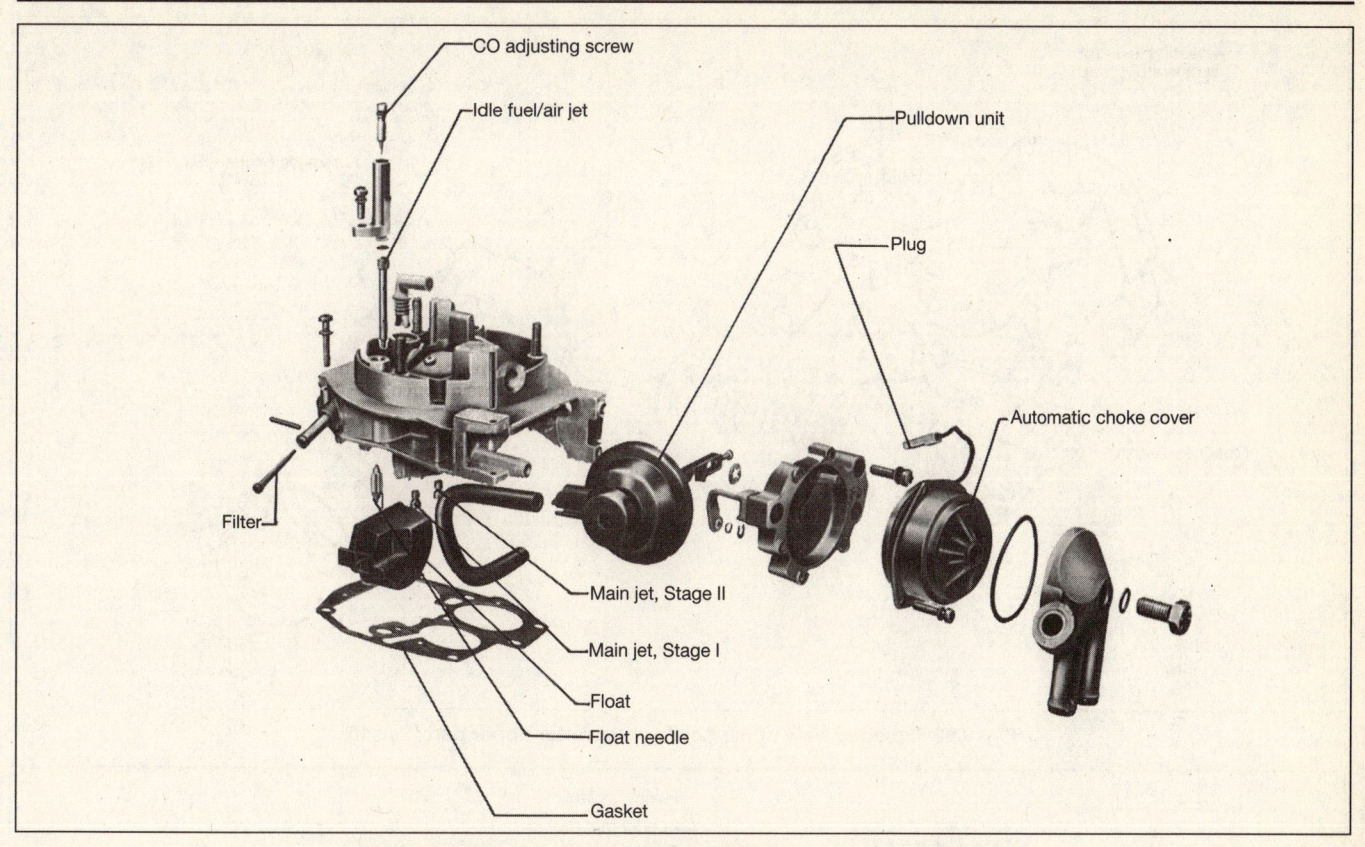

Fig. 3.10 Exploded view of the 2E2 carburettor upper part (Sec 10)

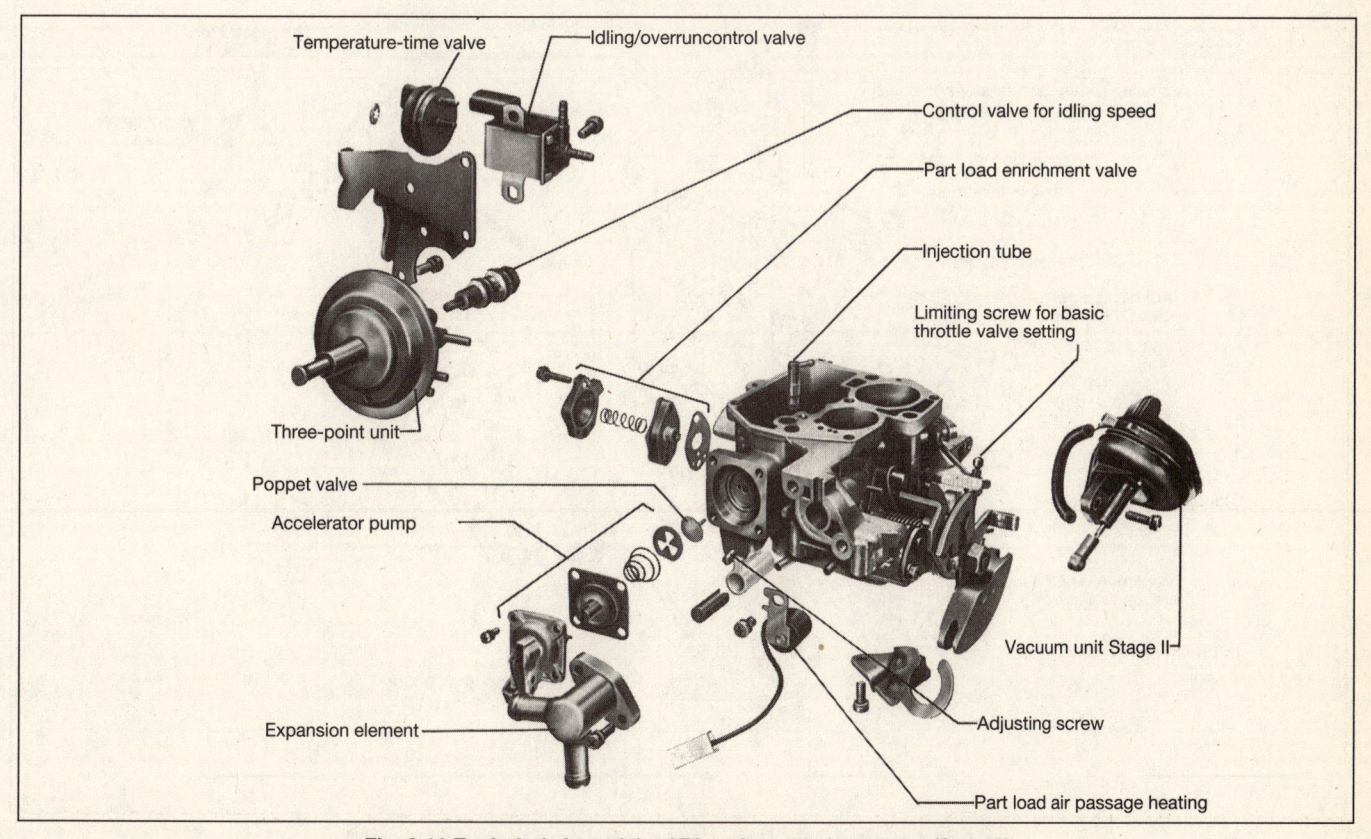

Fig. 3.11 Exploded view of the 2E2 carburettor lower part (Sec 10)

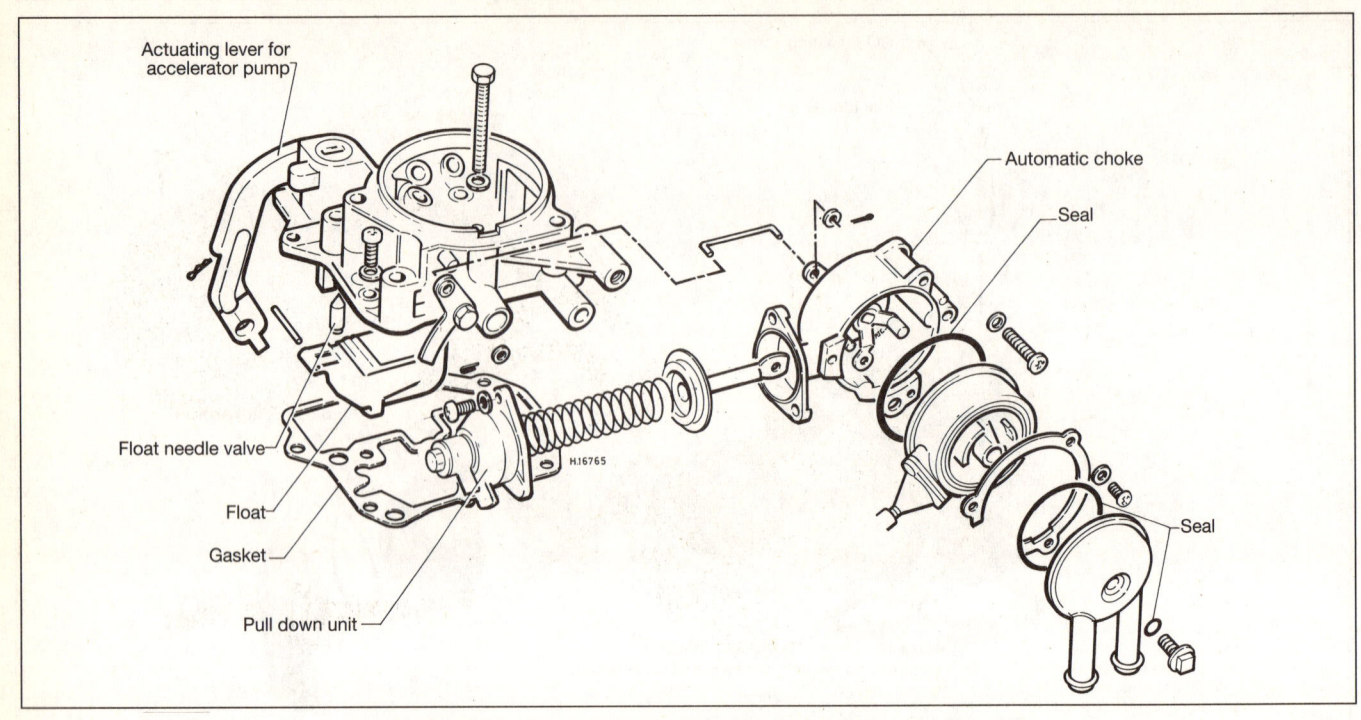

Fig. 3.12 Exploded view of the Keihin carburettor upper part (Sec 10)

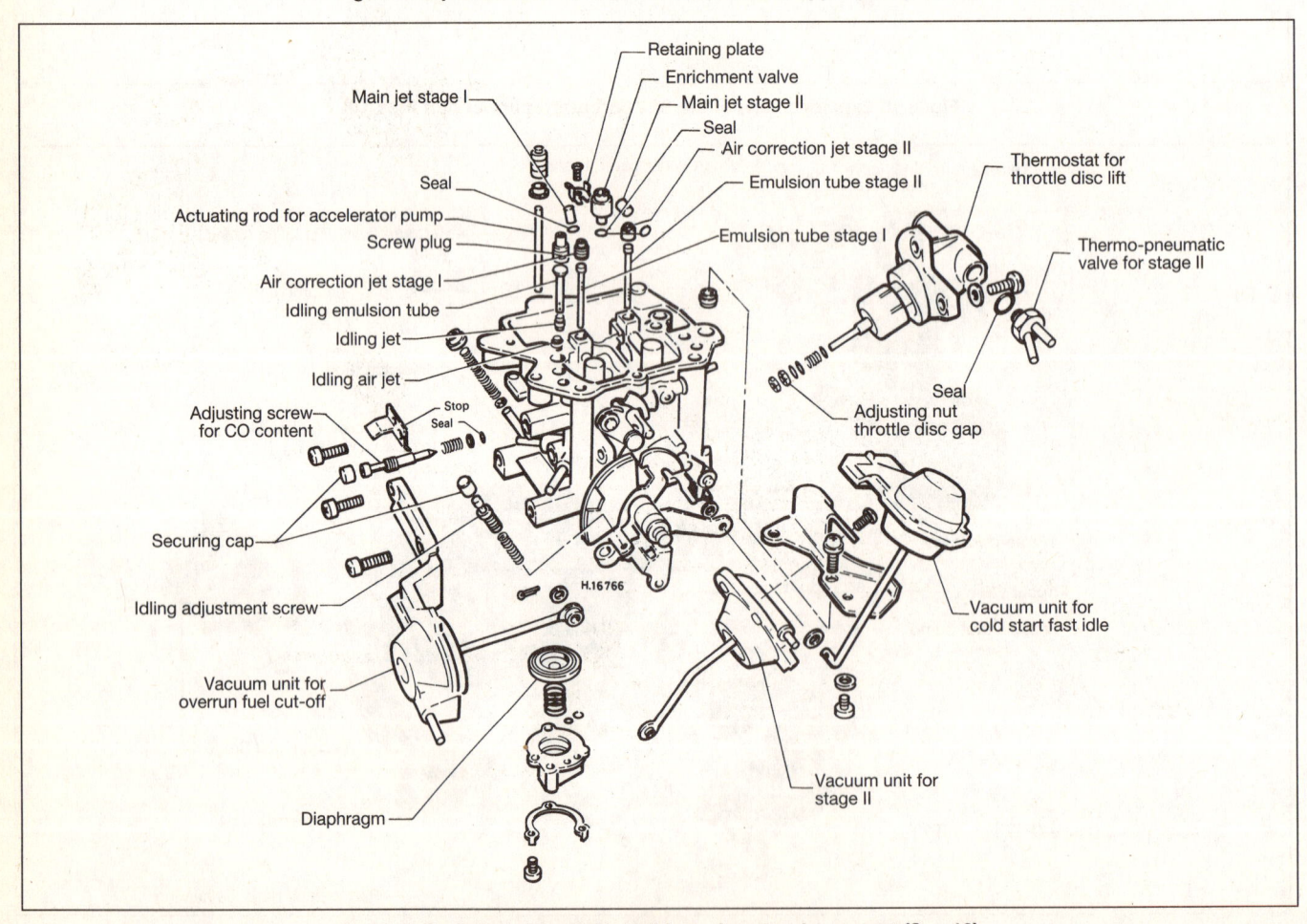

Fig. 3.13 Exploded view of the Keihin carburettor lower part (Sec 10)

1.8 and 1.9 litre carburettor models 3•11

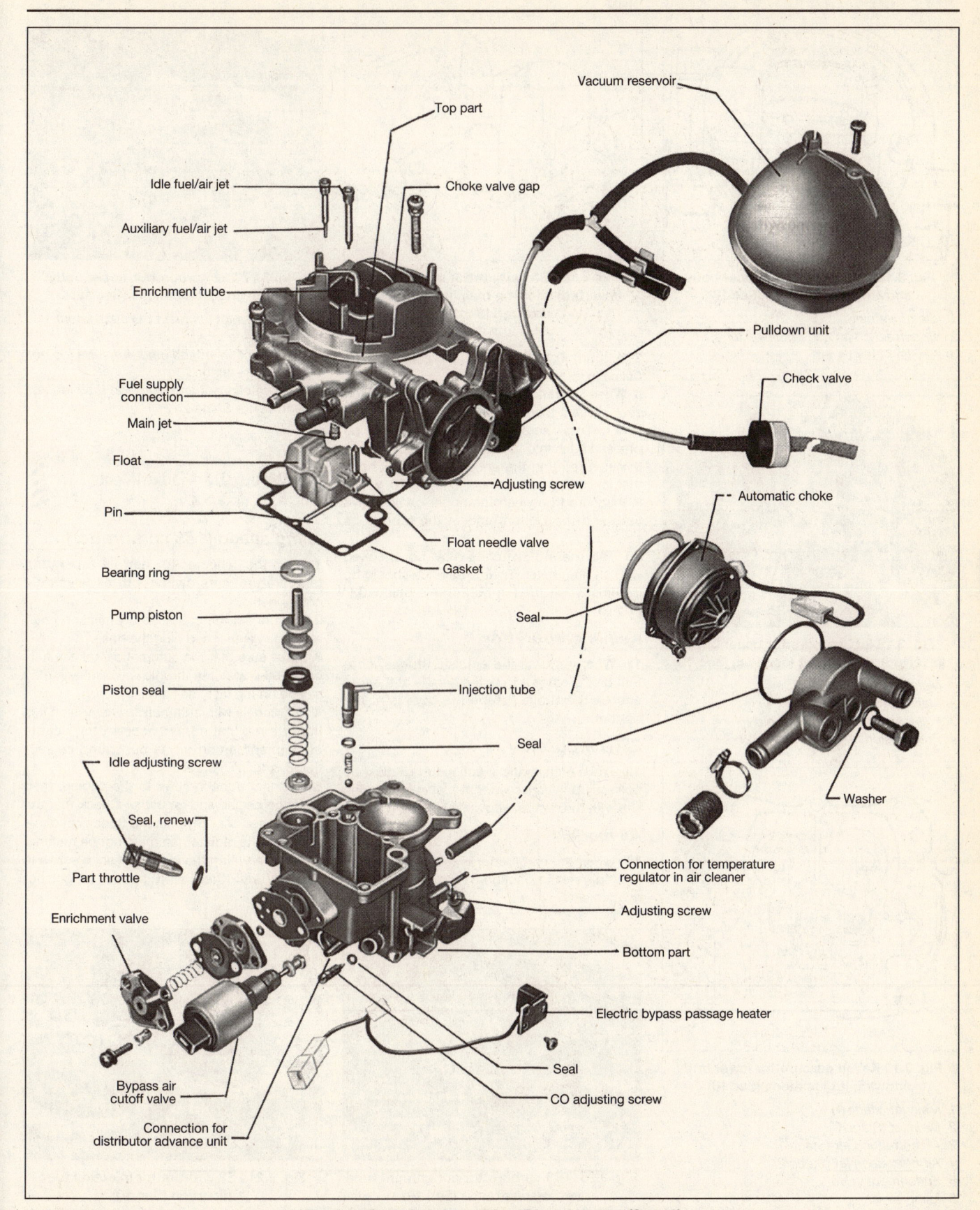

Fig. 3.14 Exploded view of the 1B3 carburettor (Sec 10)

3•12 1.8 and 1.9 litre carburettor models

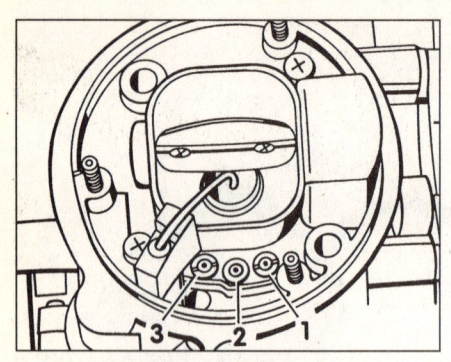

Fig. 3.15 1B3 carburettor upper body showing jet locations (Sec 10)

1 Idle fuel/air jet
2 Air correction jet and emulsion tube
3 Auxiliary fuel/air jet

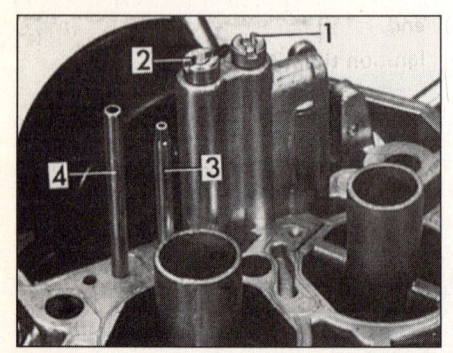

Fig. 3.18 2E2 carburettor upper body (inverted) showing jet locations (Sec 10)

1 Main jet (Stage 1)
2 Main jet (Stage 2)
3 Full load enrichment feed pipe
4 Progression feed pipe (Stage 2)

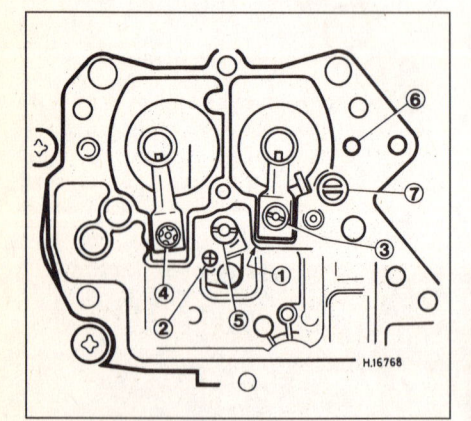

Fig. 3.19 Keihin carburettor lower body showing jet locations (Sec 10)

1 Main jet (stage 1)
2 Main jet (Stage 2)
3 Air correction jet (Stage 1)
4 Air correction jet (Stage 2)
5 Enrichment valve
6 Idling air jet
7 Idling jet (below idling emulsion tube)

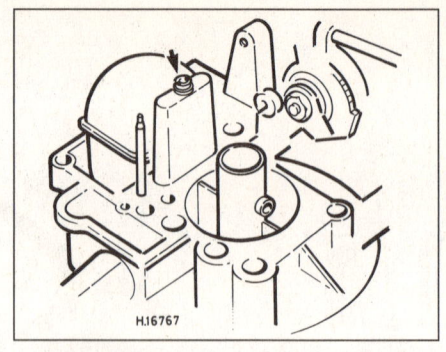

Fig. 3.16 1B3 carburettor upper body (inverted) showing main jet location – arrowed (Sec 10)

3 to 4 mm (0.12 to 0.16 in), the core must be pulled in.

8 When inserting the accelerator pump piston seal, press it towards the opposite side of the vent drilling. The piston retaining ring must be pressed flush into the carburettor body.

9 When refitting the enrichment tube check that its setting clearance, a in Fig. 3.20, which is measured between the upper choke valve face and the bottom end of the tube is as specified.

10 The thermo-switches may be checked with an ohmmeter. Their resistance should be 0 ohms when the temperature is below 33° (91° C).

Keihin carburettor

11 When refitting the emulsion tubes, note that on the stage 1 tube the bore is at the top, and on the Stage 2 tube the bore is at the bottom.

2E2 carburettor

12 When refitting the injection tube it must be correctly positioned so that fuel is sprayed in line with the recess, shown in Fig. 3.21.

All models

13 When the carburettor is reassembled and refitted, refer to Section 11 for the necessary adjustments.

Fig. 3.20 1B3 carburettor enrichment tube setting clearance (Sec 10)

a = 0.7 to 1.3 mm (0.027 to 0.051 in)

Fig. 3.17 2E2 carburettor upper body showing jet locations (Sec 10)

1 Idle fuel/air jet (beneath CO adjustment screw guide tube)
2 Air correction jet and emulsion tube (do not remove) – Stage 7
3 Air correction jet and emulsion tube (do not remove) – Stage 2

11 Carburettor – adjustments

Idling speed (1B3 carburettor)

1 Run the engine to normal operating temperature and switch off all electrical components.

2 Disconnect the crankcase ventilation hose at the air cleaner and plug the hose.

3 Make sure that the automatic choke is fully open, otherwise the throttle valve linkage may still be on the fast idle cam.

4 On models with automatic transmission it is important that the accelerator cable adjustment is correct as described in Section 8, and in Chapter 7.

5 Connect a tachometer to the engine, then start the engine and let it idle. Check that the idling speed is as given in the Specifications – note that the radiator fan must not be running. If necessary, turn the idling adjusting screw in or out until the idling speed is correct (Fig. 3.22).

Fig. 3.21 2E2 carburettor injection tube direction (Sec 10)

1.8 and 1.9 litre carburettor models 3•13

Fig. 3.22 1B3 carburettor idle adjusting screw – arrowed (Sec 11)

Fig. 3.23 1B3 carburettor CO adjusting screw – arrowed (Sec 11)

Fig. 3.24 1B3 carburettor fast idle cam (A) and adjustment screw (B) (Sec 11)

6 The CO adjustment screw is covered with a tamperproof cap which must be removed in order to adjust the mixture. However, first make sure that current regulations permit its removal (Fig. 3.23).
7 If an exhaust gas analyser is available, connect it to the exhaust system, then run the engine at idling speed and adjust the screw to give the specified CO content percentage. Alternatively, as a temporary measure, adjust the screw to give the highest engine speed, then readjust the idling speed if necessary.
8 After making the adjustment, fit a new tamperproof cap, and reconnect the crankcase ventilation hose.

Fast idling speed (1B3 carburettor)

9 With the engine at normal operating temperature and switched off, connect a tachometer and remove the air cleaner.
10 Fully open the throttle valve, then turn the fast idle cam and release the throttle valve so that the adjustment screw is positioned on the highest part of the cam (Fig. 3.24).
11 Without touching the accelerator pedal, start the engine and check that the fast idling speed is as given in the Specifications. If not, turn the adjustment screw on the linkage as necessary. If a tamperproof cap is fitted, renew it after making the adjustment.

Choke pull-down system (1B3 carburettor)

12 Remove the air cleaner cover. as described in Section 3.

13 Half open the throttle valve then completely close the choke valve.
14 Without touching the accelerator pedal, start the engine.
15 Close the choke valve by hand and check that resistance is felt over the final 4 mm (0.16 in) of travel. If no resistance is felt there may be a leak in the vacuum connections or the pull-down diaphragm may be broken.
16 Further checking of the system requires the use of a vacuum pump and a gauge, therefore this work should be entrusted to your Audi dealer.

Choke valve gap (1B3 carburettor)

17 The choke valve gap measurement and adjustment points are shown in Fig 3.25 for reference purposes only; the use of a vacuum tester and gauge is required, so this task is best left to an Audi dealer.

Throttle valve basic setting (1B3 carburettor)

18 This setting is made during manufacture and will not normally require adjustment. However, if the setting has been disturbed proceed as follows.
19 First run the engine to normal operating temperature.
20 Remove the air cleaner, as described in Section 3.
21 Disconnect the vacuum advance hose at the carburettor and connect a vacuum gauge.
22 Run the engine at idling speed, then turn the idle limiting screw on the lever until

vacuum is indicated on the gauge. Turn the screw out until the vacuum drops to zero, then turn it out a further quarter turn, (Fig. 3.26).
23 After making the adjustment, adjust the idle speed as described in paragraphs 1 to 8.

Electric bypass air heating element (1B3 carburettor)

24 Disconnect the wiring from the fuel cut-off solenoid and thermoswitch, and connect a test lamp to the heating element wire and the battery positive terminal.
25 If the lamp lights up, the heater element is in good working order.

Accelerator pump (1B3 carburettor)

26 Hold the carburettor over a funnel and measuring glass.
27 Turn the fast idle cam so that the adjusting screw is off the cam. Hold the cam in this position during the following procedure.
28 Fully open the throttle ten times, allowing at least three seconds per stroke. Divide the total quantity by ten and check that the resultant injection capacity is as given in the Specifications. If not, refer to Fig. 3.27 and loosen the cross-head screw, turn the cam plate as required, and tighten the screws.
29 If difficulty is experienced in making the adjustment. check the pump seal and make sure that the return check valve and injection tube are clear.

Fig. 3.25 1B3 carburettor choke valve gap check using drill shank (1) and adjust using socket-head bolt (2) (Sec 11)

Fig. 3.26 1B3 carburettor idle limiting screw (C) (Sec 11)

Fig. 3.27 1B3 carburettor accelerator pump adjustment (Sec 11)

a Locking screw   b Cam plate

3•14 1.8 and 1.9 litre carburettor models

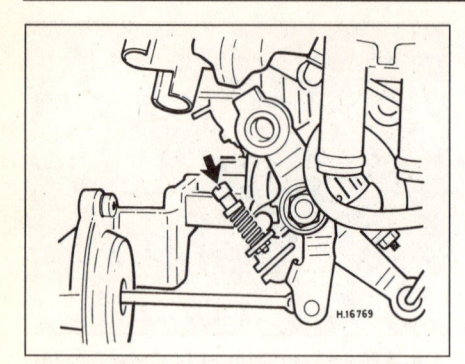

Fig. 3.28 Keihin carburettor idle adjusting screw – arrowed (Sec 11)

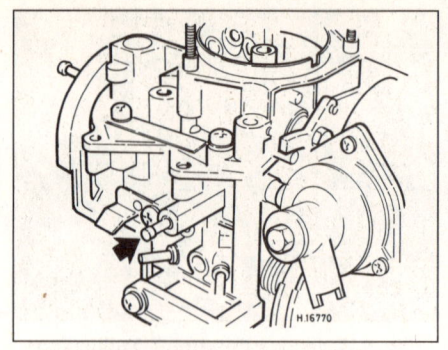

Fig. 3.29 Keihin carburettor CO adjusting screw – arrowed (Sec 11)

Fig. 3.30 Keihin carburettor vacuum hose connection (arrowed) removed for fast idle adjustment (Sec 11)

Automatic choke (1B3 carburettor)

30 The line on the cover must be in alignment with the dot on the automatic choke body.

Inlet manifold preheater (1B3 carburettor)

31 Using an ohmmeter between the disconnected lead and earth; check that the resistance of the preheater is between 0.25 and 0.50 ohms. If not, renew the unit.

Idling speed (Keihin carburettor)

32 The procedure is the same as for the 1B3 carburettor described in paragraphs 1 to 8 inclusive. The adjustment screws are shown in Figs. 3.28 and 3.29.

Fast idling speed (Keihin carburettor)

33 With the engine oil temperature at least 50°C (122°F), remove the air cleaner unit and pull free the vacuum hose from the vacuum fast idle unit. Start the engine and note the idle speed. Compare it with that specified and, if necessary, adjust accordingly by squeezing the adjuster lever together to reduce engine speed, or prising it open further to increase engine speed (Figs. 3.30, 3.31 and 3.32).

34 On completion reconnect the vacuum hose and refit the air cleaner unit.

Throttle valve gap adjustment (Keihin carburettor)

35 Using the shank of a twist drill, check the throttle lever valve-to-body clearance (starting gap) and compare it with the clearance specified. If the clearance is incorrect, prise open the adjuster lever to increase the clearance or close the adjuster lever by squeezing together using suitable pliers (Figs. 3.33 and 3.34).

36 To check the continuous running (idling gap) clearance, push the pullrod of the vacuum unit onto the stop, then fit a 9.5 mm diameter rod between the thermostat lever and the carburettor housing (a drill shank will suffice). Adjust the lever to suit the rod thickness, then measure the running clearance between the throttle valve and carburettor body using a gauge rod or drill shank. If adjustment is necessary to set the clearance to that specified, prise open the adjuster lever to reduce the clearance or compress the lever with pliers to enlarge the clearance (Fig. 3.35).

Choke valve gap adjustment (Keihin carburettor)

37 The choke valve gap is preset and should not normally need adjustment except when fitting a new upper carburettor body.

38 Remove the automatic choke unit cover

Fig. 3.31 Keihin carburettor fast idle adjustment – compress adjuster lever to reduce speed (Sec 11)

Fig. 3.32 Keihin carburettor fast idle adjustment – prise open adjuster lever to increase speed (Sec 11)

Fig. 3.33 Keihin carburettor throttle valve starting gap measurement using twist drill (Sec 11)

Fig. 3.34 Keihin carburettor throttle valve starting gap adjustment – increase by spreading adjuster lever (Sec 11)

Fig. 3.35 Keihin carburettor continuous running (idling gap) adjustment – spread adjuster lever to reduce clearance (Sec 11)

1.8 and 1.9 litre carburettor models

Fig. 3.36 Keihin carburettor choke valve gap adjustment (Sec 11)

Lever tensioned with elastic band – pulldown lever arrowed

Fig. 3.37 Keihin carburettor choke valve gap stop lever (arrowed) (Sec 11)

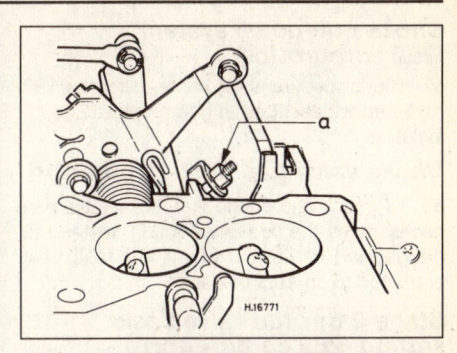

Fig. 3.38 Keihin carburettor Stage 2 basic throttle setting (Sec 11)

a Limiting screw

and, using an elastic band positioned as shown (Fig. 3.36), tension the lever against the stop, then, while pressing the operating lever of the pull-down unit onto its stop, measure the choke valve gap. Compare with that specified and, if necessary, bend the stop lever apart to enlarge the gap, or squeeze it together to reduce the gap (Fig. 3.37).

39 Remove elastic band and refit the choke cover on completion.

Basic throttle setting – Stage 2 (Keihin carburettor)

40 The limiting screw (a in Fig. 3.38) is set during manufacture. and this setting should not be altered. If the screw is turned by mistake the correct setting can be re-established by the following method.

41 With the carburettor removed, unscrew the limiting screw until there is a gap between the end of the screw and the stop.

42 Turn the limiting screw until it just contacts the stop, then screw it in by a further half a turn. Check the idling adjustments described in paragraph 32 after refitting the carburettor.

Accelerator pump adjustment (Keihin carburettor)

43 With the carburettor removed, hold the carburettor (with its float chamber full) above a funnel and measuring jar.

44 Push the thermostat lever in the 'open' direction and push the Stage 2 vacuum unit actuating rod against its stop.

45 Fit an M12 bolt between the carburettor body and the thermostat lever.

46 Open the throttle valve fully and release it slowly, taking at least three seconds to complete the operation and then repeat the cycle until ten complete strokes have been completed. Read off the amount of fuel ejected and divide by ten to obtain the quantity delivered per stroke. Compare this with the value given in Specifications

47 If adjustment is necessary, bend the stop accordingly, upwards if capacity is too low, downwards if capacity is too high. Ensure that there is no clearance between the lever and the operating rod. The injection duration is not adjustable. If the required capacity cannot be obtained then the accelerator pump diaphragm may well be at fault and should be renewed.

Choke pull-down system (Keihin carburettor)

48 The system can only be accurately checked using a vacuum pump and gauge; therefore this work should be entrusted to an Audi dealer.

Inlet manifold preheater (Keihin carburettor)

49 The procedure is the same as for the 1B3 carburettor described in paragraph 31.

Starting fast idle and overrun fuel cut-off two-way valve (Keihin carburettor)

50 To check the operation of the valve, connect a test lamp across the two terminals of the valve, which is located on the front of the engine valve cover.

51 Start the engine and allow it to idle. The test lamp should be illuminated with the engine idling. If not, switch off the engine and connect the test lamp between the valve positive terminal and earth. The bulb should be illuminated when the ignition is switch on. if the bulb does not light up there is a wiring fault in the live feed to the valve. If the lamp does light up, switch off the ignition, disconnect the wiring to the valve, and check the resistance across the valve terminals using an ohmmeter. The resistance should be 30 to 40 ohms. If this value is not obtained, renew the two-way valve. If the resistance is satisfactory, there is likely to be a fault in the wiring between the valve wiring plug and the socket for relay No 3 in the relay plate, or in the relay itself.

Thermo-pneumatic valve (Keihin carburettor)

52 A thermo-pneumatic valve is screwed into the throttle lift thermostat to control the thermo-stat vacuum supply according to temperature.

53 To check the valve without removing it from the vehicle, remove the two hoses from the valve and attach a length of tubing to one of the connections on the valve. Blow down the pipe when the engine is cold and the valve should not pass any air, or very little.

54 Run the engine until it is at normal operating temperature and again blow down the pipe. With the engine hot the valve should be open and allow free passage of air.

55 Remove the piece of tubing from the valve and re-connect the vacuum pipes to it.

Idling speed (2E2 carburettor)

56 The procedure is the same as for the 1B3 carburettor described in paragraphs 1 to 8 inclusive, but check that the fast idle adjustment screw is just making contact with the diaphragm pushrod (Fig. 3.39). The adjustment screws are shown in Fig. 3.40.

Fig. 3.39 2E2 carburettor diaphragm pushrod (A) and fast idle adjustment screw (B) (Sec 11)

Fig. 3.40 2E2 carburettor idle adjusting screw (A) and CO adjustment screw (B) (Sec 11)

3•16 1.8 and 1.9 litre carburettor models

Choke pull-down system (2E2 carburettor)

57 The procedure is the same as for the 1B3 carburettor described in paragraphs 12 to 16 inclusive.

Choke valve gap (2E2 carburettor)

58 To check and adjust the choke valve gap necessitates the use of a vacuum tester and gauge, and in view of this it is a task best entrusted to an Audi dealer.

Stage 2 throttle valve basic setting (2E2 carburettor)

59 This is made during manufacture and will not normally require adjustment. However if the setting has been disturbed proceed as follows. First remove the carburettor (Section 9).
60 Referring to Fig. 3.41, open the throttle valve and hold in this position by inserting a wooden rod or similar implement between the valve and the venturi.
61 Using a rubber band as shown, pre-tension the Stage 2 throttle valve locking lever, then unscrew the limiting screw to provide a clearance between the stop and limiting screw.
62 Now turn the limiting screw in so that it is just in contact with the stop. The limiting screw stop point can be assessed by inserting a piece of thin paper between the screw and stop, moving the paper as the limiting screw is tightened. With the stop point reached turn the screw in a further quarter of a turn then secure it with locking compound. Close both throttle valves then measure the locking lever clearances, A and B in Fig. 3.42. If the clearances are not as specified, bend the arm as necessary.

Accelerator pump (2E2 carburettor)

63 To check and adjust the accelerator pump necessitates the use of a vacuum pump and gauges, and in view of this the work should be entrusted to an Audi dealer.

Three-point unit (2E2 carburettor)

64 To check this, specialised test equipment is required and it should therefore be entrusted to your Audi dealer.

Fig. 3.41 2E2 carburettor throttle valve basic setting showing rod to hold valve open (arrowed), lock lever (1), limiting screw (2) and stop (3) (Sec 11)

Idle/overrun control valve (2E2 carburettor)

65 To check this, specialised test equipment is required and it should therefore be entrusted to your Audi dealer.

Temperature time valve (2E2 carburettor)

66 To check this, specialised test equipment is required and it should therefore be entrusted to your Audi dealer.

12 Inlet and exhaust manifolds – removal and refitting

1 Partially drain the cooling system, with reference to Chapter 2.
2 Remove the air cleaner, as described in Section 3, and the carburettor, as described in Section 9.
3 Disconnect the brake servo vacuum hose.
4 Disconnect the coolant hoses at the inlet manifold.
5 Disconnect the inlet manifold preheater lead at the connector.
6 Detach the exhaust stabiliser and manifold support brackets where fitted.

Fig. 3.42 2E2 carburettor lock lever clearance with throttle valves closed (Sec 11)

A = 0.3 to 0.5 mm (0.011 to 0.019 in)
B = 0.9 to 1.1 mm (0.035 to 0.043 in)

7 Undo the retaining bolts and withdraw the inlet manifold.
8 Undo the exhaust front pipe-to-manifold nuts, and separate the front pipe at the flange. Recover the gasket.
9 Remove the exhaust manifold retaining nuts and withdraw the manifold. Recover the gasket.
10 Refitting is the reverse sequence to removal. Use a new gasket and tighten the retaining, nuts and bolts to the specified torque.

13 Exhaust system – checking, removal and refitting

1 The exhaust system should be examined for leaks, damage and security at regular intervals (see Routine Maintenance). To do this apply the handbrake and, in a well ventilated area, allow the engine to idle. Lie down on each side of the car in turn, and check the full length of the exhaust system for leaks whilst an assistant temporarily places a wad of cloth over the end of the tailpipe. If a leak is evident. stop the engine and use a proprietary repair kit. If the leak is excessive, or damage is evident, renew the section.

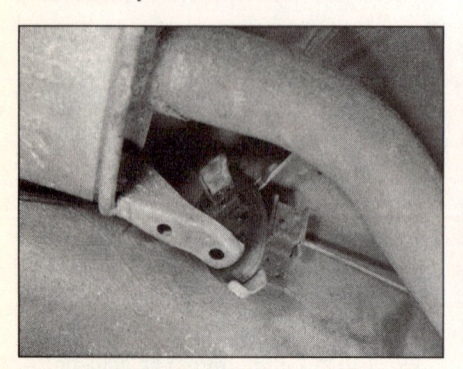

13.1A Exhaust intermediate silencer front rubber mounting . . .

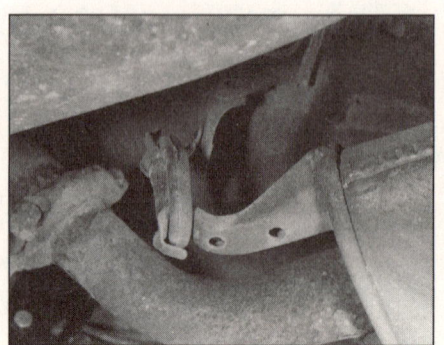

13.1B . . . rear rubber mounting . . .

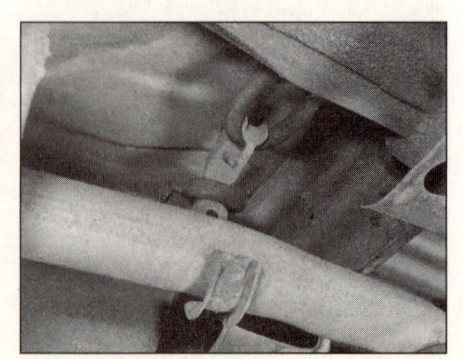

13.1C . . . and tail pipe mounting

1.8 and 1.9 litre carburettor models

Check the rubber mountings for deterioration, and renew them, if necessary (photos).
2 Before doing any dismantling work on the exhaust system, wait until the system has cooled down and then saturate the fixing bolts and joints with a proprietary anti-corrosion fluid.
3 When refitting the system, new nuts and bolts should be used, and it may be found easier to cut through the old bolts with a hacksaw, rather than unscrew them.
4 When renewing any part of the exhaust system, it is usually easier to undo the manifold-to-front pipe joint and remove the complete system from the car, then separate the various pieces of the system, or cut out the defective part, using a hacksaw.
5 Refit the system a piece at a time, starting with the front pipe. Use a new joint gasket and note that it has a flanged side. The flanged side should face towards the exhaust pipe.
6 Smear all the joints with a proprietary exhaust sealing compound before assembly. This makes it easier to slide the pieces to align them and ensures that the joints will be gas tight.
7 Tighten all exhaust fastenings to the specified torque and, while doing this, twist any movable joints as necessary so that the system remains clear of the underbody, and places an equal load on all the mountings.

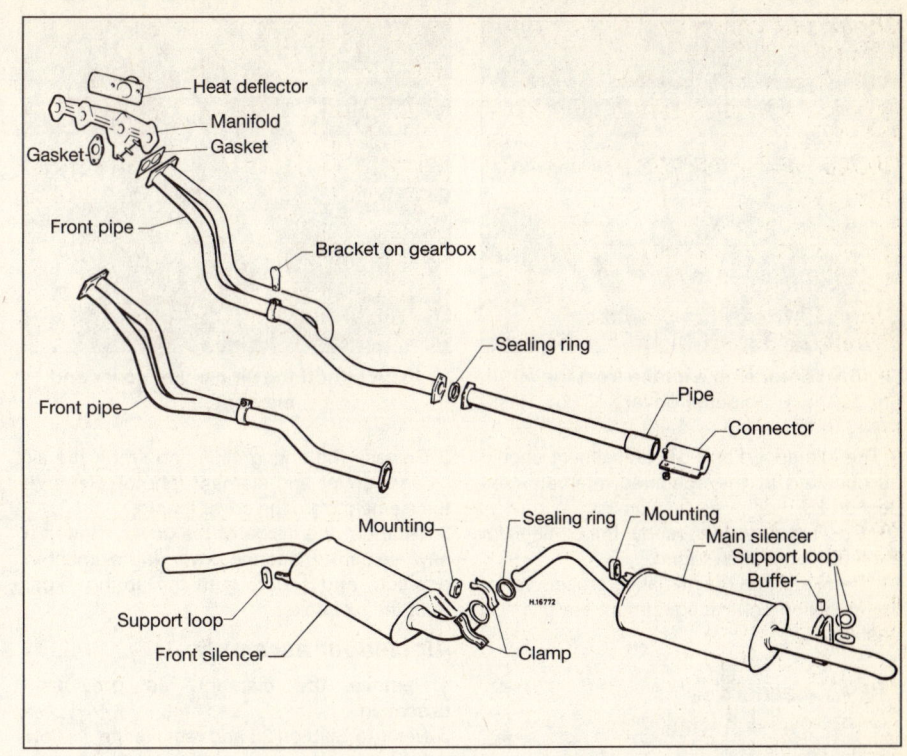

Fig. 3.43 Layout of exhaust system and manifold – 1.8 litre model shown (Secs 12 and 13)

Part B – 2.0, 2.2 and 2.3 litre fuel injection models

14 General description

Warning: *Many of the procedures in this Chapter entail the removal of fuel pipes and connections which may result in some fuel spillage. Before carrying out any operation on the fuel system refer to the precautions given in Safety First! at the beginning of this manual and follow them implicitly. Petrol is a highly dangerous and volatile liquid and the precautions necessary when handling it cannot be overstressed.*

The fuel system consists of a centrally mounted fuel tank, electric fuel pump and Bosch K or KE-Jetronic fuel injection. A turbocharged version of the 2.2 litre engine is available on certain models.
The air cleaner contains a disposable paper element, and is equipped with an intake air preheating system on certain models.
The exhaust system is in four sections, comprising twin front pipes and main and intermediate silencers according to model. The system is bolted to a cast iron manifold at the front, and suspended on flexible rubber mountings throughout its length.

15 Maintenance and inspection

1 Refer to Section 2, paragraphs 1 to 7 and note the following additional items.
2 Renew the fuel filter using the following procedure.
3 Ensure that the vehicle is in a well ventilated area, and that there are no naked flames or other possible sources of ignition.
4 Disconnect the battery negative lead.
5 While holding a rag over the union to prevent fuel from spraying out, slacken the control pressure line at the warm-up valve to release the fuel pressure in the system. The control pressure line is the one connected to the upper union on the warm-up valve (photo). Tighten the union when the fuel pressure is released.
6 Place rags under the filter, and unscrew the fuel lines at each end. Recover the washers at the outlet union (photo).
7 Undo the filter clamp bracket nut and withdraw the filter.
8 Fit the new filter with the arrow stamped on the filter body pointing in the direction of fuel flow. Tighten the fuel lines, and check for leaks with the engine running.

15.5 Control pressure line union (arrowed) at the warm-up valve

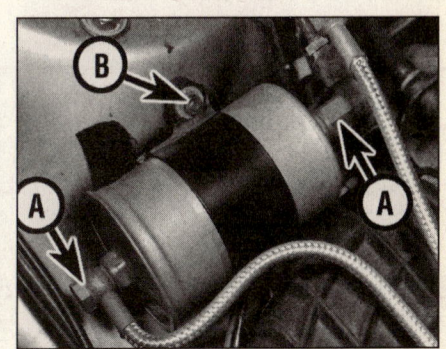

15.6 Fuel filter fuel line unions (A) and clamp bracket nut (B)

16.1 Withdraw the intake from the air cleaner cover

16.2A Lift off the air cleaner cover and element . . .

16.2B . . . and withdraw the element from the cover

9 The idle speed and CO adjustment should be checked at the specified intervals (see Section 23).
10 On Turbo models, renew the oil filter for the turbo lubrication circuit.
11 Details of the maintenance procedure for the emission control equipment are given in Section 38.

16 Air cleaners – removal and refitting

Element renewal

1 Slacken the cold air intake clamp and withdraw the intake from the air cleaner cover (photo).

2 Release the spring clips and lift off the air cleaner cover and element (photo). Remove the element from the cover (photo).
3 Wipe out the inside of the cover, then fit a new element. Place the cover and element in position, and secure with the spring clips. Refit the air intake.

Air cleaner assembly

4 Remove the element, as previously described.
5 Refer to Section 25 and remove the air-flow meter.
6 Withdraw the overrun cut-off valve from the air cleaner housing.
7 Undo the retaining bolt, disengage the air cleaner housing peg from the locating grommet, and remove the unit from the engine compartment.
8 Refitting is a reversal of the removal sequence

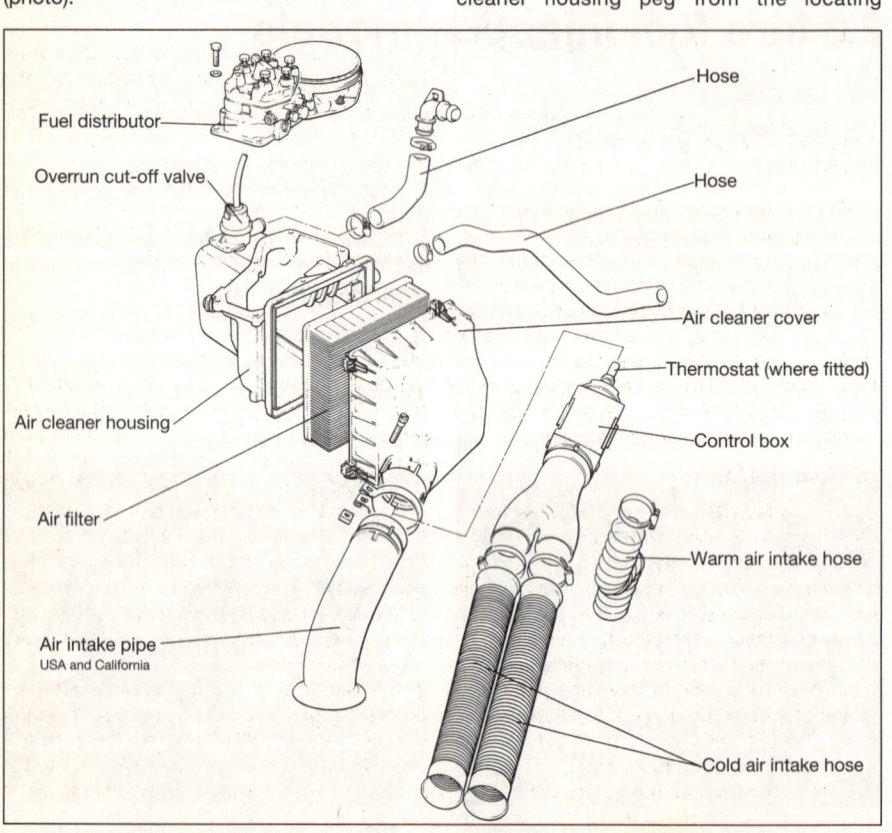

17 Automatic air temperature control – checking

1 Certain models are equipped with a thermostatically operated air temperature control device, located in a regulator box fitted in the air cleaner intake. The unit contains a flap valve, which can open or close a hot or cold air intake to maintain the intake air temperature within predetermined parameters.
2 To check the operation of the unit, remove the air intake ducts, then remove the regulator box from the air cleaner.
3 Hold the thermostat capsule in warm water (approximately 20°C, 68°F) for two minutes. Check that the flap valve has moved to a position where it is just shutting off the cold air intake. If necessary, alter the thermostat position by screwing it in or out of the adjuster as required. Secure the thermostat with sealing paint after adjustment.
4 When refitting the regulator box, ensure that the rib aligns with the groove in the air cleaner cover.

18 Fuel tank – removal and refitting

Refer to Section 6 of this Chapter, but note that the fuel pump is located in the tank along with the fuel gauge sender unit. If necessary, remove the pump, as described in Section 31.

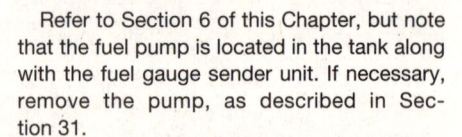

19 Fuel gauge sender unit – removal and refitting

Refer to Section 7 of this Chapter.

Fig. 3.44 Air cleaner assembly and related components (Sec 16)

2.0, 2.2 and 2.3 litre fuel injection models 3•19

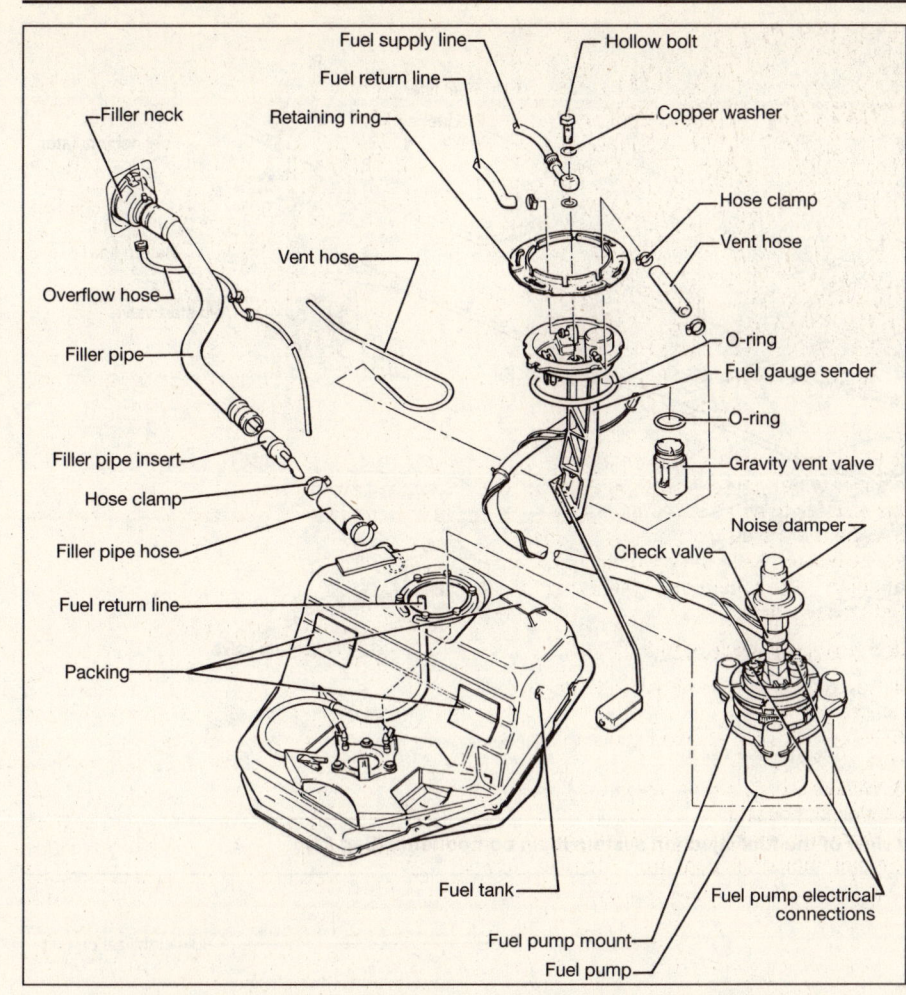

Fig. 3.45 Exploded view of the fuel tank, fuel pump and fuel gauge sender unit components (Secs 18, 19 and 31)

20.1 Accelerator cable attachment at the throttle valve housing

20 Accelerator cable – removal, refitting and adjustment

Refer to Section 8 of this Chapter, but note that it is not necessary to remove the air cleaner. The cable is secured to the lever on the throttle valve housing by a clamp bolt (photo), or ferrule.

21 Fuel injection system – general description

A Bosch K or KE-Jetronic fuel injection system is fitted to all fuel injection models covered by this manual. An exploded view of the main parts of these systems is shown in Fig. 3.46 and the accompanying illustrations show the various subsidiary components associated with the main system.

The following paragraphs describe the system and its various elements. Later Sections describe the tests which can be carried out to ensure whether a particular unit is functioning correctly, but dismantling and repair procedure of units are not generally given because repairs are not possible.

The system measures the amount of air entering the engine and determines the amount of fuel which needs to be mixed with the air to give the correct combustion mixture for the particular conditions of engine operation. The fuel is sprayed continuously by an injection nozzle to the inlet channel of each cylinder. This fuel and air is drawn into the cylinders when the inlet valves open.

Airflow meter

1 This measures the volume of air entering the engine and relies on the principle that a circular disc, when placed in a funnel through which a current of air is passing, will rise until the weight of the disc is equal to the force on its lower surface which the air creates. If the volume of air flowing is increased and the plate were to remain in the same place, the rate of flow of air through the gap between the cone and the plate would increase and the force on the plate would increase.

2 If the plate is free to move then, as the force on the plate increases, the plate rises in the cone and the area between the edge of the plate and the edge of the cone increases, until the rate of airflow and hence the force on the plate, becomes the same as it was at the former lower flow rate and smaller area. Thus the height of the plate is a measure of the volume of air entering the engine.

3 The airflow meter consists of an air funnel with a sensor plate mounted on a lever which is supported at its fulcrum. The weight of the airflow sensor plate and its lever are balanced by a counterweight and the upward force on the sensor plate is opposed by a plunger. The plunger, which moves up and down as a result of the variations in airflow, is surrounded by a sleeve having vertical slots in it. The vertical movement of the plunger uncovers a greater or lesser length of the slots, which meters the fuel to the injection valves.

4 The sides of the air funnel are not a pure cone because optimum operation of the engine requires a different air/fuel ratio under different conditions such as idling, part load and full load. By making parts of the funnel steeper than the basic shape, a richer mixture can be provided for at idling and full load. By making the funnel flatter than the basic shape, a leaner mixture can be provided.

Fuel supply

5 Fuel is pumped continuously while the engine is running by a roller cell pump running at constant speed: excess fuel is returned to the tank. The fuel pump is operated when the ignition switch is in the START position, but once the starter is released a switch connected to the air plate prevents the pump from operating unless the engine is running.

6 The fuel line to the fuel supply valve incorporates a filter and also a fuel accumulator. The function of the accumulator is to maintain pressure in the fuel system after the engine has been switched off and so give good hot restarting.

7 Associated with the fuel accumulator is a pressure regulator which is an integral part of the fuel metering device. When the engine is switched off, the pressure regulator lets the pressure to the injection valves fall rapidly to cut off the fuel flow through them and so prevent the engine from dieseling or running on. The valve closes at just below the opening

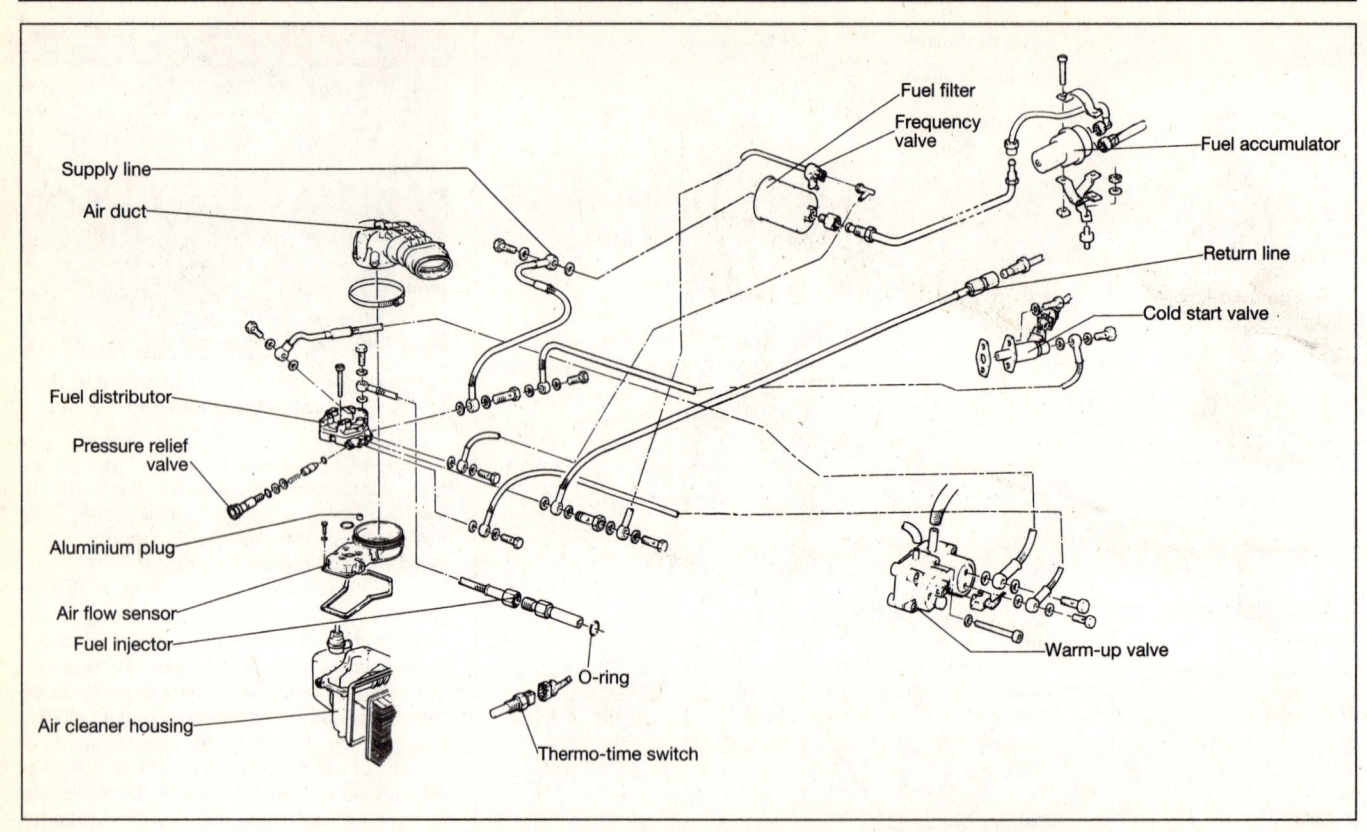

Fig. 3.46 Exploded view of the fuel injection system main components (Sec 21)

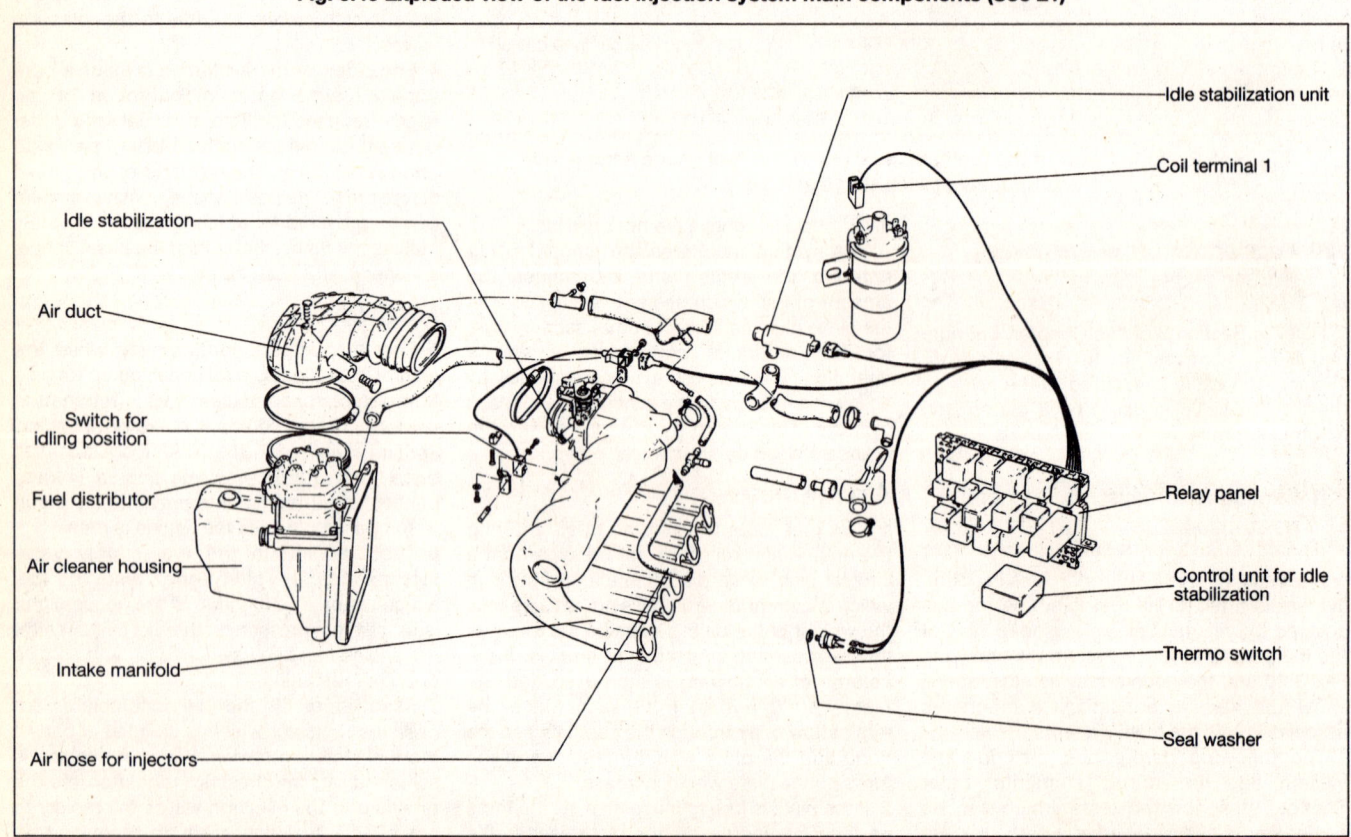

Fig. 3.47 Layout of the idle stabilisation system (Sec 21)

2.0, 2.2 and 2.3 litre fuel injection models 3•21

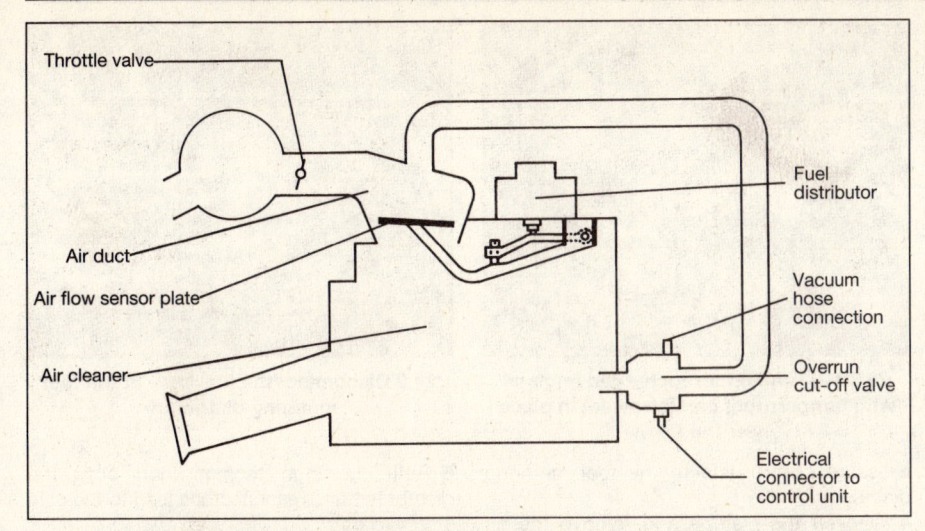

Fig. 3.48 Diagrammatic representation of the overrun fuel cut-off system (Sec 21)

pressure of the injector valves and this pressure is then maintained by the pressure accumulator.

Fuel distributor

8 The fuel distributor is mounted on the air metering device and is controlled by the vertical movement of the airflow sensor plate. It consists of a spool valve which moves vertically in a sleeve, the sleeve having as many vertical slots around its circumference as there are cylinders on the engine.

9 The spool valve is subjected to hydraulic pressure on the upper end and this balances the pressure on the air plate which is applied to the bottom of the valve by a plunger. As the spool valve rises and falls it uncovers a greater or lesser length of metering slot and so controls the column of fuel fed to each injector.

10 Each metering slot has a different pressure valve, which ensures that the difference in pressure between the two sides of the slot is always the same. Because the drop in pressure across the metering slot is unaffected by the length of slot exposed, the amount of fuel flowing depends only on the exposed area of the slots.

Compensation units

11 For cold starting and during warming-up, additional devices are required to adjust the fuel supply to the different fuel requirements of the engine under these conditions.

Cold start valve

12 The cold start valve is mounted in the intake manifold and sprays additional fuel into the manifold during cold starting. The valve is solenoid operated and is controlled by a thermotime switch in the engine cooling system. The thermotime switch is actuated for a period which depends upon coolant temperature, the period decreasing with rise in coolant temperature. If the coolant temperature is high enough for the engine not to need additional fuel for starting, the switch does not operate.

Warm-up regulator

13 While warming up, the engine needs a richer mixture to compensate for fuel which condenses on the cold walls of the inlet manifold and cylinder walls. It also needs more fuel to compensate for power lost because of increased friction losses and increased oil drag in a cold engine. The mixture is made richer during warming up by the warm-up regulator. This is a pressure regulator which lowers the pressure applied to the control plunger of the fuel regulator during warm-up. This reduced pressure causes the airflow plate to rise higher than it would do otherwise, thus uncovering a greater length of metering slot and making the mixture richer.

14 The valve is operated by a bi-metallic strip which is heated by an electric heater. When the engine is cold the bit-metallic spring pressed against the delivery valve spring to reduce the pressure on the diaphragm and enlarge the discharge cross-section. This increase in cross-section results in a lowering of the pressure fed to the control plunger.

15 When the engine is started, the electrical heater of the bi-metallic strip is switch ON. As the strip warms it rises gradually until it ultimately rises free of the control spring plate and the valve spring becomes fully effective to give normal control pressure.

Idle stabilisation

16 Various sensors on the engine monitor engine speed, temperature and throttle position and transmit the information to an electronic switch unit. If the engine idle speed varies from the design speed of the switch unit, the unit operates a control valve to increase or decrease an additional air supply around the throttle valve, and maintain the idling speed at a stablised level.

Overrun cut-off

17 In the interests of fuel economy, an additional device is used to restrict the fuel supply during engine overrun.

18 The overrun cut-off valve is located on the air cleaner housing, and is controlled by a switch unit which in turn receives information from a temperature switch, and throttle valve switch. If the coolant temperature is above 30°C (86°F). the engine speed above 1400 rpm, and the throttle in the idling position, the switch unit activates the overrun cut-off valve which is then opened by vacuum. An auxiliary air channel is opened, and intake air bypasses the airflow sensor plate, and the plate then falls. Consequently the fuel supply is cut-off until the auxiliary air channel once again closes.

22 Fuel injection system – precautions and general repair information

1 Due to the complexity of the fuel injection system, and the need for special tools and test equipment, any work should be limited to the operations described in this Chapter. Other adjustments and system checks are beyond the scope of most readers, and should be left to an Audi dealer.

2 Before disconnecting any fuel lines, unions, or components, thoroughly clean the component or connection and the adjacent area.

3 Place any removed components on a clean surface and cover them with plastic sheet or paper. Do not use fluffy rags for cleaning.

4 New parts should be left packaged until immediately before they are to be fitted.

5 The system operates under pressure at all times, and care must be taken when disconnecting fuel lines. Relieve the system pressure, as described in Section 15, paragraphs 3 to 5, before disconnecting any fuel lines under pressure. Refer to the warning note in Section 14, and always work with the battery negative lead disconnected.

6 In the event of a malfunction in the system, reference should be made to the Fault finding Section at the end of this Chapter, but first make a basic check of the system hoses, connections, fuses, and relays for any obvious and immediately visible defects.

23 Idle speed and idle mixture – adjustment

1 The engine idling speed is maintained at a predetermined value by the idle stabilisation valve, and does not normally require adjustment. In the event of unsatisfactory idling, the advice of an Audi dealer should be sought. The engine idling speed cannot be adjusted without bypassing the idle stabilisation system, and this entails the use of Audi test equipment.

3•22 2.0, 2.2 and 2.3 litre fuel injection models

23.3A Idle speed adjustment screw (arrowed) on normally aspirated fuel injection engines . . .

23.3B . . . and on turbocharged engines with tamperproof cap (arrowed) in place over the screw

24.2 Disconnect the fuel lines at the fuel metering distributor

2 The idle mixture adjustment is carried out in conjunction with the idle speed adjustment, and special Audi test equipment is also required for this operation.
3 For reference purposes the idle speed adjustment screws are shown in the photos.

24 Fuel metering distributor – removal and refitting

1 Release the fuel pressure in the system, as described in Section 15, paragraphs 3 to 5 inclusive.
2 Mark each fuel line and its port on the distributor, then disconnect the fuel lines (photo). Recover the copper washers at each union.
3 Unscrew and remove the connection of the pressure control line to the fuel metering distributor.
4 Undo the three fuel metering distributor retaining screws.
5 Lift off the fuel metering distributor, taking care that the metering plunger does not fall out. If the plunger does fall out accidentally, clean it in fuel and then re-insert it with its chamfered end downwards.
6 Before refitting the metering distributor, ensure that the plunger moves up and down freely. If the plunger sticks, the distributor must be renewed, because the plunger cannot be repaired or replaced separately.
7 Refit the distributor, using a new sealing ring, and after tightening the screws, lock them with paint.
8 Reconnect the fuel lines to their original positions.

25 Airflow meter – removal and refitting

1 Release the fuel pressure in the system, as described in Section 15, paragraphs 3 to 5 inclusive.
2 Mark each fuel line and its port on the fuel metering distributor, then disconnect the fuel lines, Recover the copper washers at each union.
3 Unscrew and remove the connection of the pressure control line to the fuel metering distributor.
4 Slacken the clamps and remove the air intake duct.
5 Remove the bolts securing the airflow meter to the air cleaner and remove the meter, complete with fuel metering distributor.
6 The fuel metering plunger should be prevented from falling out when the fuel metering distributor is removed from the airflow meter (see previous Section).
7 Refitting is the reverse of removing, but it is necessary to use a new gasket between the airflow meter and the air cleaner.

26 Pressure relief valve – removal, servicing and refitting

1 Release the pressure in the fuel system, as described in paragraphs 3 to 5 of Section 15.
2 Unscrew the non-return valve plug and remove the plug and its sealing washer.
3 Take out the O-ring, plunger and O-ring in that order.
4 When refitting the assembly, use new O-rings and ensure that all the shims which were removed are refitted.

27 Thermotime switch – checking

1 The thermotime switch energises the cold start valve for a short time on starting and the time for which the valve is switched on depends upon the engine temperature.
2 Pull the connector off the cold start valve and connect a test lamp across the contacts of the connector.
3 Pull the high tension lead off the centre of the distributor and connect the lead to earth.
4 Operate the starter for 10 seconds and note the interval before the test lamp lights and the period for which it remains alight. Reference to the graph (Fig. 3.49) will show that at a coolant temperature of 30°C (86°F) the lamp should light immediately and stay on for two seconds.
5 The check should not be carried out if the coolant temperature is above 30°C (86°F).
6 Refit the high tension lead onto the distributor, and reconnect the lead to the cold start valve.

28 Cold start valve – checking

1 Ensure that the coolant temperature is below 30°C (86°F) and that the car battery is fully charged.
2 Pull the high tension lead off the centre of the distributor and connect the lead to earth.
3 Pull the connectors off the warm-up valve and the cold start valve.
4 Remove the two bolts securing the cold start valve to the inlet manifold and remove the valve, taking care not to damage the gasket.
5 With fuel line and electrical connections connected to the valve, hold the valve over a glass jar and operate the starter for 10 seconds. The cold start valve should produce an even cone of spray during the time the thermotime switch is on.
6 After completing the checks refit the valve and reconnect the leads that were disturbed.

29 Warm-up regulator – checking

1 With the engine cold, pull the connectors off the warm-up valve.

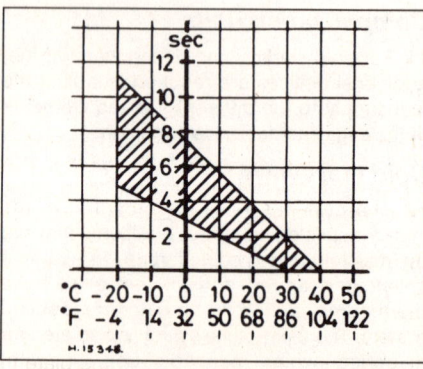

Fig. 3.49 Thermotime switch operation graph (Sec 27)

2.0, 2.2 and 2.3 litre fuel injection models 3•23

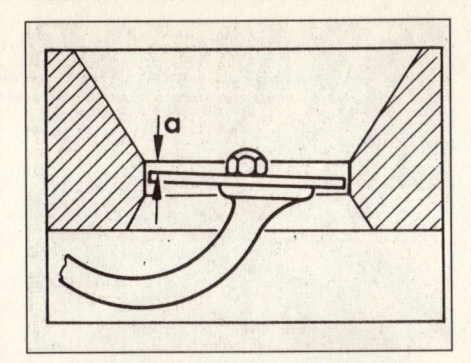

Fig. 3.50 Airflow sensor plate position relative to air cone bottom edge (Sec 30)

a = specified plate upper edge to air cone bottom edge dimension

2 Connect a voltmeter across the terminals of the warm-up valve connector and operate the starter. The voltage across the terminals should be a minimum of 8.0 volts.
3 Switch the ignition OFF and connect an ohmmeter across the terminals of the warm-up valve. If the meter does not indicate a resistance of about 20 ohms, the heater coil is defective and a new valve must be fitted.

30 Airflow sensor lever and control plunger – checking

1 For the correct mixture to be supplied to the engine it is essential that the sensor plate is central in the venturi, and that its height is correct.
2 Slacken the retaining clips and remove the air intake duct. If the sensor plate appears to be off-centre, loosen its centre screw and carefully run a 0.10 mm (0.004 in) feeler gauge round the edge of the plate to centralise it, then retighten the bolt.
3 Raise the airflow sensor plate and then quickly move it to its rest position. No resistance should be felt on the downward movement; if there is resistance the airflow meter is defective and a new one must be fitted.
4 If the sensor plate can be moved downwards easily, but has a strong resistance to upward movement, the control plunger is sticking. Remove the fuel distributor (Section 24) and clean the control plunger in fuel. If this does not cure the problem, a new fuel distributor must be fitted.
5 Check the position of the airflow sensor in relation to the air cone. On all engines except code KZ, the upper edge of the plate should be flush with the bottom edge of the air cone, or a maximum of 0.5 mm (0.020 in) below it. On code (KZ engines, the upper edge of the plate should be 1.75 to 2.05 mm (0.068 to 0.081 in) below the bottom edge of the air cone (Fig. 3.50).
6 Adjust the height of the plate by lifting it and bending the wire clips attaching the plate to the balance arm, but take care not to scratch or damage the surface of the air cone.

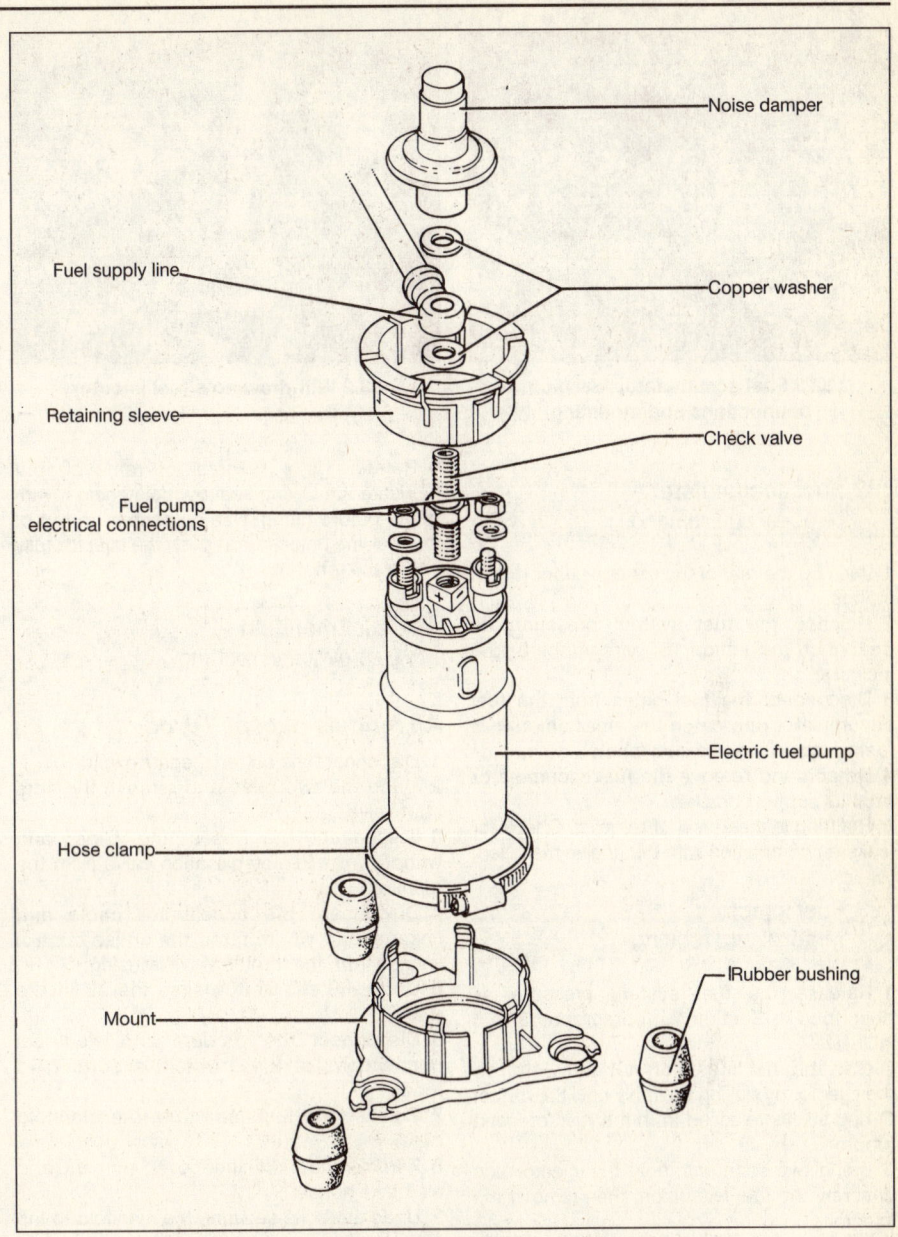

Fig. 3.51 Exploded view of the fuel pump components (Sec 31)

31 Electric fuel pump – removal and refitting

1 The electric fuel pump is located in the fuel tank and is just accessible through the sender unit opening with the sender unit removed (Section 19). The pump is a sealed unit; the only replacement part available is the check valve on the fuel outlet.
2 Before removing the pump, first ensure that the car is in a well ventilated place and that there is no danger of ignition from sparks or naked flames. Disconnect the battery negative lead.
3 With the sender unit removed, release the pump from its retaining lugs and remove it from the tank.
4 To separate the pump from the sender unit, unscrew the nuts and disconnect the wiring. Remove the noise damper from the check valve and lift off the fuel line and washers.
5 The outlet check valve may be unscrewed if necessary, but the pump body must not be held in a vice. Either grip the hexagon of the valve in the vice and turn the pump by hand, or use a spanner on the valve and a strap wrench on the pump body.
6 The pump is designed to work with all its moving parts immersed in petrol and it will be damaged irreparably if it is run without being connected to the fuel system.
7 The capacity of the pump is much greater than the fuel requirement of the engine and it is unlikely that pump output will fall to a point where it is inadequate.
8 Refitting is a reversal of removal.

3•24 2.0, 2.2 and 2.3 litre fuel injection models

32.3 Fuel accumulator fuel pipe connections and mounting

33.2 Withdrawing a fuel injector

33.5 Using a spanner to push a fuel injector fully home

32 Fuel accumulator – removal and refitting

1 Jack up the rear of the car and support it on stands.
2 Release the fuel system pressure, as described in Section 15, paragraphs 3 to 5 inclusive.
3 Disconnect the fuel pipes from the fuel accumulator and catch the small amount of fuel which will be released (photo).
4 Detach and remove the fuel accumulator from its support bracket.
5 Refitting is a reversal of removal. Check for leaks on completion with the engine restarted.

33 Fuel injectors – removal and refitting

1 Release the fuel system pressure as described in Section 15, paragraphs 3 to 5 inclusive.
2 Grip the fuel line union nut and withdraw the injector by pulling up firmly until the rubber O-ring seal is released from the injector insert (photo).
3 Using two spanners, hold the injector and unscrew the fuel line union, then remove the injector.
4 Accurate checking of the injector spray pattern and leakage requires special test equipment and should be left to an Audi dealer.

5 Refitting is a reversal of removal, but lubricate the O-ring seal by moistening it with petrol before fitting. Use a spanner on top of the fuel line union nut to push the injector fully into place (photo).

34 Inlet manifold – removal and refitting

All models except Turbo

1 Disconnect the battery negative lead.
2 Undo the two bolts and remove the cold start valve.
3 Disconnect the hoses and clips, and withdraw the idle stabilisation valve from the manifold.
4 Disconnect the accelerator cable and linkage, and where fitted the cruise control linkage from the throttle valve housing.
5 Undo the clip and release the air intake duct.
6 Disconnect the vacuum and electrical connections at the manifold according to model.
7 Release the fuel lines from the manifold clips.
8 Remove the air cleaner cover, element, and air intake hoses.
9 Undo the bolts securing the manifold to the cylinder head, and the exhaust manifold support bracket nuts (photo).
10 Withdraw the manifold from the cylinder head and remove it from under the fuel lines.

11 Refitting is a reversal of removal, but adjust the accelerator cable and linkage as described in Section 20, and Chapter 7 where automatic transmission is fitted.

Turbo models

12 Disconnect the battery negative lead.
13 Undo the clip and remove the air intake duct at the throttle valve housing.
14 Remove the air intake tube from the air cleaner, and intake duct at the airflow sensor.
15 Remove the air cleaner cover and element.
16 Remove the idle stabilisation valve, bracket, and duct (photo).
17 Release the fuel lines at the manifold clips.
18 Disconnect the accelerator cable and linkage, and where fitted the cruise control linkage at the throttle valve housing and manifold.
19 Note the locations of all electrical and vacuum connections likely to restrict removal of the manifold, and disconnect them.
20 Undo the bolts securing the manifold to the cylinder head, and the exhaust manifold support bracket nuts.
21 Withdraw the manifold from the cylinder head, and remove it from under the fuel lines.
22 Refitting is a reversal of removal, but adjust the accelerator cable and linkage as described in Section 20, and Chapter 7 where automatic transmission is fitted.

35 Turbocharger – description

2.2 litre Turbo models are equipped with an exhaust driven turbocharger, which is a device designed to increase the engine's power output without increasing exhaust emissions or adversely affecting fuel economy. It does so by utilizing the heat energy present in the exhaust gases as they exit the engine.
Basically, the turbocharger consists of two fans mounted on a common shaft. One fan is driven by the hot exhaust gases as they rush through the exhaust manifold and expand. The other pulls in fresh air and compresses it

34.9 Inlet manifold retaining bolts and exhaust manifold support brackets

34.16 Idle stabilisation valve on Turbo models

2.0, 2.2 and 2.3 litre fuel injection models 3•25

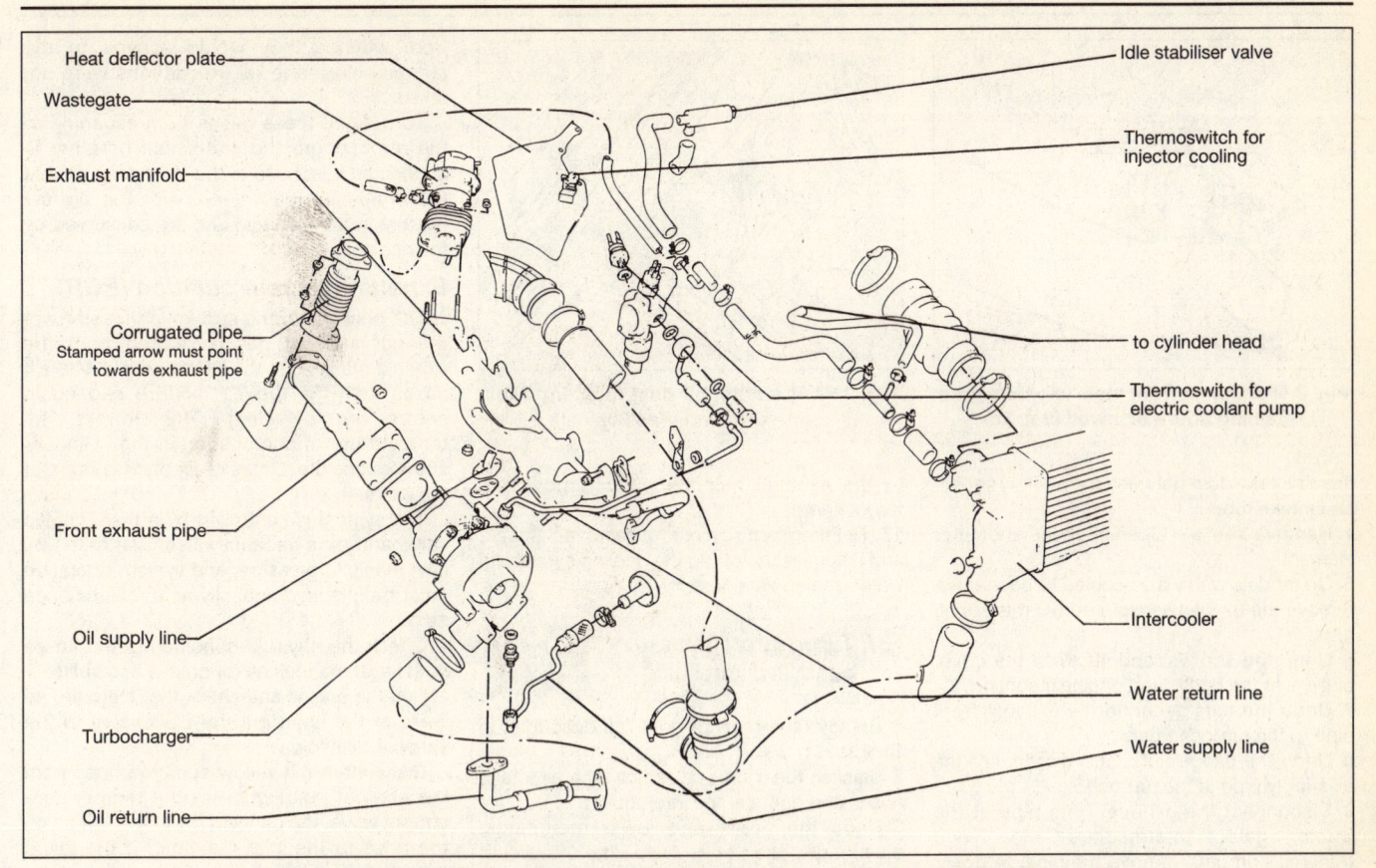

Fig. 3.52 Exploded view of the water-cooled turbocharger components (Secs 35 and 36)

before it enters the intake manifold. By compressing the air, a larger charge can be let into each cylinder and greater power output is achieved.

The temperature of the intake air is reduced, thus increasing its density, by passing it through an intercooler mounted at the front of the engine prior to It entering the manifold.

The boost pressure generated by the turbocharger is controlled by a waste gate which opens once a predetermined pressure is achieved.

The turbocharger is lubricated by oil from the engine lubrication circuit, but an additional oil filter and an oil cooler are fitted.

On later models, the turbocharger is connected into the engine coolant circuit for cooling, and an electric coolant pump, activated by a thermoswitch, operates when the coolant temperature exceeds a preset value.

The turbocharger is a close tolerance, expensive component, and servicing or repairs should be left to a dealer service department, or specialist with turbocharger repair experience. Apart from the information in the following Sections, any other work on the turbocharger or its related components is beyond the scope of the average reader.

36 Turbocharger – removal and refitting

1 Disconnect the battery negative lead.
2 Remove the air intake duct between the intercooler and throttle valve housing.
3 Disconnect the vacuum hose, then remove

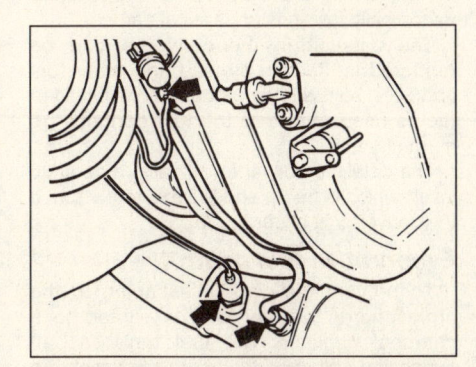

Fig. 3.53 Oxygen sensor and CO measuring tube attachments at the turbocharger (arrowed) – North American models (Sec 36)

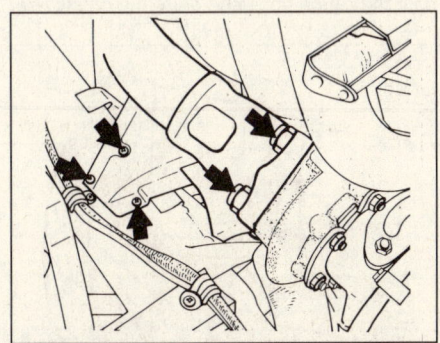

Fig. 3.54 Engine mounting cover plate screws and exhaust front pipe attachment at turbocharger – arrowed (Sec 36)

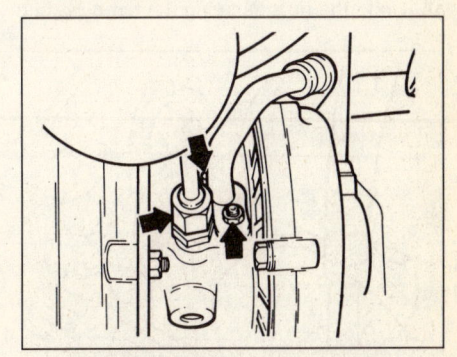

Fig. 3.55 Oil supply pipe and coolant pipe union (arrowed) at the turbocharger (Sec 36)

Fig. 3.56 Exhaust front pipe-to-waste gate retaining nuts – arrowed (Sec 36)

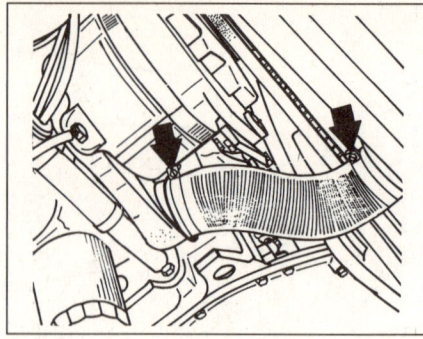

Fig. 3.57 Alternator air duct retaining clips – arrowed (Sec 36)

the air intake duct between the air-flow sensor and intake tube.
4 Remove the air cleaner cover and filter element.
5 On models with water-cooled turbocharger, remove the oxygen sensor and CO measuring tube.
6 Undo the screws, and lift away the cover plate over the right-hand engine mounting.
7 Undo the nuts securing the exhaust front pipe to the turbocharger.
8 Undo the flange nuts, and disconnect the oil supply pipe at the turbocharger.
9 Disconnect the exhaust front pipe at the waste gate, intermediate pipe and transmission, and remove the pipe. Recover the gaskets.
10 Slacken the clips, and remove the air duct to the alternator.
11 Slacken the clip, and disconnect the intercooler hose from the turbocharger.
12 Undo the flange nuts, and disconnect the oil return pipe at the turbocharger.
13 On water-cooled versions, disconnect the lower coolant pipe at the union adjacent to the oil return pipe.
14 Refer to Chapter 12 and remove the alternator, then remove the alternator mounting bracket.
15 On water-cooled versions, disconnect the upper coolant pipe and the adjacent oil supply pipe.
16 Undo the nuts securing the turbocharger to the exhaust manifold, and remove the turbocharger.
17 Refitting is a reversal of removal. Check, and if necessary top up the cooling system on water-cooled versions.

37 Turbo intercooler – removal and refitting

1 Remove the radiator grille, as described in Chapter 11.
2 Slacken the clips, and remove the air intake hoses and ducts at the intercooler.
3 Undo the upper and lower mountings, disengage the unit from its mounting grommets, and remove the intercooler from the car.
4 Refitting is a reversal of removal.

38 Emission control systems – general

Although careful attention to the correct ignition and mixture settings minimises the amount of harmful gases released by the exhaust system, the increasingly stringent legislation in some countries has made the introduction of additional systems necessary.

Crankcase ventilation system

Some of the products of combustion blow past the piston rings and enter the crankcase, from whence they would escape to the atmosphere if special precautions were not taken.
To prevent these gases from escaping to the atmosphere the crankcase breather is connected by a hose to the air cleaner so that the crankcase gases mix with the air/fuel mixture in the manifold and are consumed by the engine.

Exhaust gas recirculation (EGR)

The principle of the system is that some of the hot exhaust gas is ducted from the exhaust manifold to the inlet manifold where it mixes with the fuel/air mixture and again enters the cylinders. This lowers the temperature of combustion in the cylinders and reduces the oxides of nitrogen content of the exhaust.
The system is controlled by a thermostatic valve and by a vacuum valve, controlled by inlet manifold pressure, and system operation must be checked annually as a maintenance item.
Check the physical condition of the hoses of the system, looking for cracks and splits.
Run the engine and check that there are no leaks in the line from the EGR valve to the exhaust manifold.
Disconnect the yellow coloured hose from the straight connection of the temperature control valve and connect it to the T-piece on the hose to the inlet manifold. If the idling speed of the engine falls, or the engine stalls, the EGR valve is working properly. If the idle speed does not change, check that none of the hoses is blocked. If the hoses are clear the EGR valve is faulty and must be renewed.

Catalytic converter

This is fitted to cars intended for certain territories and it consists of an additional component in the exhaust pipe and silencer system.
The converter contains a catalyst which induces a chemical reaction to turn the carbon monoxide and hydrocarbons in the exhaust gas into carbon dioxide and water.
The converter does not require any maintenance, but should be examined periodically for signs of physical damage.
The catalyst in the converter can be rendered ineffective by lead and other fuel additives, so it is important that only unleaded fuel is used, and that the fuel contains no harmful additives.
The catalytic converter contains a ceramic insert which is fragile and is liable to fracture if the converter is hit, or dropped.

Evaporative fuel control

To prevent fuel vapour escaping to the atmosphere, the fuel tank is vented to a charcoal canister. The fuel tank has an expansion chamber and vent lines which are arranged so that no fuel or vapour can escape even though the car may be at a very high temperature, or may be driven or parked on a very steep incline.

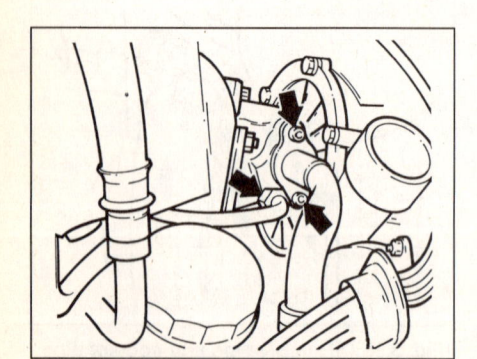

Fig. 3.58 Oil return pipe and coolant pipe union (arrowed) at the turbocharger (Sec 36)

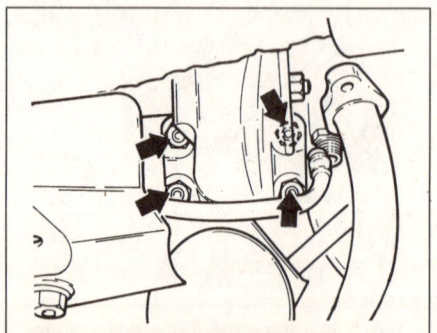

Fig. 3.59 Turbocharger retaining nuts – arrowed (Sec 36)

2.0, 2.2 and 2.3 litre fuel injection models 3•27

40.5 Exhaust manifold retaining nuts

40.6A Withdraw the manifold . . .

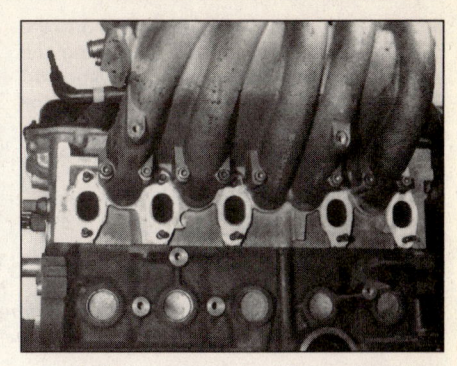

40.6B . . . and recover the gaskets

The vent lines are connected to a canister containing charcoal which absorbs the hydrocarbon vapours. When the engine is not running, fuel vapour collects in the charcoal canister. When the engine is running, fresh air is sucked through the canister and the vapours are drawn from the canister through the air cleaner and into the engine, where they are burnt.

Oxygen sensor system

This system consists of a sensor located in the exhaust manifold, an electronic control unit located in the right-hand front footwell, a thermoswitch relay, and frequency valve. An elapsed mileage odometer also illuminates a warning light on the instrument panel to indicate a maintenance check is required on the system.

The system controls the fuel/air mixture according to engine temperature and exhaust gas content, but will only be accurate if the basic mixture adjustments are correct.

39 Emission control systems – operating precautions

1 The efficiency and reliability of the emission control system is dependent upon a number of operating factors, and the following precautions must be observed.
2 Ensure that the fuel and ignition systems are serviced regularly and that only suitable fuel, free from harmful additives, is used.
3 Do not alter or remove any parts of the emission control system, or any controls which have been fitted to the vehicle to protect the environment.
4 Do not continue to use the car if it is misfiring, or showing any other symptoms of faulty operation of the engine.
5 Do not leave the car unattended when the engine is running, because any indications of improper operation will not be noticed and prolonged idling can cause the engine to overheat and be damaged.
6 If a catalytic converter is fitted, take care not to park the car on areas of dry grass or leaves, because the external temperature of the converter may be sufficient to ignite them.

7 Do not apply any additional underseaing or rustproofing material to the exhaust system, or anywhere very near to it, because this may lead to a fire.
8 If a catalytic converter is fitted, the car must never be pushed or towed to start it and the engine must not be turned off if the car is moving. To do so would allow unburnt fuel to enter the converter and damage it.
9 Always renew seals and gaskets upstream of the catalytic converter whenever they are disturbed.

40 Exhaust manifold – removal and refitting

1 Disconnect the battery negative terminal.
2 On Turbo models remove the turbocharger, as described in Section 36.
3 Undo the exhaust front pipe-to-manifold nuts, and separate the front pipe at the flange. Recover the gasket.
4 On Turbo models, undo the nuts and separate the waste gate at the manifold.

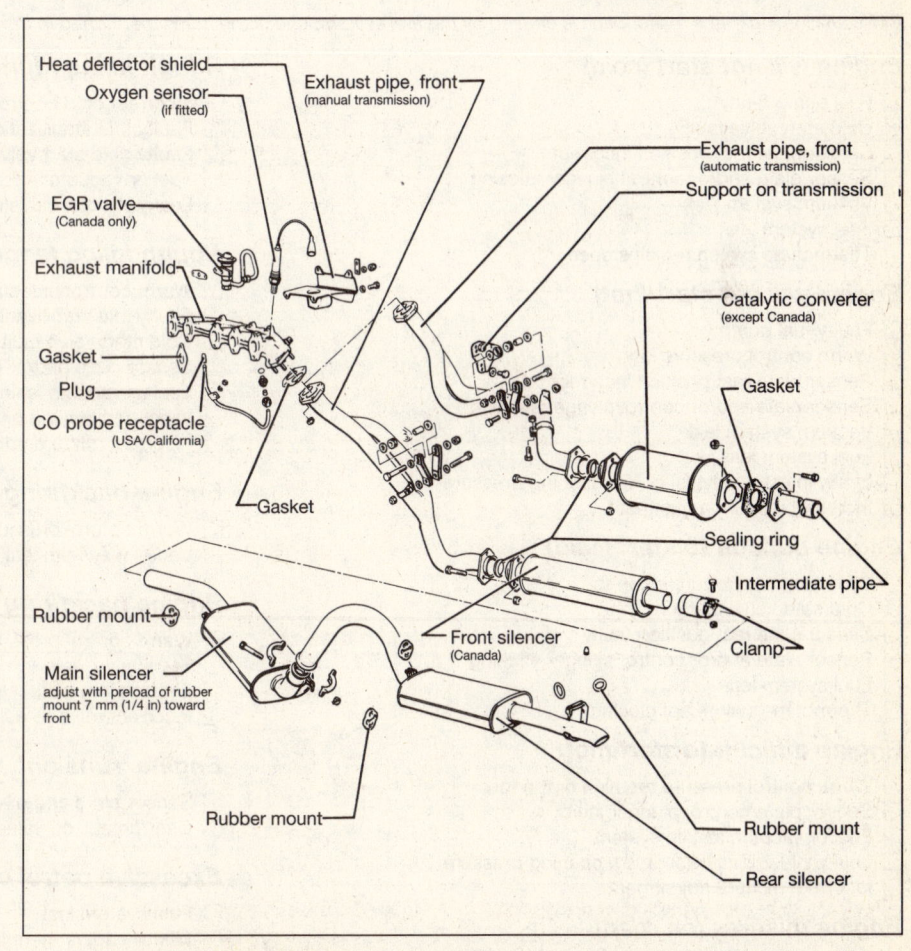

Fig. 3.60 Layout of the exhaust system fitted to North American models (Sec 41)

5 Undo the nuts securing the manifold to the cylinder head, and the bolts securing the support brackets to the inlet manifold (photo).
6 Withdraw the manifold and recover the gaskets (photos).
7 Refitting is the reverse sequence to removal.

41 Exhaust system – checking, removal and refitting

The procedures are the same as described in Section 13 of this Chapter, but refer to Fig. 3.60 for an exploded view of the system. Note that on Turbo models the front pipe is connected to the turbocharger, and an additional pipe connects the waste gate to the front pipe. If this pipe is renewed, the arrow must point towards the front pipe when refitting.

Fault finding - fuel system (carburettor models)

Note: *High fuel consumption and poor performance are not necessarily due to carburettor faults. Make sure that the ignition system is properly adjusted that the brakes are not binding and that the engine is in good mechanical condition before tampering with the carburettor*

Fuel consumption excessive
- [ ] Air cleaner choked, giving rich mixture
- [ ] Leak from tank, pump or fuel lines
- [ ] Float chamber flooding due to incorrect level or worn needle valve
- [ ] Carburettor incorrectly adjusted
- [ ] Idle speed too high
- [ ] Choke faulty (sticks on)
- [ ] Excessively worn carburettor

Lack of power, stalling or difficult starting
- [ ] Faulty fuel pump
- [ ] Leak on suction side of pump or in fuel line

- [ ] Intake manifold or carburettor flange gaskets leaking
- [ ] Carburettor incorrectly adjusted
- [ ] Faulty choke
- [ ] Emission control system defect

Poor or erratic idling
- [ ] Weak mixture
- [ ] Leak in intake manifold
- [ ] Leak in crankcase breather hose
- [ ] Leak in brake servo hose

Fault finding – fuel system (fuel injection models)

Before assuming that a malfunction is caused by the fuel system, check the items mentioned in the special note at the start of the previous Section

Engine will not start (cold)
- [ ] Fuel pump faulty
- [ ] Cold start valve faulty
- [ ] Sensor plate rest position incorrect
- [ ] Sensor plate and/or control plunger sticking
- [ ] Vacuum system leak
- [ ] Fuel system leak
- [ ] Thermotime switch remains open

Engine will not start (hot)
- [ ] Faulty fuel pump
- [ ] Warm control pressure low
- [ ] Sensor plate rest position incorrect
- [ ] Sensor plate and/or control plunger sticking
- [ ] Vacuum system leak
- [ ] Fuel system leak
- [ ] Leaky injector valve(s) or low opening pressure
- [ ] Incorrect mixture adjustment

Engine difficult to start (cold)
- [ ] Cold control pressure incorrect
- [ ] Cold start valve faulty
- [ ] Sensor plate rest position faulty
- [ ] Sensor plate and/or control plunger sticking
- [ ] Fuel system leak
- [ ] Thermotime switch not closing

Engine difficult to start (hot)
- [ ] Warm control pressure too high or too low
- [ ] Sensor plate/control plunger faulty
- [ ] Fuel or vacuum leak in system
- [ ] Leaky injector valve(s) or low opening pressure
- [ ] Incorrect mixture adjustment

Engine misfires (on road)
- [ ] Fuel system leak

Rough idling (during warm-up period)
- [ ] Incorrect cold control pressure
- [ ] Faulty idle stabilization system
- [ ] Faulty cold start valve
- [ ] Fuel or vacuum leak in system
- [ ] Leaky injector valve(s) or low opening pressure

Rough idling (engine warm)
- [ ] Warm control pressure incorrect
- [ ] Faulty idle stabilization system
- [ ] Cold start valve faulty
- [ ] Sensor plate and/or control plunger sticking
- [ ] Fuel or vacuum leak in system
- [ ] Injector(s) leaking or low opening pressure
- [ ] Incorrect mixture adjustment

Engine backfiring into intake manifold
- [ ] Warm control pressure high
- [ ] Vacuum system leak

Engine backfiring into exhaust manifold
- [ ] Warm control pressure high
- [ ] Start valve leak
- [ ] Fuel system leak
- [ ] Incorrect mixture adjustment

Engine 'runs on'
- [ ] Sensor plate and or control plunger sticking
- [ ] Overrun cut-off valve faulty

Excessive petrol consumption
- [ ] Fuel system leak
- [ ] Mixture adjustment Incorrect
- [ ] Low warm control pressure

Chapter 4 Ignition system

For modifications, and information applicable to later models, see Supplement at end of manual

Contents

Part A – Transistorised coil ignition

Distributor – dismantling, inspection and reassembly 5
Distributor – removal and refitting 4
Fault finding – ignition system . . . . See end of Chapter
General description 1
Ignition system – precautions 3
Ignition system – testing 8
Ignition timing – basic setting 6
Ignition timing – dynamic setting 7
Maintenance and inspection 2
Spark plugs – removal 9

Part B – All-electronic ignition

Distributor – dismantling, inspection and reassembly 14
Distributor – removal and refining 13
General description 10
Fault finding – ignition system . . . . See end of Chapter
Ignition system – precautions 12
Ignition system – testing 16
Ignition timing – adjustment 15
Ignition timing sender and rpm sender – removal and refitting 17
Maintenance and inspection 11
Spark plugs and HT leads – general 18

Degrees of difficulty

Easy, suitable for novice with little experience	**Fairly easy,** suitable for beginner with some experience	**Fairly difficult,** suitable for competent DIY mechanic	**Difficult,** suitable for experienced DIY mechanic	**Very difficult,** suitable for expert DIY or professional

Specifications

Part A – Transistorised coil ignition

General
System type . . . . Hall effect transistorised coil ignition
Application . . . . All models except Turbo

Distributor
Rotor rotation . . . . Clockwise
Firing order:
  Four-cylinder engines . . . . 1-3-4-2 (No 1 at timing belt end)
  Five-cylinder engines . . . . 1-2-4-5-3 (No 1 at timing belt end)

Coil
Primary resistance . . . . 0.52 to 0.76 ohm
Secondary resistance . . . . 2.4 to 3.5 kohm

Ignition timing
Vacuum hoses remain connected on all models
1.8 litre engines . . . . 17° to 19° BTDC at 700 to 800 rpm
1.9, 2.0, 2.2 and 2.3 litre engines . . . . 17° to 19° BTDC at 750 to 850 rpm

Spark plugs
Type:
  1.8 litre engines 1983 to July 1985 . . . . Champion N7YCC or N7YC
  1.8 litre engines August 1985-on . . . . Champion N7YCC or N7BYC
  1.9 litre engines . . . . Champion N7YCC or N7YC
  2.0 litre engines September 1984 to July 1985 . . . . Champion N7YCC or N7YC
  2.0 litre engines August 1985-on . . . . Champion N7YCC or N7BYC
  2.2 litre non Turbo engines . . . . Champion N7YCC or N7YC
  2.2 litre Turbo engines . . . . Champion N6YCC or N6YC
  2.3 litre engines . . . . Champion N7YCC or N7BYC
Electrode gap:
  All plug types and all engines . . . . 0.8 mm (0.032 in)

Torque wrench settings
	Nm	lbf ft
Spark plugs	20	15
Distributor clamp bolt/nut	15	11

Part B – All-electronic ignition

General
System type	Hall effect all electronic ignition with microprocessor control
Application	2.2 litre Turbo models

Distributor
Rotor rotation	Clockwise
Firing order	1-2-4-5-3 (No 1 at timing belt end)

Coil
Primary resistance	0.5 to 1.5 ohm
Secondary resistance:	
Type 1	6.8 kohm
Type 2	7.7 kohm

Ignition timing sender
Clearance between sender head and flywheel pin	0.45 to 1.25 mm (0.017 to 0.049 in)

RPM sender
Clearance between sender head and flywheel ring gear teeth	0.51 to 1.24 mm (0.020 to 0.048 in)

Spark plugs
Type	Champion N6YCC or N6YC
Electrode gap	0.8 mm (0.032 in)

Torque wrench settings
	Nm	lbf ft
Spark plugs	20	15
Distributor clamp nut	15	11

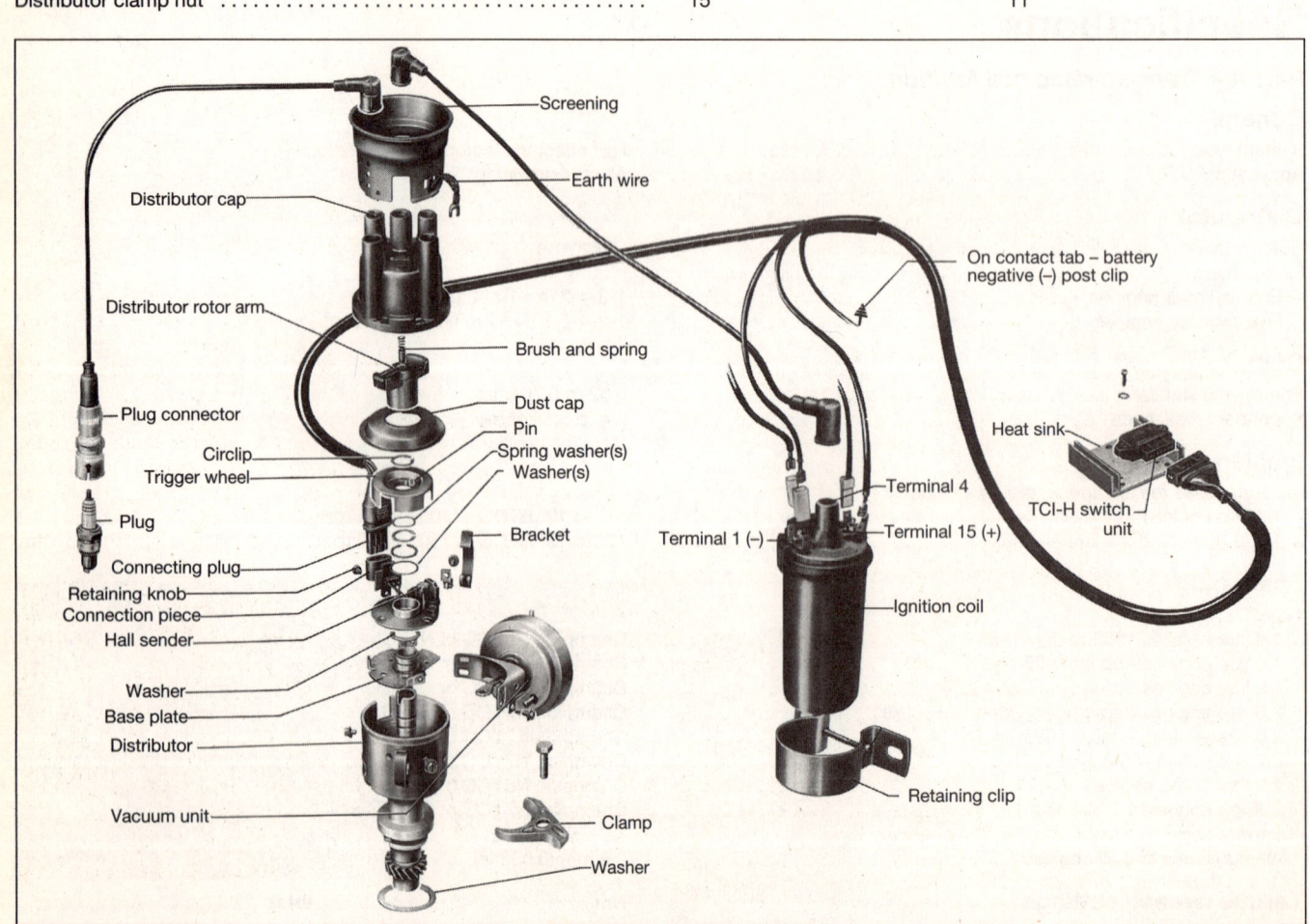

Fig. 4.1 Transistorised coil ignition components (Sec 1)

Part A – Transistorised coil ignition

1 General description

A transistorised coil ignition system (TCI-H) working on the Hall effect principle is used on all models except Turbo versions and comprises the battery, coil, distributor, ignition control unit, spark plugs and associated leads and wiring.

The system is divided into two circuits, low tension and high tension. The high tension (HT) circuit is similar to that of a conventional ignition system, and consists of the high tension coil windings, distributor, rotor arm, spark plugs and leads. The low tension (LT) circuit consists of the battery, ignition switch, low tension or primary coil windings, and a rotor and pick-up unit operating in conjunction with the control unit. The rotor and pick-up unit are located in the distributor, and perform the same function as the contact breaker points used in conventional systems.

The rotor is a four or five toothed wheel (one for each cylinder) which is fitted to the distributor shaft.

The pick-up unit is fitted to the distributor baseplate and basically consists of a coil and permanent magnet.

The control unit is located in the engine compartment and is an amplifier module which is used to boost the voltage induced by the pick-up coil.

When the ignition switch is on, the ignition primary circuit is energised. When the distributor rotor teeth approach the pick-up coil assembly, a voltage is induced which signals the amplifier to switch off the coil primary circuit, causing the magnetic field in the ignition coil to collapse, inducing a high voltage in the secondary windings. This is conducted to the distributor cap where the rotor arm directs it to the appropriate spark plug. A timing circuit in the amplifier module turns on the coil current again after the coil magnetic field has collapsed, and the process continues for each power stroke of the engine.

The distributor is fitted with centrifugal and vacuum advance mechanisms to control the ignition timing according to engine speed and load respectively.

2 Maintenance and inspection

1 At the intervals specified in Routine Maintenance at the beginning of this manual remove the distributor cap and thoroughly clean it inside and out with a dry lint-free rag. Examine the HT lead segments inside the cap. If the segments appear badly burnt or pitted, renew the cap. Make sure that the carbon brush in the centre of the cap is free to move and that it protrudes by approximately 3 mm (0.1 in) from its holder.
2 With the distributor cap removed, lift off the rotor arm and the protective plastic cover. Carefully apply two drops of engine oil to the centre of the cam spindle. Also lubricate the centrifugal advance mechanism by applying two drops of engine oil through one of the holes in the baseplate. Wipe away any excess oil and refit the plastic cover, rotor arm, and distributor cap.
3 Renew the spark plugs, as described in Section 9. If the spark plugs have been renewed within the service interval, clean them and reset the electrode gap, as described in Section 9.
4 Check the condition and security of all leads and wiring associated with the ignition system. Make sure that no chafing is occurring on any of the wires, and that all connections are secure, clean, and free of corrosion. Pay particular attention to the HT leads which should be carefully inspected for any sign of corrosion on their end fitting which, if evident, should be carefully cleaned away. Wipe clean the HT leads over their entire length before refitting.

3 Ignition system – precautions

1 To prevent personal injury and damage to the ignition system, the following precautions must be observed when working on the ignition system.
2 Do not attempt to disconnect any plug lead or touch any of the high tension cables when the engine is running, or being turned by the starter motor.
3 Ensure that the ignition is turned OFF before connecting or disconnecting any ignition wiring.
4 Ensure that the ignition is switched OFF before connecting or disconnecting any ignition testing equipment such as a timing light.
5 Do not connect a suppression condenser or test lamp to the coil negative terminal (1).
6 Do not connect any test appliance or stroboscopic lamp requiring a 12 volt supply to the coil positive terminal (15).
7 If the HT cable is disconnected from the distributor (terminal 4), the cable must be connected to earth and remain earthed if the engine is to be rotated by the starter motor, for example if a compression test is to be done.
8 If a high current boost charger is used, the charger output voltage must not exceed 16.5 volts and the time must not exceed one minute.
9 The ignition coil of a transistorised system must never be replaced with the ignition coil from a contact breaker type ignition system.
10 If an electric arc welder is to be used on any part of the vehicle, the car battery must be disconnected while welding is being done.
11 If a stationary engine is heated to above 80°C (176°F) such as may happen after paint drying, or steam cleaning, the engine must not be started until it has cooled.
12 Ensure that the ignition is switched OFF when the car is washed.
13 Where there is a known or suspected defect in the ignition system the wiring plug at the control unit must be disconnected if the vehicle is to be towed.
14 Never substitute the standard fitting 1 kohm rotor arm (marked R1) with a different type.
15 For the purposes of radio suppression, only 1 kohm spark plug HT leads with 1 kohm to 5 kohm spark plug connectors may be used.

4 Distributor – removal and refitting

1 Pull the high tension connection from the centre of the ignition coil and remove the caps from the spark plugs (photo).
2 Release the two spring clips securing the distributor cap, then remove the distributor cap with the ignition harness attached. On models with metal screening round the top of the distributor, it is necessary to remove the bonding strap connector before the cap can be taken off (photo).
3 Turn the engine using a spanner on the

4.1 Disconnecting the spark plug HT leads (five-cylinder engines)

4.2 Disconnect the earth bonding strap connector (arrowed) before removing the distributor cap (five-cylinder engines)

Fig. 4.2 Flywheel TDC O mark (arrowed) aligned with pointer in timing aperture (Sec 4)

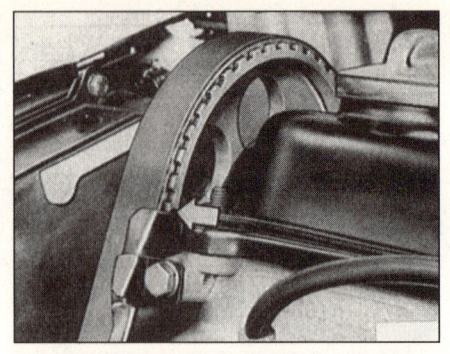

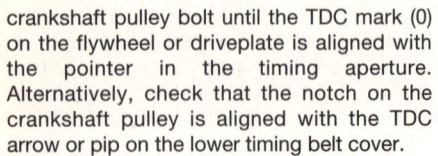

Fig. 4.3 Mark on camshaft gear (arrowed) aligned with top of timing belt rear cover – four-cylinder engines (Sec 4)

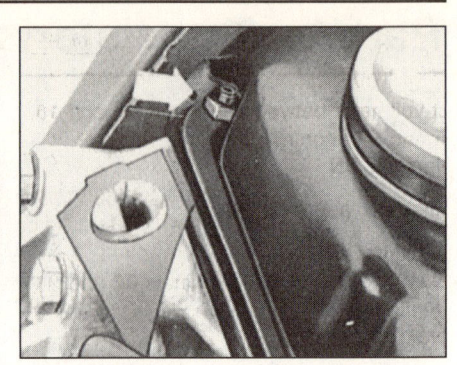

Fig. 4.4 Mark on camshaft gear (arrowed) aligned with upper surface of valve cover gasket – five-cylinder engines (Sec 4)

crankshaft pulley bolt until the TDC mark (0) on the flywheel or driveplate is aligned with the pointer in the timing aperture. Alternatively, check that the notch on the crankshaft pulley is aligned with the TDC arrow or pip on the lower timing belt cover.

4 Check that the mark on the rear of the camshaft gear is aligned with the top of the timing belt rear cover – four-cylinder engines (Fig. 4.3), or with the upper surface of the valve cover gasket – five-cylinder engines (Fig. 4.4). In this position the distributor rotor arm contact should be aligned with the mark on the rim of the distributor body.

5 Disconnect the wiring connector at the distributor pick-up unit.

6 Note the exact position of the rotor arm, so that the distributor can be fitted with the rotor arm in the same position, and also put mating marks on the distributor mounting flange and base. By marking these positions and also ensuring that the crankshaft is not moved while the distributor is off, the distributor can be refitted without upsetting the ignition timing.

7 Pull the vacuum pipe(s) from the vacuum control unit, marking the position of the pipes if there is more than one.

8 Remove the nut/bolt and washer from the distributor clamp plate and take the clamp plate off. Remove the distributor and gasket (photos).

9 When refitting the distributor always renew the gasket (photo). Provided the crankshaft has not been moved, turn the rotor arm to such a position that when the distributor is fully installed and the gears mesh, the rotor will turn and take up the position which it held before removal (photo). On the four-cylinder engine if the distributor will not seat fully, withdraw the unit and use pliers to turn the oil pump driveshaft slightly, then try again.

10 Fit the clamp plate and washer, then fit the nut/bolt and tighten it.

11 Fit the distributor cap and clip it in place, then reconnect the high and low tension wires and the earth bonding strap (if fitted).

12 If the engine has been the subject of overhaul, the crankshaft has been rotated or a new distributor is being fitted, then the procedure for installing the distributor will differ according to engine; refer to Section 6.

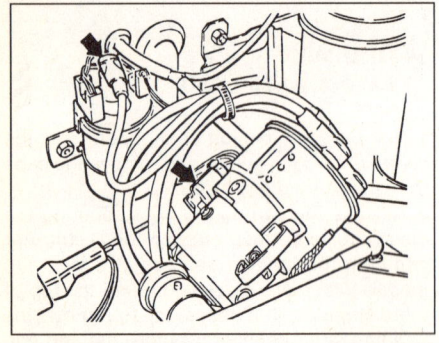

Fig. 4.5 HT lead connection at ignition coil and wiring plug location on distributor – arrowed (Sec 4)

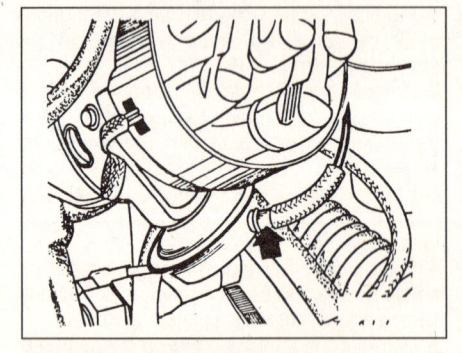

Fig. 4.6 Vacuum pipe attachment (arrowed) at distributor (Sec 4)

4.8A Remove the clamp plate and retaining bolt . . .

4.8B . . . then remove the distributor (five-cylinder engines)

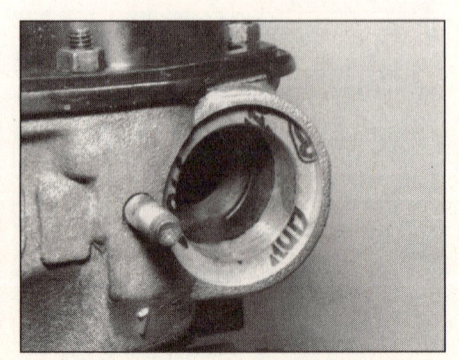

4.9A Gasket in place prior to fitting the distributor (five-cylinder engines)

4.9B Distributor fitted position with rotor arm contact (A) aligned with mark on distributor rim (B) (five-cylinder engines)

5 Distributor – dismantling, inspection and reassembly

Note: *Before commencing work check if spare parts are readily available for the distributor.*

1 Remove the distributor, as described in Section 4.
2 Pull the rotor arm off the distributor shaft, then lift off the plastic cover. Do not allow the cap retaining clips to touch the toothed rotor.
3 Mark the toothed rotor in relation to the distributor shaft, then prise out the retainer. Using two screwdrivers, carefully lever off the rotor and recover the locating pin.
4 Remove the retainer and washers, noting their location.
5 Remove the screws, and withdraw the vacuum unit and packing after disconnecting the operating arm.
6 Remove the retainer and washers from the baseplate, and also remove the screw securing the socket to the side of the distributor. Withdraw the pick-up unit and socket together.
7 Remove the screws and lift out the baseplate followed by the washer.
8 Clean all the components and examine them for wear and damage.
9 Inspect the inside of the distributor cap for signs of burning, or tracking. Make sure that the small carbon brush in the centre of the distributor cap is in good condition and can move up and down freely under the influence of its spring.
10 Check that the rotor arm is not damaged. Use an ohmmeter to measure the resistance between the brass contact in the centre of the rotor arm and the brass contact at the edge of the arm. The measured value of resistance should be between 0.6 and 1.4 kohms.
11 Suck on the pipe connection to the vacuum diaphragm and check that the operating rod of the diaphragm unit moves. Retain the diaphragm under vacuum to check that the diaphragm is not perforated.
12 Reassemble the distributor in the reverse order of dismantling, but apply a few drops of engine oil to the centrifugal advance weights and smear a little grease on the bearing surface of the baseplate.

6 Ignition timing – basic setting

1 If the distributor has been removed and the ignition timing disturbed, it will be necessary to reset the timing using the following static method before setting it dynamically, as described in Section 7.

Four-cylinder engines

2 Turn the engine using a spanner on the crankshaft pulley bolt until the TDC mark (O)

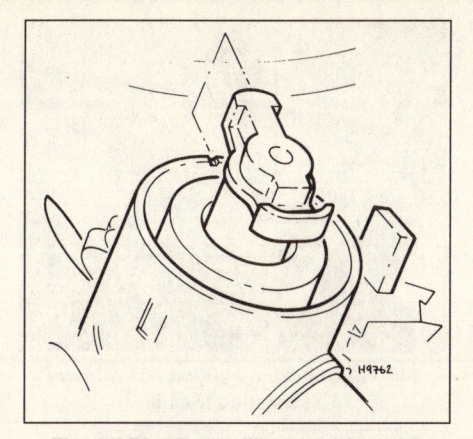

Fig. 4.7 Distributor fitted position with rotor arm aligned with notch in distributor body rim – four-cylinder engines (Sec 6)

on the flywheel or driveplate is aligned with the pointer in the timing aperture (Fig. 4.2) which is located next to the distributor.
3 Check that the mark on the rear of the camshaft gear is aligned with the top of the timing belt rear cover, as shown in Fig. 4.3. If the mark is on the opposite side of the cylinder head, turn the crankshaft forward one complete revolution, and again align the TDC mark.
4 Turn the oil pump shaft so that its lug is parallel with the crankshaft.
5 With the distributor cap removed, turn the rotor arm so that the centre of the metal contact is aligned with the mark on the rim of the distributor body.
6 Hold the distributor over its recess in the cylinder block with the vacuum unit slightly clockwise of the position shown in Fig. 4.7.
7 Insert the distributor fully. As the drivegear meshes with the intermediate shaft, the rotor will turn slightly anti-clockwise and the body can be realigned with the rotor arm to take up the final positions shown in Fig. 4.7. A certain amount of trial and error may be required for this. If the distributor cannot be fully inserted into its mounting hole, slightly reposition the oil pump driveshaft lug. Turn the distributor body until the original body-to-cylinder head marks are in alignment. Tighten the distributor clamp bolt

Five-cylinder engines

8 Turn the engine using a spanner on the crankshaft pulley bolt until the TDC mark (O) is aligned with the lug in the timing aperture in the flywheel or driveplate housing.
9 Check that the mark on the rear of the camshaft gear is aligned with the upper edge of the valve cover gasket. If the mark is on the opposite side of the cylinder head, turn the crankshaft forward one complete revolution and again align the TDC mark.
10 With the distributor cap removed, turn the rotor arm so that the centre of the metal contact is aligned with the mark on the rim of the distributor body (photo 4.9B).

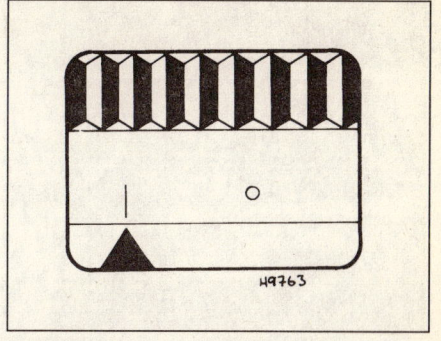

Fig. 4.8 Flywheel 18° BTDC timing mark aligned with pointer in timing aperture (Sec 7)

11 Hold the distributor over the location aperture in the rear of the cylinder head with the vacuum unit facing downwards.
12 Insert the distributor fully. As the drivegear meshes with the camshaft, the rotor will turn slightly anti-clockwise, and the body can then be realigned with the rotor arm so that the vacuum unit faces slightly to the right.
13 Fit the clamp and tighten the nut.

7 Ignition timing – dynamic setting

1 The ignition timing is adjusted dynamically with the engine at normal operating temperature, idling at the specified speed (see Chapter 3), with all electrical accessories switched off and the radiator cooling fan not running. The vacuum hose connections remain connected at the distributor.
2 The ignition timing may be checked using a digital tester connected to the TDC sensor in the flywheel or driveplate housing. However, as this equipment is not normally available to the home mechanic, the following method describes the use of a timing light.
3 Connect the timing light to the engine in accordance with the manufacturer's instructions.
4 Run the engine at idling speed and direct the timing light through the timing aperture in the flywheel or driveplate housing. The mark on the flywheel or driveplate should appear in line with the pointer or reference edge on the housing (Fig. 4.8). If adjustment is necessary, loosen the clamp and turn the distributor body until the correct position is achieved, then tighten the clamp.
5 Gradually increase the engine speed and check that the ignition advances – the centrifugal advance can be checked by pinching the vacuum hoses, and an indication of the vacuum advances can be obtained by releasing the hoses and noting that a different advance occurs.
6 After adjustment check and if necessary reset the engine idling speed, then switch off and remove the timing light.

Transistorised coil ignition

8.1 Ignition coil location on bulkhead (five-cylinder engines)

Fig. 4.9 Checking ignition coil primary resistance (Sec 8)

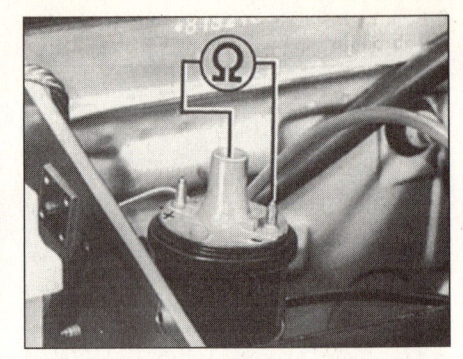

Fig. 4.10 Checking ignition coil secondary resistance (Sec 8)

8 Ignition system – testing

Ignition coil

1 It is rare for an ignition coil (photo) to fail, but if there is reason to suspect it, use an ohmmeter to measure the resistance of the primary and secondary circuits.
2 With the wiring disconnected, measure the primary resistance between the terminals 1 and 15 and the secondary resistance between the centre HT terminal and terminal 1. The correct resistance values are given in the Specifications.
3 Renew the coil if the specified values are not obtained.

Control unit

4 First check that the ignition coil is in order.
5 Disconnect the multi-plug from the control unit and measure the voltage between contacts 4 and 2 with the ignition switched on (Fig. 4.11). Note that the control unit may be located alongside the heater beneath the plastic cover in the engine compartment (photo), or under the carpet in the front footwell, according to model. If the voltage is not approximately battery voltage, check the wiring for possible breakage.
6 Switch off the ignition and reconnect the multi-plug.
7 Disconnect the multi-plug from the distributor and connect a voltmeter across the coil primary terminals. With the ignition switched on at least 2 volts must register, failing to zero after approximately 1 to 2 seconds. If this does not occur, renew the control unit and coil.
8 Connect a wire briefly between the centre terminal of the distributor multi-plug and earth. The voltage should rise to at least 2 volts on four-cylinder engines, and between 5 and 6 volts on five-cylinder engines, otherwise the control unit should be renewed.
9 Switch off the ignition and connect a voltmeter across the outer terminals of the distributor multi-plug. Switch on the ignition and check that 5 volts is registered. If not, check the wiring for possible breakage.

Pick-up unit

10 First check the ignition coil, and control unit. The following test should be made within ambient temperature extremes of 0 and 40°C (32° and 104°F).
11 Disconnect the central HT lead from the distributor cap and earth it with a bridging wire.
12 Pull back the rubber grommet on the control unit and connect a voltmeter across terminals 6 and 3 (Fig. 4.12).
13 Switch on the ignition, then turn the engine slowly in the normal direction using a spanner on the crankshaft pulley bolt. The voltage should alternate between 0 to 0.7 volts, and 1.8 volts to battery voltage, if required, the distributor cap can be removed – with a full air gap 0 to 0.7 volts should register, but when the toothed rotor covers the air gap 1.8 volts to battery voltage should register
14 If the results are not as given in paragraph 13, the pick-up unit is faulty.

9 Spark plugs – removal

Refer also to Chapter 13, Section 6

1 The correct functioning of the spark plugs is vital for the correct running and efficiency of the engine. It is essential that the plugs fitted are appropriate for the engine, and the suitable type is specified at the beginning of this Chapter. If this type is used and the engine is in good condition, the spark plugs should not need attention between scheduled renewal intervals. Spark plug cleaning is rarely necessary and should not be attempted unless specialised equipment is available as damage can easily be caused to the firing ends.
2 To remove the plugs, first open the bonnet and mark the HT leads one to four or five as applicable, to correspond to the cylinder the lead serves (number one cylinder is at the timing belt end of the engine). Pull the HT leads from the plugs by gripping the end fitting, not the lead otherwise the lead connection may be fractured.

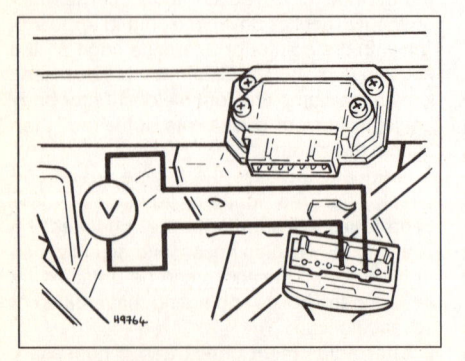

Fig. 4.11 Checking voltage at control unit plug terminals 4 and 2 (Sec 8)

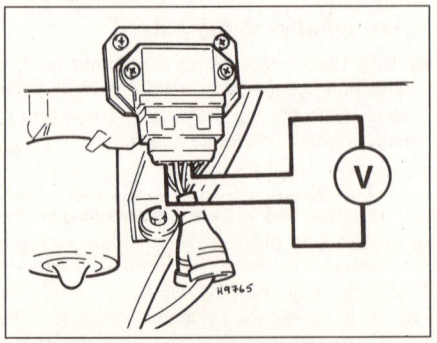

Fig. 4.12 Voltmeter connected across control unit plug terminals 6 and 3 (Sec 8)

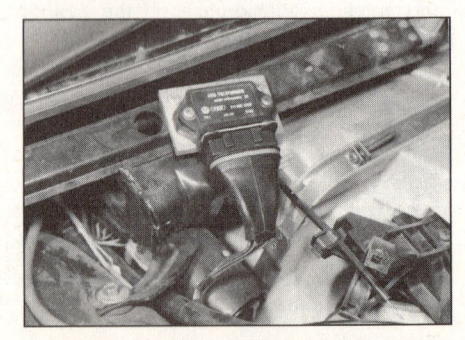

8.5 Ignition control unit location alongside heater in engine compartment (five-cylinder engines)

Transistorised coil ignition 4•7

3 It is advisable to remove the dirt from the spark plug recesses using a clean brush, vacuum cleaner or compressed air before removing the plugs, to prevent the dirt dropping into the cylinders.

4 Unscrew the plugs using a spark plug spanner, suitable box spanner or a deep socket and extension bar. As each plug is removed, examine it as follows.

5 Examination of the spark plugs will give a good indication of the condition of the engine. If the insulator nose of the spark plug is clean and white, with no deposits, this is indicative of a weak mixture or too hot a plug (a hot plug transfers heat away from the electrode slowly, a cold plug transfers heat away quickly).

6 If the tip and insulator nose are covered with hard black looking deposits, then this is indicative that the mixture is too rich. Should the plug be black and oily, then it is likely that the engine is fairly worn, as well as the mixture being too rich.

7 If the insulator nose is covered with light tan to greyish brown deposits, then the mixture is correct and it is likely that the engine is in good condition.

8 The spark plug gap is of considerable importance as, if it is too large or too small, the size of the spark and its efficiency will be seriously impaired. For the best results the spark plug gap should be set in accordance with the Specifications.

9 To set it, measure the gap with a feeler gauge, and then bend open, or close, the outer plug electrode until the correct gap is achieved. The centre electrode should never be bent, as this may crack the insulation and cause plug failure, if nothing worse.

10 Special spark plug electrode gap adjusting tools are available from most motor accessory shops.

11 Before fitting the spark plugs check that the threaded connector sleeves are tight and that the plug exterior surfaces and threads are clean .

12 Screw in the spark plugs by hand where possible, then tighten them to the specified torque. Take extra care to enter the plug threads correctly as the cylinder head is of aluminium.

13 Reconnect the HT leads in their correct order.

Part B – All-electronic ignition

10 General description

Turbo models are equipped with an all-electronic ignition system, which utilizes computer technology and electro-magnetic circuitry to simulate the main functions of a conventional ignition distributor, and also to locate and identify by visual warning any faults occurring in the system.

The all-electronic ignition comprises the battery, coil, distributor, ignition control unit, spark plugs, and associated sender units, cables and wiring (Fig. 4.13).

The distributor operates on the Hall effect principle and functions in the same manner as the unit used in the transistorised coil ignition described in Part A of this Chapter. The electronic control unit receives information on engine speed and load from the various sender units, and computes the most efficient ignition timing for the prevailing operating conditions. The control unit also continually monitors the operation of the system, and initiates a fault display made to visually warn the driver of any serious system fault by means of a warning lamp.

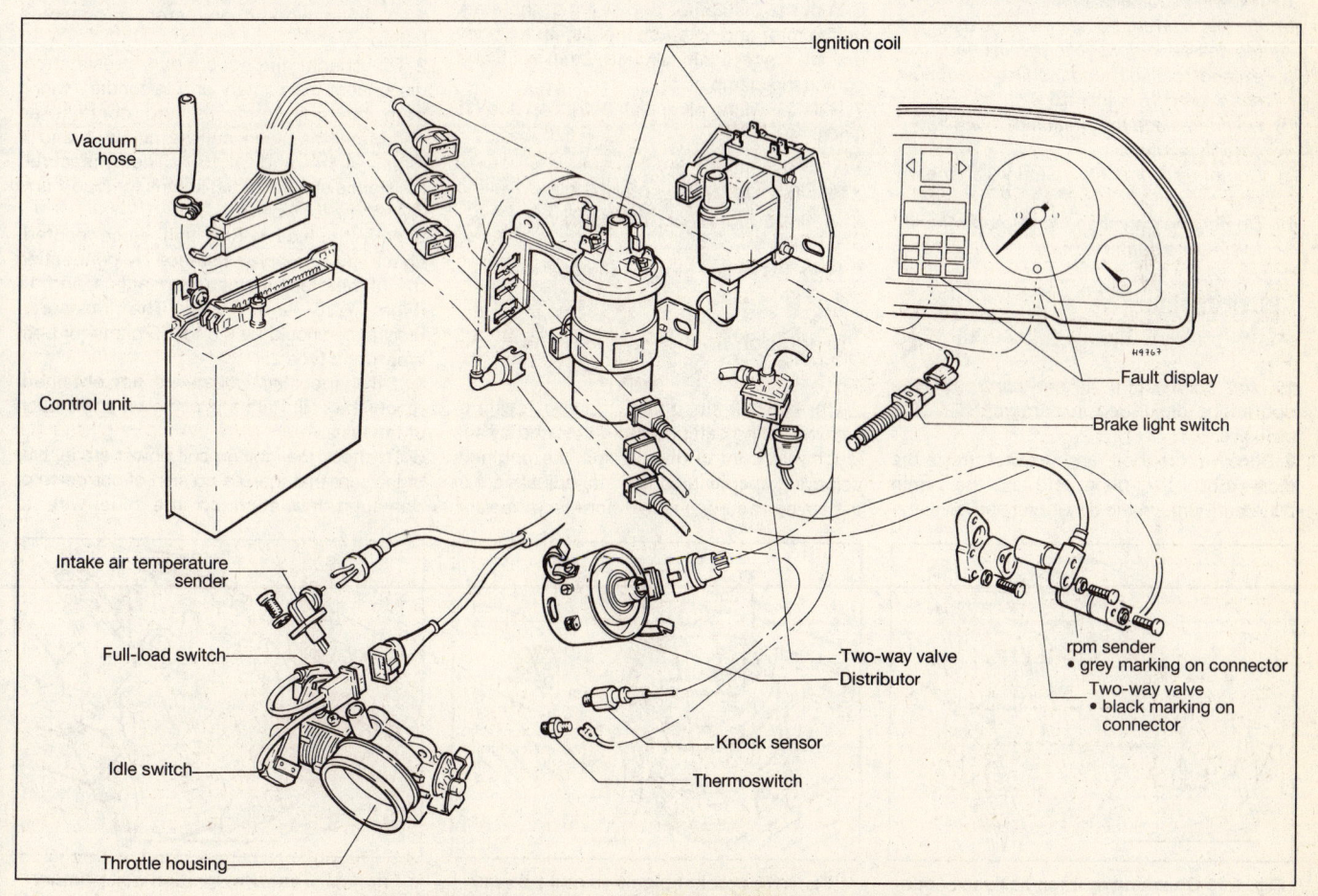

Fig. 4.13 All-electronic ignition system components (Sec 10)

4•8 All-electronic ignition

13.4 Mark on distributor toothed rotor (A) aligned with distributor body notch (B) (five-cylinder Turbo engines)

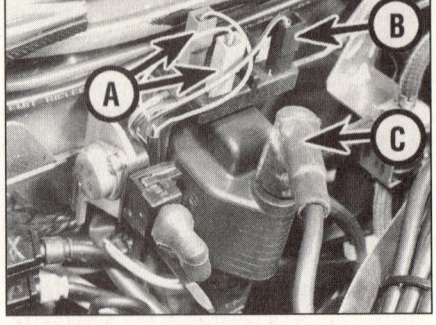

16.1 Wiring connections at the type 2 ignition coil (five-cylinder Turbo engines)
A Terminal 1   C Terminal 4
B Terminal 15   D Power stage wiring plug

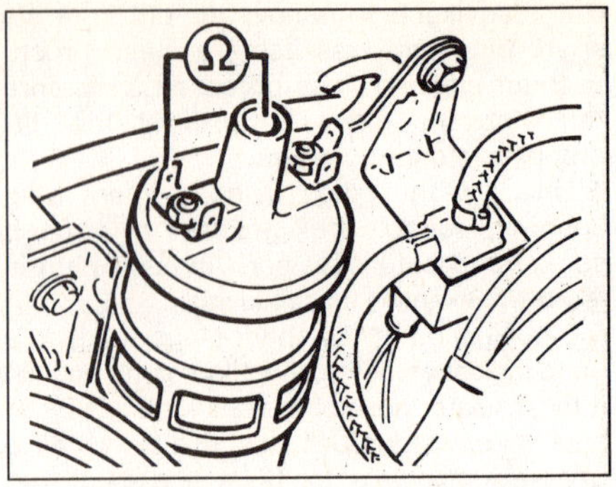

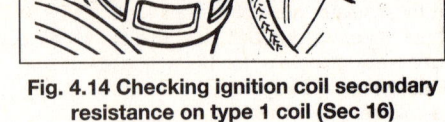

Fig. 4.14 Checking ignition coil secondary resistance on type 1 coil (Sec 16)

11 Maintenance and inspection

Refer to Section 2 of this Chapter.

12 Ignition system – precautions

Refer to Section 3 of this Chapter, but note the following additional items:
(a) If a high current boost charger is used, the charger output voltage must not exceed 76.5 volts and the time used must not exceed 15 seconds
(b) Do not replace the ignition coil with any other type of coil
(c) Do not disconnect the battery with the engine running
(d) Do not apply a voltage to the control unit to simulate output signals

13 Distributor – removal and refitting

1 Refer to Section 4 and carry out the operations described in paragraphs 1 to 5 inclusive.
2 Remove the bolt and washer from the distributor clamp plate, and take the clamp plate off. Remove the distributor and gasket.
3 Before refitting the distributor, ensure that the crankshaft is still positioned as described in Section 4.
4 Turn the distributor shaft as necessary so that the mark on the upper face of the toothed rotor is aligned with the notch on the rim of the distributor body (photo).
5 With a new gasket in position, hold the distributor so that the wiring socket is in approximately the 3 o'clock position, and insert the unit into its location.
6 Turn the distributor body so that the mark on the rotor and notch on the distributor body rim are once again aligned, then refit and tighten the clamp plate.
7 Refit the wiring plug, distributor cap and HT leads.

14 Distributor – dismantling, inspection and reassembly

Refer to Section 5 of this Chapter.

15 Ignition timing – adjustment

On the all-electronic ignition system, ignition timing settings are generated by the electronic control unit to suit the engine's prevailing operating conditions. Adjustment of the timing in service is therefore unnecessary, apart from ensuring that the distributor is positioned correctly initially after removal and refitting (See Section 13).

16 Ignition system – testing

Ignition coil

1 The ignition coil fitted may be either type 1 or type 2, as shown in Fig. 4.13. Identify the type being worked on before proceeding (photo).
2 To check the secondary resistance, disconnect the primary and secondary wiring from the coil terminals and connect an ohmmeter between coil terminals 1 and 4 (Figs. 4.14 and 4.15). The measured resistance should be 6.8 kohms for type 1 and 7.7 kohms for type 2.
3 With the coil wiring still disconnected, check the primary resistance by connecting the ohmmeter between terminals 1 and 15 (Figs. 4.16 and 4.17). The measured resistance should be 0.5 to 1.5 ohms for both type 1 and type 2.
4 If the specified values are not obtained, renew the coil. Refit the wiring on completion of the tests.
5 To check the ignition coil power stage, first make sure that there is no sign of corrosion or damaged insulation on the blue wire to

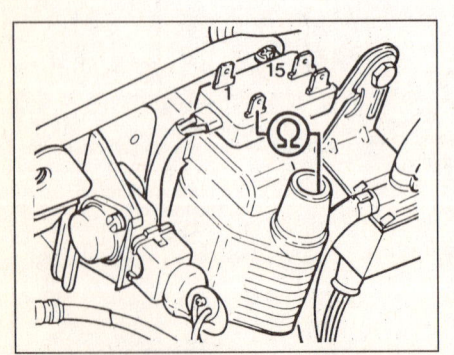

Fig. 4.15 Checking ignition coil secondary resistance on type 2 coil (Sec 16)

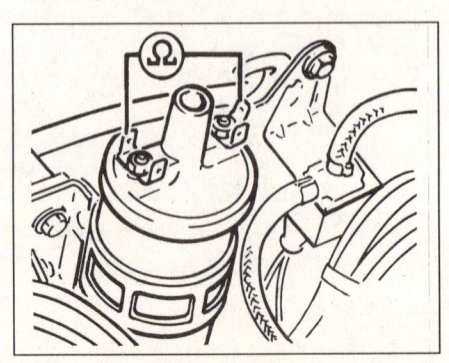

Fig. 4.16 Checking ignition coil primary resistance on type 1 coil (Sec 16)

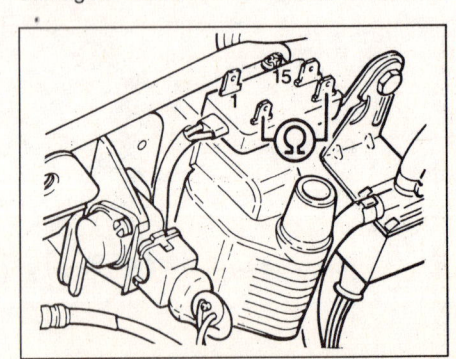

Fig. 4.17 Checking ignition coil primary resistance on type 2 coil (Sec 16)

All-electronic ignition 4•9

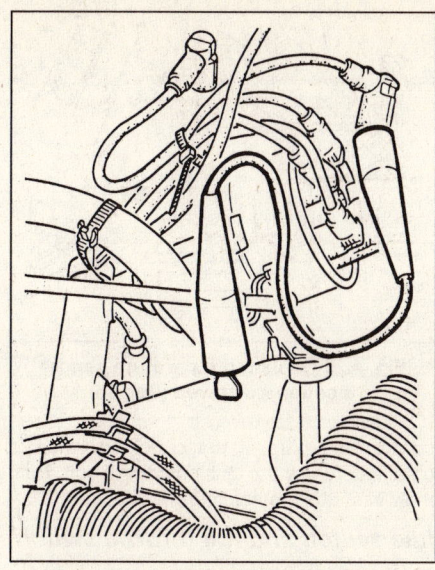

Fig. 4.18 Distributor central HT lead connected to earth with a bridging wire (Sec 16)

Fig. 4.19 Ignition coil power stage wiring plug – arrowed (Sec 16)

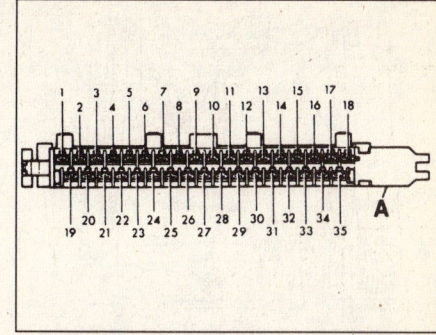

Fig. 4.20 Ignition control unit wiring plug terminal identification (Sec 16)

terminal 1 on the coil. Make good any defects found, then refit the wire.

6 Disconnect the central HT lead at the distributor cap (from coil terminal 4), and earth it with a bridging wire.

7 Disconnect the wiring plug from the power stage at the side of the ignition coil (Fig. 4.19). Identify the terminal in the wiring plug to which the green/white wire is attached. Connect a voltmeter between the green/white wire and earth, and connect a bridging wire between the other terminal and earth.

8 Crank the engine on the starter and note the voltmeter reading, which should be at least 0.2 volts.

9 If the specified voltage is not obtained, remove the cover over the ignition control unit located in the right-hand side front footwell, and disconnect the wiring plug.

10 Check the continuity of the wiring between the power stage wiring plug (green/white terminal), and terminal 22 in the control unit plug (Fig. 4.20). The reading obtained should be approximately 0 ohms. The same value should be obtained when checking between terminal 2 in the control unit plug, and the other terminal in the power stage wiring plug. If these values are not obtained: check for breaks in the wiring or poor connections in the wiring plugs. If all is satisfactory, renew the ignition control unit. Reconnect all wiring on completion of the tests.

Ignition timing sender

11 Disconnect the black plug at the wiring connector support bracket on the bulkhead (Fig. 4.21).

12 Using an ohmmeter, check the resistance between terminals 1 and 2 in the wiring socket, which should be approximately 1 kohm (Fig. 4.22). If this value is not obtained, renew the ignition timing sender.

13 If the specified reading is obtained, connect the ohmmeter between terminals 1 and 3 in the wiring socket, then between terminals 2 and 3. There should be no reading on the ohmmeter in each case. If there is, renew the ignition timing sender.

14 If the test results are satisfactory so far, check for continuity in the wiring between the ignition timing sender plug and the ignition control unit plug as follows.

15 Remove the cover over the ignition control unit located in the right-hand side front footwell and disconnect the wiring plug.

16 Check the continuity of the wiring between terminal 1 in the sender plug (Fig. 4.23) and terminal 13 in the control unit plug (Fig. 4.20) Next, check the continuity between terminal 2 in the sender plug and 12 in the control unit plug, then finally terminal 3 in the sender plug and 28 in the control unit plug. The ohmmeter readings should be 0 ohms in each case. If the specified values are not obtained, there is a break in the wiring between the two plugs. If the readings are satisfactory, check the ignition timing sender fitted position, as described in Section 17. If this is correct, renew the ignition control unit. reconnect all wiring on completion of the checks.

RPM sender

17 Disconnect the grey plug at the wiring connector support bracket on the bulkhead (Fig. 4.21).

18 Using an ohmmeter, check the resistance between terminals 1 and 2 in the wiring socket (Fig. 4.22), which should be approximately 1 kohm. If this value is not obtained, renew the rpm sender.

19 If the test results are satisfactory, check the wiring socket, then check for continuity between the sender plug and ignition control unit plug using the procedure described in paragraphs 13 to 16. When checking continuity between the two plugs, the checks are made between sender plug terminal 1, and control unit plug terminal 29, then

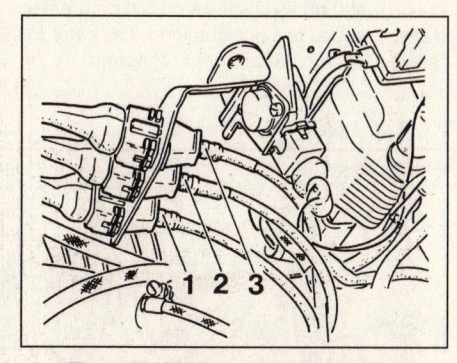

Fig. 4.21 Wiring connectors at the bulkhead support bracket (Sec 16)

1 Black plug – ignition timing sender
2 Grey plug – rpm sender
3 Red plug – knock sensor

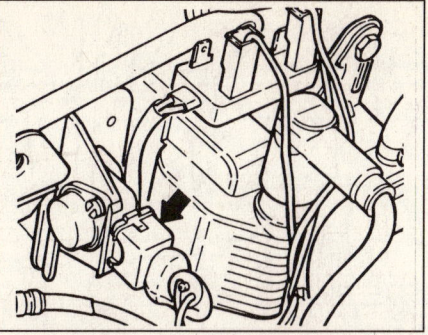

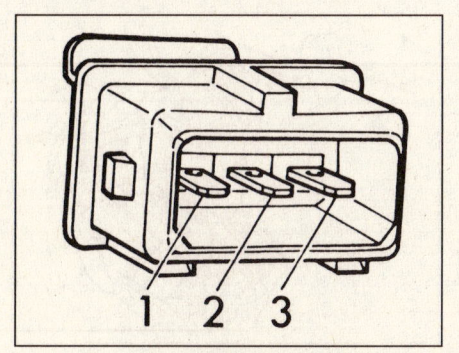

Fig. 4.22 Wiring socket terminal identification (Sec 16)

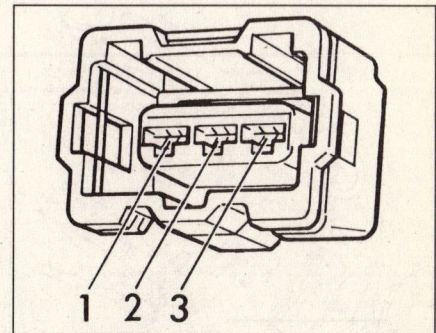

Fig. 4.23 Wiring plug terminal identification on 3-pin type (Sec 16)

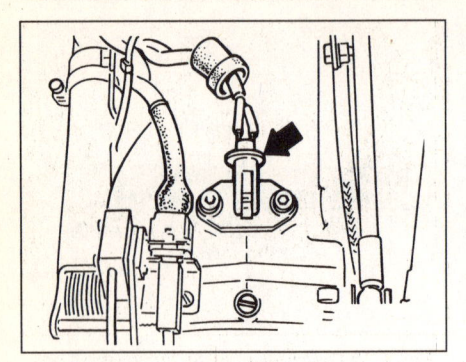

Fig. 4.24 Air intake temperature sender (arrowed) on throttle valve housing (Sec 16)

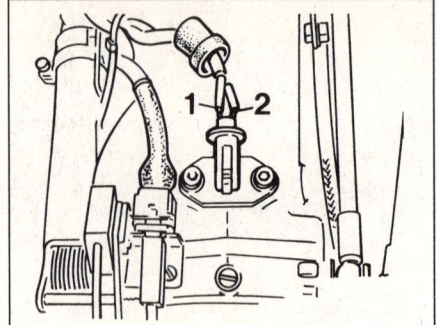

Fig. 4.25 Air intake temperature sender terminal identification (Sec 16)

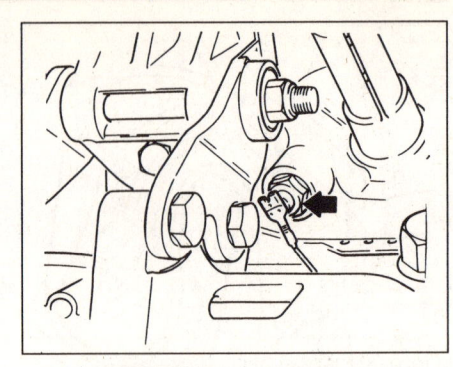

Fig. 4.26 Coolant temperature sender location – arrowed (Sec 16)

between terminal 2 and 11, and 3 and 28 in the sender plug and control unit plug respectively.

Air intake temperature sender

20 Pull back the cover over the air intake temperature sender on the throttle valve housing (Fig. 4.24).
21 Using an ohmmeter, check the resistance between the two sender contacts which should be between 450 and 650 ohms.
22 If the specified value is not obtained, remove the cover over the ignition control unit, located in the right-hand side front footwell, and disconnect the wiring plug.
23 Check the resistance of the wiring between terminal 23 in the control unit plug (Fig. 4.20) and contact 1 and contact 2 alternately on the intake temperature sender (Fig. 4.25). The readings obtained should be 0 ohms and 400 to 700 ohms respectively. Repeat this test between control unit plug terminal 24, and senser contacts 1 and 2 alternately. The readings should again be 0 ohms and between 400 and 700 ohms respectively. If the specified values are obtained, cut off the two wires at the intake air temperature sender (the sender will have to be renewed after doing this, as described below). Now recheck the resistance at the two sender contacts, which should be between 400 and 700 ohms. If this is the case, there is a fault in the wiring between the sender and the control unit plug which must be rectified before renewing the sender.
24 To renew the sender, first cut off the two wires at the contacts if not already done. Undo the bolts and remove the sender unit.
25 Fit the new unit and secure with the two bolts.
26 Fit the rubber cover and protective cover over the wiring, fit terminal lugs on the bared wires, and solder the wires to the two contacts. Fit the protective covers over the soldered wiring.
27 Refit the wiring plug to the control unit.

Coolant temperature sender

28 For the following check the coolant temperature must be above 20°C (68°F).
29 Disconnect the wire from the coolant temperature sender (Fig. 4.26), and measure the resistance between the sender terminal and earth using an ohmmeter. The value obtained should be 60 to 1000 ohms. If this is not the case, renew the sender.
30 If the specified resistance value is obtained, remove the cover over the ignition control unit, located in the right-hand side front footwell, and disconnect the wiring plug.
31 Check the continuity of the wiring by connecting the ohmmeter between the disconnected coolant temperature sender wire and terminal 10 of the control unit wiring plug (Fig. 4.20). The ohmmeter reading should be 0 ohms. If this value is not obtained, there is a fault in the wiring between the sender and control unit plug. If the specified value is obtained, renew the ignition control unit. Refit the wiring after completing the checks.

Idle switch and full throttle switch

32 To check the switch supply voltage, disconnect the wiring plug at the idle and full throttle switch on the throttle valve housing (Fig 4.27), and connect a voltmeter between terminal 2 of the plug and earth (Fig. 4.24). Switch on the ignition and check that approximately 12 volts is present at the wiring plug. If not, check for a fault in the wiring to the plug.
33 Check the idle switch by connecting an ohmmeter between terminals 1 and 2 of the idle switch wiring socket (Fig. 4.28). The value obtained should be 0 ohms. Now operate the throttle to activate the switch, and check that no reading is shown on the ohmmeter. If these values are not obtained, have the idle switch adjustment checked by an Audi dealer, then repeat the checks. If the specified readings are still not obtained, renew the idle switch. If the readings are satisfactory, check the full throttle switch as follows.
34 With the wiring plug still disconnected, check the resistance between terminals 2 and 3 in the wiring socket. There should be no reading shown on the ohmmeter scale. Now operate the throttle to activate the switch, and check that 0 ohms is shown on the ohmmeter. If these values are not obtained, have the full throttle switch adjustment checked by an

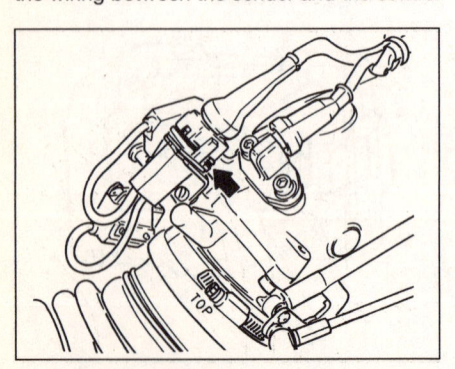

Fig. 4.27 Idle and full throttle switch wiring plug – arrowed (Sec 16)

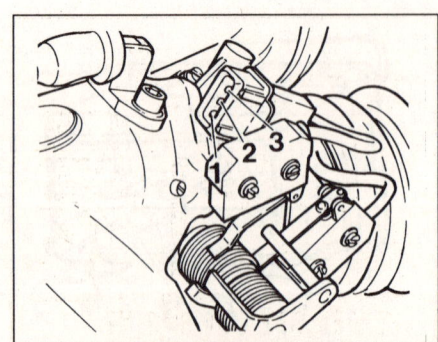

Fig. 4.28 Idle and full throttle switch socket terminal identification (Sec 16)

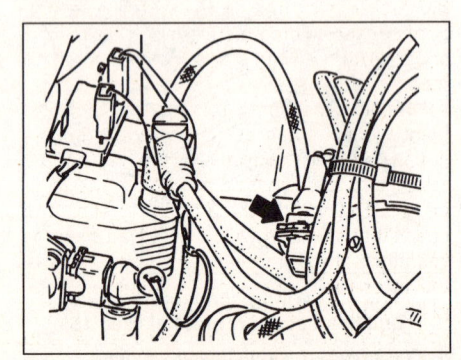

Fig. 4.29 Pick-up unit wiring plug (arrowed) on distributor (Sec 16)

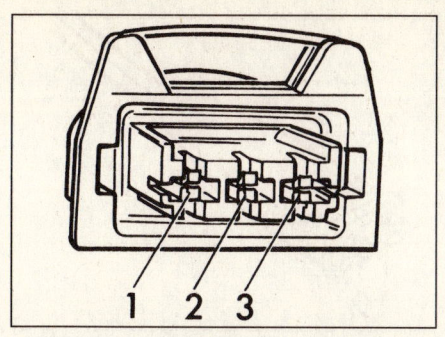

Fig. 4.30 Pick-up unit wiring plug terminal identification (Sec 16)

Fig. 4.31 Distributor rotor tooth openings positioned away from pick-up unit – arrowed (Sec 16)

Fig. 4.32 Distributor rotor tooth opening aligned with pick-up unit – arrowed (Sec 16)

Audi dealer, then repeat the checks. If the specified readings are still not obtained, renew the full throttle switch.

35 If the specified values are obtained, remove the cover over the ignition control unit, located in the right-hand side front footwell, and disconnect the wiring plug.

36 Check the continuity of the wiring by connecting the ohmmeter between terminal 1 on the idle and full throttle switch wiring plug, and terminal 20 on the control unit plug (Fig. 4.20). The specified reading should be 0 ohms. Now connect the ohmmeter between terminals 3 and 26 of the throttle and control unit plugs respectively. The reading should again be 0 ohms. If the specified readings are not obtained, check for a fault in the wiring between the two plugs. If the readings are satisfactory, renew the ignition control unit.

37 Reconnect the wiring on completion of the tests.

Pick-up unit

38 Disconnect the central HT lead at the distributor cap (from coil terminal 4), and earth it with a bridging wire.

39 Disconnect the wiring plug at the pick-up unit on the side of the distributor (Fig. 4.29), and connect a voltmeter between the two outer terminals 1 and 3 (Fig. 4.30). Switch on the ignition, and check that at least 9 volts is indicated on the voltmeter, then switch off the ignition. If the specified valve is not obtained, check for a wiring fault in the lead to the pick-up unit.

40 If the readings are satisfactory, pull back the rubber grommet on the wiring plug and connect the voltmeter between terminals 1 and 2. With the voltmeter connected, refit the plug.

41 Remove the distributor cap, rotor arm and plastic cover, then using a spanner on the crankshaft pulley, turn the engine so that the rotor tooth openings are away from the pick-up unit (Fig. 4.31). Switch on the ignition and check that at least 4 volts are indicated on the voltmeter. Now turn the engine so that one of the rotor tooth openings is in line with the pick-up unit (Fig. 4.32), and check that the voltmeter reading is now between 0 and 0.5 volts. Switch off the ignition.

42 If the specified values are not obtained, renew the pick-up unit.

43 If the specified values are obtained, remove the cover over the ignition control unit, located in the right-hand side front footwell, and disconnect the wiring plug.

44 Check the continuity of the wiring by connecting an ohmmeter between terminal 1 of the pick-up unit wiring plug and terminal 4 of the control unit wiring plug (Fig. 4.20). The specified reading should be 0 ohms. Now connect the ohmmeter between pick-up unit plug terminal 2, and control unit plug terminal 27, then pick-up plug terminal 3, and control unit plug terminal 25. The readings should again be 0 ohms in each case. If the specified values are not obtained, check for a wiring fault between the two plugs. If the readings are satisfactory, renew the control unit.

45 Reconnect all wiring and components after completing the checks.

Ignition control unit

46 To check the supply voltage to the control unit, remove the control unit cover, located in the right-hand side front footwell, and disconnect the wiring plug.

47 Connect a voltmeter between wiring plug terminals 35 and 18, and 35 and 9 (Fig. 4.20), then switch on the ignition. The values indicated should be approximately 12 volts. Switch off the ignition.

48 Connect the voltmeter between terminals 32 and 9 in the wiring plug, switch on the ignition, and depress the brake pedal. Approximately 12 volts should be indicated on the voltmeter scale. If these values are not obtained, there is a wiring fault in the supply to the control unit, or the brake light switch is faulty. Switch off the ignition.

49 Reconnect the wiring plug on completion.

50 To check the control unit output signal to the fuel pump relay, pull the fuel pump relay out of socket 10 on the relay plate, and connect a voltmeter between terminals 46 and 47 in the plate (Fig. 4.33).

51 Briefly crank the engine on the starter motor, and check that approximately 9.5 volts is indicated on the voltmeter, then switch off the ignition.

52 If the specified voltage is not present, connect the voltmeter between terminal 46 and earth, then switch on the ignition. The reading should be approximately 12 volts. If this is not the case, there is a fault in the wiring to the relay plate. If the voltage is as specified, remove the cover over the ignition control unit in the right-hand front footwell and disconnect the wiring plug.

53 Using an ohmmeter, check for continuity between terminal 21 in the control unit plug (Fig. 4.20) and terminal 41 of socket 10 in the relay plate. The ohmmeter should indicate 0 ohms. If this is not the case, there is a fault in the wiring between the relay plate and control unit plug. If the specified value is obtained, renew the control unit.

54 Refit the relay and wiring plug on completion.

55 On manual transmission models, check the control unit output signal to the overrun cut-off valve as follows.

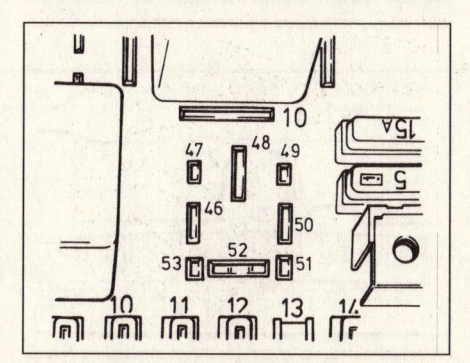

Fig. 4.33 Socket 10 terminal identification at the relay board (Sec 16)

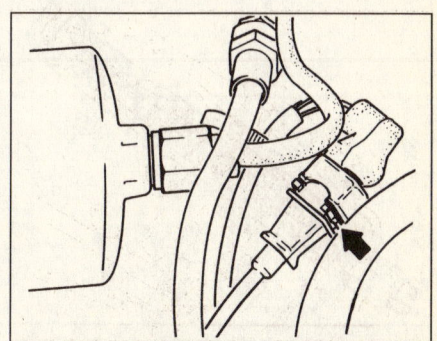

Fig. 4.34 Overrun cut-off valve wiring plug – arrowed (Sec 16)

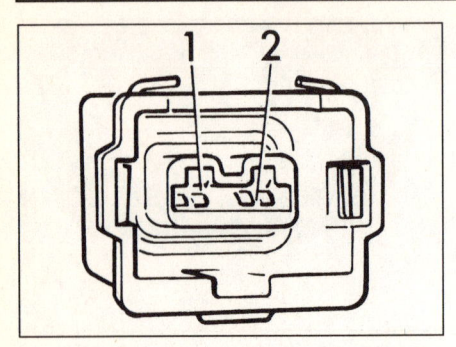

Fig. 4.35 Wiring plug terminal identification on 2-pin type (Sec 16)

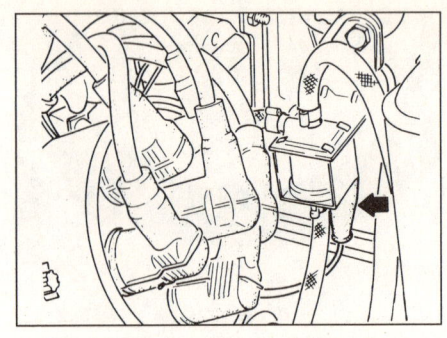

Fig. 4.36 Two-way valve wiring plug – arrowed (Sec 16)

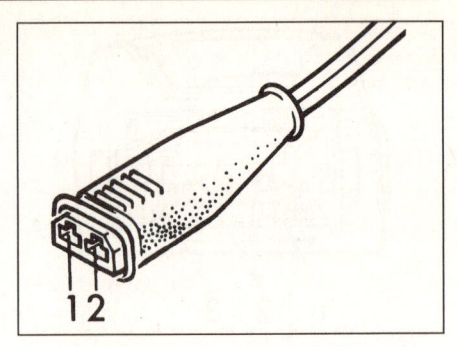

Fig. 4.37 Two-way valve wiring plug terminal identification (Sec 16)

56 Ensure that the coolant temperature is at least 50°C (122°F), then accelerate the engine to at least 2000 rpm, and close the throttle abruptly. When the throttle is closed, the air intake elbow must visibly contract under negative pressure.

57 If the elbow does not contract, switch off the engine and disconnect the overrun cut-off valve wiring plug (Fig. 4.34).

58 Connect a voltmeter between the two terminals in the plug, start the engine and accelerate the engine to at least 2000 rpm once more. Close the throttle abruptly, and check that approximately 12 volts is shown on the voltmeter. If the specified value is obtained, and if the vacuum line is connected to the overrun cut-off valve, renew the valve. If the specified reading is not obtained, check the idle switch as described earlier in this Section, then repeat the test. Switch off after checking.

59 If the specified reading is still not obtained, disconnect the ignition control unit wiring plug and, using an ohmmeter, check for continuity between terminal 1 in the cut-off valve wiring plug (Fig. 4.35), and terminal 14 in the control unit plug. (On 1985 onwards models the check is made between terminal 2 in the cut-off valve plug, and terminal 14 in the control unit plug). The ohmmeter reading should be 0 ohms. If this is not the case, there is a fault in the wiring between the cut-off valve and control unit plugs. If the reading is satisfactory, renew the control unit.

60 To check the control unit output signal to the two-way valve, first ensure that the coolant temperature is at least 80°C (176°F), then run the engine at idle.

61 Operate the full throttle switch by hand, and listen for an audible indication that the two-way valve is operating. If this is not the case, switch off the engine and disconnect the wiring plug at the two-way valve (Fig. 4.36).

62 Connect a voltmeter between the two plug terminals, and check that approximately 12 volts is indicated on the voltmeter scale. If the specified value is obtained, renew the two-way valve.

63 If the specified value is not obtained, connect the voltmeter between terminal 1 (blue/black wire) in the wiring plug, and earth. Switch on the ignition and check that approximately 12 volts is indicated, the switch off the ignition. If this figure is not obtained, check for a fault in the wiring to plug terminal 1.

64 If the specified value is obtained, disconnect the ignition control unit wiring plug, and check the wiring continuity between terminal 2 (yellow/black wire) in the two-way valve plug, and terminal 8 of the control unit wiring plug. The ohmmeter should indicate 0 ohms. If the specified value is not obtained, there is a fault in the wiring between the control unit plug and the valve plug. If the specified value is obtained, renew the control unit.

65 To check the control unit output signal to the tachometer, remove the cover over the ignition control unit in the right-hand side front

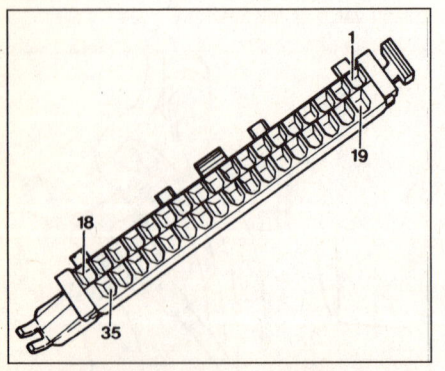

Fig. 4.38 Ignition control unit wiring plug terminal identification viewed from rear of plug (Sec 16)

Fig. 4.39 Flywheel pin centred in the ignition timing sender opening (Sec 17)

footwell. Pull back the rubber boot on the wiring plug, and connect a voltmeter between terminal 7 of the wiring plug, and earth (Fig. 4.38). Note that the plug remains connected for this test.

66 Connect a suitable tachometer to the engine following the manufacturer's instructions.

67 Start the engine, and increase the speed to 2000 rpm. Check that the indicated voltage is approximately 1.3 volts. If this is not the case, renew the ignition control unit.

68 If the specified voltage is obtained, but the vehicle tachometer does not agree with the test tachometer, there is a possible fault in the wiring from plug terminal 7 to the wiring plug in the instrument panel, or a fault in the tachometer.

69 Switch off the engine and reconnect the wiring on completion.

17 Ignition timing sender and rpm sender – removal and refitting

1 The ignition timing sender and rpm sender are located on the side of the cylinder block in line with the flywheel, and transmit information on engine speed and crankshaft position to the ignition control unit.

2 To remove either unit, disconnect its wiring plug at the wiring connector support bracket on the bulkhead (black plug for timing sender and grey plug for rpm sender – Fig. 4.21).

3 Using an Allen key, undo the retaining bolt, and remove the unit from its holder.

4 Refitting is the reversal of removal.

5 To check the fitted depth of the senders, as part of a test or fault finding procedure, it will first be necessary to remove the transmission (Chapters 6 or 7) to gain access to the flywheel or driveplate.

6 Undo the bolts securing the sender unit mounting bracket, and remove the bracket and senders.

7 Turn the engine over using a spanner on the crankshaft pulley, until the pin on the flywheel or driveplate is centered in the sender opening (Fig. 4.39).

8 Refit the sender bracket with senders and, using feeler gauges, measure the clearance

between the end of the ignition timing sender and the pin on the flywheel (Fig. 4.40), and the clearance between the rpm sender and the flywheel ring gear teeth (Fig. 4.41). If the measured clearances are outside the tolerance range given in the Specifications, check each unit for damage or distortion of the sensor end, and renew the unit as necessary. If the specified clearance still cannot be obtained, use packing shims to increase the clearance, or carefully file the sender bracket to decrease the clearance.

18 Spark plugs and HT leads – general

Refer to Section 9 of this Chapter.

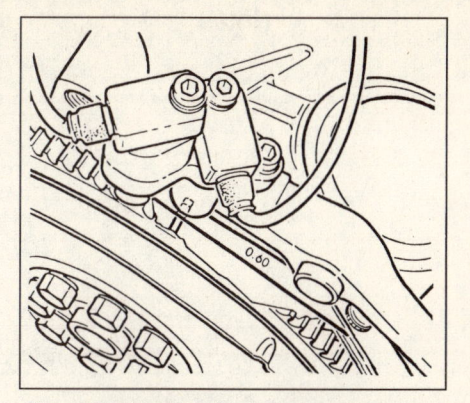

Fig. 4.40 Checking ignition timing sender-to-pin clearance (Sec 17)

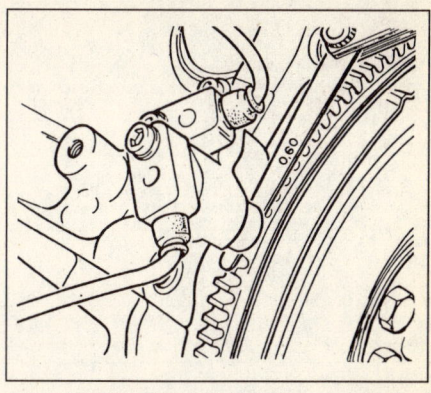

Fig. 4.41 Checking rpm sender-to-flywheel ring gear clearance (Sec 17)

Fault finding – ignition system

> **Warning: When carrying out fault finding tests or any checks on the ignition system, do not disconnect any wiring or leads (including spark plug HT leads) with the engine running or the ignition switched on.**

1 There are two distinct symptoms of ignition faults. Either the engine will not start or fire, or it starts with difficulty and does not run normally.
2 If the starter motor spins the engine satisfactorily, there is adequate fuel supply and yet the engine will not start, the fault is likely to be in the LT or primary side.
3 If the engine starts, but does not run satisfactorily, it is more likely to be an HT or secondary circuit fault.

Engine fails to start

4 If the starter motor spins the engine satisfactorily, but the engine does not start, first check that the fuel supply to the engine is in order, with reference to Chapter 3.
5 Check for obvious signs of broken or disconnected wires or wiring plugs, particularly those to the coil and distributor, and for damp distributor cap and HT leads.
6 If the engine fails to start due to either damp HT leads or distributor cap, a moisture dispersant can be very effective.
7 For vehicles with transistorised coil ignition, follow the procedure described in Section 8. For vehicles with all-electronic ignition, follow the procedure described in Section 16, with particular emphasis on the ignition coil, pick-up unit, and ignition control unit.

Engine starts but misfires

8 Bad starting and intermittent misfiring can be caused by an LT fault, such as intermittent connection of either the distributor or coil LT wiring connections or plugs.
9 If these are satisfactory, look for signs of tracking or burning inside the distributor cap, then check the rotor arm, HT leads, spark plug caps, and plug insulators.
10 If the engine misfires regularly, it indicates that the fault is on one particular cylinder. This can often be confirmed by removing the spark plugs and checking to see if any are badly sooted or even wet, indicating that that particular spark plug is not firing. If this is the case, renew the HT lead, or try a lead known to be satisfactory. If the fault persists. check once again for tracking in the distributor cap. If these tests fail to cure the problem, there may be an internal engine fault on that cylinder, such as low cylinder compression.
11 If the misfire is of a more irregular nature, follow the test procedures described in Section 8 for vehicles with transistorised coil ignition, and Section 16 for vehicles with all-electronic ignition.

Notes

Chapter 5 Clutch

For modifications, and information applicable to later models, see Supplement at end of manual

Contents

Clutch – adjustment	2
Clutch – removal, inspection and refitting	9
Clutch cable – removal and refitting	3
Clutch hydraulic system – bleeding	11
Clutch master cylinder – overhaul	6
Clutch master cylinder – removal and refitting	5
Clutch pedal – removal and refitting	4
Clutch release bearing and mechanism – removal, inspection and refitting	10
Clutch slave cylinder – overhaul	8
Clutch slave cylinder – removal and refitting	7
Fault finding – clutch	See end of Chapter
General description	1

Degrees of difficulty

Easy, suitable for novice with little experience

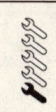

Fairly easy, suitable for beginner with some experience

Fairly difficult, suitable for competent DIY mechanic

Difficult, suitable for experienced DIY mechanic

Very difficult, suitable for expert DIY or professional

Specifications

Type .... Single dry plate, diaphragm spring with hydraulic or cable operation according to model

Clutch disc
Diameter .... 210 mm (8.27 in), 215 mm (8.47 in), 228 mm (8.98 in), or 240 mm (9.45 in) according to model
Maximum run-out .... 0.5 mm (0.020 in)

Pressure plate
Maximum distortion (inner edge to outer edge) .... 0.3 mm (0.012 in)
Maximum diaphragm spring finger scoring depth .... 0.3 mm (0.012 in)

Clutch adjustment
Free play (cable operated clutch) .... 15 mm (0.6 in) maximum at pedal
Pedal height (hydraulically operated clutch) .... 10 mm (0.4 in) above brake pedal

Clutch fluid type/specification (hydraulic clutch) ..... Hydraulic fluid to FMVSS 116 DOT 4

Torque wrench settings	Nm	lbf ft
Pressure plate (clutch cover) retaining bolts	25	18
Clutch release lever clamp bolt (cable operated clutch)	25	11
Release shaft retaining bolt (cable operated clutch)	15	11
Release lever retainer (hydraulically operated clutch)	15	11
Master cylinder retaining bolts	5	18
Pedal mounting bracket retaining bolts	25	18

5•2 Clutch

1 General description

All manual transmission models are equipped with a single dry plate diaphragm spring clutch. The unit consists of a steel cover which is bolted to the flywheel and contains the pressure plate and diaphragm spring.

The clutch disc is free to slide along the splined gearbox input shaft, and is held in position between the flywheel and the pressure plate by the pressure of the diaghragm spring. Friction lining material is riveted to the clutch disc, which has a spring cushioned hub to absorb transmission shocks and help ensure a smooth take-up of the drive.

Depending on vehicle specification, the clutch may be operated either mechanically by a cable or hydraulically by a master and slave cylinder. The clutch release mechanism consists of a release shaft on the cable operated type, or release lever on the hydraulically operated type, together with a release bearing, mounted in the clutch housing on the end of the gearbox.

2 Clutch – adjustment

1 The clutch operation and adjustment should be checked at the intervals given in Routine Maintenance using the following procedure according to clutch type.

Cable operated clutch

2 To check the adjustment, measure the free play at the clutch pedal which should be as given in the Specifications.
3 If adjustment is necessary, open the bonnet to gain access to the adjuster, which is either secured to a bracket attached to the left-hand engine mounting, or located midway along the cable.
4 Slacken the two locknuts, and turn the threaded cable ferrule in or out as necessary to achieve the specified free play. When the adjustment is correct, tighten the two locknuts (photo).

2.4 Clutch cable ferrule and end fitting

Hydraulically operated clutch

5 Remove the parcel shelf (see Chapter 11, Section 23) to gain access to the clutch master cylinder.
6 Release the locknut behind the clevis on the clutch master cylinder operating rod and turn the rod until the correct pedal height is achieved .
7 Depress the clutch pedal and then release it to ensure that the overcentre spring returns the pedal properly. After the pedal has returned, check that the pedal is clear of the pedal stop. If the pedal is against the pedal stop in the rest position, premature wear of the clutch facing will result.
8 When the operation of the pedal is satisfactory, tighten the clevis locknut and refit the parcel shelf.

3 Clutch cable – removal and refitting

1 Disconnect the battery negative terminal.
2 Remove the parcel shelf (see Chapter 11, Section 23) to gain access to the upper end of the clutch pedal.
3 Release the two locknuts on the clutch cable adjuster in the engine compartment and slide the cable assembly out of its anchorage.
4 Unhook the clutch cable connection from the hook on the upper end of the clutch pedal and from the hook on the end of the clutch operating lever.
5 Pull the clutch cable through the front bulkhead into the engine compartment and remove the assembly.
6 When fitting a new cable, fit the pedal end first and when installation has been completed, check and if necessary adjust the pedal freeplay.

4 Clutch pedal – removal and refitting

1 Disconnect the battery negative terminal.
2 Remove the parcel shelf (see Chapter 11, Section 23) to gain access to the pedal attachments.

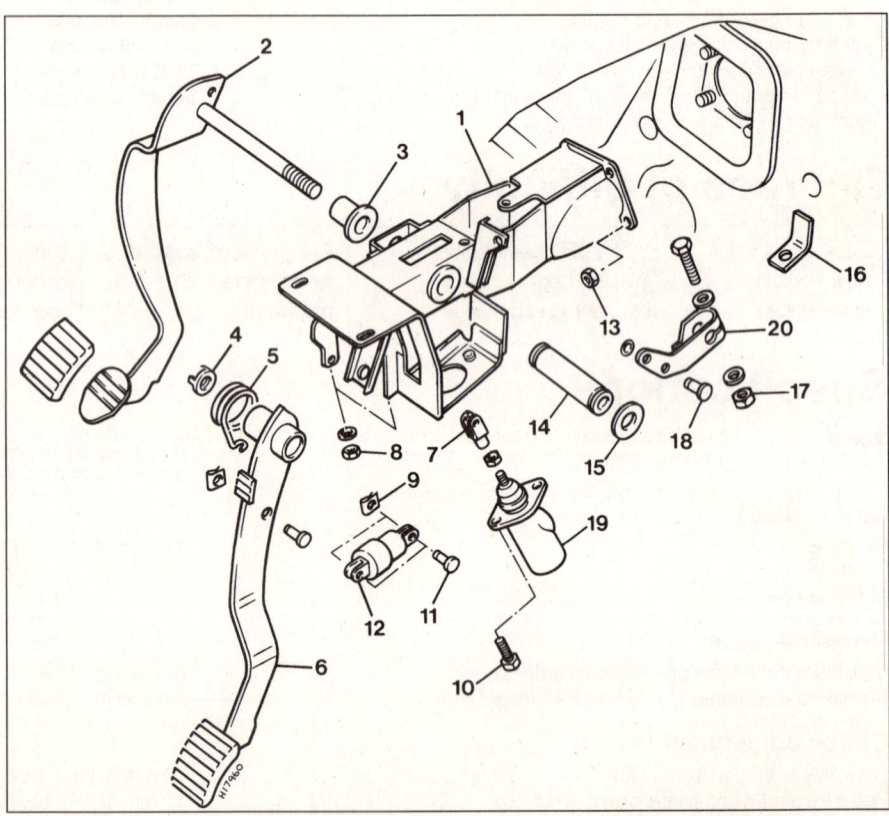

Fig. 5.1 Clutch pedal and associated components – RHD vehicles (Sec 4)

1 Pedal bracket
2 Clutch pedal
3 Bush
4 Washer
5 Spring
6 Brake pedal
7 Clevis
8 Nut
9 Clips
10 Clutch master cylinder bolt
11 Clevis pins
12 Over-centre spring
13 Nut
14 Tube
15 Washer
16 Bracket (cruise control)
17 Clamp nut
18 Clevis pin
19 Clutch master cylinder
20 Clutch pedal lever

Hydraulic clutch shown, cable clutch is similar

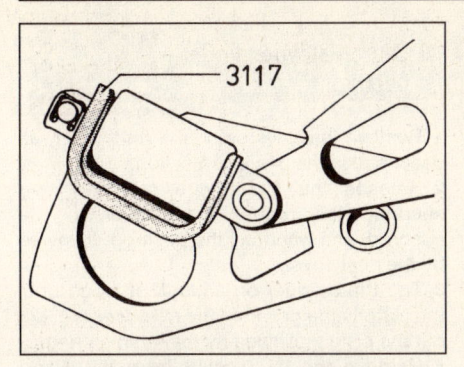

Clutch 5•3

Fig. 5.2 Clutch pedal over-centre spring with tool 3117 fitted (Sec 4)

3 On models equipped with a cable operated clutch. disconnect the cable at the pedal with reference to Section 3.
4 On models equipped with a hydraulically operated clutch, disconnect the master cylinder clevis pin at the pedal, then remove the master cylinder from its mounting bracket.
5 Disconnect the brake servo pushrod Clevis pin at the brake pedal.
6 Disconnect the brake light switch wires, and any additional wiring or fittings according to model or optional equipment fitted.
7 Undo the retaining nuts and bolts, and remove the pedal bracket assembly, complete with pedals, from the car.
8 Extract the circlips and clevis pins, and remove the clutch pedal over-centre spring. To facilitate removal and refitting of the over-centre spring, use tool 3117, or a suitable alternative made up from steel channel, to retain the over-centre spring in the compressed position.
9 Remove the clamp nut and bolt from the clutch pedal lever. Note the position of the lever, then pull it off the splines. Release the brake pedal return spring and pull the clutch pedal and pivot shaft out of the pedal bracket. Recover the washers, bushes, etc.
10 Where necessary, the pedal pivot bushes can be removed by punching them out with a drift, and pressing in new bushes between vice jaws.
11 Before reassembly, smear all contact surfaces with grease, and renew all locknuts and circlips. Reassemble and refit the pedals using the reverse sequence to removal. On completion check the clutch adjustment, as described in Section 2.

5 Clutch master cylinder – removal and refitting

On models equipped with a hydraulically operated clutch, the master cylinder is located inside the car, at the base of the clutch and brake pedal mounting bracket. Hydraulic fluid for the unit is supplied from the brake master cylinder reservoir.

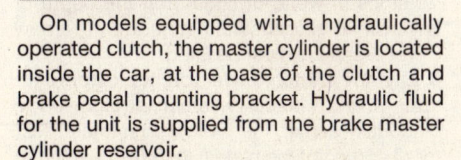

1 Disconnect the battery negative terminal.
2 Remove the parcel shelf (see Chapter 11, Section 23) to gain access to the master cylinder.
3 Cover the floor beneath the pedals to protect against hydraulic fluid spillage.
4 Carefully pull the hydraulic fluid supply hose off the outlet on the cylinder, and quickly plug the hose with an old bolt or rod of suitable diameter.
5 Unscrew the hydraulic pipe union at the base of the cylinder, and carefully ease out the pipe.
6 Extract the circlip, and withdraw the clevis pin securing the master cylinder pushrod to the clutch pedal.
7 Undo the two retaining bolts, and remove the cylinder from the car.
8 Refitting is the reverse sequence to removal. Bleed the clutch hydraulic system, as described in Section 11, and check the clutch adjustment, as described in Section 2.

6 Clutch master cylinder – overhaul

1 Remove the master cylinder from the car, as described in the previous Section.
2 Remove the dust cover from the master cylinder then extract the pushrod retaining circlip and washer, Remove the pushrod.
3 Tap the end of the cylinder on a block of wood until the piston emerges from the end of the cylinder bore.
4 Withdraw the piston from the cylinder, together with the return spring. Carefully remove the spring from the piston and recover the spring retainer.
5 Remove the primary and secondary cup seals from the piston, noting which way round they are fitted.

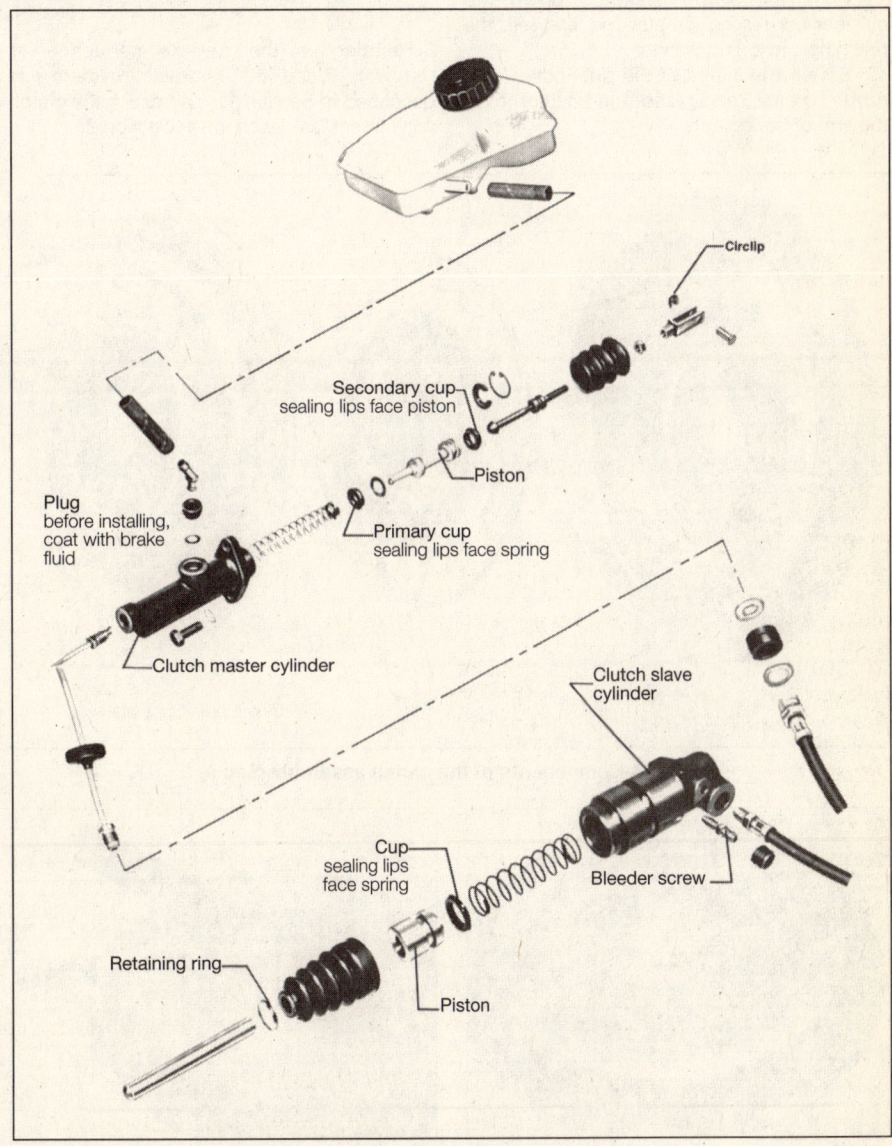

Fig. 5.3 Exploded view of the clutch master cylinder and slave cylinder – hydraulically operated clutch (Secs 6 and 8)

5•4 Clutch

6 Wash all the components in clean hydraulic fluid, then wipe dry with a lint-free cloth.

7 Examine the cylinder bore and piston carefully for signs of scoring or wear ridges. If these are apparent, renew the complete master cylinder. If the condition of the components appears satisfactory, a new set of rubber seals must be obtained. Never re-use the old seals.

8 Begin reassembly by thoroughly lubricating the internal components and the cylinder bore, using clean hydraulic fluid.

9 Using fingers only, place the primary and secondary cup seals in position, with the lip of the seals facing towards the spring.

10 Place the spring retainer and spring in position over the piston, and carefully insert this assembly into the cylinder bore. Take care not to allow the lips of the seals to roll over as they are inserted.

11 Push the piston assembly down the cylinder bore using the pushrod, and refit the retaining circlip and washer.

12 Smear the inside of the dust cover with rubber grease, and place it in position over the end of the cylinder.

7 Clutch slave cylinder – removal and refitting

1 From under the car, withdraw the tensioning wire from the slave cylinder and from the retaining roll pin hole on top of the gearbox.

2 Using a suitable punch, drive out the roll pin, then withdraw the cylinder, complete with pushrod, rearwards away from its mounting location.

3 Unscrew the flexible hydraulic pipe by holding the pipe union with a spanner and unscrewing the slave cylinder off the pipe. Recover the sealing washer and plug the pipe to prevent fluid loss and dirt entry.

4 Remove the slave cylinder from under the car.

5 Refitting is the reverse sequence to removal, Bleed the hydraulic system, as described in Section 11, and check the clutch adjustment, as described in Section 2.

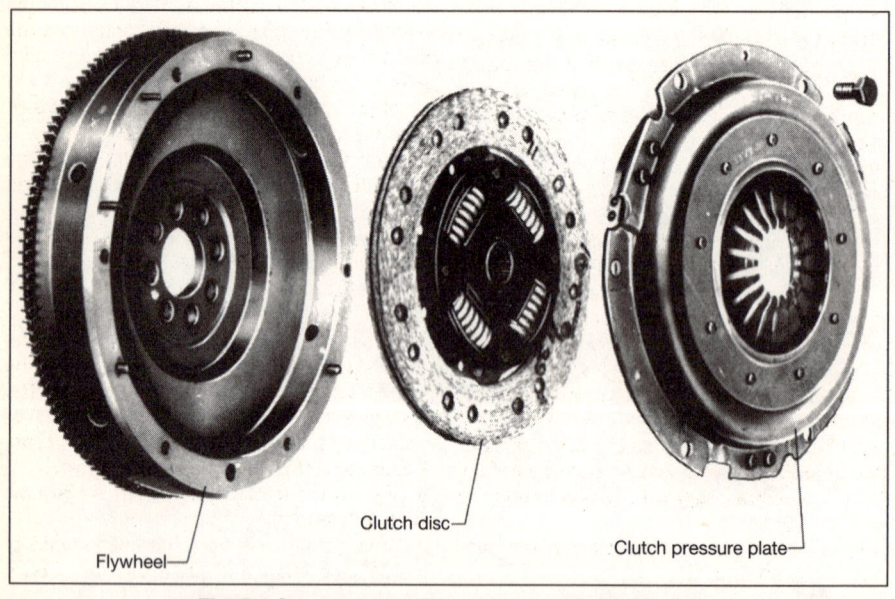

8 Clutch slave cylinder – overhaul

1 Remove the slave cylinder from the car, as described in the previous Section.

2 Release the small wire retaining ring securing the rubber dust cover to the pushrod, and withdraw the pushrod, followed by the dust cover.

3 Tap the cylinder on a block of wood until the piston emerges from the cylinder bore. Lift out the piston followed by the return spring.

4 Remove the dust cover from the bleed screw, then unscrew the bleed screw from the cylinder.

5 Remove the cup seal from the piston, then wash the components in clean hydraulic fluid. Wipe dry with a lint-free cloth.

6 Carry out a careful inspection of the slave cylinder components with reference to Section 6, paragraph 7. If the cylinder is in a satisfactory condition, fit a new cup seal to the piston, with the sealing lip towards the spring. Thoroughly lubricate the parts in clean hydraulic fluid, and re-assemble the cylinder using the reverse sequence to dismantling.

9 Clutch – removal, inspection and refitting

1 Access to the clutch is obtained either by removing the engine (Chapter 1) or by removing the gearbox (Chapter 6). If the clutch requires attention and the engine is not in need of a major overhaul, it is preferable to gain access to the clutch by removing the gearbox, provided that either a pit is available, or the car can be put on ramps to give a good ground clearance.

2 Put a mark on the rim of the clutch pressure plate cover and a corresponding mark on the flywheel so that the clutch can be refitted in exactly the same position.

3 Slacken the clutch cover retaining bolts a turn at a time, working in diagonal pairs round the casing. When all the bolts have been loosened enough to release the tension of the diaphragm spring, remove the bolts and lift off the clutch cover and the disc.

4 Clean the parts with a damp cloth. ensuring that the dust is not inhaled. *Because the dust produced by the wearing of the clutch facing may contain asbestos, which is dangerous to health, parts should not be blown clean or brushed to remove dust.*

5 Examine the fingers of the diaphragm spring for signs of wear, or scoring. If the depth of any scoring exceeds 0.3 mm (0.012 in), a new cover assembly must be fitted.

6 Lay the clutch cover on its diaphragm spring end, place a steel straight-edge diagonally across the pressure plate and test for distortion of the plate (Fig. 5.6). If a 0.3 mm (0.012 in) feeler gauge can be inserted in any gap beneath the straight-edge, the clutch

Fig. 5.4 Components of the clutch assembly (Sec 9)

Fig. 5.5 Checking clutch diaphragm spring fingers – arrowed (Sec 9)

Fig. 5.6 Checking for distortion of the pressure plate (Sec 9)

Clutch 5•5

Fig. 5.7 Checking clutch disc run-out (See 9)

cover must be discarded and a new one fitted. The check for distortion should be made at several points round the plate.
7 Check that the pressure plate is not badly scored, and shows no signs of cracking, or burning
8 Inspect the clutch disc and fit a new disc if the surface of the friction material left is approaching the level of the rivets. Discard the disc if the friction material has become impregnated with oil, or shows signs of breaking into shreds.
9 Examine the clutch disc splined hub for signs of damage, or wear. Check that when the hub is on the gearbox input shaft, the hub slides smoothly along the shaft and that the radial clearance between the gearbox shaft and clutch hub is small.
10 If there is reason to suspect that the clutch hub is not running true, it should be checked by mounting the hub between centres and checking it with a dial gauge. Unless you have the proper equipment, get your local dealer to make this check
11 Do not re-use any part which is suspect. Having gone to the trouble of dismantling the clutch, it is well worth ensuring that when

9.13 Fit the clutch disc with the torsion springs toward the pressure plate . . .

reassembled it will operate satisfactorily for a long time. Cheek the flywheel for scoring and tiny cracks caused by overheating; refinish or renew as necessary.
12 Ensure that all the parts are clean, free of oil and grease and are in a satisfactory condition before reassembling.
13 Fit the clutch disc so that the torsion spring cages are towards the pressure plate (photo).
14 Fit the clutch cover to the flywheel ensuring (where applicable) that the marks made before dismantling are lined up, and insert all bolts finger tight to hold the cover in position (photo).
15 Centralise the clutch disc either by using a proprietary tool, or by making-up a similar tool to hold the clutch disc concentric with the hole in the end of the crankshaft (photo).
16 With the centraliser holding the clutch disc in position, tighten all the clutch cover bolts a turn at a time in diagonal sequence until the specified torque is achieved.
17 Remove the centring tool and smear the hub splines with molybdenum disulphide grease.
18 Cheek the release bearing in the front of the gearbox for wear and smooth operation, and if necessary renew it, with reference to Section 10.
19 Refit the engine or gearbox with reference to Chapters 1 or 6.

9.14 . . . then fit the cover assembly

10 Clutch release bearing and mechanism – removal, inspection and refitting

1 With the gearbox removed from the car, proceed as follows according to type.

Cable operated clutch

2 To remove the release bearing, either lift the release arm to disengage the forks from the spring clips, or extract the clips from each side of the bearing, noting how they are fitted (photos). The bearing can then be withdrawn from the guide sleeve.
3 Mark the release lever in relation to the shaft then unscrew the clamp bolt and withdraw the lever.
4 On four-cylinder models, remove the dowel bolt from the rear of the bellhousing. The bolt engages a groove in the end of the release shaft.
5 On all models, note the position of the release shaft return spring in relation to the ground projection cast in the bellhousing. The spring end fits either in the groove, or adjacent to it, according to gearbox type. Record the fitted position before removal.
6 Unhook the return spring from the release shaft fork (photo).
7 Extract the circlip from the splined end of the release shaft and prise out the rubber

9.15 Using a proprietary tool to centralise the clutch disc

10.2A Clutch release bearing and release shaft

10.2B Release bearing retaining clip fitment

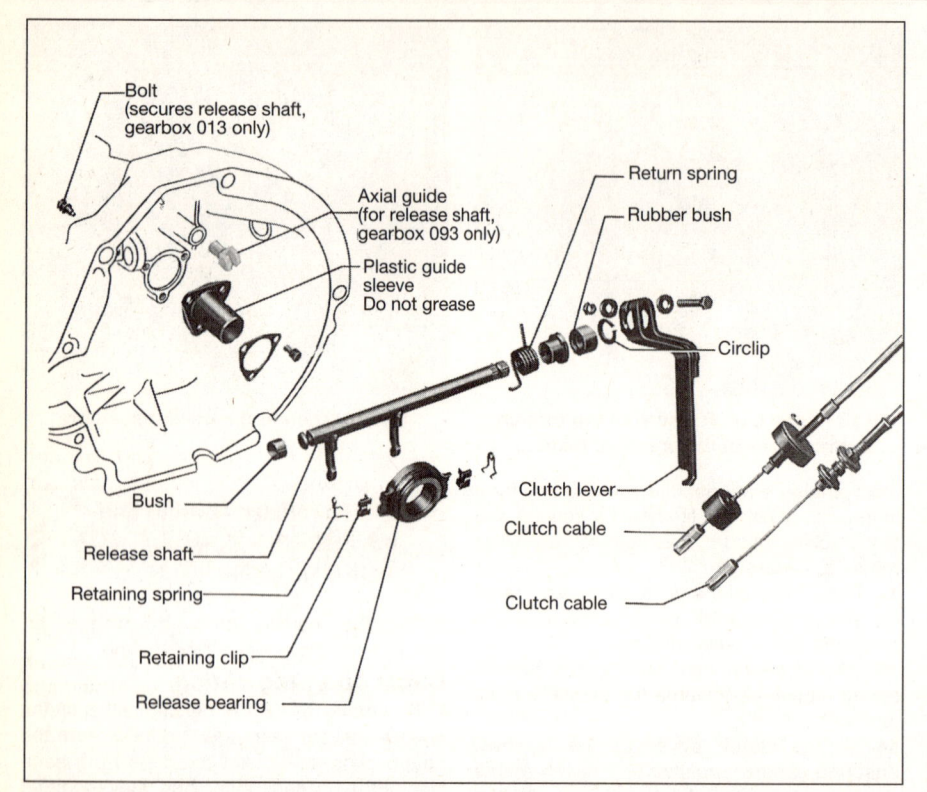

5•6 Clutch

Fig. 5.8 Exploded view of the clutch release bearing and mechanism – cable operated clutch (Sec 10)

Labels: Bolt (secures release shaft, gearbox 013 only); Axial guide (for release shaft, gearbox 093 only); Plastic guide sleeve Do not grease; Bush; Release shaft; Retaining spring; Retaining clip; Release bearing; Return spring; Rubber bush; Circlip; Clutch lever; Clutch cable; Clutch cable

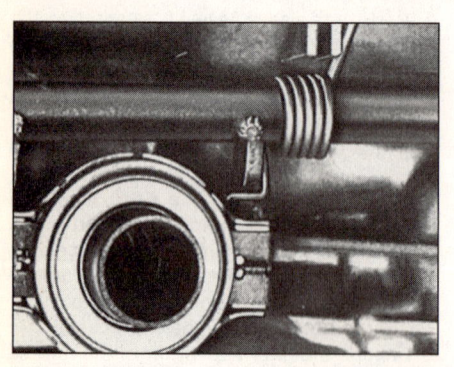

Fig. 5.9 Clutch release shaft return spring positioned adjacent to bellhousing cast projection (Sec 10)

Fig. 5.10 Inserting the dowel bolt (A) on four-cylinder models – press in the release shaft to compress the rubber bush to 18 mm (0.7 in) (Sec 10)

Fig. 5.11 Release lever fitting dimension – cable operated clutch (Sec 10)

a = 185 mm (7.28 in)

10.6 Unhooking the release shaft return spring

10.7 Removing the release shaft flanged bush

10.8 Removing the release shaft

bush (where fitted) and the flanged bush (photo).

8 Turn the release shaft so that the forks are free of the guide sleeve, then remove the inner end from the bush and withdraw the shaft from inside the bellhousing (photo).

9 Clean the release bearing with a dry cloth. Do not wash the bearing in solvent, because this will cause its lubricant to be washed out. If the bearing is noisy, or has excessive wear, discard it and obtain a new one.

10 Inspect the release shaft and its bushes for wear. Do not remove the inner bush unless a new one has to be fitted. If a new inner bush is required, the old one will need a special extractor to remove it.

11 Before refitting the release shaft, coat the bearing surfaces with molybdenum disulphide grease and ensure that the return spring is fitted to the shaft.

12 Refitting is a reversal of removal. However, on four-cylinder models press in the release shaft until the rubber bush is compressed to approximately 18 mm (0.7 in) (photo) before inserting and tightening the dowel bolt. If a new release lever is being fitted, position it on the splined shaft as shown in Fig. 5.11 (photo). Coat all bearing surfaces with high melting-point grease, except for the plastic guide sleeve.

Hydraulically operated clutch

13 Remove the release bearing, as described in paragraph 2.

Clutch 5•7

10.12A Checking the release shaft rubber bush dimension

10.12B Checking the release lever fitted dimension

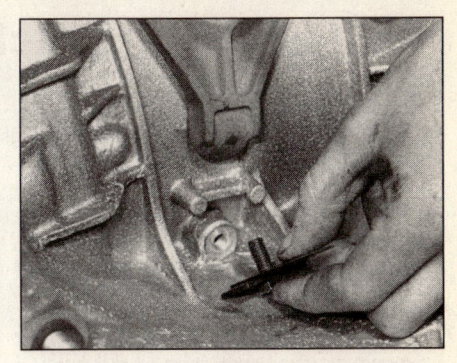

10.14 Removing the retainer and leaf spring

14 Unscrew and remove the bolt securing the clutch release lever retainer and leaf spring (photo). Remove the retainer and spring, then take out the clutch release lever.

15 Clean the release bearing, as described in paragraph 9. Coat the top of the ball cap inside the bellhousing and also all the working surfaces of the clutch operating lever with molybdenum disulphide grease and refit the arm and release bearing by reversing the removal procedure.

11 Clutch hydraulic system – bleeding

1 If any part of the hydraulic system is dismantled, or if air has accidentally entered the system, the system will need to be bled. The presence of air is characterised by the pedal having a 'spongy' feel (which lessens if the pedal is pumped a few times) and it results in difficulty in changing gear.

2 The design of the clutch hydraulic system does not allow bleeding to be carried out using the conventional method of pumping the clutch pedal. In order to remove all air present in the system, it is necessary to use pressure bleeding equipment. This is available from auto accessory shops at relatively low cost.

3 The pressure bleeding equipment should be connected to the hydraulic system in accordance with the manufacturer's instructions. The system is normally bled through the bleed screw of the clutch slave cylinder, which is located at the top of the gearbox housing.

4 The system is bled until the fluid being ejected is free from air bubbles. The bleed screw is then closed and the bleeding equipment disconnected and removed.

5 Check the operation of the clutch to see that it is satisfactory. If air still remains in the system, repeat the bleeding operation.

6 Discard any fluid which is bled from the system, even if it looks clean. Hydraulic fluid absorbs water and its re-use can can cause internal corrosion of the master and slave cylinders, leading to excessive wear and failure of the seals.

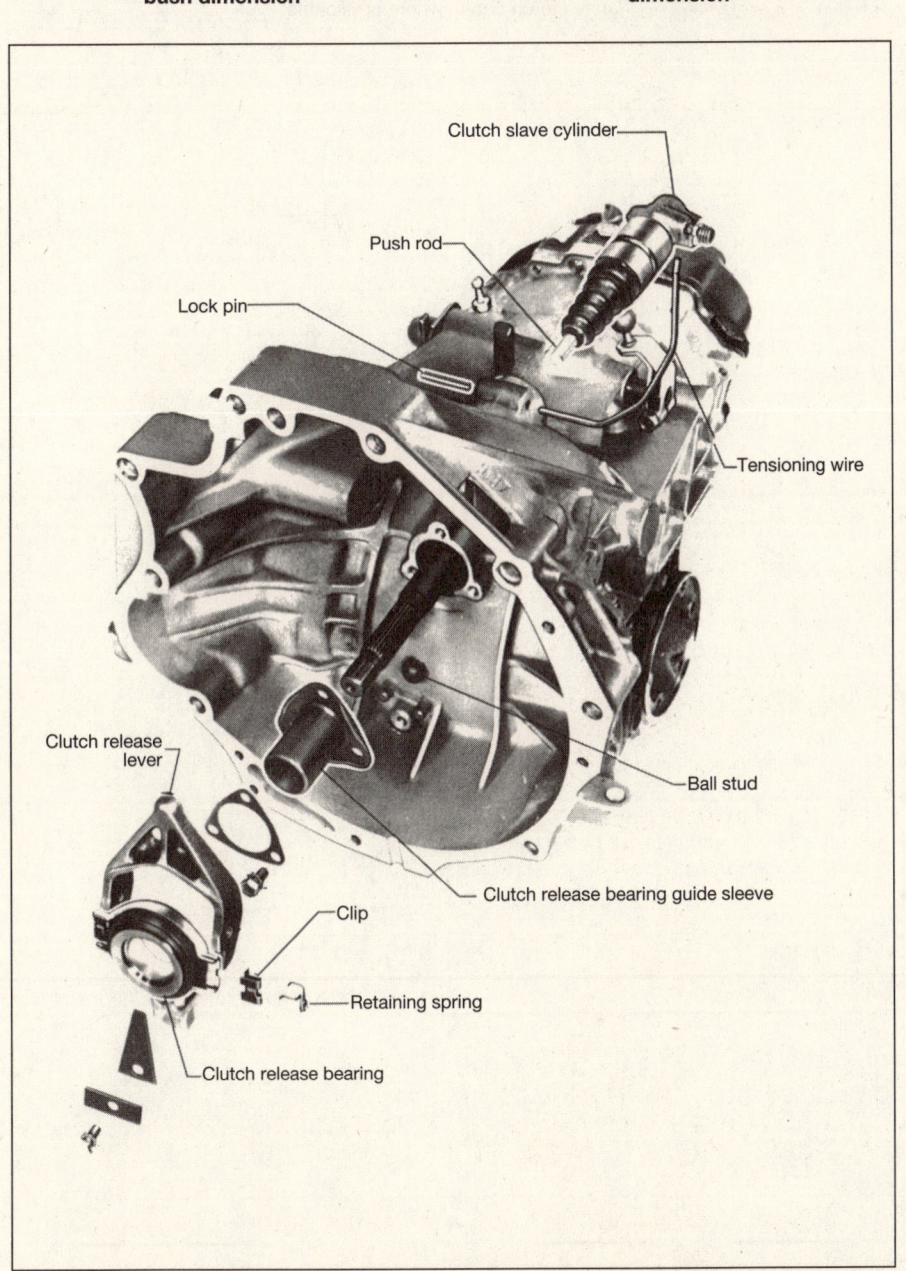

Fig. 5.12 Exploded view of the clutch release bearing and mechanism – hydraulically operated clutch (Sec 10)

Clutch slave cylinder
Push rod
Lock pin
Tensioning wire
Clutch release lever
Ball stud
Clutch release bearing guide sleeve
Clip
Retaining spring
Clutch release bearing

Fault finding – clutch

Judder when taking up drive
☐ Oil or grease contamination of friction linings
☐ Worn friction linings
☐ Excessive clutch disc run-out
☐ Clutch disc sticking on input shaft splines
☐ Faulty pressure plate or diaphragm spring
☐ Worn or broken engine/gearbox mountings
☐ Clutch cable sticking (where applicable)

Clutch slip
☐ Incorrect adjustment
☐ Friction linings worn or contaminated
☐ Weak or broken diaphragm spring

Clutch drag (failure to disengage)
☐ Incorrect adjustment
☐ Clutch disc sticking on input shaft splines
☐ Clutch disc sticking to flywheel
☐ Input shaft seized in spigot bearing
☐ Broken clutch cable (where applicable)
☐ Air in clutch hydraulic system (where applicable)
☐ Faulty clutch master cylinder (where applicable)

Noise evident when depressing clutch pedal
☐ Dry or worn release bearing
☐ Dry clutch pedal or release shaft bushes
☐ Faulty clutch cable (where applicable)

Chapter 6 Manual gearbox

For modifications, and information applicable to later models, see Supplement at at end of manual

Contents

Fault finding - manual gearbox .... See end of Chapter
Gearbox – removal and refitting 3
Gearbox – overhaul 4
Gearshift lever (013 and 093) – removal, refitting and adjustment .. 7
Gearshift lever (014) – removal, refitting and adjustment 5
Gearshift lever (016) – removal, refitting and adjustment 9
Gearshift linkage (013 and 093) – dismantling and reassembly 8
Gearshift linkage (014) – dismantling and reassembly 6
Gearshift linkage (016) – dismantling and reassembly 10
General description 1
Maintenance and inspection 2

Degrees of difficulty

| Easy, suitable for novice with little experience | Fairly easy, suitable for beginner with some experience | Fairly difficult, suitable for competent DIY mechanic | Difficult, suitable for experienced DIY mechanic | Very difficult, suitable for expert DIY or professional |

Specifications

Type .... Four or five forward speeds and reverse, with synchromesh on all forward speeds; integral final drive

Identification
Gearbox code number:
- 014 .... Four-speed gearbox fitted to 1.8 litre four-cylinder models
- 013 .... Five-speed gearbox fitted to 1.8 litre four-cylinder models
- 093 .... Five-speed gearbox fitted to 1.9 litre five-cylinder models
- 016 .... Five-speed gearbox fitted to 2.0, 2.2 and 2.3 litre five-cylinder models

Ratios

Gearbox 014:

	QN	4X
Final drive	4.11 : 1	4.11 : 1
1st	3.46 : 1	3.46 : 1
2nd	1.79 : 1	1.79 : 1
3rd	1.07 : 1	1.07 : 1
4th	0.70 : 1	0.70 : 1
Reverse	3.17 : 1	3.17 : 1

Gearbox 013:

	3T	HE	HF
Final drive	4.11 : 1	4.11 : 1	4.11 : 1
1st	3.46 : 1	3.46 : 1	3.46 : 1
2nd	1.79 : 1	1.79 : 1	1.79 : 1
3rd	1.07 : 1	1.13 : 1	1.13 : 1
4th	0.78 : 1	0.83 : 1	0.83 : 1
5th	0.60 : 1	0.68 : 1	0.68 : 1
Reverse	3.17 : 1	3.17 : 1	3.17 : 1

Gearbox 093:

	3Q
Final drive	5.22 : 1
1st	2.84 : 1
2nd	1.52 : 1
3rd	0.90 : 1
4th	0.64 : 1
5th	0.48 : 1
Reverse	3.16 : 1

Gearbox 016:

	AAZ	3V	3K	5N	3U
Final drive	3.89 : 1	3.89 : 1	3.89 : 1	4.11 : 1	3.89 : 1
1st	3.60 : 1	3.60 : 1	3.60 : 1	3.60 : 1	3.60 : 1
2nd	2.13 : 1	2.13 : 1	2.13 : 1	2.13 : 1	1.88 : 1
3rd	1.46 : 1	1.46 : 1	1.36 : 1	1.36 : 1	1.19 : 1
4th	1.07 : 1	1.07 : 1	0.97 : 1	0.97 : 1	0.84 : 1
5th	0.86 : 1	0.83 : 1	0.78 : 1	0.73 : 1	0.64 : 1
Reverse	3.50 : 1	3.50 : 1	3.50 : 1	3.50 : 1	3.50 : 1

Synchro-ring wear limit
All gearboxes .... 0.5 mm (0.02 in)

Lubrication
Oil type/specification .... VW/Audi gear oil G50, viscosity SAE 75W/90

Torque wrench settings

	Nm	lbf ft
Gearbox to engine	55	41
Gearbox mountings to subframe:		
013 and 014	45	33
093 and 016	40	30
Mounting brackets to gearbox (093 and 016)	40	30
Gearshift linkage sideplate bolt (014, 013 and 093)	30	22
Gearshift linkage adaptor lockbolt (014, 013 and 093)	20	15
Gearshift linkage support bar (014, 013 and 093)	25	18
Gearshift linkage shift rod clamp bolt (014, 013, 093 and 016)	15	11
Shift rod to gearshift lever (014, 013, 093 and 016)	10	7
Gearshift lever housing to floor (014, 013, 093 and 016)	10	7
Gearshift lever stop. cover plate and lever bearing (014, 013, 093 and 016)	10	7
Pushrod clamp plate (016 later version)	20	15
Filler and drain plugs (014, 013, 093 and 016)	25	18
Final drive cover (014, 013, 093 and 016)	25	18
Drive flange bolts:		
014	20	15
013, 093 and 016	25	18
Pinion output shaft nut (014, 013 and 093)	100	74
Fifth speed driven and driving gear bolts (013. 093 and 016)	70	52
Gearshift housing and bearing carrier (014, 013, 093 and 016)	25	18
Selector shaft cover (016)	10	7
Reverse relay lever bolt (014, 013 and 093)	35	26

1 General description

The manual gearbox may be either a four-speed type or one of three variations of five-speed type, according to model.

The gearbox is bolted to the rear of the engine in conventional manner but, because of the front wheel drive configuration, drive is transmitted to a differential unit located at the front of the earbox and then through the driveshafts to the front wheels. All forward gears incorporate synchromesh engagement, and reverse gear is obtained by engaging a spur type idler gear with the 1st/2nd synchro sleeve on the pinion shaft and a spur gear on the input shaft.

Gearshift is by means of a floor-mounted lever, and a single rod and linkage clamped to the selector rod which protrudes from the rear of the gearbox. The selector rod incorporates a finger which engages the other selector rods in the bearing carrier.

2 Maintenance and inspection

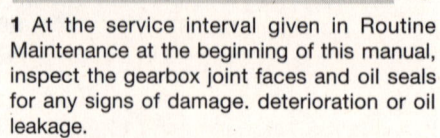

1 At the service interval given in Routine Maintenance at the beginning of this manual, inspect the gearbox joint faces and oil seals for any signs of damage. deterioration or oil leakage.

2 Also check and, if necessary, top up the gearbox oil. The filler plug is located on the left-hand side of the final drive housing and the oil level should be maintained up to the level of the filler plug orifice (photos). The oil drain plug is located just below the filler plug, but note that draining and refilling of the gearbox oil is not a service requirement.

3 Gearbox – removal and refitting

1 Position the front of the car over an inspection pit, or on ramps or axle stands and apply the handbrake firmly.
2 Disconnect the battery negative lead.
3 Unscrew and remove the upper bolts attaching the gearbox to the engine, noting the location of any brackets.

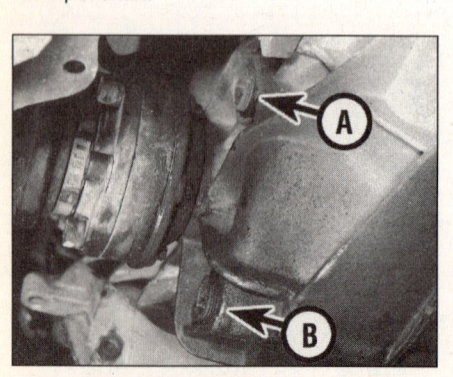

2.2A Gearbox filler plug (A) and drain plug (B) (016 gearbox shown)

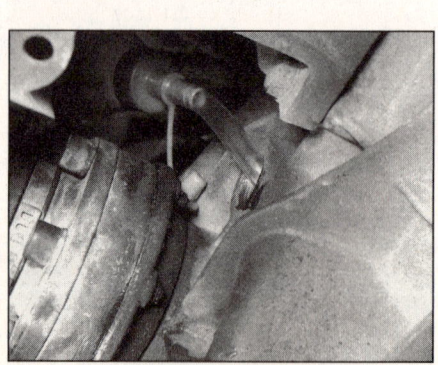

2.2B Topping-up the gearbox oil

Fig. 6.1 Support bar required when removing the gearbox on five-cylinder models (Sec 3)

Manual gearbox 6•3

3.4 Speedometer cable attachment

3.9 Econometer switch wiring (016 gearbox shown)

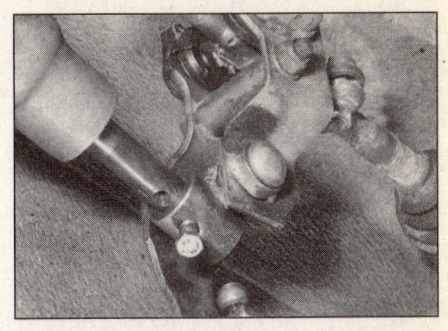

3.14 Disconnecting the selector linkage from the rear of the gearbox (013 gearbox shown)

4 Disconnect the speedometer cable from the differential cover (photo).
5 On models equipped with a cable-operated clutch, detach the clutch cable from the gearbox with reference to Chapter 5.
6 On models equipped with a hydraulically-operated clutch, remove the slave cylinder from the gearbox, leaving the hydraulic hose attached, with reference to Chapter 5.
7 If working on the 016 type gearbox, refer to Chapter 3 and remove the air cleaner.
8 Remove the exhaust front pipe from the manifold and exhaust system, with reference to Chapter 3.
9 Disconnect the wiring to the econometer switch and remove the cable clip (photo). Disconnect any additional gearbox wiring where fitted.

10 On five-cylinder engine models, support the front of the engine with a hoist or bar arrangement similar to that shown in Fig. 6.1.
11 Unbolt and remove the gearbox front cover.
12 Remove the starter motor, as described in Chapter 12.
13 Disconnect the driveshafts from the drive flanges, with reference to Chapter 8, and tie them to one side.
14 Unscrew the lockbolt securing the selector adaptor to the selector rod on the rear of the gearbox (photo). Press the support rod from the balljoint and withdraw the adaptor from the selector lever. Remove the shift rod and, where fitted, the pushrod (016 gearbox).
15 If working on the 016 type gearbox, remove the guard plates from the subframe.
16 Support the gearbox with a trolley jack or stand.
17 Unscrew and remove the lower bolts attaching the gearbox to the engine.
18 If working on the 016 type gearbox remove the subframe rear mounting bolts (photo).
19 Undo the bolts securing the gearbox mountings to the subframe and where necessary remove the mounting brackets from the gearbox to clear the subframe (photo).

3.18 Subframe rear mounting bolt (A) and gearbox mounting-to-subframe bolt (B) (016 gearbox shown)

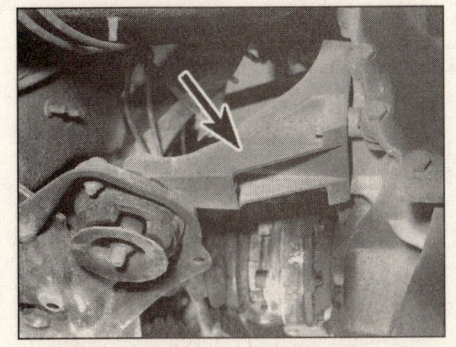

3.19 Gearbox mounting bracket (arrowed) (016 gearbox shown)

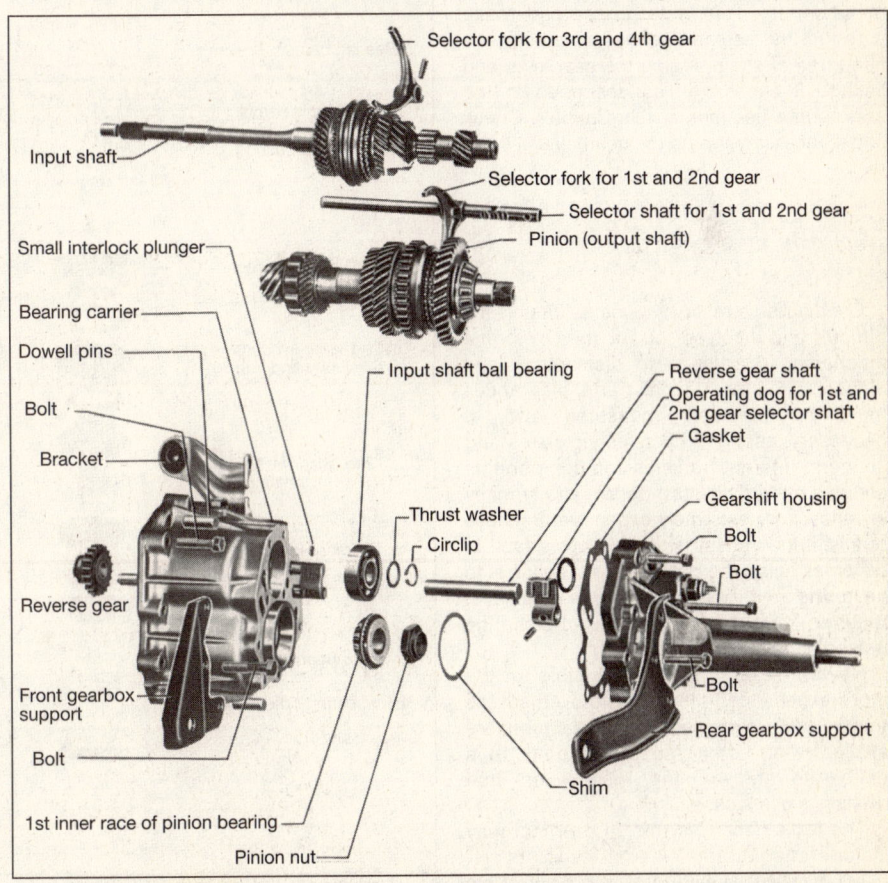

Fig. 6.2 Exploded view of the gearbox major assemblies – 014 gearbox (Sec 4)

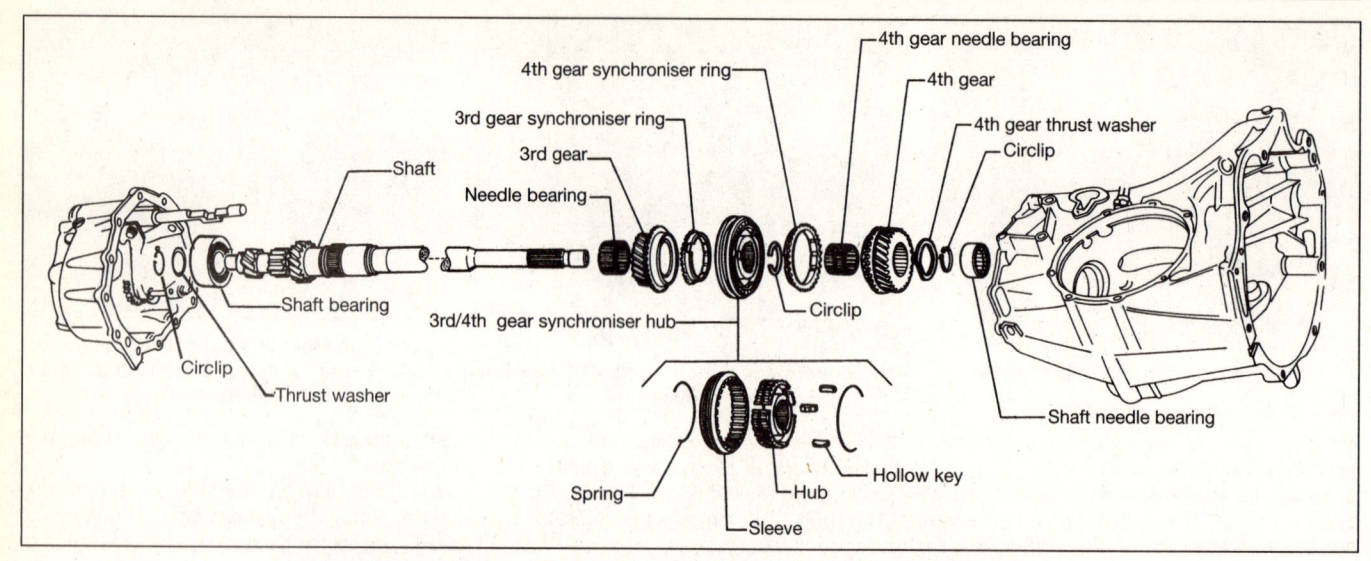

Fig. 6.3 Exploded view of the input shaft components – 014 gearbox (Sec 4)

20 With the help of an assistant, withdraw the gearbox from the engine; making sure that the input shaft does not hang on the clutch. Lower the gearbox to the ground and remove it from under the car.

21 Refitting is a reversal of removal, but lightly lubricate the input shaft splines and clutch release bearing front face with molybdenum disulphide grease and make sure that the engine/gearbox mountings are fitted free of strain. Adjust the gear lever and linkage if necessary, as described in the appropriate Sections of this Chapter. Check and if necessary top up the gearbox oil.

4 Gearbox – overhaul

Overhauling a manual transmission unit is a difficult and involved job for the DIY home mechanic. In addition to dismantling and reassembling many small parts, clearances must be precisely measured and, if necessary, changed by selecting shims and spacers. Internal transmission components are also often difficult to obtain, and in many instances, are extremely expensive. Because of this, if the transmission develops a fault or becomes noisy, the best course of action is to have the unit overhauled by a specialist repairer, or to obtain an exchange reconditioned unit.

Nevertheless, it is not impossible for the more experienced mechanic to overhaul the transmission, provided the special tools are available, and that the job is done in a deliberate step-by-step manner so that nothing is overlooked.

The tools necessary for an overhaul may include internal and external circlip pliers, bearing pullers, a slide hammer, a set of pin punches, a dial test indicator, and possibly a

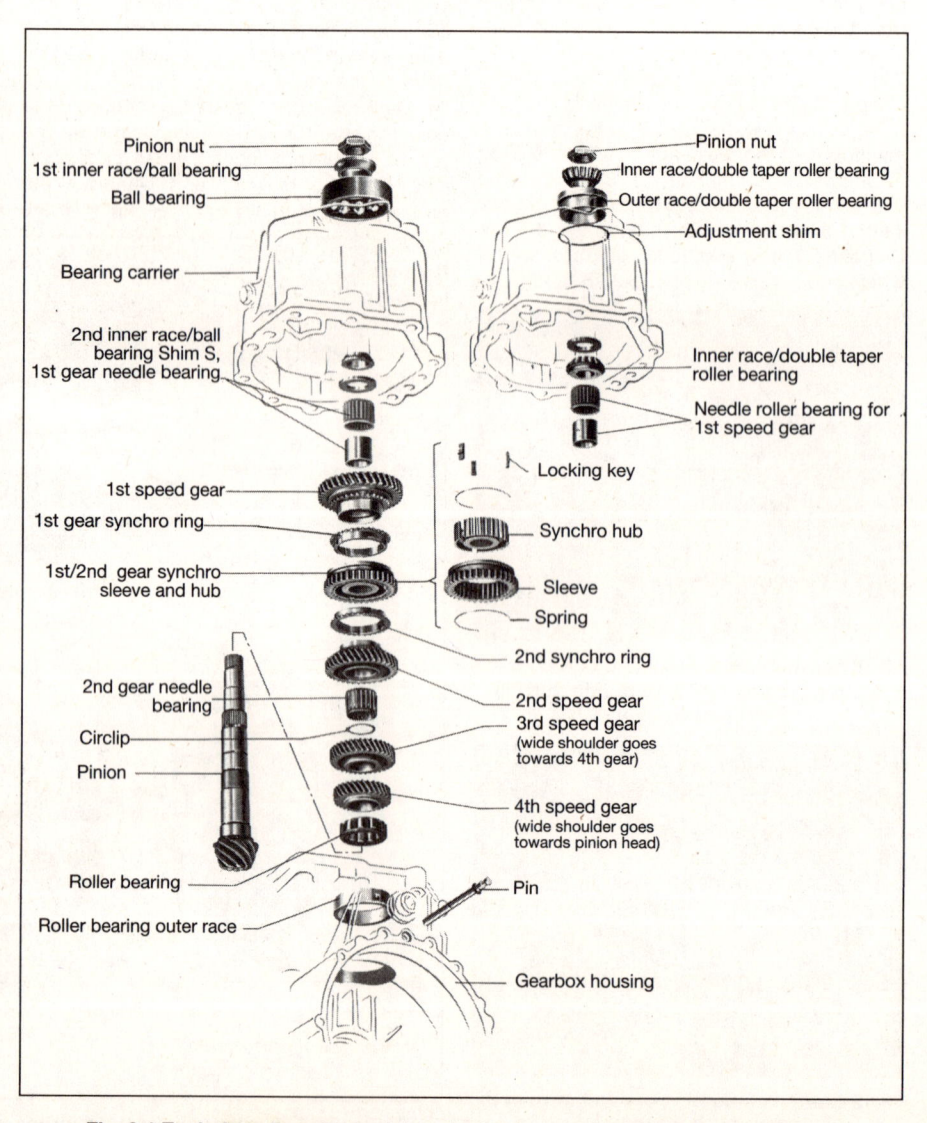

Fig. 6.4 Exploded view of the pinion shaft components – 014 gearbox (Sec 4)

Manual gearbox 6•5

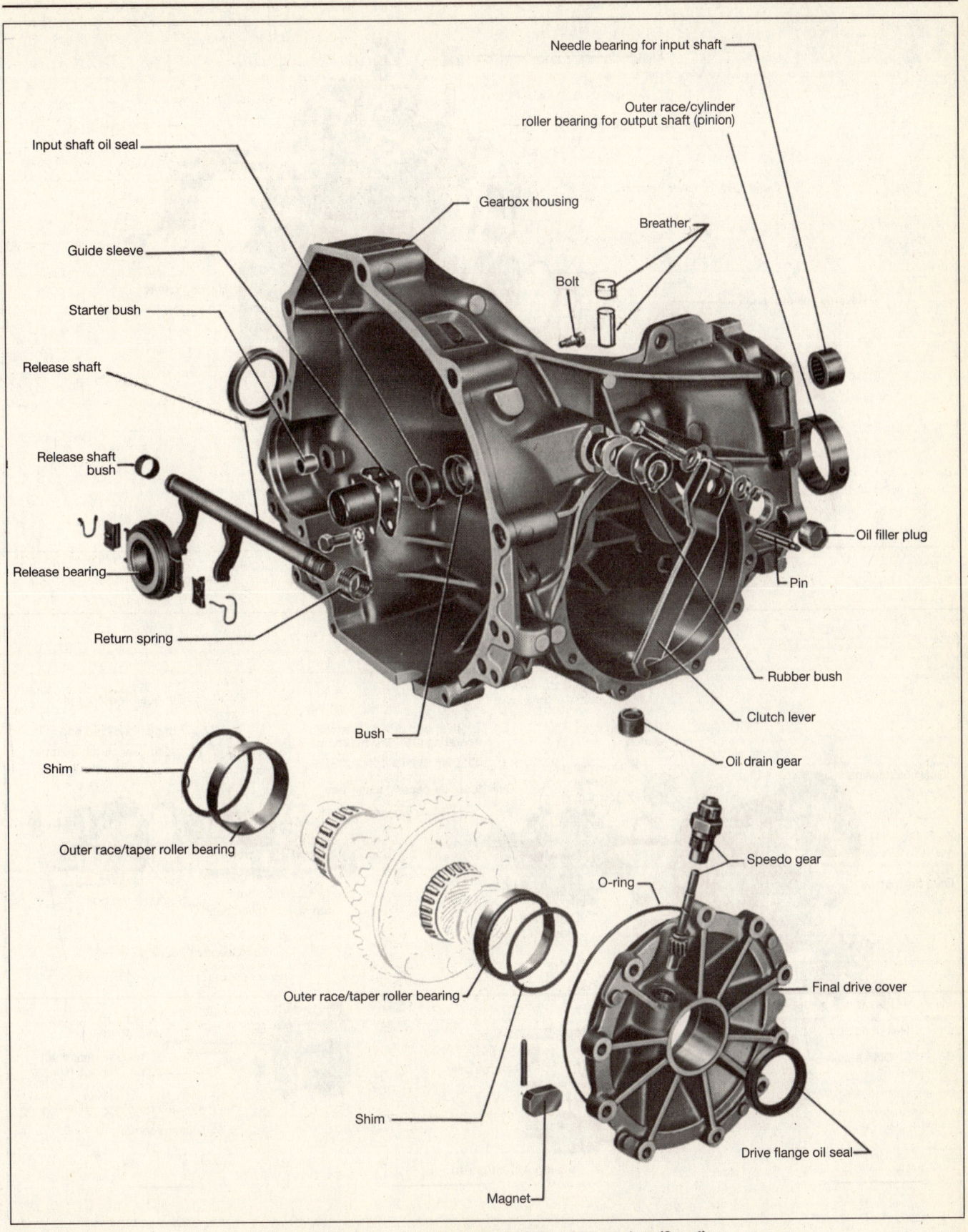

Fig. 6.5 Final drive housing components – 014 gearbox (Sec 4)

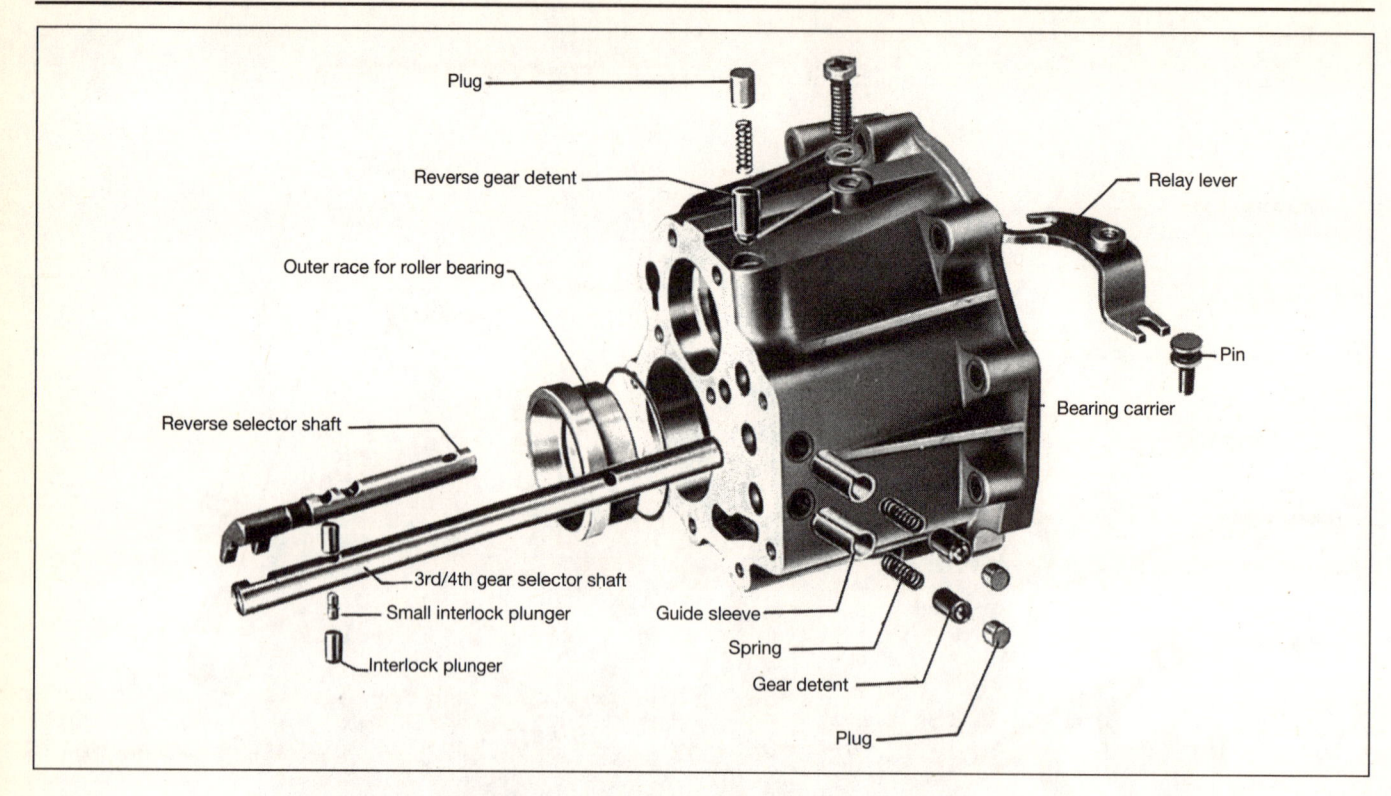

Fig. 6.6 Gear carrier components – 014 gearbox (Sec 4)

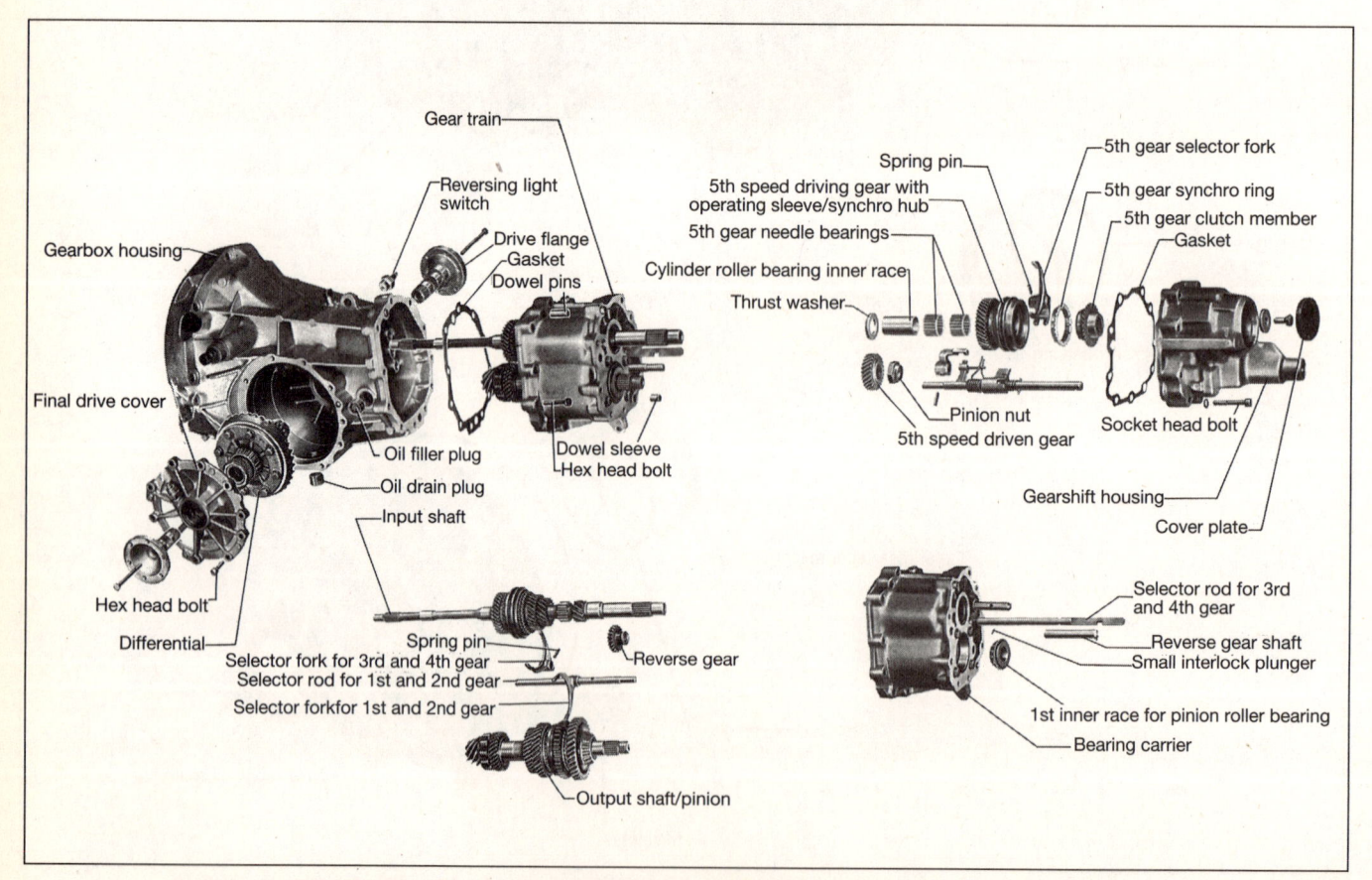

Fig. 6.7 Exploded view of the gearbox major assemblies – 013 gearbox (Sec 4)

Manual gearbox 6•7

Fig. 6.9 Exploded view of the pinion shaft components – 013 and 093 gearboxes (Sec 4)

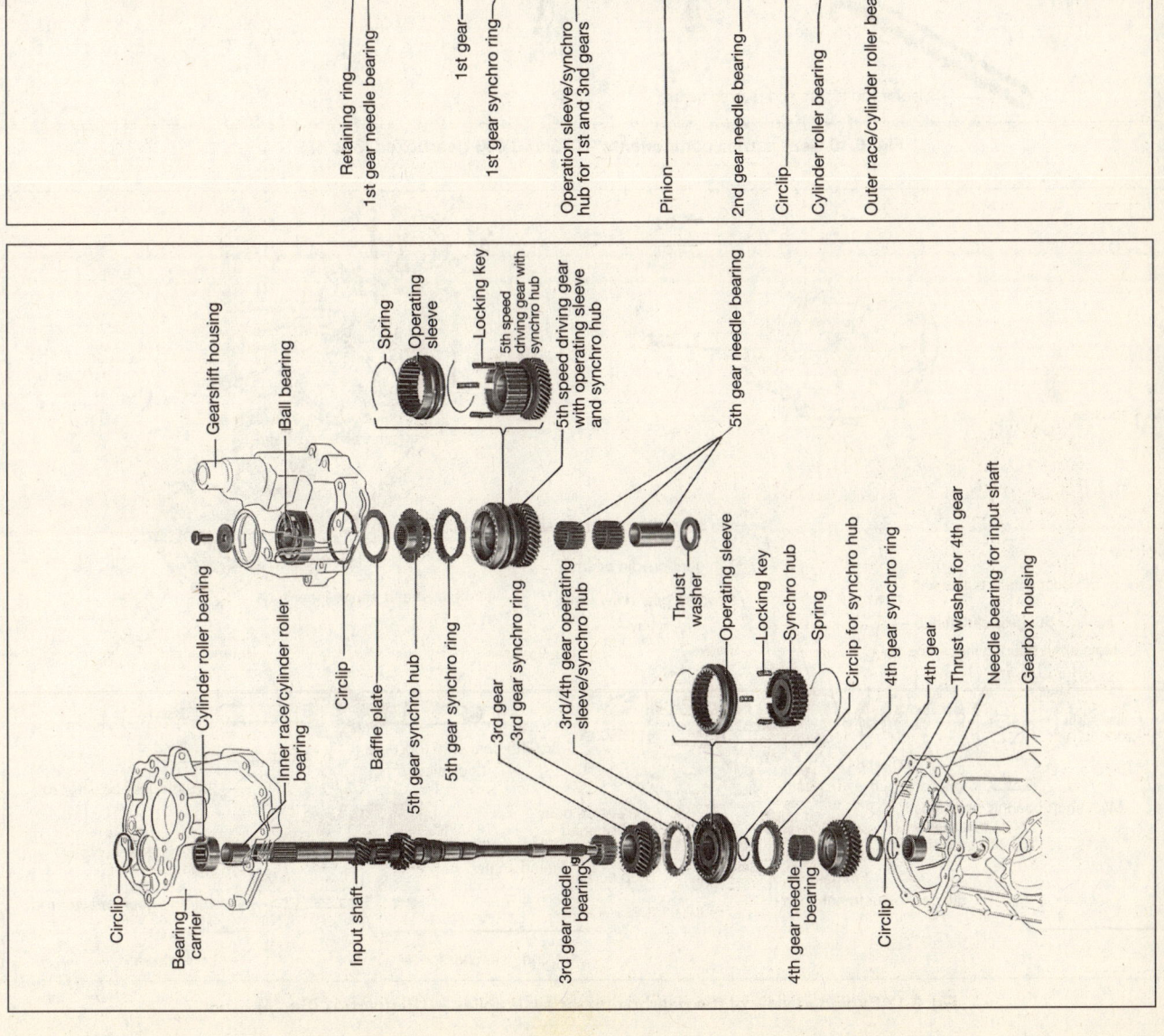

Fig. 6.8 Exploded view of the input shaft components – 013 and 093 gearboxes (Sec 4)

6•8 Manual gearbox

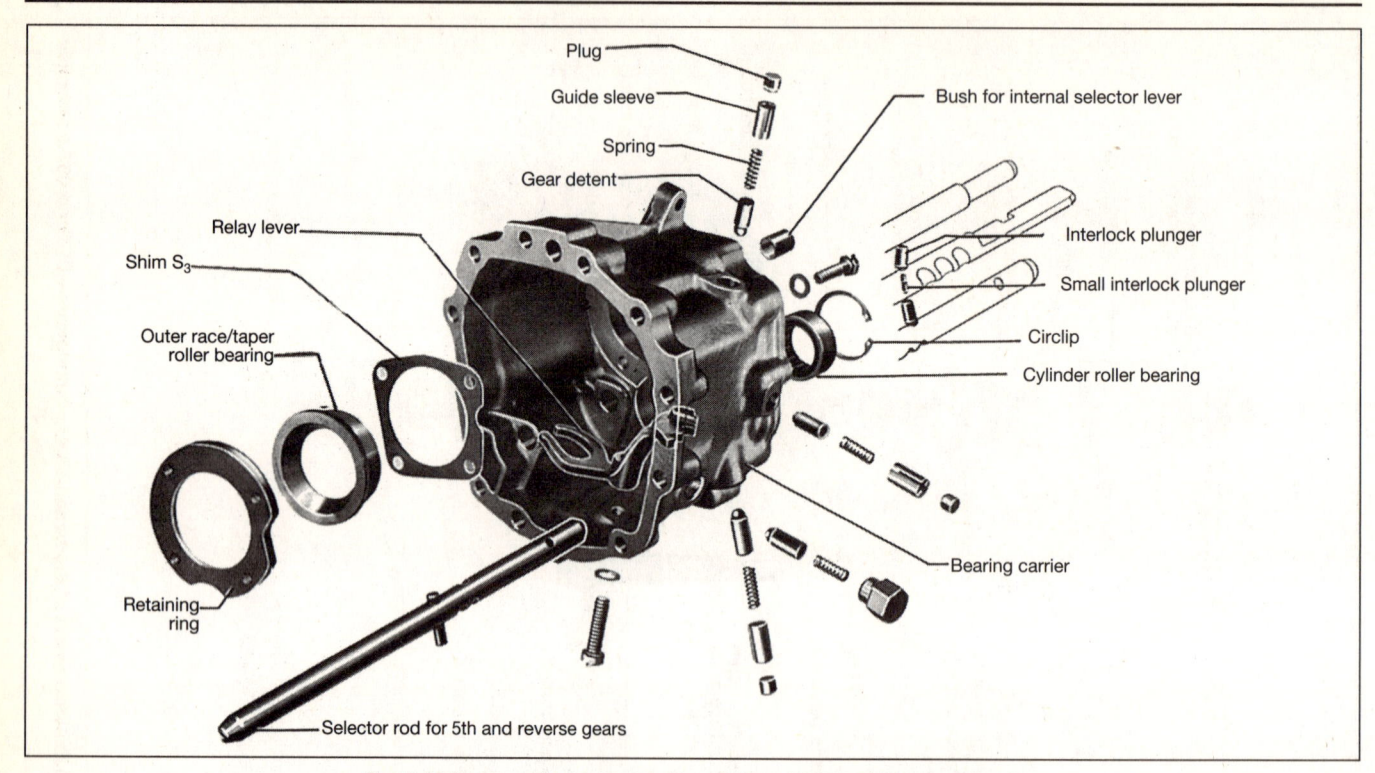

Fig. 6.10 Gear carrier components – 013 and 093 gearboxes (Sec 4)

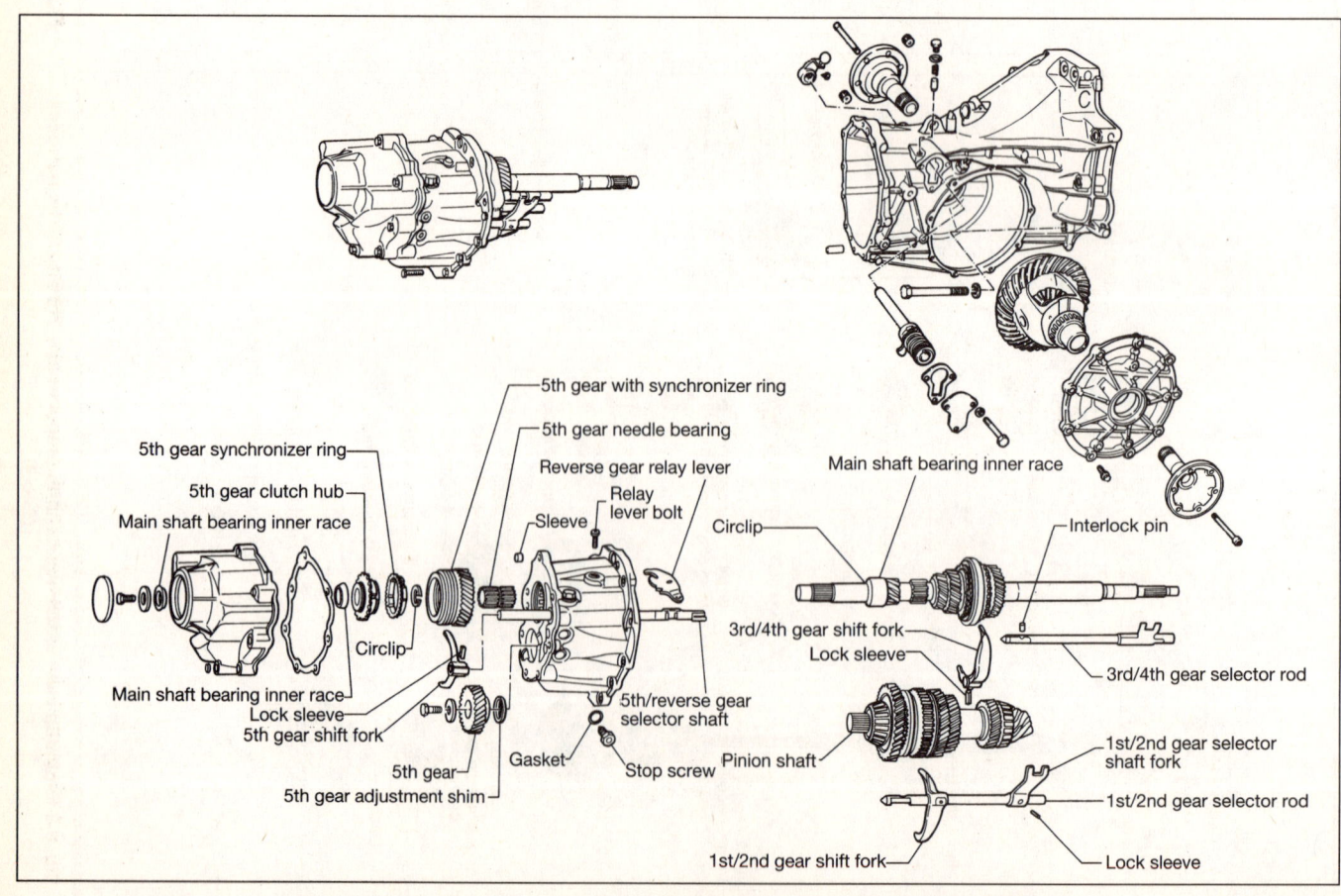

Fig. 6.11 Exploded view of the gearbox major assemblies – 016 gearbox (Sec 4)

Manual gearbox 6•9

Fig. 6.13 Exploded view of the pinion shaft components – 016 gearbox (Sec 4)

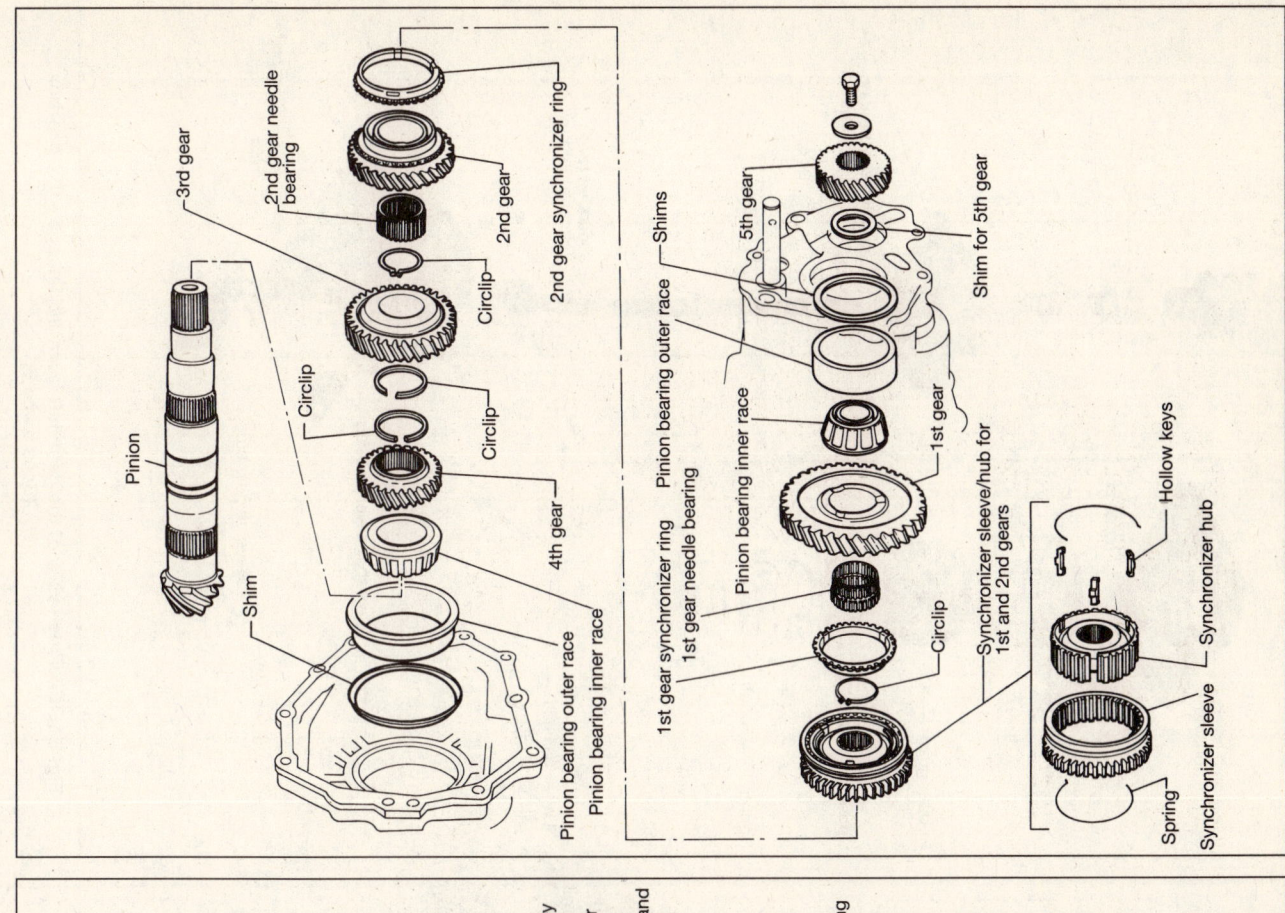

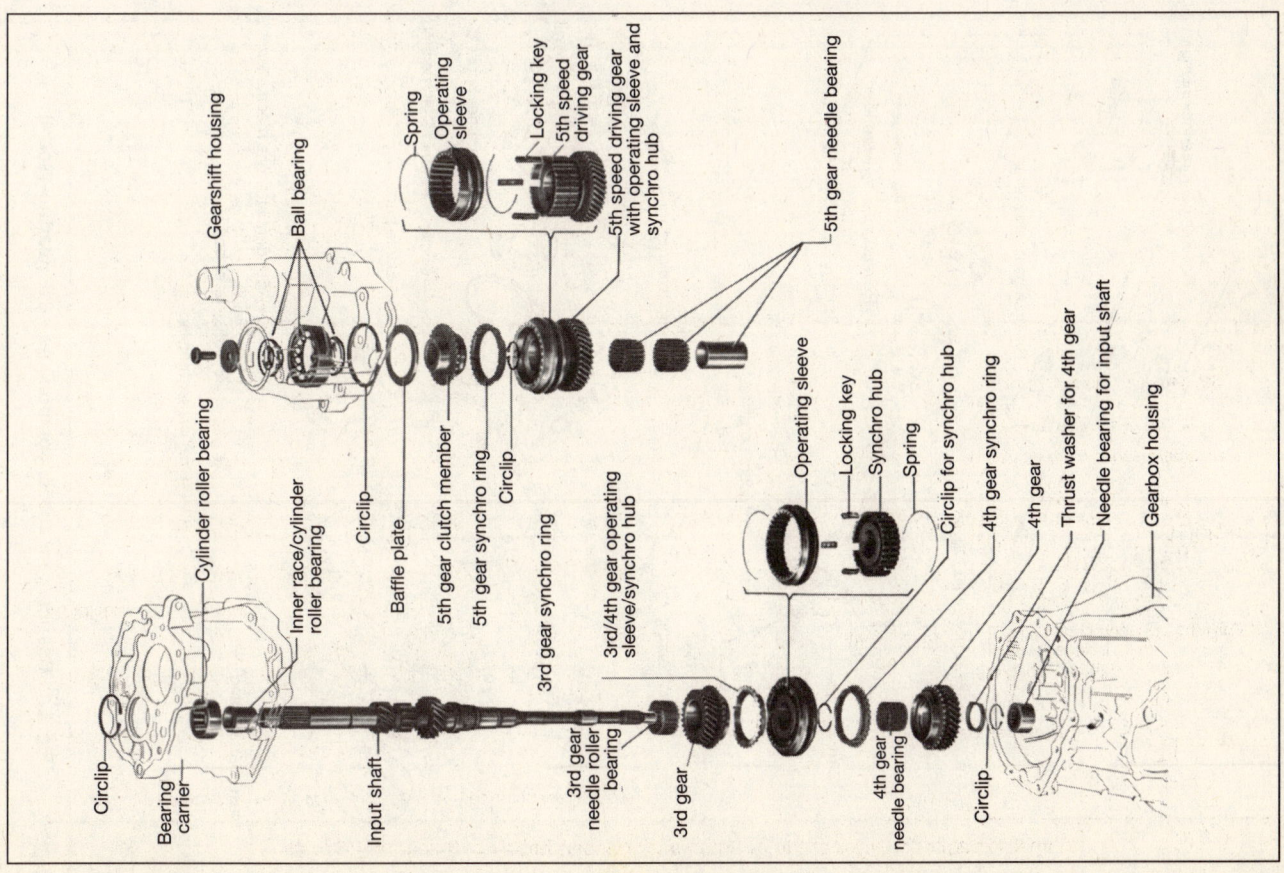

Fig. 6.12 Exploded view of the input shaft components – 016 gearbox (Sec 4)

6•10 Manual gearbox

Fig. 6.15 Exploded view of the gearshift lever and linkage – 014 gearbox (Secs 5 and 6)

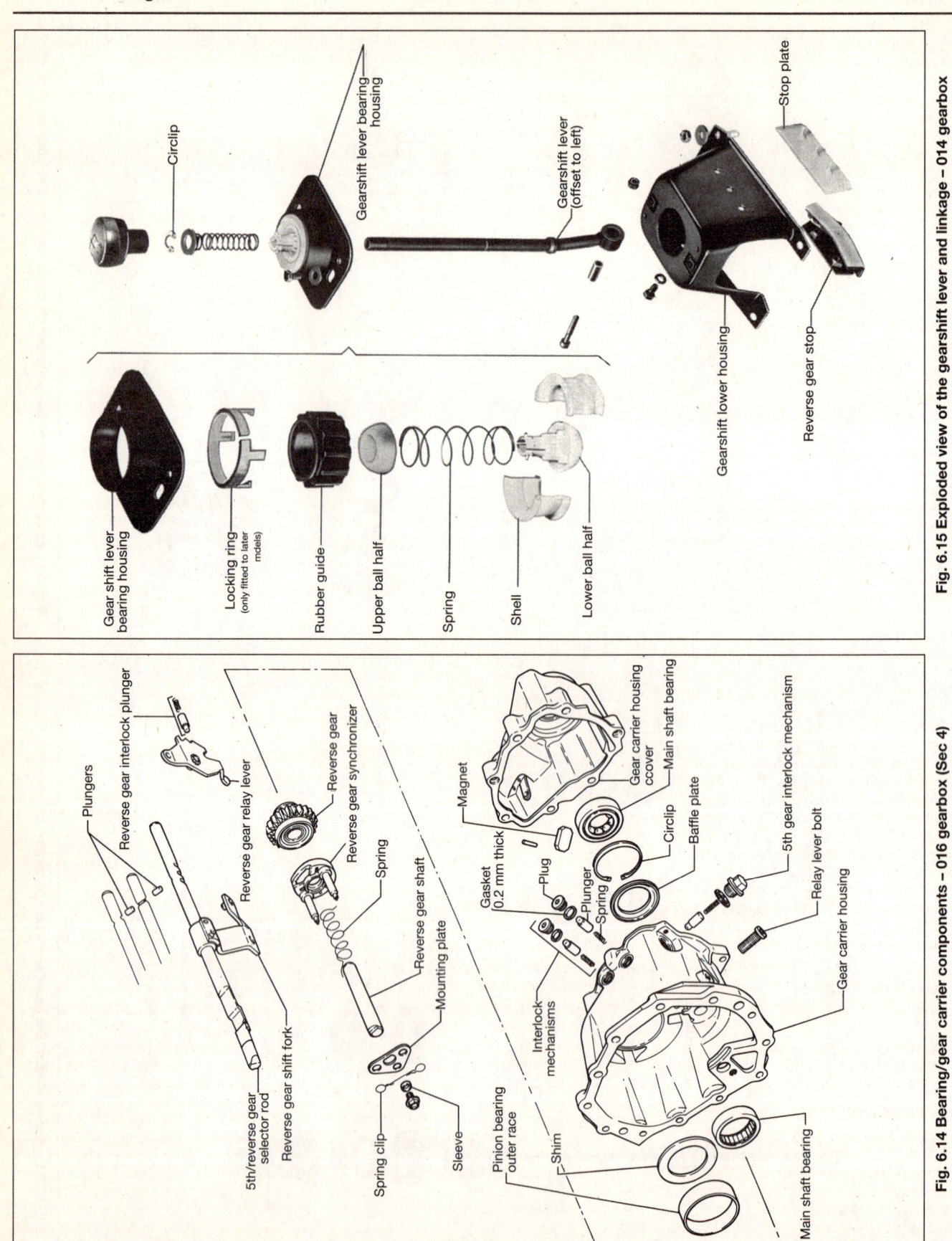

Fig. 6.14 Bearing/gear carrier components – 016 gearbox (Sec 4)

hydraulic press. In addition, a large, sturdy workbench and a vice will be required.

During dismantling of the transmission, make careful notes of how each component is fitted, to make reassembly easier and accurate.

Before dismantling the transmission, it will help if you have some idea which area is malfunctioning. Certain problems can be closely related to specific areas in the gearbox, which can make component examination and replacement easier.

5 Gearshift lever (014) – removal, refitting and adjustment

1 The adjustment of the gearshift linkage requires a special tool, so if the linkage is undone it is very important to mark the position of the shift rod in the shift finger before separating them.
2 Put a mark to show how far the shift rod is inserted into the clamp, and also mark a horizontal line on both the shift finger and the shift rod so that they can be reconnected without any rotational change.
3 Release the bolt on the clamp and separate the shift rod from the shift finger.
4 From inside the car, remove the centre console, as described in Chapter 11, undo the four nuts and washers securing the lever housing to the car floor and remove the gear lever assembly and shift rod.
5 To separate the shift rod from the gear lever, undo and remove the shift rod clevis bolt.
6 After refitting the gear lever, by reversing the removal operations, the basic setting of the linkage should be tested by engaging 1st gear and then moving the gear lever as far to the left as it will go. Hold the gear lever with one finger and allow it to spring back slowly to the pressure point. Measured at the gear lever knob the movement must be at last 5 to 10 mm (0.2 to 0.4 in). If the movement is insufficient, slacken the lever bearing retaining bolts and move the bearing to the right to reduce the gear lever movement, or to the left to increase it, then tighten the nuts. If gear selection is still unsatisfactory the adjustment should be checked by an Audi dealer.

6 Gearshift linkage (014) – dismantling and reassembly

1 The gearshift linkage consists of two principal parts, the shift rod coupling assembly and the lever assembly.

Gear lever assembly

2 Remove the gear lever, as described in Section 5.
3 Dismantle the assembly by unscrewing the gear knob, removing the circlip from the gear lever and lifting off the washer and spring. The gear lever can then be pulled down out of the lever bearing assembly.

4 Before separating the lever bearing assembly from the lever housing, mark round the lever bearing plate with a scriber so that it can be returned to exactly the same position, then remove the two screws and washer from the plate.
5 Do not dismantle the bearing unless it is necessary to grease it. Push the rubber guide and locking ring (if fitted) down out of the housing plate, then prise the plastic shells apart and remove the ball halves and spring – the shells can then be removed from the rubber guide.
6 When reassembling, have the rubber guide with its shouldered end uppermost and press the two shells into it. Press the lower ball half into the shells, then the spring and finally press in the upper ball half, pushing the shells slightly apart if necessary.
7 After assembling the parts into the rubber guide, push the assembly up into the lever bearing plate, together with the locking ring, where fitted.
8 When inserting the lever into the bearing, note that the lever is cranked to the left, and when refitting the lever bearing plate to the housing, take care to line up the plate with the scribed mark made before dismantling.

Shift rod coupling

9 To dismantle the shift rod coupling, remove the bolt from the end of the support rod. Mark the position of the adaptor on the gearbox selector lever, then loosen the bolt and remove the shift rod coupling assembly.
10 Prise the ball coupling of the support off its mounting on the side plate. Remove the bolt which clamps the two side plates together and extract the shift finger and its bushes.
11 When reassembling the shift rod coupling, note that the adaptor should be fitted so that the hole for the clamp bolt is towards the front and the groove for the clamp bolt on the shift finger is on the left-hand side. Make sure that the holes in the two side plates are exactly in line, so that the coupling is assembled without any strain.
12 All the joints and friction surfaces of the shift rod coupling should be lubricated with special grease AOS 126 000 05.

7 Gearshift lever (013 and 093) – removal, refitting and adjustment

1 The procedure is basically the same as that described for the 014 gearbox in Section 5. However, after checking the return distance in 1st gear, engage 5th gear and move the lever to the right as far as possible. Hold the gear lever with one finger and allow it to spring back slowly to the pressure point. The return distance should be the same as measured in the 1st gear position and, on these gearboxes, should be at least 5 mm (0.2 in). If the movement is not the same in both positions move the gear lever bearing within the travel allowed by its elongated holes: to the right for more movement in 5th gear or to the left for more movement in 1st gear. If gear selection is still unsatisfactory the adjustment should be checked by an Audi dealer.

8 Gearshift linkage (013 and 093) – dismantling and reassembly

The procedure is identical to that for the 014 gearbox described in Section 6. However, the bottom of the gear lever is not cranked and can therefore be fitted either way round.

9 Gearshift lever (016) – removal, refitting and adjustment

1 Two types of gearshift lever assembly and gearshift linkage are used on Audi models fitted with the 016 gearbox. The early type utilizes a single shift rod and is shown in Fig. 6.16. The later type utilizes a shift rod and also a pushrod to prevent movement of the engine/gearbox assembly from causing the gear lever to move. This later type is shown in Fig. 6.17; Although minor adjustment of the gearshift lever can be carried out without special tools, a setting gauge is needed to first establish a basic setting and this can only be done by an Audi dealer. For this reason it is very important to mark the fitted depth and angular position of the shift rods and, on later models, the pushrod before slackening any of the clamps.
2 To remove the early type gearshift lever first remove the centre console, as described in Chapter 11.
3 Undo the nut and bolt securing the shift rod to the gearshift lever and the four bolts securing the gear lever base to the car floor. Separate the shift rod and remove the gearshift lever assembly.
4 To remove the later type gearshift lever first remove the centre console, as described in Chapter 11.
5 Undo the nut and bolt securing the shift rod to the gearshift lever and the bolt and clamping plate securing the front and rear pushrods together.
6 Undo the four nuts and lift off the stop and cover plate. Disengage the rear pushrod bearing pin from the rubber mounting and withdraw the gearshift lever assembly. Recheck the gearshift operation. If it is unsatisfactory remove the adjusting rod by prising it off the ball-stud and shift lever on the gearbox and check that its length between balljoint centres is 134 mm (5.28 in). Adjust the rod length if necessary and try the gearshift action once more. If it is still unsatisfactory the only course of action is to try a long trial and error process by altering the position of the front and rear shift rods at the clamp or by having an Audi dealer adjust the linkage with the setting gauge.

6•12 Manual gearbox

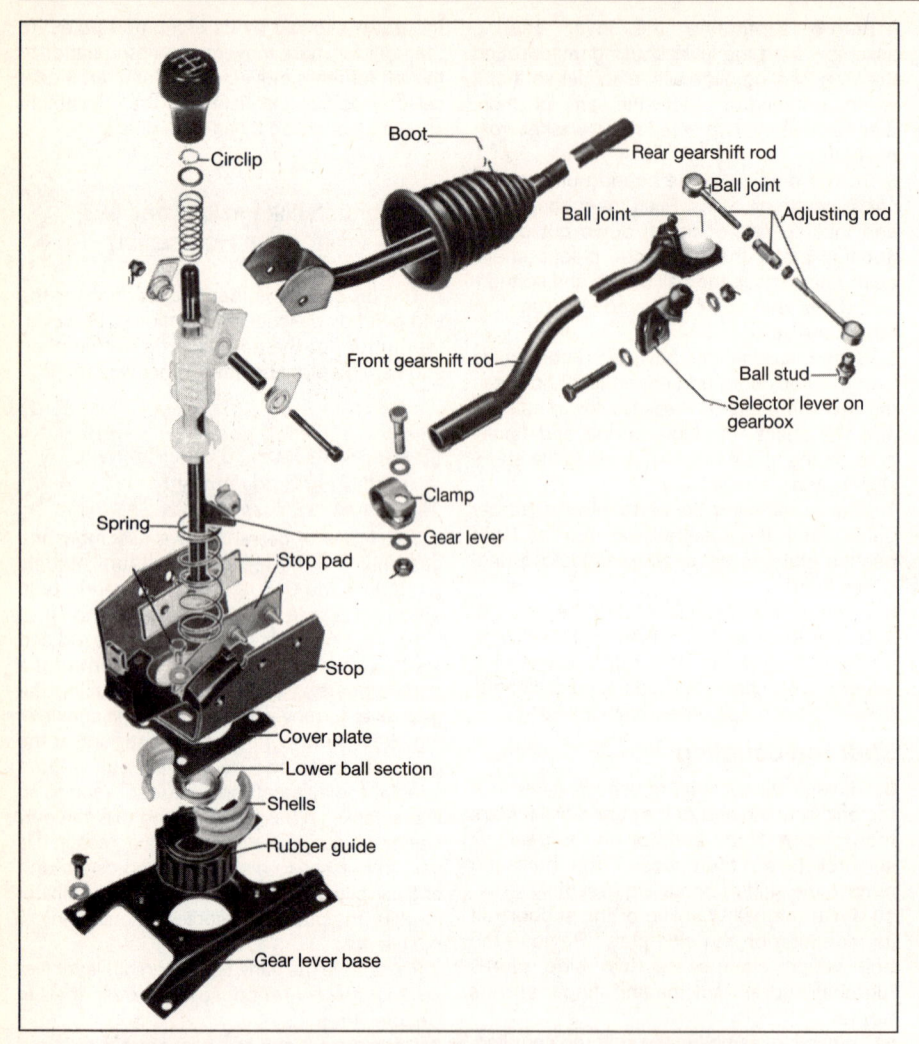

Fig. 6.16 Early type gearshift lever and linkage assembly – 016 gearbox (Secs 9 and 10)

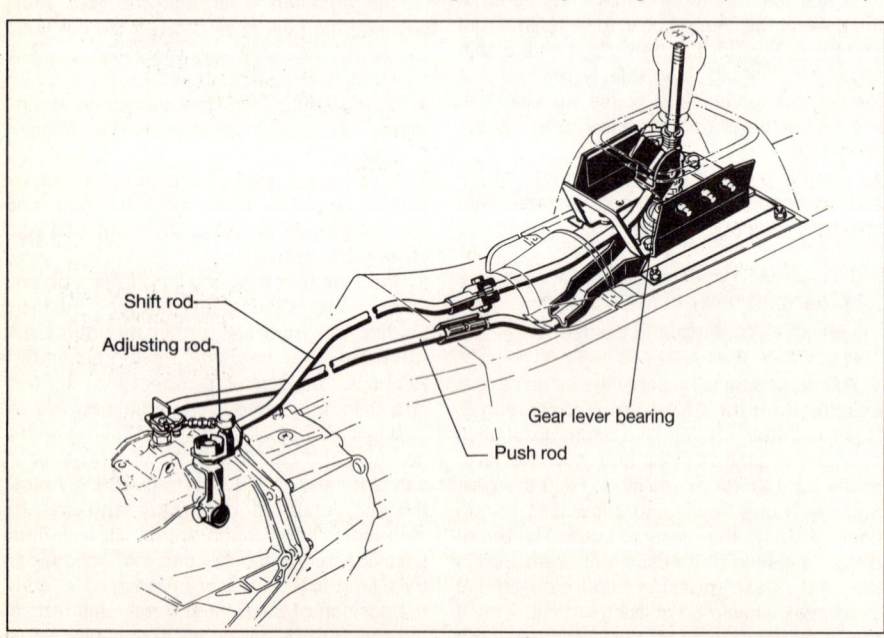

Fig. 6.17 Later type gearshift lever and linkage assembly – 018 gearbox (Sec 9)

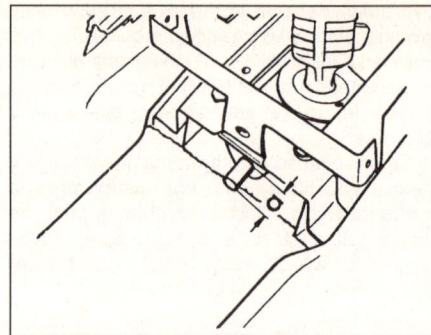

Fig. 6.18 Gearshift lever bearing pin protrusion 'a' on later type assemblies – 016 gearbox (Sec 9)

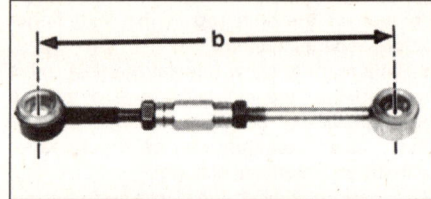

Fig. 6.19 Adjusting rod setting dimension – 016 gearbox (Sec 9)

b = 134 mm (5.28 in)

10 Gearshift linkage (016) – dismantling and reassembly

Note: *before proceeding refer to Section 9, paragraph 1.*

1 The gearshift linkage consists of two principle parts, the gearshift lever assembly and the linkage rods.

Gearshift lever assembly

2 Remove the gearshift lever, as described in Section 9.

3 Unscrew the lever knob, remove the circlip and withdraw the spring from the gearshift lever.

4 On early versions mark the relationship of the stop to the cover plate then remove the four bolts and separate the stop, cover plate and gear lever base. Do not dismantle the lower bearing unless it is necessary to grease it. Push the rubber guide out of the gear lever base then prise the plastic shells apart and remove the gearshift lever and upper ball section and the lower ball section. On later versions it will be necessary to release the peening around the lower bearing then the metal ring and rubber guide can be removed and dismantled as previously described.

5 When reassembling, lubricate all the friction surfaces with special grease AOS 126 000 OS.

6 When reassembling the rubber guide, position it with the shouldered end uppermost

and press the two shells into it. Press the lower ball half into the shells then the spring and finally press in the upper ball half, pushing the shells apart if necessary.

7 Push the rubber gauge into the gear lever base or, on later versions, the rear pushrod. On later versions refit the metal ring and secure the assembly by peening in three places

8 Reassemble the stop, cover plate and gear lever base, lining up the previously made marks.

9 Refit the spring and circlip then screw on the gearshift, knob.

10 Refit the gearshift lever assembly, as described in Section 9.

Linkage rods

11 To remove the front shift rod, prise the adjusting rod balljoint off the shift rod then release the shift rod from the shift lever. Slacken the clamp, withdraw the front shift rod from the rear shift rod (photo) and remove from under the car. Refit in the reverse sequence to removal.

12 To remove the rear shift rod, remove the centre console, as described in Chapter 11 then undo the nut and bolt securing the rod to the gearshift lever. Slacken the clamp, withdraw the rear shift rod from the front shift rod and remove the rod upwards and into the car. Refit in the reverse sequence to removal.

13 To remove the adjusting rod, prise it off the front shift rod and gearbox shift lever ball-studs then remove it from under the car. Whenever the adjusting rod is removed, check its length which should be 134 mm (5.28 in) and reset if necessary. Refit the adjusting rod by pushing it back onto the ball-studs.

14 On later versions the front pushrod can be removed after removing the locking clip at the gearbox and the clamp bolt and plate at the rear pushrod attachment. Refit in the reverse sequence to removal.

15 The rear pushrod on later versions is removed in conjunction with the gearshift lever (Section 9).

10.11 Front-to-rear shift rod clamp

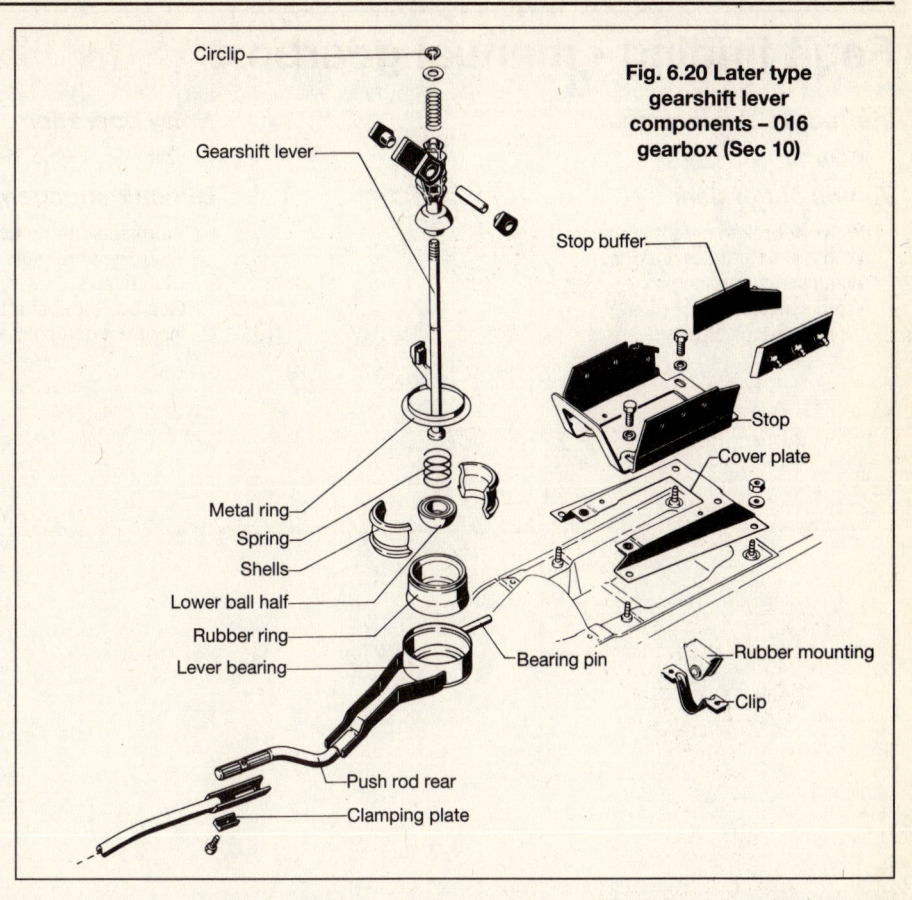

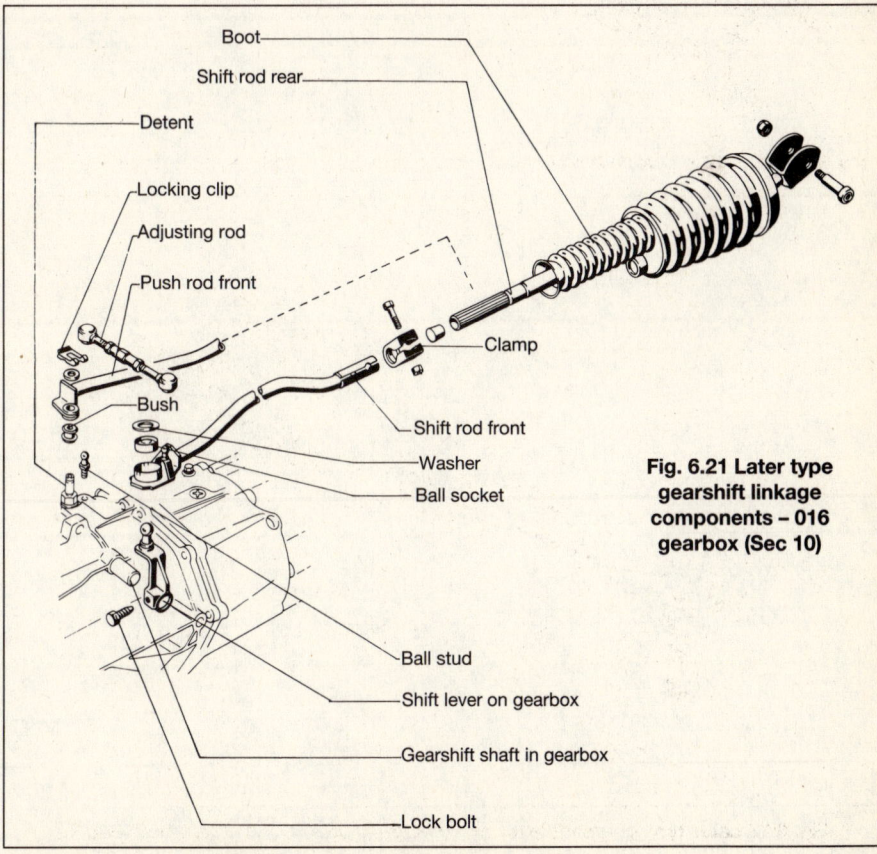

Fig. 6.20 Later type gearshift lever components – 016 gearbox (Sec 10)

Fig. 6.21 Later type gearshift linkage components – 016 gearbox (Sec 10)

Fault finding - manual gearbox

Ineffective synchromesh
☐ Worn synchro rings

Jumps out of gear
☐ Weak or broken detent spring
☐ Worn selector forks or dogs
☐ Weak synchro springs
☐ Worn synchro unit or gears
☐ Worn bearings or gears

Noisy operation
☐ Worn bearings or gears

Difficult engagement of gears
☐ Worn selector components
☐ Worn synchro units
☐ Clutch fault
☐ Gearbox input shaft spigot bearing seized in end of crankshaft
☐ Incorrect gearshift adjustment

Chapter 7 Automatic transmission

For modifications, and information applicable to later models, see Supplement at at end of manual

Contents

Accelerator pedal and linkage – adjustment 6
Automatic transmission – removal and refitting 4
Automatic transmission fluid – draining and refilling 3
Fault finding – automatic transmission .... See end of Chapter
General description 1
Maintenance and inspection 2
Selector lever and cable – removal, refitting and adjustment 7
Starter inhibitor switch – removal, refitting and adjustment 8
Torque converter checking and draining 5

Degrees of difficulty

| **Easy,** suitable for novice with little experience | **Fairly easy,** suitable for beginner with some experience | **Fairly difficult,** suitable for competent DIY mechanic | **Difficult,** suitable for experienced DIY mechanic | **Very difficult,** suitable for expert DIY or professional |

Specifications

Type .... Three-speed planetary gearbox with hydrodynamic torque converter and integral final drive assembly

Identification
Transmission code number:
- 087 .... Fitted to five-cylinder models
- 089 .... Fitted to four-cylinder models

Ratios

	087	089
Final drive	3.08:1. 3.25:1 or 3.45:1 (according to model and engine)	3.42:1
1st	2.71:1	2.71:1
2nd	1.50:1	1.50:1
3rd	1.00:1	1.00:1
Reverse	2.43:1	2.43:1

Lubrication
Transmission .... Dexron II type ATF
Final drive:
- 3-speed .... Gear oil, viscosity SAE 90, to API GL5
- 4-speed .... VW/Audi gear oil G50, viscosity SAE 75W/90

Torque converter
Maximum diameter of bush .... 34.12 mm (1.34 in)
Maximum out-of-round of bush .... 0.03 mm (0.001 in)

Torque wrench settings

	Nm	lbf ft
Torque converter to driveplate	30	22
Transmission to engine	55	41
Mounting to transmission	40	30
Mounting to body	60	44
Oil pan bolts	20	15
Oil strainer cover	3	2
Selector cable clamp bolt	8	6

1 General description

The automatic transmission consists of three main assemblies, these being the torque converter, which is directly coupled to the engine; the final drive unit which incorporates the differential assembly; and the planetary gearbox with its hydraulically operated multi-disc clutches and brake bands. The gearbox also houses a rear mounted oil pump, which is coupled to the torque converter impeller, and this pump supplies automatic transmission fluid to the planetary gears, hydraulic controls and torque converter. The fluid performs a triple function by lubricating the moving parts, cooling the automatic transmission system and providing a torque transfer medium. The final drive lubrication is separate from the transmission lubrication system, unlike the manual gearbox where the final drive shares a common lubrication system.

The torque converter is a sealed unit which cannot be dismantled. It is bolted to the crankshaft driveplate and replaces the clutch found on an engine with manual transmission.

The gearbox is of the planetary type with epicycle gear trains operated by brakes and clutches through a hydraulic control system. The correct gear is selected by a combination of three control signals; a manual valve operated by the gearshift cable, a manual valve operated by the accelerator pedal, and a governor to control hydraulic pressure. The gearshift cable and selector lever allow the driver to select a specific gear and override the automatic control, if desired. The accelerator control determines the correct gear for the desired rate of acceleration, and the governor determines the correct gear in relation to engine speed.

Because of the need for special test equipment, the complexity of some of the parts and the need for scrupulous cleanliness when servicing automatic transmissions, the amount which the owner can do is limited, but those operations which can reasonably be carried out are detailed in the following Sections. Repairs to the final drive differential are also not recommended.

2 Maintenance and inspection

1 At the intervals specified in Routine Maintenance the automatic transmission fluid level and the final drive differential oil level should be checked and if necessary topped up using the following procedures.
2 The fluid level should be checked when the transmission is at normal operating temperature (this will be reached after a journey of approximately 6 miles/10 km when starting from cold).
3 With the car standing on level ground and with the engine idling and the selector lever in the N (Neutral) position, withdraw the fluid dipstick and wipe it on a clean, lint-free rag. Reinsert the dipstick, withdraw it immediately and observe the fluid level which should be between the two marks.
4 If topping-up is necessary, switch off the engine and add the required quantity of the specified fluid through the dipstick tube. Take care not to overfill the transmission; noting that the difference between the upper and lower marks on the dipstick is 0.4 litre (0.75 Imp pt, 0.42 US quarts).
5 The final drive differential oil level is checked by means of the filler plug located just to the rear of the driveshaft flange on the left-hand side of the transmission. Access is easiest from below the car.
6 With the car level, unscrew the filler plug using a suitable hexagonal key and check that the level is up to the filler plug orifice.
7 If topping-up is necessary, add the specified lubricant through the filter orifice until the level is correct, then refit the plug.
8 At the less frequent intervals specified in Routine Maintenance the automatic transmission fluid should be drained and fresh fluid added, using the procedures described in Section 3. It is not necessary to drain and refill the final drive differential oil as part of the normal servicing procedures.

3 Automatic transmission fluid – draining and refilling

1 This job should not be attempted unless clean, dust free conditions can be achieved.
2 With the car standing on level ground, place a container of suitable capacity beneath the oil pan of the transmission. For working room beneath the car, jack it up and support it with axle stands, or use car ramps.
3 Unscrew the union nut securing the dipstick tube to the oil pan, pull out the tube and allow the fluid to drain out.
4 Remove the retaining screws and withdraw the oil pan. Remove the gasket.
5 Remove the screws and withdraw the cover, strainer, and gasket.
6 Clean the pan and strainer with methylated spirit and allow to dry.
7 Refit the strainer, cover and pan in reverse order using new gaskets and tightening the screws to the specified torque.
8 Insert the dipstick tube and tighten the union nut.
9 Wipe round the top of the dipstick tube, then remove the dipstick.
10 With the car on level ground, fill the transmission with the correct quantity and grade of fluid, using a clean funnel if necessary.
11 Start the engine and, with the handbrake applied, select every gear position once. With the engine idling and the transmission in N (Neutral), check the level of the fluid on the dipstick, and if necessary top up to the lower mark.
12 Road test the car for approximately 6 miles (10 km) then recheck the fluid level, as described in Section 2.

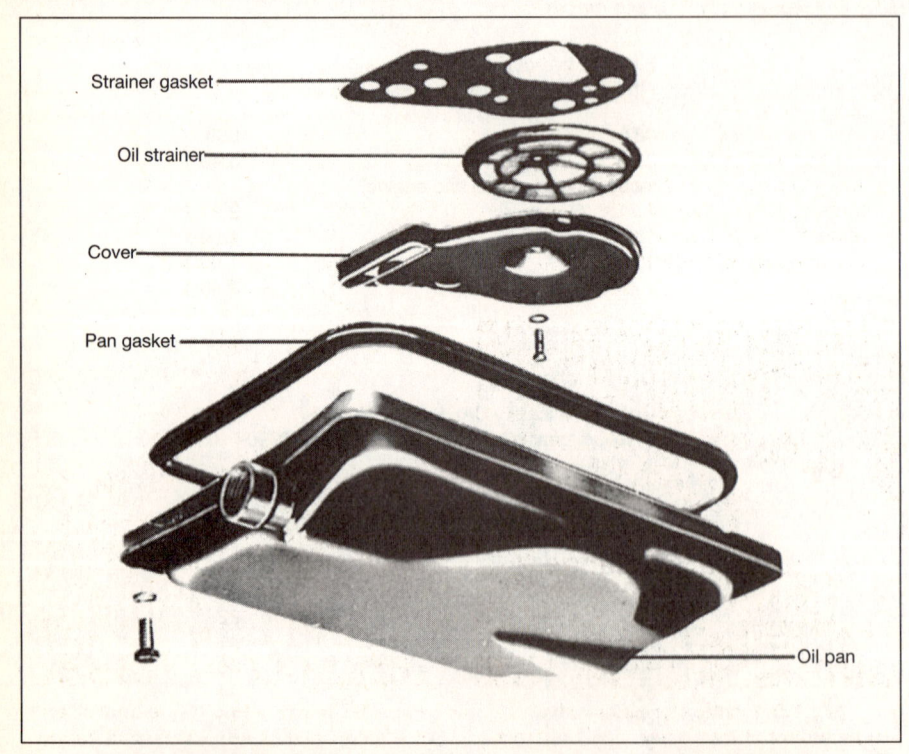

Fig. 7.1 Automatic transmission oil pan and strainer components (Sec 3)

Strainer gasket
Oil strainer
Cover
Pan gasket
Oil pan

Automatic transmission 7•3

Fig. 7.2 Using a special tool to support the front of the engine (Sec 4)

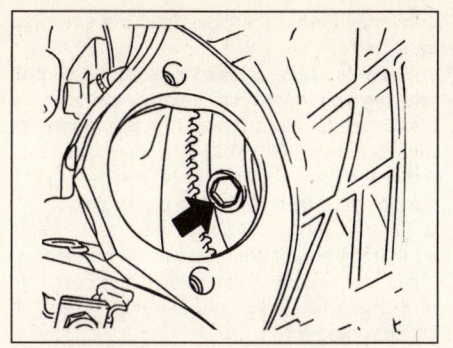

Fig. 7.3 A torque converter-to-driveplate bolt viewed through the starter aperture (Sec 4)

Fig. 7.4 Selector lever cable holder at the rear of the transmission (Sec 4)

4 Automatic transmission – removal and refitting

1 Position the car over an inspection pit or on car ramps or axle stands. Apply the handbrake and chock the wheels.
2 Disconnect the battery negative terminal.
3 Drain the cooling system, as described in Chapter 2.
4 Disconnect the two coolant hoses from the transmission fluid cooler.
5 Disconnect the speedometer cable at the transmission end.
6 Support the front of the engine using a hoist or support bar. Fig. 7.2 shows the Audi tool designed for this purpose and can be used as a guide for making up a similar apparatus if a hoist is not available.
7 Remove the starter motor, as described in Chapter 12.
8 Working through the starter aperture, unscrew the bolts securing the torque converter to the driveplate while holding the starter ring gear stationary with a screwdriver. It will be necessary to rotate the crankshaft to bring each bolt to an accessible position in the starter aperture.
9 Refer to Chapter 8 and separate the driveshaft inner constant velocity joints from the transmission drive flanges.
10 Remove the selector lever cable holder from the rear of the transmission. Extract the circlip and disconnect the selector lever cable from the transmission lever.
11 On the 087 transmission remove the accelerator linkage pushrod.
12 Disconnect the accelerator pedal cable and detach the cable at the transmission support bracket.
13 Place a suitable container beneath the transmission and unscrew the dipstick tube union nut at the oil pan. Withdraw the tube from the pan and allow the fluid to drain.
14 Unscrew and remove the upper engine-to-transmission bolts.
15 On the 089 transmission unscrew the throttle cable support bracket bolts, release the cable end locking clip and separate the cable and bracket from the transmission.
16 Support the transmission with a suitable trolley jack.
17 Unscrew and remove the lower engine-to-transmission bolts.
18 Remove the transmission mounting retaining bolts then remove the mounting supports.
19 With the help of an assistant, withdraw the transmission from the engine, making sure that the torque converter remains fully engaged with the transmission splines.
20 Lower the transmission and remove it from under the car.
21 Refitting is the reverse sequence to removal, bearing in mind the following points:
(a) *Ensure that the torque converter is correctly positioned, and fully engaged with the pump shaft splines before installing the transmission*
(b) *Reconnect the driveshafts, with reference to Chapter 8, and refit the starter, with reference to Chapter 12*
(c) *Refill the cooling system, with reference to Chapter 2*
(d) *After refitting adjust the accelerator, throttle, selector lever and cables with reference to Sections 6 and 7, and fill the transmission with reference to Section 3*

Fig. 7.5 Accelerator pedal cable attachment at the transmission support bracket (Sec 4)

5 Torque converter – checking and draining

1 The torque converter is a welded unit and if it is faulty the complete unit must be replaced. Only the bush can be renewed.
2 Examine the bush for signs of scoring and wear. To check for wear requires an internal micrometer or dial gauge; if one is available measure the bore diameter to see if it exceeds the wear limit given in the Specifications
3 To remove the bush requires a commercial extractor and a slide hammer. After fitting a new bush, its diameter must be within the limit given; if not the bush must be removed and another one fitted. For this reason the job is really one for an Audi agent.
4 Check that the cooling vanes on the converter are secure.
5 Fit the turbine shaft into the converter and check that the turbine turns freely.
6 If the fluid was dirty when drained from the oil pan, drain the fluid from the torque

Fig. 7.6 Checking the torque converter bush internal diameter with a dial gauge (Sec 5)

7•4 Automatic transmission

Fig. 7.7 Syphoning the fluid from the torque converter (Sec 5)

converter before the automatic transmission is refitted.

7 Have ready a container of about 2 litre (3.5 Imp pints. 2.1 US quarts) capacity, a plastic bottle and a piece of plastic tubing of not more than 8 mm (0.32 in) outside diameter.
8 Put the torque converter on the bench and support it so that it is tipped up slightly.
9 Cut one end of the plastic tube on an angle so that the end of the tube will not be blocked if it comes against a flat surface and push this end into the torque converter hub until it touches the bottom.
10 Connect the spout of the plastic bottle to the other end of the tube, hold the bottle below the level of the torque converter and squeeze the bottle. As the bottle expands again, fluid will be sucked into it; as soon as the fluid begins to syphon, pull the tube end off the bottle and rest the tube end in the larger container. Syphon as much fluid as possible from the torque converter. On reassembly and installation, the converter will fill with fluid as soon as the engine is started

6 Accelerator pedal and linkage – adjustment

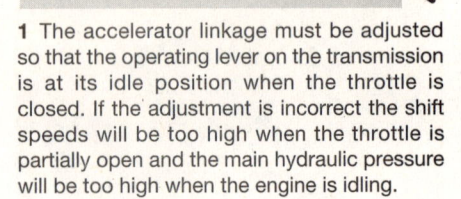

1 The accelerator linkage must be adjusted so that the operating lever on the transmission is at its idle position when the throttle is closed. If the adjustment is incorrect the shift speeds will be too high when the throttle is partially open and the main hydraulic pressure will be too high when the engine is idling.

087 transmission

2 Before carrying out any adjustments ensure that the engine is at normal operating temperature and that, on carburettor engines, the automatic choke is fully open.
3 Working in the engine compartment, disconnect the linkage pullrod and pushrod and, where fitted, the cruise control linkage.
4 Move the pullrod lever to its stop and check that the end fitting on the rod will fit easily on the ball-stud without opening the linkage. If necessary screw the pullrod end fitting in or out as necessary to achieve this condition.
5 Refit the pullrod and pushrod end fittings to the linkage.
6 From under the car slacken the clamp bolt at the transmission end of the pushrod.
7 With the transmission operating lever in

Fig. 7.9 Pullrod end fitting adjustment – 087 transmission (Sec 6)

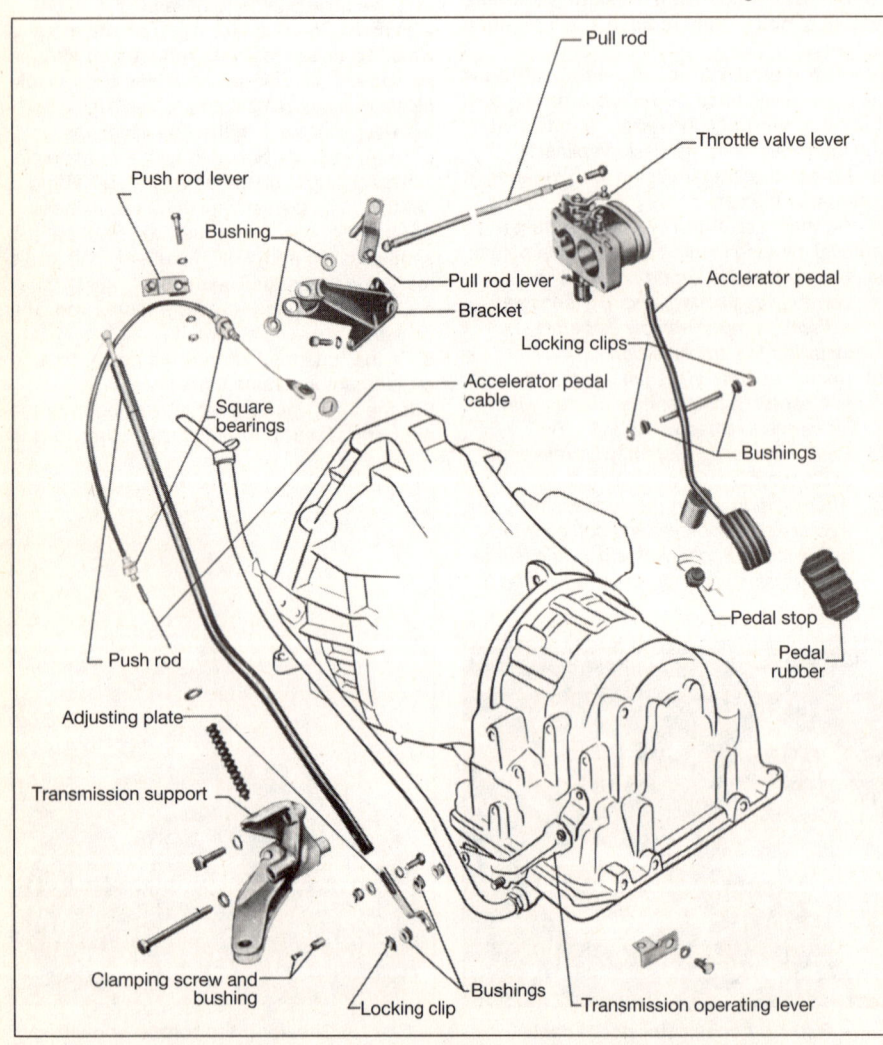

Fig. 7.8 Layout of the throttle and accelerator pedal cables on the 087 transmission (Sec 6)

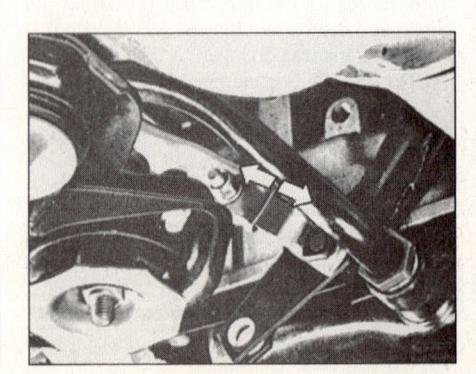

Fig. 7.10 Pushrod adjustment at the clamp bolt – 087 transmission (Sec 6)

Automatic transmission 7•5

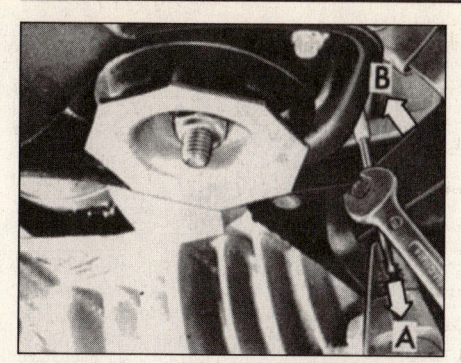

Fig. 7.11 Pull the accelerator pedal cable in direction A while pushing operating lever B against stop – 087 transmission (Sec 6)

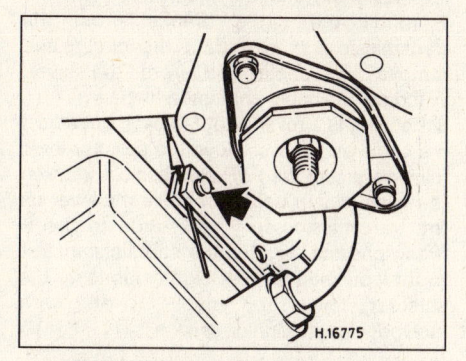

Fig. 7.12 Accelerator pedal cable attachment at transmission operating lever clamp bolt – 089 transmission (Sec 6)

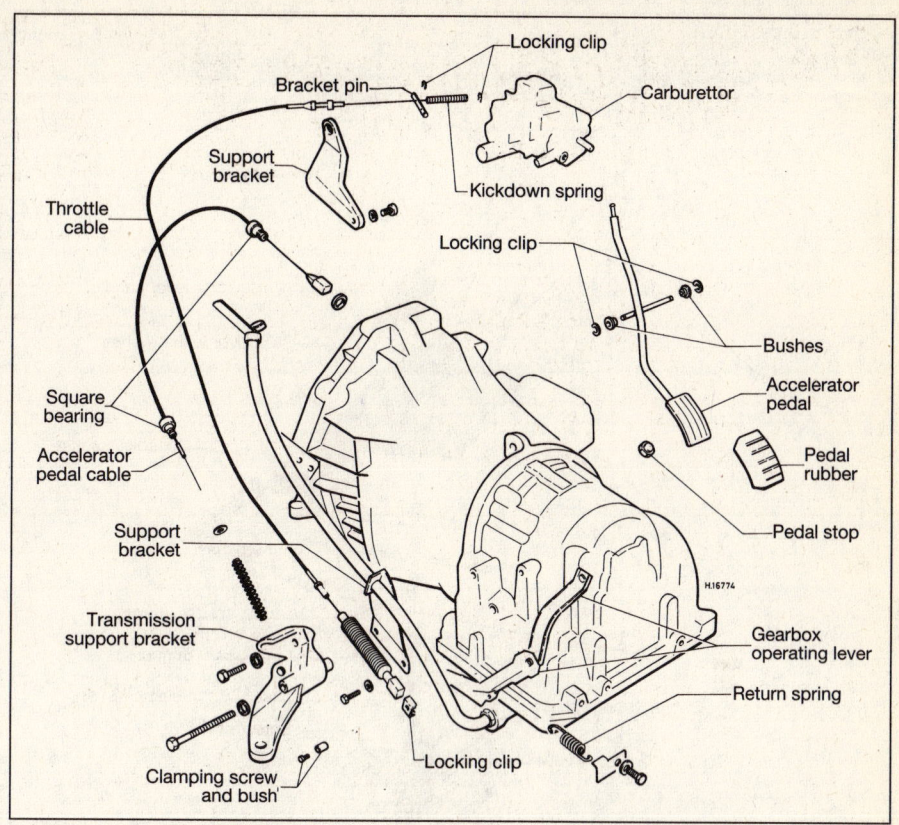

Fig. 7.13 Layout of the throttle and accelerator pedal cables on the 089 transmission (Sec 6)

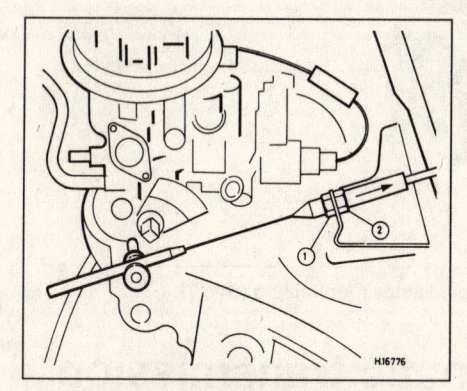

Fig. 7.14 Throttle cable adjusting nuts 1 and 2 at the carburettor support bracket – 089 transmission (Sec 6)

Pull outer cable in direction of arrow to eliminate free play

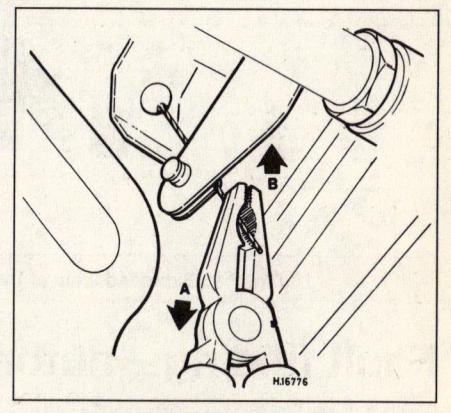

Fig. 7.15 Pull the accelerator pedal cable in direction of arrow A while holding operating lever B against stop – 089 transmission (Sec 6)

contact with the no-throttle stop and the throttle lever in contact with the idle stop, tighten the pushrod clamp bolt.

8 Extract the locking clip and slip the pushrod end off the transmission operating lever. Unhook the return spring.
9 Have an assistant fully depress the accelerator pedal and hold it in this position.
10 Push the transmission operating lever against the kickdown stop and hold it in this position.
11 Slacken the accelerator pedal cable clamp bolt on the transmission operating lever, grip the cable end with pliers and pull the cable as shown in Fig. 7.11. Hold the cable end and tighten the clamp bolt.
12 Refit the pushrod to the operating lever and reconnect the return spring.

089 transmission

13 Note the adjustment criterion detailed in paragraph 2.
14 From under the car slacken the clamp bolt and disconnect the accelerator pedal cable from the transmission operating lever.
15 Slacken the two throttle cable adjusting nuts at the carburettor support bracket.
16 Hold the carburettor linkage closed and pull the outer cable through the bracket to eliminate all the free play. Hold the cable in this position and tighten the adjusting nuts.
17 At the transmission, unhook the operating lever return spring.
18 Have an assistant fully depress the accelerator pedal and hold it in this position.
19 Push the transmission operating lever against the kickdown stop and hold it in this position.
20 Slacken the accelerator pedal cable clamp bolt on the transmission operating lever, grip the cable end with pliers and pull the cable as shown in Fig. 7.15. Hold the cable end and tighten the clamp bolt.
21 Refit the return spring.
22 To check the adjustment, depress the accelerator pedal until resistance is felt at the full throttle position. Do not go into the kickdown position. Check that the throttle lever on the carburettor linkage is in contact with the full throttle stop and the kickdown spring is not compressed.
23 Now depress the accelerator pedal fully. Check that the transmission operating lever is in contact with the kickdown stop and the kickdown spring at the carburettor is compressed approximately 8 mm (0.32 in).

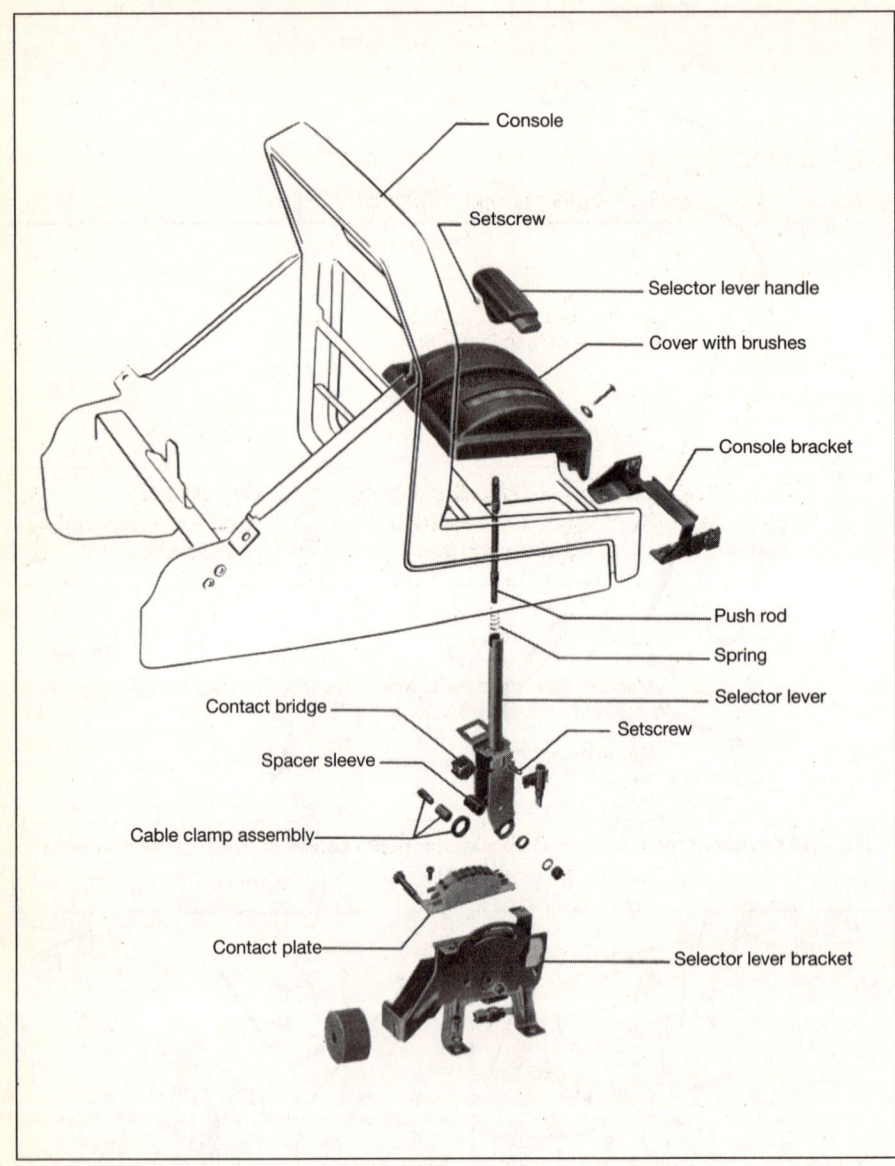

Fig. 7.16 Exploded view of the selector mechanism (Sec 7)

Labels: Console; Setscrew; Selector lever handle; Cover with brushes; Console bracket; Push rod; Spring; Selector lever; Setscrew; Contact bridge; Spacer sleeve; Cable clamp assembly; Contact plate; Selector lever bracket

7 Selector lever and cable – removal, refitting and adjustment

1 Disconnect the battery negative terminal.
2 If the selector lever or cable are to be removed, refer to Chapter 11 and remove the centre console. If adjustment only is being carried out, proceed to paragraph 8.
3 Disconnect the wiring from the starter inhibitor switch and selector illumination bulb.
4 Undo the retaining bolts and remove the console front mounting bracket.
5 Unscrew the cable clamp bolt and the nut securing the cable to the lever bracket.
6 Undo the bolts and remove the bracket and lever assembly from the floor.
7 Unbolt the cable bracket from the transmission, then extract the circlip and remove the cable end from the lever. Withdraw the cable from under the car.
8 Refitting is a reversal of removal, but adjust the cable as follows. Move the selector lever fully forward to the P (Park) position. Slacken the cable clamp bolt then move the lever on the transmission fully rearwards to the P (Park) position. Tighten the cable clamp bolt to the specified torque. Lightly lubricate the selector lever and cable pivots with molybdenum disulphide grease.

8 Starter inhibitor switch – removal, refitting and adjustment

1 Disconnect the battery negative terminal.
2 Refer to Chapter 11 and remove the centre console.
3 Disconnect the wiring from the starter inhibitor switch then remove the screws and withdraw the switch.
4 Refitting is a reversal of removal, but before fitting the console check that it is only possible to start the engine with the selector lever in positions N (Neutral) or P (Park). If necessary, reposition the switch within the elongated screw holes.

Fault finding – automatic transmission

1 Before the automatic transmission is removed for repair of a suspected malfunction, it is imperative that the cause be traced and confirmed. To do this requires specialist experience and various tools and gauges not normally found in the DIY mechanic's workshop.
2 If any fault arises that cannot be cured by attention to the fluid level and the adjustments described in this Chapter, take the vehicle to an Audi dealer for diagnosis and repair.

Chapter 8 Driveshafts

For modifications, and information applicable to later models, see Supplement at end of manual

Contents

Driveshafts – overhaul 4
Driveshafts – removal and refitting 3
Fault finding – driveshafts .... See end of Chapter
General description 1
Maintenance and inspection 2

Degrees of difficulty

Easy, suitable for novice with little experience	**Fairly easy,** suitable for beginner with some experience	**Fairly difficult,** suitable for competent DIY mechanic	**Difficult,** suitable for experienced DIY mechanic	**Very difficult,** suitable for expert DIY or professional

Specifications

Type .... Tubular steel driveshafts with inner and outer ball and cage type constant velocity joints

Length (excluding constant velocity joints)

	Right-hand	Left-hand
Four-cylinder engine models:		
With manual transmission	579.2 mm (22.82 in)	540.7 mm (21.30 in)
With automatic transmission	540.7 mm (21.30 in)	598.5 mm (23.58 in)
Five-cylinder engine models:		
With manual transmission	550.9 mm (21.70 in)	550.9 mm (21.70 in)
With automatic transmission	529.1 mm (20.84 in)	582.8 mm (22.96 in)

Constant velocity joint lubricant .... Audi G6 grease

Torque wrench settings

	Nm	lbf ft
Inner constant velocity joint retaining bolts:		
M8 bolts	45	33
M10 bolts	80	59
Driveshaft retaining nut	280	207

1 General description

Drive is transmitted from the differential to the front wheels by means of two tubular steel driveshafts. Both driveshafts are fitted with ball and cage type constant joints at each end. The outer joints are splined to accept the driveshaft and wheel hub while the inner joints are splined to accept the driveshaft and bolted to the differential drive flanges.

2 Maintenance and inspection

1 At the intervals given in Routine Maintenance at the beginning of this manual, carry out a thorough inspection of the driveshafts and constant velocity joints as follows.
2 Jack up the front of the car and support it securely on axle stands.
3 Slowly rotate the roadwheel and inspect the condition of the outer joint rubber boots. Check for signs of cracking, splits or deterioration of the rubber which may allow the grease to escape and lead to water and grit entry into the joint. Also check the security and condition of the retaining clamps. Repeat these checks on the inner constant velocity joints (photo). If any damage or deterioration is found, the joints should be attended to, as described in Section 4.
4 Continue rotating the roadwheel and check for any distortion or damage to the driveshafts. Check for any free play in the joints by holding the driveshaft firmly and attempting to rotate the wheel. Repeat this check whilst holding the differential drive flange. Any noticeable movement indicates wear in the joints, wear in the driveshaft splines, or loose joint retaining bolts or hub nut.
5 Road test the car and check for any noticeable slackness in the driveline when changing from acceleration to overrun and *vice versa*, or for vibration felt through the car when accelerating. Problems of this nature usually indicate wear in the constant velocity joints.

2.3 Checking the driveshaft inner joint rubber boot

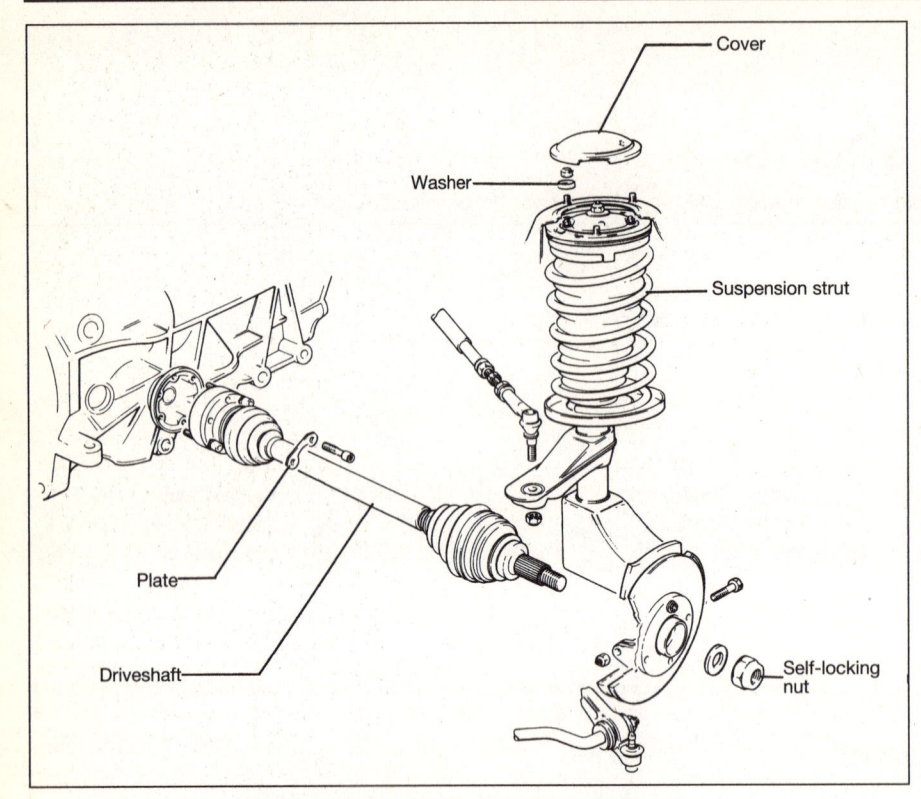

8•2 Driveshafts

Fig. 8.1 Driveshaft attachment details (Sec 3)

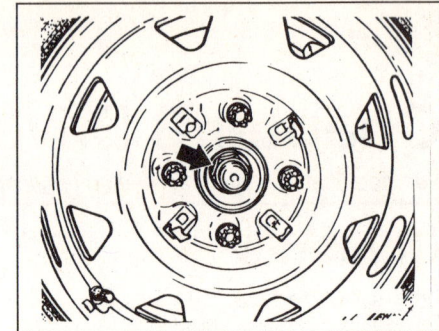

Fig. 8.2 Driveshaft retaining nut – arrowed (Sec 3)

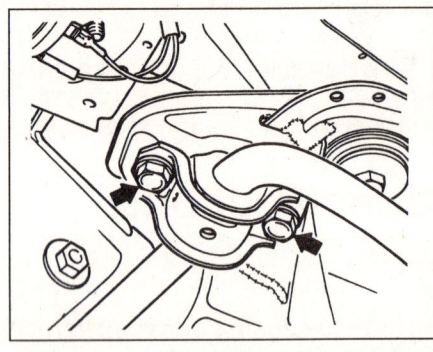

Fig. 8.3 Anti-roll bar clamp bolts – arrowed (Sec 3)

3 Driveshafts – removal and refitting

Manual transmission models

1 Remove the wheel trim then unscrew the driveshaft retaining nut. This is tightened to a very high torque and no attempt to loosen it must be made unless the full weight of the car is on the roadwheels.
2 Loosen the four roadwheel retaining bolts.
3 Jack up the front of the car and securely support it on axle stands. Remove the roadwheel.
4 If working on the right-hand driveshaft, remove the exhaust front pipe, referring to Chapter 3 if necessary, and also the heat shield below the inner constant velocity joint.
5 Using a suitable multi-tooth socket bit, unscrew the inner constant velocity joint retaining bolts then remove the bolts, together with the spreader plates (photo). Separate the inner constant velocity joint from the differential drive flange then angle the driveshaft upwards alongside the transmission.
6 Turn the steering onto full left lock if working on the left-hand driveshaft or right lock if working on the right-hand driveshaft.
7 Attach a suitable puller to the front hub using the roadwheel retaining bolts.
8 Using the puller, press the driveshaft out of the front hub then withdraw the shaft assembly from under the car (photo).

Automatic transmission models

9 Carry out the operations described in paragraphs 1 to 4 inclusive.
10 Undo the two bolts securing the anti-roll bar clamp to the crossmember on the side being worked on.
11 Undo the nut and remove the clamp bolt securing the track control arm balljoint to the suspension strut. Lever the track control arm downward and separate the balljoint from the strut (photo).
12 Using a suitable multi-tooth socket bit, unscrew the inner constant velocity joint retaining bolts then remove the bolts, together with the spreader plates. Separate the inner constant velocity joint from the differential drive flange.

3.5 Removing the inner joint retaining bolts

3.8A Press out the driveshaft using a puller . . .

3.8B . . . then remove it from the rear of the hub

Driveshafts 8•3

3.11 Track control arm balljoint clamp bolt

3.16A Applying locking compound to the constant velocity joint splines

3.16B Tighten the driveshaft retaining nut with the car on its wheels

13 Attach a suitable puller to the front hub using the roadwheel retaining bolts.
14 Move the suspension strut outwards at the bottom and press the driveshaft out of the front hub using the puller. Withdraw the driveshaft from under the car.

All models

15 Do not move the car with the driveshaft removed, otherwise the front wheel bearing will be damaged.
16 Refitting is the reverse sequence to removal, bearing in mind the following points:

(a) Ensure that the splines and thread on the outer constant velocity joint are clean, then apply a locking compound in a 6 mm (0.25 in) band around the end of the splines before refitting the driveshaft (photo).
(b) Always use a new driveshaft retaining nut, inner joint-to-drive flange gasket, and where applicable control arm balljoint clamp bolt and nut.
(c) Tighten all nuts and bolts to the specified torque (photo).

4 Driveshafts – overhaul

1 Remove the driveshaft from the car, as described in the previous Section.
2 To remove the inner constant velocity joint, remove the rubber boot retaining clamps and slide the boot down the shaft and off the joint.
3 Using a suitable drift, drive the protective cap off the constant velocity joint.
4 Extract the circlip from the end of the driveshaft (photo).

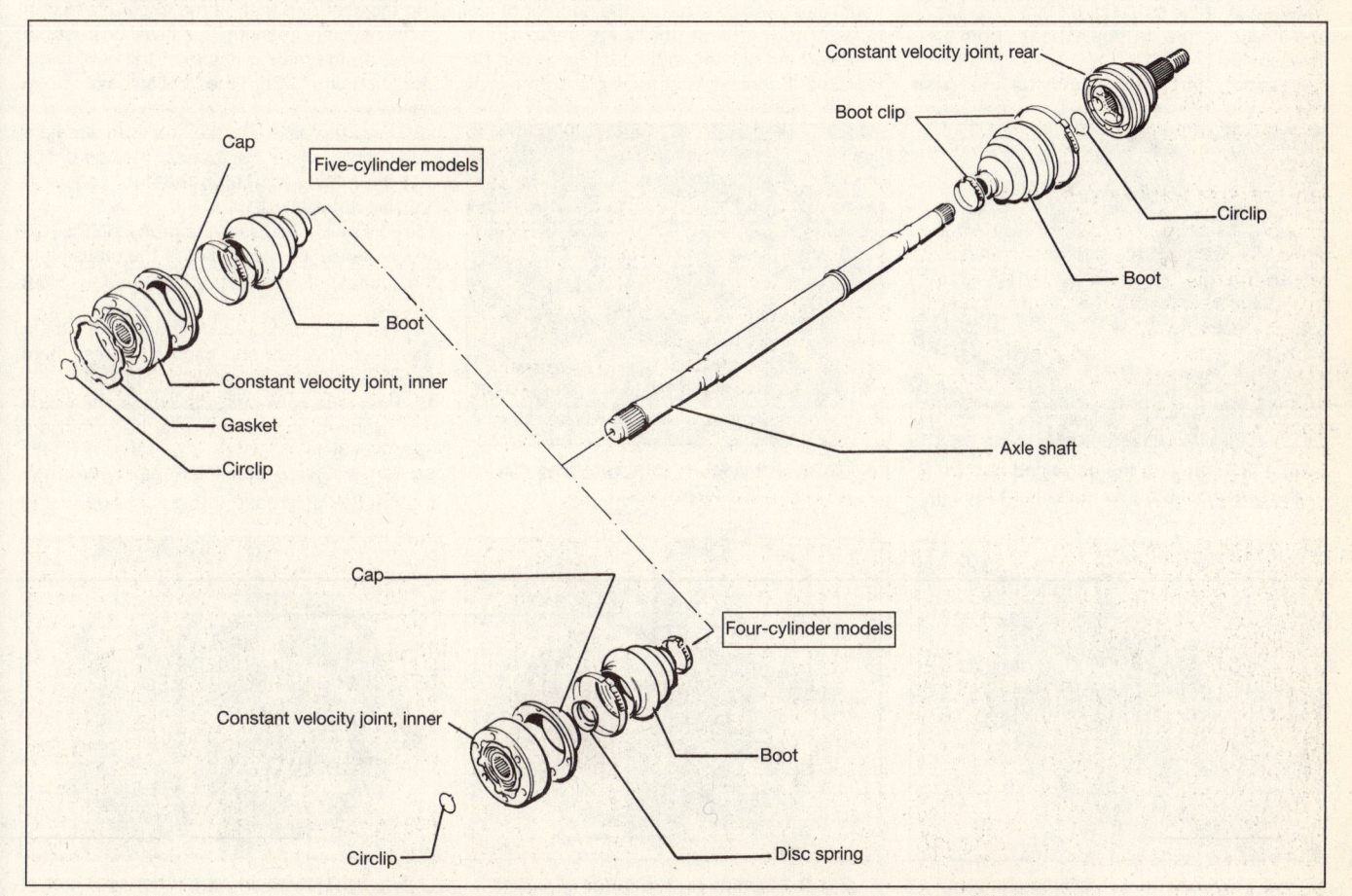

Fig. 8.4 Exploded view of the driveshaft and constant velocity joints (Sec 4)

8•4 Driveshafts

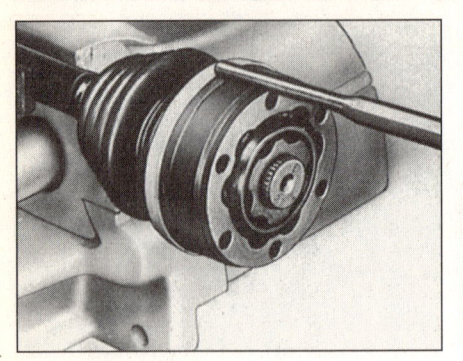

Fig. 8.5 Removing the protective cap from the inner joint (Sec 4)

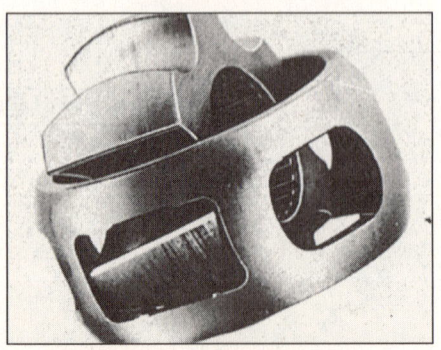

Fig. 8.6 Removing the outer constant velocity joint (Sec 4)

A Circlip
B Drive off the hub in the direction shown

Fig. 8.7 Removing the balls from the outer constant velocity joint (Sec 4)

5 Support the underside of the ball cage and remove the driveshaft by pressing it out.
6 Withdraw the rubber boot and protective cap from the driveshaft, together with the dished washer, where fitted.
7 To remove the outer constant velocity joint, remove the two rubber boot retaining clamps and slide the boot down the shaft and off the joint (photo).
8 Spread the retaining circlip and tap the joint off the shaft using a soft metal drift against the inner edge of the hub (Fig. 8.6).
9 Withdraw the rubber boot from the driveshaft.
10 Before starting to dismantle the outer joint, mark the position of the hub in relation to the cage and housing. Because the parts are hardened this mark will either have to be done with a grinding stone, or with paint.
11 Swivel the hub and cage and take out the balls one at a time.
12 Turn the cage until the two rectangular openings align with the housing and then remove the cage and hub.
13 Turn the hub until one segment can be pushed into one of the rectangular openings in the cage and then swivel the hub out of the cage. The parts of the joint make up a matched set and no individual parts can be replaced. If there is excessive play in the joint which is noticeable when changing from acceleration to overrun, or *vice versa,* a new joint must be fitted, but do not renew a joint because the parts have been polished by wear and the track of the balls is clearly visible.
14 When reassembling the joint. clean off all the old grease and use a new circlip, rubber boot and clamps. Use only the special grease recommended by Audi for packing the joints – see Specifications.
15 Press half a sachet of grease (45 g, 1.6 oz) into the joint and then fit the cage and hub in to the housing, ensuring that it will be possible to line up the mating marks of the hub, cage, and housing after the balls have been inserted.
16 Press the balls into the hub from alternate sides, when all six have been inserted check that the mating marks on the hub, cage and housing are aligned.
17 Fit a new circlip into the groove in the hub and squeeze the remainder of the grease into the joint so that the total amount is 90 g (3.2 oz).
18 The inner joint is dismantled in a similar way. Pivot the hub and cage and press them out of the housing as shown in Fig. 8.10.
19 Press the balls out of the cage, then align two grooves and remove the hub from the cage (Fig. 8.11).
20 When reassembling the joint, press half the charge of grease into each side of the

Fig. 8.8 Removing the cage and hub from the outer constant velocity joint (Sec 4)

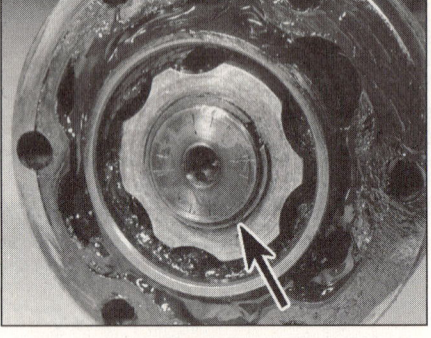

4.4 Constant velocity joint retaining circlip (arrowed)

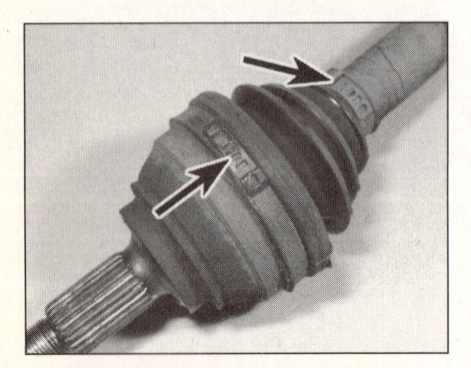

4.7 Rubber boot retaining clamps (arrowed)

Fig. 8.9 Removing the outer constant velocity joint hub from the cage (Sec 4)

Fig. 8.10 Removing the inner constant velocity joint hub and cage (Sec 4)

Driveshafts 8•5

Fig. 8.11 Removing the inner constant velocity joint hub from the cage (Sec 4)
Arrows indicate grooves

Fig. 8.12 Reassembling the inner constant velocity joint (Sec 4)

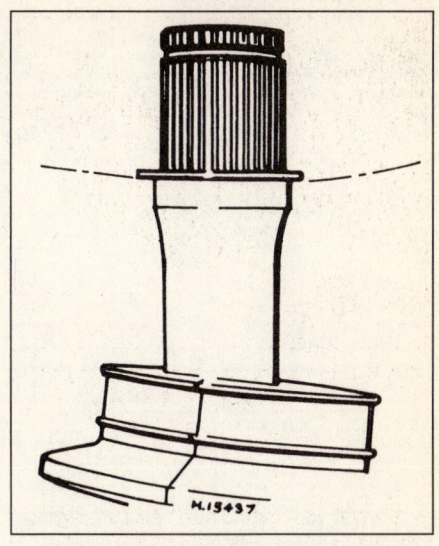

Fig. 8.13 Correct location of the dished washer on the inner end of the driveshaft (Sec 4)

joint. Note that on 4-cylinder engine models the total amount of grease used in each inner joint is 90g (3.2 oz) and on 5-cylinder engine models it is 120g (4.2 oz). Ensure that the chamfer on the splined hub is towards the larger diameter side of the outer member. It will be necessary to pivot the joint hub when reassembling in order to align the balls with the grooves.

21 It is advisable to fit new rubber boots to the shaft; a defective boot will soon lead to the need to fit a new joint due to wear caused by grit entering the joint. Fit the boots to the shaft and put any residual grease into the boots.

22 Fit the dished washer, where applicable, to the inner end of the driveshaft and locate the protective cap on the boot. Note that the concave side of the dished washer must face the joint.

23 Press the inner joint onto the shaft and secure it with a new circlip.

24 Tap the protective cap onto the outer member.

25 Place the outer joint in position against the end of the driveshaft and, using a mallet, drive it onto the shaft until the circlip engages the groove.

26 Fit new clamps to each end of the rubber boots. locate the boots over the joints and tighten the clamps. If the rubber boot fitted to the inner joint is of the type incorporating a breather hole, the inner (smaller) clamp should not be fitted.

27 Where applicable, fit a new gasket to the mating face of the inner joint by peeling off the protective film and sticking the gasket to the joint face.

Fault finding – driveshafts

Vibration and noise on lock
☐ Worn driveshaft joints

Noise on taking up drive or between acceleration and overrun
☐ Worn driveshaft joints
☐ Worn front wheel hub and driveshaft splines
☐ Loose driveshaft bolts or nut

Notes

Chapter 9 Braking system

For modifications, and information applicable to later models, see Supplement at end of manual

Contents

Anti-lock braking system – description and operation 27	Hydraulic brake pipes and hoses – removal and refitting 16
Anti-lock braking system – precautions 28	Hydraulic servo unit – description and testing 24
Anti-lock braking system components – removal and refitting 29	Hydraulic servo unit – removal and refitting 25
Brake drum – inspection and renewal 9	Hydraulic system – bleeding 17
Brake pedal – removal and refitting 18	Maintenance and inspection 2
Brake pressure regulator – testing and adjustment 15	Master cylinder – removal and refitting 14
Fault finding – braking system . . . . See end of Chapter	Pressure accumulator – removal and refitting 26
Front brake disc – removal and refitting 6	Rear brake disc – removal and refining 13
Front disc caliper – overhaul 5	Rear brake shoes – inspection and renewal 7
Front disc caliper – removal and refitting 4	Rear disc caliper – overhaul 12
Front disc pads – inspection and renewal 3	Rear disc caliper – removal and refitting 11
General description 1	Rear disc pads – inspection and renewal 10
Handbrake – adjustment 19	Rear wheel cylinder – removal, overhaul and refitting 8
Handbrake cable – removal and refitting 21	Vacuum servo unit – description and testing 22
Handbrake lever – removal and refitting 20	Vacuum servo unit – removal and refitting 23

Degrees of difficulty

Easy, suitable for novice with little experience	**Fairly easy,** suitable for beginner with some experience	**Fairly difficult,** suitable for competent DIY mechanic	**Difficult,** suitable for experienced DIY mechanic	**Very difficult,** suitable for expert DIY or professional

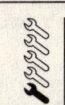

Specifications

System type . . . . Diagonally split, servo-assisted dual circuit hydraulic with pressure regulator in rear hydraulic circuit and cable-operated handbrake. Anti-lock braking system available on certain models

Rear brakes

Type . . . . Single leading shoe drum, or disc with single piston sliding calipers

Drum brakes:
  Drum diameter:
    New . . . . 230.0 mm (9.055 in)
    Wear limit . . . . 231.0 mm (9.094 in)
  Maximum drum diameter after machining . . . . 230.5 mm (9.075 in)
  Maximum drum radial run-out . . . . 0.1 mm (0.004 in)
  Maximum drum lateral run-out at wheel contact face . . . . 0.2 mm (0.008 in)
  Brake shoe minimum lining thickness . . . . 2.5 mm (0.10 in)
  Wheel cylinder piston diameter . . . . 17.46 mm (0.687 in)

Disc brakes:
  Make . . . . Girling or Teves
  Disc diameter . . . . 245.0 mm (9.646 in)
  Disc thickness:
    New . . . . 10.0 mm (0.40 in)
    Wear limit . . . . 8.0 mm (0.315 in)
  Minimum disc thickness after machining . . . . 8.5 mm (0.335 in)
  Maximum disc run-out . . . . 0.06 mm (0.002 in)
  Minimum disc pad thickness . . . . 7.0 mm (0.27 in) including backing

9•2 Braking system

Front brakes
Type	Disc with single piston sliding calipers
Make	Girling or Teves
Disc diameter	256.0 mm (10.08 in)
Disc thickness:	
New	22.0 mm (0.866 in)
Wear limit	20.0 mm (0.787 in)
Minimum disc thickness after machining	20.5 mm (0.807 in)
Maximum disc run-out	0.06 mm (0.002 in)
Minimum disc pad thickness	7.0 mm (0.27 in) including backing

Brake fluid type/specification
Hydraulic fluid to FMVSS 116 DOT 4

Torque wrench settings
	Nm	lbf ft
Caliper guide pin bolts (Girling)	35	26
Caliper guide pins (Teves)	25	18
Front caliper carrier bracket to suspension strut	125	92
Rear caliper carrier bracket to rear axle	65	48
Rear brake backplate to stub axle (drum brakes)	30	22
Master cylinder to servo	25	18
Servo unit to bulkhead	25	18
Pressure regulator spring mounting	25	18

1 General description

The braking system is of the servo-assisted, dual circuit hydraulic type with disc brakes at the front and drum or disc brakes at the rear, according to model. A diagonally split dual circuit hydraulic system is employed in which each circuit operates one front and one diagonally opposite rear brake from a tandem master cylinder. Under normal conditions both circuits operate in unison; however; in the event of hydraulic failure in one circuit, full braking force will still be available at two wheels. A brake pressure regulator is incorporated in the rear brake hydraulic circuit. This unit regulates the pressure applied to each rear brake and reduces the possibility of the rear wheels locking under heavy braking.

The front disc brakes are operated by single piston sliding type calipers. On models equipped with rear drum brakes, leading and trailing brake shoes are operated by twin piston wheel cylinders and are self-adjusting by footbrake application. On models equipped with rear disc brakes, single piston sliding type calipers, similar to those used at the front, are employed. On all models a cable-operated handbrake provides an independent mechanical means of rear brake application.

The brake servo unit is of the conventional vacuum operated type on models with manual steering or hydraulically operated on models with power-assisted steering. System pressure for the hydraulic servo is generated by the power steering pump and contained in a pressure accumulator. This is then supplied to the hydraulic servo unit on demand to reduce pedal effort when the brakes are applied.

An anti-lock braking system (ABS) is also available as standard or optional equipment, according to model. Further information on this system will be found in the relevant Sections of this Chapter.

> **Warning:** *On models equipped with anti-lock braking systems (ABS) certain precautions must be observed when working on the braking system. Refer to Section 28 before carrying out any of the operations described in this Chapter.*

2 Maintenance and inspection

1 At the intervals given in Routine Maintenance at the beginning of this manual the following service operations should be carried out on the braking system components.

2 Check the brake hydraulic fluid level and, if necessary, top up with the specified fluid to the MAX mark on the master cylinder reservoir (photos). Any need for frequent topping-up indicates a fluid leak somewhere in the system which must be investigated and rectified immediately.

3 Check the front disc pads and the rear disc pads or brake shoe linings, as applicable, and inspect the condition of the discs and drums. Details will be found in Sections 3, 10 and 7 respectively.

4 Check the condition of the hydraulic pipes and hoses, as described in Section 16. At the same time check the condition of the handbrake cables, lubricate the exposed cables and linkages (photo) and, if necessary, adjust the handbrake, as described in Section 19.

5 Renew the brake hydraulic fluid at the specified intervals by draining the system and refilling with fresh fluid, as described in Section 17.

2.2A Top up the master cylinder reservoir . . .

2.2B . . . until the level is up to the MAX mark (arrowed)

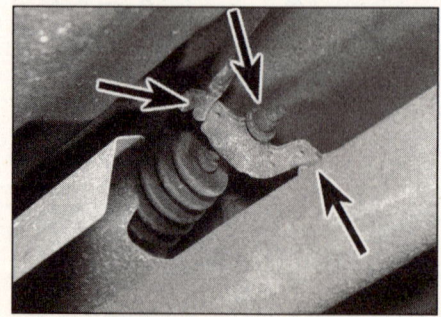

2.4 Lubricate the handbrake exposed cables and linkages (arrowed) with multi-purpose grease

3 Front disc pads – inspection and renewal

1 Jack up the front of the car and support it on stands. Remove both front roadwheels.
2 Check the thickness of the disc pads by viewing through the slot in the front of the caliper body. If the lining thickness on any of the pads is at, or below, the minimum specified thickness all four pads must be renewed as a complete set.

Girling caliper

3 Disconnect the pad wear indicator wiring connector and using a suitable spanner, unscrew the lower guide pin bolt while holding the guide pin with a second spanner.
4 Pivot the caliper body upwards. withdraw the two disc pads and remove the piston heat shield. If the pads are to be re-used, suitably identify them so that they can be refitted in their original positions.
5 Brush the dust and dirt from the caliper, piston, disc and pads, but **do not inhale it,** as it is injurious to health.
6 Rotate the brake disc by hand and scrape away any rust and scale. Carefully inspect the entire surface of the disc and if there are any signs of cracks, deep scoring or severe abrasions, the disc must be renewed. Also inspect the caliper for signs of fluid leaks around the piston, corrosion, or other

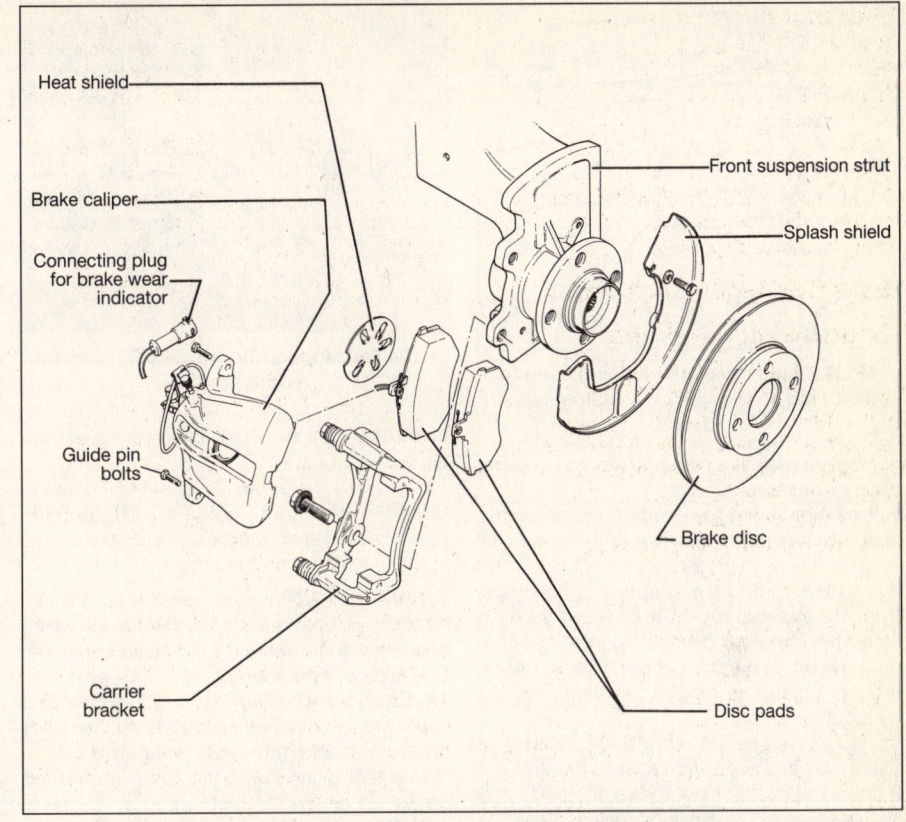

Fig. 9.1 Exploded view of the Girling front brake components (Secs 3 and 4)

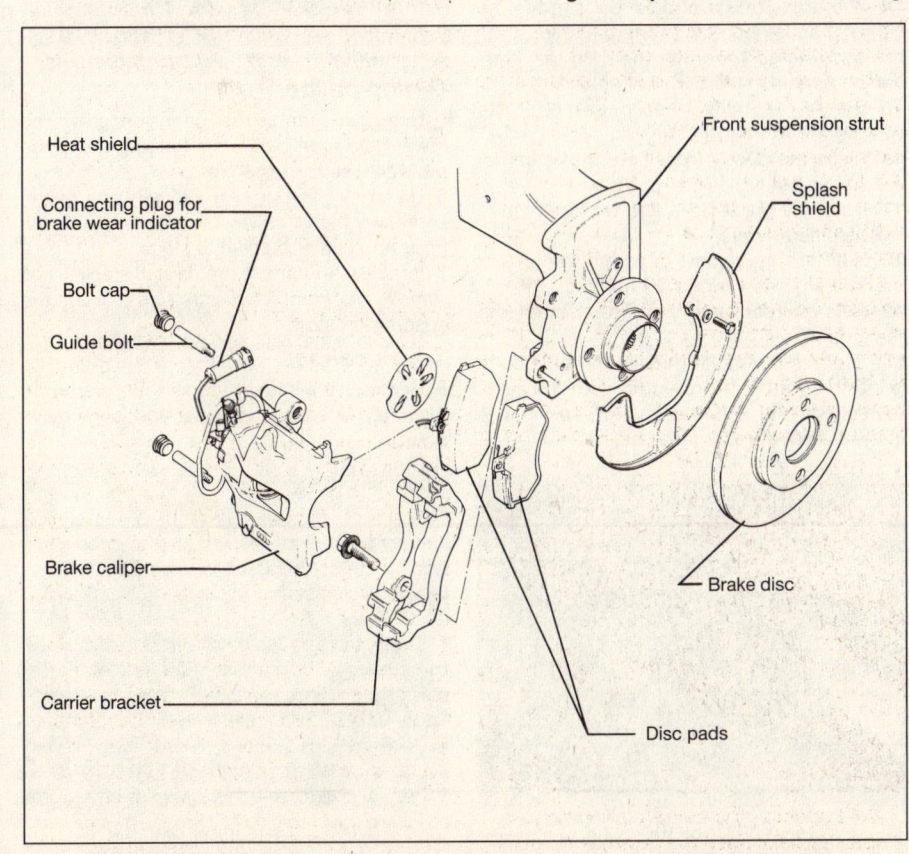

Fig. 9.2 Exploded view of the Teves front brake components (Secs 3 and 4)

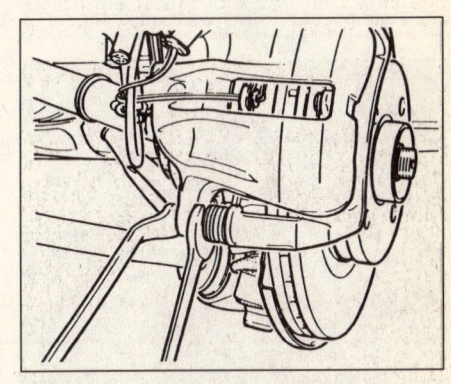

Fig. 9.3 Lower guide pin bolt removal – Girling caliper (Sec 3)

Fig. 9.4 Pivot the caliper body upwards to remove the pads – Girling caliper (Sec 3)

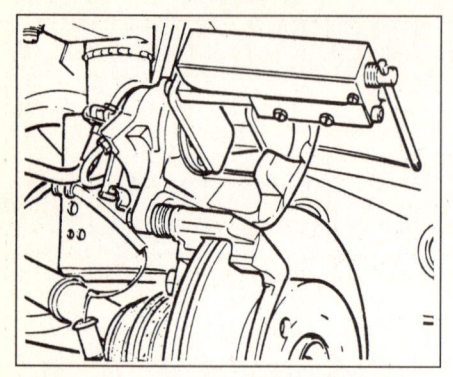

9•4 Braking system

Fig. 9.5 Audi special tool being used to retract the caliper piston – Girling caliper (Sec 3)

damage. Renew the piston seals or the caliper body as necessary.
7 If new pads are to be fitted, first push the piston back into its bore using a G-clamp or suitable blocks of wood as levers. While doing this, check that brake fluid will not overflow from the reservoir, and if necessary use a clean flexible plastic bottle to extract some fluid. **Note:** Brake fluid is poisonous and no attempt should be made to syphon the fluid by mouth.
8 Place a new heat shield on the piston then place the pads in position against the disc.
9 Swing the caliper body over the pads and secure using a new guide pin bolt tightened to the specified torque.
10 Reconnect the pad wear indicator wiring

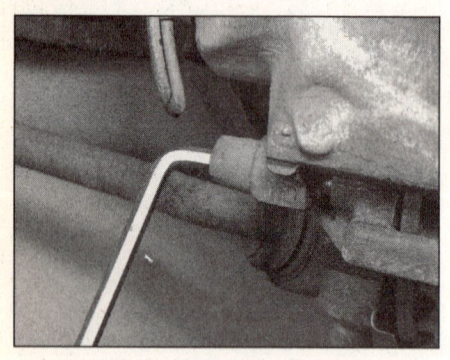

3.13A Unscrew the guide bolts . . .

3.12A Disconnect the warning light wiring connector . . .

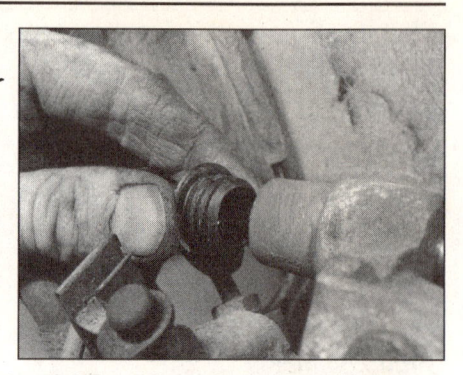

connector, refit the roadwheels and lower the car to the ground.
11 Depress the brake pedal several times to bring the piston into contact with the pads then check and, if necessary, top up the fluid in the master cylinder reservoir.

Teves caliper

12 Disconnect the pad wear indicator wiring connector then remove the plastic caps over the guide bolts (photos).
13 Using an Alien key, undo the upper and lower guide bolts and lift off the caliper body (photos). Suspend the caliper from a convenient place under the wheel arch using string or wire. Do not allow it to hang unsupported.
14 Withdraw the two disc pads from the carrier bracket (photos). If the pads are to be re-used, suitably identify them so that they can be refitted in their original positions.
15 Before refitting the pads refer to paragraphs 5, 6 and 7.
16 Place the pads in position on the carrier bracket and fit the caliper body.
17 Insert the guide bolts and tighten them to the specified torque.
18 Refit the guide bolt caps and reconnect the wear indicator wiring connector.
19 Refit the roadwheels and lower the car to the ground.
20 Depress the brake pedal several times to bring the piston into contact with the pads then check and, if necessary, top up the fluid in the master cylinder reservoir.

3.14A Withdraw the outer . . .

3.12B . . . then remove the guide bolt plastic caps

4 Front disc caliper – removal and refitting

Note: *On models equipped with an anti-lock braking system, refer to Section 28 before proceeding.*

1 Jack up the front of the car and support it on stands. Remove the appropriate front roadwheel.
2 Disconnect the pad wear indicator wiring connector.
3 Using a brake hose clamp, or self-locking wrench with protected jaws, clamp the flexible brake hose. This will minimise brake fluid loss during subsequent operations.
4 Unscrew the brake pipe-to-hose union at the caliper body then extract the retaining clip and lift away the hose.

Girling caliper

5 Using a suitable spanner, unscrew the lower guide pin bolt while holding the guide pin with a second spanner.
6 Unscrew the upper guide pin bolt in the same way then lift away the caliper leaving the pads and carrier bracket in place.
7 If necessary unbolt the carrier bracket and remove it, complete with pads, from the suspension strut.

Teves caliper

8 Remove the plastic caps then, using an Allen key, unscrew the upper and lower guide bolts.

3.13B . . and lift off the caliper body

3.14B . . . and inner disc pads

Braking system 9•5

9 Lift off the caliper leaving the pads and carrier bracket in place.

10 If necessary unbolt the carrier bracket and remove it, complete with pads, from the suspension strut.

Girling and Teves calipers

11 Refitting is the reversal of removal, but make sure all mating faces are clean and tighten the bolts and unions to the specified torque. Use new guide pin bolts on the Girling caliper.

12 Bleed the hydraulic system as described in Section 17, on completion.

5 Front disc caliper – overhaul

1 Remove the caliper, as described in Section 4, and clean it externally, taking care not to allow any foreign matter to enter the brake pipe aperture.

2 Use a foot pump, or a compressed air supply to blow the piston out of the cylinder, but place a block of wood inside the frame to prevent damage to the piston. Remove the dust cap.

3 Use a blunt screwdriver to prise the seal out of the caliper bore, taking great care not to scratch the bore walls.

4 Clean the caliper components thoroughly with methylated spirit and allow to dry.

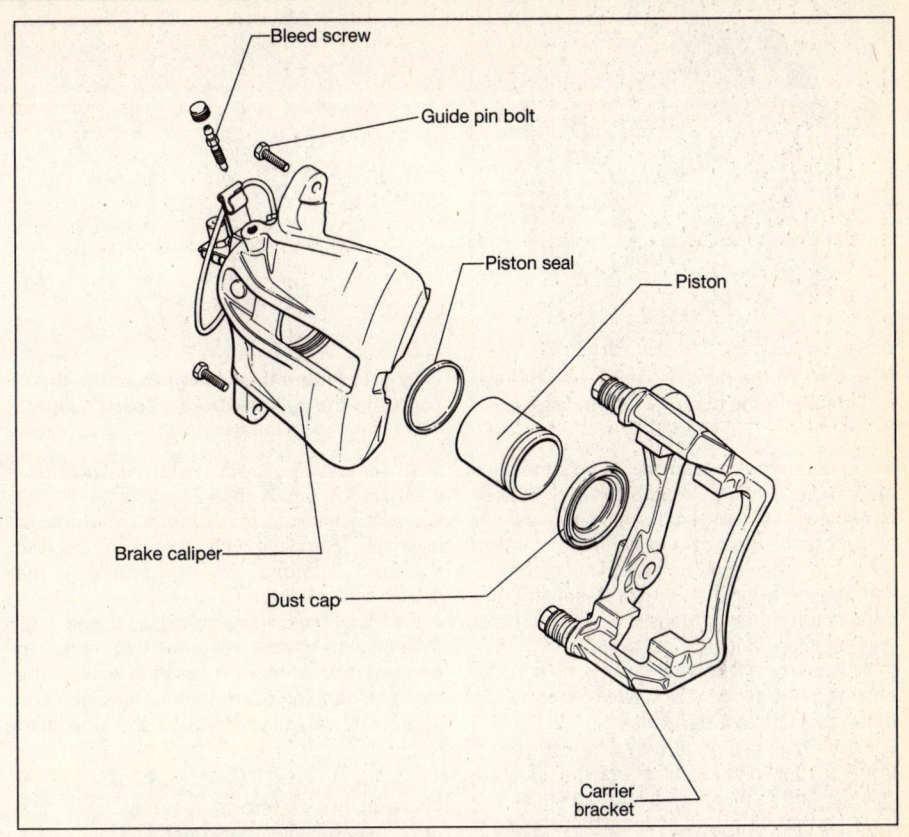

Fig. 9.6 Exploded view of the Girling front brake caliper assembly (Sec 5)

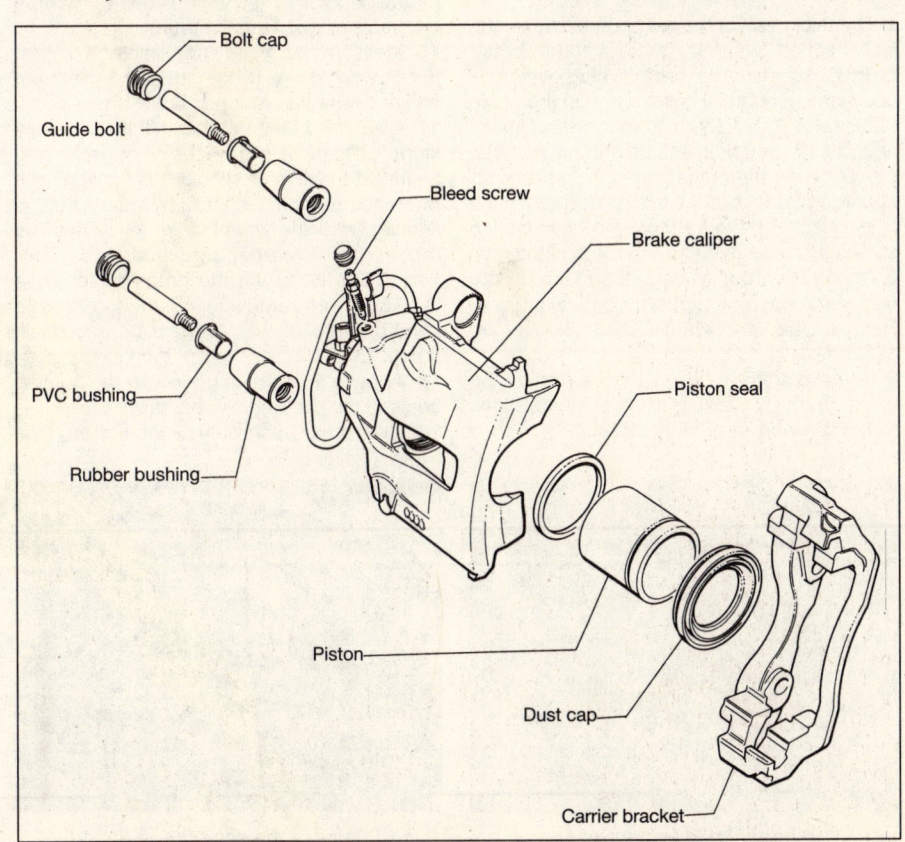

Fig. 9.7 Exploded view of the Teves front brake caliper assembly (Sec 5)

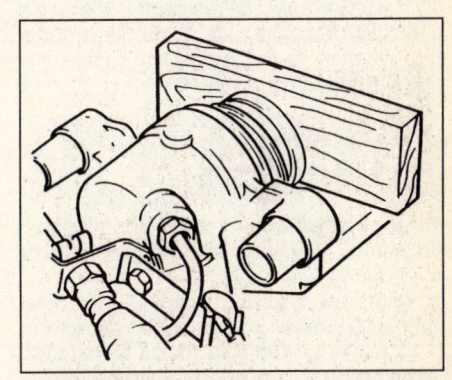

Fig. 9.8 Using compressed air to remove the caliper piston – Teves caliper (Sec 5)

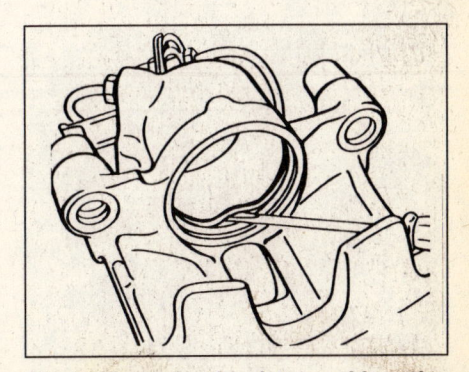

Fig. 9.9 Removing the piston seal from the caliper – Teves caliper (Sec 5)

Fig. 9.10 Fit the dust cap as shown before installing the piston – Teves caliper (Sec 5)

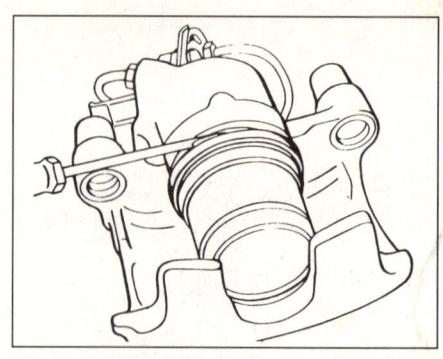

Fig. 9.11 Fitting the sealing lip of the dust cap into the cylinder bore – Teves caliper (Sec 5)

5 Inspect the piston and caliper bore for signs of damage, scuffing or corrosion and, if these conditions are evident, renew the caliper assembly. Also renew the guide pins and/or bushings if they show any sign of damage.
6 If the components are in a satisfactory condition a repair kit consisting of new seals and dust cap should be obtained.
7 Fit a new seal into the groove in the cylinder bore. Apply a thin coat of brake cylinder paste to the seal and to the cylinder.
8 Fit the dust cap on to the piston, as shown in Fig. 9.10, and then offer the piston up to the cylinder and fit the sealing lip of the dust cap into the groove of the cylinder bore using a screwdriver.
9 Smear brake cylinder paste over the piston and then press the piston into the cylinder until the outer lip of the dust cap springs into place in the piston groove.

6 Front brake disc – removal and refitting

1 Jack up the front of the car and support it on stands. Remove the appropriate front roadwheel.
2 Rotate the disc and examine it for deep scoring or grooving. Light scoring is normal, but if excessive the disc should be removed and renewed, or ground by a suitably qualified engineering works. Use a micrometer in several positions to check the disc thickness.
3 To remove the disc, undo the two bolts securing the brake caliper carrier bracket to the suspension strut. Withdraw the caliper assembly, complete with pads, from the disc and place it to one side. Avoid straining the flexible brake hose.
4 Withdraw the disc from the hub flange.
5 Refitting is the reverse sequence to removal. Ensure that the mating face of the disc and hub flange are thoroughly clean and tighten all retaining bolts to the specified torque.

7 Rear brake shoes – inspection and removal

1 The thickness of the rear brake linings can be checked without removing the brake drums. Remove the rubber plug which is above the handbrake cable entry on the brake backplate. Use a torch to increase visibility and check the thickness of friction material remaining on the brake shoes. If the amount remaining is close to the minimum given in the Specifications, a more thorough examination should be made by removing the brake drum.
2 Chock the front wheels, then jack up the rear of the car and support it on axle stands. Remove the rear wheels, and release the handbrake.
3 Remove the cap from the centre of the brake drum by tapping it on alternate sides with a screwdriver or blunt chisel.
4 Extract the split pin and remove the locking ring.
5 Unscrew the nut and remove the thrust washer.
6 Withdraw the brake drum, making sure that the outer wheel bearing does not fall out. If the brake drum binds on the shoes, insert a small screwdriver through a wheel bolt hole and lever up the wedged key in order to release the shoes.
7 Note the position of the brake shoes and springs and mark the webs of the shoes, if necessary, to aid refitting.
8 Using pliers, depress the spring retainer caps, turn them through 90° and remove them, together with the springs (photo).
9 Unhook the lower return spring from the shoes (photo).
10 Detach the bottom of the shoes from the bottom anchor, then release the top of the shoes from the wheel cylinder and swivel down to reveal the rear of the shoes (photo).
11 Disconnect the handbrake cable, then clamp the bottom of the shoes in a vice.
12 Unhook the upper return spring and the wedged key spring.
13 Separate the trailing shoe from the leading shoe and pushrod.
14 Unhook the tensioning spring and remove the pushrod from the leading shoe together with the wedged key.
15 Brush the dust from the brake drum, brake shoes, and backplate, but **do not inhale it**, as it is injurious to health. Scrape any scale or rust from the drum.
16 Measure the brake shoe lining thickness. If it is worn down to the specified minimum amount, renew all four rear brake shoes.
17 Clean the brake backplate. If there are any signs of loss of grease from the rear hub bearings, the oil seal should be renewed, with reference to Chapter 10. If hydraulic fluid is leaking from the wheel cylinder, it must be repaired or renewed, as described in Section 8. Do not touch the brake pedal while the shoes are removed. Position an elastic band over the wheel cylinder pistons to retain them.
18 Apply a little brake grease to the contact areas of the pushrod and handbrake lever.
19 Clamp the pushrod in a vice, then hook

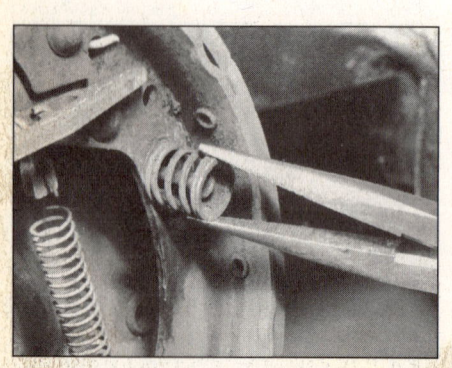

7.8 Remove the spring retainer caps and springs

7.9 Unhook the lower return spring (arrowed) from the brake shoes

7.10 Release the shoe upper locations from the wheel cylinder

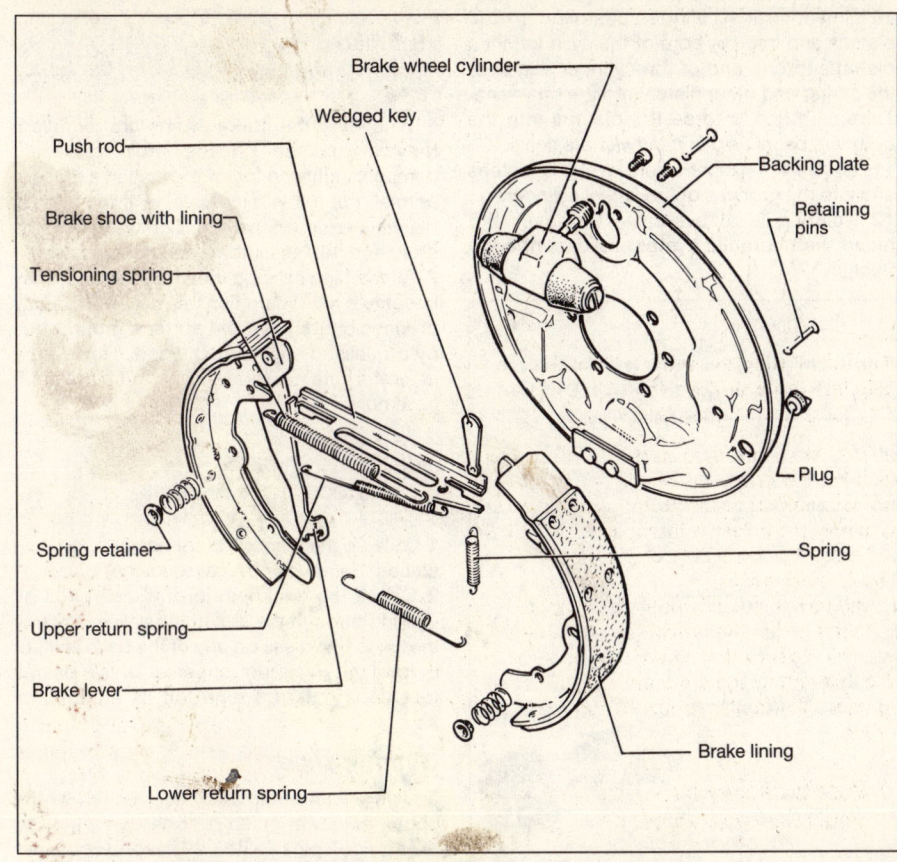

Braking system 9•7

Fig. 9.12 Exploded view of the rear drum brake components (Sec 7)

Labels: Push rod; Brake shoe with lining; Tensioning spring; Spring retainer; Upper return spring; Brake lever; Lower return spring; Wedged key; Brake wheel cylinder; Backing plate; Retaining pins; Plug; Spring; Brake lining

7.24 Brake shoe self-adjusting wedged key and spring (arrowed)

8 Rear wheel cylinder – removal, overhaul and refitting

1 Remove the brake shoes, as described in Section 7.
2 Remove the master cylinder reservoir filler cap and top up the reservoir fully. Place a piece of polythene over the filler neck and secure the polythene with an elastic band. This will minimise brake fluid loss during subsequent operations. Alternatively clamp the flexible brake hose between the rear axle and body using a brake hose clamp or self-locking wrench with protected jaws.
3 Loosen the brake pipe union on the rear of the wheel cylinder.
4 Using an Allen key, unscrew the wheel cylinder mounting bolts.
5 Unscrew the brake pipe union and withdraw the wheel cylinder from the backplate. Plug the end of the hydraulic pipe, if necessary.
6 Clean the exterior of the wheel cylinder, taking care not to allow any foreign matter to enter the hydraulic pipe aperture.
7 Remove the rubber boots from the ends of the cylinder and extract the two pistons and the spring between them.
8 Inspect the cylinder bore for signs of scoring and corrosion and the pistons and seals for wear. If the cylinder is satisfactory a

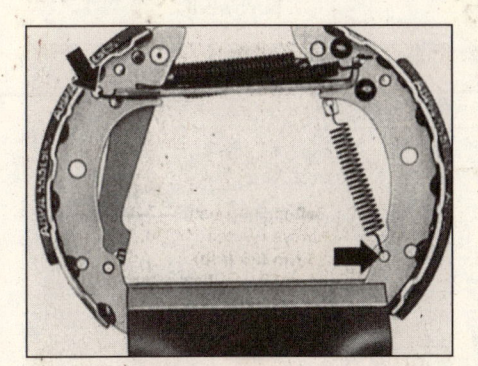

the tensioning spring on the pushrod and leading shoe and position the shoe slot over the pushrod.
20 Fit the wedged key between the shoe and pushrod.
21 Locate the handbrake lever on the trailing shoe in the pushrod, and fit the upper return spring.
22 Connect the handbrake cable to the handbrake lever, swivel the shoes upward and locate the top of the shoes on the wheel cylinder pistons.
23 Fit the lower return spring to the shoes, then lever the bottom of the shoes onto the bottom anchor.
24 Fit the spring to the wedged key and leading shoe (photo).
25 Fit the retaining springs and caps.
26 Press the wedged key upwards to give the maximum shoe clearance.
27 Fit the brake drum and adjust the wheel bearings, with reference to Chapter 10.
28 Depress the brake pedal once firmly in order to adjust the rear brakes.
29 Repeat the procedure on the remaining rear brake, then lower the car to the ground.

Fig. 9.13 Brake shoe upper return spring and wedged key spring removal (Sec 7)

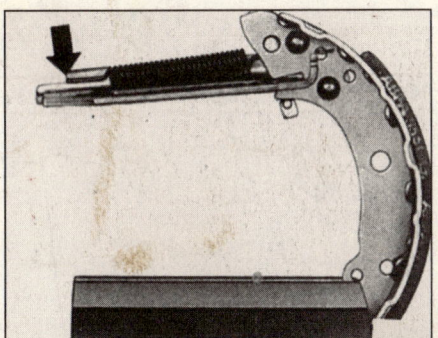

Fig. 9.14 Removal of tensioning spring end (arrowed) and pushrod from the leading brake shoe (Sec 7)

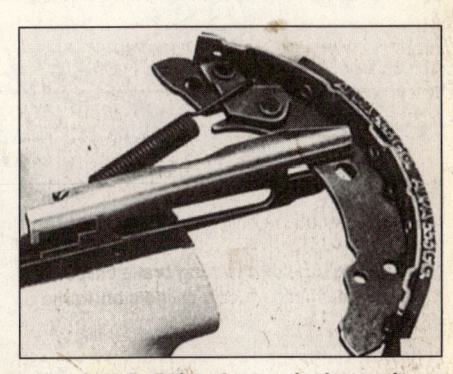

Fig. 9.15 Refitting the tensioning spring and leading brake shoe to the pushrod (Sec 7)

9•8 Braking system

repair kit can be used; otherwise the cylinder should be discarded and a new complete assembly fitted. If servicing a cylinder, use all the parts in the repair kit. Clean all the metal parts, using methylated spirit if necessary, *but never petrol or similar solvents,* then leave the parts to dry in the air, or dry them with a lint-free cloth.

9 Apply brake cylinder paste to the seals and fit them so that their larger diameter end is nearest to the end of the piston.

10 Smear brake cylinder paste on to the pistons and into the bore of the cylinder. Fit a piston into one end of the cylinder and then the spring and other piston into the other end. Take care not to force the pistons into the cylinders because this can twist the seals.

11 Locate the rubber boots over the pistons and into the grooves of the wheel cylinder.

12 Refitting is a reversal of removal, but bleed the hydraulic system as described in Section 17.

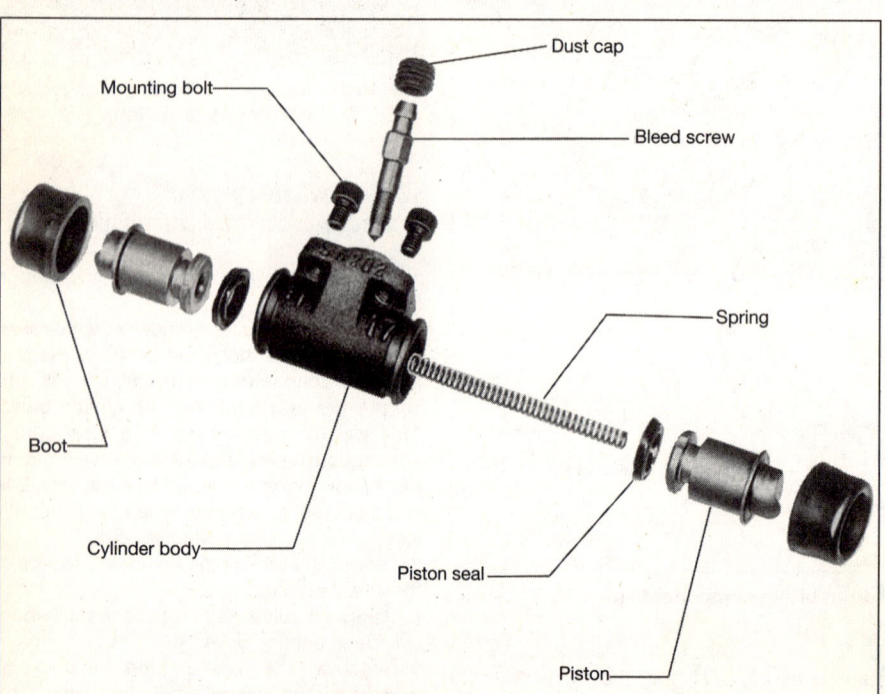

9 Brake drum – inspection and renewal

1 Whenever the brake drums are removed, they should be checked for wear and damage. Light scoring of the friction surface is normal, but if it is excessive, or if the internal diameter exceeds the specified wear limit, the drum and hub assembly should be renewed.

2 After a high mileage the friction surface may become oval. Where this has occurred, it may be possible to have the surface ground true by a qualified engineering works. However, it is preferable to renew the drum and hub assembly.

10 Rear disc pads – inspection and renewal

1 Jack up the rear of the car and support it on stands. Remove both rear roadwheels.

2 Check the thickness of the disc pads by viewing through the slot in the caliper body. If the lining thickness on any of the pads is at, or below, the minimum specified thickness all four pads must be renewed as a complete set.

Girling caliper

3 Using a suitable spanner, unscrew the upper and lower guide pin bolts while holding the guide pins with a second spanner (photos).

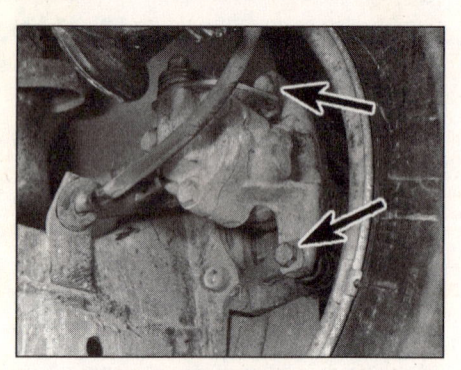

Fig. 9.16 Exploded view of the rear drum brake wheel cylinder (Sec 8)

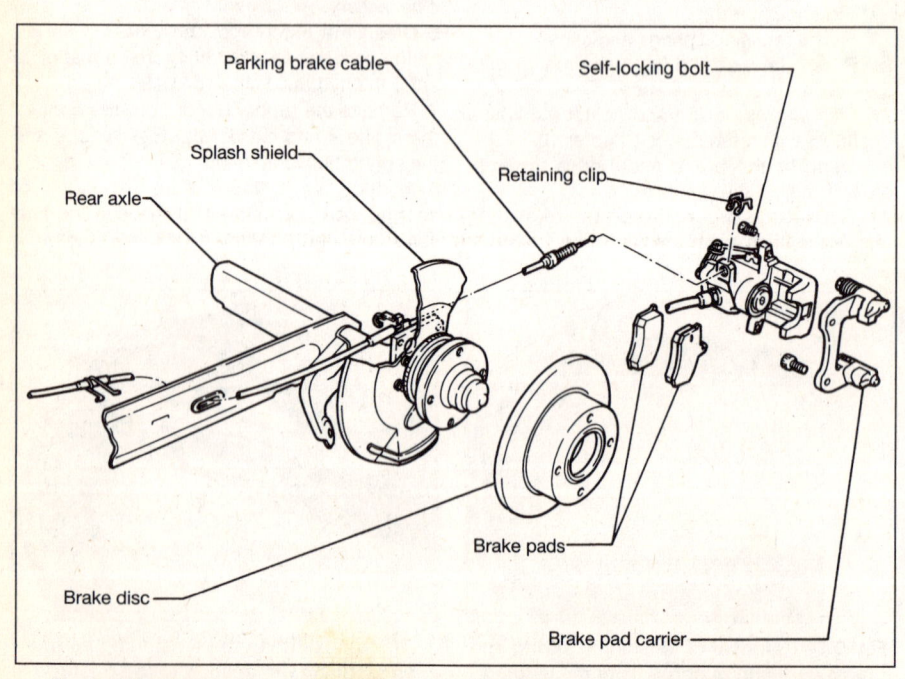

Fig. 9.17 Exploded view of the Girling rear disc brake components (Secs 10 and 11)

10.3A Rear caliper guide pin bolts (arrowed)

10.3B Removing the caliper upper guide pin bolt

Braking system 9•9

10.4 Lift off the caliper body

10.5A Remove the outer . . .

10.5B . . . and inner disc pads

4 Lift off the caliper body and place it to one side, but avoid straining the flexible brake hose (photo).

5 Withdraw the disc pads from the carrier bracket (photos). If the pads are to be re-used, suitably identify them so that they can be refitted in their original positions.

6 Brush the dust and dirt from the caliper, piston, disc and pads, but **do not inhale it,** as it is injurious to health.

7 Rotate the brake disc by hand and scrape away any rust and scale. Carefully inspect the entire surface of the disc and if there are any signs of cracks, deep scoring or severe abrasions, the disc must be renewed. Also inspect the caliper for signs of fluid leaks around the piston, corrosion, or other damage. Renew the piston seals or the caliper body as necessary.

8 If new pads are to be fitted, retract the piston into its bore by turning the piston clockwise with a suitable Allen key and at the same time pushing in firmly (photo). While doing this, check that brake fluid will not overflow from the reservoir, and if necessary use a clean flexible plastic bottle to extract some fluid. **Note:** Brake fluid is poisonous and no attempt should be made to syphon the fluid by mouth.

9 Place the pads in position on the carrier bracket then locate the caliper body over the pads.

10 Fit and tighten new guide pin bolts to the specified torque.

Teves caliper

11 Remove the plastic caps over the guide bolts then unscrew the bolts using an Allen key. Only unscrew the bolts sufficiently to free the caliper; do not remove them completely.

12 Pull the caliper body away from the centre of the car, then swivel it rearwards and lift it off the pads. Place the caliper to one side but avoid straining the flexible brake hose.

13 Withdraw the pads from the carrier

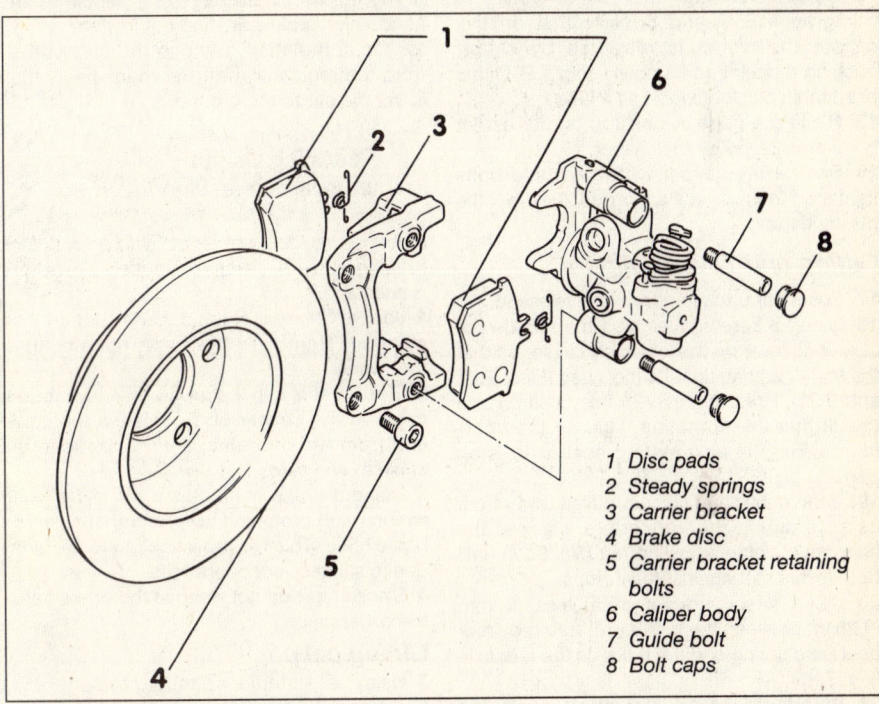

1 Disc pads
2 Steady springs
3 Carrier bracket
4 Brake disc
5 Carrier bracket retaining bolts
6 Caliper body
7 Guide bolt
8 Bolt caps

Fig. 9.18 Exploded view of the Teves rear disc brake components (Secs 10 and 11)

10.8 Engage a suitable Allen key in the piston hexagonal slot then turn clockwise to retract the piston

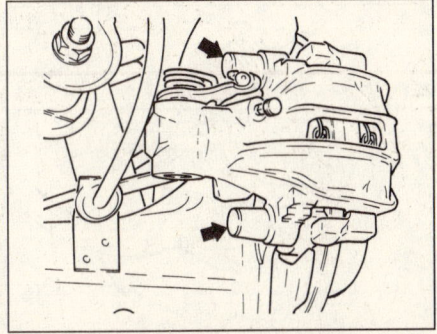

Fig. 9.19 Guide bolt plastic caps (arrowed) – Teves caliper (Sec 10)

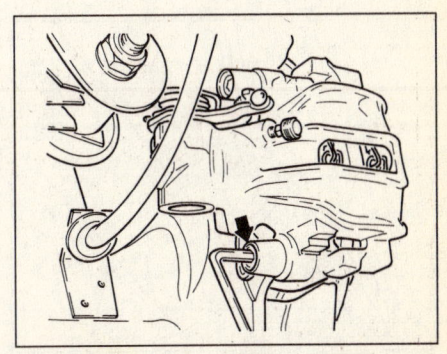

Fig. 9.20 Lower guide bolt removal using an Allen key (arrowed) – Teves caliper (Sec 10)

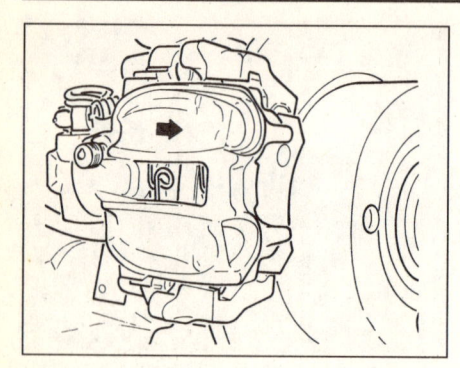

9•10 Braking system

Fig. 9.21 Pull the caliper in the direction of the arrow, swivel rearwards and remove – Teves caliper (Sec 10)

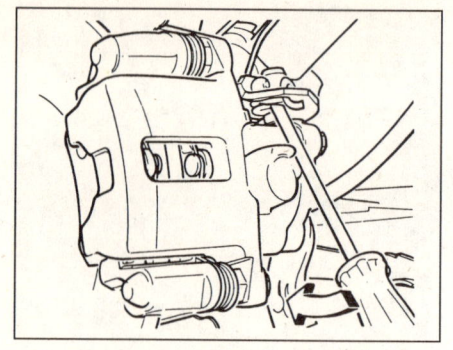

Fig. 9.22 Press the handbrake operating lever on the caliper against its stop using a screwdriver (Sec 10)

Fig. 9.23 Handbrake operating lever stop peg (arrowed) on rear caliper (Sec 10)

bracket. If the pads are to be re-used, suitably identify them so that they can be refitted in their original positions.

14 Before refitting the pads, refer to paragraphs 6, 7 and 8. Note that on this caliper the piston is retracted by simply pushing it back into its bore using a G-clamp or suitable block of wood as a lever.

15 Place the pads in position on the carrier bracket followed by the caliper.

16 Secure the caliper with the guide bolts tightened to the specified torque, then refit the plastic caps.

Girling and Teves calipers

17 Ensure that the handbrake is released.

18 Using a screwdriver, pull the handbrake operating lever on the left-hand caliper so that the lever rests against its stop peg (Figs. 9.22 and 9.23). Hold the lever in this position and check that the operating lever on the right-hand caliper is also resting against its stop peg.

19 If the right-hand lever is pulled away from its stop during this procedure, slacken the handbrake cable adjusting nut (Fig. 9.24) until both levers rest against their stops.

20 Insert a screwdriver of at least 6 mm (0.25 in) between the brake pressure regulator operating spring and the roller on the rear axle (Fig. 9.25).

21 With the engine switched off, pump the brake pedal approximately 40 times using moderate pressure then check that both rear discs are free to turn with the pedal released. If this is not the case repeat the procedure in paragraphs 18 to 21 but slacken the handbrake cable adjusting nut further.

22 On completion, remove the screwdriver from the regulator, refit the roadwheels then lower the car to the ground.

11 Rear disc caliper – removal and refitting

Note: *On models equipped with an anti-lock braking system, refer to Section 28 before proceeding.*

1 Jack up the rear of the car and support it on stands. Remove the appropriate rear roadwheel.

2 Extract the clip securing the handbrake cable to the caliper body, release the cable end from the operating lever and move the cable to one side.

3 Using a brake hose clamp, or self-locking wrench with protected jaws, clamp the flexible brake hose. This will minimise brake fluid loss during subsequent operations.

4 Slacken but do not remove the brake hose-to-caliper union.

Girling caliper

5 Using a suitable spanner, unscrew the upper and lower guide pin bolts while holding the guide pins with a second spanner.

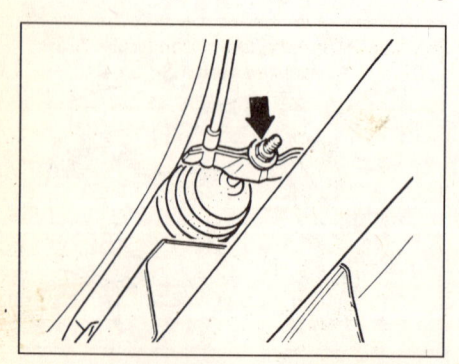

Fig. 9.24 Handbrake cable adjusting nut – arrowed (Sec 10)

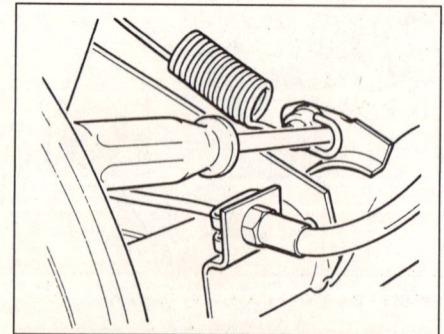

Fig. 9.25 Screwdriver inserted between brake pressure regulator spring and spring mounting roller (Sec 10)

6 Lift away the caliper, hold the brake hose and unscrew the caliper from the hose.

7 If necessary unbolt the carrier bracket and remove it, complete with pads, from the rear axle.

Teves caliper

8 Remove the plastic caps over the guide bolts then unscrew the two guide bolts using an Allen key. Only unscrew the guide bolts sufficiently to free the caliper; do not remove them completely.

9 Pull the caliper body away from the centre of the car then swivel it to the rear and lift it off the pads. Hold the brake hose and unscrew the caliper from the hose.

10 If necessary unbolt the carrier bracket and remove it. complete with pads, from the rear axle.

Girling and Teves calipers

11 Refitting is the reversal of removal, but make sure all mating faces are clean and tighten the bolts and unions to the specified torque. Use new guide pin bolts on the Girling caliper.

12 Bleed the hydraulic system, as described in Section 17, then carry out the rear brake basic adjustment procedure described in Section 1 paragraphs 17 to 22 inclusive.

12 Rear disc caliper – overhaul

1 Remove the caliper, as described in Section 11, and clean it externally, taking care not to allow any foreign matter to enter the brake hose aperture.

Girling caliper

2 Using a suitable Allen key, unscrew the piston from the cylinder and remove the piston dust cap.

3 Use a blunt screwdriver to prise the seal out of the cylinder bore, taking great care to avoid scratching the bore walls.

4 Clean the caliper components thoroughly with methylated spirit and allow to dry.

5 Inspect the piston and caliper bore for signs of damage, scuffing or corrosion and, if these

Braking system 9•11

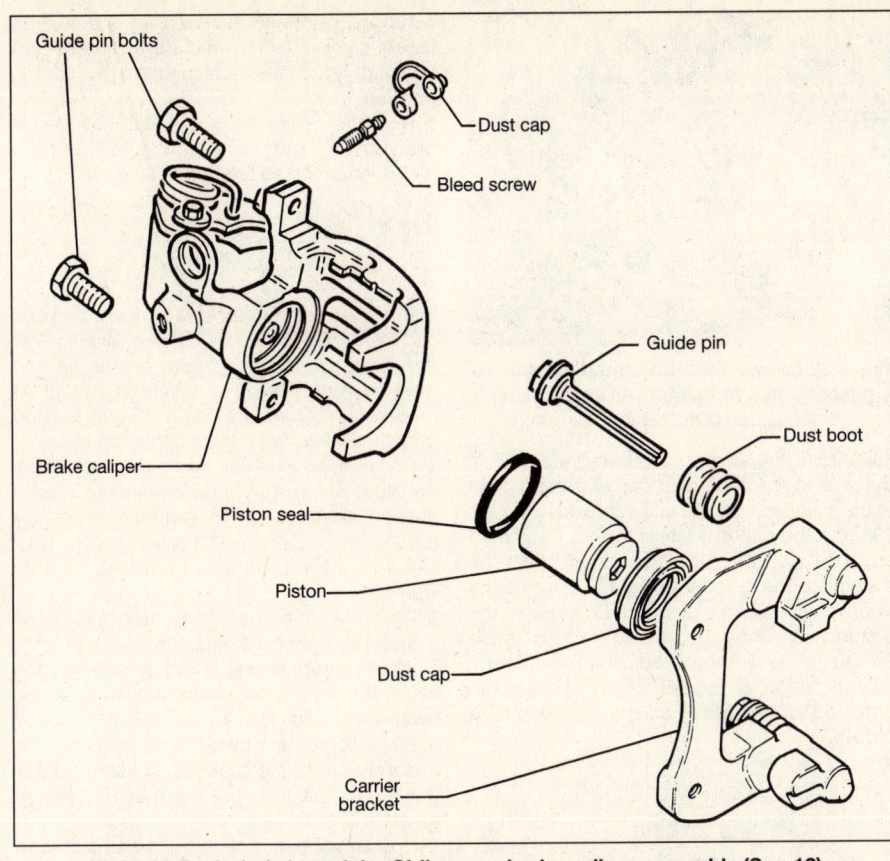

Fig. 9.26 Exploded view of the Girling rear brake caliper assembly (Sec 12)

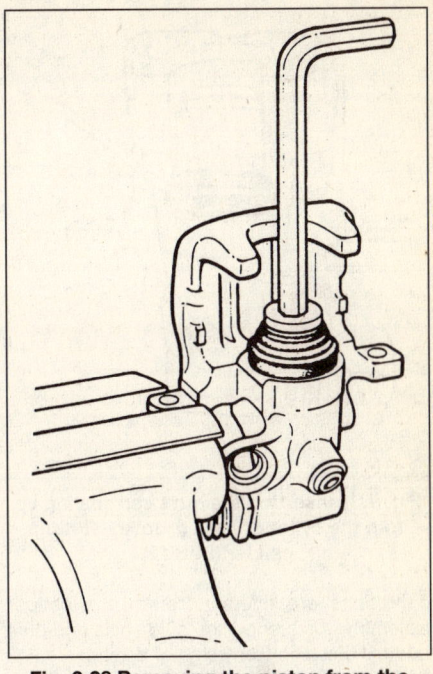

Fig. 9.28 Removing the piston from the caliper using an Allen key – Girling caliper (Sec 12)

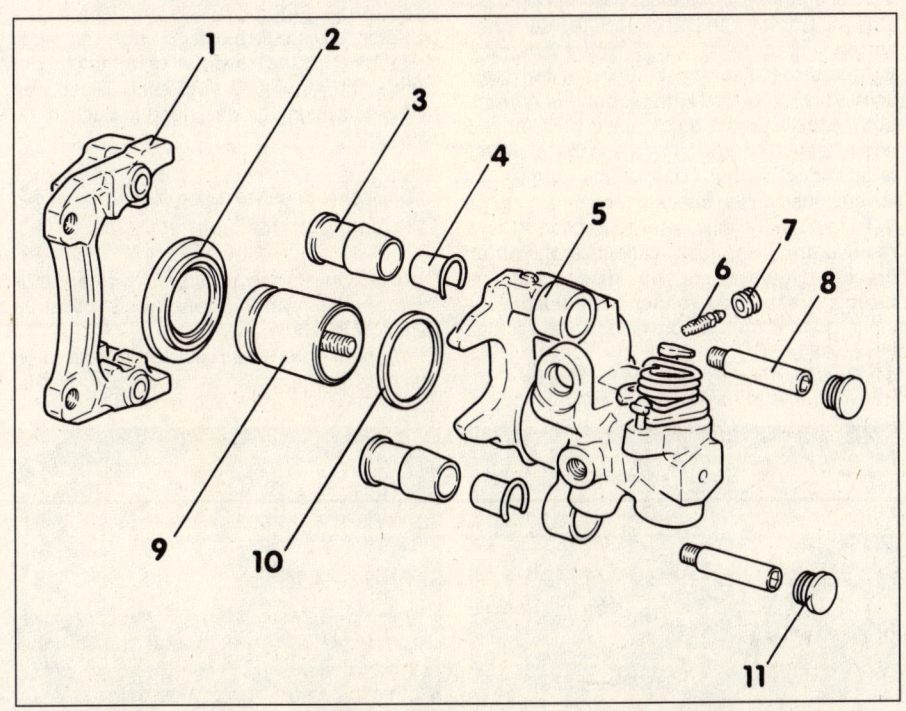

Fig. 9.27 Exploded view of the Teves rear brake caliper assembly (Sec 12)

1 Carrier bracket	5 Brake caliper	9 Piston
2 Dust cap	6 Bleed screw	10 Piston seal
3 Rubber bush	7 Cap	11 Bolt cap
4 Teflon bush	8 Guide bolt	

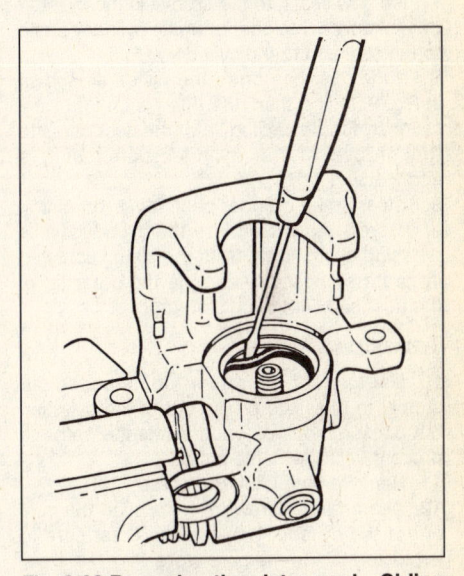

Fig. 9.29 Removing the piston seal – Girling caliper (Sec 12)

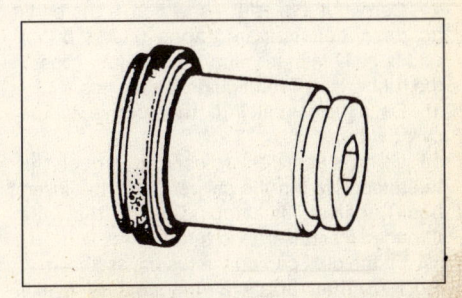

Fig. 9.30 Correct positioning of dust cap prior to fitting piston – Girling caliper (Sec 12)

9•12 Braking system

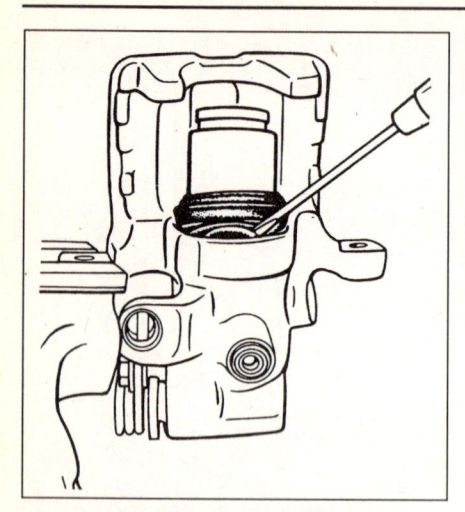

Fig. 9.31 Inserting the dust cap sealing lip into the cylinder bore groove – Girling caliper (Sec 12)

conditions are evident, renew the caliper assembly. Also renew the guide pins and dust boots if they show any sign of damage.
6 If the components are in a satisfactory condition a repair kit consisting of new seals and dust cap should be obtained.
7 Fit a new seal into the groove in the cylinder bore. Apply a thin coat of brake cylinder paste to the seal and to the cylinder.
8 Fit the dust cap on to the piston as shown in Fig. 9.30 and then offer the piston up to the cylinder. Fit the sealing lip of the dust cap into the groove of the cylinder bore using a screwdriver.
9 Smear brake cylinder paste over the piston and screw the piston into the cylinder while pressing down firmly. With the piston screwed in as far as possible engage the outer lip of the dust cap with the piston groove.

Teves caliper

10 Use a foot pump or compressed air supply to blow the piston out of the cylinder, but place a block of wood inside the frame to prevent damage to the piston.
11 Remove the piston dust cap.
12 Use a blunt screwdriver to prise the seal out of the cylinder bore, taking great care to avoid scratching the bore walls.
13 Clean the caliper components thoroughly with methylated spirit and allow to dry.
14 Carry out a careful inspection of the parts as described in paragraphs 5 and 6 but additionally inspect, and if necessary renew, the rubber and Teflon guide pin bushes.
15 Fit a new seal into the groove in the cylinder bore.
16 Using a screwdriver inserted through the threaded insert in the caliper, push the insert back against its stop. Ensure that the threaded insert is free to turn.
17 Fit the dust cap on the piston, as shown in Fig. 9.3 then apply a thin coat of brake cylinder paste to the piston, seal and cylinder bore.

Fig. 9.32 Ensure that the threaded insert is pushed back to its stop – Teves caliper (Sec 12)

18 Offer the piston up to the cylinder and fit the sealing lip of the dust cap into the groove of the cylinder bore using a screwdriver.
19 Turn the piston slightly so that the thread engages with the threaded insert. Push the piston into the cylinder using a G-clamp or by levering with a block of wood. Ensure that the piston is pushed back squarely to avoid damaging the automatic adjuster mechanism. As the piston is pushed back, engage the outer lip of the dust cap with the piston groove.

13 Rear brake disc – removal and refitting

1 Jack up the rear of the car and support it on stands. Remove the appropriate rear road wheel.
2 Rotate the disc and examine it for deep scoring or grooving. Light scoring is normal, but if excessive the disc should be removed and renewed, or ground by a suitably qualified engineering works. Use a micrometer in several positions to check the disc thickness.
3 To remove the disc, refer to Section 11 and remove the rear disc caliper and carrier bracket. However, do not disconnect the flexible brake hose suspend the caliper by string or wire from a convenient place under the wheel arch.
4 Withdraw the disc from the hub flange.

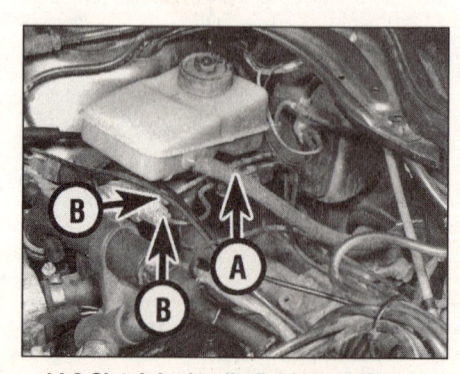

14.3 Clutch hydraulic fluid hose (A) and brake pipe connections (B) on left-hand side of master cylinder

5 Before refitting, ensure that the mating faces of the disc and hub flange are thoroughly clean then place the disc in position.
6 Refit the caliper assembly, as described in Section 11, but note that it will not be necessary to bleed the hydraulic system.

14 Master cylinder – removal and refitting

Note: *The master cylinder is a sealed unit and cannot be dismantled for repair or overhaul. In the event of master cylinder failure the unit must be renewed as a complete assembly. On models equipped with an anti-lock braking system, refer to Section 28 before proceeding.*
1 Remove the reservoir filler cap and draw off the fluid using a syringe or flexible plastic bottle. Take care not to spill fluid on the car paintwork – if some is spilled, wash it off immediately with copious amounts of cold water.
2 Refit the filler cap, but disconnect the warning light wiring connector.
3 Where applicable, detach the clutch hydraulic fluid hose from the side of the reservoir (photo).
4 Place some rags beneath the cylinder then unscrew the brake pipe union nuts and pull the pipes just clear of the master cylinder (photo).
5 Unscrew the mounting bolts and withdraw the master cylinder from the servo unit. Recover the O-ring seal. Do not depress the brake pedal with the master cylinder removed.
6 Refitting is the reversal of removal, but always fit a new O-ring seal. Bleed the hydraulic system. as described in Section 17, after fitting.

15 Brake pressure regulator – testing and adjustment

Note: *On models equipped with an anti-lock braking system, refer to Section 28 before proceeding*
1 The brake pressure regulator is located on the left-hand side of the rear axle, and is

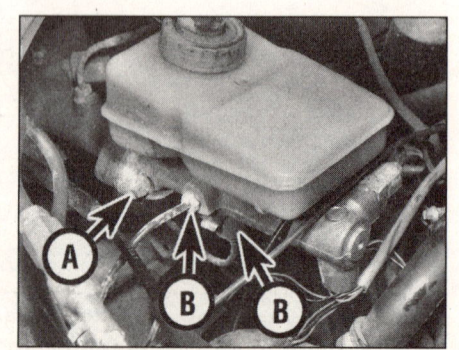

14.4 Master cylinder retaining bolt (A) and right-hand side brake pipe connections (B)

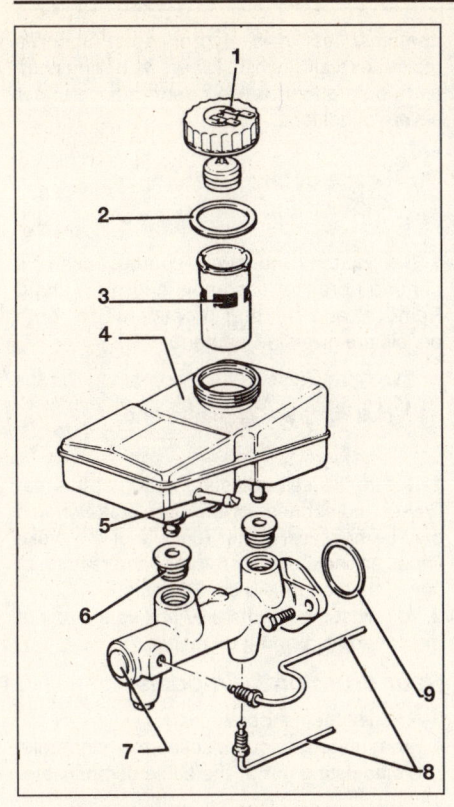

Braking system 9•13

Fig. 9.33 Brake master cylinder and reservoir components (Sec 14)

1 Control pin
2 Gasket
3 Strainer
4 Brake fluid reservoir
5 Connection for hydraulic clutch operation
6 Plug
7 Brake master cylinder
8 Brake lines
9 O-ring

15.5 Pressure regulator spring mounting (arrowed)

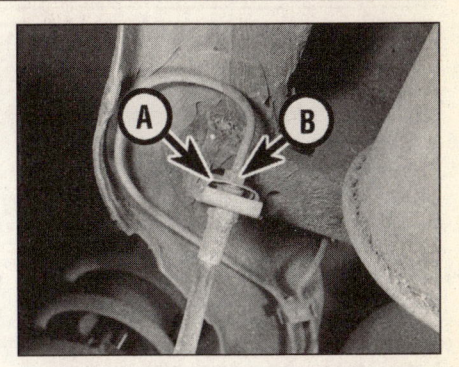

16.3 Brake hose pipe union nut (A) and retaining clip (B)

controlled by the up-and-down movement of the rear axle.
2 To test the operation of the regulator, have an assistant depress the footbrake firmly then release it quickly. With the weight of the car on the suspension the arm on the regulator should move, indicating that the unit is not seized.
3 To test the regulator for leakage, pressure gauges must be connected to the left-hand front caliper and right-hand rear wheel cylinder or caliper. As the equipment will not normally be available to the home mechanic, this work should be entrusted to an Audi dealer. However, an outline of the procedure is as follows. Depress the brake pedal so that the pressure in the left-hand front caliper is 100 bar (1450 lbf/in²). Hold this pressure for 5 seconds and check that the pressure in the right-hand rear wheel cylinder or caliper varies by no more than 10 bar (145 lbf/in²).
4 To adjust the regulator, the pressure gauges must be connected as described in paragraph 3, and the car must be at kerb weight with a full fuel tank and driver. Bounce the rear suspension several times. then depress the brake pedal so that the pressure in the left-hand front caliper is 50 bar (725 lbf/in²) - the pressure in the rear wheel cylinder or caliper should be 32.5 to 42.5 bar (471 to 616 lbf/in²). With the front caliper pressure at 100 bar (1450 lbf/in²) the rear wheel cylinder or caliper pressure should be 54.0 to 71.5 bar (783 to 1037 lbf/in²).
5 If the rear wheel cylinder or caliper pressure is too high, loosen the spring mounting on the rear axle and move the mounting forwards to release the tension. If the pressure is too low, move the mounting rearwards to increase the tension (photo).

16 Hydraulic brake pipes and hoses – removal and refitting

Note: *On models equipped with an anti-lock braking system, refer to Section 28 before proceeding.*
1 Before removing a brake pipe or hose unscrew the master cylinder reservoir filler cap and top up the reservoir fully. Place a piece of polythene over the filler neck and secure with an elastic band. This will minimise brake fluid loss during subsequent operations.
2 To remove a rigid brake pipe, unscrew the union nuts at each end, prise open the support clips and withdraw the pipe. Refitting is a reversal of removal.
3 To remove a flexible brake hose, unscrew the union nut securing the rigid brake pipe to the end of the flexible hose while holding the hose end stationary. Remove the retaining clip and withdraw the hose from the bracket. Unscrew the remaining end from the component or rigid pipe, according to position, release any retaining clips or brackets and remove the hose from the car. Refitting is a reversal of removal (photo).
4 Bleed the hydraulic system as described in Section 17, after fitting a rigid pipe or flexible hose, and whenever a pipe or hose union is disconnected.

17 Hydraulic system – bleeding

Note: *On models equipped with an anti-lock braking system, refer to Section 28 before proceeding*
1 The correct functioning of the brake hydraulic system is only possible after removal of all air from the components and circuit; this is achieved by bleeding the system. Note that clean unused brake fluid which has remained unshaken for at least 24 hours must be used.
2 If there is any possibility of incorrect fluid being used in the system, the brake lines and components must be completely flushed with uncontaminated fluid and new seals fitted to the components.
3 *Never re-use* brake fluid which has been bled from the system.
4 During the procedure, do not allow the level of brake fluid to drop more than halfway down the reservoir.
5 Before starting work, check that all pipes and hoses are secure, unions tight and bleed screws closed. Take great care not to allow brake fluid to come into contact with the car paintwork, otherwise the finish will be seriously damaged. Wash off any spilled fluid immediately with cold water.
6 There are a number of one-man, do-it-yourself, brake bleeding kits currently available from motor accessory shops. Always follow the instructions supplied with the kit. It is recommended that one of these kits is used wherever possible, as they greatly simplify the bleeding operation and also reduce the risk of expelled air and fluid being drawn back into the system. If one of these kits is not available, it will be necessary to gather together a clean jar and a suitable length of clear plastic tubing which is a tight fit over the bleed screw, and also to engage the help of an assistant.
7 If brake fluid has been lost from the master cylinder due to a leak in the system, ensure that the cause is traced and rectified before proceeding further.

9•14 Braking system

8 If the hydraulic system has only been partially disconnected and suitable precautions were taken to prevent further loss of fluid it should only be necessary to bleed that part of the system.
9 If the complete system is to be bled then it should be done in the following sequence:
(1) Right-hand rear wheel cylinder or brake caliper
(2) Left-hand rear wheel cylinder or brake caliper
(3) Right-hand front brake caliper
(4) Left-hand front brake caliper

Note: *If the system is being bled after removal and refitting of the master cylinder it will also be necessary to bleed the clutch system on models with a hydraulically operated clutch. This should be done **first**, as described in Chapter 5.*

10 To bleed the system, first clean the area around the bleed screw and fit the bleed tube. If necessary, top up the master cylinder reservoir with brake fluid.
11 If the system incorporates a vacuum servo, destroy the vacuum by giving several applications of the brake pedal in quick succession.

Bleeding – two-man method

12 Gather together a clean jar and a length of rubber or plastic tubing which will be a tight fit on the brake bleed screws.
13 Engage the help of an assistant.
14 Push one end of the bleed tube onto the first bleed screw and immerse the other end in the jar which should contain enough hydraulic fluid to cover the end of the tube.
15 Open the bleed screw one half turn and have your assistant depress the brake pedal fully then slowly release it. Tighten the bleed screw at the end of each pedal downstroke to obviate any chance of air or fluid being drawn back into the system.
16 Repeat this operation until clean hydraulic fluid, free from air bubbles, can be seen coming through into the jar.
17 Tighten the bleed screw at the end of a pedal downstroke and remove the bleed tube. Bleed the remaining screws in a similar way.

Bleeding – using a one-way valve kit

18 There are a number of one-man, one-way brake bleeding kits available from motor accessory shops. It is recommended that one of these kits is used wherever possible as it will greatly simplify the bleeding operation and also reduce the risk of air or fluid being drawn back into the system, quite apart from being able to do the work without the help of an assistant.
19 To use the kit, connect the tube to the bleed screw and open the screw one half turn.
20 Depress the brake pedal fully and slowly release it. The one-way valve in the kit will prevent expelled air from returning at the end of each pedal downstroke. Repeat this operation several times to be sure of ejecting all air from the system. Some kits include a translucent container which can be positioned so that the air bubbles can be seen being ejected from the system.
21 Tighten the bleed screw, remove the tube and repeat the operations on the remaining brakes.
22 On completion, depress the brake pedal. If it still feels spongy repeat the bleeding operations, as air must still be trapped in the system.

Bleeding – using a pressure bleed kit

23 These kits are also available from motor accessory shops and are usually operated by air pressure from the spare tyre.
24 By connecting a pressurised container to the master cylinder fluid reservoir, bleeding is then carried out by simply opening each bleed screw in turn and allowing the fluid to run out, rather like turning on a tap, until no air is visible in the expelled fluid.
25 By using this method, the large reserve of hydraulic fluid provides a safeguard against air being drawn into the master cylinder during bleeding which often occurs if the fluid level in the reservoir is not maintained.
26 Pressure bleeding is particularly effective when bleeding 'difficult' systems or when bleeding the complete system at the time of routine fluid renewal.

All methods of bleeding

27 When bleeding is completed, check and top up the fluid level in the master cylinder reservoir.
28 Check the feel of the brake pedal. If it feels at all spongy, air must still be present in the system and further bleeding is indicated. Failure to bleed satisfactorily after a reasonable repetition of the bleeding operations may be due to worn master cylinder seals.
29 Discard brake fluid which has been expelled. It is almost certain to be contaminated with moisture, air and dirt making it unsuitable for further use. Clean fluid should always be stored in an airtight container as it is hygroscopic (absorbs moisture readily) which lowers its boiling point and could affect braking performance under severe conditions.

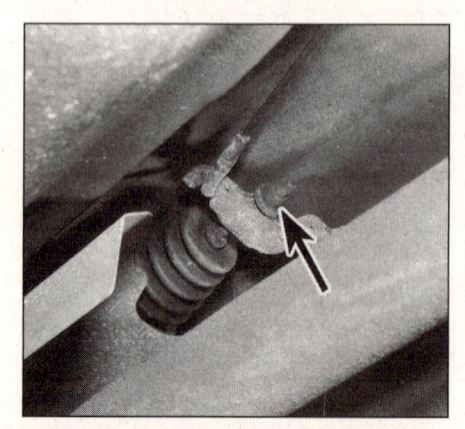

18 Brake pedal – removal and refitting

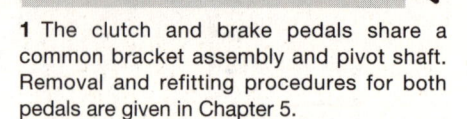

1 The clutch and brake pedals share a common bracket assembly and pivot shaft. Removal and refitting procedures for both pedals are given in Chapter 5.

19 Handbrake – adjustment

1 Due to the self-adjusting action of the rear brakes, adjustment of the handbrake should only be necessary after renewal of the brake shoes or pads, or after removal and refitting of any of the handbrake components.
2 To adjust the handbrake, jack up the rear of the car and support it on stands.

Rear drum brake models

3 Release the handbrake fully.
4 From under the car, slacken the handbrake cable adjusting nut at the cable compensator (photo).
5 Depress the brake pedal firmly once then release it.
6 Pull the handbrake lever up to the third notch of the ratchet.
7 Tighten the cable adjusting nut until both rear brakes are dragging, but can still just be turned by hand.
8 Release the handbrake and check that the rear drums are free to turn.
9 Lubricate the adjusting nut threads and compensator with multi-purpose grease then lower the car to the ground.

Rear disc brake models

10 Remove both rear roadwheels then ensure that the handbrake is released fully.
11 From under the car tighten the handbrake cable adjusting nut at the cable compensator (photo 19.4) until the handbrake operating levers on both rear calipers just move off their stop pegs (Fig. 9.23).
12 Now slacken the handbrake adjusting nut two complete turns.
13 Using a screwdriver, pull the handbrake operating lever on the left-hand caliper so that the lever rests against its stop peg (Figs. 9.22 and 9.23). Hold the lever in this position and check that the operating lever on the right-hand caliper is also resting against its stop peg. if this is not the case, slacken the cable adjusting nut further until both levers rest against their stops.
14 Lubricate the adjusting nut threads and compensator with multi-purpose grease, refit the roadwheels and lower the car to the ground.

19.4 Handbrake cable adjusting nut (arrowed)

20 Handbrake lever – removal and refitting

1 Chock the front wheels, jack up the rear of the car and support it on stands. Release the handbrake.
2 From under the car, unscrew the handbrake cable adjusting nut (photo 19.4), remove the washer and slide the compensator off the adjusting rod.
3 From inside the car, slide up the gaiter to gain access to the lever mechanism.
4 Disconnect the warning light wiring at the lever switch.
5 Extract the circlip, withdraw the pivot bolt and remove the lever assembly.
6 If necessary. the ratchet may be dismantled by grinding off the rivet heads and removing the internal parts (Fig. 9.34).
7 Refitting is the reversal of removal, but lubricate the pivots and compensator with multi-purpose grease. Finally adjust the handbrake, as described in Section 19.

21 Handbrake cable – removal and refitting

1 Chock the front wheels, jack up the rear of the car and support it on stands. Remove the appropriate rear roadwheel then release the handbrake fully.
2 Slacken the handbrake cable adjusting nut at the cable compensator then remove the cable end from the compensator arm.
3 On models with rear drum brakes, remove the brake drum, as described in Section 7, slip the cable end off the brake shoe lever and withdraw the cable from the backplate.
4 On models with rear disc brakes, extract the clip securing the handbrake cable to the caliper body then release the cable end from the operating lever.
5 On all models, withdraw the cable and grommet from the trailing arm, release the retaining clips and wire loop then remove the cable from under the car.
6 Refitting is the reversal of removal, but adjust the cable as described in Section 19 on completion.

22 Vacuum servo unit – description and testing

1 The vacuum servo unit is located between the brake pedal and the master cylinder and provides assistance to the driver when the brake pedal is depressed. The unit operates by vacuum from the inlet manifold, and on some models, the vacuum is increased by incorporating a vacuum booster in the vacuum supply.
2 The unit basically comprises a diaphragm and non-return valve. With the brake pedal released, vacuum is channelled to both sides of the diaphram but when the pedal is depressed, one side is opened to the atmosphere. The resultant unequal pressures are harnessed to assist in depressing the master cylinder pistons.
3 Normally, the vacuum servo unit is very reliable, but if the unit becomes faulty, it should be renewed. In the event of a failure, the hydraulic system is in no way affected, except that higher pedal pressures will be necessary.
4 To test the vacuum servo unit, depress the brake pedal several times with the engine switched off to dissipate the vacuum. Apply moderate pressure to the brake pedal then start the engine. The pedal should move down slightly if the servo unit is operating correctly.

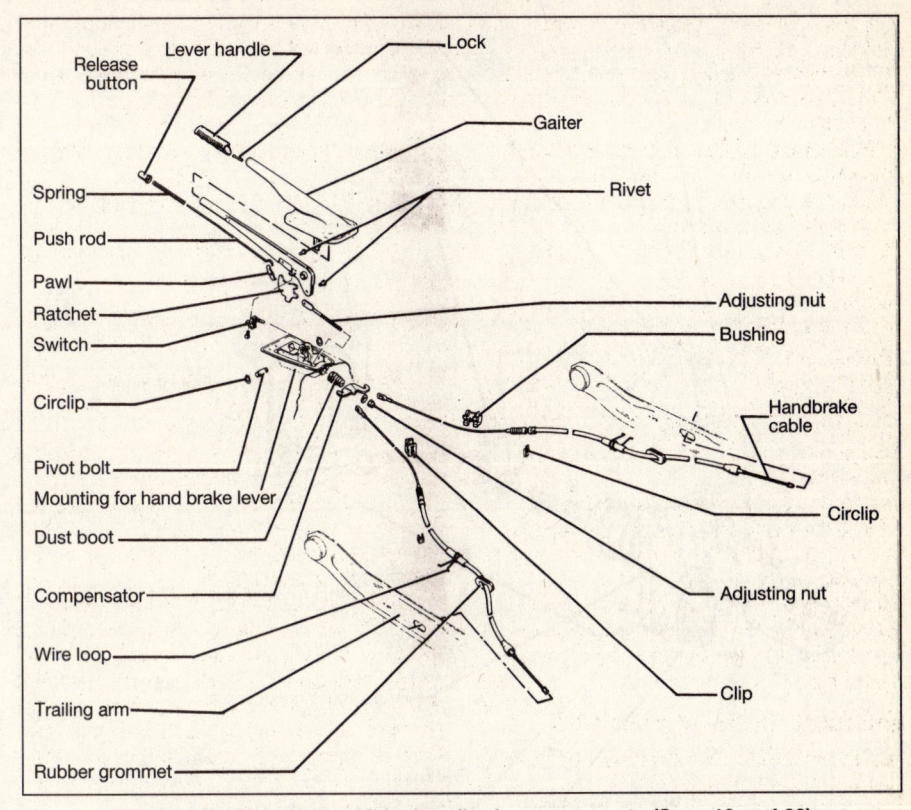

Fig. 9.34 Exploded view of the handbrake components (Secs 19 and 20)

23 Vacuum servo unit – removal and refitting

1 Remove the master cylinder, as described in Section 14.
2 Remove the parcel shelf (see Chapter 11, Section 23) to gain access to the pedal attachments.
3 Disconnect the servo pushrod from the brake pedal, but note in which of the two holes in the pushrod the clevis pin is inserted.
4 From within the engine compartment, pull the non-return valve and vacuum hose from the servo unit body.
5 Unscrew the mounting nuts and withdraw the servo unit from the bulkhead into the engine compartment.
6 Refitting is a reversal of removal. Tighten the mounting nuts to the specified torque and refit the master cylinder as described in Section 14.

24 Hydraulic servo unit – description and testing

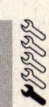

1 On models equipped with power-assisted steering a hydraulic servo unit is used to provide assistance to the driver when the brake pedal is depressed. The servo is located between the master cylinder and brake pedal and operated under hydraulic pressure from a pressure accumulator, generated by the power steering pump.
2 Normally the hydraulic servo unit is very reliable, but if the unit becomes faulty, renewal is necessary as repairs are not possible. In the event of failure the brake hydraulic system is in no way affected, except that higher pedal pressures will be necessarv.
3 To test the unit ensure that the engine is switched off then unscrew the return line union at the servo unit. With the return line disconnected it is normal for a few drops of oil to escape from the servo but if hydraulic oil escapes in a continuous flow, the unit is faulty and must be renewed.

9•16 Braking system

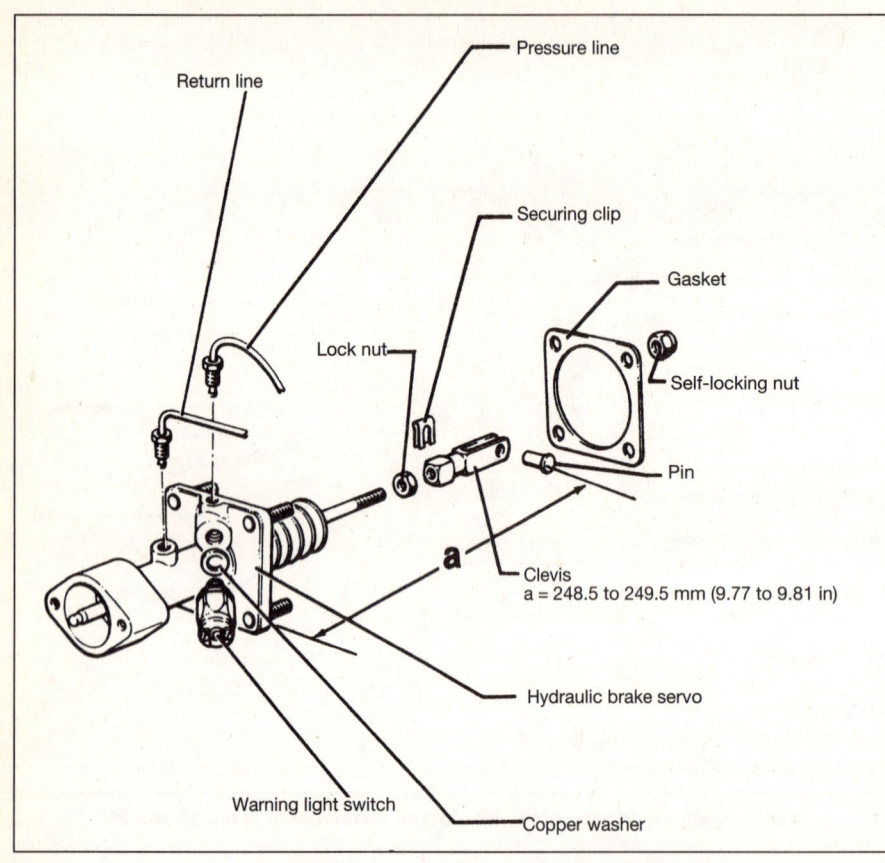

Fig. 9.35 Hydraulic servo unit mounting details (Sec 25)

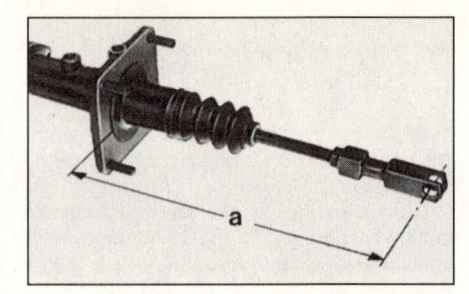

Fig. 9.36 Hydraulic servo pushrod setting dimension (Sec 25)

a = 248.5 to 249.5 mm (9.77 to 9.81 in)

25 Hydraulic servo unit – removal and refitting

1 With the engine switched off, depress the brake pedal approximately 20 times to exhaust the residual pressure in the system.
2 Remove the master cylinder, as described in Section 14.
3 Remove the parcel shelf (see Chapter 11, Section 23) to gain access to the pedal attachments.
4 Disconnect the wiring at the warning light switch.
5 Undo the two union nuts and withdraw the pressure line and return line from the servo unit.
6 From inside the car, disconnect the servo pushrod from the brake pedal and unscrew the four servo mounting nuts.
7 Withdraw the servo unit from the bulkhead into the engine compartment. Recover the flange gasket.
8 Refitting is a reversal of removal, but bear in mind the following points:
(a) Check the servo pushrod length, as shown in Fig. 9.36, and adjust if necessary by altering the position of the clevis on the threaded pushrod.
(b) Always use a new flange gasket and mounting nuts, and tighten the nuts to the specified torque.
(c) Refit the master cylinder as described in Section 14.
(d) After fitting, refer to Chapter 10 and bleed the power steering system.

26 Pressure accumulator – removal and refitting

1 With the engine switched off, depress the brake pedal approximately 20 times to exhaust the residual pressure in the system.
2 Wipe clean the area around the pressure line union on the side of the accumulator body (photo). Unscrew the union nut, withdraw the pipe and plug its end to prevent loss of hydraulic oil.
3 Unscrew the damper hose at the in-line pipe-to-hose union just below the power steering pump. Plug both hose ends.

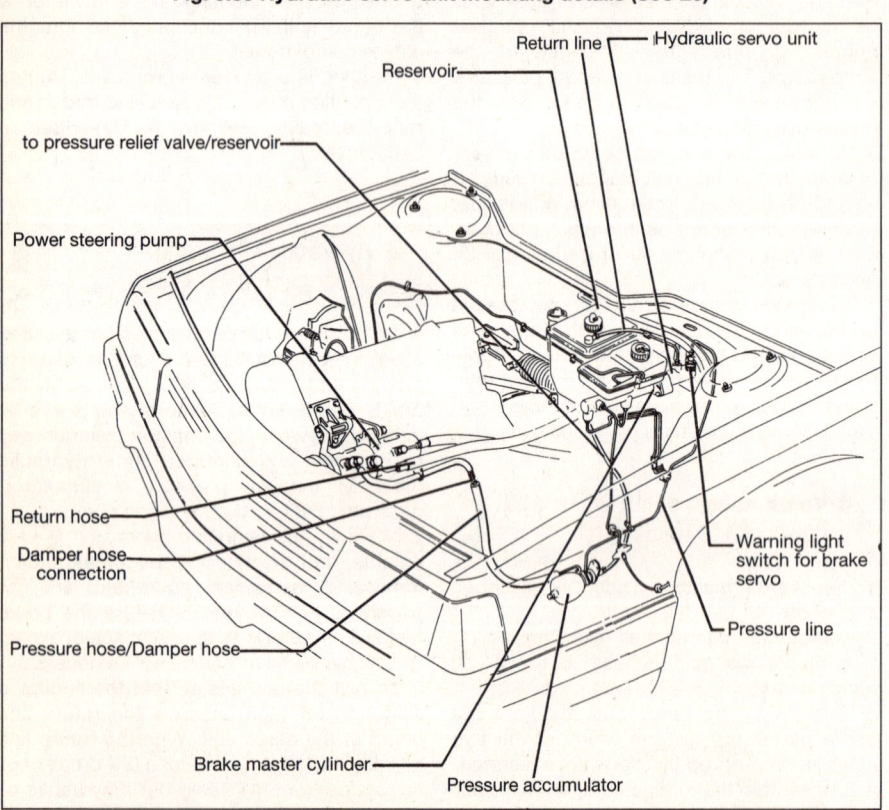

Fig. 9.37 Hydraulic servo unit and pressure accumulator layout (Secs 25 and 26)

Braking system 9•17

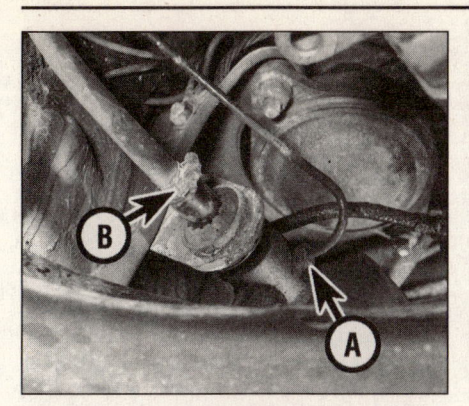

26.2 Pressure accumulator pressure line union (A) and return hose (B)

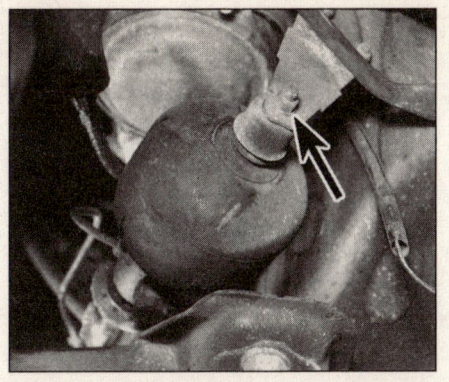

26.5 Pressure accumulator front mounting nut (arrowed)

4 Slacken the clamp and detach the return hose at the connection on the end of the accumulator. Plug the hose end.

5 Unscrew the two nuts securing the rear mounting bracket to the body and slacken the nut securing the front mounting to the bracket. Withdraw the accumulator from its mounting and remove it from the engine compartment (photo).

6 Refitting is the reverse sequence to removal, but refer to Chapter 10 and bleed the power steering system on completion. If the pressure accumulator has been renewed, render the old unit safe before discarding by drilling a 3 mm (0.12 in) hole in the accumulator body to release the pressure. Take great care when doing this and always wear safety glasses.

27 Anti-lock braking system – description and operation

Certain models covered by this manual are equipped with an anti-lock braking system (ABS) as standard or optional equipment. The system can be switched on or off under driver control and is used in conjunction with the normal braking system to provide greater stability, improved steering control and shorter stopping distances under all braking conditions. A brief description of the system operation is as follows.

Each wheel is provided with a wheel speed sensor which monitors the wheel rotational speed. The sensor consists of a magnetic core and coil and is mounted at a predetermined distance from a toothed rotor. The rotors for the front wheels are pressed onto the driveshaft outer constant velocity joints and the rotors for the rear wheels are pressed onto the rear hubs. When each hub turns it alters the magnetic field of the sensor thus inducing an alternating voltage, the frequency of which varies according to wheel speed.

Signals from the wheel speed sensors are sent to an electronic control unit which can accurately determine whether a wheel is accelerating or decelerating in relation to a reference speed. Information from the electronic control unit is sent to the hydraulic modulator which contains four solenoids, each operating one inlet and one exhaust valve for one brake, and all working independently of each other in three distinct phases:

Pressure build-up phase: The solenoid inlet valves are open and brake pressure from the master cylinder is applied directly to the brake calipers.

Constant pressure phase: The solenoid inlet and exhaust valves are closed and brake pressure at the calipers is maintained at a constant level even though master cylinder pressure may increase.

Pressure reduction phase: The solenoid inlet valve is closed to prevent further brake pressure reaching the caliper and, in addition, the exhaust valve is open to reduce existing pressure and release the brake. Fluid is returned to the master cylinder in this phase via the return pump in the hydraulic modulator.

The braking cycle for one wheel is therefore as follows and will be the same for all four wheels, although independently.

Wheel rotational speed is measured by the wheel speed sensors and processed by the electronic control unit. By comparing the signals received from each wheel the control unit can determine a reference speed, and detect any variation from this speed, which would indicate a locking brake. Should a lock-up condition be detected the control unit initiates the constant pressure phase and no further increase in brake pressure is applied to the affected brake. If the lock-up condition is still detected the pressure reduction phase is initiated to allow the wheel to turn. The control unit returns to the constant pressure phase until the wheel rotational speed exceeds a predetermined value then the cycle repeats with the control unit re-initiating the pressure build-up phase. This control cycle is continuously and rapidly repeated until the brake pedal is released or the car comes to a stop.

Additional circuitry within the electronic control unit monitors the functioning of the system and informs the driver of any fault condition by means of a warning light. Should a fault occur, the system switches off allowing normal braking, without ABS, to continue.

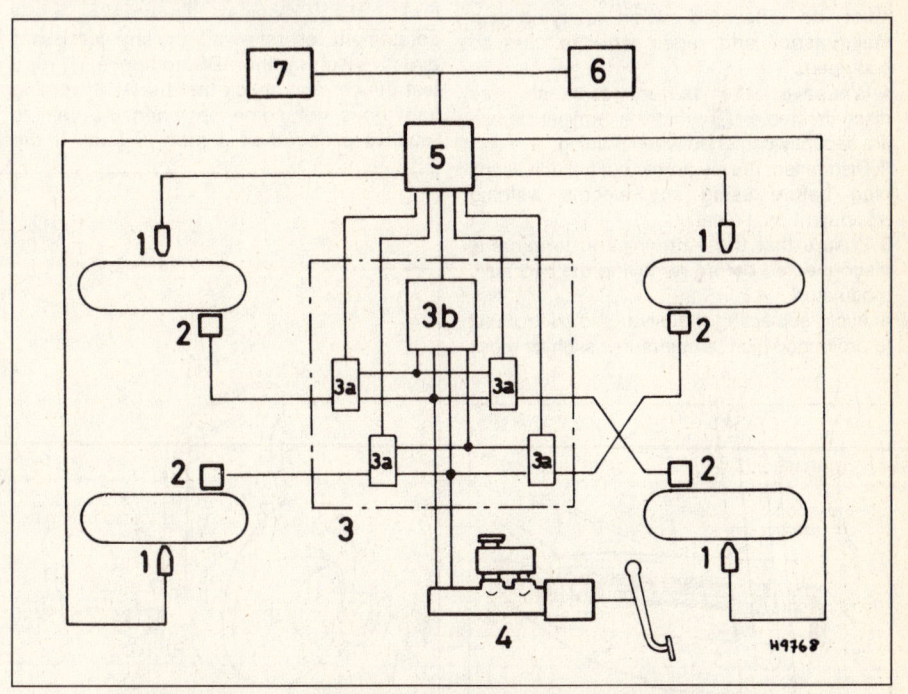

Fig. 9.38 Diagrammatic layout of the anti-lock braking system (Sec 27)

1 Wheel speed sensors
2 Brake calipers
3 Hydraulic modulator
3a Solenoid valves
3b Return pump
4 Brake master cylinder
5 Electronic control unit
6 Indicator light
7 ABS switch

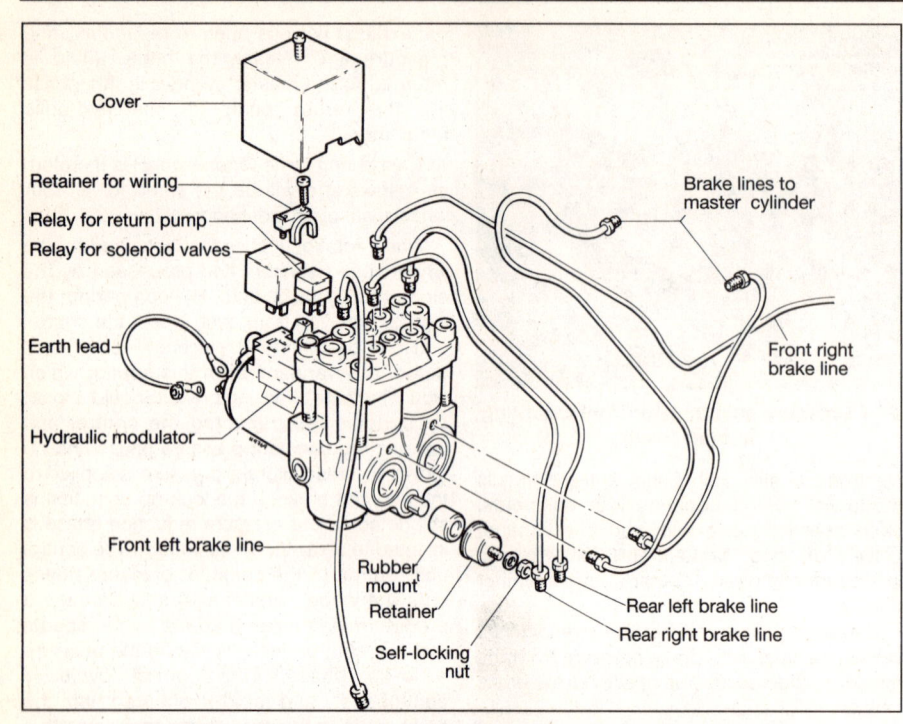

Fig. 9.39 Hydraulic modulator and related component details (Sec 29)

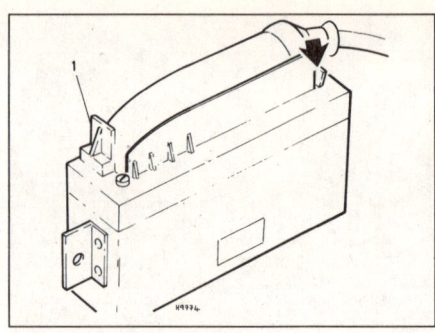

Fig. 9.40 Electronic control unit wiring plug spring tag (arrowed) and locating tab (1) (Sec 29)

28 Anti-lock braking system – precautions

Due to the complex nature of the anti-lock braking system the following precautions must be observed when carrying out maintenance and repair work to cars so equipped.
1 Whenever the battery terminals are disconnected ensure that the terminal clamps are securely tightened when refitting.
2 Disconnect the electronic control unit wiring plug before using any electric welding equipment on the car.
3 Ensure that the battery earth terminal is disconnected before removing the hydraulic modulator.
4 Avoid subjecting the electronic control unit to prolonged high temperatures such as those experienced in a paint spray oven. Maximum acceptable temperatures are 95°C (203°F) for very short periods or 85°C (185°F) for up to two hours.
5 After any general maintenance or simple repair operation such as brake pad renewal, brake disc renewal, handbrake cable adjustment or renewal, or any work not directly involving the ABS components, road test the car and check that the ABS warning light does not come on when the vehicle reaches a speed of 4 mph (6 kph). If the warning light illuminates there is a fault in the system and the advice of an Audi dealer should be sought.
6 If it is necessary to bleed the brake hydraulic system after a repair operation the system must be bled using a pressure bleeding device (see Section 17). It will also be necessary to have the complete system checked by a suitably equipped Audi dealer if the repair work involved disturbing any of the ABS components.

29 Anti-lock braking system components – removal and refitting

Note: *Before proceeding refer to Section 28*

Hydraulic modulator

1 Disconnect the battery earth terminal.
2 To remove the modulator control relays undo the screw and lift off the plastic cover. Remove the relays by pulling them out of their location. The large relay controls the solenoid valve operation and the small relay controls

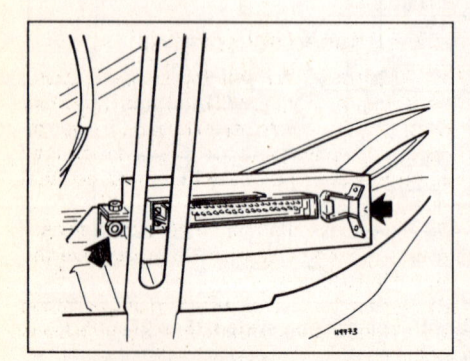

Fig. 9.41 Electronic control unit retaining screws – arrowed (Sec 29)

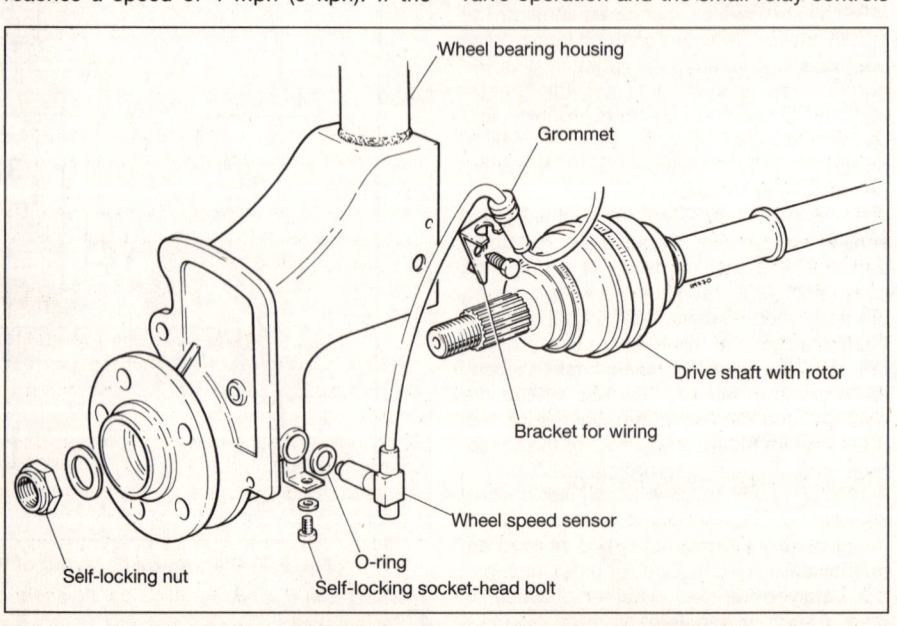

Fig. 9.42 Front wheel speed sensor mounting details (Sec 29)

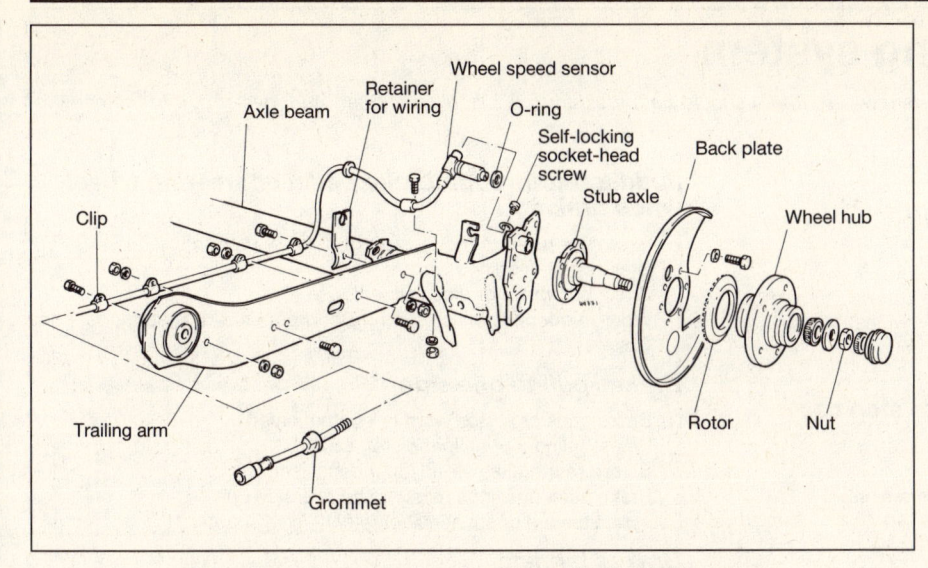

Fig. 9.43 Rear wheel speed sensor mounting details (Sec 29)

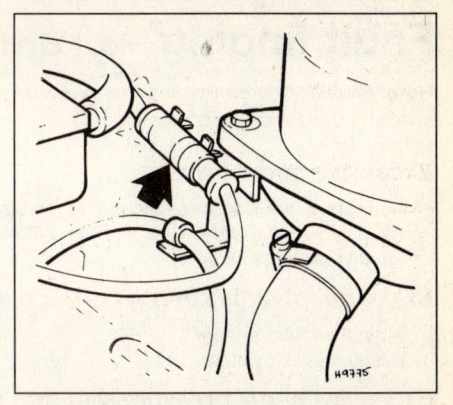

Fig. 9.44 Front wheel speed sensor wiring connector in engine compartment – arrowed (Sec 29)

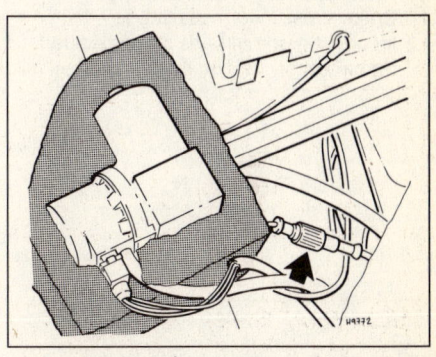

Fig. 9.45 Rear wheel speed sensor wiring connector (arrowed) under rear seat (Sec 29)

the return pump operation. Refitting is the reversal of removal.
3 To remove the complete modulator unit remove the relay cover, unscrew the cable clamp and disconnect the modulator wiring. Disconnect the earth lead on the modulator body.
4 Mark each brake pipe and its location as an aid to refitting. Unscrew each brake pipe union, withdraw the pipe and immediately plug its end and the modulator orifice.
5 Undo the modulator mounting nuts and retainers and remove the unit from its location. Do not attempt to dismantle the modulator as it is a sealed unit and no repairs are possible.
6 Refitting is the reverse sequence to removal. Bleed the hydraulic system with reference to Sections 17 and 28.

Electronic control unit

7 Disconnect the battery earth terminal.
8 Remove the rear seat, as described in Chapter 11. The control unit is located under the seat on the left-hand side.
9 Disconnect the control unit wiring plug by depressing the spring tag at the cable end. Lift the plug up at the cable end then disengage the tab at the other end.
10 Undo the retaining nuts and withdraw the control unit from its location.
11 Refitting is the reverse sequence to removal, but ensure that the wiring plug engages securely and with an audible click from the spring tag.

Front wheel speed sensor

12 Jack up the front of the car and support it on stands. Remove the appropriate front roadwheel.
13 Using an Allen key, undo the retaining bolt and withdraw the sensor from the front suspension strut.
14 Release the cable grommets from the support clips on the suspension strut and under the wheel arch.
15 From within the engine compartment, release the wiring connector from its holder and separate the connector. The left-hand connector is located just to the rear of the radiator expansion tank, and the right-hand connector is located behind the windscreen washer reservoir.
16 Pull the wiring through to the wheel arch and remove the speed sensor assembly.
17 Refitting is the reverse sequence to removal. When refitting the sensor to the suspension strut carefully push it in as far as it will go so that the tip just touches the rotor on the constant velocity joint. Hold the sensor in this position and tighten the retaining bolt. Ensure that all grommets are located in their support clips.

Rear wheel speed sensor

18 Jack up the rear of the car and support it on stands. Remove the appropriate rear roadwheel.
19 Press the handbrake cable spacer off the rear axle flange to gain access to the sensor.
20 Using an Allen key, undo the retaining bolt and withdraw the sensor from the rear axle flange.
21 Undo the retaining bolts and release the sensor wiring harness from the trailing arm.
22 Remove the rear seat, as described in Chapter 11.
23 Locate the sensor wiring harness connectors, situated in the well beneath the rear seat and separate the connectors. If working on the right-hand side connector, it will also be necessary to carefully move aside the underseat padding and the pump assembly for the central door locking system to gain access to the connector.
24 Release the grommets and pull the wiring through the floor then remove the sensor from under the car.
25 Before refitting the wheel speed sensor check and, if necessary, adjust the rear hub bearing play, as described in Chapter 10. Also obtain a new sensor O-ring seal.
26 Refitting is the reverse sequence to removal. Coat the sensor all round with brake cylinder paste then push it into its location as far as it will go so that the tip just touches the rotor on the rear hub. Hold the sensor in this position and tighten the retaining bolt. Ensure that all wiring clips and grommets are correctly located on the trailing arm and in the floor panel.

Wheel speed sensor rotor

27 The rotors for the front wheel speed sensors are an integral part of the driveshaft outer constant velocity joint and cannot be renewed separately. If the rotor is in any way unserviceable a new outer joint must be fitted (see Chapter 8).
28 To remove the rear wheel speed sensor rotors, refer to Chapter 10 and remove the rear hub assembly.
29 Mount the hub in a vice and knock off the rotor using a punch inserted through the holes in the hub.
30 Press on a new rotor then refit the hub assembly, as described in Chapter 10.

Fault finding – braking system

Note: *Fault finding on the anti-lock braking system (where fitted) should be entrusted to a suitably equipped Audi dealer due to the need for special gauges and test equipment*

Excessive pedal travel
- [ ] Rear brake self-adjust mechanism inoperative
- [ ] Air in hydraulic system
- [ ] Faulty master cylinder

Brake pedal feels spongy
- [ ] Air in hydraulic system
- [ ] Faulty master cylinder

Excessive pedal pressure required to stop car
- [ ] Faulty servo unit
- [ ] Wheel cylinder(s) or caliper piston seized
- [ ] Brake pads or brake shoe linings worn or contaminated
- [ ] Brake shoes incorrectly fitted
- [ ] Incorrect grade of pads or linings fitted
- [ ] Primary or secondary hydraulic circuit failure

Judder felt through brake pedal or steering wheel when braking
- [ ] Excessive run-out or distortion of discs or rear drums
- [ ] Brake pads or linings worn
- [ ] Brake backplate or disc caliper loose
- [ ] Wear in suspension or steering components or mountings – see Chapter 10

Brakes pull to one side
- [ ] Brake pads or linings worn or contaminated
- [ ] Wheel cylinder or caliper piston seized
- [ ] Seized rear brake self-adjust mechanism
- [ ] Brake pads or linings renewed on one side only
- [ ] Tyre, steering or suspension defect – see Chapter 10

Brakes binding
- [ ] Wheel cylinder or caliper piston seized
- [ ] Handbrake incorrectly adjusted
- [ ] Faulty master cylinder

Chapter 10 Suspension and steering

For modifications, and information applicable to later models, see Supplement at end of manual

Contents

Anti-roll bar – removal and refitting 6
Fault finding – suspension and steering .... See end of Chapter
Front hub bearings – removal and refitting 5
Front suspension strut – dismantling and reassembly 4
Front suspension strut – removal and refitting 3
Front track control arm – removal and refitting 7
Front wheel alignment and steering angles 29
General description 1
Maintenance and inspection 2
Panhard rod – removal, overhaul and refitting 11
Power-assisted steering gear – bleeding 25
Power-assisted steering gear – checking for leaks 26
Power-assisted steering pump – removal and refitting 28
Power-assisted steering pump drivebelt – removal, refitting
  and adjustment 27
Rear axle – removal and refitting 8
Rear hub bearings – removal, refitting and adjustment 12
Rear suspension strut/shock absorber – dismantling and
  reassembly 10
Rear suspension strut/shock absorber – removal and refitting 9
Self-levelling suspension – general description 13
Self-levelling suspension regulator valve – linkage adjustment 15
Self-levelling suspension regulator valve – testing 14
Self-levelling suspension reservoirs – removal and refitting 17
Self-levelling suspension strut units – removal and refitting 16
Steering column – removal, overhaul and refitting 19
Steering damper – testing, removal and refitting 22
Steering gear – adjustment 24
Steering gear – removal and refitting 21
Steering gear gaiter – renewal 23
Steering wheel – removal and refitting 18
Tie-rod – removal and refitting 20
Wheels and tyres – general care and maintenance 30

Degrees of difficulty

| **Easy,** suitable for novice with little experience | **Fairly easy,** suitable for beginner with some experience | **Fairly difficult,** suitable for competent DIY mechanic | **Difficult,** suitable for experienced DIY mechanic | **Very difficult,** suitable for expert DIY or professional |

Specifications

Front suspension
Type .... Independent, with coil spring struts incorporating telescopic shock absorbers, lower track control arm and anti-roll bar

Rear suspension
Type .... Transverse torsion axle incorporating trailing arms, Panhard rod and coil spring struts with telescopic shock absorbers. Self-levelling facility fitted to certain models

Steering
Type .... Manual or power-assisted rack-and-pinion. Steering damper fined to manual steering models

Front wheel alignment
Toe setting .... 0° +5' (toe-in) –10' (toe-out)
Camber .... – 30' ± 30'
Maximum camber difference between sides .... 30'
Castor:
  Manual steering models .... – 15' ± 40'
  Power-assisted steering models without self-levelling suspension .. +50' ± 40'
  Power-assisted steering models with self-levelling suspension .... + 1°5' ± 40'
Maximum castor difference between sides .... 1°

Rear wheel alignment
Camber .... – 40' ± 30'
Maximum camber difference between sides .... 30'
Toe setting at each wheel:
  Up to Chassis No EA 085 288 or EA 082 448 .... +15' ± 10' (toe-in)
  All other models .... +10' ± 5' (toe-in)

10•2 Suspension and steering

Wheels
Type .... Pressed steel or light alloy
Size .... 51/2J x 14, 6J x 14, 6J x 15

Tyres
Size .... 165 SR 14, 185/70 SR 14, 185/70 HR 14, 205/60 VR 15
Pressures .... Refer to handbook or pressure data sticker inside fuel tank flap for pressures according to model and territory

Power-assisted steering fluid type/specification ..... VW/Audi hydraulic oil G 002 000

Torque wrench settings

	Nm	lbf ft
Front suspension		
Strut upper mounting and bearing plate nuts*	30	22
Strut piston retaining nut*	60	44
Shock absorber screw cap	180	133
Suspension balljoint to strut	65	48
Track control arm to subframe	85	63
Subframe mounting to subframe	20	15
Subframe mounting to body	110	81
Anti-roll bar to track control arm	110	81
Rear suspension		
Panhard rod*	90	66
Trailing arm to body	95	70
Shock absorber to rear axle*	90	66
Shock absorber to body	20	15
Shock absorber upper retaining nut	20	15
Stub axle to rear axle	30	22
Self-levelling suspension linkage nuts	10	7
Self-levelling suspension reservoir	20	15
Steering		
Steering wheel retaining nut	40	30
Flange tube to steering gear pinion	25	18
Steering column clamp to safety bracket	35	26
Steering gear to body	25	18
Damper to steering gear and body	40	30
Tie-rods to steering gear and suspension strut	60	44
Tie-rod adjuster locknuts	40	30
Power-assisted steering pump mounting and adjustment nuts:		
Four-cylinder engine	25	18
Five-cylinder engine	20	15
Power-assisted steering pump pulley nuts (four-cylinder engine)	20	15
Wheels		
Wheel bolts	110	81

*Use new nuts every time

1 General description

The front suspension is of independent type, incorporating coil spring struts and lower track control arm. The struts are fitted with telescopic shock absorbers, and both front suspension units are mounted on a subframe. An anti-roll bar is fitted to the track control arms and also provides fore and aft location of each strut assembly.

The rear suspension comprises a transverse torsion axle with trailing arms rubber bushed to the body. The axle is attached to the lower ends of the rear shock absorber which act as struts, since they incorporate mountings for the coil springs. Side-to-side movement of the axle is controlled by a Panhard rod. A self-levelling system is used on certain models which utilizes gas and hydraulic pressure acting on the rear struts to keep the car at the same height irrespective of load.

The steering is of rack and pinion type mounted on the engine compartment bulkhead. The tie-rods are attached centrally to a common bracket which is itself bolted to the steering rack. Power assistance is used on certain models and a steering damper is used on those versions with manual steering.

2 Maintenance and inspection

1 At the intervals given in Routine Maintenance at the beginning of this manual a thorough inspection of all suspension and steering components should be carried out using the following procedure as a guide.

Front suspension and steering

2 Apply the handbrake, jack up the front of the car and support it securely on axle stands.
3 Visually inspect the lower balljoint dust covers and the steering rack and pinion gaiters for splits, chafing, or deterioration. If the balljoint dust covers are damaged they can be renewed separately, as described in Section 7. If the rack-and-pinion gaiters require attention, refer to Section 23.
4 Grasp the roadwheel at the 12 o'clock and 6 o'clock positions and try to rock it. Very slight free play may be felt, but if the movement is appreciable further investigation is necessary to determine the source. Continue rocking the wheel while an assistant depresses the footbrake. If the movement is

Suspension and steering 10•3

2.8A Fill the reservoir with hydraulic oil up to the MAX mark (arrowed) . . .

2.8B . . . through the reservoir filler neck

now eliminated or significantly reduced, it is likely that the hub bearings are at fault. If the free play is still evident with the footbrake depressed, then there is wear in the suspension joints or mountings. Pay close attention to the lower balljoint and track control arm mounting bushes. Renew any worn components. as described in the appropriate Sections of this Chapter.

5 Now grasp the wheel at the 9 o'clock and 3 o'clock positions and try to rock it as before. Any movement felt now may again be caused by wear in the hub bearings or the steering tie-rod inner or outer balljoints. If the movement is eliminated with the footbrake depressed
 the tie-rod joints are suspect. Removal and refitting of the tie-rod assemblies is described in Section 20.

6 Using a large screwdriver or flat bar check for wear in the anti-roll bar mountings and track control arm mountings by carefully levering against these components. Some movement is to be expected, as the mountings are made of rubber, but excessive wear should be obvious. Renew any bushes that are worn.

7 With the car standing on its wheels. have an assistant turn the steering wheel back and forth about one eighth of a turn each way. There should be no lost movement whatever between the steering wheel and roadwheels. If this is not the case, closely observe the joints and mountings previously described, but in addition check the steering column

joints for wear and also the rack-and-pinion steering gear itself. Any wear should be visually apparent and must be rectified, as described in the appropriate Sections of this Chapter.

8 On models equipped with power-assisted steering, check the hydraulic oil level in the reservoir. Carry out this check with the vehicle unladen and with the engine running and the steering in the straight-ahead position. If necessary add the specified hydraulic oil, to bring the level up to the MAX mark (photo). Check the condition of the power steering pump drivebelt and renew it or adjust its tension, where necessary, as described in Section 27.

Rear suspension

9 Chock the front wheels, jack up the rear of the car and support it securely on axle stands.
10 Visually inspect the rear suspension components, attachments and linkages for any visible signs of wear or damage.
11 Grasp the roadwheel at the 12 o'clock and 6 o'clock positions and try to rock it. Any excess movement here indicates maladjusted hub bearings which should be checked, as described in Section 12.

Wheels and tyres

12 Carefully inspect each tyre, including the spare, for signs of uneven wear, lumps, bulges or damage to the sidewalls or tread face. Refer to Section 30 for further details.
13 Check the condition of the wheel rims for distortion, damage and excessive run-out. Also make sure that the balance weights are secure with no obvious signs that any are missing. Check the torque of the wheel bolts and check the tyre pressures.

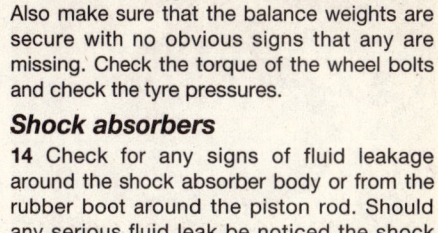

Shock absorbers

14 Check for any signs of fluid leakage around the shock absorber body or from the rubber boot around the piston rod. Should any serious fluid leak be noticed the shock absorber is defective internally and renewal is necessary.
15 The efficiency of the shock absorber may be checked by bouncing the car at each corner. Generally speaking the body will return to its normal position and stop after being depressed. If it rises and returns on a rebound, the shock absorber is probably suspect. Examine also the shock absorber upper and lower mountings for any sign of wear. Renewal procedures are contained in Sections 4 and 10.

3 Front suspension strut – removal and refitting

1 Remove the wheel trim, then unscrew the driveshaft retaining nut. This is tightened to a very high torque and no attempt to loosen it must be made unless the full weight of the car is on its roadwheels.
2 Loosen the four roadwheel retaining bolts.
3 Jack up the front of the car and securely support it on stands. Remove the roadwheel.
4 Remove the brake caliper and carrier bracket, with reference to Chapter 9, but do not disconnect the hydraulic hose. Support the caliper without straining the hose.
5 Detach the brake pad wear warning light wire from the strut (photo) and, where fitted, the wheel speed sensor and wiring for the anti-lock braking system (see Chapter 9).
6 Unscrew and remove the suspension balljoint clamp bolt and nut (photo) noting that its head faces rearwards.
7 Using a balljoint separator tool, as described in Section 20, unscrew the nut and disconnect the tie-rod end from the suspension strut.
8 Unscrew the driveshaft nut then lever the

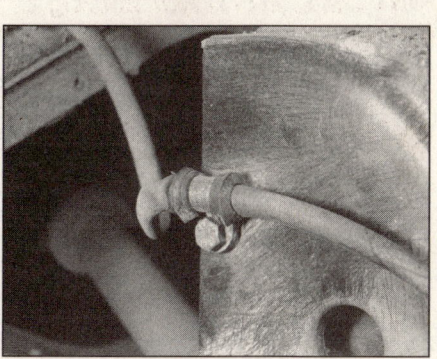

3.5 Brake pad warning light wire attachment on front strut

3.6 Remove the suspension balljoint clamp bolt and nut (arrowed)

Fig. 10.1 Levering the track control arm down to release the balljoint from the strut (Sec 3)

10•4 Suspension and steering

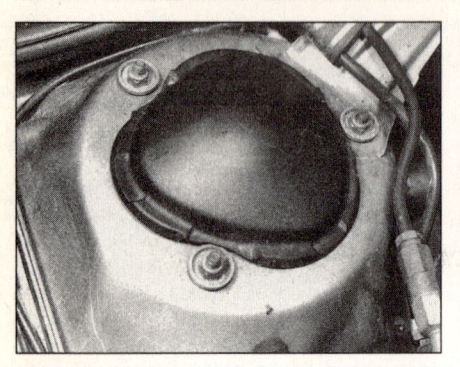

3.10 Lift off the cover over the strut upper mounting . . .

3.11 . . . then unscrew the strut upper mounting retaining nuts (arrowed)

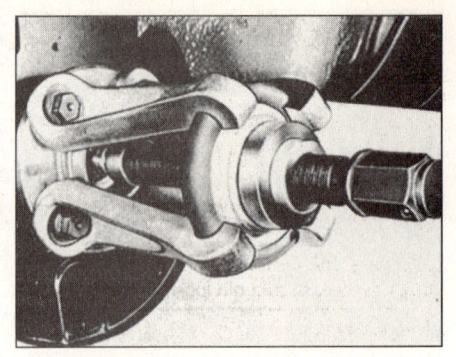

Fig. 10.2 Using a puller to release the driveshaft from the hub (Sec 3)

track control arm down to release the balljoint from the strut.
9 Attach a suitable puller to the front hub using the roadwheel retaining bolts and press the driveshaft out of the hub assembly.
10 From within the engine compartment, lift off the plastic cover over the strut upper mounting (photo).
11 Support the suspension strut from below and unscrew the three outer nuts securing the strut upper mounting to the body (photo).
12 Lower the strut and remove it from under the wheel arch.
13 Refitting is the reverse sequence to removal. Refer to Chapter 8 when installing the driveshaft, and Chapter 9 when installing the brake caliper. Tighten all nuts and bolts to the specified torque. If the strut has been dismantled the front camber angle must be checked, as described in Section 29.

4 Front suspension strut – dismantling and reassembly

Refer to Chapter 13, Section 12

1 Do not attempt to dismantle the suspension strut unless a spring compressor has been fitted over the coils of the spring. If such a tool is not available take the strut to a suitably equipped garage for dismantling.
2 With the spring compressor in place on the spring, mount the strut assembly in a vice.
3 Compress the spring until the upper spring retainer is free of tension then remove the nut and washer from the top of the piston.
4 Pull off the bearing plate, complete with strut bearing, upper spring retainer, protective ring and damping ring. **Do not** loosen the nuts securing the strut mounting to the bearing plate, otherwise the camber setting will be lost.
5 With the compressor still in place, remove the spring, boot and cover, followed by the bump stop.
6 Unscrew and remove the screw cap which retains the shock absorber in the suspension strut and pull out the shock absorber.
7 With the shock absorber removed, examine it for oil leaks and obvious signs of damage. Hold the shock absorber vertically and check its operation by pulling the piston rod out fully, then push it in fully by hand several times. Resistance should be even and the movement smooth over the entire stroke. If a shock

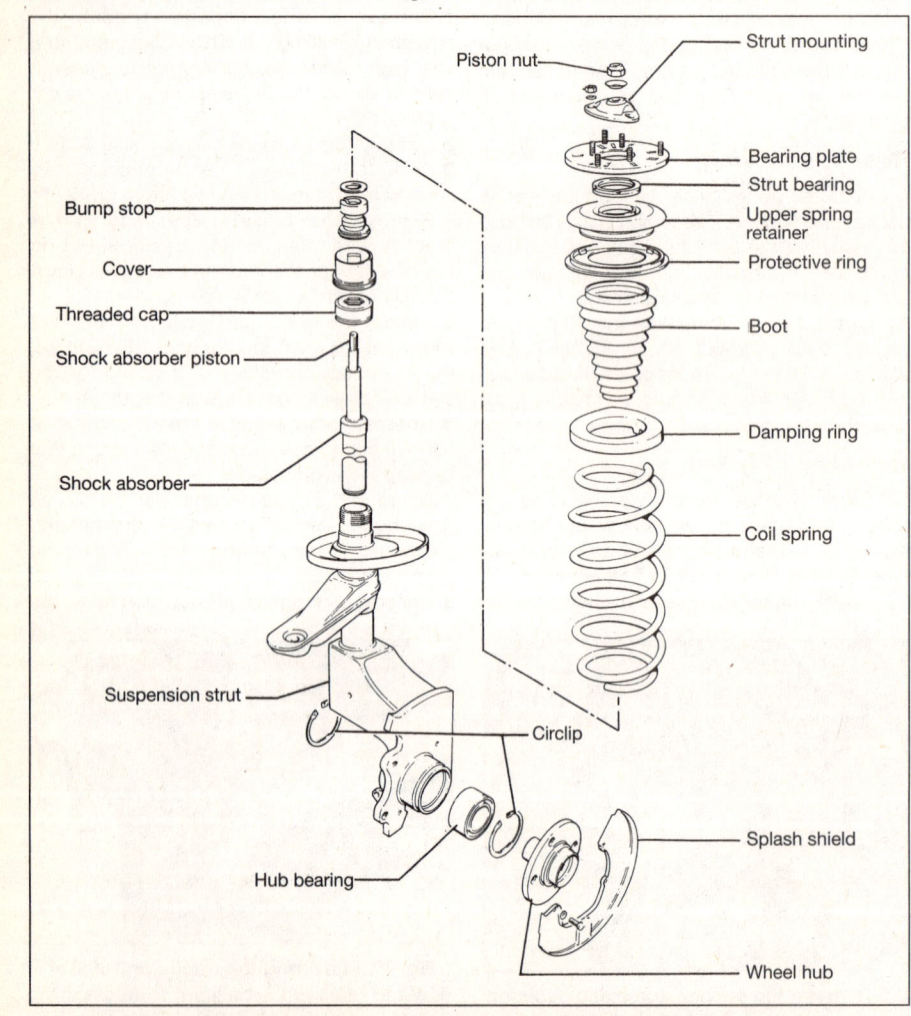

Fig. 10.3 Exploded view of the front suspension strut and hub bearings (Secs 3, 4 and 5)

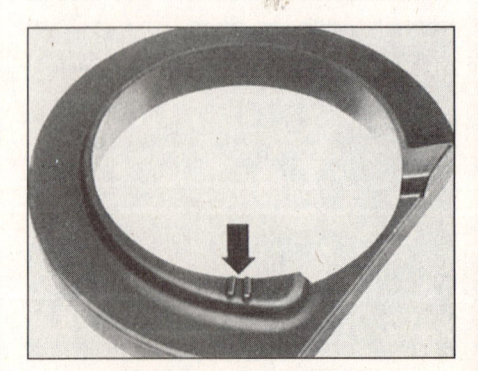

Fig. 10.4 Damping ring identification projections – arrowed (Sec 4)

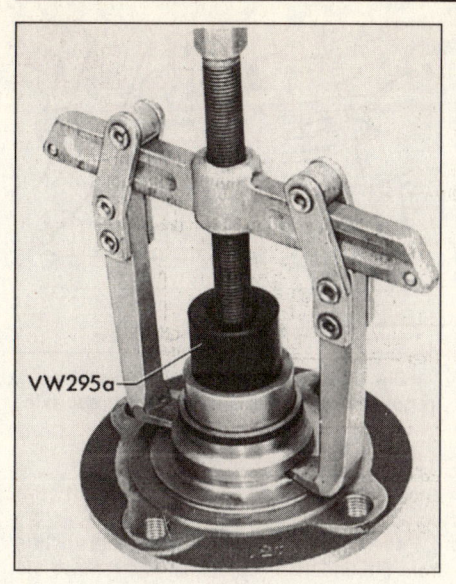

Suspension and steering 10•5

Fig. 10.5 Using a puller to remove the hub bearing inner race (Sec 5)

6.2 Anti-roll bar bracket attachments (arrowed) . . .

6.3 . . . and end mounting at track control arm (arrowed)

absorber has not been in use for a long time, it may require pumping up and down several times before it becomes effective.

8 If there has been excessive leakage of oil from the shock absorber it may be ineffective on the rebound stroke, but if there is only a slight oil seepage it may be refitted.

9 Clean out the bore of the suspension strut before fitting the shock absorber, so that the shock absorber slides in easily. Do not drive the shock absorber into the strut.

10 Refit the screw cap and tighten to the specified torque.

11 Reassemble the spring and mounting using a reversal of the dismantling procedure. If a new damping ring is being fitted note that the underside of the ring has either one, two or three projections moulded in which denote the ring thickness (Fig. 10.4). Ensure that the new ring has the same number of projections as the old one unless the spring has been changed, or there is a difference in ride height between the right and left-hand sides of the car which is being corrected.

5 Front hub bearings – removal and refitting

1 Remove the front suspension strut, as described in Section 3.
2 Remove the brake disc from the hub.
3 Remove the screws and withdraw the splash guard.
4 Support the suspension strut with the hub facing downward, and press or drive out the hub using a suitable mandrel. The bearing inner race will remain on the hub, and therefore, once removed, it is not possible to re-use the bearing. Use a puller to remove the inner race from the hub.
5 Extract the circlips, then, while supporting the suspension strut press or drive out the bearing, using a mandrel on the outer race.
6 Clean the recess in the housing, then smear it with a little general purpose grease.
7 Fit the outer circlip, then support the strut and press or drive in the new bearing, using a metal tube *on the outer race only*.
8 Fit the inner circlip making sure that it is correctly seated.
9 Position the hub with its bearing shoulder facing upward, then press or drive on the bearing and housing, using a metal tube *on the inner race only*.
10 Refit the splash guard and brake disc, then refit the front suspension strut, as described in Section 3.

6 Anti-roll bar – removal and refitting

1 If the anti-roll bar is distorted, or damaged, it must not be straightened, but a new one must be fitted.
2 Remove the two bolts from each of the two brackets which secure the anti-roll bar to the subframe and remove the brackets (photo).
3 Remove the nut and washer from each end of the anti-roll bar (photo).
4 Bounce the front suspension up and down with the vehicle standing on its wheels, at the same time pulling the anti-roll bar out of the bushes on the track control arms.

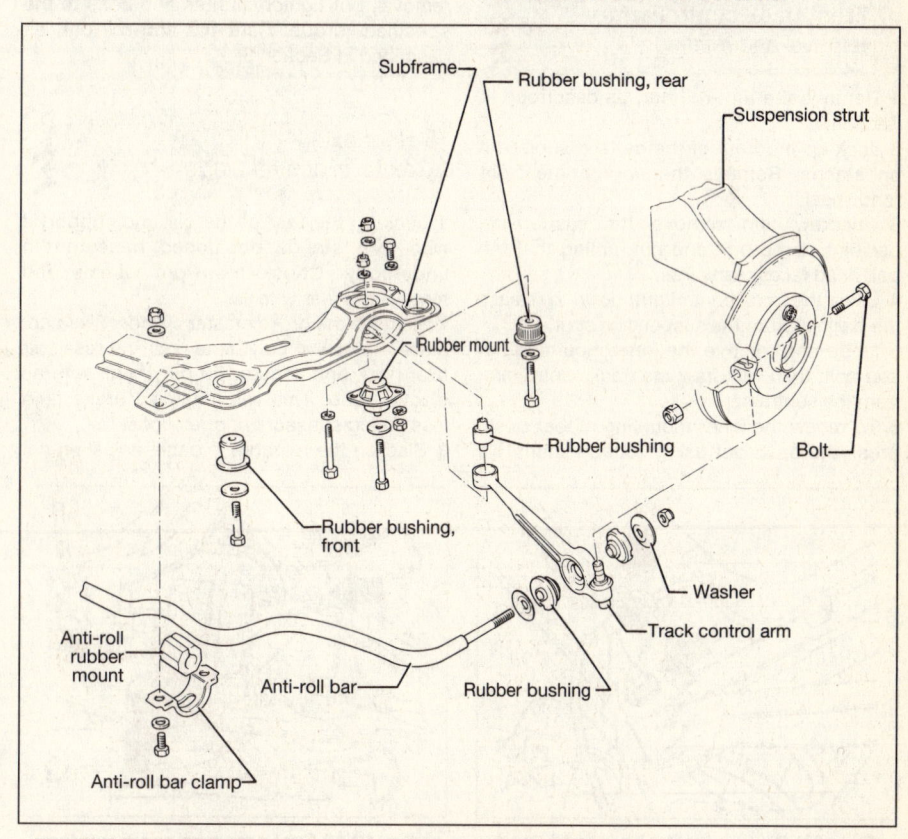

Fig. 10.6 Exploded view of the anti-roll bar, track control arm and subframe mountings (Secs 6 and 7)

10•6 Suspension and steering

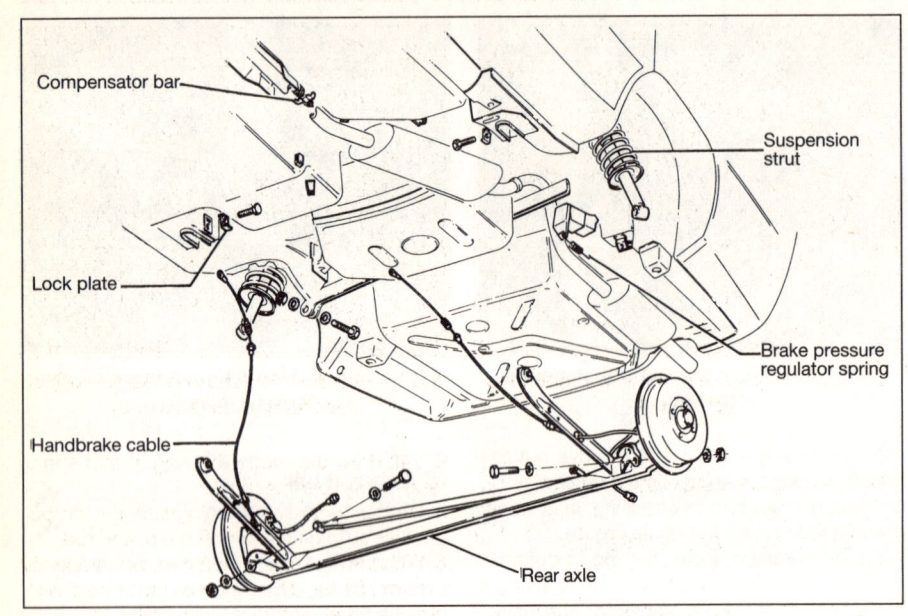

Fig. 10.7 Rear axle removal details (Sec 8)

Compensator bar
Suspension strut
Lock plate
Brake pressure regulator spring
Handbrake cable
Rear axle

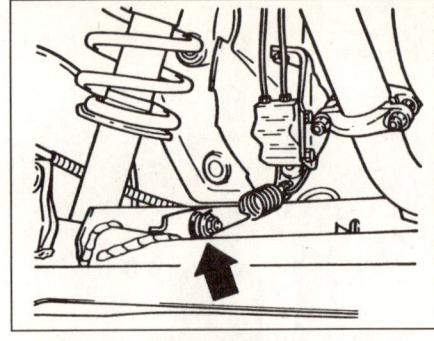

Fig. 10.8 Detach the brake pressure regulator spring (arrowed) at the rear axle (Sec 8)

5 Refitting is the reverse of removal. The front suspension should be bounced up and down while inserting the anti-roll bar into the bushes of the track control arms. Tighten the mountings to the specified torque.

7 Front track control arm – removal and refitting

1 Remove the anti-roll bar, as described in Section 6.
2 Jack up the front of the car and support it on stands. Remove the appropriate front roadwheel.
3 Unscrew and remove the suspension balljoint clamp bolt and nut, noting that the bolt head faces rearwards.
4 Lever the track control arm down to release the balljoint from the suspension strut.
5 Undo and remove the inner mounting nut and bolt, then withdraw the track control arm from the subframe.
6 To renew the inner mounting rubber bush, press the bush out using suitable mandrels and press in a new bush until flush. The outer balljoint is an integral part of the track control arm and if worn a new arm must be obtained. The dust cover may, however, be obtained separately.
7 Refitting is the reverse sequence to removal, but tighten all nuts and bolts to the specified torque. Refit the anti-roll bar, as described in Section 6.

8 Rear axle – removal and refitting

1 Jack up the rear of the car and support it with axle stands positioned beneath the underbody. Chock the front wheels and remove the rear wheels.
2 Remove the brake master cylinder filler cap, place a piece of polythene over the reservoir filler neck and secure the polythene with an elastic band. This will minimise brake fluid loss during subsequent operations.
3 Slacken the handbrake cable adjusting nut and slip the two cable ends off the compensator.
4 Prise the handbrake cable guide bushes from the underbody brackets and remove the cables from the rear brackets.
5 Unhook the brake pressure regulator spring from the rear axle.
6 Disconnect both rear flexible brake hoses at their unions with the rigid brake pipes. Plug the pipes and hoses after disconnection.
7 On cars fitted with an anti-lock braking system, remove the rear wheel speed sensors and wiring from the rear axle and trailing arms, as described in Chapter 9.
8 On cars equipped with self-levelling suspension, disconnect the regulator valve linkage at the rear axle.
9 Unscrew the two nuts and move the fuel pressure accumulator with mounting bracket to one side (where fitted). Do not disconnect the fuel lines at the accumulator.
10 Loosen the nuts on the pivot bolts at the front of the trailing arms (photo).
11 Unbolt the Panhard rod from the rear axle.
12 Support the rear axle with a trolley jack, and place axle stands beneath the trailing arms.
13 Unscrew and remove the rear shock absorber lower mounting bolts.
14 Unscrew the nuts and remove the pivot bolts from the trailing arms.
15 With the help of an assistant, if necessary, lower the rear axle to the ground.

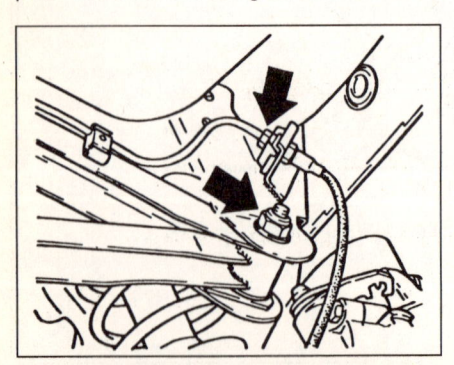

Fig. 10.9 Brake pipe-to-hose union and Panhard rod mounting – arrowed (Sec 8)

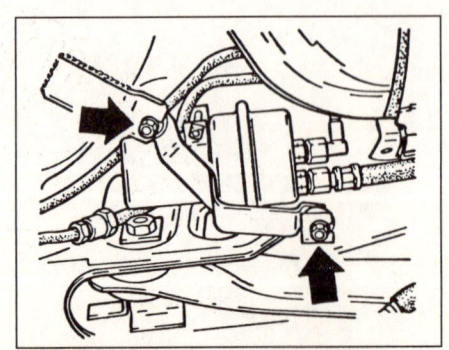

Fig. 10.10 Fuel pressure accumulator mounting nuts – arrowed (Sec 8)

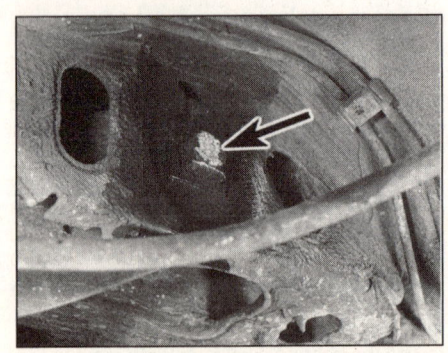

8.10 Trailing arm pivot bolt location (arrowed)

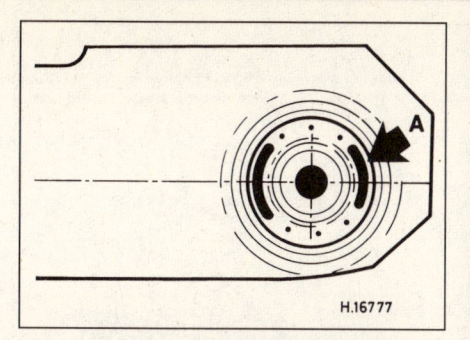

Suspension and steering 10•7

Fig. 10.11 Correct positioning of trailing arm pivot bush with larger gap (A) towards the front (Sec 8)

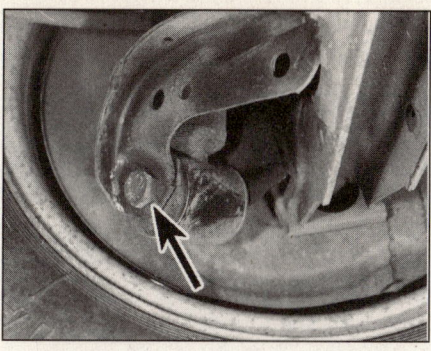

9.4 Strut/shock absorber lower mounting (arrowed)

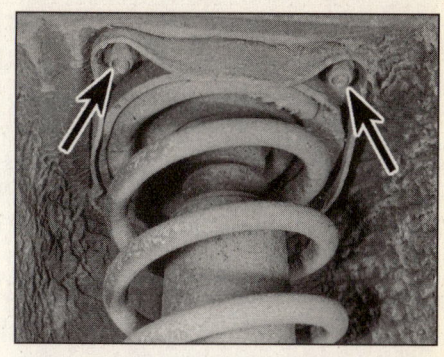

9.5 Two of the strut/shock absorber upper mounting nuts (arrowed)

16 If necessary, remove the stub axles, also remove the brake lines and handbrake cables, if required. The pivot bushes may be renewed using a long bolt and nut, metal tube, and packing washers, but make sure that the bush gaps are in line with the trailing arms and with the larger bush gap at the front, then press the bushes in flush.
17 Refitting is a reversal of removal, but delay tightening the rear axle, shock absorber and Panhard rod mounting bolts until the weight of the car is on the suspension. Bleed the hydraulic system and adjust the handbrake cable, as described in Chapter 9.

9 Rear suspension strut/shock absorber – removal and refitting

1 Jack up the rear of the car and support it on stands. Chock the front wheels and remove the appropriate rear wheel.
2 Place a jack beneath the rear axle on the side being worked on and just take the weight of the axle.
3 On cars with self-levelling suspension locate the three-way connector in the hydraulic pressure line to the rear suspension reservoirs (Fig. 10.20). Attach a suitable hose to the bleed screw on the three-way connector and place the other end of the hose in a container. Open the bleed screw to release the pressure then close it again and remove the hose. Disconnect the hydraulic pipe union at the strut unit.
4 Unscrew the nut and remove the bolt securing the shock absorber lower mounting (photo).
5 Undo the three upper mounting nuts and remove the suspension strut/shock absorber from under the wheel arch (photo).
6 Refitting is the reverse sequence to removal, but tighten all nuts and bolts to the specified torque. On cars with self-levelling suspension, top up the power steering reservoir to the MAX mark with the engine running and the steering in the straight-ahead position. If, however, the reservoir was allowed to run dry when the strut was removed, refer to Section 25 for filling and bleeding procedures.

10 Rear suspension strut/shock absorber – dismantling and reassembly

1 Do not attempt to dismantle the suspension strut unless a spring compressor has been fitted over the coils of the spring. If such a tool is not available take the strut to a suitably equipped garage for dismantling.
2 With the spring compressor in place on the spring, mount the strut assembly in a vice.
3 Compress the spring until the upper spring retainer is free of tension, then hold the piston rod and unscrew the upper self-locking retaining nut.
4 Withdraw the rubber bearing, upper spring retainer and damper ring.
5 On cars with self-levelling suspension pull the hydraulic connector off the piston rod.
6 Withdraw the spring, with the compressor still in place, followed by the bump stop and sleeve, protection cap and lower spring retainer.
7 With the shock absorber removed, examine it for oil leaks and obvious signs of damage. Hold the shock absorber vertically and check its operation by pulling the piston rod out fully, then push it in fully by hand several times. Resistance should be even and the movement smooth over the entire stroke. If a shock absorber has not been in use for a long time, it may require pumping up and down several times before it becomes effective.

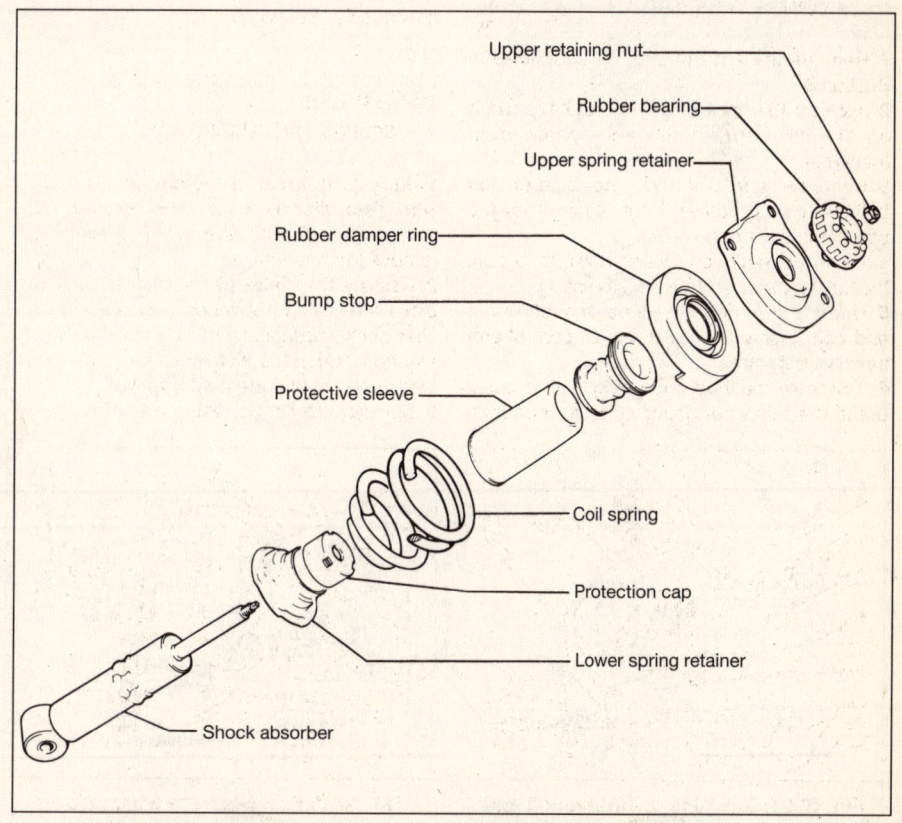

Fig. 10.12 Exploded view of the rear suspension strut/shock absorber (Sec 10)

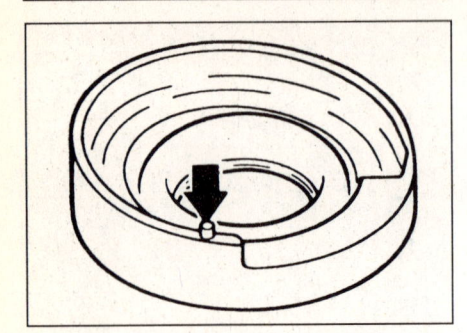

10•8 Suspension and steering

Fig. 10.13 Rubber damping ring identification projection – arrowed (Sec 10)

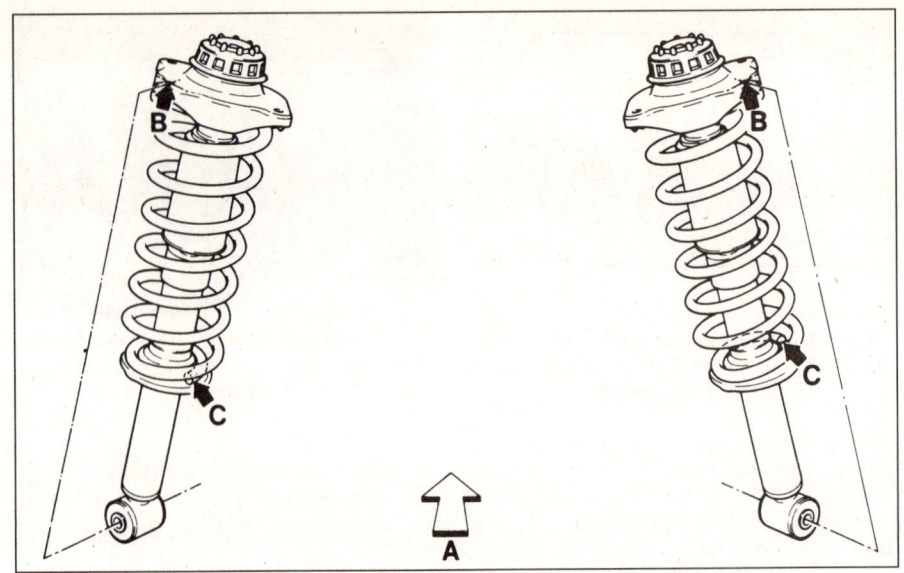

8 If there has been excessive leakage of oil from the shock absorber it may be ineffective on the rebound stroke, but if there is only a slight oil seepage, it may be refitted. Defective shock absorbers normally make a rumbling sound when the car is driven and this can also be used as a guide to the serviceability of the unit

9 Obtain new parts, as necessary, then reassemble the strut using the reverse sequence to dismantling with regard to the following.

10 If a new rubber damper ring is being fitted note that the underside of the ring may or may not have a small moulded in projection which identifies the thickness of the ring. Rings with a projection are thicker than those without, and it is necessary to obtain replacements of similar thickness (Fig. 10.13).

11 Note the fitted positions of the coil spring and upper spring retainer when reassembling, as shown in Fig. 10.14.

12 On cars with self-levelling suspension, push the hydraulic connector onto the piston rod so that the threaded connection faces the hole in the upper spring retainer. Do not turn the connector once it is in place on the piston rod.

13 Apply talcum powder to the damper ring before fitting and tighten a new upper self-locking retaining nut to the specified torque.

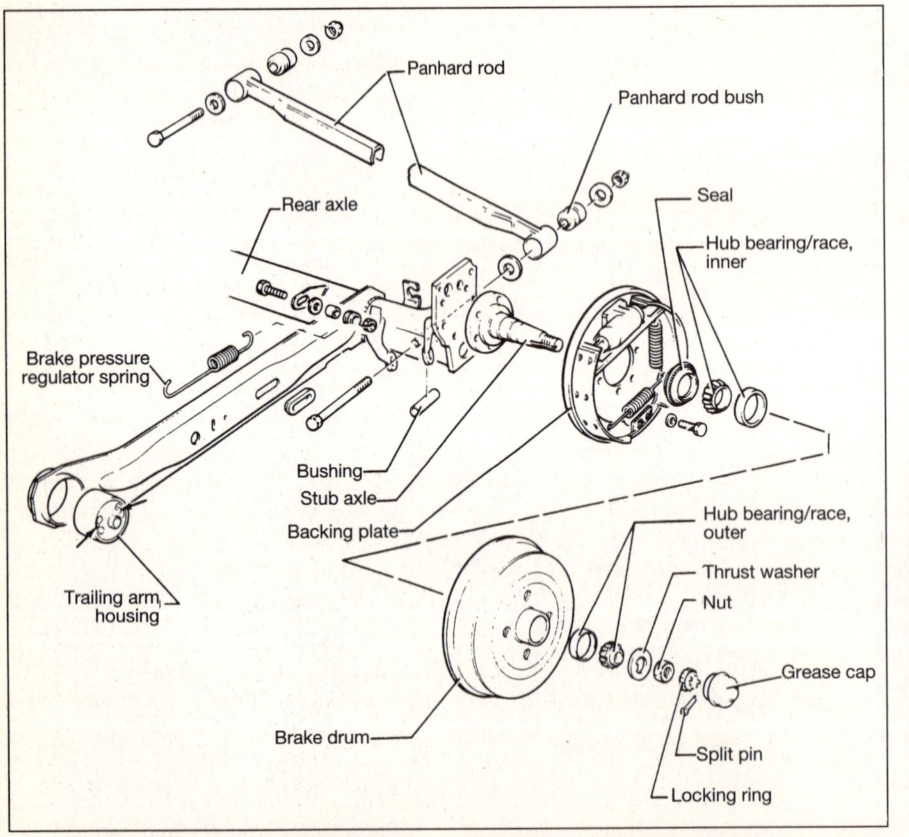

Fig. 10.14 Rear coil spring and upper spring retainer positioning (Sec 10)

A Driving direction   B Centre hole in upper spring retainer   C Lower end of coil spring

11 Panhard rod – removal, overhaul and refitting

1 Jack up the rear of the car and support it on axle stands. Chock the front wheels.

2 Unscrew and remove the bolts attaching the Panhard rod to the underbody and rear axle, noting which way round the bolts are fitted (photos). Withdraw the Panhard rod.

3 Examine the rod and bushes for damage and deterioration. If necessary, the bushes can be renewed, using a long bolt together with a metal tube and washers – dip the new bushes in soapy water before installing them.

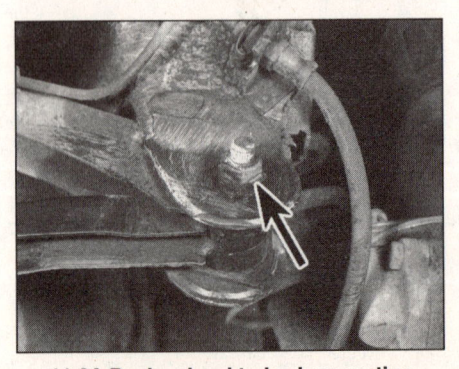

Fig. 10.15 Exploded view of the rear axle components and attachments (Secs 11 and 12)

11.2A Panhard rod to body mounting (arrowed) ...

Suspension and steering 10•9

11.2B ... and attachment to rear axle (arrowed)

12.8 Remove the cap from the centre of the hub ...

12.9 ... then extract the split pin and locking ring

4 Refitting is a reversal of removal, but delay tightening the mounting bolts until the weight of the car is on the suspension.

12 Rear hub bearings – removal, refitting and adjustment

1 Chock the front wheels, then jack up the rear of the car and support it on stands. Remove the appropriate rear roadwheel and release the handbrake.

Rear drum brake models

2 Remove the cap from the centre of the brake drum by tapping it on alternate sides with a screwdriver or blunt chisel.
3 Extract the split pin and remove the locking ring.
4 Unscrew the nut and remove the thrust washer.
5 Withdraw the brake drum, making sure that the outer bearing does not fall out. If the brake drum binds on the shoes, insert a small screwdriver through a wheel bolt hole and lever up the wedged key in order to release the shoes – refer to Chapter 9, if necessary.

Rear disc brake models

6 Remove the brake caliper and carrier bracket, with reference to Chapter 9, but do not disconnect the hydraulic hose. Support the caliper without straining the hose.
7 Withdraw the brake disc from the hub.
8 Remove the cap from the centre of the hub by tapping it on alternate sides with a screwdriver or blunt chisel (photo).
9 Extract the split pin and remove the locking ring (photo).
10 Unscrew the nut and remove the thrust washer.
11 Withdraw the hub, making sure that the outer bearing does not fall out.

All models

12 Remove the outer bearing inner race and rollers from the brake drum/hub.
13 Lever the oil seal from the inner side of the brake drum/hub and withdraw the inner bearing inner race and rollers.
14 Using a soft metal drift, drive the outer races from each side of the brake drum/hub.
15 Clean the bearings and brake drum/hub with paraffin, and also wipe the stub axle clean. Examine the tapered rollers, inner and outer races, brake drum/hub. and stub axle for wear and damage. If the bearing surfaces are pitted, renew them. Obtain a new oil seal.
16 Pack the bearing cages and tapered rollers with a lithium based grease, and also pack the grease into the brake drum/hub inner cavity.
17 Using a length of metal tube, drive the outer races fully into the brake drum/hub.
18 Insert the inner bearing inner race and rollers, then locate the oil seal with the sealing lip facing inwards. and drive it in with a block of wood until flush. Smear a little grease on the oil seal lip then wipe clean the outer face of the seal.
19 Locate the brake drum/hub on the stub axle and fit the outer wheel bearing, followed by the thrust washer and nut (photo).
20 Tighten the nut firmly while turning the drum/hub, then back off the nut until the thrust washer can just be moved by pressing on it with a screwdriver. Do not lever or twist the screwdriver in an attempt to move the thrust washer (photo).
21 Fit the locking ring without moving the nut, and install a new split pin.
22 Tap the grease cap onto the drum/hub.
23 Where applicable refit the disc followed by the caliper assembly, with reference to Chapter 9.
24 Refit the roadwheel and lower the car to the ground.

13 Self-levelling suspension – general description

The self-levelling system is hydraulically operated and keeps the rear of the car at a constant ride height irrespective of load.

The power steering pump is used to provide hydraulic pressure to a regulator valve which controls the pressure applied to the two rear suspension strut units. The struts perform the same function as shock absorbers, but with the addition of the variable ride height capability. The regulator valve is connected to the rear axle by an adjustable linkage and a gas charged suspension reservoir is provided between the regulator valve and each strut unit.

As the load on the rear axle varies the hydraulic pressure in the strut units is increased, or decreased, thus raising or lowering the rear of the car.

The hydraulic operation of the system is such that pressure gauges and special test equipment are required when undertaking most repair, overhaul or fault finding operations. Apart from the procedures described in the following Sections, all other repair operations should be entrusted to an Audi dealer suitably equipped to carry out the work.

12.19 Fitting the rear hub outer bearing

12.20 Checking the hub bearing adjustment

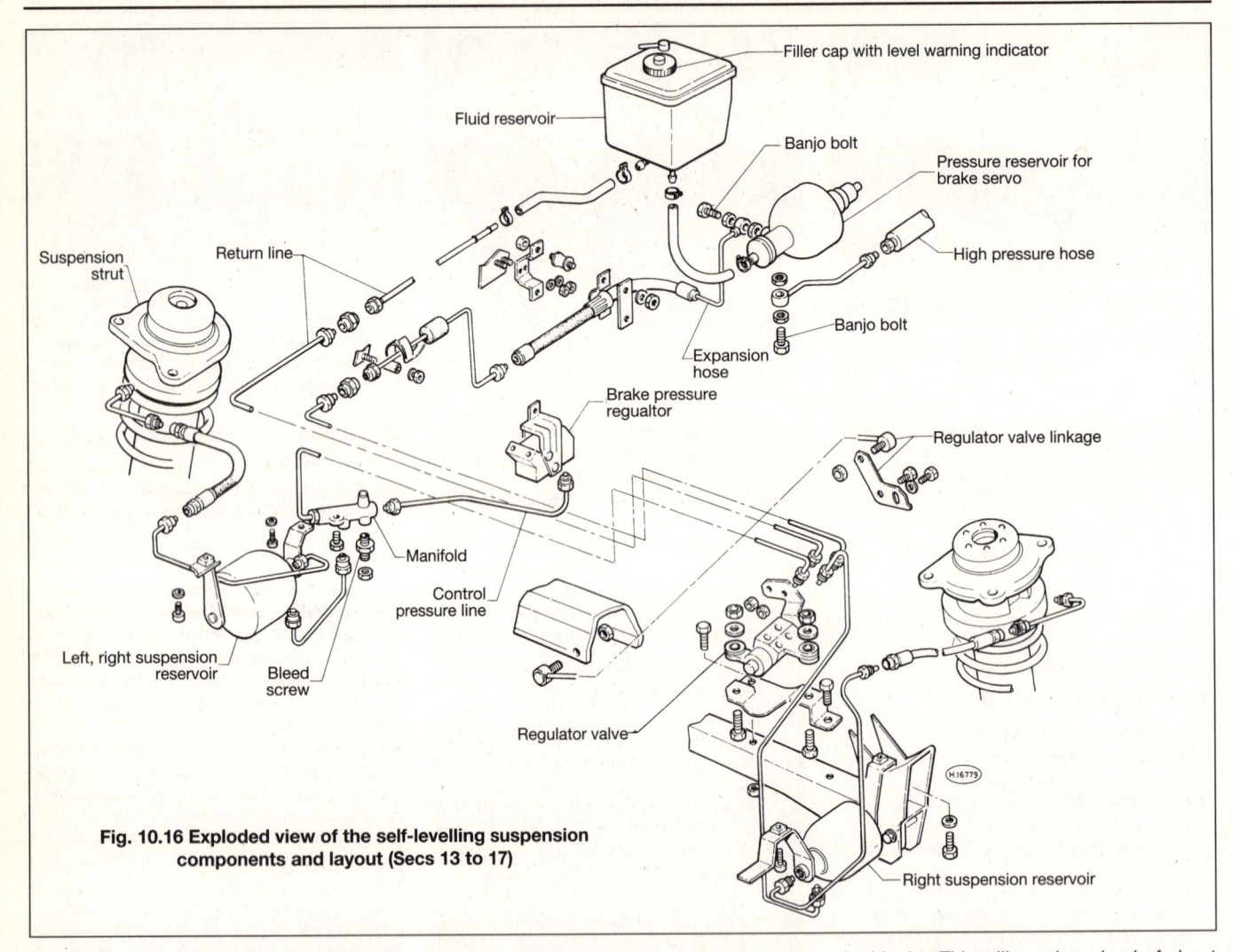

10•10 Suspension and steering

Fig. 10.16 Exploded view of the self-levelling suspension components and layout (Secs 13 to 17)

14 Self-levelling suspension regulator valve – testing

1 With the vehicle standing on its wheels, and with the engine running at idling speed, measure the height above the ground of the sill at the rear jacking point.
2 Load the vehicle by having two people sit on the rear seat and after waiting about a minute so that the system has time to operate, check the height from the ground at the same point.
3 Unload the vehicle and, after allowing the same time interval, check the height again to see that the levelling system has lowered the suspension system to counteract the rise caused by unloading.

15 Self-levelling suspension regulator valve – linkage adjustment

1 Cut two wooden blocks 341 mm (13.43 in) long from a piece of 50 x 50 mm (2.0 x 2.0 in) timber.
2 If possible have the vehicle over a pit, or on ramps to make access to the regulator valve easier and place the blocks at the measuring points shown in Fig. 10.17.
3 Load the luggage compartment so that the measuring points only just touch the ends of the blocks. This will require a load of about 100 kg (220 lb).
4 Loosen the two clamp bolts on the regulator linkage (Fig. 10.18) and then set the regulator valve by pushing a short piece of welding rod, or thick wire through the hole in the arm and into the locating hole on the valve body.
5 With the valve set, tighten the clamp bolts and then remove the wire from the locating hole.

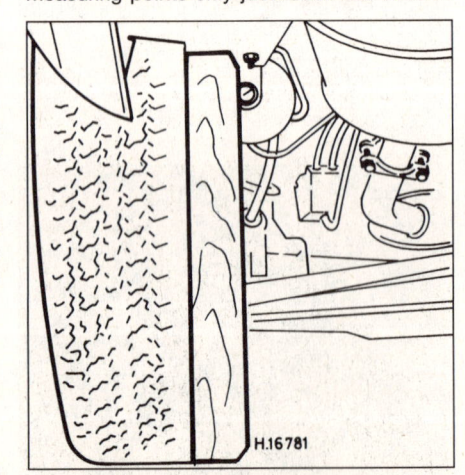

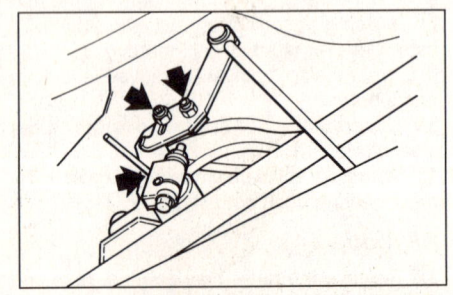

Fig. 10.17 Wooden blocks positioned for self-levelling suspension regulator valve linkage adjustment (Sec 15)

Fig. 10.18 Regulator valve linkage adjustment (Sec 15)

Linkage clamp bolts and wire rod in locating hole arrowed

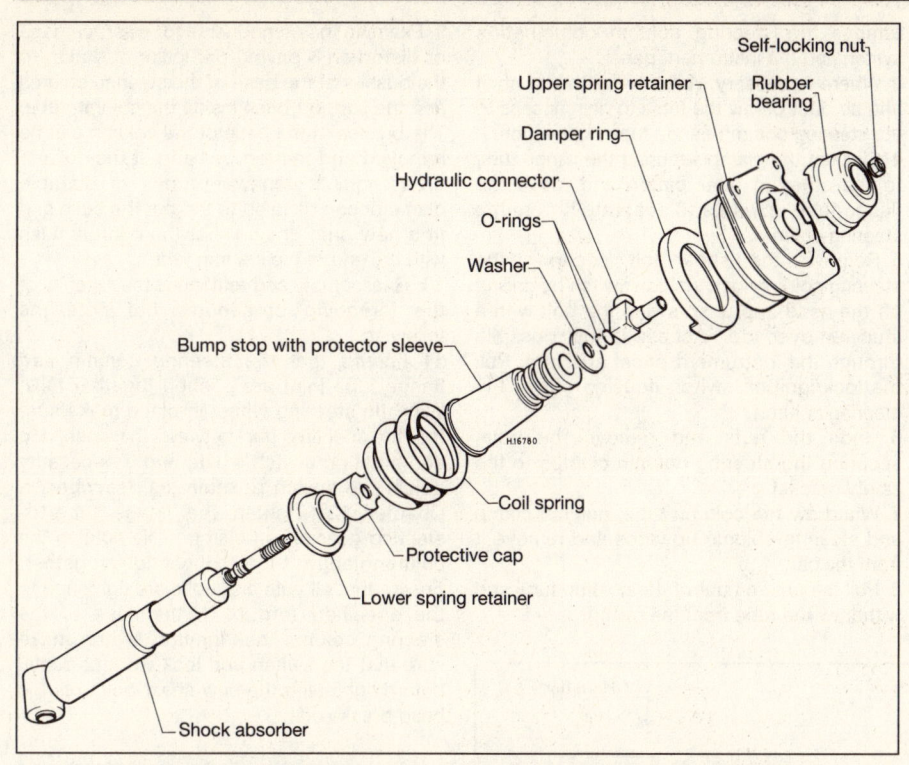

Suspension and steering 10•11

Fig. 10.19 Exploded view of the self-levelling suspension strut (Sec 16)

Labels: Self-locking nut; Upper spring retainer; Rubber bearing; Damper ring; Hydraulic connector; O-rings; Washer; Bump stop with protector sleeve; Coil spring; Protective cap; Lower spring retainer; Shock absorber

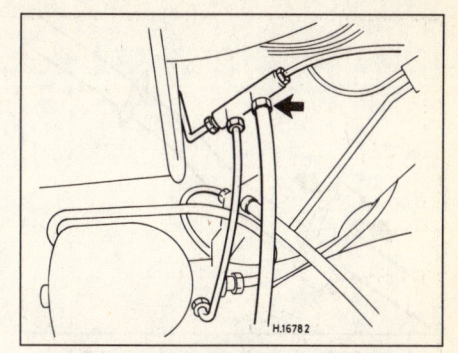

Fig. 10.20 Self-levelling suspension reservoir pipe connector (arrowed) with hose attached to bleed screw (Sec 17)

16 Self-levelling suspension strut units – removal and refitting

1 Apart from the hydraulic connection the procedure is the same as for conventional suspension and the procedures are covered in Sections 9 and 10, but refer to Fig. 10.19.

17 Self-levelling suspension reservoirs – removal and refitting

1 The suspension reservoirs are gas pressurised and a loss of gas pressure will result in heavy knocks from the rear axle when the vehicle is driven.
2 Testing of the reservoirs is carried out with them in position on the car, but it is not a job which can be done by the home mechanic. If the gas pressure is low the reservoir must be renewed.
3 To replace a reservoir which is known to be defective, remove the dust cap from the bleed screw on the pipe connector and fit a piece of plastic tube over the screw (Fig. 10.20).
4 With the open end of the tube in a jar to catch the expelled oil, open the bleed screw until the residual pressure has been released and oil flow ceases. Close the screw, remove the pipe and fit the dust cap.
5 Disconnect the two hydraulic pipes from the reservoir and cover their open ends to prevent the entry of dirt and loss of oil.
6 Remove the two mounting nuts and washers and lift the reservoir clear.
7 Refitting is the reverse sequence to removal, but fill the system with hydraulic oil using the procedure described in Section 25.

If a reservoir has been renewed, render the old unit safe before discarding by drilling a 3 mm (0.12 in) diameter hole in the reservoir body to release the residual pressure. Take care when doing this and always wear safety glasses.

18 Steering wheel – removal and refitting

Note: *No attempt should be made to remove the steering wheel on vehicles fitted with an air bag safety system*

1 Pull the horn bar from the centre of the steering wheel – the retainers are quite strong and quite an effort is required to release the bar (photo).
2 Disconnect the horn wiring and withdraw the bar (photo).
3 Set the front wheel in the straight-ahead position, and the turn signal lever in neutral.
4 Mark the steering wheel and inner column in relation to each other, then unscrew and remove the retaining nut and washer (photo).
5 Withdraw the steering wheel from the inner column splines. If it is tight, ease it off by rocking from side to side.
6 Refitting is a reversal of removal, but align the previously made marks, and tighten the retaining nut to the specified torque. Make sure that the turn signal lever is in neutral, otherwise the switch arm may be damaged.

18.1 Pull the horn bar from the centre of the steering wheel ..

18.2 . . . and disconnect the horn wiring

18.4 Steering wheel retaining nut (arrowed)

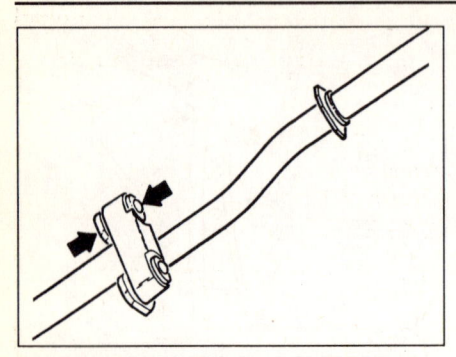

10•12 Suspension and steering

remove the steering column combination switch and the instrument panel.

3 Where necessary, remove the parcel shelf and air duct below the facia to gain access to the steering column/flange tube connection.

4 Slacken the clamp securing the flange tube to the steering gear pinion and move the flange tube upwards to separate it from the steering column.

5 Remove the shear-bolt securing the steering column lock/ignition switch by drilling off the head and unscrewing the bolt with a stud remover tool. Access is just possible through the instrument panel aperture. Pull the lock/ignition switch housing out of the steering column.

6 Undo the nuts and remove the bolts securing the steering column clamps to the safety bracket.

7 Withdraw the column tube, column clamp and steering column upwards and remove it from the car.

8 Pull the column out of the column tube and withdraw the tube from the clamp.

9 Examine the components for wear, damage or distortion – paying particular attention to the bushes at the base of the steering column and the support bush inside the column tube. The bushes at the base of the column can be removed and refitted by hand. If the column tube requires renewal, tubes of suitable diameter can be used to tap out the bush and fit a new one. Ensure that the bush is flush with the end of the column tube.

10 Reassembly and refitting is the reversal of the foregoing procedures but note the following.

11 Ensure that the steering column and flange tube joint are pushed together fully. With the steering wheel in place make sure that the specified gap between the wheel and combination switch exists and if necessary adjust the switch position, as described in Chapter 12. Tighten the flange tube-to-steering gear pinion clamp while holding the column/flange tube connection together. Ensure that all nuts and bolts are tightened to the specified torque. In the case of the steering column lock/ignition switch make sure that the switch and lock work correctly before tightening the new shear-bolt until the head breaks off.

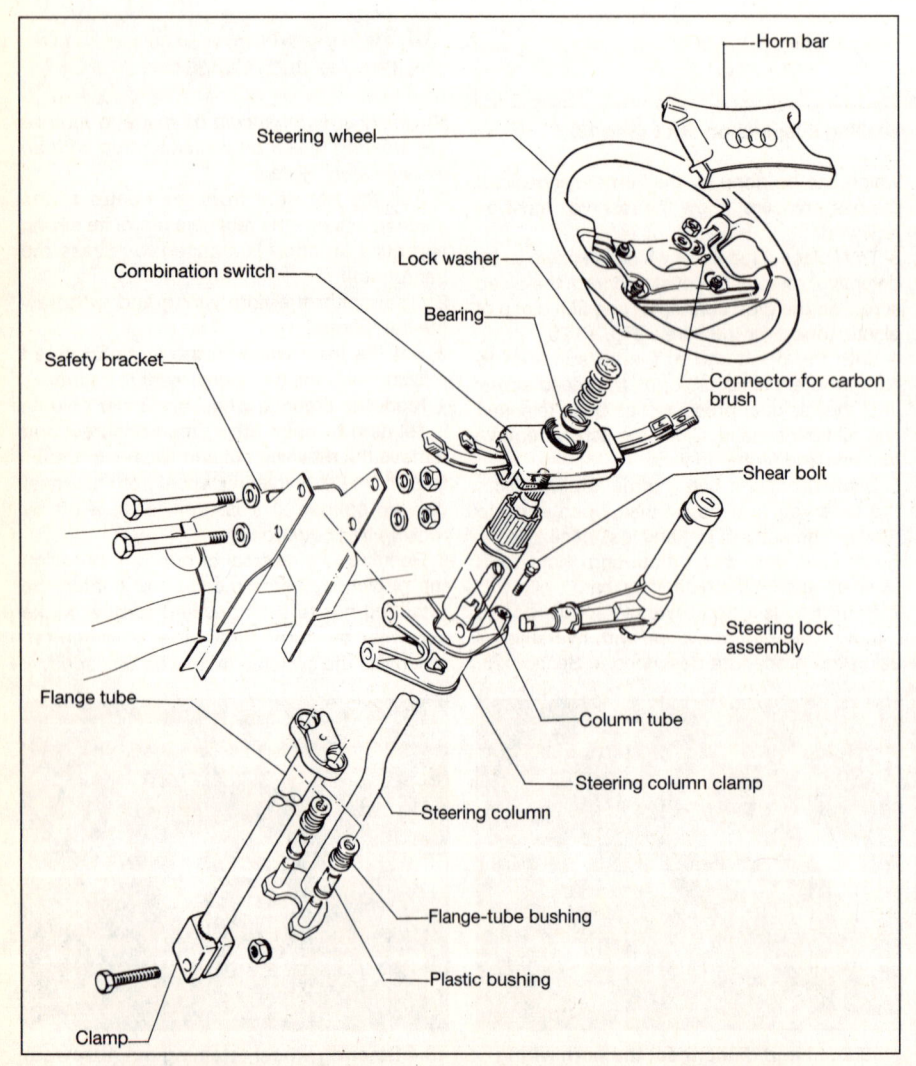

Fig. 10.21 Ensure that column and flange tube joint (arrowed) are pushed tightly together when refitting column (Sec 19)

19 Steering column – removal, overhaul and refitting

1 Disconnect the battery negative terminal
2 Remove the steering wheel, as described in Section 18, then refer to Chapter 12 and

20 Tie-rod – removal and refitting

1 Apply the handbrake, jack up the front of the car, and support it on axle stands. Remove the roadwheel.

2 Unscrew the balljoint nut from the outer end of the tie-rod, and use a separator tool to detach the tie-rod from the strut (photo).

3 At the inner end of the tie-rod, flatten the lockplate. unscrew the bolt and withdraw the tie-rod. If the remaining tie-rod is to be removed as well, refit the removed bolt first, otherwise it will be difficult to refit the bolts.

4 If renewing the end of a tie-rod, measure the distance between the two ends before screwing the old tie-rod end out, and then screw in the new one to the same dimension, otherwise the front wheel alignment will be disturbed.

5 Refitting is a reversal of removal, but renew

Fig. 10.22 Exploded view of the steering column assembly (Sec 19)

20.2 Using a separator tool to detach the tie-rod balljoint

Suspension and steering 10•13

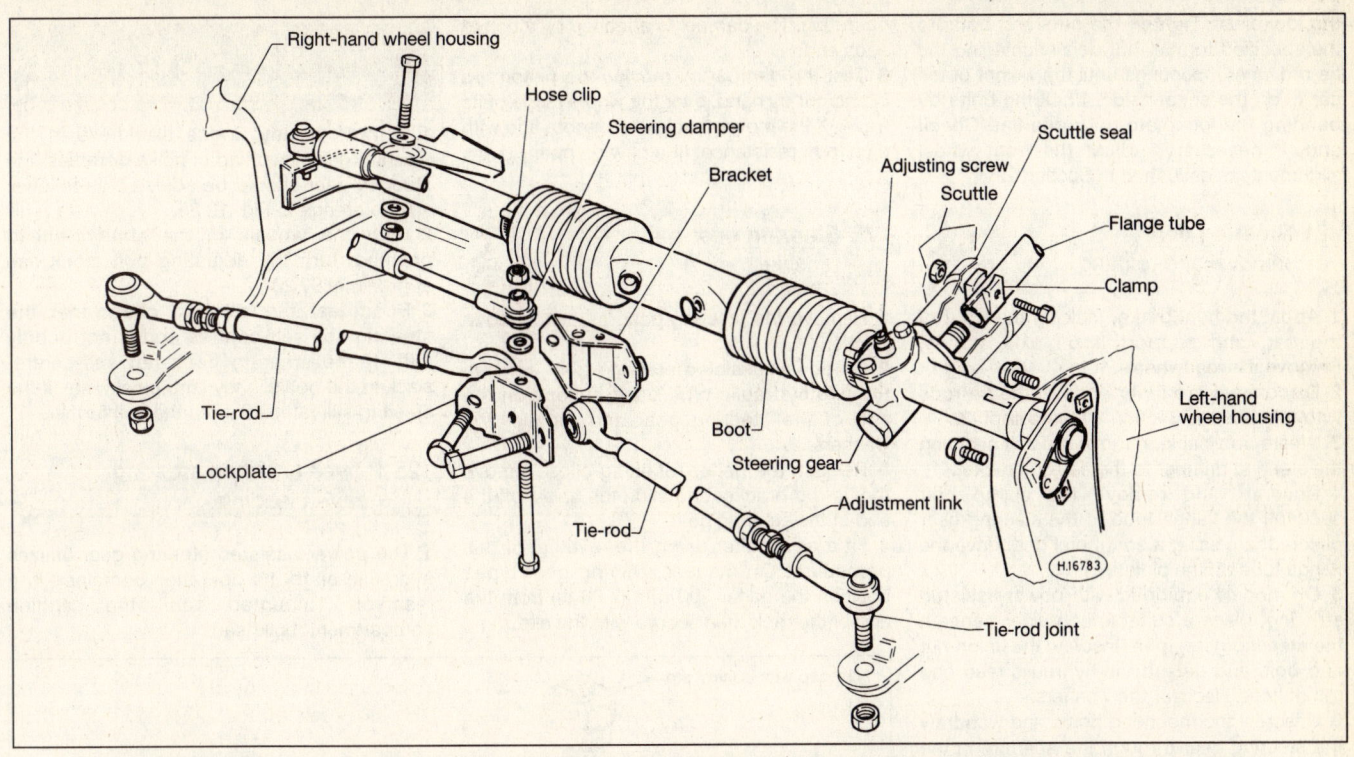

Fig. 10.23 Exploded view of the tie-rods, steering damper and manual steering gear attachments (Secs 20, 21 and 22)

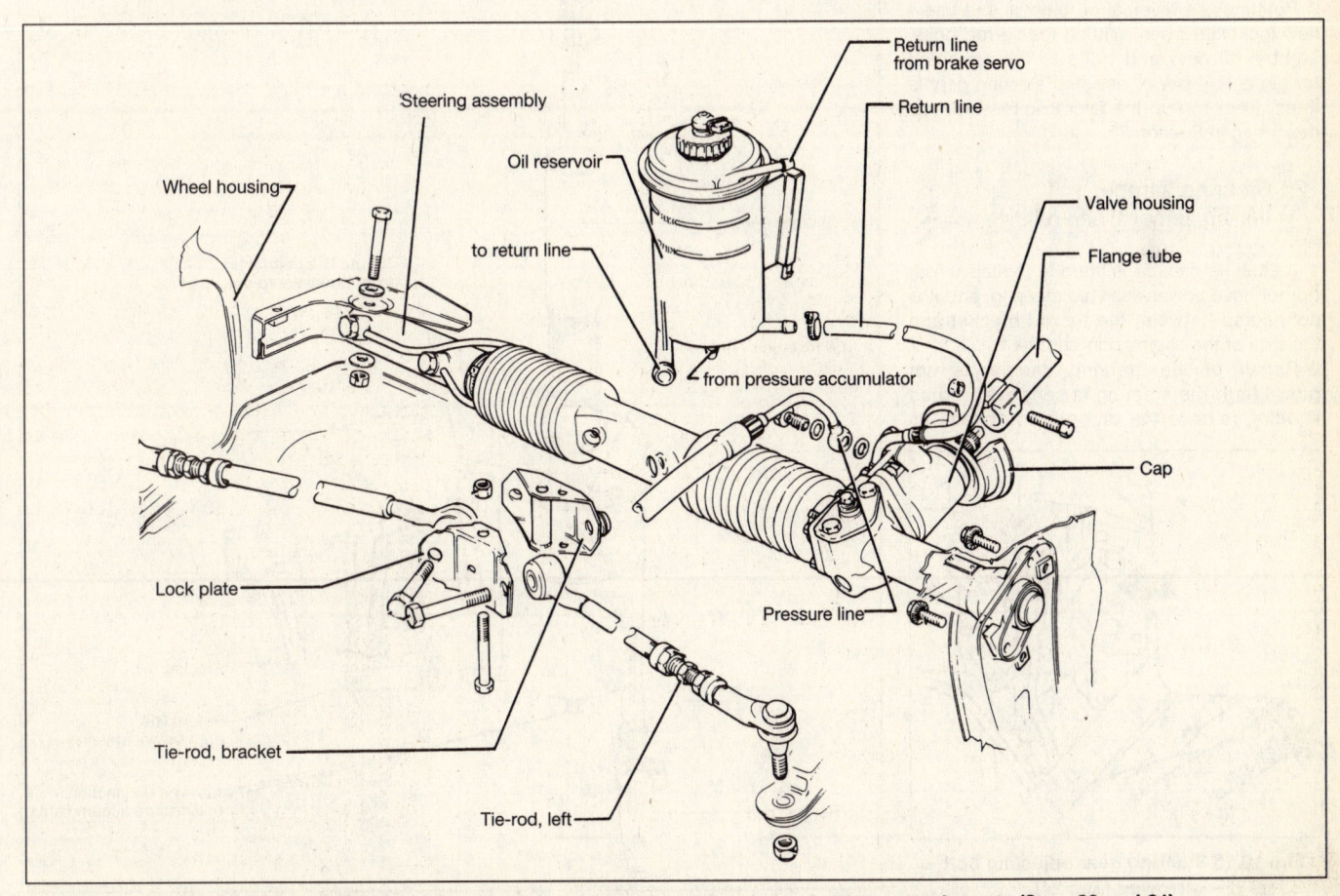

Fig. 10.24 Exploded view of the tie-rods and power-assisted steering gear attachments (Secs 20 and 21)

10•14 Suspension and steering

the lockplate. Tighten the nuts and bolts to the specified torque, but delay tightening the tie-rod inner mountings until the weight of the car is on the suspension. Lock the bolts by bending the lockplate onto one flat. Check and, if necessary, adjust the front wheel alignment, as described in Section 29

21 Steering gear – removal and refitting

1 Apply the handbrake, jack up the front of the car, and support it on axle stands. Remove the roadwheels.
2 Disconnect the inner ends of the tie-rods with reference to Section 20, paragraph 3.
3 Where applicable, remove the bolt securing the steering damper to the tie-rod bracket.
4 Unscrew and remove the clamp bolt securing the flange tube to the steering gear pinion, then, using a soft metal drift, drive the flange tube off the pinion.
5 On models equipped with power-assisted steering, place a suitable container beneath the steering gear, then unscrew the union nut and bolt, and detach the hydraulic feed and return lines. Recover the washers.
6 Unscrew the mounting bolts. and withdraw the steering gear through the aperture in the side panel.
7 Refitting is a reversal of removal, but use a new lockplate when refitting the tie-rod bolts. Tighten all nuts and bolts to the specified torque and, if power-assisted steering gear is fitted, fill or top up the hydraulic reservoir, as described in Section 25.

22 Steering damper – testing. removal and refitting

1 A steering damper is fitted to models which do not have power-assisted steering, and it is connected between the tie-rod bracket and the side of the engine compartment.
2 Repair of the steering damper is not possible. If the steering is sensitive to road shocks, remove the damper and check its operation. The damper is attached by a bolt at each end.
3 Test the damper by moving the piston rod in and out by hand, over the whole range of its travel. If the movement is not smooth and with a uniform resistance, fit a new damper.

23 Steering gear gaiter – renewal

1 Remove the steering gear, as described in Section 21.
2 On power-assisted steering gear, remove the two hydraulic pipe banjo unions on the end of the steering gear and recover the washers.
3 Release the gaiter retaining clips, remove the tie-rod bracket and slide the gaiter off the end of the steering gear.
4 Fit a new gaiter using the reversal of this procedure. On manual steering gear types position the gaiter 200 mm (7.88 in) from the end of the rack then secure with the clip.

24 Steering gear – adjustment

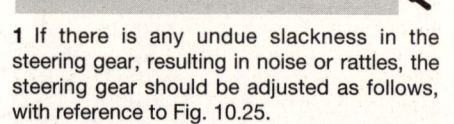

1 If there is any undue slackness in the steering gear, resulting in noise or rattles, the steering gear should be adjusted as follows, with reference to Fig. 10.25.
2 With the wheels in the straight-ahead position, turn the adjusting bolt clockwise approximately 20°.
3 Road test the car and check that the steering still self-centres and is not unduly stiff. If the steering does not self-centre, slacken the bolt slightly (anti-clockwise). if the steering still rattles tighten the bolt further.

25 Power-assisted steering gear – bleeding

1 The power-assisted steering gear utilizes hydraulic oil for its operation contained in a reservoir mounted on the engine compartment bulkhead.

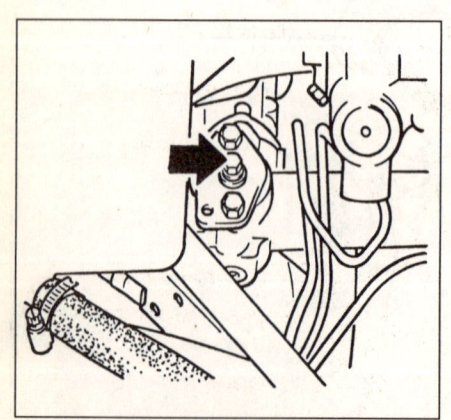

Fig. 10.25 Steering gear adjusting bolt – arrowed (Sec 24)

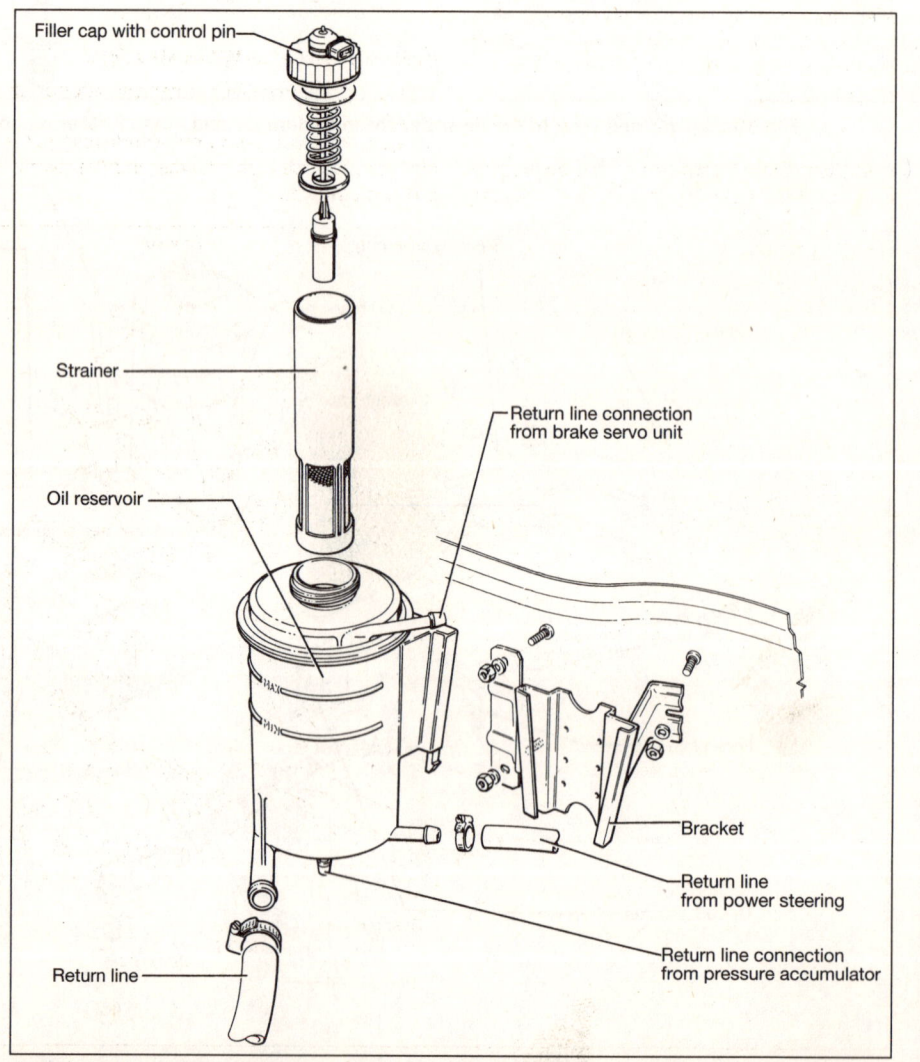

Fig. 10.26 Power-assisted steering gear hydraulic reservoir (round type) details (Sec 25)

Suspension and steering 10•15

2 The power steering pump is also the central hydraulic pump for all other hydraulic systems on the car such as the braking system, anti-lock braking system and self-levelling suspension. If the hydraulic connections of any of these systems have been disturbed the following procedure should be used to fill and bleed the system.

3 If the system is only being topped up. and the oil level in the reservoir has not fallen below the MIN mark, set the steering in the straight-ahead position and, with the vehicle unladen, start the engine. Add the specified hydraulic oil to the reservoir to bring the level up to the MAX mark then refit the filler cap and switch off the engine.

4 If the system is being refilled after a repair operation or if the level in the reservoir has fallen below the MIN mark first remove the oil strainer from the filler cap assembly and clean it in petrol. Dry the strainer and refit it to the cap.

5 Jack up the front of the car so that the wheels are just clear of the ground and support it on stands.

6 Fill the reservoir with the specified oil to the MAX mark and with the engine switched off turn the steering quickly from lock to lock several times.

7 Top up the reservoir to the MAX mark once more.

8 Start the engine and continue adding oil until the level remains constant and no more bubbles appear when the steering is turned.

9 Switch off the engine, check the oil level once more then refit the filler cap and lower the car to the ground.

26 Power-assisted steering gear – checking for leaks

1 With the engine running, turn the steering to full lock on one side and hold it in this position to allow maximum pressure to build up in the system.

2 With the steering still at full lock check all joints and unions for signs of leaks and tighten if necessary. To check the steering rack seal remove the inner end of the rack gaiter from the steering gear, and pull it back to reveal the seal.

3 Turn the wheel to full lock on the other side and again check for leaks.

27 Power-assisted steering pump drivebelt – removal refitting and adjustment

Four-cylinder engine models

1 Jack up the front of the car and support it on stands.

2 Undo the three pump pulley retaining nuts and remove the outer shims and the pump pulley outer half.

3 Remove the drivebelt from the pump and crankshaft pulley

4 Examine the belt for cracks fraying or other signs of deterioration and renew it if worn.

5 To refit and adjust the belt, first place all the original shims together with the pulley inner half over the pump flange studs.

6 Fit the drivebelt to the crankshaft pulley and over the shims on the pump pulley then place the pulley outer half over the studs.

7 Place the spare shims over the studs and refit the three pulley retaining nuts.

8 Tighten the nuts while turning the pulley so that the belt does not jam between the two pulley halves.

9 Apply moderate thumb pressure to the belt midway between the crankshaft and pump pulleys. When the belt is correctly adjusted the deflection should be approximately 10 mm (0.4 in). If the belt is slack, remove the pulley outer half take out a shim refit the outer half and check the deflection again. Repeat until the tension is correct. If the belt is too tight add a shim between the pulley halves using one of the spare shims. Store the spare shims between the pulley outer half and the retaining nuts.

10 After adjustment lower the car to the ground.

Five-cylinder engine models

11 If the drivebelt is to be renewed refer to Chapter 12 and remove the alternator drivebelt.

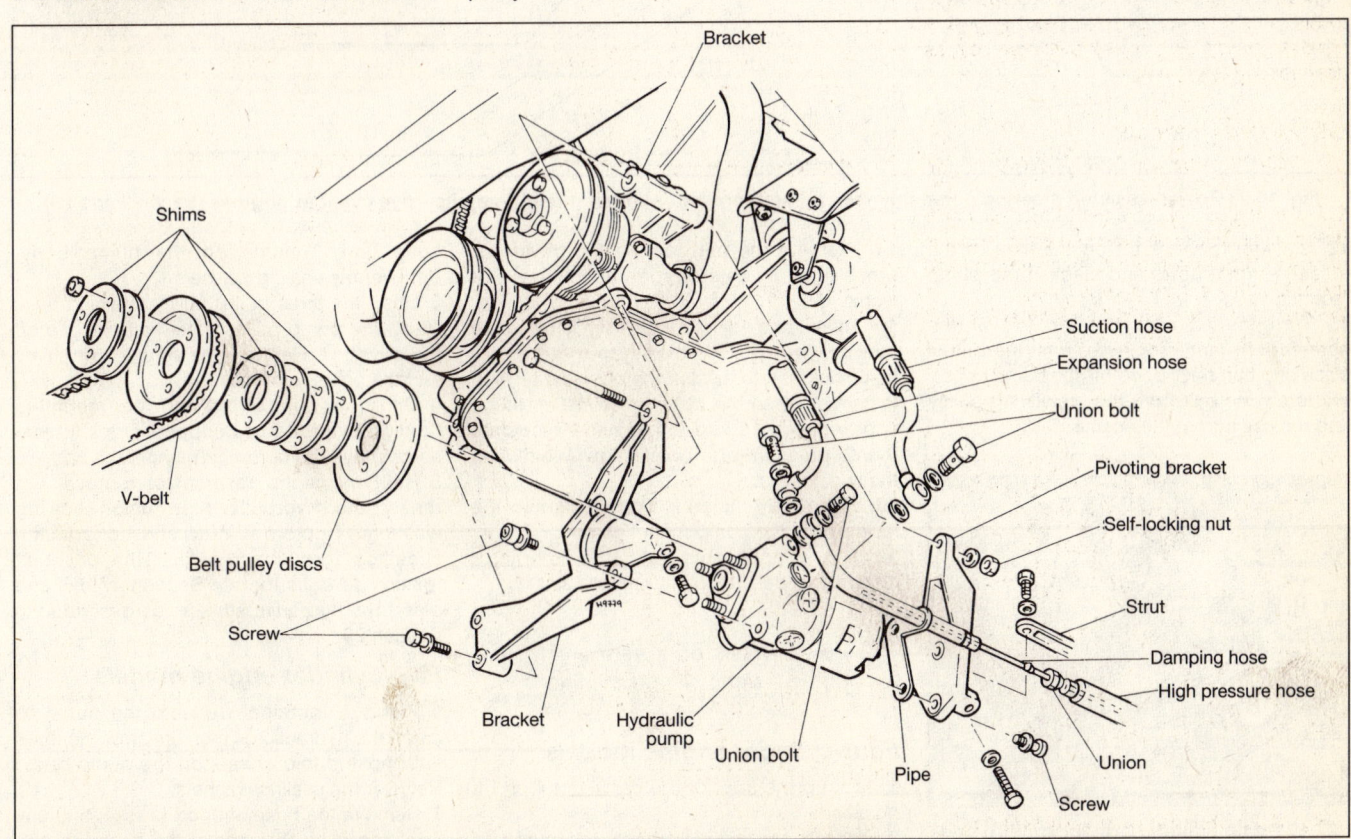

Fig. 10.27 Power-assisted steering pump drivebelt adjustment and pump mounting details – four-cylinder engines (Sec 27 and 28)

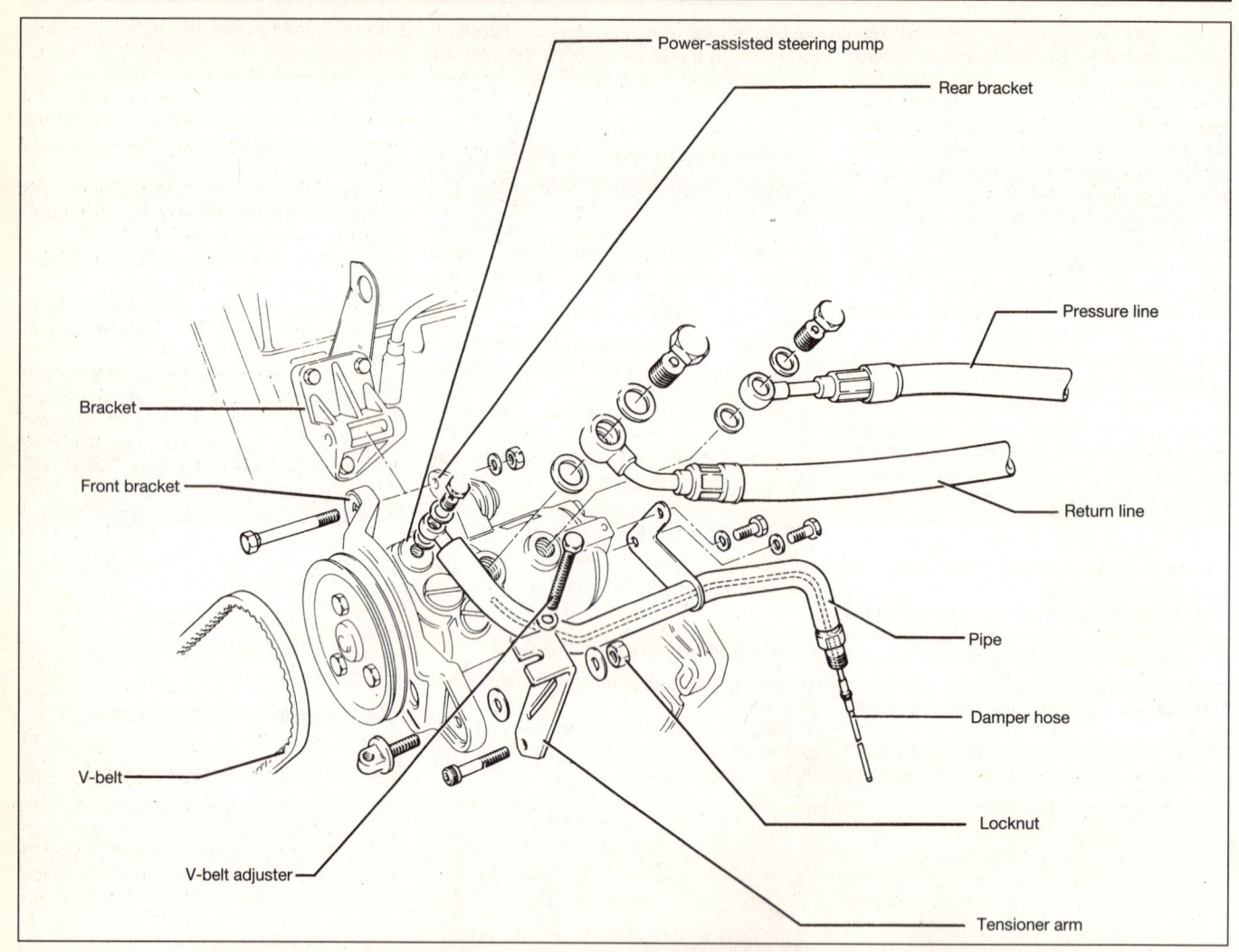

10•16 Suspension and steering

Fig. 10.28 Power-assisted steering pump drivebelt adjustment and pump mounting details – five cylinder engines (Secs 27 and 28)

12 Slacken the locknut on the side of the adjuster arm (photo) and slacken the pump mounting bolt.
13 Turn the adjuster bolt on top of the adjuster arm anti-clockwise until the belt is slack and can be slipped off the pump pulley. Withdraw the belt from the crankshaft pulley and remove it from the engine.

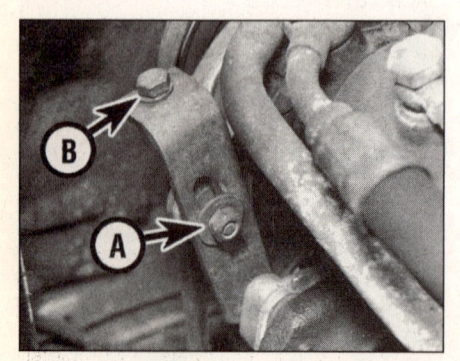

14 Examine the belt for cracks, fraying or other signs of deterioration and renew it if worn.
15 To refit and adjust the belt slip it into place over the two pulleys then turn the adjuster bolt clockwise to tension the belt. The tension is correct when the belt can be deflected by approximately 10 mm (0.4 in) under moderate thumb pressure at a point midway between the two pulleys.
16 When the tension is correct tighten the locknut and the pump mounting bolt.
17 Where applicable refit the alternator drivebelt as described in Chapter 12.

28 Power-assisted steering pump – removal and refitting

Four-cylinder engine models

1 Jack up the front of the car and support it on stands.
2 Place a container beneath the pump to catch the hydraulic oil then unscrew the fluid

hose banjo unions on the pump body. Recover the sealing washers.
3 Undo the three pump pulley retaining bolts lift off the pump pulley outer half and slip off the drivebelt. Remove the adjustment shims and the pulley inner half.
4 Undo the pump front and rear mounting bolts, move the hose support bracket clear and remove the pump from under the car.
5 Refitting is the reversal of removal but renew the hydraulic pipe union sealing washers. Tighten all nuts and bolts to the specified torque and adjust the drivebelt tension as described in Section 27. Fill and bleed the hydraulic system, as described in Section 25.

Five-cylinder engine models

6 Place a container beneath the pump to catch the hydraulic oil then unscrew the three fluid hose banjo unions on the pump body. Recover the sealing washers.
7 Remove the hose support bracket and any retaining clips then move the hoses to one side.

27.12 Pump adjuster arm locknut (A) and adjuster bolt (B)

Suspension and steering 10•17

Fig. 10.29 Suspension strut upper mounting bolts for camber adjustment – arrowed (Sec 29)

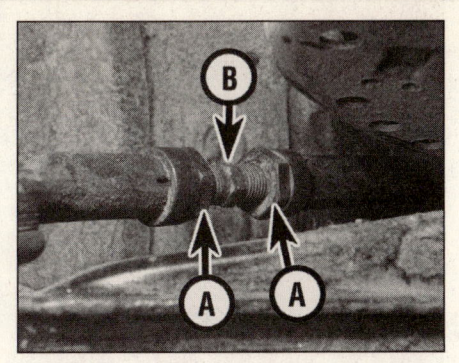

29.7 Tie-rod locknuts (A) and threaded adjuster (B)

8 Slacken the drivebelt adjuster as described in Section 27 and slip the belt off the pump pulley.
9 Unscrew the bolt securing the adjuster arm to the engine, remove the pump mounting bolt and lift away the pump.
10 Refitting is the reversal of removal but renew the hydraulic pipe union sealing washers. Tighten all nuts and bolts to the specified torque and adjust the drivebelt tension as described in Section 27. Fill and bleed the hydraulic system as described in Section 25.

29 Front wheel alignment and steering angles

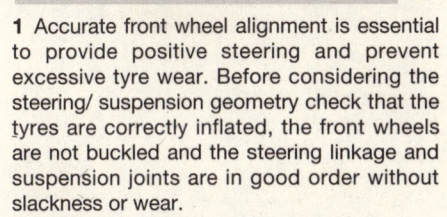

1 Accurate front wheel alignment is essential to provide positive steering and prevent excessive tyre wear. Before considering the steering/ suspension geometry check that the tyres are correctly inflated, the front wheels are not buckled and the steering linkage and suspension joints are in good order without slackness or wear.
2 Wheel alignment consists of four factors:
Camber is the angle at which the front wheels are set from the vertical when viewed from the front of the car. 'Positive camber' is the amount (in degrees) that the wheels are tilted outward at the top from the vertical.
Castor is the angle between the steering axis and a vertical line when viewed from each side of the car. 'Positive castor' is when the steering axis is inclined rearward.
Steering axis inclination is the angle (when viewed from the front of the car) between the vertical and an imaginary line drawn between the suspension strut upper mounting and the lower suspension arm balljoint.
Toe setting is the amount by which the distance between the front inside edges of the roadwheels (measured at hub height) differs from the diametrically opposite distance measured between the rear inside edges of the front roadwheels.
3 Castor and steering axis inclination are set in production and cannot be altered.
4 Camber is adjustable by slackening the three suspension strut top mounting nuts and moving the strut within the limits of the elongated mounting plate holes. Without special gauges adjustment should not be attempted but left to a dealer.
5 Two methods are available to the home mechanic for checking the toe setting. One method is to use a gauge to measure the distance between the front and rear inside edges of the roadwheels. The other method is to use a scuff plate in which each front wheel is rolled across a movable plate which records any deviation or scuff of the tyre from the straight-ahead position as it moves across the plate. Relatively inexpensive equipment of both types is available from accessory outlets to enable these checks and subsequent adjustments to be carried out at home.
6 If after checking the toe setting using whichever method is preferable it is found that adjustment is necessary, proceed as follows.
7 Slacken the two nuts on each tie-rod and turn the threaded adjusters as necessary to achieve the desired setting (photo). Turn both adjusters by equal amounts. but only approximately one quarter of a turn each time, then recheck the setting using the gauges or scuff plate. Tighten the clamps when the setting is correct.

30 Wheels and tyres – general care and maintenance

Wheels and tyres should give no real problems in use provided that a close eye is kept on them with regard to excessive wear or damage. To this end the following points should be noted
Ensure that tyre pressures are checked regularly and maintained correctly. Checking should be carried out with the tyres cold and not immediately after the vehicle has been in use. If the pressures are checked with the tyres hot, an apparently high reading will be obtained owing to heat expansion. Under no circumstances should an attempt be made to reduce the pressures to the quoted cold reading in this instance, or effective underinflation will result.
Underinflation will cause overheating of the tyre owing to excessive flexing of the casing, and the tread will not sit correctly on the road surface. This will cause a consequent loss of adhesion and excessive wear, not to mention the danger of sudden tyre failure due to heat build-up.
Overinflation will cause rapid wear of the centre part of the tyre tread coupled with reduced adhesion, harsher ride and the danger of shock damage occurring in the tyre casing.
Regularly check the tyres for damage in the form of cuts or bulges especially in the sidewalls. Remove any nails or stones embedded in the tread before they penetrate the tyre to cause deflation. If removal of a nail *does* reveal that the tyre has been punctured refit the nail so that its point of penetration is marked. Then immediately change the wheel and have the tyre repaired by a tyre dealer. Do *not* drive on a tyre in such a condition. In many cases a puncture can be simply repaired by the use of an inner tube of the correct size and type. If in any doubt as to the possible consequences of any damage found. consult your local tyre dealer for advice.
Periodically remove the wheels and clean any dirt or mud from the inside and outside surfaces. Examine the wheel rims for signs of rusting, corrosion or other damage. Light alloy wheels are easily damaged by kerbing whilst parking and similarly steel wheels may become dented or buckled. Renewal of the wheel is very often the only course of remedial action possible.
The balance of each wheel and tyre assembly should be maintained to avoid excessive wear not only to the tyres but also to the steering and suspension components. Wheel imbalance is normally signified by vibration through the vehicle's bodyshell although in many cases it is particularly noticeable through the steering wheel. Conversely, it should be noted that wear or damage in suspension or steering components may cause excessive tyre wear. Out-of-round or out-of-true tyres, damaged wheels and wheel bearing wear/ maladjustment also fail into this category. Balancing will not usually cure vibration caused by such wear.
Wheel balancing may be carried out with the wheel either on or off the vehicle if balanced on the vehicle ensure that the wheel-to-hub relationship is marked in some way prior to subsequent wheel removal so that it may be refitted in its original position.
General tyre wear is influenced to a large degree by driving style – harsh braking and acceleration or fast cornering will all produce more rapid tyre wear. Interchanging of tyres may result in more even wear but this should only be carried out where there is no mix of tyre types on the vehicle. However it is worth bearing in mind that if this is completely effective the added expense of replacing a complete set of tyres simultaneousiy is

10•18 Suspension and steering

incurred which may prove financially restrictive for many owners.

Front tyres may wear unevenly as a result of wheel misalignment. The front wheels should always be correctly aligned according to the settings specified by the vehicle manufacturer.

Legal restrictions apply to the mixing of tyre types on a vehicle. Basically this means that a vehicle must not have tyres of differing construction on the same axle. Although it is not recommended to mix tyre types between front axle and rear axle, the only legally permissible combination is crossply at the front and radial at the rear. When mixing radial ply tyres, textile braced radials must always go on the front axle. with steel braced radials at the rear. An obvious disadvantage of such mixing is the necessity to carry two spare tyres to avoid contravening the law in the event of a puncture.

In the UK. the Motor Vehicles Construction and Use Regulations apply to many aspects of tyre fitting and usage. It is suggested that a copy of these regulations is obtained from your local police if in doubt as to the current legal requirements with regard to tyre condition minimum tread depth, etc.

Fault finding – suspension and steering

Note: *More detailed fault finding on the power-assisted steering gear and self-levelling suspension (where fitted) entails the use of special test equipment. Apart from the general references listed below, faults on these systems should be referred to an Audi dealer*

Excessive play in steering
☐ Worn steering gear
☐ Worn tie-rod end balljoints
☐ Worn tie-rod bushes
☐ Incorrect rack adjustment
☐ Worn suspension balljoints

Wheel wobble and vibration
☐ Roadwheels out of balance
☐ Roadwheels damaged
☐ Weak shock absorbers
☐ Worn hub bearings

Excessive tyre wear
☐ incorrect tyre pressures
☐ Roadwheels out of balance

Wanders or pulls to one side
☐ Incorrect wheel alignment
☐ Worn tie-rod end balljoints
☐ Worn suspension balljoints
☐ Uneven tyre pressures
☐ Weak shock absorber
☐ Broken or weak coil spring

Heavy or stiff steering
☐ Seized steering or suspension balljoint
☐ Incorrect wheel alignment
☐ Low tyre pressures
☐ Leak of lubricant in steering gear
☐ Power steering faulty (where applicable)
☐ Power steering pump drivebelt broken (where applicable)

Chapter 11 Bodywork

For modifications, and information applicable to later models, see Supplement at end of manual

Contents

Air conditioner – precautions and maintenance 31	General description 1
Air conditioner drivebelt – removal, refitting and adjustment 32	Heater blower motor (without air conditioning) – removal
Bonnet – removal, refitting and adjustment 12	and refitting 29
Bonnet lock cable – removal, refitting and adjustment 14	Heater controls (without air conditioning) – removal and refitting . . . 30
Bonnet support struts – removal and refitting 13	Heater unit (without air conditioning) – removal and refitting 28
Boot lid – removal, refitting and adjustment 15	Maintenance – bodywork and underframe 2
Boot lid lock – removal, refitting and adjustment 16	Maintenance – upholstery and carpets 3
Bumpers – removal and refitting 21	Major body damage – repair 5
Central door locking system – general 26	Minor body damage – repair 4
Centre console – removal and refitting 24	Power-operated windows – general 27
Door exterior handle – removal and refitting 8	Radiator grille and ventilation grille – removal and refitting 22
Door inner trim panel – removal and refitting 6	Seats – removal and refitting 25
Door locks – removal and refitting 7	Sunroof – general 20
Doors – dismantling and reassembly 9	Tailgate (Avant models) – removal, refitting and adjustment 17
Doors – removal and refitting 10	Tailgate lock (Avant models) – removal, refitting and adjustment . . 18
Door striker – adjustment 11	Windscreen, rear window and fixed window glass – removal
Facia – removal and refitting 23	and refitting 19

Degrees of difficulty

Easy, suitable for novice with little experience	Fairly easy, suitable for beginner with some experience	Fairly difficult, suitable for competent DIY mechanic	Difficult, suitable for experienced DIY mechanic	Very difficult, suitable for expert DIY or professional

1 General description

The body is of unitary all-steel construction, and incorporates computer calculated impact crumple zones at the front and rear, with a central safety cell passenger compartment. During manufacture the body is undersealed and treated with cavity wax injection. In addition all open box members are sealed.

There are two body styles, the four-door Saloon and the five-door Avant, and there are a number of trim options on the Saloon version.

2 Maintenance – bodywork and underframe

The general condition of a vehicle's bodywork is the one thing that significantly affects its value. Maintenance is easy, but needs to be regular. Neglect, particularly after minor damage, can lead quickly to further deterioration and costly repair bills. It is important also to keep watch on those parts of the vehicle not immediately visible, for instance the underside, inside all the wheel arches, and the lower part of the engine compartment.

The basic maintenance routine for the bodywork is washing - preferably with a lot of water, from a hose. This will remove all the loose solids which may have stuck to the vehicle. It is important to flush these off in such a way as to prevent grit from scratching the finish. The wheel arches and underframe need washing in the same way, to remove any accumulated mud, which will retain moisture and tend to encourage rust. Paradoxically enough, the best time to clean the underframe and wheel arches is in wet weather, when the mud is thoroughly wet and soft. In very wet weather, the underframe is usually cleaned of large accumulations automatically, and this is a good time for inspection.

Periodically, except on vehicles with a wax-based underbody protective coating, it is a good idea to have the whole of the underframe of the vehicle steam-cleaned, engine compartment included, so that a thorough inspection can be carried out to see what minor repairs and renovations are necessary. Steam-cleaning is available at many garages, and is necessary for the removal of the accumulation of oily grime, which sometimes is allowed to become thick in certain areas. If steam-cleaning facilities are not available, there are some excellent grease solvents available which can be brush-applied; the dirt can then be simply hosed off. Note that these methods should not be used on vehicles with wax-based underbody protective coating, or the coating will be removed. Such vehicles should be inspected annually, preferably just prior to Winter, when the underbody should be washed down, and any damage to the wax coating repaired. Ideally, a completely fresh coat should be applied. It would also be worth considering the use of such wax-based protection for injection into door panels, sills, box sections, etc, as an additional safeguard against rust damage, where such protection is not provided by the vehicle manufacturer.

After washing paintwork, wipe off with a chamois leather to give an unspotted clear finish. A coat of clear protective wax polish will give added protection against chemical pollutants in the air. If the paintwork sheen has dulled or oxidised, use a cleaner/polisher combination to restore the brilliance of the shine. This requires a little effort, but such dulling is usually caused because regular washing has been neglected. Care needs to be taken with metallic paintwork, as special non-abrasive cleaner/polisher is required to avoid damage to the finish. Always check that the door and ventilator opening drain holes and pipes are completely clear, so that water can be drained out. Brightwork should be treated in the same way as paintwork. Windscreens and windows can be kept clear of the smeary film which often appears, by the use of proprietary glass cleaner. Never use any form of wax or other body or chromium polish on glass.

3 Maintenance - upholstery and carpets

Mats and carpets should be brushed or vacuum-cleaned regularly, to keep them free of grit. If they are badly stained, remove them from the vehicle for scrubbing or sponging, and make quite sure they are dry before refitting. Seats and interior trim panels can be kept clean by wiping with a damp cloth. If they do become stained (which can be more apparent on light-coloured upholstery), use a little liquid detergent and a soft nail brush to scour the grime out of the grain of the material. Do not forget to keep the headlining clean in the same way as the upholstery. When using liquid cleaners inside the vehicle, do not over-wet the surfaces being cleaned. Excessive damp could get into the seams and padded interior, causing stains, offensive odours or even rot.

> **HAYNES HINT**: *If the inside of the vehicle gets wet accidentally, it is worthwhile taking some trouble to dry it out properly, particularly where carpets are involved. Do not leave oil or electric heaters inside the vehicle for this purpose.*

4 Minor body damage - repair

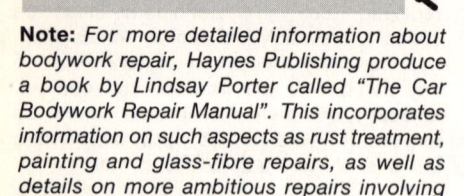

Note: *For more detailed information about bodywork repair, Haynes Publishing produce a book by Lindsay Porter called "The Car Bodywork Repair Manual". This incorporates information on such aspects as rust treatment, painting and glass-fibre repairs, as well as details on more ambitious repairs involving welding and panel beating.*

Repairs of minor scratches in bodywork

If the scratch is very superficial, and does not penetrate to the metal of the bodywork, repair is very simple. Lightly rub the area of the scratch with a paintwork renovator, or a very fine cutting paste, to remove loose paint from the scratch, and to clear the surrounding bodywork of wax polish. Rinse the area with clean water.

Apply touch-up paint to the scratch using a fine paint brush; continue to apply fine layers of paint until the surface of the paint in the scratch is level with the surrounding paintwork. Allow the new paint at least two weeks to harden, then blend it into the surrounding paintwork by rubbing the scratch area with a paintwork renovator or a very fine cutting paste. Finally, apply wax polish.

Where the scratch has penetrated right through to the metal of the bodywork, causing the metal to rust, a different repair technique is required. Remove any loose rust from the bottom of the scratch with a penknife, then apply rust-inhibiting paint to prevent the formation of rust in the future. Using a rubber or nylon applicator, fill the scratch with bodystopper paste. If required, this paste can be mixed with cellulose thinners to provide a very thin paste which is ideal for filling narrow scratches. Before the stopper-paste in the scratch hardens, wrap a piece of smooth cotton rag around the top of a finger. Dip the finger in cellulose thinners, and quickly sweep it across the surface of the stopper-paste in the scratch; this will ensure that the surface of the stopper-paste is slightly hollowed. The scratch can now be painted over as described earlier in this Section.

Repairs of dents in bodywork

When deep denting of the vehicle's bodywork has taken place, the first task is to pull the dent out, until the affected bodywork almost attains its original shape. There is little point in trying to restore the original shape completely, as the metal in the damaged area will have stretched on impact, and cannot be reshaped fully to its original contour. It is better to bring the level of the dent up to a point which is about 3 mm below the level of the surrounding bodywork. In cases where the dent is very shallow anyway, it is not worth trying to pull it out at all. If the underside of the dent is accessible, it can be hammered out gently from behind, using a mallet with a wooden or plastic head. Whilst doing this, hold a suitable block of wood firmly against the outside of the panel, to absorb the impact from the hammer blows and thus prevent a large area of the bodywork from being "belled-out".

Should the dent be in a section of the bodywork which has a double skin, or some other factor making it inaccessible from behind, a different technique is called for. Drill several small holes through the metal inside the area - particularly in the deeper section. Then screw long self-tapping screws into the holes, just sufficiently for them to gain a good purchase in the metal. Now the dent can be pulled out by pulling on the protruding heads of the screws with a pair of pliers.

The next stage of the repair is the removal of the paint from the damaged area, and from an inch or so of the surrounding "sound" bodywork. This is accomplished most easily by using a wire brush or abrasive pad on a power drill, although it can be done just as effectively by hand, using sheets of abrasive paper. To complete the preparation for filling, score the surface of the bare metal with a screwdriver or the tang of a file, or alternatively, drill small holes in the affected area. This will provide a really good "key" for the filler paste.

To complete the repair, see the Section on filling and respraying.

Repairs of rust holes or gashes in bodywork

Remove all paint from the affected area, and from an inch or so of the surrounding "sound" bodywork, using an abrasive pad or a wire brush on a power drill. If these are not available, a few sheets of abrasive paper will do the job most effectively. With the paint removed, you will be able to judge the severity of the corrosion, and therefore decide whether to renew the whole panel (if this is possible) or to repair the affected area. New body panels are not as expensive as most people think, and it is often quicker and more satisfactory to fit a new panel than to attempt to repair large areas of corrosion.

Remove all fittings from the affected area, except those which will act as a guide to the original shape of the damaged bodywork (eg headlight shells etc). Then, using tin snips or a hacksaw blade, remove all loose metal and any other metal badly affected by corrosion. Hammer the edges of the hole inwards, in order to create a slight depression for the filler paste.

Wire-brush the affected area to remove the powdery rust from the surface of the remaining metal. Paint the affected area with rust-inhibiting paint, if the back of the rusted area is accessible, treat this also.

Before filling can take place, it will be necessary to block the hole in some way. This can be achieved by the use of aluminium or plastic mesh, or aluminium tape.

Aluminium or plastic mesh, or glass-fibre matting, is probably the best material to use for a large hole. Cut a piece to the approximate size and shape of the hole to be filled, then position it in the hole so that its edges are below the level of the surrounding bodywork. It can be retained in position by several blobs of filler paste around its periphery.

Aluminium tape should be used for small or very narrow holes. Pull a piece off the roll, trim it to the approximate size and shape required, then pull off the backing paper (if used) and stick the tape over the hole; it can be overlapped if the thickness of one piece is insufficient. Burnish down the edges of the tape with the handle of a screwdriver or similar, to ensure that the tape is securely attached to the metal underneath.

Bodywork repairs - filling and respraying

Before using this Section, see the Sections on dent, deep scratch, rust holes and gash repairs.

Many types of bodyfiller are available, but generally speaking, those proprietary kits which contain a tin of filler paste and a tube of resin hardener are best for this type of repair. A wide, flexible plastic or nylon applicator will be found invaluable for imparting a smooth and well-contoured finish to the surface of the filler.

Mix up a little filler on a clean piece of card or board - measure the hardener carefully (follow the maker's instructions on the pack), otherwise the filler will set too rapidly or too slowly. Using the applicator, apply the filler paste to the prepared area; draw the applicator across the surface of the filler to achieve the correct contour and to level the surface. As soon as a contour that approximates to the correct one is achieved, stop working the paste - if you carry on too long, the paste will become sticky and begin to "pick-up" on the applicator. Continue to add thin layers of filler paste at 20-minute intervals, until the level of the filler is just proud of the surrounding bodywork.

Once the filler has hardened, the excess can be removed using a metal plane or file. From then on, progressively-finer grades of abrasive paper should be used, starting with a 40-grade production paper, and finishing with a 400-grade wet-and-dry paper. Always wrap the abrasive paper around a flat rubber, cork, or wooden block - otherwise the surface of the filler will not be completely flat. During the smoothing of the filler surface, the wet-and-dry paper should be periodically rinsed in water. This will ensure that a very smooth finish is imparted to the filler at the final stage.

At this stage, the "dent" should be surrounded by a ring of bare metal, which in turn should be encircled by the finely "feathered" edge of the good paintwork. Rinse the repair area with clean water, until all of the dust produced by the rubbing-down operation has gone.

Spray the whole area with a light coat of primer - this will show up any imperfections in the surface of the filler. Repair these imperfections with fresh filler paste or bodystopper, and once more smooth the surface with abrasive paper. Repeat this spray-and-repair procedure until you are satisfied that the surface of the filler, and the feathered edge of the paintwork, are perfect. Clean the repair area with clean water, and allow to dry fully.

> **HAYNES HiNT** *If bodystopper is used, it can be mixed with cellulose thinners, to form a really thin paste which is ideal for filling small holes.*

The repair area is now ready for final spraying. Paint spraying must be carried out in a warm, dry, windless and dust-free atmosphere. This condition can be created artificially if you have access to a large indoor working area, but if you are forced to work in the open, you will have to pick your day very carefully. If you are working indoors, dousing the floor in the work area with water will help to settle the dust which would otherwise be in the atmosphere. If the repair area is confined to one body panel, mask off the surrounding panels; this will help to minimise the effects of a slight mis-match in paint colours. Bodywork fittings (eg chrome strips, door handles etc) will also need to be masked off. Use genuine masking tape, and several thicknesses of newspaper, for the masking operations.

Before commencing to spray, agitate the aerosol can thoroughly, then spray a test area (an old tin, or similar) until the technique is mastered. Cover the repair area with a thick coat of primer; the thickness should be built up using several thin layers of paint, rather than one thick one. Using 400-grade wet-and-dry paper, rub down the surface of the primer until it is really smooth. While doing this, the work area should be thoroughly doused with water, and the wet-and-dry paper periodically rinsed in water. Allow to dry before spraying on more paint.

Spray on the top coat, again building up the thickness by using several thin layers of paint. Start spraying at one edge of the repair area, and then, using a side-to-side motion, work until the whole repair area and about 2 inches of the surrounding original paintwork is covered. Remove all masking material 10 to 15 minutes after spraying on the final coat of paint.

Allow the new paint at least two weeks to harden, then, using a paintwork renovator, or a very fine cutting paste, blend the edges of the paint into the existing paintwork. Finally, apply wax polish.

Plastic components

With the use of more and more plastic body components by the vehicle manufacturers (eg bumpers. spoilers, and in some cases major body panels), rectification of more serious damage to such items has become a matter of either entrusting repair work to a specialist in this field, or renewing complete components. Repair of such damage by the DIY owner is not really feasible, owing to the cost of the equipment and materials required for effecting such repairs. The basic technique involves making a groove along the line of the crack in the plastic, using a rotary burr in a power drill. The damaged part is then welded back together, using a hot-air gun to heat up and fuse a plastic filler rod into the groove. Any excess plastic is then removed, and the area rubbed down to a smooth finish. It is important that a filler rod of the correct plastic is used, as body components can be made of a variety of different types (eg polycarbonate, ABS, polypropylene).

Damage of a less serious nature (abrasions, minor cracks etc) can be repaired by the DIY owner using a two-part epoxy filler repair material. Once mixed in equal proportions, this is used in similar fashion to the bodywork filler used on metal panels. The filler is usually cured in twenty to thirty minutes, ready for sanding and painting.

If the owner is renewing a complete component himself, or if he has repaired it with epoxy filler, he will be left with the problem of finding a suitable paint for finishing which is compatible with the type of plastic used. At one time, the use of a universal paint was not possible, owing to the complex range of plastics encountered in body component applications. Standard paints, generally speaking, will not bond to plastic or rubber satisfactorily. However, it is now possible to obtain a plastic body parts finishing kit which consists of a pre-primer treatment, a primer and coloured top coat. Full instructions are normally supplied with a kit, but basically, the method of use is to first apply the pre-primer to the component concerned, and allow it to dry for up to 30 minutes. Then the primer is applied, and left to dry for about an hour before finally applying the special-coloured top coat. The result is a correctly-coloured component, where the paint will flex with the plastic or rubber, a property that standard paint does not normally posses.

5 Major body damage – repair

Where serious damage has occurred, or large areas need renewal due to neglect, it means that the complete new panels will need welding in, and this is best left to professionals. If the damage is due to impact, it will also be necessary to check completely the alignment of the bodyshell, and this can only be carried out accurately by an Audi dealer using special jigs. If the body is left misaligned, it is primarily dangerous as the car will not handle properly, and secondly, uneven stresses will be imposed on the steering, suspension and possibly transmission, causing abnormal wear, or complete failure, particularly to such items as the tyres.

6 Door inner trim panel – removal and refitting

1 Undo the screws and lift off the door front pillar trim (photos). Unscrew the door lock button.

2 Carefully prise off the door pull trim then undo the screws and remove the handle (photos).

6.1A Door pillar trim retaining screw (arrowed)

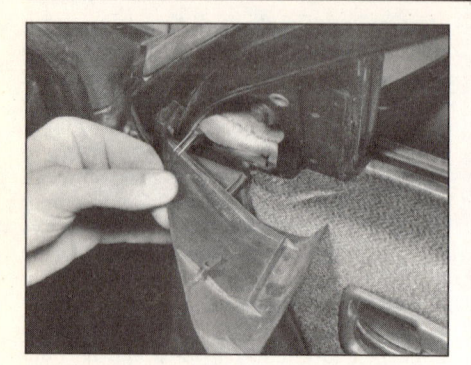

11•4 Bodywork

6.1B Removing the door pillar trim

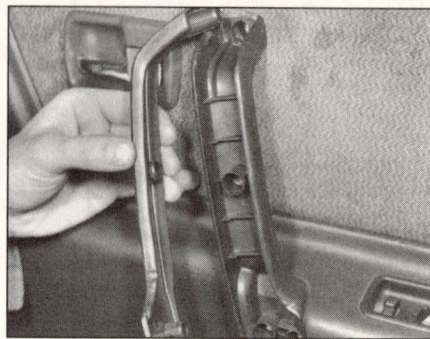

6.2A Remove the trim over the door pull . . .

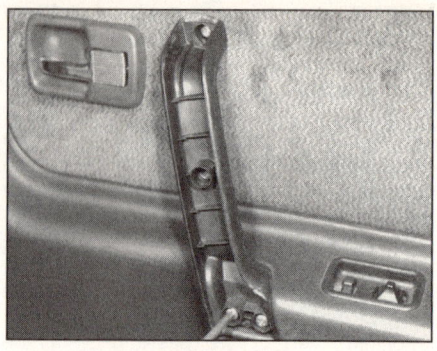

6.2B . . . then undo the screws and remove the door pull

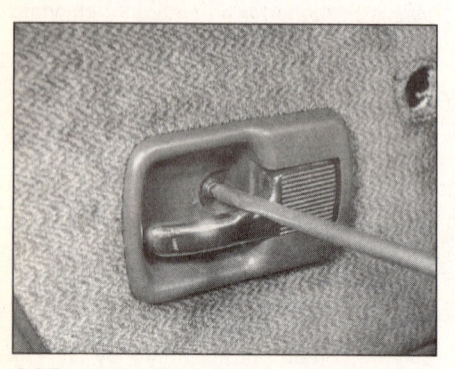

6.3 Removing the interior handle trim plate

6.5A Trim panel upper retaining screw (arrowed)

6.5B Trim panel retaining screw accessible through the door pull opening

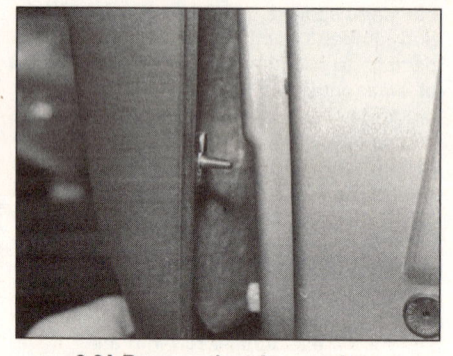

6.6A Remove the trim panel . . .

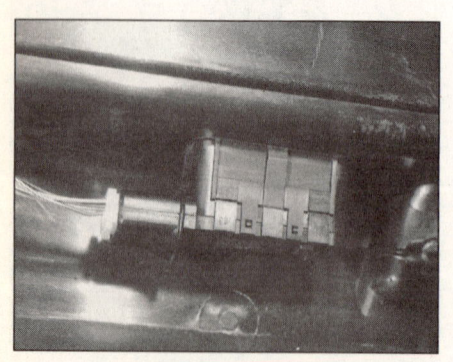

6.6B . . . and disconnect the power window switch wiring (where applicable)

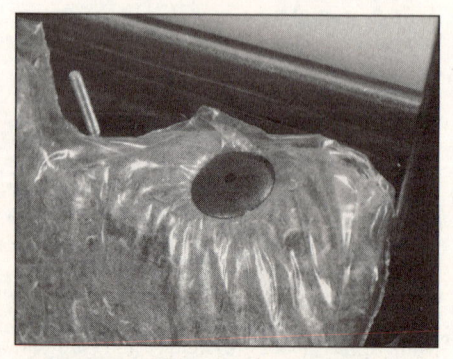

6.7 Insulation panel retaining clip

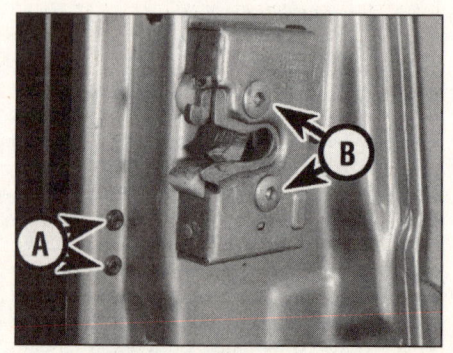

3 Undo the interior handle trim plate screw and remove the trim plate (photo).
4 Where manually-operated windows are fitted, prise off the window crank handle trim, undo the screw and remove the handle On later models the crank handle trim is removed by pressing the retaining lug at the knob end with a screwdriver, then pulling off (Fig. 11.1).
5 Undo the two upper screws at each end of the trim panel and the screw accessible through the door pull opening (photos).
6 Using a suitable flat tool, carefully prise the trim panel off the door, then pull the panel up and remove it from the door (photo). Where power windows are fitted, disconnect the wiring connector at the operating switch (photo).
7 To remove the inner insulation panel, remove the upper clips and lift the panel off the door (photo).
8 Refitting is a reversal of removal.

7 Door locks – removal and refitting

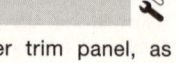

1 Remove the door inner trim panel, as described in Section 6.
2 Undo the two screws on the edge of the door securing the interior handle cable support (photo).
3 Undo the two door lock retaining screws using an Allen key.

7.2 Interior handle cable support screws (A) and lock retaining screws (B)

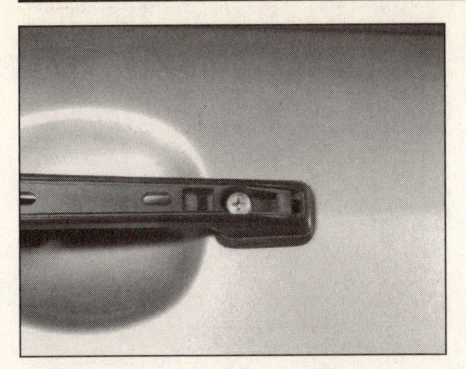

Bodywork 11•5

8.3 Door exterior handle retaining screw

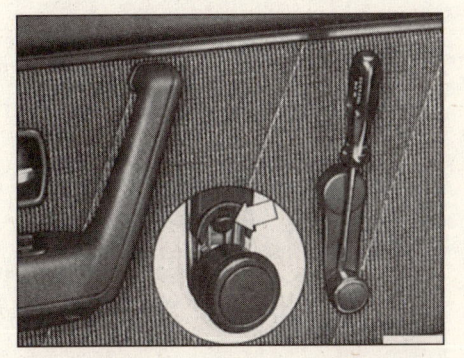

Fig. 11.1 Removal of the later type window crank handle trim by depressing lug (arrowed) with screwdriver (Sec 9)

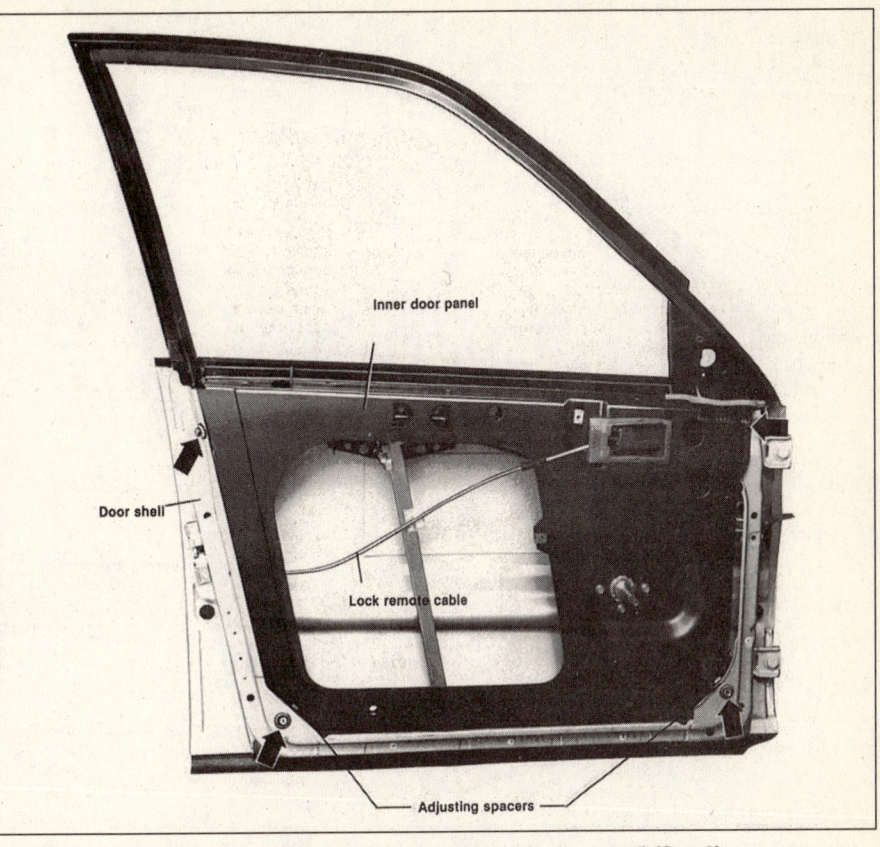

Fig. 11.2 Inner door panel retaining bolts (arrowed) (Sec 9)

4 Disconnect the operating rods and cable, then withdraw the lock from the door.
5 Refitting is a reversal of removal.

8 Door exterior handle – removal and refitting

1 Remove the door inner trim panel, as described in Section 6.
2 Carefully prise off the plastic insert using a screwdriver.
3 Disconnect the operating rods, undo the two screws and withdraw the handle from the door (photo).
4 Refitting is a reversal of removal.

9 Doors – dismantling and reassembly

1 Remove the inner trim panel, door lock and door exterior handle, as described in Sections 6, 7 and 8.
2 Disconnect the wiring connector on models with power windows.
3 Refer to Fig. 11.2 and undo the four bolts securing the inner door panel to the outer door panel. Note the adjusting spacers on two lower bolts.
4 Withdraw the complete inner door panel with the glass and frame from the outer door panel.
5 Undo the bolts securing the window regulator to the door panel (photos), and the clip securing the regulator slide to the window glass. Withdraw the regulator from the inner door panel.
6 Remove the window glass by sliding it down and out of the guide channels.
7 Refitting is a reversal of removal, but adjust the window glass as follows before refitting the inner door panel to the outer door panel.
8 Move the window to its lowest position using the regulator handle or by temporarily reconnecting the power window wiring.
9 View down the guide channel and check that the lower guide pin is located in the centre of the guide. If not, slacken the

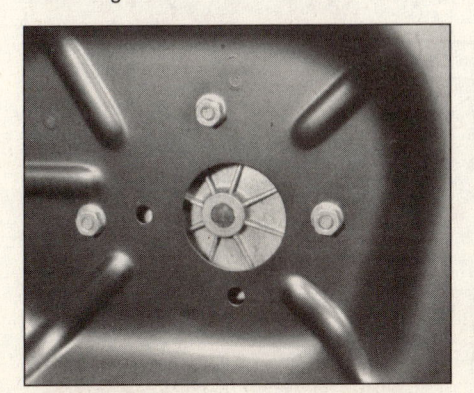

9.5A Window regulator retaining nuts . . .

9.5B . . . and regulator frame upper . . .

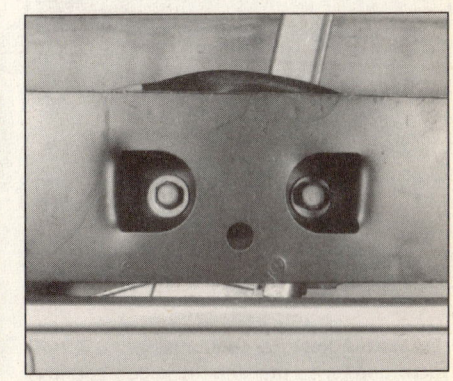

9.5C . . . and lower retaining bolts

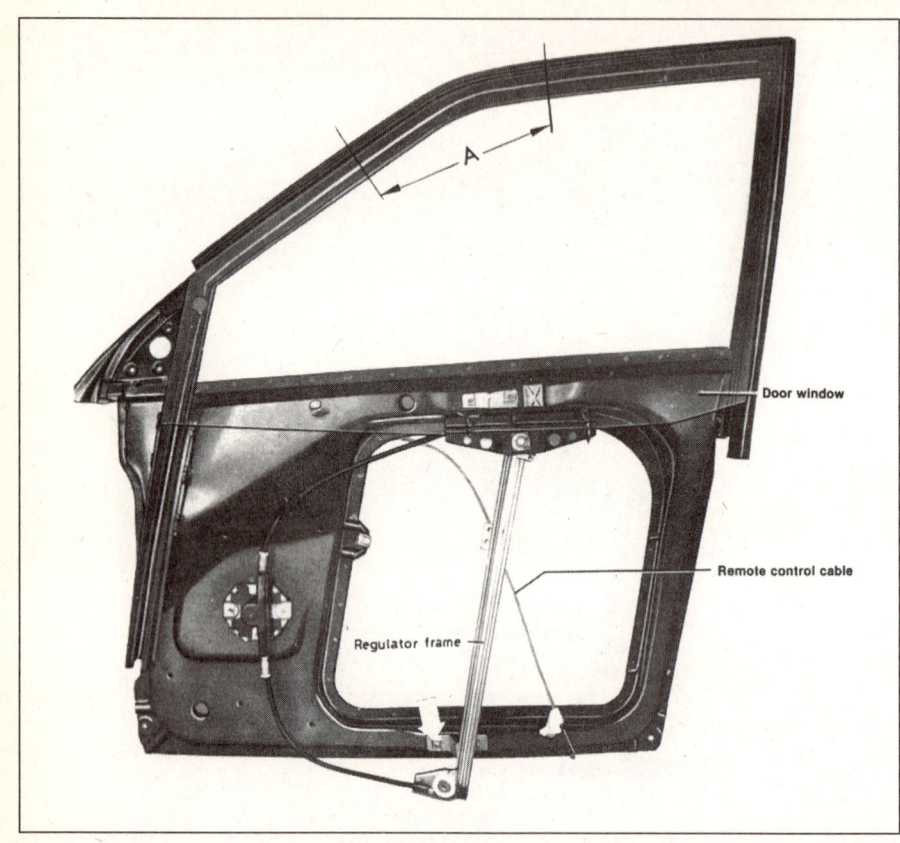

Fig. 11.3 Window regulator with lower mounting (arrowed) as viewed from inside the inner door panel (Sec 9)

A Door-to-body critical sealing area

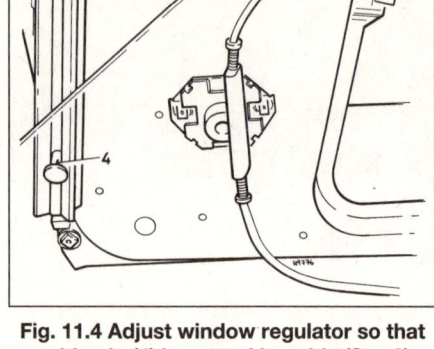

Fig. 11.4 Adjust window regulator so that guide pin (4) is central in guide (Sec 9)

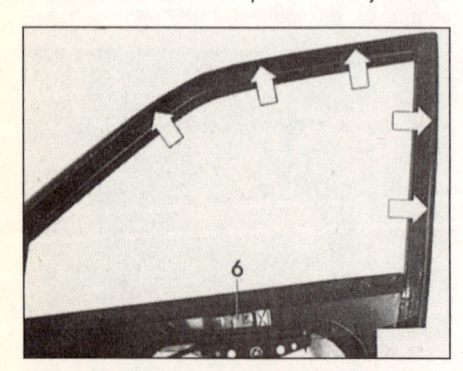

Fig. 11.5 Adjust the regulator frame upper mounting (6) so that the glass contacts the seal evenly at the points indicated (Sec 9)

Fig. 11.6 Regulator slide stop screw (arrowed) for additional adjustment of glass position (Sec 9)

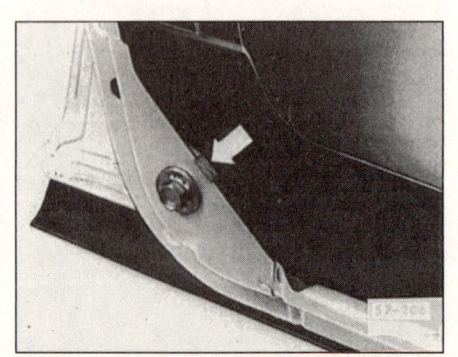

Fig. 11.7 Door inner panel lower mounting spacer location – arrowed (Sec 9)

regulator retaining bolts and move the regulator within the elongated holes until the guide pin is centralised.
10 Raise the window and adjust the regulator frame upper mounting so that the glass contacts the seal evenly at the points indicated in Fig. 11.5. It may also be necessary to turn the stop screw on the regulator slide as required (Fig. 11.6).
11 With the inner and outer door panels assembled, adjust the inner panel as follows.
12 Check the closure of the door and the fit of the door in the door aperture. If adjustment is necessary, slacken all four bolts securing the inner panel to the outer panel. Move the panel as necessary noting the following:
(a) The elongated holes in the upper mountings allow height adjustment
(b) The elongated holes in the lower mountings allow height and side adjustment
(c) By changing the thickness of the spacers at the lower mountings (two thicknesses available) lateral adjustment of the panel at the top of the window frame is allowed
(d) The most critical sealing area of the door is midway along the window frame at the top (Fig. 11.3) and attention should be paid to the fit and adjustment of the door in this area.

10 Doors – removal and refitting

1 Remove the inner trim panel, as described in Section 6.
2 If the same door is being refitted, mark round the hinges on the door to simplify realignment.
3 Disconnect the electrical and vacuum connections inside the door, as applicable, and remove the wiring and hoses from the door. If an electric mirror is fitted, disconnect the wiring plug in the footwell – see Chapter 13, Section 13.
4 Drill off the lower part of the door check strap retaining rivet then remove the rivet using a drift.
5 Support the door, undo the hinge retaining bolts (photo) and remove the door from the car.
6 Refitting is a reversal of removal, but peen over the bottom of a new check strap rivet to retain it in place. Adjust the striker, as described in Section 11, and adjust the inner door panel, as described in Section 9, if a satisfactory fit of the door cannot be achieved at the striker.

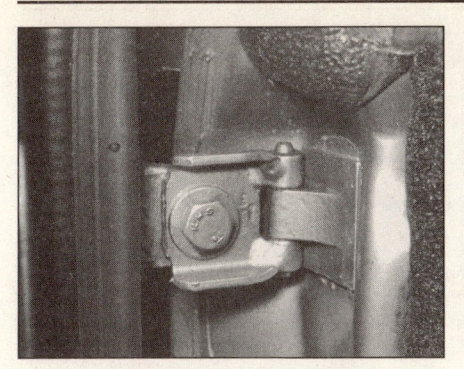

Bodywork 11•7

10.5 Door hinge retaining bolt

11.1 Front door striker pin

12.2A Windscreen washer hose connector . . .

11 Door striker – adjustment

1 Mark round the door striker (photo) with a pencil, or a fine ballpoint pen.
2 Fit a spanner to the hexagon on the striker and unscrew the striker about one turn so that the striker moves when tapped with a soft-headed hammer.
3 Tap the striker towards the inside of the car if the door rattles, or towards the outside of the car if the door fits too tightly, but be careful to keep the striker in the same horizontal line, unless it also requires vertical adjustment. Only move the striker a small amount at a time; the actual amount moved can be checked by reference to the pencil mark made before the striker was loosened.
4 When a position has been found in which the door closes firmly, but without difficulty, tighten the striker.
5 If a satisfactory adjustment cannot be achieved at the striker, check the adjustment of the inner door panel, as described in Section 9.

12 Bonnet – removal, refitting and adjustment

1 Support the bonnet in its open position and place some rags in the corners by the hinges
2 Disconnect the windscreen washer hose

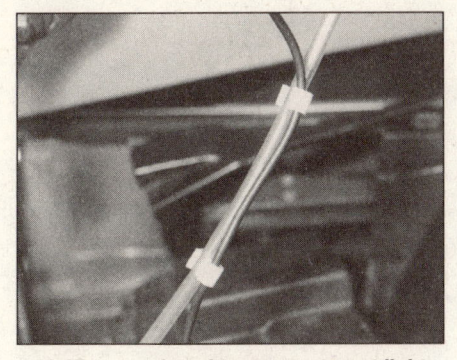

12.2B . . . and engine compartment light wiring clipped to hose

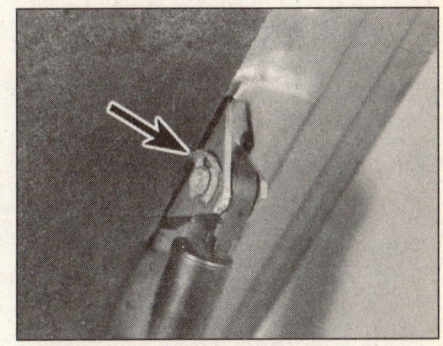

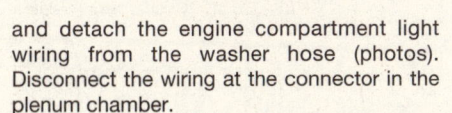

and detach the engine compartment light wiring from the washer hose (photos). Disconnect the wiring at the connector in the plenum chamber.
3 Mark around the hinges to facilitate realignment when refitting.
4 Extract the retaining clips from the support strut upper retaining pins (photo) and withdraw the pins.
5 Undo the four bonnet hinge retaining bolts and, with the help of an assistant, lift the bonnet off the car (photo).
6 Refitting is a reversal of removal, but adjust the hinges to their original positions so that the bonnet edge gap remains constant. If necessary adjust the two strikers on the front of the bonnet to achieve satisfactory closure.

12.4 Support strut pin retaining clip (arrowed)

13 Bonnet support strut – removal and refitting

1 Support the bonnet in the open position.
2 Extract the retaining clip from the support strut upper retaining pin and withdraw the pin.
3 If the strut lower mounting is of the plastic ball socket type, withdraw the retaining clip approximately 4.0 mm (0.15 in) using a screwdriver and pull the strut lower mounting off the ball-stud. Do not remove the clip fully or it will be damaged.
4 If the lower mounting is of the metal ball socket type, pull out the retaining pin using pliers and remove the strut lower mounting from the ball-stud.
5 Refitting is a reversal of removal.

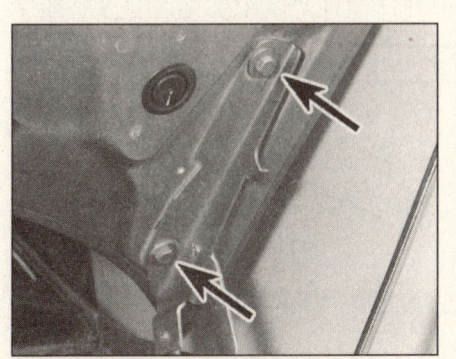

12.5 Bonnet hinge retaining bolts (arrowed)

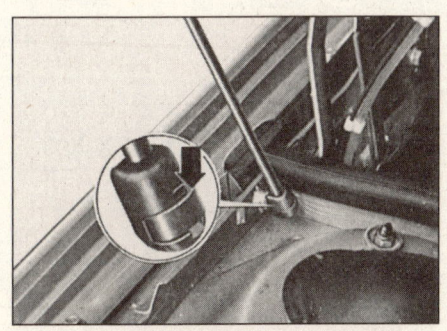

Fig. 11.8 Retaining clip (arrowed) on bonnet support strut with plastic ball socket (Sec 13)

Fig. 11.9 Retaining pin (arrowed) on bonnet support strut with metal ball socket (Sec 13)

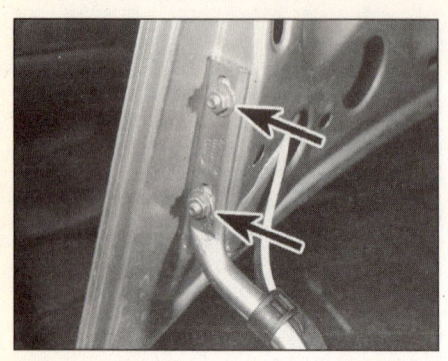

15.2 Boot lid hinge retaining nuts (arrowed)

14 Bonnet lock cable – removal, refitting and adjustment

1 Remove the radiator grille, as described in Section 22.
2 Undo the clamp bolt and disconnect the cable end from the nipple.
3 Release the cable from the locking levers, sleeves and cable clips in the engine compartment.
4 Undo the two screws securing the cable release lever assembly inside the car, pull the cable through the bulkhead and remove it from inside the car.
5 Refitting is a reversal of removal, but adjust the cable to take up the free play at the nipple without tensioning the locking levers.

15 Boot lid – removal, refitting and adjustment

1 Support the boot lid in its open position, and place some rags beneath the corners by the hinges.
2 Disconnect the wiring loom and vacuum hose, as necessary, then mark the location of the hinges with a pencil (photo).
3 With the help of an assistant, unscrew the nuts and withdraw the boot lid from the car.
4 Refitting is a reversal of removal, but adjust the hinges to their original positions so that the boot lid is level with the surrounding bodywork.

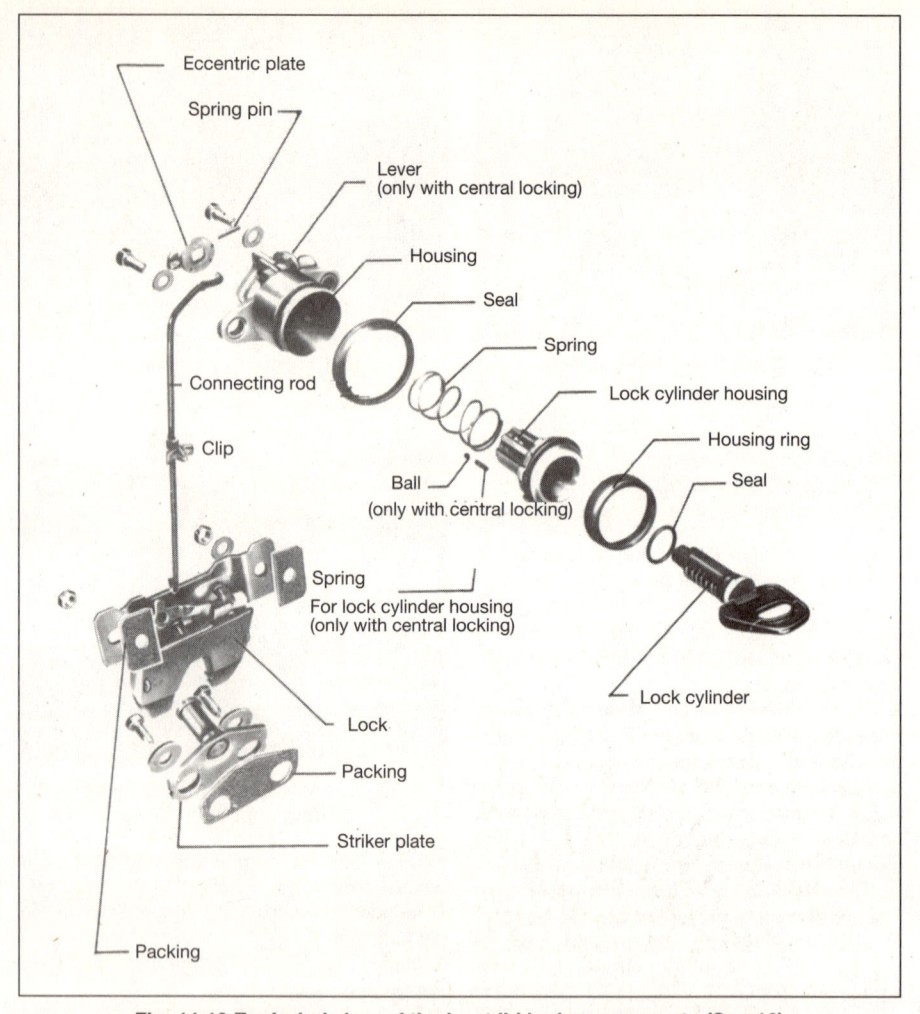

Fig. 11.10 Exploded view of the boot lid lock components (Sec 16)

Eccentric plate
Spring pin
Lever (only with central locking)
Housing
Seal
Spring
Lock cylinder housing
Housing ring
Seal
Lock cylinder
Connecting rod
Clip
Ball (only with central locking)
Spring For lock cylinder housing (only with central locking)
Lock
Packing
Striker plate
Packing

16 Boot lid lock – removal, refitting and adjustment

1 Open the boot lid, undo the two bolts and withdraw the lock cylinder from the boot lid (photo).
2 Twist the lock to release it from the connecting rod and remove it from the car.
3 Undo the two nuts and withdraw the lock mechanism off the studs (photo). Recover the packing, where fitted.
4 Disconnect the connecting rod and remove the lock from the car.
5 Refitting is a reversal of removal, but adjust the closure of the boot lid and the operation of the lock by adjusting the striker plate as necessary (photo).

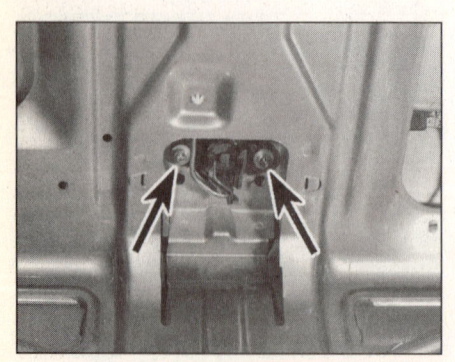

16.1 Boot lid lock cylinder retaining bolts (arrowed)

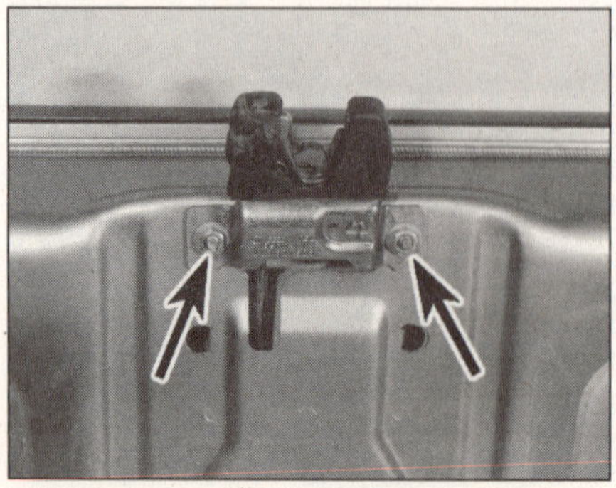

16.3 Boot lid lock mechanism retaining nuts (arrowed)

16.5 Boot lid striker plate retaining bolts (arrowed)

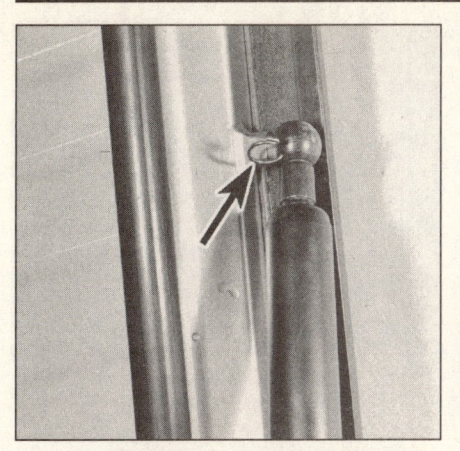

Bodywork 11•9

17.3 Tailgate support strut locking clip (arrowed)

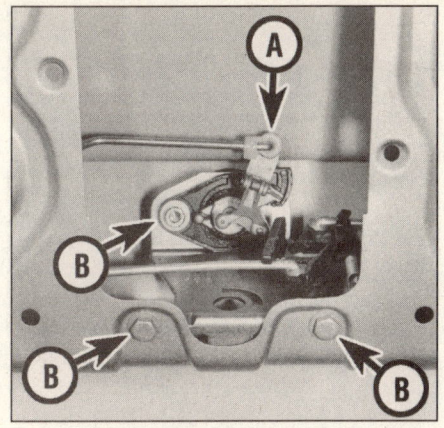

18.2 Tailgate lock connecting rod clip (A) and retaining bolts (B)

17 Tailgate (Avant models) – removal, refitting and adjustment

1 Disconnect the battery negative lead. Open the tailgate and support it.
2 Disconnect the wiring, vacuum and washer hose, as applicable, and withdraw the wiring and hoses from the tailgate.
3 Extract the locking clip and remove the support struts from the tailgate ball-studs (photo).
4 Mark the outline of the tailgate hinges.
5 Undo the four hinge plate retaining bolts and with the help of an assistant, remove the tailgate from the car.
6 Refitting is a reversal of removal, but adjust the position of the tailgate hinges to provide an even gap down both sides, together with satisfactory closing.

18 Tailgate lock (Avant models) – removal, refitting and adjustment

1 Open the tailgate and remove the inner trim to gain access to the lock assemblies.
2 Detach the clip and disengage the connecting rod from the lock cylinder arm (photo).
3 Undo the bolt securing the lock cylinder to the tailgate and the two bolts securing the lock carrier plate to the tailgate.
4 Disconnect the two pullrods and remove the assembly through the tailgate aperture.
5 To remove the two lock mechanisms undo the retaining bolts, withdraw the mechanism into the tailgate and disengage the pullrod. Remove the lock from the car.
6 Refitting is the reversal of removal, but if necessary adjust the striker plate to give satisfactory closure of the tailgate and operation of the lock.

19 Windscreen, rear window and fixed window glass – removal and refitting

All fixed windows are attached by direct flush bonding to the bodywork, and the removal and refitting of glass should be left to your Audi dealer or a specialist glass replacement company.

20 Sunroof – general

A steel sunroof, either mechanically or electrically operated, is available on all models.
The sunroof is maintenance-free, but any adjustment or removal and refitting of the component parts should be entrusted to a dealer due to the complexity of the unit and the need to remove much of the interior trim and headlining to gain access. The latter operation is involved, and entails the use of special tools.

21 Bumpers – removal and refitting

Front bumper

1 Where fitted, remove the front foglights and/or direction indicators from the bumper, as described in Chapter 12.
2 Lever off the edging strip along the top edge of the bumper below the headlights.
3 Undo the screws below the radiator grille securing the centre trim strip, then carefully lever up the strip at both ends (photo) and remove it.
4 Refer to Section 22 and remove the radiator grille and ventilation grille.
5 Undo the two upper and one lower bolt on each side (photos) and pull the bumper forwards slightly.
6 Detach the headlamp washer hose, where applicable, then pull the bumper forwards out of the side guides and remove it from the car.
7 Refitting is a reversal of removal.

Rear bumper

8 From within the luggage compartment, undo the two bolts each side securing the bumper mounting brackets, pull the bumper rearwards out of the side guides and remove it from the car.
9 Refitting is a reversal of removal.

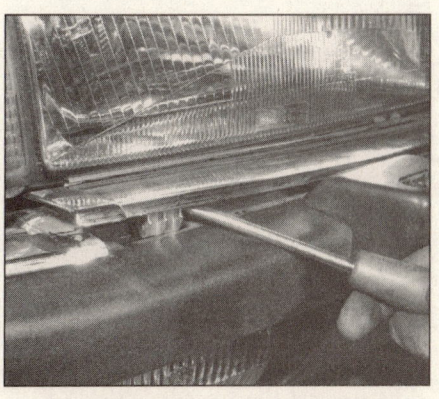

21.3 Removing the bumper centre trim strip (Audi 100 shown)

21.5A Front bumper upper right-hand retaining bolts

21.5B Front bumper lower right-hand retaining bolt (arrowed)

11•10 Bodywork

22.1 Removing the radiator grille centre retaining screw

22.2 Releasing the radiator grille side retaining catches

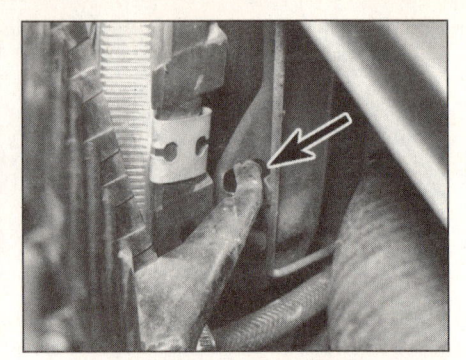

22.3 Radiator grille lower retaining lug (arrowed)

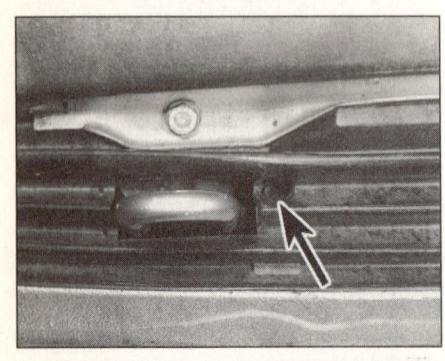

22.4 Ventilation grille retaining screw (arrowed)

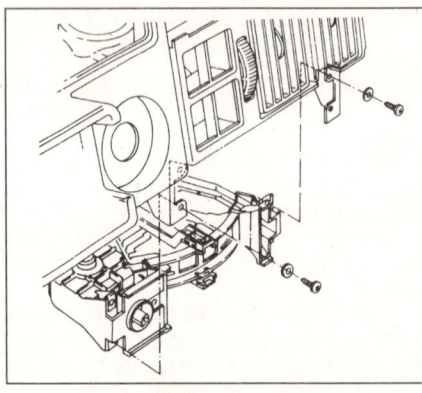

Fig. 11.11 Heater control panel attachments at the facia – Audi 100 and Audi 5000S (Sec 23)

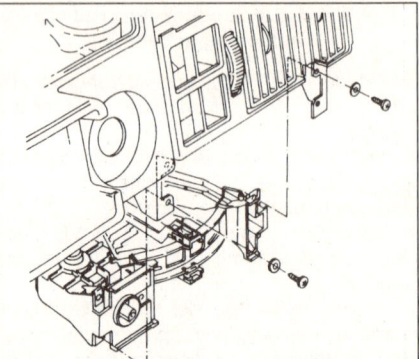

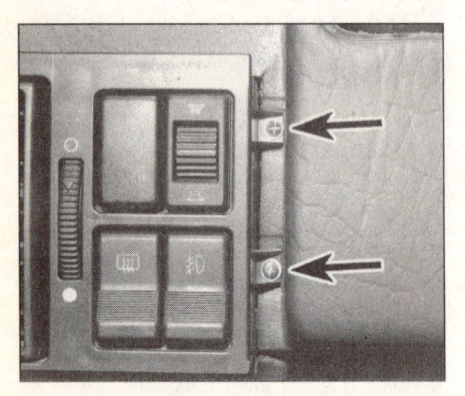

23.5 Upper switch and vent panel retaining screws (arrowed)

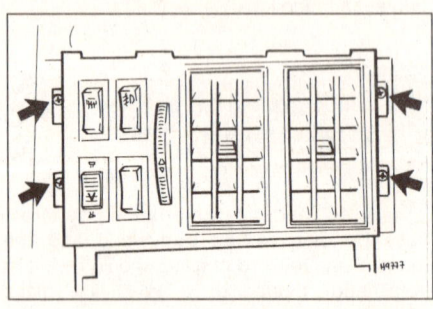

Fig. 11.12 Switch and vent panel retaining screws (arrowed) – Audi 100 and Audi 5000S (Sec 23)

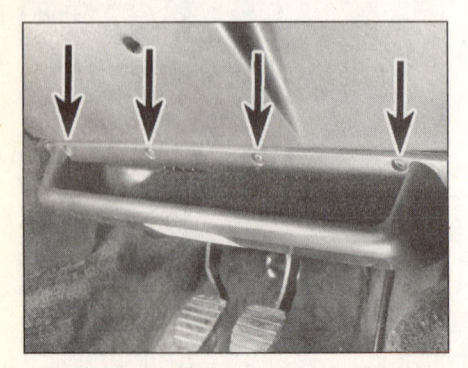

23.6 Driver's side parcel shelf retaining screws (arrowed)

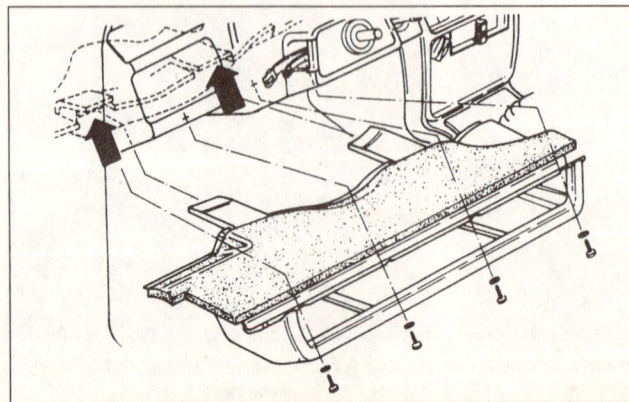

Fig. 11.13 Driver's side parcel shelf attachments – Audi 100 and Audi 5000S (Sec 23)

22 Radiator grille and ventilation grille – removal and refitting

1 Open the bonnet and undo the radiator grille centre retaining screw (photo).
2 Release the catches on each side of the grille and pull it forwards (photo).
3 Disengage the lower lugs and remove the radiator grille from the car (photo).
4 To remove the ventilation grille below the bumper, undo the screws each side (photo) and withdraw the grille.
5 Refitting is a reversal of removal.

23 Facia – removal and refitting

Audi 100 and Audi 5000S models

1 Remove the steering wheel, as described in Chapter 10.
2 Remove the combination switch and instrument panel, as described in Chapter 12.
3 Remove the centre console, as described in Section 24 of this Chapter.
4 Undo the four screws at the side of the heater control panel and lower the panel.
5 Undo the four screws at the side of the upper switch and vent panel (photo), withdraw the panel and disconnect the wiring at the rear after labelling the connectors. Remove the panel.

Bodywork 11•11

6 Undo the parcel shelf retaining screws on the driver's side, lower the shelf and detach it from its guides. Remove the shelf (photo).
7 Undo the parcel shelf retaining screws on the passenger's side, lower the shelf and detach it from its guides. Remove the shelf.
8 Disconnect the air ducts at the heater blower under the facia.
9 Undo the two screws each side (photo) and one through the instrument panel aperture securing the facia to its brackets. Detach the wiring harness at the cable clips and cable binder, and pull the facia out of its location. Remove the facia from the car.
10 Refitting is a reversal of removal.

Audi 200 and Audi 5000 Turbo models

11 Remove the steering wheel, as described in Chapter 10.
12 Remove the combination switch and instrument panel, as described in Chapter 12.
13 Undo the screw securing the left-hand hinge of the glove compartment to the facia. Disengage the glove compartment from the right-hand hinge and remove it from the facia.
14 Press out the side moulding lower clip, undo the three screws and remove the side moulding by lowering it to disengage the upper tags (Fig. 11.18).
15 Undo the screws, disengage the tags and remove the cover under the facia on the driver's side.
16 Remove the gear lever knob or selector

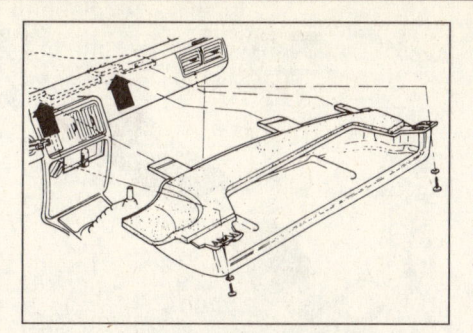

Fig. 11.14 Passenger's side parcel shelf attachments – Audi100 and Audi 5000S (Sec 23)

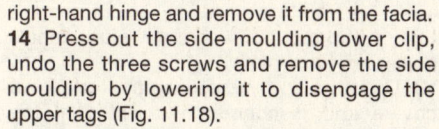

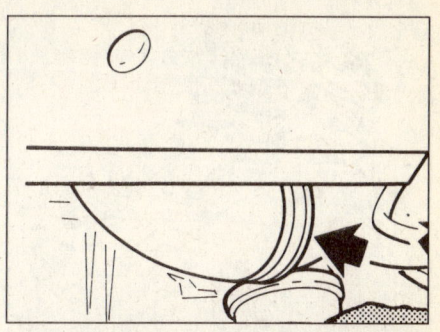

Fig. 11.15 Air duct attachments beneath the facia (arrowed) – Audi 100 and Audi 5000S (Sec 23)

23.9 Facia right-hand side retaining screws

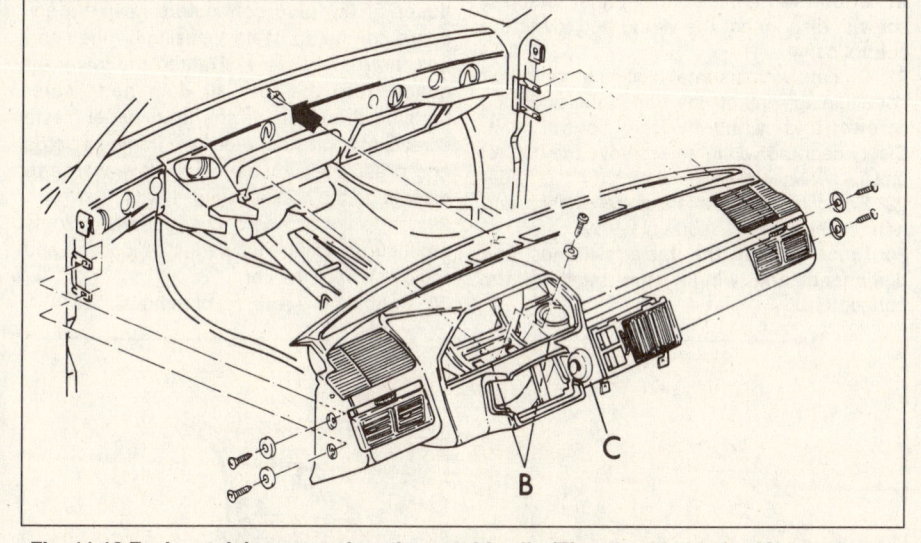

Fig. 11.16 Facia retaining screw locations, cable clip (B) and cable binder (C) locations – Audi 100 and Audi 5000S (Sec 23)

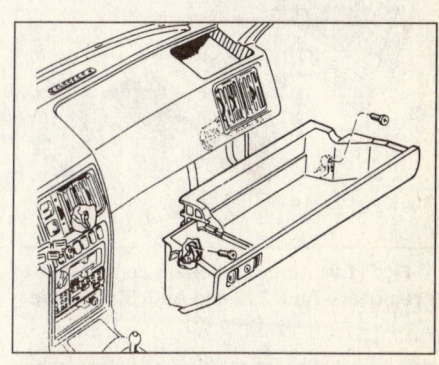

Fig. 11.17 Glove compartment removal – Audi 200 and Audi 5000 Turbo (Sec 23)

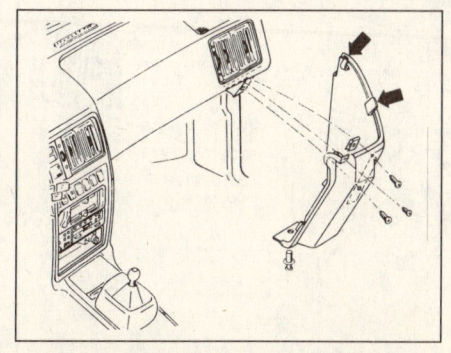

Fig. 11.18 Side moulding retaining screws and upper tags (arrowed) – Audi 200 and Audi 5000 Turbo (Sec 23)

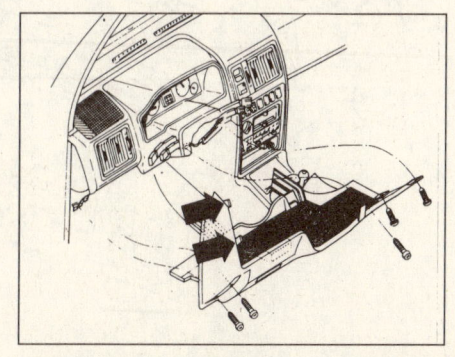

Fig. 11.19 Driver's side cover under facia retaining screws and tags (arrowed) – Audi 200 and Audi 5000 Turbo (Sec 23)

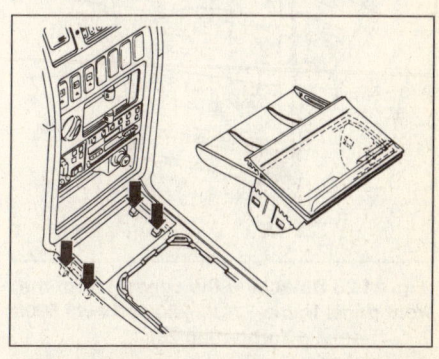

Fig. 11.20 Ashtray insert retaining tabs (arrowed) – Audi 200 and Audi 5000 Turbo (Sec 23)

11•12 Bodywork

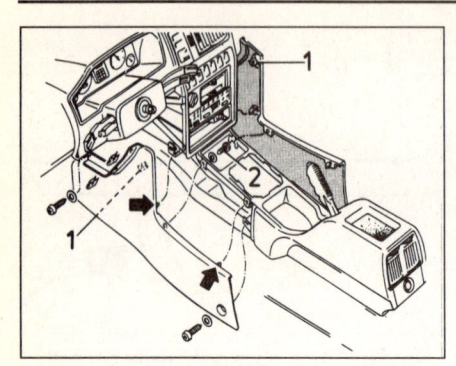

Fig. 11.21 Centre console side panel removal – Audi 200 and Audi 5000 Turbo (Sec 23)

1 Upper retaining clips
2 Inner retaining screw
Side retaining clip locations arrowed

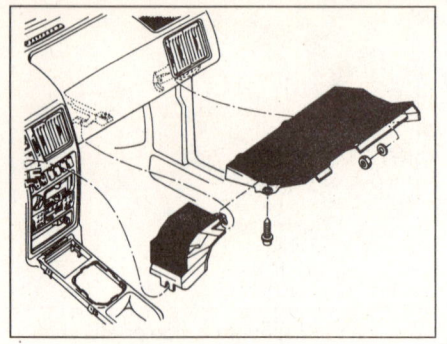

Fig. 11.22 Facia inner cover removal – Audi 200 and Audi 5000 Turbo (Sec 23)

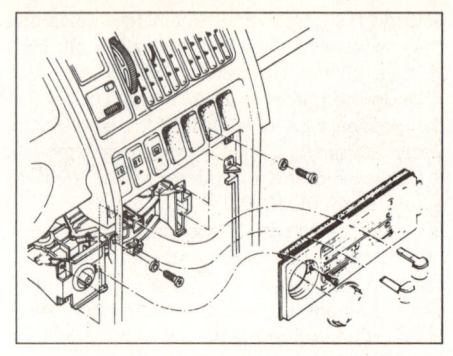

Fig. 11.23 Heater control panel faceplate removal – Audi 200 and Audi 5000 Turbo (Sec 23)

lever handle then disengage the gear lever or selector lever trim from the clips by pulling it upwards.

17 Press the ashtray insert retaining tabs outwards and press out the ashtray insert through the gear lever trim aperture in the console.

18 Undo the screws and disengage the clips then withdraw both console side panels downwards to remove.

19 Undo the screws securing the facia inner covers and disconnect the wiring at the adjacent control units. Remove the covers and control units.

20 Pull off the heater control knobs, undo the heater control faceplate screw and remove the faceplate.

21 Undo the heater control panel retaining screws, disconnect the wiring and lower the control panel.

22 On cars with automatic climate control/air conditioning, pull off the trim plate, undo the screws and withdraw the control unit. Disconnect the wiring and remove the control unit.

23 Refer to Chapter 12 if necessary and remove the radio/cassette player.

24 Press out all the facia switches and disconnect the wiring after labelling the connectors.

25 Remove the on-board computer after disconnecting and labelling the wiring connectors.

26 Detach the wiring harness, plug connectors and auxiliary relay panel from the facia and console.

27 Pull the wiring harness out of the facia.

28 On cars with air conditioning, disconnect the wiring at the sensor in the centre of the facia. Disconnect the air conditioning vacuum hoses at the plug connectors near the on-board computer, heater housing on the right, and instrument panel. Detach the lower air hoses from the rear air duct and heater housing then remove the front panel frame screws at each side, press the frame forwards and press the console cover downwards to disengage the retainers (Fig. 11.25).

29 Undo the screws securing the facia to its mountings, pull the facia from its location and remove it from the car.

30 Refitting is a reversal of removal.

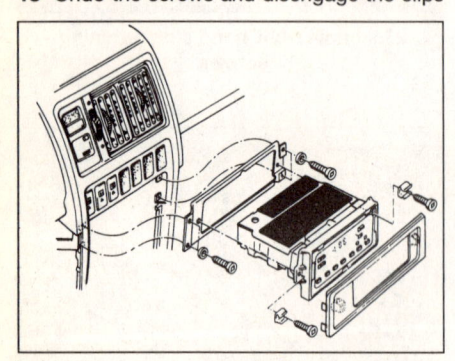

Fig. 11.24 Air conditioning control unit removal – Audi 200 and Audi 5000 Turbo (Sec 23)

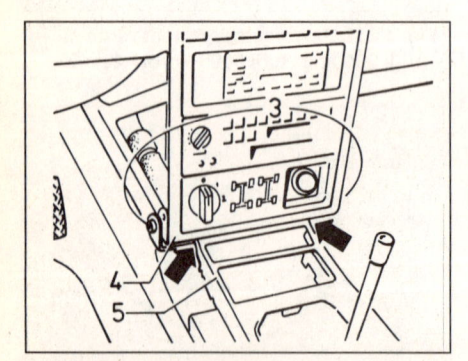

Fig. 11.25 Detaching the console from the front panel frame – Audi 200 and Audi 5000 Turbo (Sec 23)

3 Retaining screws
4 Front panel
5 Console
Console to front panel retaining tags arrowed

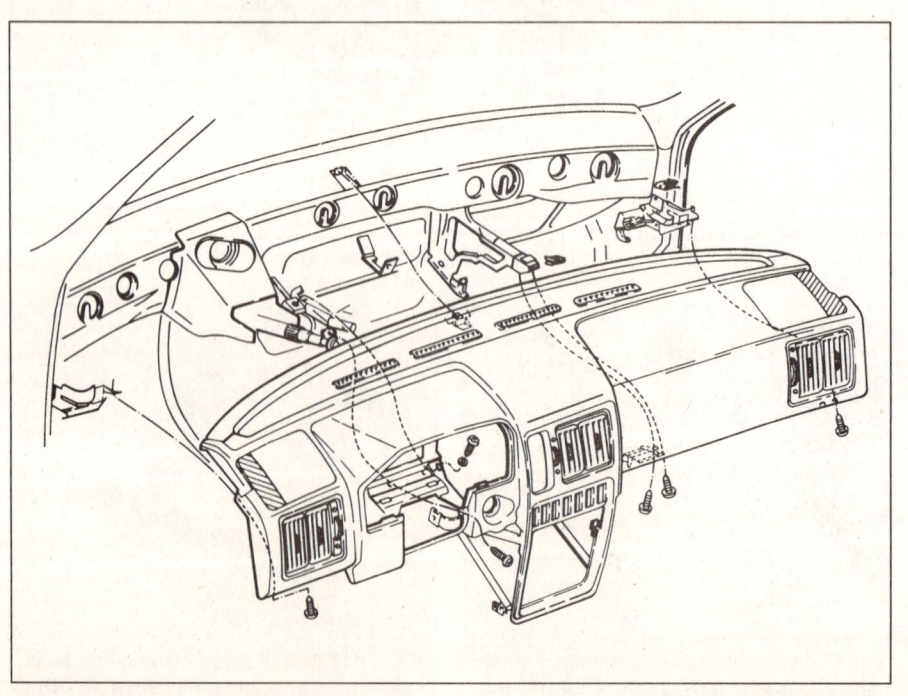

Fig. 11.26 Facia retaining screw locations – Audi 200 and Audi 5000 Turbo (Sec 23)

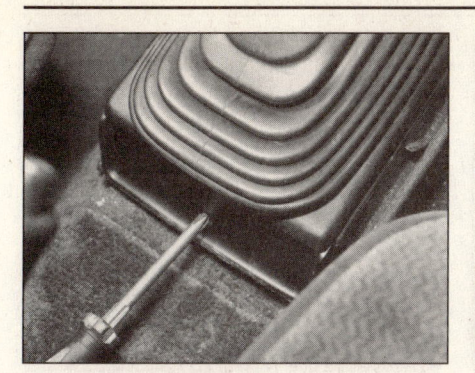

Bodywork 11•13

24.2 Removing the centre console cover trim retaining screw

24.3 Console trim surround rear retaining screw (arrowed)

24.4 Console trim surround front retaining screw (arrowed)

24 Centre console – removal and refitting

Audi 100 and Audi 5000S models

1 Disconnect the battery negative lead.
2 Remove the gear lever knob then undo the screw at the rear and remove the cover trim (photo).
3 Undo the two rear screws securing the console trim surround (photo).
4 Remove the ashtray and undo the two screws at the front accessible through the ashtray aperture (photo).
5 Lift the trim surround up at the rear, disengage it from the retaining tags and remove it from the console (photo).
6 Remove the radio/cassette player, as described in Chapter 12, or the trim over the radio aperture if a radio/cassette player is not fitted.
7 Pull off the heater control knobs (photos), then undo the screw securing the heater control panel and remove the panel (photos).
8 If switches are fitted below the radio aperture, push them out and disconnect the wiring after noting their locations and labelling the wiring.
9 Disconnect the wiring at the cigarette lighter.
10 Undo the console retaining screws and withdraw the console from its location.
11 Refitting is a reversal of removal.

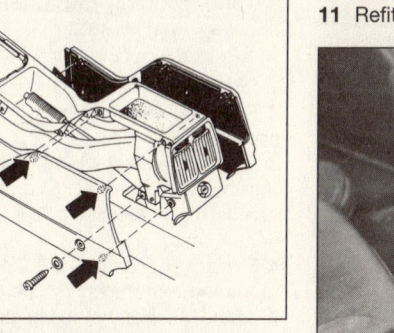

Audi 200 and Audi 5000 Turbo models

12 Disconnect the battery negative lead.
13 Remove the gear lever knob or selector lever handle. Remove the trim around the handle or lever by pulling up to disengage the clips.
14 Remove the ashtray by pressing the retaining tabs outwards then press out the ashtray insert through the gear or selector lever aperture (Fig. 11.20).
15 Undo the screws and disengage the clips, then withdraw both console side panels downwards to remove (Fig. 11.21).
16 Undo the screws, disengage the clips and withdraw both rear side panels.
17 Undo the screws, disconnect the wiring

Fig. 11.27 Centre console rear side panel removal – Audi 200 and Audi 5000 Turbo (Sec 24)

Retaining clip locations arrowed

24.5 Removing the console trim surround

24.7A Pull off the heater control rotary ...

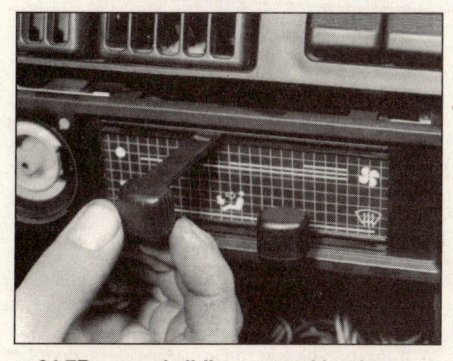

24.7B ... and sliding control knobs ...

24.7C ... undo the control panel retaining screw (arrowed)

24.7D ... and remove the control panel

11•14 Bodywork

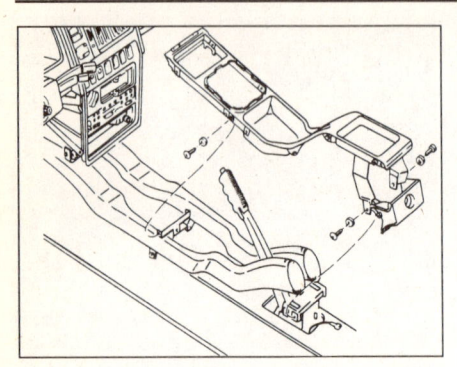

Fig. 11.28 Centre console upper section removal – Audi 200 and Audi 5000 Turbo (Sec 24)

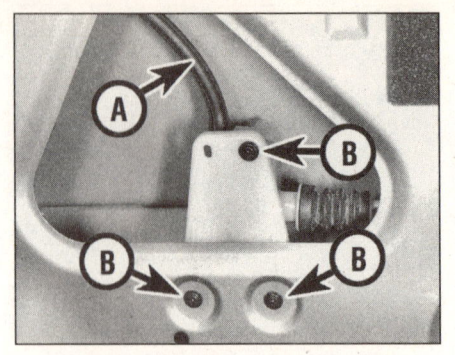

26.2 Central locking actuator vacuum hose (A) and retaining screws (B) in the Avant tailgate

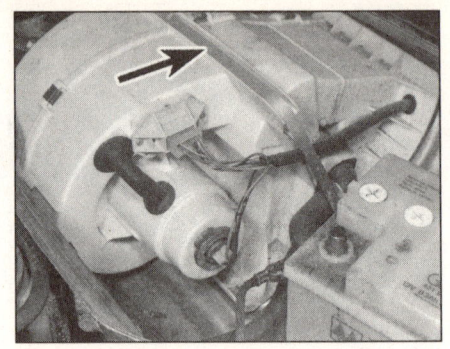

28.6 Heater unit retaining strap (arrowed)

and withdraw the console upper section rearwards to remove.
18 Refitting is a reversal of removal.

25 Seats – removal and refitting

Front seat

1 Push the seat fully forward.
2 Remove the screw where fitted, then pull the trim piece from the seat runner.
3 Pull the cap from the seat runner side-member.
4 At the front of the seat unscrew the stop nut.
5 Pull up the lever and slide the seat off the rear of the runners. Remove the seat through the door aperture.
6 Where electrically-operated front seats are fitted, disconnect the battery negative lead, disconnect the wiring and undo the bolts securing the seat frame to the floor (see also Chapter 12).
7 Refitting is a reversal of removal.

Rear seat

8 To remove the cushion, remove the two screws, one each side below the front edge, lift up the cushion at the front and pull it upwards and out.
9 To remove the seat back on Saloon models, remove the cushion then undo the two screws at the bottom of the seat back, lift it up and out to remove. (See also Chapter 13, Section 13.)
10 To remove the seat back on Avant models, remove the trim as necessary to gain access to the hinges.
11 Undo the hinge retaining bolts and remove the seat back from the car.
12 Refitting is a reversal of removal.

26 Central door locking system – general

1 Certain models are equipped with a central door locking system which automatically locks all doors and the rear boot lid/tailgate in unison with the manual locking of either front door. The system is vacuum-operated, and the vacuum for the system is generated by an electric pump located under the rear seat.
2 Any fault in the system is most likely to be caused by a leak in one of the hoses, in which case the hose and connection should be checked and repaired as necessary. Access to the relevant actuator is straightforward after removal of the appropriate trim panel (photo). Removal and refitting of the actuator entails disconnecting the vacuum hose and operating rod, then undoing the retaining screws. Refitting is a reversal of removal. If a fault develops on the vacuum pump repair should be entrusted to an Audi dealer, but first check that a fuse has not blown.

27 Power operated windows – general

1 Certain models are equipped with power (electric) operated windows which can be raised or lowered when the ignition is switched on.
2 If a fault develops, first check that the system fuse has not blown.
3 Access to the electric motors and regulator mechanism is gained by removing the door panels, as described in Section 9.

28 Heater unit (without air conditioning) – removal and refitting

1 Disconnect the battery negative lead.
2 Drain the cooling system, as described in Chapter 2.
3 Disconnect the heater hoses at the engine compartment bulkhead.
4 Refer to Section 24 or Section 23 and remove the centre console or facia components, as applicable, sufficiently to release the heater controls from their attachments, and the air ducts and wiring from the heater and facia.
5 Remove the black plastic cover over the plenum chamber in the engine compartment.
6 Undo the screw and free the heater retaining strap (photo).
7 Withdraw the heater upwards from its location and remove it, complete with heater controls and wiring loom, from the engine compartment.
8 Refitting is a reversal of removal, but renew the self-adhesive seals on the heater assembly before installing.

29 Heater blower motor (without air conditioning) – removal and refitting

1 Disconnect the battery negative lead.
2 Remove the heater unit as described above.
3 Disconnect the wiring plug on the end of the blower motor and extract the motor ventilating hose elbow from the motor and heater case.
4 Extract the circlip, retaining washer and grommet from the end of the motor.
5 At the other end of the heater unit, withdraw the intake duct and air flap then pull the motor and fan out of the heater case.
6 Refitting is a reversal of removal.

30 Heater controls (without air conditioning) – removal and refitting

1 Disconnect the battery negative lead.
2 Refer to Section 24 or Section 23 and remove the centre console or facia components, as applicable, sufficiently to release the heater controls from their attachments.
3 Release the clips securing the control cables to the control unit then disconnect the cable ends from the operating levers. Remove the control unit.
4 If the cables are to be removed, disconnect them at the heater then pull through the bulkhead to remove.

Bodywork 11•15

5 Refitting is a reversal of removal. To adjust the cables, connect them to the heater first then pull the inner cables out as far as they will go. Attach the inner cables to the control unit levers, set the levers and rotary knob in their end positions and secure the outer cables with the retaining clips.

31 Air conditioning – precautions and maintenance

1 Never disconnect any part of the air conditioner refrigeration circuit unless the system has been discharged by your Audi dealer or a qualified refrigeration engineer.
2 Where the compressor or condenser obstruct other mechanical operations such as engine removal, then it is permissible to unbolt their mountings and move them to the limit of their flexible hose deflection, but not to disconnect the hoses. If there is still insufficient room to carry out the required work then the system must be discharged before disconnecting and removing the assemblies.
3 The system will, of course, have to be recharged on completion.
4 Regularly check the condenser for clogging with flies or dirt. Hose clean with water or compressed air.
5 Check the drivebelt condition and if necessary adjust the belt tension, as described in Section 32.

32 Air conditioner drivebelt – removal, refitting and adjustment

1 Remove the alternator and/or power-assisted steering pump drivebelt, as necessary, to allow removal of the drivebelt.
2 Slacken the compressor mounting and adjustment nuts, move the compressor towards the engine and slip the drivebelt off.
3 Fit a new belt over the pulleys and tension the belt by levering the compressor away from the engine until it is just possible to deflect the belt by 10 mm (0.4 in) under thumb pressure at a point midway between the pulleys. Hold the compressor in this position and tighten the adjustment and mounting nuts.

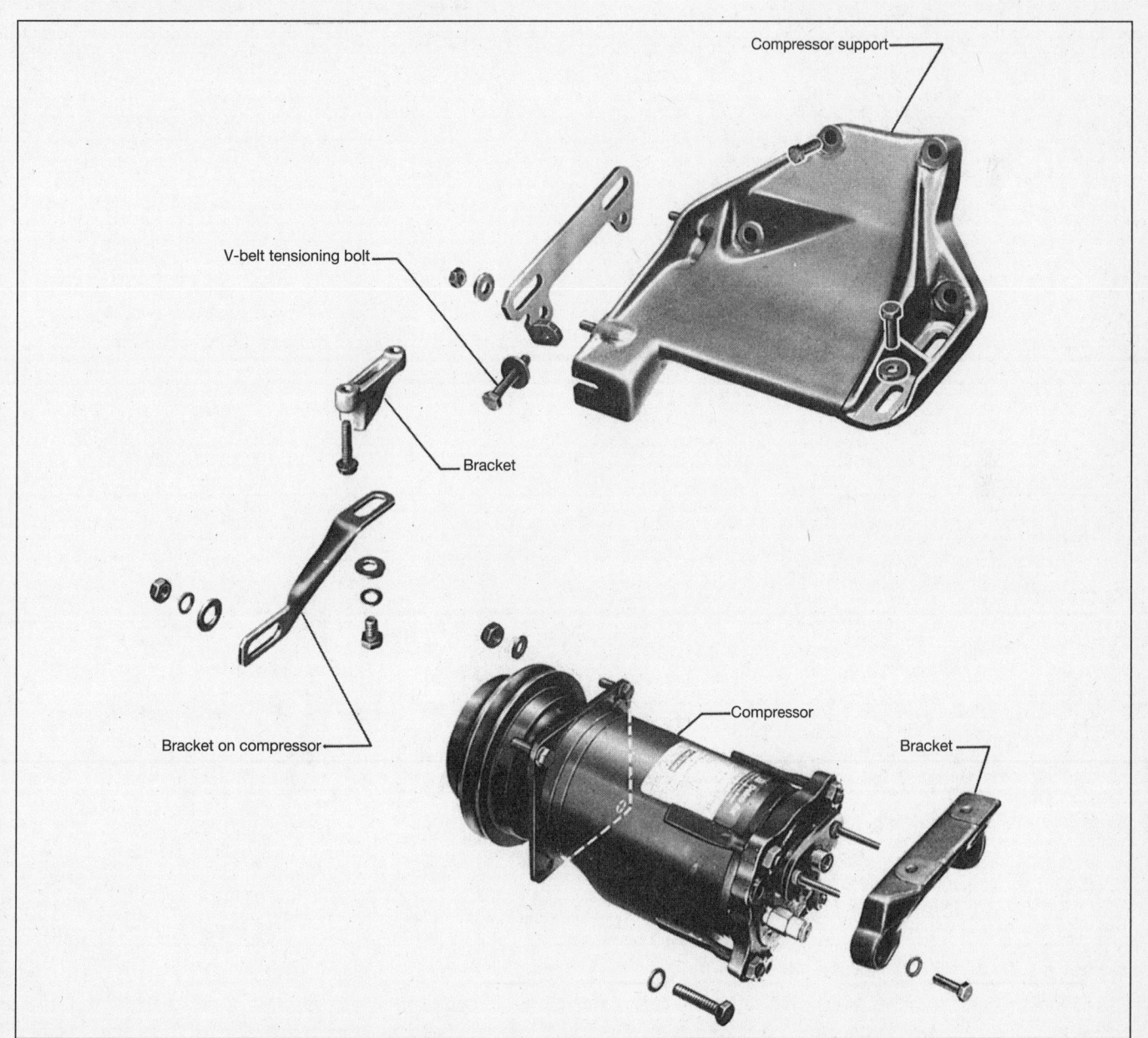

Fig. 11.29 Air conditioning compressor mounting and adjustment details (Sec 32)

Notes

Chapter 12 Electrical system

For modifications, and information applicable to later models, see Supplement at end of manual

Contents

Alternator – removal and refitting 6	Horn – removal and refitting 28
Alternator – servicing 8	Ignition switch/steering column lock – removal and refitting ... 13
Alternator drivebelt – removal and adjustment 7	Instrument panel – removal and refitting 17
Auto-check system – general 33	Instruments – removal, testing and refitting 18
Battery – charging 5	Maintenance and inspection 3
Battery – removal and refitting 4	On-board computer – general 32
Bulbs and lamp units – removal and refitting 22	Radio/cassette player and speakers – removal and refitting .. 30
Centre console and facia switches – removal and refitting .. 15	Speedometer cable – removal and refitting 19
Combination switch – removal and refitting 14	Starter motor – overhaul 11
Courtesy light switches – removal and refitting 16	Starter motor – removal and refitting 10
Cruise control system – removal and refitting of components . 31	Starter motor – testing in the car 9
Electrically-operated front seats – general 34	Tailgate wiper blades and arm (Avant models) – removal
Electrical system – precautions 2	and refitting 26
Fault finding – electrical system .... See end of Chapter	Tailgate wiper motor (Avant models) – removal and refitting . 27
Fuses, relays and control units – general 12	Windscreen washer system – removal, refitting and adjustment . 25
General description 1	Windscreen wiper blades and arms – removal and refitting ... 23
Headlamps – alignment 21	Windscreen wiper linkage and motor – removal and refitting . 24
Headlamps and headlamp bulbs – removal and refitting 20	Wiring diagrams .... See end of Manual
Headlamp washers – removal and refitting 29	

Degrees of difficulty

Easy, suitable for novice with little experience	Fairly easy, suitable for beginner with some experience	Fairly difficult, suitable for competent DIY mechanic	Difficult, suitable for experienced DIY mechanic	Very difficult, suitable for expert DIY or professional

Specifications

System type .... 12 volt negative earth

Battery
Capacity .... 45, 54 or 63 Ah

Alternator
Type .... Bosch
Output .... 65 or 90 amp
Minimum brush length .... 5.0 mm (0.2 in)
Stator winding resistance .... 0.1 ohm maximum
Diode resistance .... 50 to 80 ohm
Rotor winding resistance .... 3.0 to 4.0 ohm

Starter motor
Type .... Bosch pre-engaged, 0.95 or 1.1 kW rating
Commutator minimum diameter:
   0.95 kw starter .... 33.5 mm (1.32 in)
   1.1 kw starter .... 31.2 mm (1.23 in)
Commutator maximum run-out .... 0.03 mm (0.001 in)
Commutator insulation undercut .... 0.5 to 0.8 mm (0.02 to 0.03 in)
Armature axial play:
   0.95 kw starter .... 0.1 to 0.3 mm (0.004 to 0.012 in)
   1.1 kw starter .... 0.05 to 0.4 mm (0.002 to 0.016 in)
Minimum brush length:
   0.95 kw starter .... 11.5 mm (0.45 in)
   1.1 kw starter .... 8.0 mm (0.32 in)

Wiper blades .... Champion CS 5301

12•2 Electrical system

Fuses

Fuse	Function	Rating (amps)
1	Front and rear fog lights (UK models)	15
2	Hazard warning lights, air conditioner	15
3	Horn, brake lights	25
4	Interior lights, courtesy lights, luggage compartment light, front cigarette lighter, or on-board computer, radio	15
5	Vacant	
6	Right-hand tail and parking lights	5
7	Left-hand tail and parking lights	5
8	Right-hand headlight main beam, main beam warning light	10
9	Left-hand headlight main beam	10
10	Right-hand headlight dipped beam	10
11	Left-hand headlight dipped beam	10
12	Instruments, reversing lights, Auto-check system	15
13	Electric fuel pump	15
14	Number plate light, glovebox light, engine compartment light, heater controls, ashtray lighting	5
15	Direction indicators, windscreen wipers/washers	25
16	Rear window heater, on-board computer lights, clock	30
17	Fresh air blower	30
18	Electric sliding roof (UK models) rear window wiper/washer, electrically heated seats (North American models)	30
19	Central locking system, electric mirrors	10
20	Electrically heated seats (UK models)	30
21	Rear cigarette lighter	25
22	Vacant	

Additional fuses on fusebox inside wall

Fuse	Function	Rating (amps)
23	Passenger's seat adjustment, seat memory control unit	30
27	Electric sliding roof (North American models)	20

Bulbs

	Wattage
Headlamps	55/60
Front foglights/additional driving lights	55
Sidelights	4
Direction indicators	21
Rear foglights	21
Brake lights	21
Tail lights	5 and 10
Reversing lights	21
Number plate light	5
Interior lights	10
Ashtray illumination	1.2
Heater control illumination	1.2
Instrument panel illumination	3
Instrument panel warning lights	1.2 and 2
Glovebox light	2
Engine compartment light	10
Luggage compartment light	5
Reading lights	5
Vanity mirror light	3

Torque wrench settings

	Nm	lbf ft
Alternator mounting bolts	35	26
Alternator adjustment bolts	20	15
Alternator pulley nut	35	26
Starter motor to engine	60	44
Windscreen wiper arm to spindle	16	12
Wiper frame	7	5
Wiper motor	4	3
Wiper motor crankarm nut	5	4

1 General description

Caution: *Before carrying out any work on the vehicle electrical system, read through the precautions given in Safety First! at the beginning of this manual and in Section 2 of this Chapter.*

The electrical system is of the 12 volt negative earth type, and consists of a 12 volt battery, alternator, starter motor and related electrical accessories, components and wiring. The battery is charged by an alternator which is belt-driven from the crankshaft pulley. The starter motor is of the pre-engaged type incorporating an integral solenoid. On starting, the solenoid moves the drive pinion into engagement with the flywheel ring gear before the starter motor is energised. Once the engine has started, a one-way clutch prevents the motor armature being driven by the engine until the piston disengages from the flywheel.

Further details of the major electrical systems are given in the relevant Sections of this Chapter.

2.7 Battery with negative terminal disconnected

2 Electrical system – precautions

It is necessary to take extra care when working on the electrical system to avoid damage to semi-conductor devices (diodes and transistors), and to avoid the risk of personal injury. In addition to the precautions given in Safety First! at the beginning of this manual, observe the following items when working on the system.

1 *Always remove rings, watches, etc, before working on the electrical system.* Even with the battery disconnected, capacitive discharge could occur if a component live terminal is earthed through a metal object. This could cause a shock or nasty burn.

2 *Do not reverse the battery connections.* Components such as the alternator or any other having semi-conductor circuitry could be irreparably damaged.

3 If the engine is being started using jump leads and a slave battery, connect the batteries *positive to positive* and *negative to negative.* This also applies when connecting a battery charger.

4 Never disconnect the battery terminals, or alternator wiring when the engine is running.

5 The battery leads and alternator wiring must be disconnected before carrying out any electric welding on the car.

6 Never use an ohmmeter of the type incorporating a hand cranked generator for circuit or continuity testing.

7 Always ensure that the battery negative lead is disconnected (photo) when working on the electrical system.

3 Maintenance and inspection

1 At regular intervals (see Routine Maintenance) carry out the following maintenance and inspection operations on the electrical system components.

2 Check the operation of all the electrical equipment, ie, wipers, washers, lights, direction indicators, horn, etc. Refer to the appropriate Sections of this Chapter if any components are found to be inoperative.

3 Visually check all accessible wiring connections, harnesses and retaining clips for security, or any signs of chafing or damage. Rectify any problems encountered.

4 Check the alternator drivebelt for cracks, fraying or damage. Renew the belt if worn or,

Electrical system 12•3

3.7A Top up the windscreen washer reservoir . . .

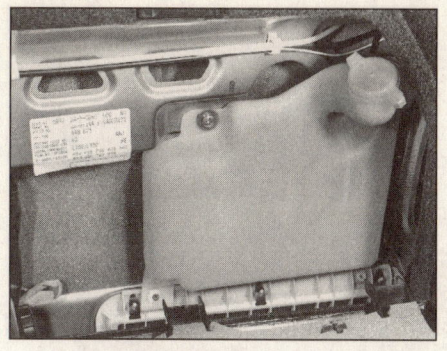

3.7B . . . and the rear window washer reservoir on Avant models

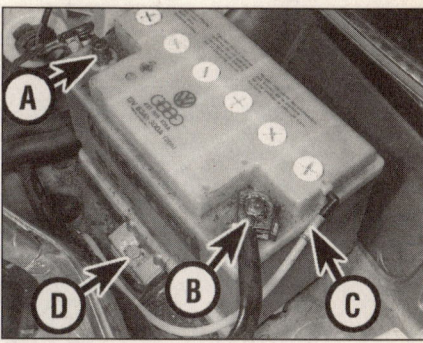

4.2 Battery negative terminal (A), positive terminal (B), vent hose (C) and clamp bolt (D)

if satisfactory, check and adjust the belt tension, as described in Section 7.
5 Check the condition of the wiper blades and if they are cracked or show signs of deterioration, renew them, as described in Sections 23 and 26. Check the operation of the windscreen rear window and headlamp washers (if fitted). Adjust the nozzles using a pin, if necessary.
6 Check the battery terminals, and if there is any sign of corrosion disconnect and clean them thoroughly. Smear the terminals and battery posts with petroleum jelly before refitting the plastic covers. If there is any corrosion on the battery tray, remove the battery, clean the deposits away and treat the affected metal with an anti-rust preparation. Repaint the tray in the original colour after treatment.
7 Top up the washer reservoirs and check the security of the pump wires and water pipes (photos).
8 Check the electrolyte level in the battery by viewing the side of the translucent case. Maintain the level between the MIN and MAX marks by adding distilled or de-ionized water as necessary.
9 It is advisable to have the headlight aim adjusted using optical beam setting equipment.
10 While carrying out a road test check the operation of all the instruments and warning lights, and the operation of the direction indicator self-cancelling mechanism.

4 Battery – removal and refitting

1 The battery may be located at the rear of the engine compartment under a black plastic cover or under the rear seat bench according to model.
2 Slacken the negative terminal clamp and disconnect the lead (photo).
3 Slacken the positive terminal clamp and disconnect the lead.
4 Detach the battery vent hose.
5 Unscrew the bolt and remove the battery holding clamp.
6 Lift the battery out of its location taking care to keep it upright.
7 Refitting is a reversal of removal, but make sure that the polarity is correct before connecting the leads and do not overtighten the clamps.

5 Battery – charging

1 In winter when a heavy demand is placed on the battery, such as when starting from cold and using more electrical equipment, it is a good idea to have the battery fully charged occasionally from an external source at a rate of 10% of the battery capacity (ie 6.3 amp for a 63 Ah battery). It is advisable to disconnect the battery leads when charging.

2 Continue to charge the battery until no further rise in specific gravity is noted over a four hour period.
3 Alternatively, a trickle charger, charging at a rate of 1.5 amp can be safely used overnight.
4 Special rapid 'boost' charges, which are claimed to restore the power of the battery in 1 to 2 hours, can be dangerous unless they are thermostatically controlled, as they can cause serious damage to the battery plates through overheating.
5 While charging the battery, ensure that the temperature of the electrolyte never exceeds 37.8°C (100°F) and loosen the vent caps (where applicable).

6 Alternator – removal and refitting

1 Disconnect the battery negative lead.
2 On five-cylinder engines undo the nuts and remove the cover plate from the rear of the alternator (photo). On some models it will first be necessary to remove the cooling air hose.
3 Slacken the alternator mounting and adjustment bolts and slip the drivebelt off the pulley (photo).
4 Note the location of the wiring then disconnect it from the rear of the alternator (photo).
5 Undo the mounting and adjustment bolts and remove the alternator from the engine.
6 Refitting is a reversal of removal, but adjust the drivebelt as described in Section 7.

6.2 Alternator rear cover plate on five-cylinder engines

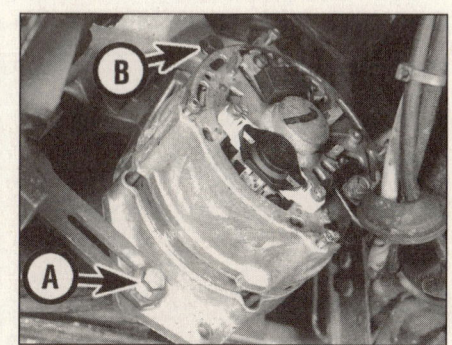

6.3 Alternator adjustment bolt (A) and mounting bolt (B) on five-cylinder engines

6.4 Wiring connections at the rear of the alternator on five-cylinder engines

12•4 Electrical system

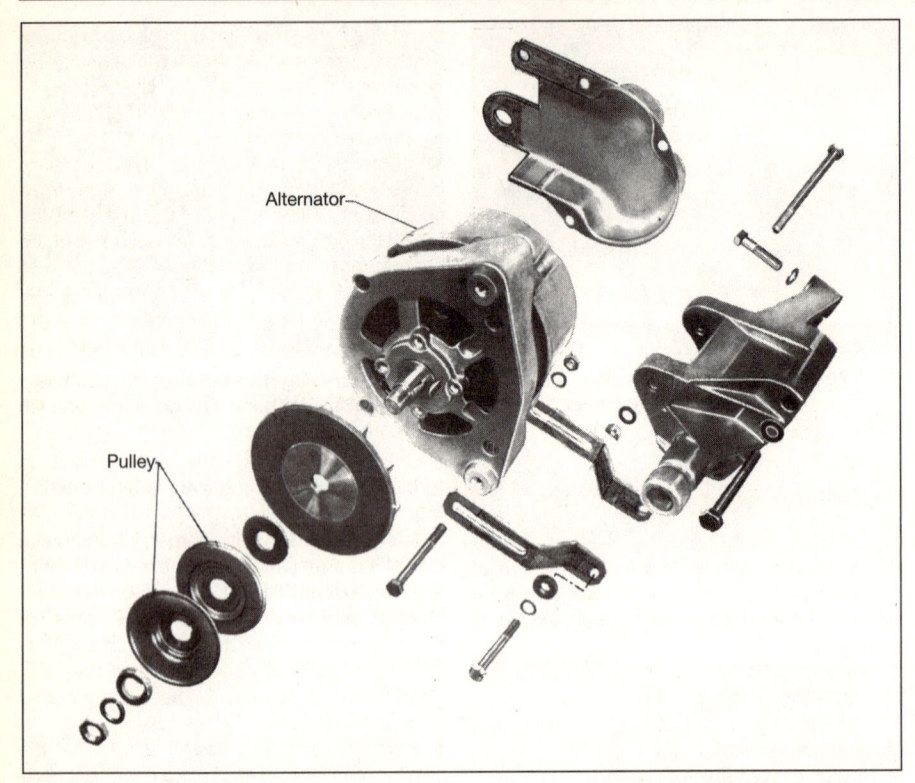

Fig. 12.1 Alternator pulley and mounting details – five-cylinder engines (Sec 6)

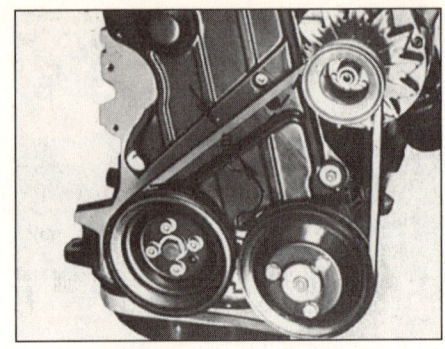

Fig. 12.2 Drivebelt adjustment point – four-cylinder engines (Sec 7)

a *Specified drivebelt deflection*

7 Alternator drivebelt – removal and adjustment

1 At the intervals specified in Routine Maintenance the drivebelt should be checked for condition and re-tensioned. If there are any signs of cracking or deterioration, the drivebelt should be renewed.
2 To remove the drivebelt, first remove the air conditioner drivebelt (Chapter 11) and/or power-assisted steering pump drivebelt (Chapter 10) as necessary.
3 Slacken the alternator mounting and adjustment arm bolts so that the alternator is free to move, then push the unit towards the engine. Slip the drivebelt off the pulleys and remove it from the engine.
4 Slip the new drivebelt over the pulleys then lever the alternator from the engine until it is just possible to deflect the belt under moderate thumb pressure by 10 to 15 mm (0.4 to 0.6 in) at a point midway between the alternator and crankshaft pulleys (photo). Hold the alternator in this position and tighten the mounting and adjustment bolts. Note that on later models the adjustment bolt incorporates an inner toothed nut which engages with teeth in the adjustment arm in the form of a rack and pinion arrangement. Turn the nut using a spanner or socket until the tension is correct then tighten the adjusting bolt.
5 Refit the other belts, where applicable, as described in the relevant Chapters, then run the engine for several minutes. Switch off then recheck the tension and adjust if necessary.

8 Alternator – servicing

Note: *The voltage regulator and brushes can be removed without removing the alternator. However, the following complete dismantling procedure assumes that the alternator is on the bench.*

1 Clean the exterior of the alternator.
2 Remove the screws and withdraw the voltage regulator and brushes. If the brushes are worn below the specified minimum length, they must be renewed, complete with the voltage regulator, as an assembly.
3 Mark the end housings and stator in relation to each other.
4 Grip the pulley in a vice then unscrew the nut and withdraw the washer, pulley and fan, together with any spacers. Prise out the key.
5 Unscrew the through-bolts and tap off the front housing, together with the rotor.
6 Using a mallet or puller, remove the rotor from the front housing and remove the spacers.
7 Remove the screws and retaining plate. Drive the bearing from the front housing with a soft metal drift.
8 Using a suitable puller, remove the bearing from the slip ring end of the rotor, but take care not to damage the slip rings.
9 Remove the screw, disconnect the lead,

7.4 Using a screwdriver to tension the alternator drivebelt on five-cylinder engines

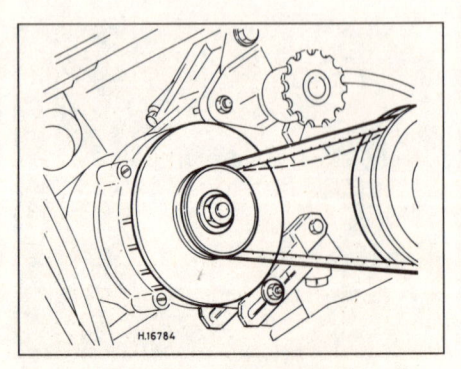

Fig. 12.3 Drivebelt adjustment point – five-cylinder engines (Sec 7)

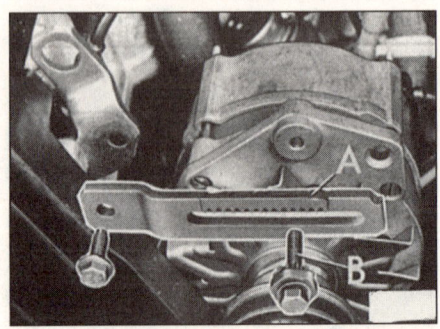

Fig. 12.4 Later type alternator adjustment components (Sec 7)

A Toothed adjustment arm
B Toothed adjusting nut

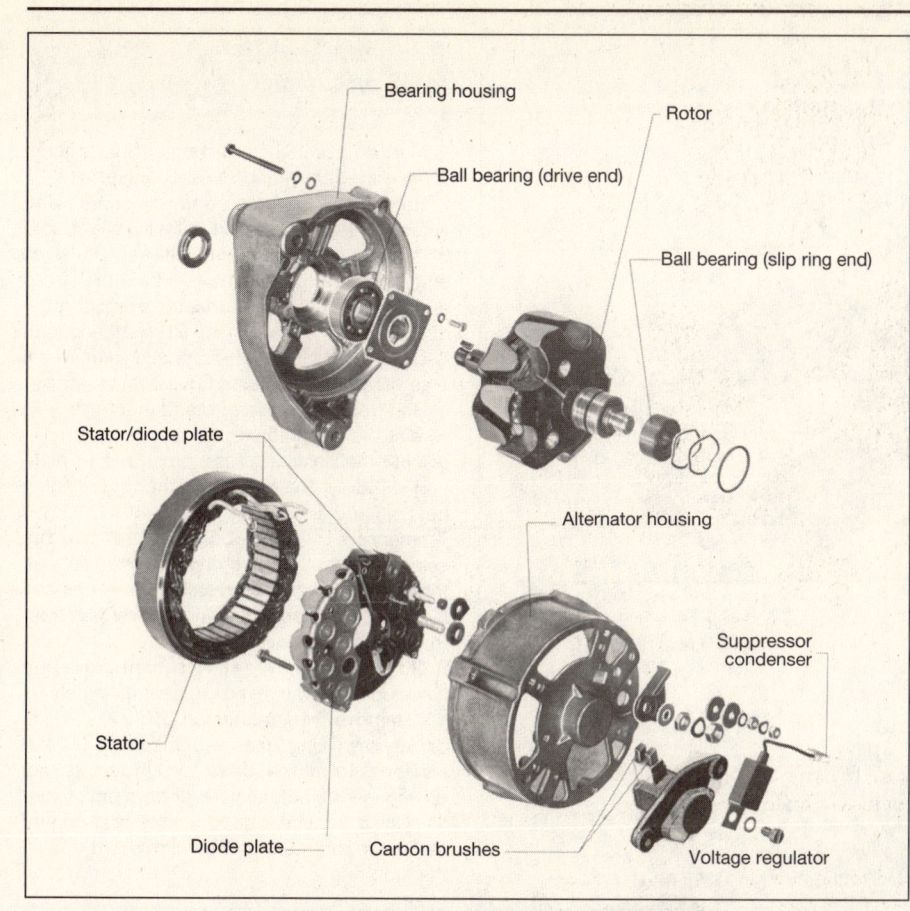

Electrical system 12•5

core Check that the internal resistance of the winding is as given in the Specifications using an ohmmeter between the two slip rings.
17 Clean all the components and obtain new bearings, brushes, etc, as required.
18 Reassembly is a reversal of dismantling, but when fitting the bearing to the front housing, drive it in using a metal tube *on the outer race* making sure that the open end of the bearing faces the rotor. When fitting the rear bearing to the rotor, drive it on using a metal tube *on the inner race,* making sure that the open end of the bearing faces the rear housing.

9 Starter motor – testing in the car

1 If the starter motor fails to respond when the starter switch is operated, first check that the fault is not external to the starter motor.
2 Connect a test lamp between chassis earth and the large terminal on the starter solenoid, terminal 30. This terminal is connected directly to the battery and the test lamp should light whether or not the ignition switch is operated.
3 Remove the test lamp connection from the large terminal (30) and transfer it to the smaller terminal (50) on the solenoid. The lamp should light only when the starter switch is in its Start position.
4 If both these tests are satisfactory the fault is in the starter motor.
5 If the starter motor is heard to operate, but the engine fails to start, check the battery terminals, the starter motor leads and the engine-to-body earth strap for cleanliness and tightness.

10 Starter motor – removal and refitting

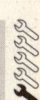

1 Disconnect the battery negative lead.
2 Note the location of the wires on the starter solenoid, then disconnect them (photo).
3 Unscrew the mounting bolts and withdraw the starter motor (photo).
4 Refitting is a reversal of removal, but make sure that the mating faces are clean and tighten the mounting bolts to the specified torque.

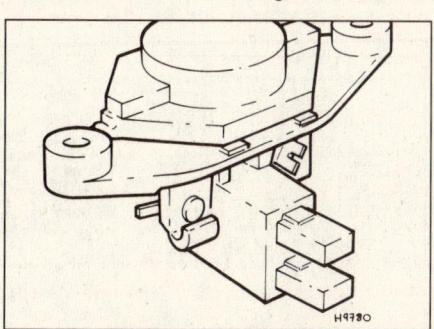

Fig. 12.5 Exploded view of the alternator (Sec 8)

and withdraw the suppressor condenser from the rear housing.
10 Unscrew the terminal nut(s), then remove the washers, and remove the insulator from the rear housing.
11 Carefully separate the stator from the rear housing without straining the wires. Identify each wire for location, then unsolder them using the minimum of heat to avoid damage to the diodes. Long-nosed pliers may be used as a heat sink.
12 Remove the screws and separate the diode plate from the rear housing.
13 Remove the wave washer from the rear housing.
14 Check the stator windings for a short to ground by connecting an ohmmeter or test bulb between each wire and the outer ring. Check that the internal resistance between the wires is as given in the Specifications using an ohmmeter between wires 1 and 2, then 1 and 3 and 2 and 3 – the numbering of the wires is of no importance.
15 Using the ohmmeter check that the resistance of each diode is as given in the Specifications when the ohmmeter is connected across the diode in one direction. Reverse the wires and check that there is now no resistance.
16 Check the rotor windings for a short to ground by connecting an ohmmeter or test bulb between each slip ring and the winding

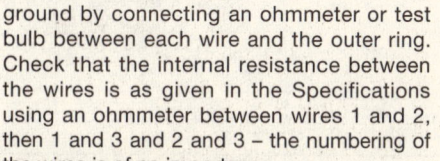

Fig. 12.6 Alternator voltage regulator with integral brushes (Sec 8)

10.2 Wiring connections at the starter solenoid

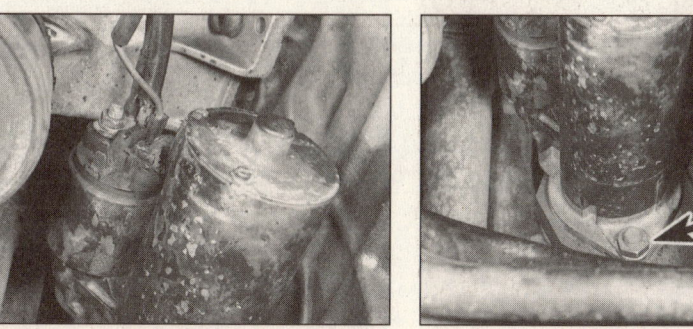

10.3 Starter motor lower mounting bolt (arrowed)

12•6 Electrical system

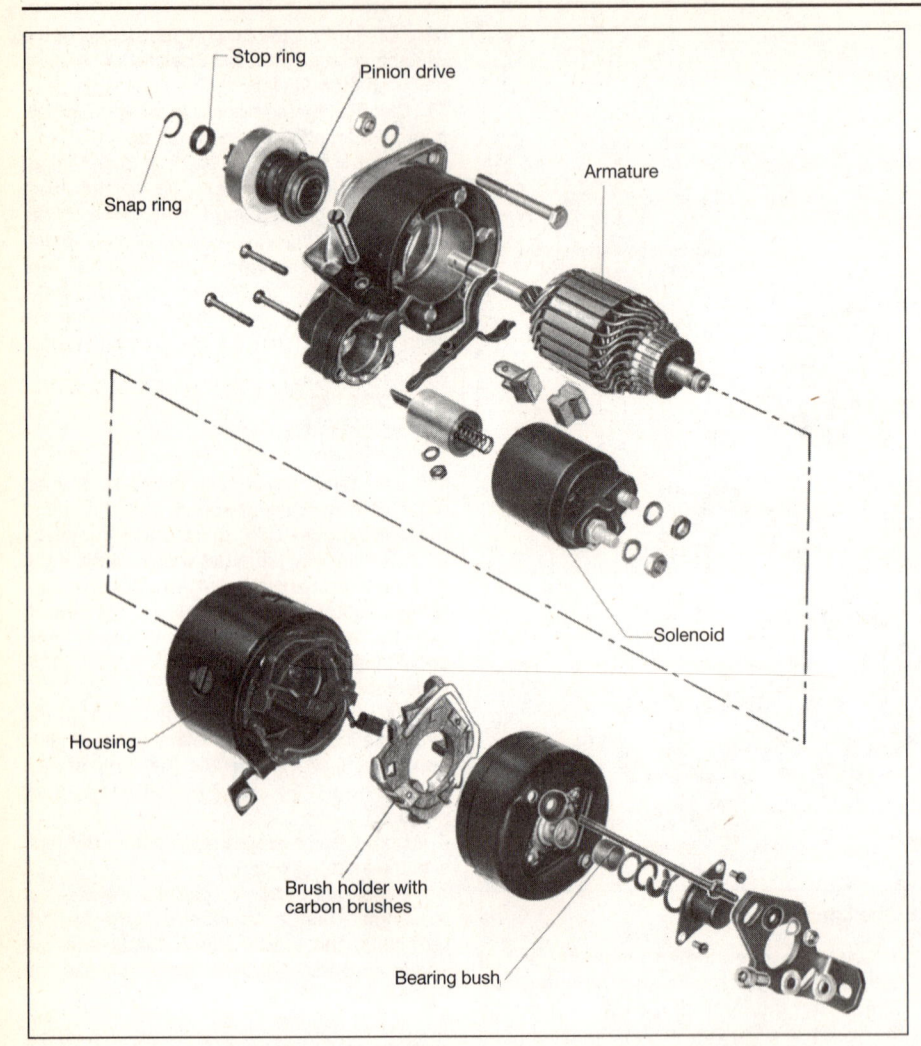

Fig. 12.7 Exploded view of the Bosch 0.95 kW starter motor (Sec 11)

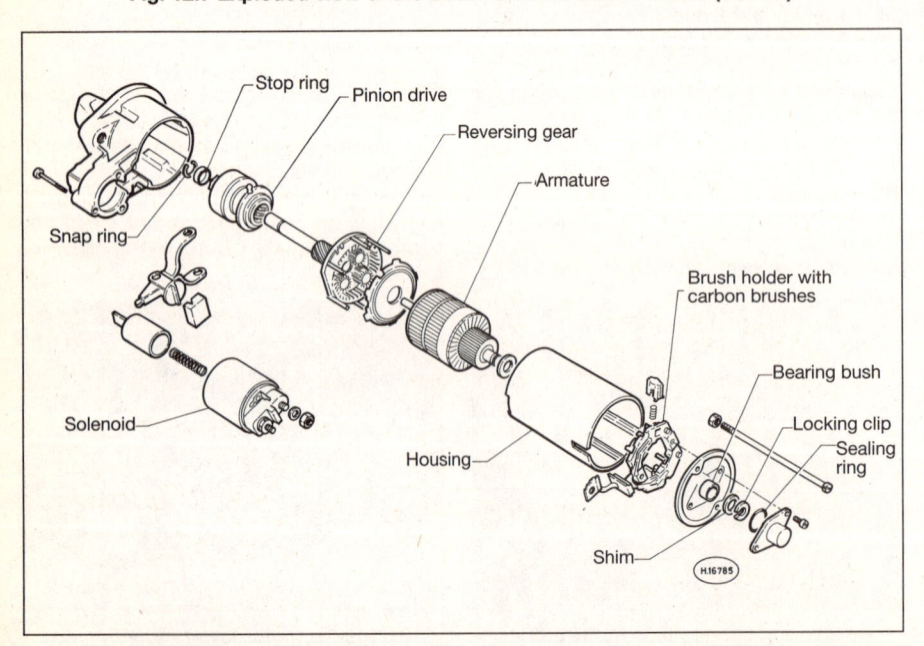

Fig. 12.8 Exploded view of the Bosch 1.1 kW starter motor (Sec 11)

11 Starter motor – overhaul

1 Mark the housings and mounting bracket (where fitted) in relation to each other.
2 Remove the nuts and washers and withdraw the end support plate (where fitted).
3 Remove the screws and withdraw the small end cover and gasket, then extract the circlip and remove the shims. Note the exact number of shims, as they determine the shaft endfloat.
4 Unscrew the through-bolts and remove the commutator end bearing housing.
5 Unscrew the nut and disconnect the field wire at the solenoid.
6 Note the position of the brush holder plate and withdraw the plate from the field winding housing and armature.
7 Unscrew the three bolts and remove the solenoid from the drive end housing. Unhook the solenoid from the actuating lever.
8 Prise out the actuating lever cover pad from the drive end housing.
9 On the 1.1 kW starter, withdraw the armature from the reversing gear assembly.
10 Remove the armature on 0.95 kW starters, or the reversing gear assembly on 1.1 kW starters, from the drive end housing and disengage the actuating lever from the pinion.
11 Using a metal tube, drive the stop ring off the circlip, then extract the circlip and pull off the stop ring.

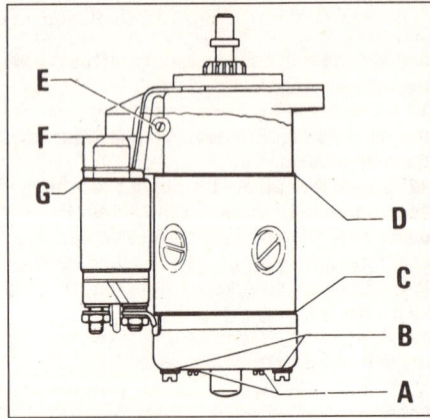

Fig. 12.9 Sealing points on the 0.95 kW starter motor (Sec 11)

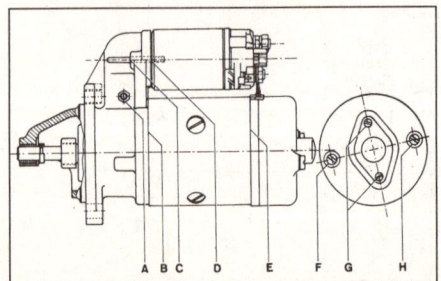

Fig. 12.10 Sealing points on the 1.1 kW starter motor (Sec 11)

Electrical system 12•7

12 Withdraw the pinion drive from the armature or reversing gear.

13 Clean all the components in paraffin and wipe dry, then examine them for wear and damage. Check the pinion drive for damaged teeth and make sure that the one-way clutch only rotates in one direction. If the shaft bushes are worn they can be removed using a soft metal drift and new bushes installed. However, the new bushes must first be soaked in hot oil for approximately five minutes. Clean the commutator with a rag moistened with a suitable solvent. Minor scoring can be removed with fine glasspaper, but deep scoring will necessitate the commutator being skimmed in a lathe and then being undercut. Commutator refinishing is a job which is best left to a specialist. On the 1.1 kW starter do not dismantle the reversing gear assembly, but renew it as a unit if it was rough or noisy in operation.

14 Measure the length of the brushes. If less than the minimum given in the Specifications, renew the brush holder plate as an assembly. To do this on the 0.95 kW starter, cut off the copper braid next to the brush holder and solder it to the new holder.

15 Reassembly is a reversal of the dismantling procedure, but note the following. To fit the brush assembly over the commutator, either hook the brush springs on to the edge of the brush holder, or bend pieces of wire to hold the springs off the brushes until the brush assembly has been fitted. As soon as this has been done, release the brush springs and position them so that they bear on the centres of the brushes. Apply a little molybdenum disulphide grease to the splines of the pinion drive. Fit a new circlip to the pinion end of the shaft and ensure that the circlip groove is not damaged. Any burrs on the edges of the groove should be removed with a fine file. During reassembly apply sealing compound to the points indicated in Figs. 12.9 and 12.10.

12 Fuses, relays and control units – general

Fuses

1 The fusebox is situated at the rear of the engine compartment on the right or left-hand side of the plenum chamber – according to model. To gain access to the fuses, release the fusebox cover from its clips and lift off. The fuse locations, current rating and circuits protected are listed on the inside of the cover (photo). Each fuse is colour-coded and has its rating stamped on it (photo).

2 To remove a fuse from its location, hook it out using the small plastic removal tool provided. This is located, together with the spare fuses, in the fusebox tray. Hook the tool over the fuse and pull up to remove. Refit the fuse by pressing it firmly into its location.

3 Always renew a fuse with one of an

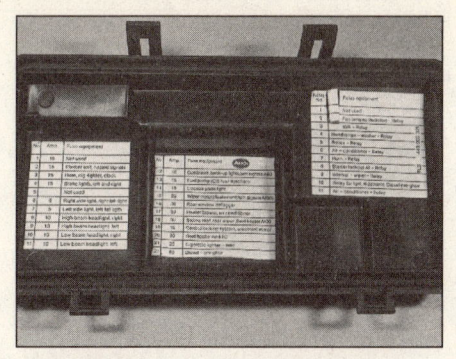

12.1A Fuse and relay positions shown on the inside of the fusebox cover

12.1B Fuses and relays in the fusebox

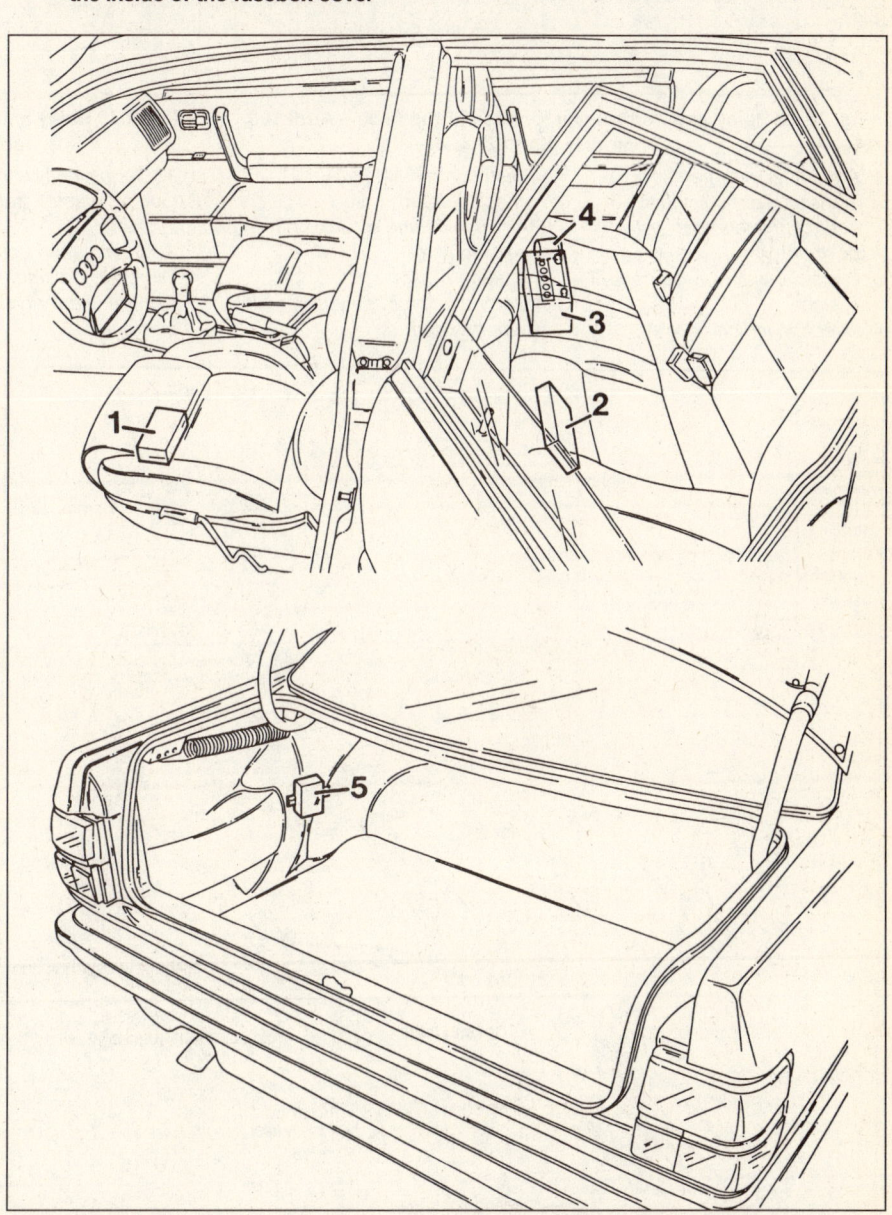

Fig. 12.11 Control unit locations in the car interior and luggage compartment (Sec 12)

1 Control unit for electrically-operated front seats
2 Anti-lock braking system control unit
3 Battery
4 Central locking system pump motor
5 Bulb monitoring control unit

12•8 Electrical system

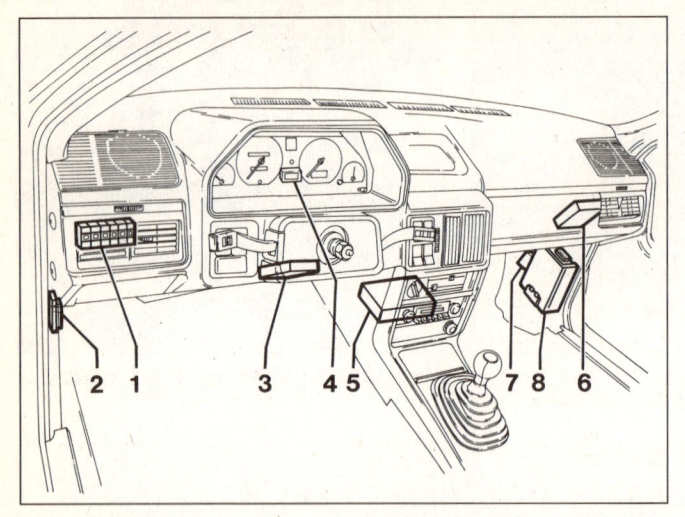

Fig. 12.12 Relay and control unit location at the facia – Audi 100 models (Sec 12)

1 Additional relay carrier
2 Transistorized coil ignition control unit (alternative position)
3 Control unit for cruise control system
4 Direction indicator relay
5 Main control unit for Auto-check system
6 Air conditioning control unit and regulator
7 Altitude sensor
8 Control unit for KE-Jetronic fuel injection system

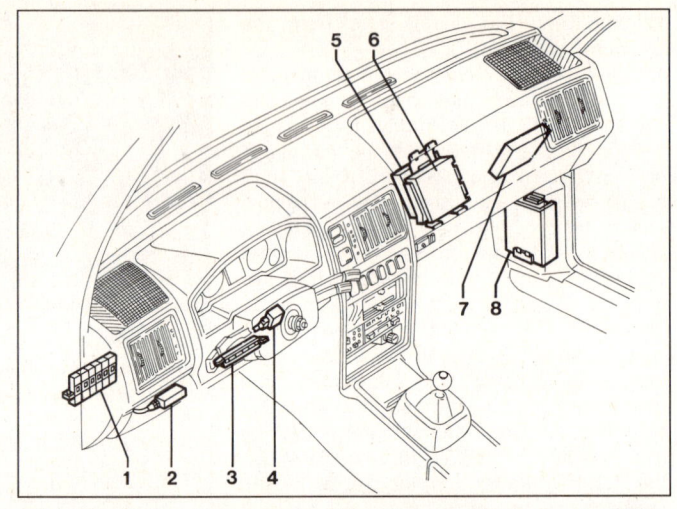

Fig. 12.13 Relay and control unit locations at the facia – Audi 200 and Audi 5000 models (Sec 12)

1 Additional relay carrier (1)
2 Control unit for cruise control system
3 Additional relay carrier (2)
4 Direction indicator relay
5 Control unit for on-board computer
6 Main control unit for Auto-check system
7 Air conditioning control unit and regulator
8 All electronic ignition system control unit

Relays and control units

4 The main relays are located alongside the fuses in the fusebox and there is an additional relay carrier located under the left-hand side of the facia.

5 The relays can be removed by simply pulling them from their respective locations. If a system controlled by a relay becomes inoperative, and the relay is suspect, operate the system and if the relay is functioning it should be possible to hear it click as it is energised. If this is the case, the fault lies with the components of the system. If the relay is not being energised then the relay is not receiving a main supply voltage, a switching voltage or the relay itself is faulty.

6 Control units for the various systems will be found situated throughout the car; depending on equipment and options fitted, and territory of export. The control unit locations are shown in Figs. 12.11, 12.12 and 12.13.

13 Ignition switch/steering column lock – removal and refitting

1 Remove the instrument panel, as described in Section 17.
2 Working through the instrument panel aperture, disconnect the wiring plug at the rear of the ignition switch.
3 Scrape away the paint over the retaining screw, undo the screw and withdraw the ignition switch.

Fig. 12.14 Exploded view of the ignition switch/steering column lock and combination switch components (Secs 13 and 14)

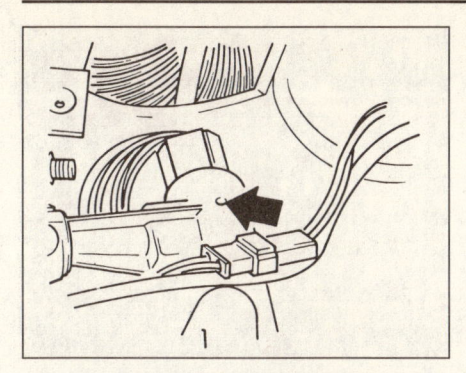

Electrical system 12•9

Fig. 12.15 Ignition switch retaining screw location – arrowed (Sec 13)

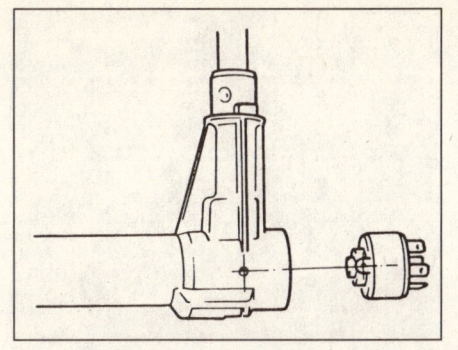

Fig. 12.16 Alignment of ignition switch and housing locating holes (Sec 13)

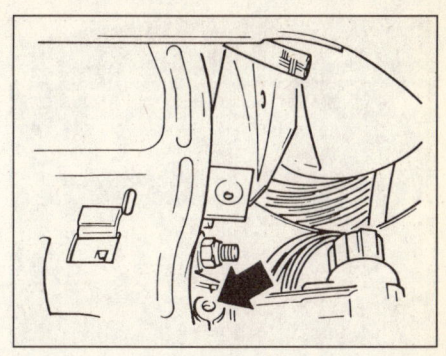

Fig. 12.17 Lock housing shear-bolt location – arrowed (Sec 13)

4 Refit the switch with the hole in the housing and switch aligned. then refit the screw and seal with paint.
5 To remove the steering column lock, first remove the combination switch, as described in Section 14.
6 Using a 2.5 mm diameter drill bit, drill out the lock housing shear-bolt then remove the remains of the shear-bolt with a stud extractor.
7 Undo the two nuts and remove both steering column upper mounting bolts.
8 Remove the trim under the facia and the air ducting sufficiently to allow the column to be lowered.
9 Push the steering column down and withdraw the lock housing from the column.
10 Using a 3 mm diameter drill, drill into the lock housing at the point shown in Fig. 12.18. Take care when doing this, otherwise the drill will damage the lock once it penetrates the lock housing wall.
11 Depress the retaining pin through the drilled hole and withdraw the lock from the lock housing.
12 Refit the lock by pushing it into the housing until the pin springs into the hole.
13 Refit the lock housing to the column using a new shear-bolt. Check the operation of the lock before tightening the shear-bolt until the head breaks off.
14 The remainder of refitting is a reversal of removal. Refit the instrument panel, as described in Section 17, and the combination switch, as described in Section 14.

14 Combination switch – removal and refitting

1 Disconnect the battery negative lead.
2 Remove the steering wheel, as described in Chapter 10.
3 Withdraw the trim end cappings from the combination switch stalks (photo).
4 Insert a screwdriver through the opening under the switch and slacken the switch clamp screw (photo).
5 Withdraw the switch assembly from the steering column, disconnect the wiring connectors and remove the combination switch (photos)
6 Refitting is a reversal of removal. Check that the gap between the switch and steering wheel is 3 mm (1/5 in), if necessary adjust the switch position.

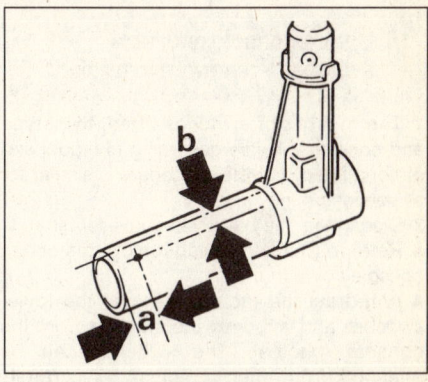

Fig. 12.18 Lock housing drilling point for lock removal (Sec 13)

a = 12.5 mm (0.5 in)   b = 8.0 mm (0.3 in)

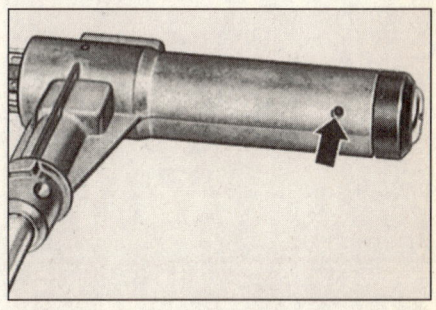

Fig. 12.19 Depress the pin (arrowed) and withdraw the lock from the housing (Sec 13)

14.3 Withdraw the combination switch trim end cappings

14.4 Slacken the combination switch clamp screw

14.5A Withdraw the combination switch assembly . . .

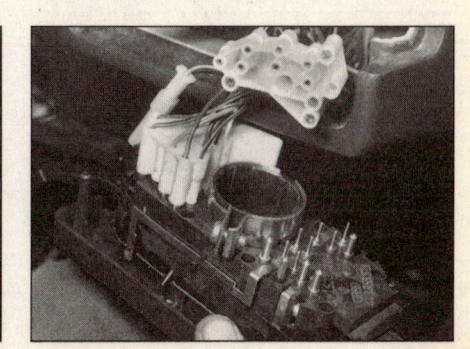

14.5B . . . and disconnect the wiring connectors

12•10 Electrical system

15.4A Withdraw the facia plate . . .

15.4B . . . then push out the console switches

15.6 Facia switch removal

15 Centre console and facia switches – removal and refitting

1 The number of switches fitted, their type and position will vary according to model and options fitted, but the procedure is similar for all versions.
2 Disconnect the battery negative terminal.
3 Refer to Chapter 11 and remove the centre console cover trim.
4 Withdraw the facia plate over the lower switches and withdraw the switches from the console (photos). The switches can be released from their opening by carefully prising out with a screwdriver or, if access permits, by pushing out the switch from behind.
5 Disconnect the switch wiring plug and remove the switch.
6 The upper console and facia switches are removed by carefully prising them out at the top then withdrawing from their location (photo). Disconnect the wiring plug and remove the switch.
7 Refitting is a reversal of removal.

16 Courtesy light switches – removal and refitting

1 Disconnect the battery negative lead.
2 Undo the screw securing the switch in position (photos), withdraw the switch and disconnect the wiring.
3 Refitting is a reversal of removal.

17 Instrument panel – removal and refitting

1 Disconnect the battery negative lead.
2 Refer to Chapter 10 and remove the steering wheel.
3 Undo the two screws securing the instrument panel to the facia hood (photo) and pull the instrument out slightly.
4 Reach behind the panel and disconnect the speedometer cable (bayonet fitting) then withdraw the panel.
5 Mark the location of the wiring connectors and vacuum hose then disconnect them from the rear of the panel (photo). Remove the instrument panel from the car.
6 Refitting is a reversal of removal.

18 Instruments – removal, testing and refitting

1 Remove the instrument panel, as described in Section 17.
2 Remove the relevant instrument, component or printed circuit with reference to Figs. 12.20 and 12.21.
3 Much of the instrument testing entails the use of an Audi tester, but the following can be carried out without the use of specialist equipment.
4 To test the voltage stabilizer, reconnect the

16.2A Interior courtesy light switch on door pillar

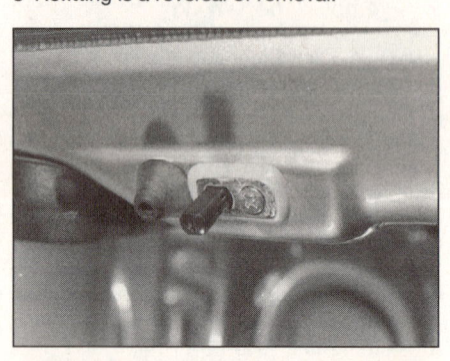

16.2B Luggage compartment light switch on boot lid

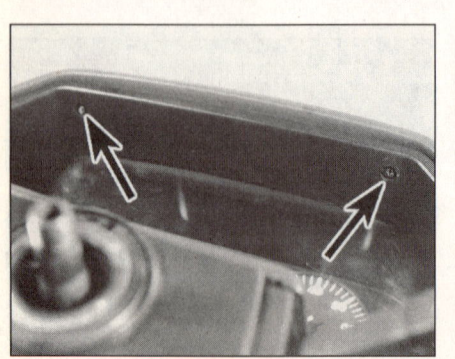

17.3 Instrument panel retaining screws (arrowed)

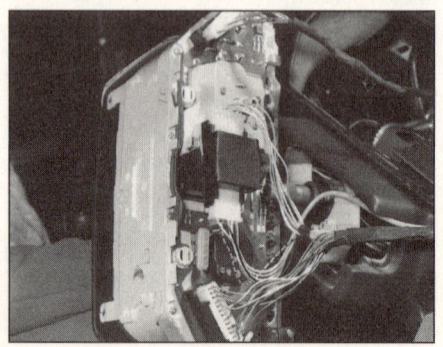

17.5 Instrument panel removal

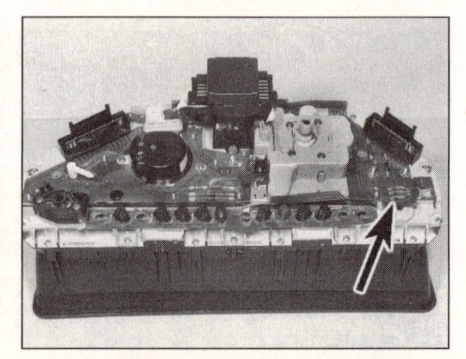

18.5 Voltage stabilizer connections (arrowed) on the instrument panel

Electrical system 12•11

instrument wiring plugs and reconnect the battery negative lead.

5 Connect a voltmeter between the voltage stabilizer positive connection and earth (Fig. 12.22) (photo). Switch on the ignition and check that approximately battery voltage is shown on the voltmeter. If not, check for a wiring fault in the feed to the stabilizer.

6 Check the stabilizer output voltage by connecting the voltmeter between connection 3 (positive output) and 1 (earth), as shown in Fig. 12.24. With the ignition switched on a voltage of between 9.75 and 10.25 volts should be indicated. If not, renew the voltage stabilizer. Switch off the ignition after completing the checks.

7 The accuracy of the fuel gauge can be checked after removing all fuel from the tank by syphon or hand pump (ensure a well ventilated area is available for this) then filling with exactly 12.0 litres (2.64 Imp gal/3.17 US gal) of fuel.

8 Switch on the ignition and wait two minutes for the gauge reading to stabilize. After this time the needle should be aligned with the upper edge of the red reserve zone. If necessary turn the adjusting screw below the gauge to correct the reading.

9 Reassembly of the instrument panel is the reverse of removal.

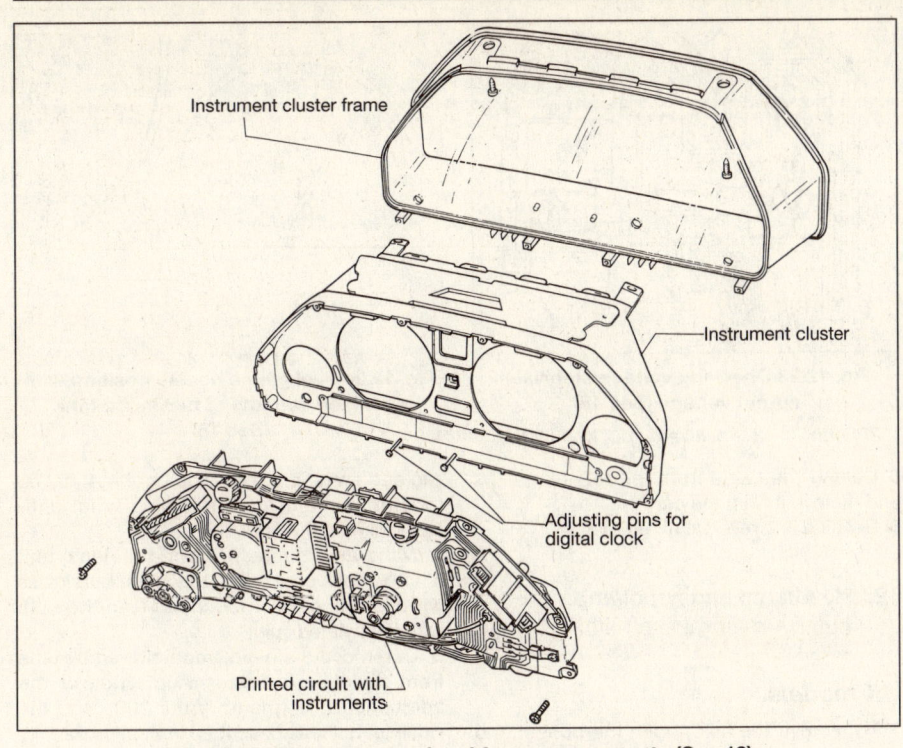

Fig. 12.20 Instrument panel and frame components (Sec 18)

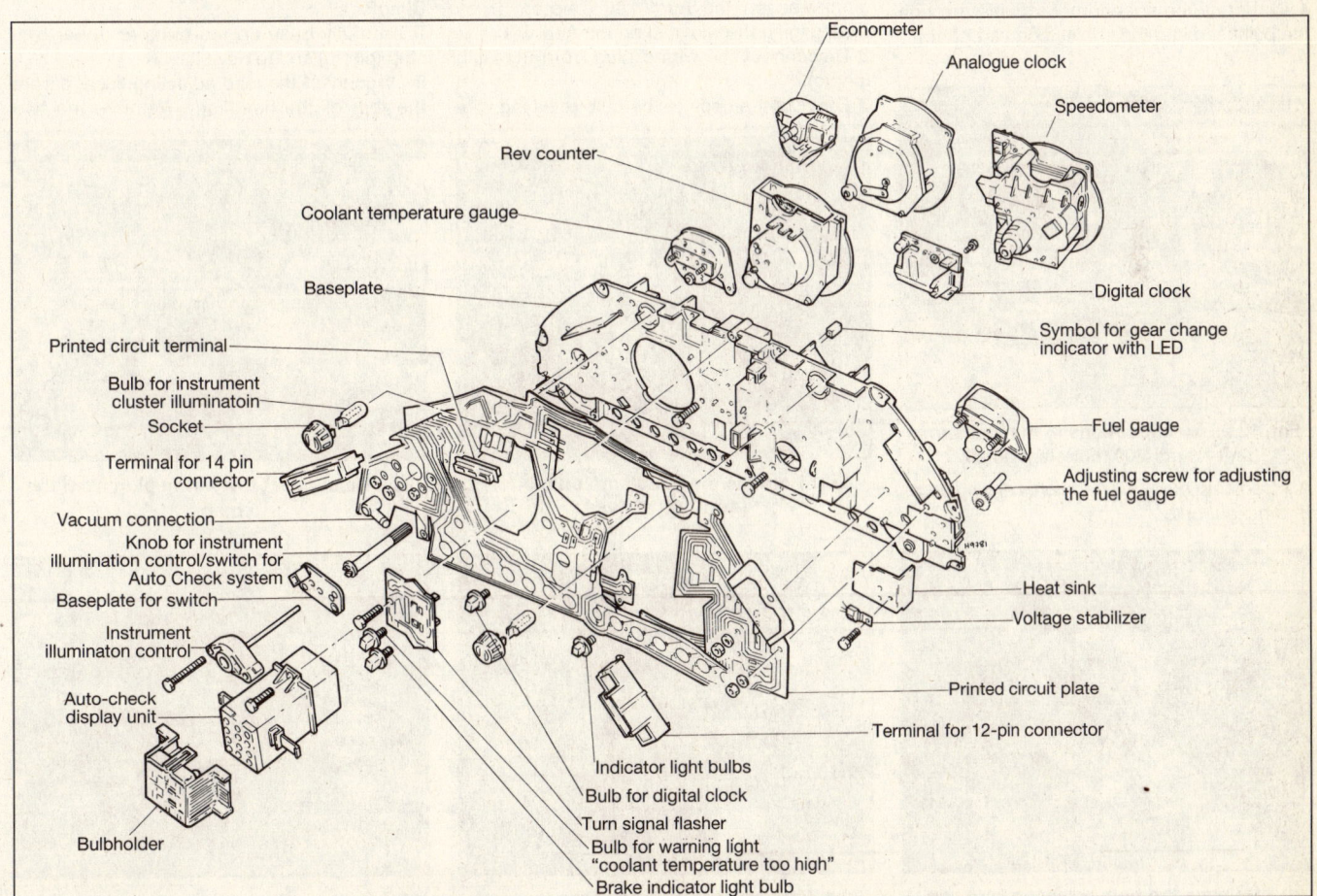

Fig. 12.21 Exploded view of the instrument panel (Sec 18)

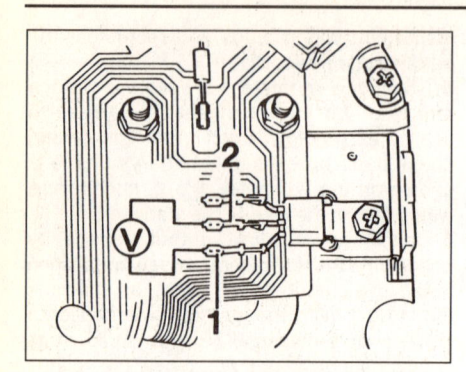

12•12 Electrical system

Fig. 12.22 Checking voltage stabiliser supply voltage (Sec 18)

1 Positive supply connection   2 Earth

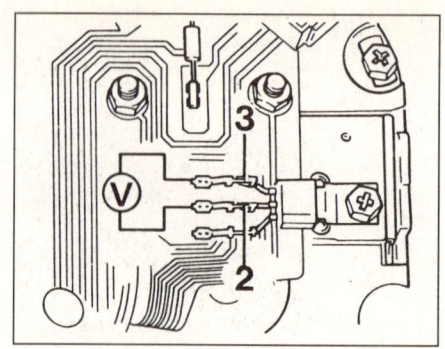

Fig. 12.23 Checking voltage stabiliser output voltage (Sec 18)

2 Earth   3 Positive output connection

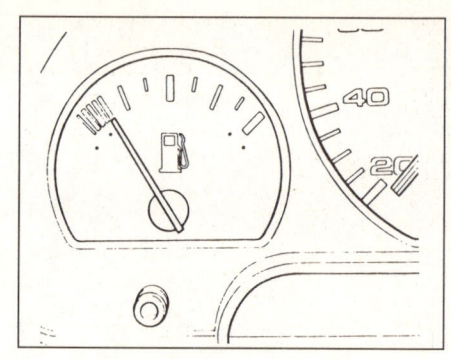

Fig. 12.24 Fuel gauge needle position with specified quantity of fuel in the tank (Sec 18)

19 Speedometer cable – removal and refitting

1 Disconnect the battery negative lead.
2 Remove the two screws and withdraw the instrument panel just sufficiently to allow the speedometer cable to be disconnected from behind (bayonet fitting).
3 Working in the engine compartment disconnect the speedometer cable from the transmission.
4 Withdraw the speedometer cable through the bulkhead into the engine compartment.
5 Detach the cable from the retaining clips and remove it from the car.
6 Refitting is a reversal of removal.

20 Headlamp and headlamp bulbs – removal and refitting

UK models

1 To remove the bulb, open the bonnet and remove the bulb cover by turning it anti-clockwise on the Audi 100 (photo), or by disengaging the wire clip on the Audi 200.
2 Disconnect the wiring plug from the bulb (photo).
3 Depress the ends of the bulb retaining wire clip and swing it to one side on the Audi 100 (photo), or turn the retaining ring anti-clockwise on the Audi 200.
4 Withdraw the bulb from the lens unit (photo). Take care not to touch the bulb glass with your fingers; if touched clean the bulb with methylated spirit.
5 To remove the headlamp unit, remove the front direction indicator (Audi 100), or the additional driving lamp (Audi 200), and the sidelight bulb, as described in Section 22.
6 Remove the radiator grille, as described in Chapter 11.
7 Carefully prise up the bumper upper trim strip (photo) and remove it.
8 Disconnect the load adjusting linkage from the rear of the headlight. Remove the two

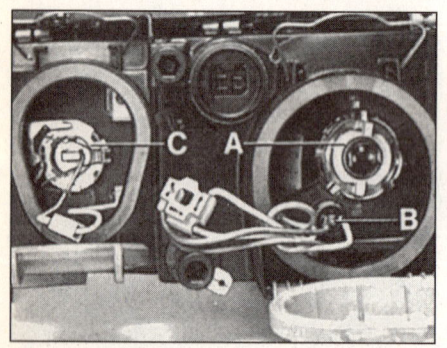

Fig. 12.25 Bulb locations in the headlamp unit – Audi 200 models (Sec 20)

A Headlamp bulb   C Additional driving lamp
B Sidelight bulb

20.1 Remove the headlamp bulb cover (Audi 100 shown)

20.2 Disconnect the wiring plug from the bulb

20.3 Release the bulb retaining wire clip – arrowed (Audi 100 shown)

20.4 Withdraw the bulb from the lens unit

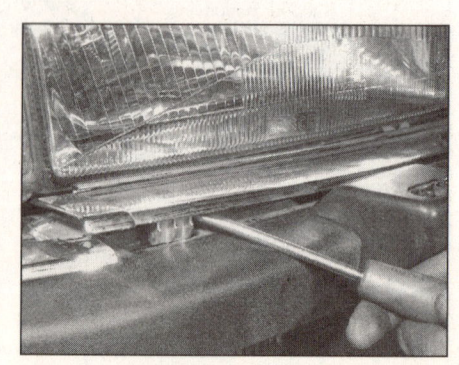

20.7 Remove the bumper upper trim strip (Audi 100 shown)

Electrical system 12•13

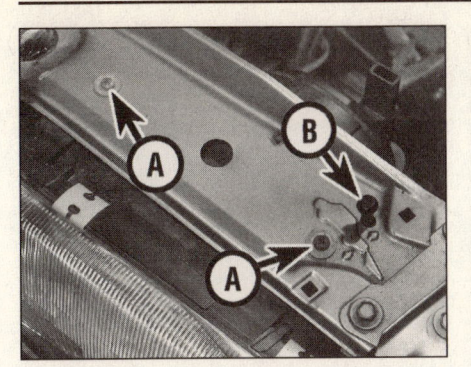

20.8A Headlamp unit upper retaining screws (A), and load adjustment button (B)

20.8B Removing a headlamp unit lower retaining screw

Fig. 12.26 Headlamp trim surround retaining screws (arrowed) – North American models (Sec 20)

upper and two lower retaining screws, and withdraw the unit from the car (photos).
9 Refitting the bulb and headlamp unit is a reversal of removal.

North American models

10 To remove the sealed beam headlamp bulb, open the bonnet and disconnect the wiring plug at the rear of the bulb.
11 Remove the side marker lamp bulbholder.
12 Remove the two trim surround retaining screws (Fig. 12.26) push out the trim and withdraw it from the guides.
13 Remove the four screws securing the headlamp bulb retainer, withdraw the retainer and take out the sealed beam bulb.
14 To remove the headlamp support frame, remove both sealed beam bulb units on the side to be removed.
15 Undo the four mounting frame retaining screws and withdraw the frame from the car.
16 Refitting the sealed beam bulbs and mounting frame is a reversal of removal.

21 Headlamps – alignment

1 At the intervals specified in Routine Maintenance the headlamp aim should be checked and, if necessary, adjusted.
2 Due to the light pattern of the homofocal headlamp lenses fitted, optical beam setting equipment must be used to achieve satisfactory aim of the headlamps. It is recommended, therefore, that this work is entrusted to an Audi dealer.

22 Bulbs and lamp units – removal and refitting

Front sidelights – UK models

1 From within the engine compartment, remove the cover at the rear of the headlamp by turning it anti-clockwise (photo).

22.1 Remove the headlamp bulb cover . . .

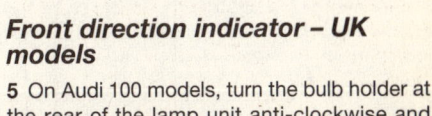

2 Withdraw the sidelight bulbholder from the headlamp then push and twist the bulb to remove it (photo).

Front side marker lights – North American models

3 From within the engine compartment, remove the rubber boot and bulb holder from the side marker light.
4 Push and turn the bulb to remove it.

Front direction indicator – UK models

5 On Audi 100 models, turn the bulb holder at the rear of the lamp unit anti-clockwise and

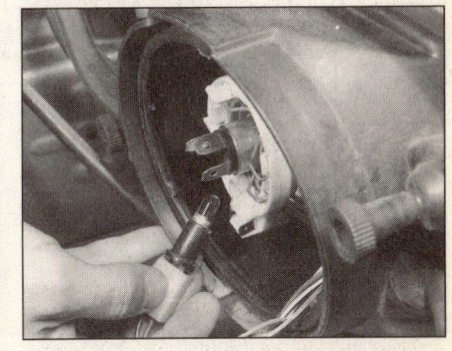

22.2 . . . and remove the sidelight bulb and holder (Audi 100 shown)

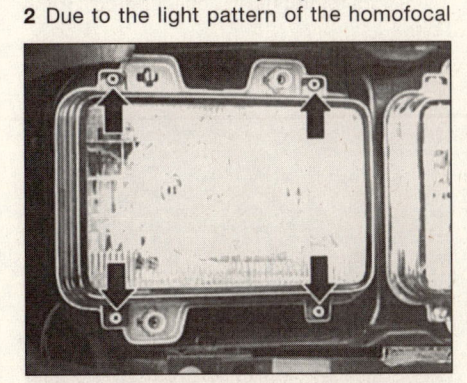

Fig. 12.27 Headlamp bulb retainer screws (arrowed) – North American models (Sec 20)

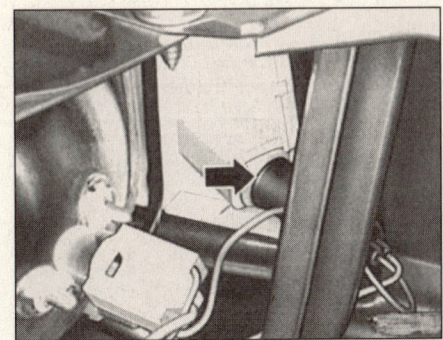

Fig. 12.28 Front side marker light bulbholder (arrowed) – North American models (Sec 22)

Fig. 12.29 Front direction indicator lamp lens – Audi 200 models (Sec 22)

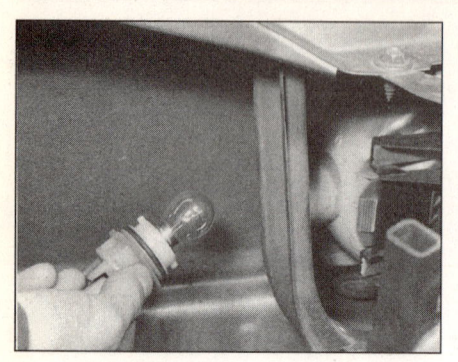

12•14 Electrical system

22.5 Front direction indicator bulb and holder (Audi 100 shown)

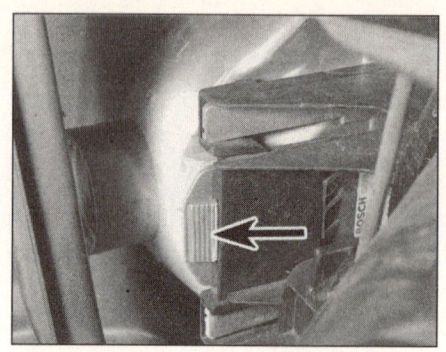

22.6A Depress the plastic tag . . .

22.6B . . . and remove the direction indicator lamp unit (Audi 100 shown)

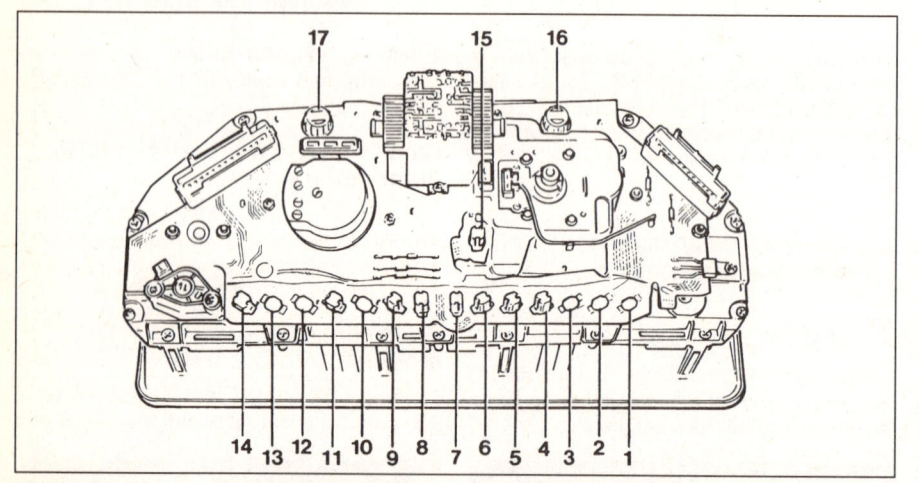

Fig. 12.30 Bulb locations at the rear of the instrument panel (Sec 22)

1 Anti-lock braking system warning light (UK only)
2 Seat belt warning light (UK only)
3 Cold coolant temperature warning light (UK only)
4 Handbrake warning light
5 Alternator charge warning light
6 Oil pressure warning tight (UK)/OXS system warning light (North America)
7 Trailer turn signal warning light (UK)/left direction indicator light (North America)
8 Hazard light indicator (UK)/right direction indicator light (North America)
9 Headlamp mainbeam warning lamp
10 Rear foglight warning lamp
11 Heated rear window warning lamp
12 Heated front seat warning lamp
13 Direction indicator warning lamp (UK only)
14 Seat belt warning lamp (North America only)
15 Digital clock illumination
16 Instrument panel right-hand illumination
17 Instrument panel left-hand illumination

Additional for certain UK models, not shown on illustration – brake warning lamp and hot coolant temperature warning lamp – located in the centre of the panel

withdraw it (photo). Push and twist the bulb to renew it.
6 To remove the direction indicator lamp unit on the Audi 100, depress the plastic tag on the side and withdraw the unit forwards from the car (photos)
7 On Audi 200 models, renew the bulb by undoing the two screws at the front of the lens and removing the lens. Push and twist the bulb to remove it.
8 To remove the lamp unit, disconnect the wiring at the connector, undo the retaining screws at the rear and remove the unit from the bumper.

Additional driving lamps – Audi 200 UK models

9 From within the engine compartment, disengage the cover retaining clip, swing the clip upwards and remove the cover.
10 Pull the wiring plug off the bulb, disengage the bulb retaining clip and remove the bulb.

Front foglamp – UK models

11 Withdraw the trim surround (where fitted) from the front of the lamp unit (photo).
12 Undo the two retaining screws and pull out the lamp unit (photo).
13 Disengage the wire retaining clip at the rear of the bulb (photo), then lift the bulb holder out of the lamp unit (photo).
14 Remove the bulb by pulling it out of the holder.

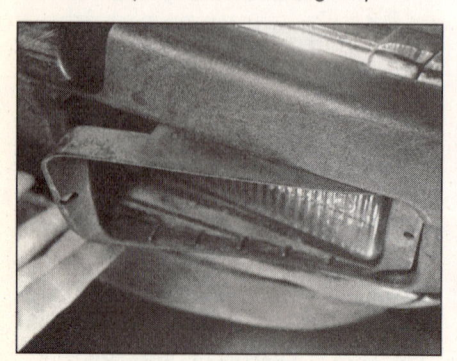

22.11 Withdraw the foglamp trim surround

22.12 Undo the two foglamp retaining screws (arrowed)

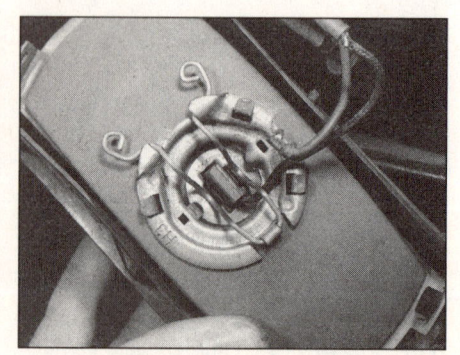

22.13A Disengage the wire retaining clip . . .

Electrical system 12•15

22.13B . . . and lift out the bulb and bulb holder

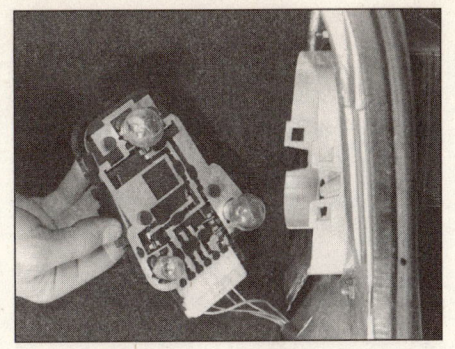

22.16 Rear lamp cluster bulb plate

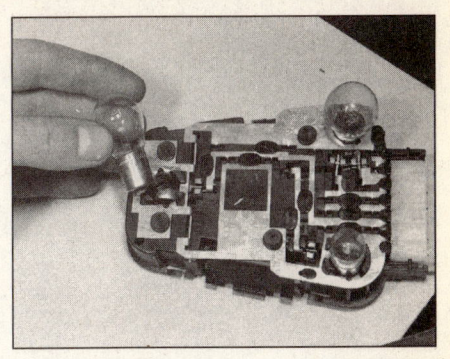

22.17 Rear lamp cluster bulb renewal

Rear lamp cluster

15 Working in the luggage compartment, undo the two knurled nuts and remove the cover at the rear of the lamp cluster.
16 Depress the catches on each side of the bulb plate and withdraw the bulb plate from the lamp cluster (photo).
17 Push and twist the bulbs to remove (photo).
18 To remove the lamp cluster, undo the four retaining nuts and washers then carefully prise the unit off the body (photo) The unit will be found stuck quite firmly in place, due to the mastic sealing, and considerable effort is needed to initially break the seal. When refitting, ensure that the mastic sealant is spread evenly around the groove in the lamp cluster (photo).

Boot lid/trunk lid/tailgate lights

19 Open the boot/trunk/tailgate and, using a screwdriver, carefully prise off the trim panel at the rear of the light unit (photos).
20 Turn the bulb holder anti-clockwise and withdraw it from the light unit (photo).
21 Push and twist the bulbs to remove.

Number plate/licence plate light

22 Open the boot/trunk/tailgate and undo the two screws securing the lens cover (photo).
23 Withdraw the lens and lamp unit then remove the bulb by pushing and twisting (photo).

22.18A Removing the rear lamp cluster lens assembly

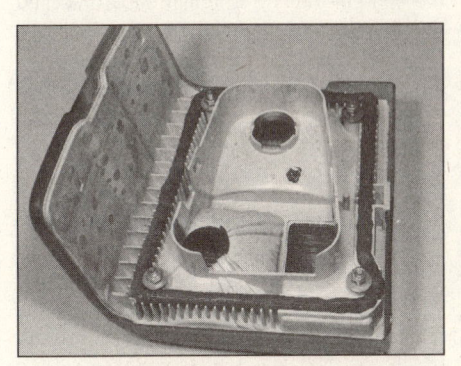

22.18B Sealing mastic evenly spread in lamp cluster groove

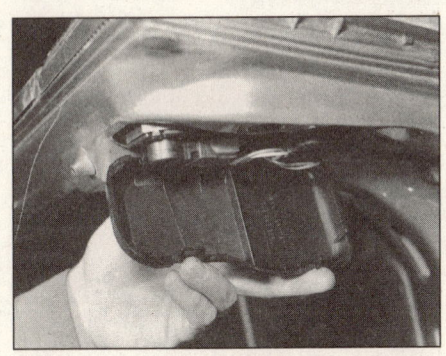

22.19A Removing the boot lid trim cover on Saloon models . . .

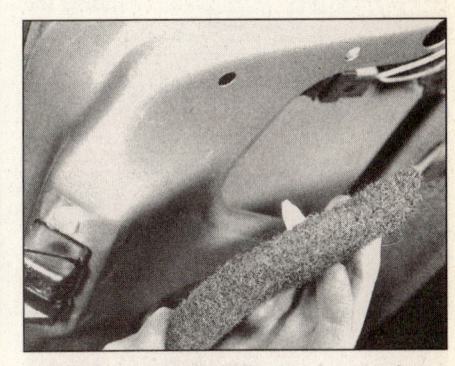

22.19B . . . and the tailgate trim panel on Avant models

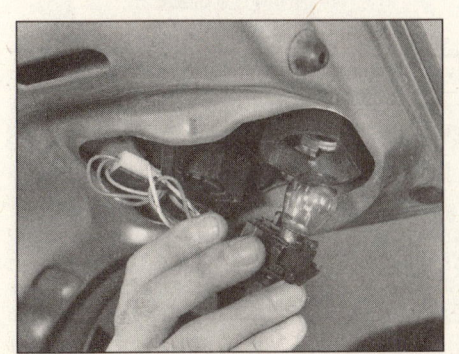

22.20 Removing the bulbholder from the boot lid

22.22 Number plate light retaining screws

22.23 Number plate light bulb renewal

22.25 Removing the interior light lens and bulb

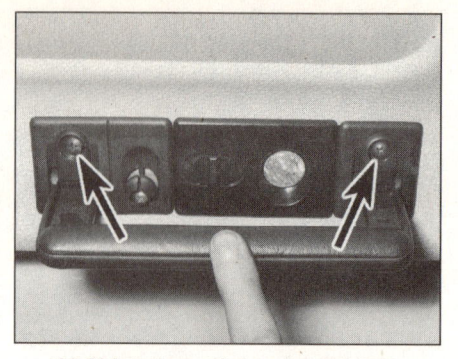

22.26 Interior grab handle and light retaining screws (arrowed)

22.28 Interior light lens and bulb

Interior light

24 Press the clip on the edge of the light lens opposite the switch carefully inwards, using a screwdriver.
25 Withdraw the lens and remove the festoon type bulb from the contacts (photo).

Interior reading light

26 Pull down the handle and undo the two screws above the handle hinges (photo).
27 Using a screwdriver, carefully prise off the cap over the coat hook.
28 Undo the coat hook screw and withdraw the bulb holder (photo).
29 Push and twist the bulb to remove.

Luggage compartment light

30 Using a screwdriver, carefully prise out the bulb holder and lens.

31 Withdraw the festoon type bulb from the contacts.

Instrument panel lamps

32 Remove the instrument panel, as described in Section 17.
33 Turn the bulb holder through 90° and remove it from the instrument panel (photos).
34 Pull out the wedge type bulb.

Glovebox lamp

35 Open the glovebox and prise out the switch/bulbholder.
36 Push and twist the bulb to remove it.

All lamp units

37 Refitting is a reversal of removal.

23 Windscreen wiper blades and arms – removal and refitting

Wiper blades

1 Lift the wiper blade and arm from the windscreen.
2 Depress the plastic clip and lift the blade from the hooked end of the arm (photo).
3 Insert the new blade, making sure the plastic clip is engaged.

Wiper arms

4 Prise the trim button off the top of the arm (photo).
5 Unscrew the nut securing the arm to the spindle (photo).
6 Insert a dowel rod or bolt into the hole on the edge of the arm to retain the arm locked against spring pressure (photo).

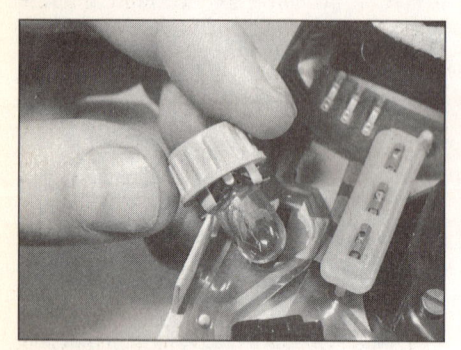

22.33A Removing an instrument panel illumination bulb . . .

22.33B . . . and warning light bulb

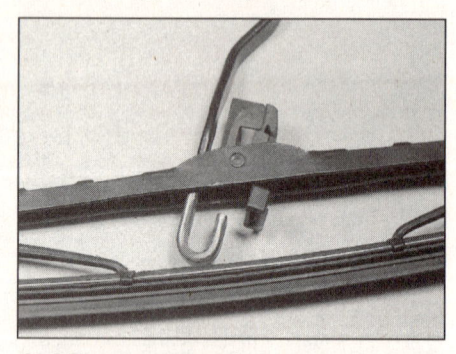

23.2 Disengage the wiper arm hooked end from the blade

23.4 Remove the wiper arm trim button . . .

23.5 . . . then unscrew the retaining nut

23.6 Lock the wiper arm in the closed position using a bolt or dowel prior to removal from the spindle

Electrical system 12•17

7 Carefully lever off the wiper arms.
8 Refitting is a reversal of removal, but install the arm so that the blade is parallel and approximately 20 mm (0.78 in) below the black edging of the windscreen when the wipers are parked.

24 Windscreen wiper linkage and motor – removal and refitting

1 Disconnect the battery negative lead.
2 Remove the wiper arms, as described in Section 23.
3 Remove the black plastic cover trim over the plenum chamber at the rear of the engine compartment.
4 Disconnect the wiring plug at the wiper motor.
5 Undo the bolts securing the wiper linkage frame and wiper motor to the body (photo) then remove the linkage and motor assembly from the plenum chamber.
6 Detach the linkage arms from the motor and remove the motor.
7 Refitting is a reversal of removal.

25 Windscreen washer system – removing, refitting and adjustment

1 The windscreen washer reservoir is located at the front right-hand side on UK models and at the rear of the engine compartment on North American models. The washer pump is attached to the reservoir on all models except those for the UK with headlamp washers, in which case it is remotely sited. On UK models with headlamp washers the reservoir serves both systems, and the pump attached to the reservoir is for the headlamp system.
2 To remove the reservoir, lift it out of its retaining bracket or remove the retaining screws (photo).
3 The pump is a push-fit in the reservoir and can be removed by carefully prising out. The pump is a sealed unit and cannot be repaired.
4 If the washer jets require cleaning, do not use a needle or piece of wire because this will damage the orifice. Jets can be cleaned without damage by using a brush bristle or a piece of nylon line.
5 Adjust the jets to give the spray pattern shown in Fig. 12.32.

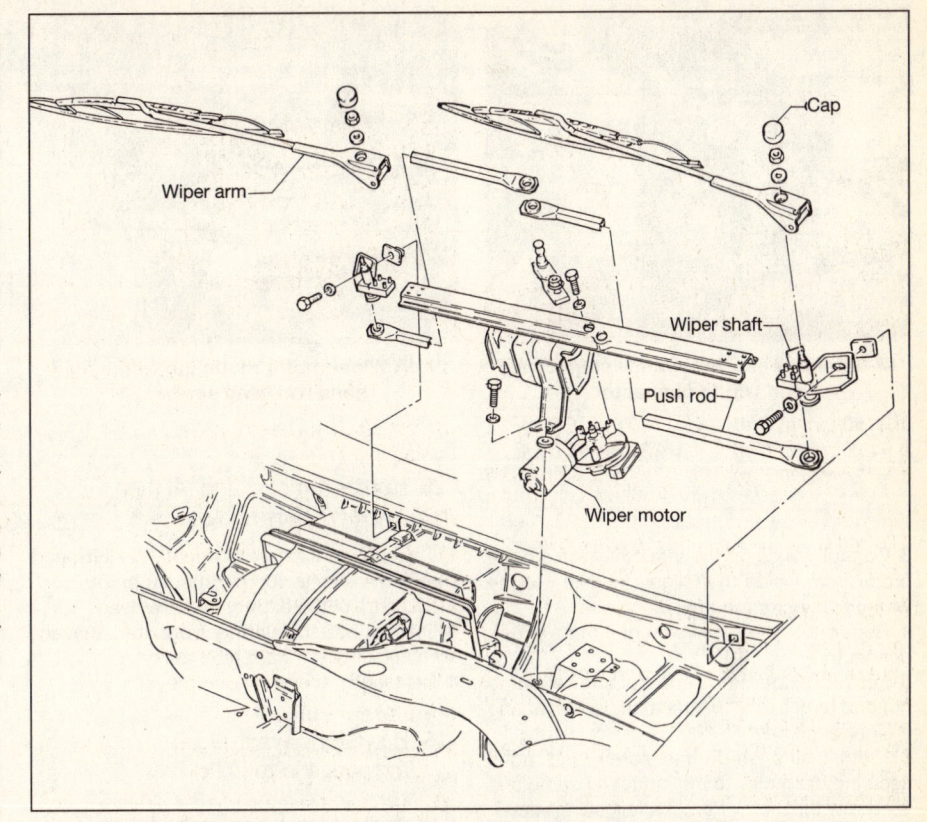

26 Tailgate wiper blades and arm (Avant models) – removal and refitting

Wiper blades

1 The procedure is the same as for the windscreen wiper blades described in Section 23.

Wiper arm

2 Flip up the cover and unscrew the arm retaining nut.
3 Carefully lever the arm off the spindle.
4 Refitting is a reversal of removal, but position the arm as near as possible to the bottom edge of the window with the wiper motor in the park position.

27 Tailgate wiper motor (Avant models) – removal and refitting

1 Disconnect the battery negative lead.
2 Remove the wiper arm, as described in Section 26.

Fig. 12.31 Exploded view of the windscreen wiper motor and linkage (Sec 24)

24.5 Wiper linkage frame left-hand retaining bolt (arrowed)

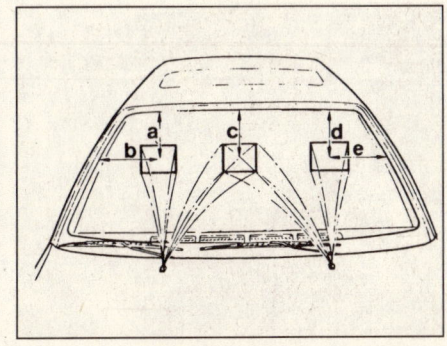

Fig. 12.32 Windscreen washer jet aiming diagram (Sec 25)

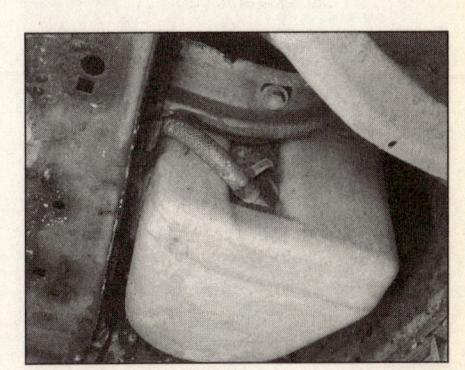

25.2 Windscreen washer reservoir, pump and mounting

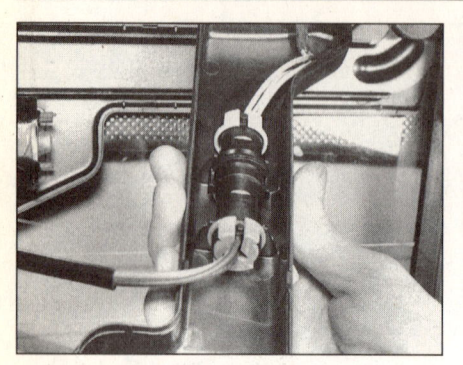

12•18 Electrical system

27.3 Remove the wiper motor trim cover and wiring connector

a = 160 mm (6.3 in)   d = 160 mm (6.3 in)
b = 220 mm (8.6 in)   e = 220 mm (8.6 in)
c = 120 mm (4.7 in)

27.6A Wiper motor mounting frame right-hand retaining screw . . .

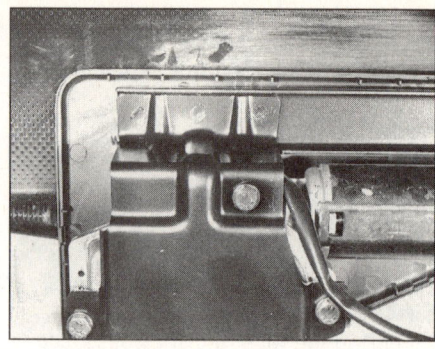

27.6B . . . and motor securing bolts

3 Carefully prise off the trim cover around the motor from inside the tailgate and lift out the wiring connector (photo).
4 Separate the halves of the wiring connector.
5 From outside, undo the spindle retaining nut and remove the washers and seals; noting their arrangement.
6 From inside, undo the screw and bolts securing the motor to the mounting frame and withdraw the motor from the tailgate (photos).
7 Refitting is a reversal of removal.

28 Horn – removal and refitting

1 The horns are located beneath the left-hand side of the engine compartment (photo).
2 Disconnect the battery negative lead.
3 Disconnect the wiring from the relevant horn and unbolt it from the bracket.
4 Refitting is a reversal of removal.

29 Headlamp washers – removal and refitting

1 Carefully prise out the edge trim over the front bumper.
2 Undo the two nuts securing the washer assembly to the bumper (photo).
3 Withdraw the washer assembly and disengage the hose valve from the grommet.
4 Refitting is a reversal of removal. Adjust the jets so that the water strikes the headlamp glass at two points roughly equidistant from the centre of the glass and with the outer water jet slightly lower than the inner water jet.

30 Radio/cassette player and speakers – removal and refitting

1 Disconnect the battery negative lead.
2 Refer to Chapter 11 and remove the centre console cover trim.

3 Remove the control knobs and front facia plate (photo).
4 According to equipment type fitted, either remove the retaining screws, or wire retaining clips, and withdraw the radio from the console (photo).
5 Disconnect the relevant wiring at the rear of the radio and remove the unit from the car.
6 Refitting is a reversal of removal.
7 Removal and refitting of the speakers simply entails undoing the retaining screws and removing the relevant speaker after first removing the covers and wiring. The arrangement of the audio system is shown in Fig. 12.33.

31 Cruise control system – removal and refitting of components

The cruise control system automatically maintains a desired speed when actuated above approximately 22 mph (35 km/h). When engaged, the system controls the position of the throttle linkage by means of a vacuum-operated servo unit, and maintains a constant road speed. The servo unit is controlled by an electronic control unit which in turn receives information from various sensors. The system can be overridden by the driver by means of the function switch or whenever the clutch or brake pedal are depressed.

28.1 Horn mountings and wiring connections

29.2 Headlamp washer retaining nuts (arrowed)

30.3 Remove the radio facia plate (Audi 100 shown)

30.4 Radio removal (Audi 100 shown)

Electrical system 12•19

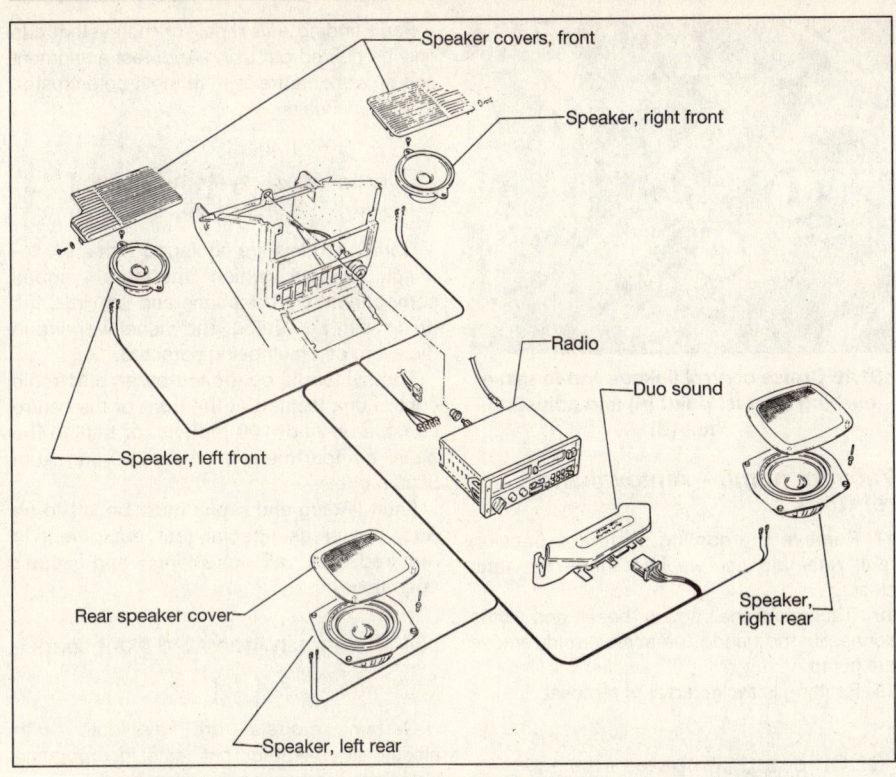

Fig. 12.33 Layout of the radio/cassette player and speakers (Sec 30)

Control unit – removal and refitting

1 Disconnect the battery negative lead.
2 On Audi 100 models, remove the trim under the facia on the driver's side. On Audi 200 and Audi 5000 models, remove the cover and trim below the facia on the driver's side and take out the parcel shelf.
3 Disconnect the wiring, remove the retaining screws and remove the control unit.
4 Refitting is a reversal of removal.

Control switch – removal and refitting

5 The control switch is part of the steering column combination switch and removal and refitting procedures are contained in Section 14.

Clutch/brake pedal vent valves

6 Disconnect the battery negative lead.
7 Remove the facia trim or parcel shelf, as necessary, to gain access to the clutch and brake pedals.
8 Disconnect the wiring and vacuum hose to the relevant vent valve then prise the unit out of its holder. Audi tool 2041 is available for removal of the valves, but even with the

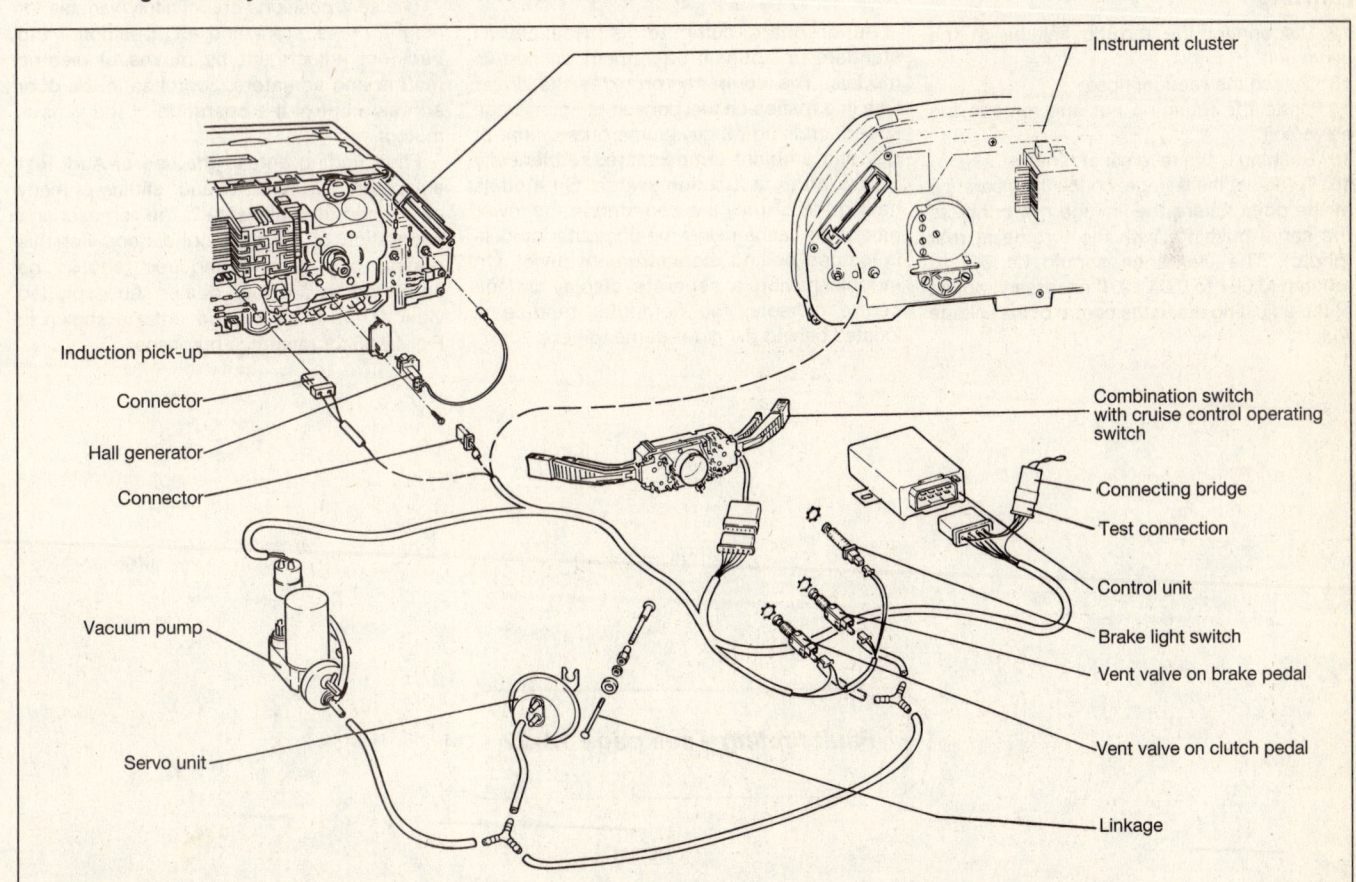

Fig. 12.34 Layout of the cruise control components, wiring and vacuum connections (Sec 31)

12•20 Electrical system

Fig. 12.35 Removal of the clutch pedal vent valve (1) using tool 2041 (Sec 31)

2 Brake pedal vent valve

special tool the valves must be discarded after removal as the threads will be damaged.
9 To fit new valves, place them in position and push them into their holders as far as they will go using a 10 mm socket.
10 Pull up on the clutch or brake pedal as far as it will go to set the valve adjustment.
11 Refit the trim and reconnect the battery.

Vacuum servo unit – removal and refitting

12 Disconnect the throttle linkage at the servo unit.
13 Detach the vacuum hose.
14 Undo the retaining nut and remove the servo unit.
15 Refitting is the reversal of removal.
16 To adjust the linkage, check the clearance at the point where the linkage rod contacts the servo bushing, with the throttle at rest (photo). The clearance should be 0.1 to 1.0 mm (0.004 to 0.04 in). If necessary, adjust at the adjusting nut in the centre of the linkage rod.

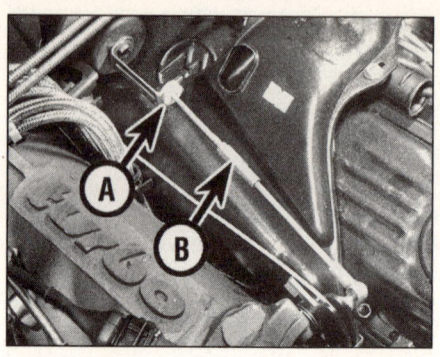

31.16 Cruise control linkage rod to servo bushing contact point (A) and adjusting nut (B)

Vacuum pump – removal and refitting

17 Remove the cooling system expansion tank retaining screws and move the tank clear.
18 Disconnect the vacuum hoses and wiring connector then undo the screws and remove the pump.
19 Refitting is the reversal of removal.

32 On-board computer – general

An on-board computer is available as standard or optional equipment on certain models. The computer provides the driver with information on fuel consumption, average speed, cruising range, journey time, time of day and ambient temperature; sequentially controlled by a function switch. On models having the display incorporated in the lower part of the tachometer, the computer module is located behind the instrument panel. On models having a separate display on the centre console, the computer module is located behind the glove compartment.

Fault finding and repair of the system can only be carried out using Audi test equipment and all work on the system must be entrusted to an Audi dealer.

33 Auto-check system – general

Certain models are equipped with an Auto-check system which monitors various components and functions and provides the driver with an audible and visual warning in the event of a fault being detected.
The system is controlled by an electronic control unit located at the front of the centre console on Audi 100 models, or behind the glove compartment on Audi 200 and Audi 5000 models.
Fault finding and repair must be left to an Audi dealer as special test equipment is required for all checking and repair operations.

34 Electrically-operated front seats – general

Certain models are available with electrically-operated front seats; incorporating a position memory on the driver's seat.
The seat positions are infinitely variable for height, rake, fore-and-aft position, and backrest adjustment by means of electric motors and actuators. Switches in the door armrest control the operation of the various motors.
Fault finding entails the use of Audi test equipment and removal and refitting of many of the components entails the removal and separation of the seat upholstery. For this reason any repairs required should be entrusted to an Audi dealer. An exploded view of the main components is shown in Fig. 12.36 for reference purposes.

Fault finding – see page 12•22

Electrical system 12•21

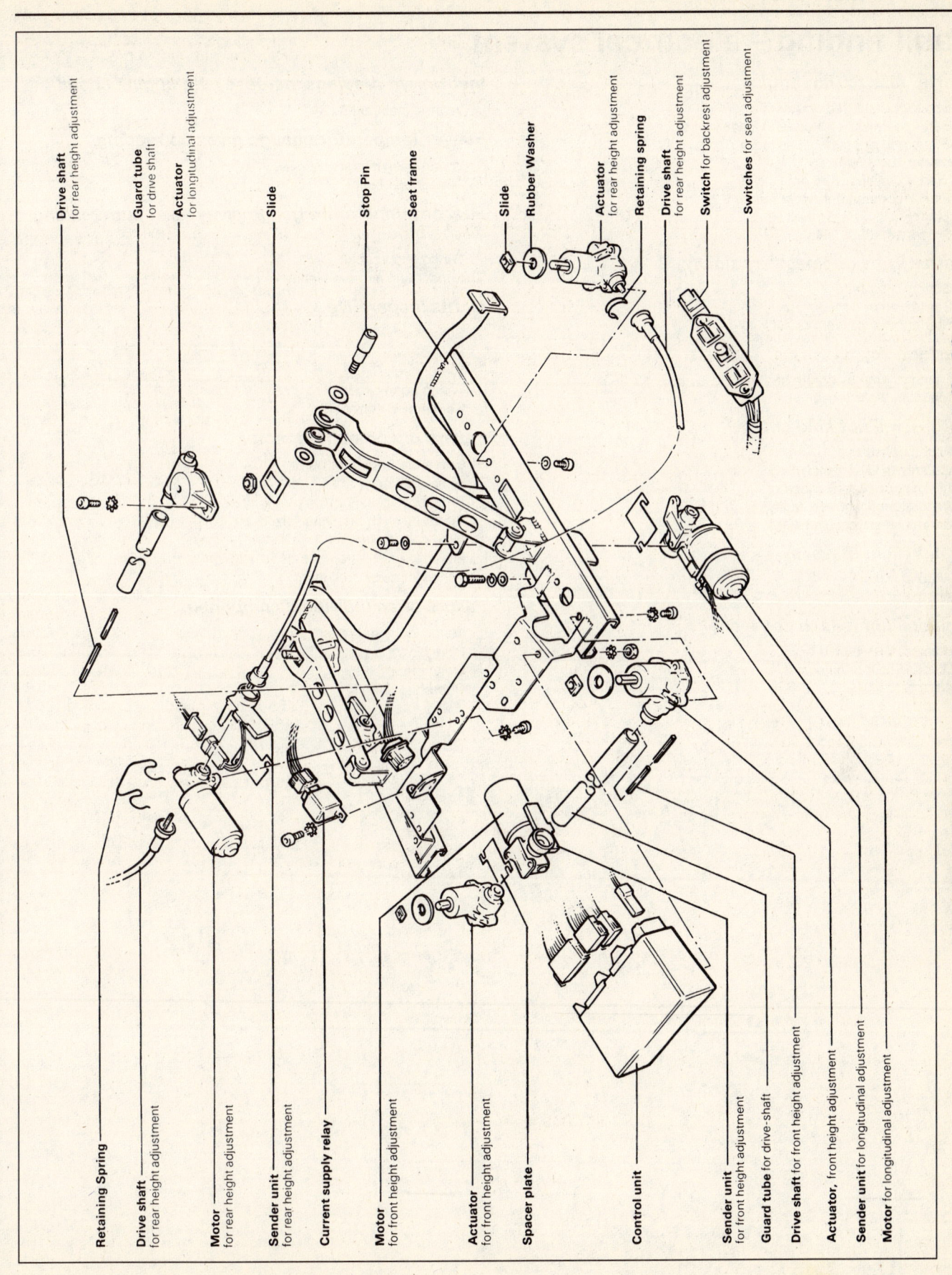

Fig. 12.36 Exploded view of the electrically-operated front seat components (Sec 34)

Fault finding – electrical system

Starter fails to turn engine
☐ Battery discharged or defective
☐ Battery terminal and/or earth leads loose
☐ Starter motor connections loose
☐ Starter solenoid faulty
☐ Starter brushes worn or sticking
☐ Starter commutator dirty or worn
☐ Starter field coils earthed
☐ Starter armature faulty

Starter turns engines very slowly
☐ Battery discharged
☐ Starter motor connections loose
☐ Starter brushes worn or sticking

Starter noisy
☐ Pinion or ring gear teeth badly worn
☐ Mounting bolts loose

Battery will not hold charge
☐ Plates defective
☐ Electrolyte level too low
☐ Alternator drivebelt slipping
☐ Alternator or regulator faulty
☐ Short in electrical circuit

Ignition light stays on
☐ Alternator faulty
☐ Alternator drivebelt broken

Ignition light fails to come on
☐ Warning bulb blown
☐ Warning light open circuit
☐ Alternator faulty

Instrument readings increase with engine speed
☐ Voltage stabilizer faulty

Fuel or temperature gauge gives no reading
☐ Wiring open circuit
☐ Sender unit faulty

Fuel or temperature gauge gives maximum reading all the time
☐ Wiring short circuit
☐ Sender unit or gauge faulty

Lights inoperative
☐ Bulb blown
☐ Fuse blown
☐ Switch faulty
☐ Wiring open circuit
☐ Connection corroded

Failure of component motor
☐ Commutator dirty or burnt
☐ Armature faulty
☐ Brushes sticking or worn
☐ Armature shaft bearings seized
☐ Field coils faulty
☐ Fuse blown
☐ Wiring loose or broken

Failure of an individual component
☐ Wiring loose or broken
☐ Fuse blown
☐ Switch faulty
☐ Component faulty

Chapter 13 Supplement:
Revisions and information on later models

Contents

Introduction 1
Specifications 2
Engine 3
   Engine oil specification – 1986-on
   Hydraulic tappets (four-cylinder engines, 1986-on)
   Camshaft (four-cylinder engines, 1986-on) – removal and refitting
   Crankshaft gear bolt (four-cylinder engines) – tightening torque
   Piston ring end gap (four-cylinder engines)
   Exchange cylinder heads/engines (four-cylinder engines)
   Cylinder head (four-cylinder engines) – renewal
   Engine (four-cylinder engines) – realignment after refitting
   Pistons (four-cylinder engines) – identification
   Hydraulic tappets (all models) – testing and renewal
   Flywheel/driveplate (models with transistorised ignition) – renewal
   Flywheel/driveplate (models with electronic ignition) – renewal
   Valve cover (all engines) – leakage
   Valve cover (five-cylinder engines, 1989-on) – removal and refitting
   Cylinder head (all engines) – refitting
   Big-end bearing caps (five-cylinder engines) – checking
   Crankshaft and needle roller bearing (five-cylinder engines) renewal
   Reworked engine (2.2 litre, code MC) – identification
Cooling system 4
   Coolant (all models) – general
Fuel and exhaust systems 5
   Operation on unleaded fuel – general
   Accelerator cable (four-cylinder engines, code DR and DS, later models) – adjustment
   Fuel tank (1988-on) – removal and refitting
   Fuel gauge sender unit (1988-on) – removal and refitting
   Fuel pump (1988-on) – removal and refitting
   K and KE-Jetronic fuel injection systems – modifications
   Thermotime switch (K and KE-Jetronic, later models) – checking
   Cold start valve (K and KE-Jetronic, later models) – checking
   Diaphragm pressure switch (K and KE-Jetronic, later models) – general
   Fuel injectors (K and KE-Jetronic, later models) – removal and refitting
   Difficult starting when hot (K and KE-Jetronic models)
   K and KE-Jetronic Lambda closed loop system (engine codes MC and RT, 1989-on)
   KE III-Jetronic fuel injection system – general description
   KE III-Jetronic fuel injection system – testing
   KE III-Jetronic fuel injection system – idle speed and CO adjustment
   KE III-Jetronic fuel injection system – component renewal
   Inlet manifold (fuel injection models, 1989-on) – removal and refitting
   Emission control system (later models) – general
   Exhaust manifold (1989-on) – removal and refitting
   Catalytic converter – removal and refitting

Ignition system 6
   Spark plugs (all models) – renewal
   Fully Electronic Ignition system (FEI) (later models) – general description
   Fully Electronic Ignition system – safety precautions
   Ignition timing (FEI) – adjustment
Clutch 7
   Clutch pedal (all models with hydraulic clutch) – failure to return
   Clutch slave cylinder (016 gearbox, 1988-on) – modifications
Manual transmission 8
   Gearshift leader (016 gearbox, 1988-on) – adjusting
   Electronic speedometer sender (016 gearbox, 1988-on) – removal and refitting
   Front gearshift rod (models with Procon-ten system) removal and refitting
   Procon-ten safety system
   Manual gearbox (012) – general description
   Manual gearbox (012) – removal and refitting
   Gear lever (012) gearbox – removal, overhaul and refitting
   Gear shift linkage (012 gearbox) – adjustment
Automatic transmission 9
   Selector modification (1987 models)
   Selector modification, August 1988-on – adjustment
   Selector lever illumination bulb (1988-on) – renewal
Driveshafts 10
   Driveshafts (engine code NF with automatic transmission, 1989-on) – removal, refitting and overhaul
Braking system 11
   Twin piston front disc brake calipers – general
   Brake pad renewal (models with twin piston front disc brakes)
   Rear disc caliper (1989-on) – overhaul
   Rear brake caliper (all models with rear disc brakes) – refitting
   Vacuum servo unit – pushrod adjustment
   Anti-lock braking system relays – general
   Brake light switch (all models) – removal and refitting
Suspension and steering 12
   Front suspension strut top mounting modification
   Front shock absorber (all models) – removal and refitting
   Rear anti-roll bar – general
   Power steering fluid (models with self-levelling suspension) – level checking
   Air bag safety system – general description
   Air bag safety system – testing
   Air bag safety system – precautions

Degrees of difficulty

| **Easy,** suitable for novice with little experience | **Fairly easy,** suitable for beginner with some experience | **Fairly difficult,** suitable for competent DIY mechanic | **Difficult,** suitable for experienced DIY mechanic | **Very difficult,** suitable for expert DIY or professional |

13•2 Supplement: Revisions and information on later models

Bodywork and fittings 13
   Sunroof drain hoses (all models)
   Seat belts (all models) – general care and maintenance
   Seat belts (all models) – removal and refitting
   Rear seat (Saloon with head restraints) – removal and refitting
   Head restraints (all models) – removal and refitting
   Interior mirror (all models) – removal and refitting
   Door mirror glass (all models) – renewal
   Door mirror (manually adjusted type) – removal and refitting
   Door mirror (electrically adjusted type) – removal and refitting
   Air conditioning – further precautions and maintenance
   Fully automatic air conditioning – general
   Procon-ten safety system – general description
   Procon-ten safety system – inspection
   Procon-ten system components – removal and refitting
   Heater controls (rotary, 1988-on) – removal and refitting
   Heater control assembly and cables (rotary, 1988-on) – removal and refitting
   Interior door trim panel (1988-on) – removal and refitting
   Boot lid lock (1988-on) – general
   Centre console (1988-on) – removal and refitting

Electrical system 14
   Starter motor (1.1 kW with reversing gear) – overhaul
   Bulb failure warning system – general
   Dim-dip lighting system – description
   Ambient air temperature indicator – removal and refitting
   Ambient air temperature sensor – removal and refitting
   Alternator drivebelt tension (engine code DR and DS) – adjustment
   Side repeater lamp – bulb renewal
   Heater control panel illumination bulb (1988-on models) – renewal
   Headlamp beam adjustment (mechanical) – general
   Headlamp beam adjustment (electric) – general
   Headlamp beam adjustment (electric) – servicing
   Radio/cassette player (DIN fitting) – removal and refitting
   Radio aerial (1987-on models) – general
   Rear loudspeaker and audio controls (Saloon) – removal and refitting

1 Introduction

This supplement contains information about UK models which have become available since the book was first written. Most of the information applies to 1986 and later models, although some of the information applies to earlier models.

The Sections in the Supplement are arranged in the same order as the Chapters to which they relate. All the Specifications are grouped together for convenience, but they too follow Chapter order.

To use the Supplement to its best advantage, it should be referred to before the main Chapters. Any relevant information can then be noted for incorporation into the procedures given in Chapters 1 to 12.

Project vehicle

The vehicles used in the preparation of this Supplement, and appearing in many of the photographic sequences were a 1987 Audi 100 CC Saloon and a 1989 Audi 100 2.0 E.

2 Specifications

These specifications are revisions of, or supplementary to, those at the beginning of the previous Chapters.

Part A – four-cylinder engines

Pistons and rings
Piston ring end gap (engine code DR and DS):
  Oil scraper ring:
    Two-part .... 0.25 to 0.45 mm (0.010 to 0.018 in)
    Three-part .... 0.25 to 0.50 mm (0.010 to 0.020 in)

Valves (1986-on)
Length (with hydraulic tappets):
  Inlet .... 91.0 mm (3.583 in)
  Exhaust .... 90.8 mm (3.575 in)

Torque wrench setting
	Nm	lbf ft
Oil pressure switch	25	18

Part B – five-cylinder engines

Specifications as for equivalent size engines as given in Chapter 1, except for the following.

General
Code letters:
  1994 cc (121.6 cu in) .... RT
  2226 cc (135.7 cu in) .... 1B, 2B and MC
  2309 cc (140.8 cu in) .... NF
Power output:
  RT .... 85 kW (115 bhp) at 5400 rpm
  1B .... 147 kW (191 bhp) at 5800 rpm
  2B .... 140 kW (182 bhp) at 5800 rpm
  MC .... 121 kW (157 bhp) at 5500 rpm
  NF .... 100 kW (130 bhp) at 5600 rpm

General (continued)

Torque:
- RT .... 172 Nm (126 lbf ft) at 4000 rpm
- 1 B, 2B .... 270 Nm (199 lbf ft) at 3000 rpm
- MC .... 240 Nm (176 lbf ft) at 3000 rpm
- NF .... 190 Nm (140 lbf ft) at 4000 rpm

Bore: NF .... 82.5 mm (3.25 in)
Stroke: NF .... 86.4 mm (3.40 in)

Compression ratio:
- RT 10.0:1
- 1B, 2B 8.6:1
- MC, up to 9/1988 .... 7.8:1
- MC, 10/1988-on 8.4:1
- NF 10:1

Cylinder compression

Compression pressure (warm engine, throttle open):
- Engine code KP, KU, RT and NF .... 11 to 16 bar (159 to 232 lbf/in^2)
- Engine code KG, 1B, 2B also MC with two knock sensors .. 9 to 13 bar (130 to 188 lbf/in^2)
- Engine code MC with one knock sensor .... 8 to 11 bar (116 to 159 lbf/in^2)
- Maximum permissible difference between cylinders ...... 2 bar (29 lbf/in^2)

Crankshaft

Endplay (new) – 1984-on .... 0.07 to 0.23 mm (0.003 to 0.009 in)

Big-end bearing journal diameter (2.0 litre engines from 7/1983 and non-Turbo engines from 7/1984):
- Standard .... 47.76 to 47.78 mm (1.8817 to 1.8825 in)
- 1st undersize .... 47.51 to 47.53 mm (1.8718 to 1.8825 in)
- 2nd undersize .... 47.26 to 47.28 mm (1.8620 to 1.8628 in)
- 3rd undersize .... 47.01 to 47.03 mm (1.8521 to 1.8529 in)

Pistons and rings

Piston size (engine code NF):

	Piston diameter	Bore diameter
Standard size	82.48 mm (3.2497 in)	82.51 mm (3.2508 in)
1st oversize	82.74 mm (3.2599 in)	82.76 mm (3.2607 in)
2nd oversize	82.98 mm (3.2694 in)	83.01 mm (3.2705 in)

Camshaft

Camshaft bearing maximum radial clearance .... 0.1 mm (0.0039 in)

Valves

Valve timing (at 1.0 mm lift and zero clearance):

Engine code 1B/2B up to 1989:
- Inlet opens at .... TDC
- Inlet closes at .... 41° ABDC
- Exhaust opens at .... 40° BBDC
- Exhaust closes at .... 1° BTDC

Engine code RT 1988-on:
- Inlet opens at .... 2° ATDC
- Inlet closes at .... 31° ABDC
- Exhaust opens at .... 31° BBDC
- Exhaust closes at .... 1° BTDC

Engine code NF 1985 to 1989:
- Inlet opens at .... 0° BTDC
- Inlet closes at .... 41.1° ABDC
- Exhaust opens at .... 40° BBDC
- Exhaust closes at .... 1.1° ATDC

Engine code NF 1989-on:
- Inlet opens at .... 3.9° ATDC
- Inlet closes at .... 41.2° ABDC
- Exhaust opens at .... 45.9° BBDC
- Exhaust closes at .... 4.9° BTDC

Engine code MC up to 9/1988:
- Inlet opens at .... 0° BTDC
- Inlet closes at .... 41° ABDC
- Exhaust opens at .... 40° BBDC
- Exhaust closes at .... 10 ATDC

Engine code MC 10/1988-on:
- Inlet opens at .... 4° ATDC
- Inlet closes at .... 41° ABDC
- Exhaust opens at .... 46° BBDC
- Exhaust closes at .... 5° BTDC

Torque wrench settings

	Nm	lbf ft
Valve cover nuts:		
Stage 1	5	4
Stage 2	10	7
Stage 3	12	9
Engine to transmission:		
M8 bolts	20	15
M10 bolts	45	33
M12 bolts	65	48

Cooling system

Torque wrench setting

	Nm	lbf ft
Cooling fan thermoswitch (in radiator on four-cylinder engines):		
Engine codes DR and DS	35	25

Fuel and exhaust systems

Fuel injection system

System pressure, July, 1986-on .... 5.6 to 6.0 bar (81.2 to 87.0 lbf/in^2)

Fuel octane rating

All engines 1987-on .... 98 RON leaded or 95 RON unleaded

Note: *Refer to 'Operation on unleaded fuel' in Section 5 of this Supplement*

Ignition system

Fully Electronic Ignition (FEI)

System type .... Hall effect, fully electronic ignition system with micro-processor control
Application .... Engine code RT (from 9/1989) and engine Codes NF and MC

Coil

Primary resistance:
  Engine code RT .... 0.52 to 0.76 ohms
  Engine code NF .... 0.50 to 1.50 ohms
  Engine code MC .... 0.50 to 0.70 ohms
Secondary resistance:
  Engine code RT .... 2.4 to 3.5 kohms
  Engine code NF .... 5.0 to 9.0 kohms
  Engine code MC .... 5.0 to 9.0 kohms

Ignition timing

Engine code RT .... 17 to 19° BTDC
Engine code NF .... 14 to 16° BTDC
Engine code MC .... non-adjustable

Spark plugs

Engine codes RT and NF .... Champion N7YCC or N7BYC
Engine codes MC, 1B or 2B .... Champion N9YCC or N9BYC
Electrode gap (all plug types) .... 0.8 mm (0.032 in)

Clutch

Torque wrench setting

	Nm	lbf ft
Clutch slave cylinder bolt (016 gearboxes, 1988-on)	25	18

Manual gearbox

Gearbox 012

Type .... Five forward speeds and reverse, synchromesh on all gears, integral final drive

Ratios (code letters AMK)

Final drive 3.888:1
1st 3.545:1
2nd 2.105:1
3rd 1.429:1
4th 1.029:1
5th 0.838:1
Reverse 3.500:1

Supplement: Revisions and information on later models

Torque wrench settings (1988 on)	Nm	lbf ft
Shift linkage coupling bolt	20	15
Shift linkage clamp bolt	25	18
Gear lever shift fork nut	10	7
Gear lever mounting plate	10	7
Electronic speedometer sensor lock bolt	25	18
5th/reverse gear catch	10	7
Multi-function connector	10	7
Selector shaft cover	20	15
Final drive cover	25	18
Clutch release guide sleeve	35	26
Relay shaft Torx bolt	40	30
Detent Torx bolt	25	18
Rear housing to main housing	25	18
Reverse gear shaft	35	26

Braking system

Front brakes (solid discs) 100 models:
Disc thickness:
  New .... 13.0 mm (0.512 in)
  Wear limit .... 11.0 mm (0.433 in)

Front brakes (15 inch wheels, from January 1986)
Caliper type .... Twin piston
Disc diameter .... 276.0 mm (10.87 in)
Disc thickness:
  New .... 25.0 mm (0.984 in)
  Wear limit .... 23.0 mm (0.906 in)

Suspension and steering

Front wheel alignment
Castor (manual steering models from chassis No 43 GA 024 419) ..... + 50' ± 40'

Rear wheel alignment
Toe setting at each wheel:
  Up to Chassis No EA 085 288 (Drum brakes) or EN 082 448 (Disc brakes) .... + 15' ± 10' (toe-in)
  From Chassis No EA 085 289 (Drum brakes) or EA 082 449 (Disc brakes) .... + 10' ± 5' (toe-in)

Bodywork and fittings (all models)

Torque wrench settings	Nm	lbf ft
Seat belt mountings:		
Front mountings and inertia reel to B-pillar	50	37
Front buckle to seat frame	60	44
Rear mountings to floor	50	37
Rear inertia reel to cross panel	40	30
Height adjustable type (August 1985-on):		
Adjuster-to-B pillar bolt	24	18
Belt buckle-to-adjuster nut	55	40
Procon-ten system		
Cable tensioner to manual gearbox:		
Front bolts	40	30
Rear bolts	65	48
Cable tensioner to automatic transmission:		
Bolts	40	30
Nuts	40	30
Guide bracket bolts	75	55
Anchor bracket bolts	75	55

Electrical system

Torque wrench settings	Nm	lbf ft
Alternator drivebelt adjuster (engine code DR and DS):		
New belt	8	6
Used belt	4	3

13•6 Supplement: Revisions and information on later models

3.1 Topping-up the engine oil

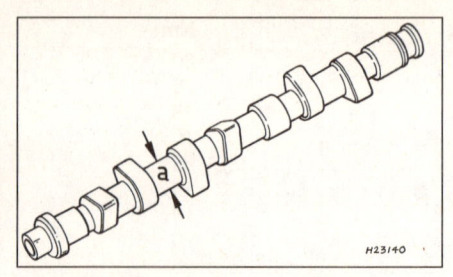

Fig. 13.1 Camshaft size identification (four-cylinder engines) (Sec 3)

a = 26.00 mm (1.024 in), normal size
a = 25.75 mm (1.014 in), undersize (also has yellow paint spot on VW-Audi sign)

3 Engine

Engine oil specification – 1986-on

1 The manufacturers strongly recommend the use of high performance oils, to specification VW 500 00. In the absence of such oils, 'improved lubricity' oil (to the same specification), or reputable multigrade oil to API-SF or higher may be used (photo).

Hydraulic tappets (four-cylinder engines, 1986-on)

2 From 1986 model year, hydraulic tappets are fitted to the 4-cylinder 66 kW engine (code DS). Adjustment of the valve clearances is therefore no longer necessary.

Camshaft (four-cylinder engines, 1986-on) – removal and refitting

3 With the introduction of hydraulic tappets, No 4 camshaft bearing has been deleted. The camshaft bearing caps should therefore be removed and refitted as described for the 5-cylinder engine in Chapter 1, Sections 37 and 45.

Crankshaft gear bolt (four-cylinder engines) – tightening torque

4 Note that there are two types of crankshaft gear bolt one with a hexagon head, and one with a double hexagon head. The torque loading figure for each is different.
5 With the hexagon head type, a washer is used and the threads of the bolt should be oiled before fitting. With the double hexagon type, no washer is used, the bolt must be renewed every time it is removed, and the thread and shoulder of the new bolt should be oiled before fitting.

Piston ring end gap (four-cylinder engines)

6 Note the revised piston ring end gap for two and three-part oil scraper rings given in the Specifications.

Exchange cylinder heads/engines (four-cylinder engines)

7 Exchange cylinder heads/engines may be supplied with bearing shells for normal and undersize camshafts.
8 An undersize camshaft is not available as a service part. Where applicable, a normal size camshaft with the appropriate bearing shells must be used. Refer to an Audi dealer for bearing specification.

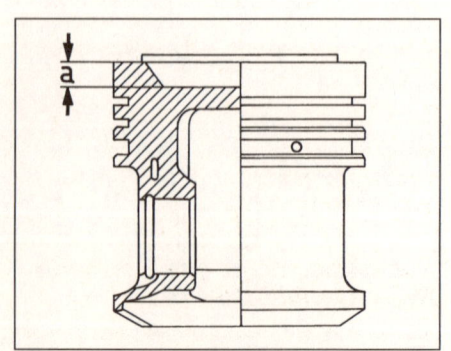

Cylinder head (four-cylinder engines) – renewal

9 Whenever a new or exchange cylinder head is fitted, the coolant in the cooling system must also be renewed.

Engine (four-cylinder engines) – realignment after refitting

10 Realignment of the engine/gearbox should only be necessary if either the engine or gearbox have been removed from their bonded rubber mountings.
11 If only the engine has been removed, the engine mountings and engine bearer bolts must be finally tightened to the specified torque while the engine is idling.
12 To carry out the realignment, slacken both bonded rubber securing nuts.
13 Rock the engine and gearbox on their mountings to align the assembly longitudinally.
14 Once the correct alignment is obtained (see Fig. 13.2), tighten the mounting bolts to the specified torque.

Pistons (four-cylinder engines) – identification

15 The pistons fitted to code DR engines differ from those fitted to code DS engines and can be identified by the depth of the hollow in the piston crown (see Fig. 13.3).

Hydraulic tappets (all models) – testing and renewal

16 To identify a noisy hydraulic tappet with the engine stopped, remove the valve cover and turn the crankshaft until a pair of cam lobes point upwards.
17 Using a tapered wooden or plastic rod, gently depress the tappet to feel for free play before the valve begins to open. If this free play exceeds 0.1 mm, then the tappet must be renewed.
18 Turn the crankshaft to bring the other pairs of cam lobes in position for checking the remaining tappets.
19 Where new tappets are being fitted, it is

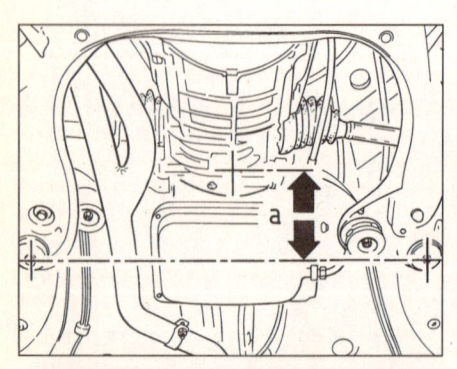

Fig. 13.2 Engine/gearbox alignment on four-cylinder engines (Sec 3)

a = 99.0 to 102.0 mm (3.9 to 4.01 in) manual gearbox
a = 152.0 to 155.0 mm (5.9 to 6.0 in) automatic transmission

Fig. 13.3 Piston identification (four-cylinder engines) (Sec 3)

a = 8.1 mm (0.319 in) engine code DR
a = 44 mm (0.173 in) engine code DS

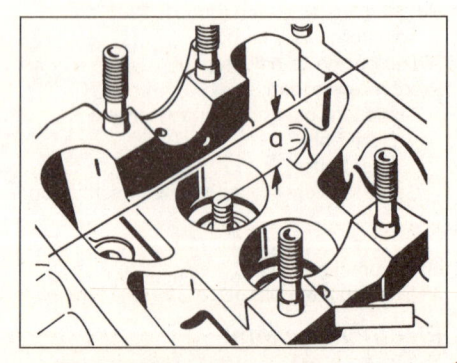

Fig. 13.4 Valve stem to cylinder head dimension (a) (Sec 3)

Inlet = 33.8 mm (1.33 in) minimum
Exhaust = 34.1 mm (1.34 in) minimum

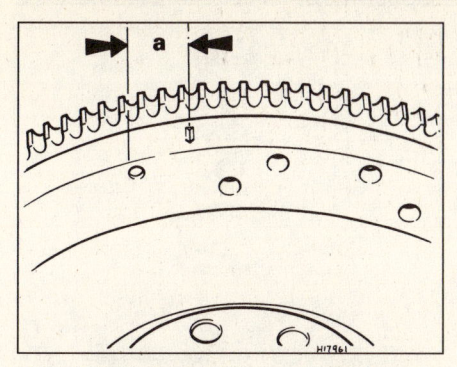

Fig. 13.5 Distance (a) between TDC mark and ignition timing mark on flywheel (five-cylinder engines) (Sec 3)

3° ATDC = 7.3 mm (0.29 in) to right of TDC
6° BTDC = 14.5mm (0.57in) to left of TDC
15° BTDC = 365 mm (1.44 in) to left of TDC
18°BTDC = 43.5mm (1.71 in) to left of TDC

important that the distance between the end of the valve stem and the surface of the cylinder head around the tappet bore is measured with a depth gauge. If the dimension is less than that specified in Fig. 13.4 then the valve and/or cylinder head will have to be renewed.

20 After new tappets have been fitted, the engine must not be started for at least 30 minutes. This is to allow the new tappets to compress. Failure to observe this time period could result in piston-to-valve contact with subsequent engine damage.

Flywheel/driveplate (models with transistorised ignition) – renewal

21 A new flywheel or driveplate only bears a TDC mark (usually a '0').
22 The ignition timing marks must therefore be scribed (preferably) or painted on the flywheel or driveplate the appropriate distance from the TDC mark (see Fig. 13.5).
23 When carrying out the measurement, allow for the radius of the flywheel or driveplate.

Flywheel/driveplate (models with electronic ignition) – renewal

24 A new flywheel/driveplate is supplied without the ignition timing pin(s). These must be removed from the old flywheel and knocked in to the new flywheel until they are flush with their shoulders.

Valve cover (all engines) – leakage

25 If a valve cover fitted with a cork/rubber compound gasket develops leaks, the problem may be rectified by fitting an all rubber gasket, obtainable from VAG dealers, but note the following:
26 There are two types of valve cover retaining studs (screwed into the cylinder head), one type with a collar, and one type without a collar. Similarly, there are two types of rubber gasket, one for use on studs with a collar, and one for use on studs without a collar. Ensure the correct gasket is obtained and fitted.
27 When fitting a rubber gasket for the first time a new valve cover must also be fitted.
28 Observe the three stage torque tightening sequence of the valve cover retaining nuts when refitting the valve cover.

Valve cover (five-cylinder engines, 1989-on) – removal and refitting

29 Before the valve cover on 1989-on models with a modified inlet manifold can be removed, the upper section of the inlet manifold must be removed as described in Section 5.

Cylinder head (all engines) – refitting

30 Before refitting the cylinder head as described in Sections 16 and 44, of Chapter 1, turn the crankshaft so that the piston of No 1 cylinder is at TDC, then turn the crankshaft back again until all the pistons are a uniform distance from the top of the bores.

Big-end bearing caps (five-cylinder engines) – checking

31 When checking big-end bearing cap radial clearance where the cap nuts are notched, tighten the nuts to the specified torque, but do not tighten by a further 1/4 turn (90°).

Crankshaft and needle roller bearing (five-cylinder engines) – renewal

32 Replacement crankshafts are supplied with the needle roller bearing at the flywheel end already fitted.
33 The needle roller bearing is not used on vehicles with automatic transmission and therefore must be removed as described in Chapter 1, Section 27.
34 If the needle roller bearing is being renewed on manual gearbox models, refer to Chapter 12, Section 27, but note the fitted depth dimension given in Section 55 of the same Chapter.

Reworked engine (2.2 litre, code MC) – identification

35 In October 1988 a modified version of the 2.2 litre engine was introduced but still carrying the original MC engine code. The modified versions can be identified by the presence of two knock sensors, instead of a single sensor on the original engine.

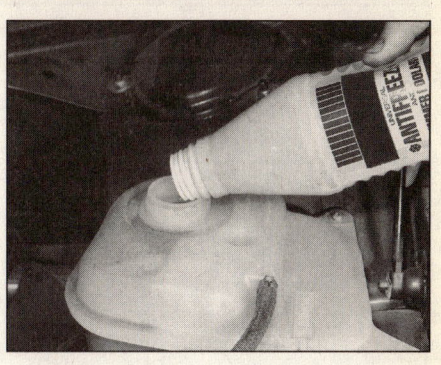

4.2 Topping-up the cooling system

4 Cooling system

Coolant (all models) – general

1 Whenever a new or reconditioned cylinder head Is fitted, or the engine is completely overhauled, the manufacturers recommend that the coolant is completely renewed.
2 Always use good quality ethylene glycol based antifreeze, and not one based on methanol. Be sure that the correct concentration of antifreeze is used, and top-up the system with the same concentration on completion (photo).

5 Fuel and exhaust systems

Operation on unleaded fuel – general

1 All models fitted with a catalyst **must be operated on unleaded fuel only**. Leaded fuel will destroy the catalyst element and render it ineffective.
2 For all other models, consult a VAG dealer as to suitability and for the possible need for ignition timing adjustment.

Accelerator cable (four-cylinder engines, code DR and DS, later models) – adjustment

3 The procedure is basically as described in Chapter 3, Part A, Section 8, but adjustment is made by moving the retaining clip up or down the serrated cable-end fitting to achieve the specified clearance between the throttle lever and stop.

Fuel tank (1988-on) – removal and refitting

4 From 1988 model year, the fuel tank and associated components have been modified. The procedure for removal and refitting are still basically the same as described in Chapter 3, Section 18, but the vacuum hose to the charcoal filter on models with a catalytic converter must also be disconnected.

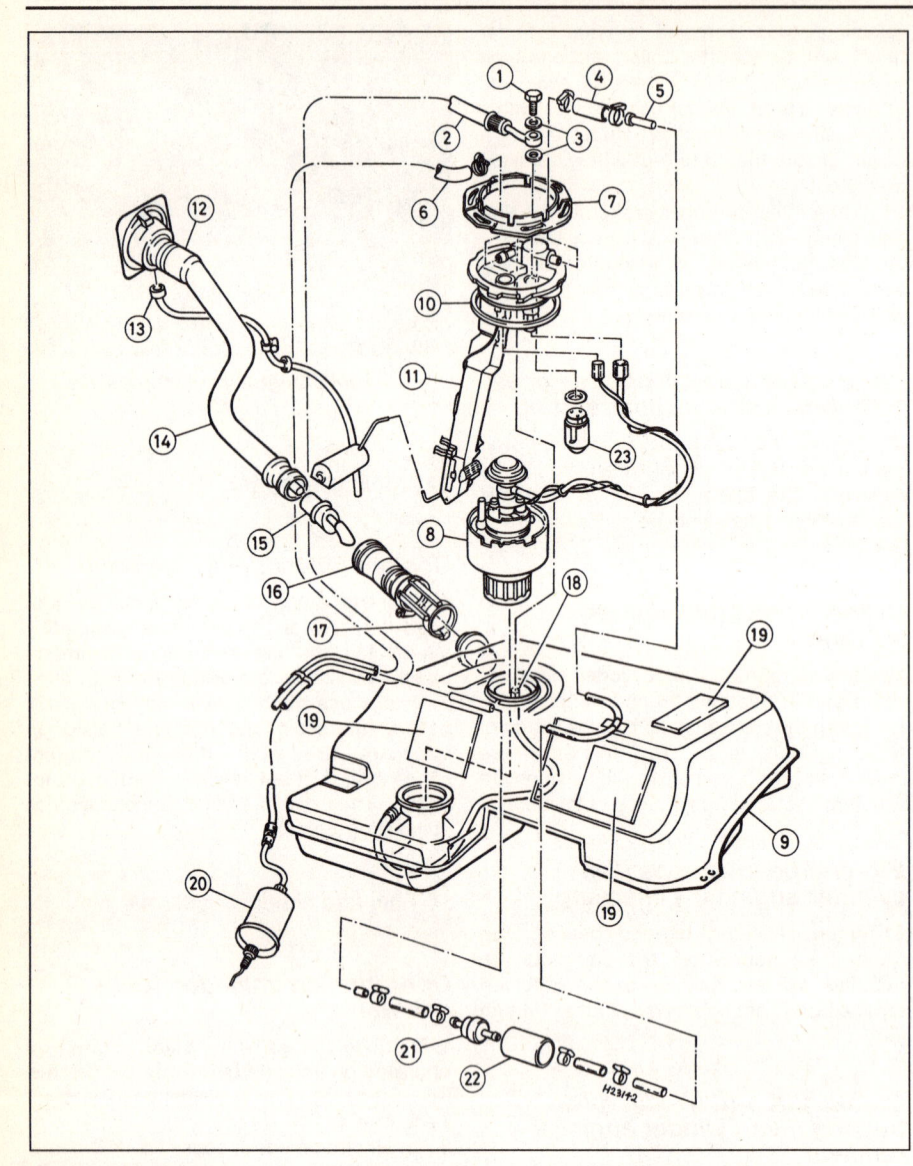

Fig. 13.6 Exploded view of the 1988-on fuel tank assembly (Sec 5)

1 Banjo bolt
2 Fuel supply pipe
3 Sealing rings
4 Breather pipe connection
5 Breather pipe to charcoal filter (where fitted)
6 Fuel return pipe
7 Retaining ring
8 Fuel pump
9 Fuel tank
10 Sealing ring
11 Fuel gauge sender unit
12 Filler neck
13 Overflow hose
14 Filler pipe
15 Filler pipe insert
16 Filler pipe hose
17 Clip
18 Return pipe
19 Packing
20 Fuel filter
21 Vent and breather valve
22 Support hose
23 Gravity valve

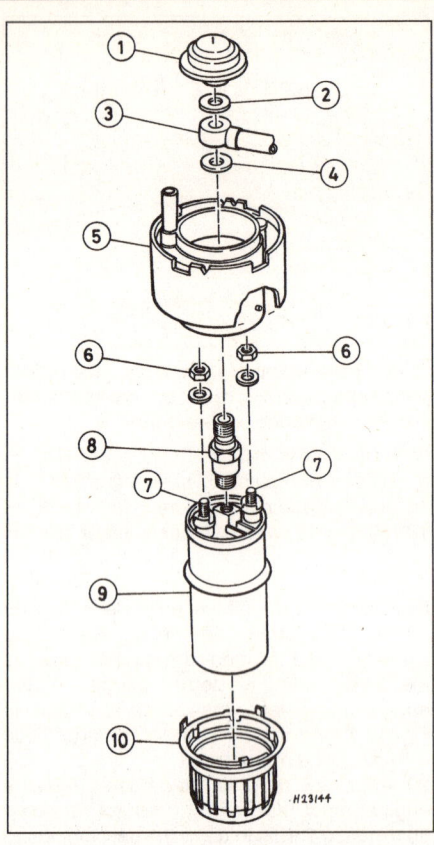

Fig. 13.7 Exploded view of the 1988-on fuel pump (Sec 5)

1 Noise damper
2 Seal
3 Supply hose
4 Seal
5 Upper housing
6 Nuts and washers
7 Electrical connections M6 positive (+) M5 earth (−)
8 Non-return valve
9 Pump body
10 Strainer

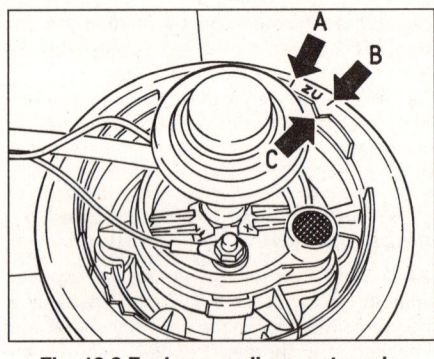

Fig. 13.8 Fuel pump alignment marks (1988-on) (sec 5)

A First mark
B Second mark
C Notch on locking ring

5 An exploded view of the assembly appears in Fig. 13.6.

Fuel gauge sender unit (1988-on) – removal and refitting

6 Again, on 1988-on models, the fuel level sender unit is of modified design to earlier models, although the basic removal procedure as described in Chapter 3, Section 7, applies.

7 Care should be exercised when removing the sender not to bend the float arm as the sender is withdrawn from the tank.

Fuel pump (1988-on) – removal and refitting

8 The fuel pump on 1988-on models has been modified along with the sender unit and tank. The removal and refitting procedure given in Chapter 3, Section 31, is still basically the same, but note the following:

9 A special tool (VAG 3214) is needed to turn the pump approximately 15 mm (0.5 in) to the left in order to release the pump from the in-tank housing, although it may be possible to use two crossed-over screwdrivers in lieu.

10 When refitting, insert the pump in the housing so that the notch in the pump locking ring aligns with the first mark on the housing rim. Turn the pump to the right using the special tool so that the notch aligns with the second mark (see Fig. 13.8).

Supplement: Revisions and information on later models

K and KE-Jetronic fuel injection systems – modifications

11 From July 1986, minor modifications have been made to the K and KE fuel injection systems. These modifications are as follows:
(a) Higher system pressure and injector opening pressure
(b) Rigid instead of flexible fuel lines supplying the injectors
(c) Conical seat, instead of banjo fuel line connections
(d) Modified pressure accumulator and thermotime switch
(e) Modified operation of cold start valve

12 Except as noted in the Specifications and elsewhere in this Section, testing and repair procedures are unchanged.

Thermotime switch (K and KE-Jetronic, later models) – checking

13 On models produced from July 1986, the operation graph for the thermotime switch is shown in Fig. 13.9. Otherwise the procedure is as given in Chapter 3, Section 27.

Cold start valve (K and KE-Jetronic, later models – checking)

14 On models with the modified thermotime switch described above, the cold start valve will continue to spray short bursts of fuel all the time that the starter motor is operated, following the period of continuous spray controlled by the thermotime switch. The procedure is otherwise as given in Chapter 3, Section 28.

Diaphragm pressure switch (K and KE-Jetronic, later models) – general

15 Fitted to later models, the diaphragm pressure switch is located next to the ignition coil (photo). It is involved with the control of acceleration enrichment and is not to be confused with the diaphragm pressure switch of the emission control system.

16 As with other fuel injection components, testing should be left to a VAG dealer.

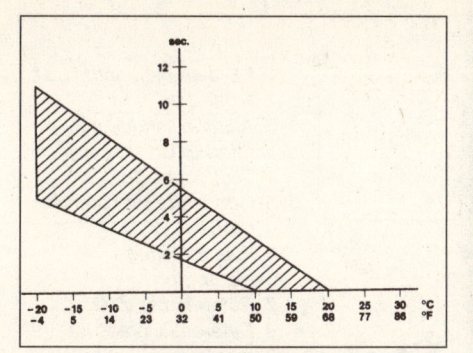

Fig. 13.9 Thermotime switch operation graph for later models (Sec 5)

Fuel injectors (K and KE-Jetronic, later models) – removal and refitting

17 Release the pressure in the fuel lines (Chapter 3, Section 15, paragraphs 3 to 5).
18 Remove the injector securing rail, retained by two Allen bolts (photo).
19 Release the fuel lines from the bracket on the inlet manifold.
20 Clean the unions on the injectors before undoing the union nuts (photo).
21 Pull the injectors from the cylinder head. Grip the injectors by the hexagon portion, not the threads (photo).
22 Refitting is the reversal of removal, using new O-ring seals lubricated with fuel.

Difficult starting when hot (K and KE-Jetronic models)

23 If problems are experienced when hot starting, first check the ignition system. Ensure the spark plugs are of the specified type and in good condition, and that the ignition timing is correct.
24 Checks should next be performed on the fuel injection system. Apart from the checks described in Chapter 3, this work must be performed by a VAG dealer.
25 If the ignition and fuel injection systems are in order, measures must be taken to reduce under-bonnet temperatures. Such measures include modifying the electric cooling fan circuitry so that it continues to run after the engine has been switched off, and the installation of an auxiliary fan and ducting to cool the injectors. Consult a VAG dealer for details.

5.15 The fuel injection diaphragm pressure switch

K and KE-Jetronic Lambda closed loop system (engine codes MC and RT, 1989-on)

General description

26 To enable models fitted with K and KE-Jetronic fuel injection to operate with a catalyst with Lambda closed loop control system, additional components are fitted to the fuel injection system.
27 These components include the Lambda probe, which is screwed into the exhaust manifold upstream of the catalyst, a frequency valve (which is in effect a variable restrictor) fitted in the fuel return line from the fuel distributor, and modified internal components of the fuel distributor.
28 The Fully Electronic Ignition system control unit receives input signals from the Lambda probe, and in turn sends control signals to the frequency valve which controls the return flow of fuel from the fuel distributor, thereby controlling the air/fuel ratio of the injected fuel/air mixture.

Testing

29 Testing of the Lambda closed loop system requires the use of specialist test equipment and is best left to VAG dealers.

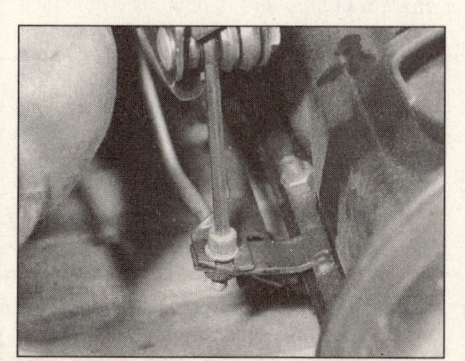

5.18 Removing a fuel injector rail securing bolt

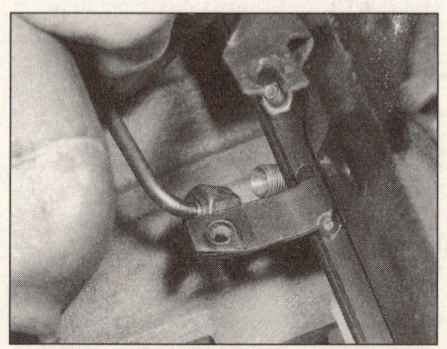

5.20 Disconnecting the fuel line from the injector

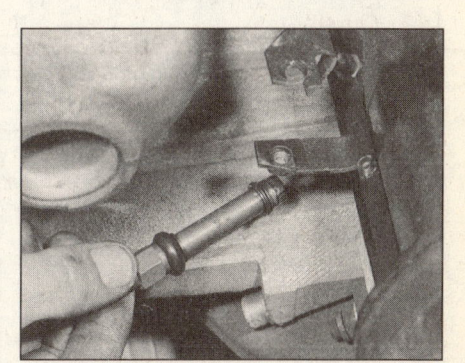

5.21 Removing the injector

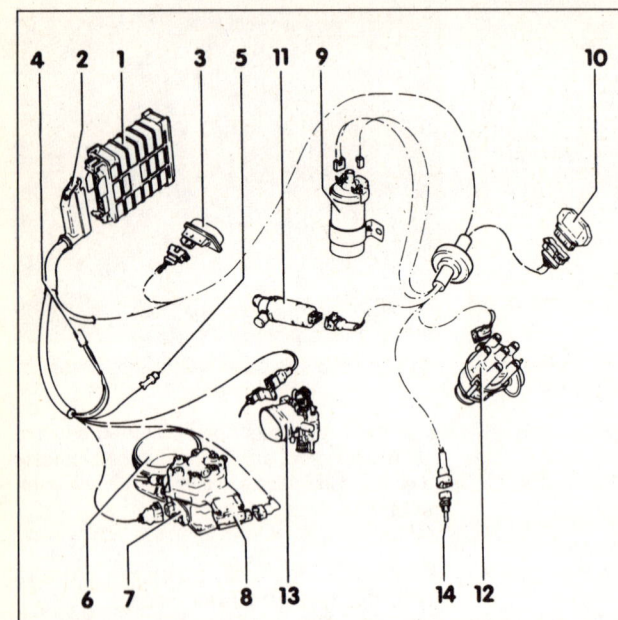

13•10 Supplement: Revisions and information on later models

1 KE-Jetronic control unit
2 Multi-plug
3 Altitude sender (not fitted to UK models)
4 Test connection
5 Connector for Lambda probe
6 Fuel metering distributor
7 Potentiometer G7
8 Differential pressure regulator
9 Ignition coil
10 TCI-H switch unit (not fitted on UK models)
11 Idling stabilisation valve
12 Distributor with Hall sender
13 Throttle valve housing
14 Coolant temperature sensor

Fig. 13.10 Electronic engine control for engine code RT with Lambda closed loop and Fully Electronic Ignition (Sec 5)

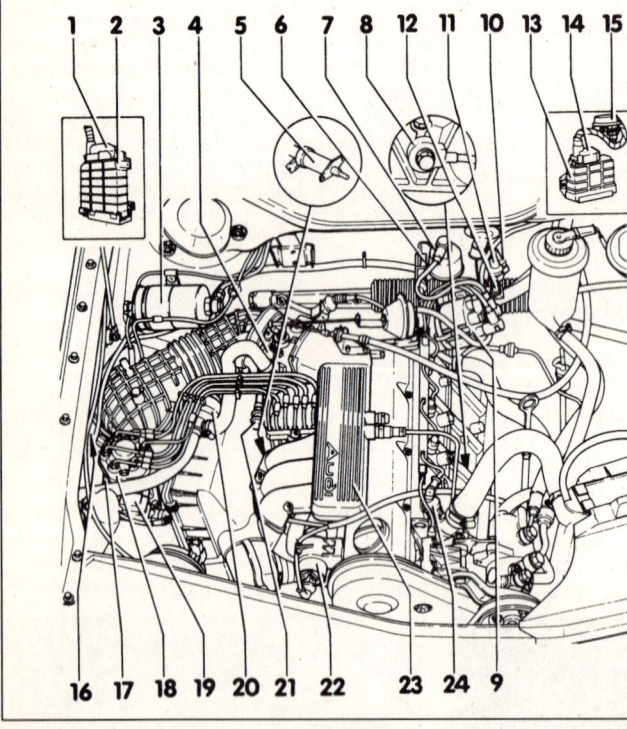

Fig. 13.11 Layout of the KE III-Jetronic fuel Injection system fitted to 1989-on models (engine code NF) (Sec 5)

1 Connector plug
2 Control unit (right-hand A-pillar)
3 Fuel filter
4 Throttle valve housing
5 Cold start valve
6 Power end stage (coil)
7 Coil
8 Knock sensor
9 Distributor
10 Connector (knock sensor)
11 Connector (Lambda sensor heating)
12 Connector (Lambda sensor)
13 FEI control unit (left-hand A-pillar)
14 Connector
15 Altitude sensor
16 Pressure regulator (early versions)
17 Potentiometer
18 Fuel metering distributor
19 Differential pressure regulator
20 Charcoal filter solenoid valve
21 Sealing cap
22 Idle speed stabilisation valve
23 Inlet manifold
24 Coolant temperature sensor

Servicing

30 Refer to later paragraphs on KE III-Jetronic fuel injection.

KE III-Jetronic fuel injection system – general description

31 The KE III-Jetronic fuel injection system is fitted to all 2.3E models (engine code NF) from 1989-on. The system is basically similar to the earlier systems described in Chapter 3, with the addition of an integrated electronically controlled engine management system, Lambda closed loop catalytic converter, and Fully Electronic Ignition (FEI) system, more fully described in Section 6. A charcoal filter and solenoid valve is fitted to control petrol vapour discharge from the fuel tank. The layout of the system is shown in Fig. 13.11.

32 The control unit, receiving signals from the various engine sensors, and in conjunction with the FEI system, controls the fuel/air ratio at the optimum level for all conditions of engine load and speed.

33 The Lambda sensor of the closed loop catalytic converter system is screwed into the exhaust manifold upstream of the catalyst and senses exhaust gas oxygen content. The design of the sensor is such that a voltage is produced across the sensor proportional to oxygen content. This voltage is used to send a signal to the control unit which adjusts the fuel/air ratio to maintain the exhaust gases at the 'cleanest' level.

34 The FEI system control unit, receiving signals from its various sensors, simultaneously controls ignition timing at the optimum level for all engine conditions.

KE III-Jetronic fuel injection system – testing

35 The KE III-Jetronic control unit is equipped with a self-diagnostic memory, the interrogation of which requires the use of specialist test equipment. For this reason, fault finding and subsequent rectification is best left to a VAG dealer unless specialist knowledge and equipment is available to the user.

36 The component renewal procedures which follow are given to enable component renewal to be undertaken to allow substitution where a component is obviously defective, and a serviceable item fitted in its place, and to allow other servicing work to be carried out.

37 It must be understood, however, that correct adjustment of the system to enable it to function efficiently can only be done using specialist equipment, and after renewal of a component the system must be checked by a VAG dealer.

KE III-Jetronic fuel injection system – idle speed and CO adjustment

38 CO adjustment requires the use of special test equipment, and the CO adjustment screw is sealed. Idle speed is controlled by the electronic engine management system.

Supplement: Revisions and information on later models

5.43 Cold start valve location on KE III-Jetronic fuel injection system (arrowed)

5.52 Idle stabilisation valve location on KE III-Jetronic fuel injection system

5.61 General view of the 1989-on modified inlet manifold

KE III-Jetronic fuel injection system – component renewal

Note: Only the procedures for those components which are different to earlier systems described in Chapter 3 are given here. Where a component is not specifically mentioned, the procedure is the same as, or very similar to, that given in Chapter 3.

Control unit

39 Remove the trim panel from the lower part of the A panel trim on the driver's side footwell.
40 Remove the control unit securing screw and withdraw the control unit.
41 Disconnect the multi-plug and remove the unit.
42 Refit in reverse order.

Cold start valve

43 Refer to Chapter 3, noting that the valve is located between the two tracts of the inlet manifold (photo).

Altitude sensor (when fitted)

44 The altitude sensor is located above the control unit in the A pillar.
45 Removal and refitting are self evident after removal of the control unit.

Charcoal filter solenoid valve

46 The valve is located by the air intake duct.
47 To remove it, disconnect the electrical and hose connections.
48 Refit in reverse order.

Charcoal filter

49 The charcoal filter is located in the right-hand inner wing.
50 To remove it, disconnect the hose, undo the filter fixings and withdraw the filter.
51 Refit in reverse order.

Idle speed stabilisation valve

52 The valve is located on the front, right-hand side of the cylinder head (photo).
53 To remove it, disconnect the electrical connection and air hoses.
54 Undo the bolt from the rubber mounting and withdraw the valve.
55 Refit in reverse order.

Fuel injectors

56 The procedure is basically as described in Chapter 3, but the upper section of the inlet manifold must first be removed for access, as described in this Section. Where fitted, the air shroud over the injectors must also be removed.

Lambda sensor

57 Disconnect the electrical connection at the bracket on the bulkhead.
58 Unscrew the Lambda sensor from the exhaust manifold.
59 Whilst the sensor is removed, take care not to damage it or allow oil, grease or dirt to come into contact with the probe.
60 Refitting is a reversal of removal, carefully applying a little G5 grease to the sensor threads.

Inlet manifold (fuel injection models, 1989-on) – removal and refitting

61 From 1989-on, the inlet manifold has been redesigned, and curves up over the valve cover (photo).
62 To remove the inlet manifold, first disconnect all vacuum hoses (these vary according to model).
63 Disconnect the air inlet duct at the throttle housing.
64 Disconnect the accelerator cable (manual gearbox) or pull rod (automatic transmission).
65 Disconnect the EGR valve.
66 Disconnect the throttle valve switch and vacuum hoses from the throttle valve housing.
67 Disconnect any earth leads bolted to the manifold.
68 Either disconnect the two fuel lines from the warm up regulator, or unbolt the regulator from the cylinder block leaving the hoses connected, and lay it to one side.
69 Remove the bolts securing the upper part of the inlet manifold to the lower part. Separate the two, then carefully manoeuvre the upper manifold off. The bracket which secures the fuel lines to the injectors will have been freed allowing movement of the fuel lines to enable the upper manifold to be withdrawn.
70 Remove the idle stabilisation valve.
71 Disconnect and unscrew the injectors.
72 If required, to give more access, the air cleaner cover and filter may be removed.
73 Disconnect or remove the cold start valve.
74 Unbolt the lower part of the manifold from the cylinder block.
75 Refit in reverse order, using new gaskets on all joint faces.

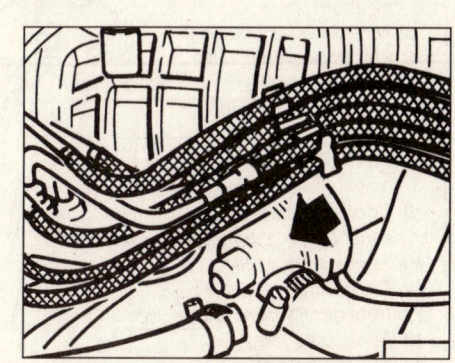

Fig. 13.12 Charcoal filter solenoid valve location (arrowed) (Sec 5)

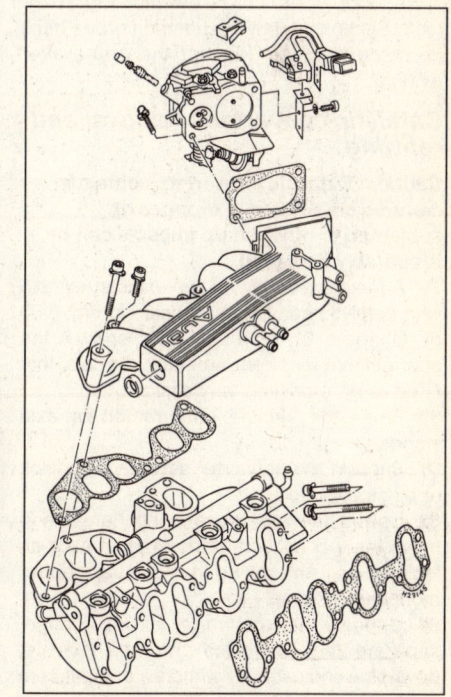

Fig. 13.13 Exploded view of the 1989-on inlet manifold (Sec 5)

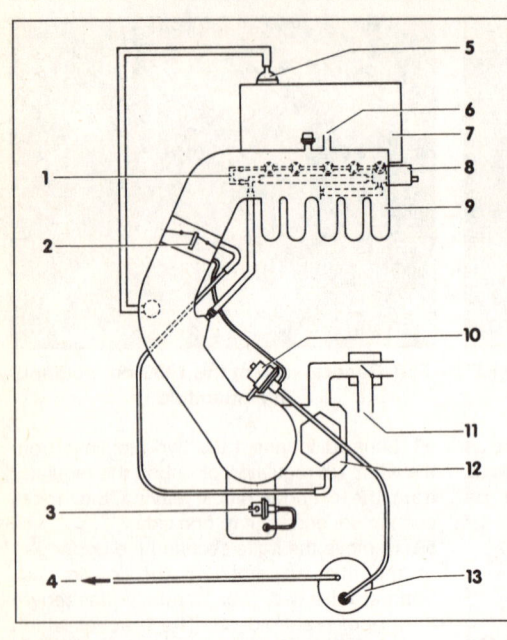

Fig. 13.14 Diagrammatic view of typical vacuum hoses on later type emission control systems (1990-model shown) (Sec 5)

1 Air shrouded injectors
2 Throttle valve housing
3 Diaphragm pressure regulator
4 To fuel tank
5 Crankcase breather
6 To air conditioner and differential lock (where fitted)
7 Cylinder head
8 Idle stabilisation valve
9 Inlet manifold
10 Charcoal filter solenoid valve
11 Inlet air pre-heating
12 Fuel metering distributor
13 Charcoal filter

5.77 Diaphragm pressure regulator fitted to later crankcase ventilation systems

Emission control system (later models) – general

76 The layout of the crankcase ventilation system fitted to later models is shown in Fig. 13.14.
77 The diaphragm pressure regulator is mounted on the air inlet elbow (photo).

Exhaust manifold (1989-on) – removal and refitting

78 The procedure for removing the exhaust manifold on 1989-on models with a Lambda closed loop system is as described in Chapter 3, Section 40, but the Lambda probe must be disconnected. Connect the probe after refitting.

Catalytic converter – removal and refitting

Caution: Catalytic converters contain a ceramic core which, if dropped or subjected to other sharp impacts can be irreparably damaged.

79 An exploded view of the exhaust system with catalytic converters appears in Fig. 3.60 of Chapter 3. Although this shows the arrangement for North American models, that fitted to UK models is very similar.
80 Raise the vehicle onto ramps or axle stands.
81 Support the converter securely on a jack or blocks of wood.
82 Unbolt the rear connecting flange and move the rear section of the exhaust back an inch or so, unhooking it from the rubber mountings as required.
83 Unbolt the converter front flange, separate the converter from the exhaust downpipe and carefully withdraw the unit from beneath the vehicle.
84 Refit in reverse order, using new gaskets and self-locking nuts.

6 Ignition system

Spark plugs (all models) – renewal

1 Ensure that the ignition is switch off, then open the bonnet.
2 Remove any air trunking or similar items which obstruct access to the plugs and leads.
3 Disconnect the HT lead from one plug at a time by pulling on the connector or metal shroud. Do not pull on the lead itself. Use pliers on the shroud if it is tight.
4 Brush or blow away any debris from around the plug seat, so that no dirt falls into the cylinder as the plug is removed.
5 Unscrew the spark plug using the correct size box spanner or socket or the longer end of the wheelbrace from the vehicle tool kit (photo;.
6 Commence fitting new spark plugs by screwing them into their threads by hand initially to avoid cross-threading them (photo). If resistance is felt, do not force the plug in, but unscrew it and start again. If a plug is cross-threaded and tightened down with a spanner it is the cylinder head which will be damaged and not the plug.
7 Carry out final tightening of the plug with a

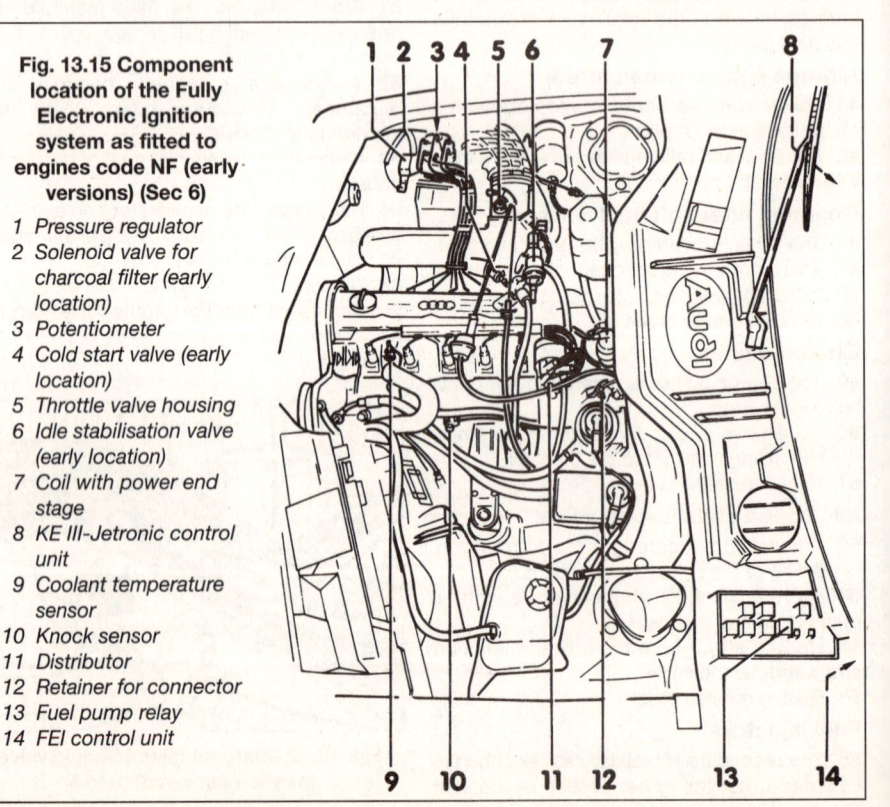

Fig. 13.15 Component location of the Fully Electronic Ignition system as fitted to engines code NF (early versions) (Sec 6)

1 Pressure regulator
2 Solenoid valve for charcoal filter (early location)
3 Potentiometer
4 Cold start valve (early location)
5 Throttle valve housing
6 Idle stabilisation valve (early location)
7 Coil with power end stage
8 KE III-Jetronic control unit
9 Coolant temperature sensor
10 Knock sensor
11 Distributor
12 Retainer for connector
13 Fuel pump relay
14 FEI control unit

Supplement: Revisions and information on later models 13•13

6.5 Unscrewing a spark plug using the spanner provided

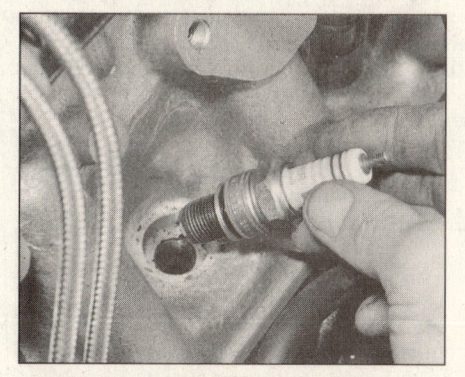

6.6 Fitting a spark plug, initially by hand

plug spanner. The use of a torque wrench is strongly recommended – see Chapter 4 Specifications for the correct torque. In the absence of a torque wrench, tighten the plug by no more than a quarter turn after the plug washer contacts the plug seat in the cylinder head.
8 Reconnect the HT lead, pushing the connector firmly onto the plug.
9 Repeat the above operations on all the remaining plugs, or as required.
10 Refit any air trunking or other disturbed items, then start and run the engine to confirm that the operation has been successfully completed.

Fully Electronic Ignition system (FEI) (later models) – general description

11 On later models a Fully Electronic Ignition system is fitted which is basically similar to the All Electronic Ignition system described in Chapter 4, although some of the components may have been modified or re-located.
12 The FEI is equipped with an electronic memory in which any intermittent or other faults are stored. For this reason, and the requirement for special test equipment, major testing, fault finding, and rectification work should be left to a VAG dealer.
13 Note that on later versions of engines with code letters MC there are two knock sensors screwed into the cylinder block and not one.

Fig. 13.16 Fully Electronic Ignition system as fitted to engines code letters RT (1989-on) (Sec 6)

1 Ignition lead
2 Suppression connector
3 Screen
4 Distributor cap
5 Carbon brush with cap
6 Spark plug connector
7 Spark plug
8 Protective cap
9 Terminal 4
10 Terminal 1 (–)
11 Terminal 15 (+)
12 Ignition coil
13 Rotor arm
14 Connector ring
15 Distributor
16 O-ring
17 Loom
18 Clamp
19 Bolt
20 Connector plug
21 Vacuum pipe from throttle valve housing
22 Valve housing
23 Bolt
24 Knock sensor
25 Power end stage of coil
26 Self diagnostic fault lamp

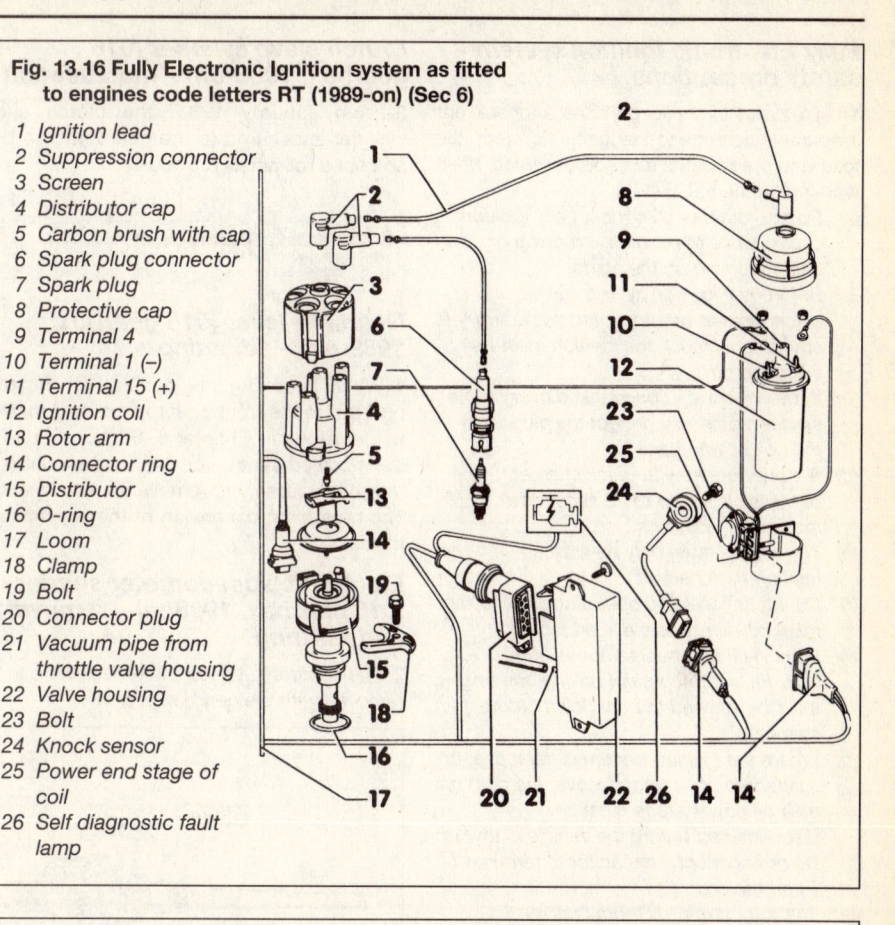

Fig. 13.17 Fully Electronic Ignition system with Lambda control as fitted to engine code letters MC with one knock sensor (Sec 6)

1 FEI control unit
2 Connector plug
3 Vacuum hose
4 Connector (black) – firing point sender
5 Connector (grey) – engine speed sensor
6 Connector (red) – knock sensor
7 Connector (black) – Lambda probe heating (located on mixture control unit on engines with one knock sensor)
8 Connector – Lambda probe
9 Connector bracket
10 Ignition timing sender
11 Engine speed sender
12 Knock sensor
13 Lambda probe
14 Frequency valve (Lambda regulation)

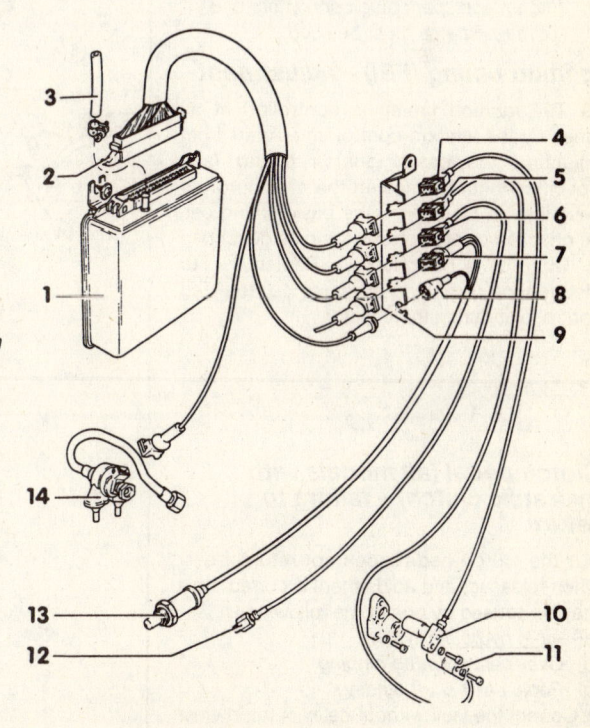

Fully Electronic Ignition system – safety precautions

14 To avoid injury to persons and prevent irreparable damage to the ignition system, the following precautions must be observed when working on the FEI system:
(a) Do not touch or disconnect any ignition cables while the engine is running or being cranked on the starter
(b) Before any ignition system cables are disconnected or connected (including test equipment leads), the ignition must be switched off
(c) If the engine is to be cranked over on the starter motor, disconnect the plug from the coil power stage
(d) A starter boost with quick charger is only permissible for up to 15 seconds at maximum 16.5 volts
(e) The engine must only be washed with the ignition switched off
(f) During any welding operations the battery must be completely disconnected
(g) If the vehicle is heated above 80°C (176°F), as during paint baking, the engine must be allowed to cool down before it is started
(h) Where the ignition system is defective, or suspected of being defective, the plug on the coil power stage must be disconnected before the vehicle is towed
(i) Do not connect a capacitor to terminal 1 (–) on the coil
(j) The rotor arm of 1/kohm (marked R1), must not be replaced with any other type, even for radio suppression
(k) For suppression purposes, suppressors of 1 kohm and spark plug connectors of 5 kohm resistance must be used

Ignition timing (FEI) – adjustment

15 The ignition timing is controlled at all times by the ignition control unit. Apart from adjusting the basic ignition timing (see Specifications) by moving the distributor as described in Chapter 4, the basic timing can be checked using a strobe lamp as described in Chapter 4, Section 7. Remember to disconnect the vacuum hose to the FEI control unit during the check.

7 Clutch

Clutch pedal (all models with hydraulic clutch) – failure to return

1 if the clutch pedal does not return freely when released, and adjustment is correct, this may be caused by one of the following:
(a) Air in hydraulic system
(b) Over-centre spring binding
(c) Pedal pivot shaft binding
2 Correct the fault without delay or rapid wear of the clutch may result.

Clutch slave cylinder (016 gearbox, 1988-on) – modification

3 From January 1988, the clutch slave cylinder is secured to the gearbox by a bolt and not a roll pin as previously.

8 Manual transmission

Gearshift lever (016 gearbox, 1988-on) – adjusting

1 When adjusting the position of the rear pushrod in the front pushrod on later models as described in Chapter 6, Section 9, due to the modified centre console front mounting it may be necessary to remove the rear bracket. The protrusion dimension of the pin remains the same.

Electronic speedometer sender (016 gearbox, 1988on) – removal and refitting

2 The electronic speedometer sender can be removed with the gearbox in situ.
3 Depress the retaining clip and carefully swing the sender out.
4 Similarly, the speedometer drive wheel can also be removed with the gearbox in situ.
5 Remove the drive flange shaft and oil seal as described in Chapter 6.
6 Remove the electronic speedometer sender as described previously.
7 Working through the drive flange aperture, carefully lever out the speedometer gear using a screwdriver.
8 Refitting of both the speedometer gear and the sender is a reversal of removal, but always use a new oil seal.

Front gearshift rod (models with Procon-ten system) – removal and refitting

9 On models with the Procon-ten system the cable tensioner is bolted to the gearbox above the front shift rod.
10 To remove the front shift rod, undo the clamp bolt and separate the front rod from the rear.
11 Lever the front rod from the gear lever and adjusting rod and withdraw the rod forwards from under the cable catcher.

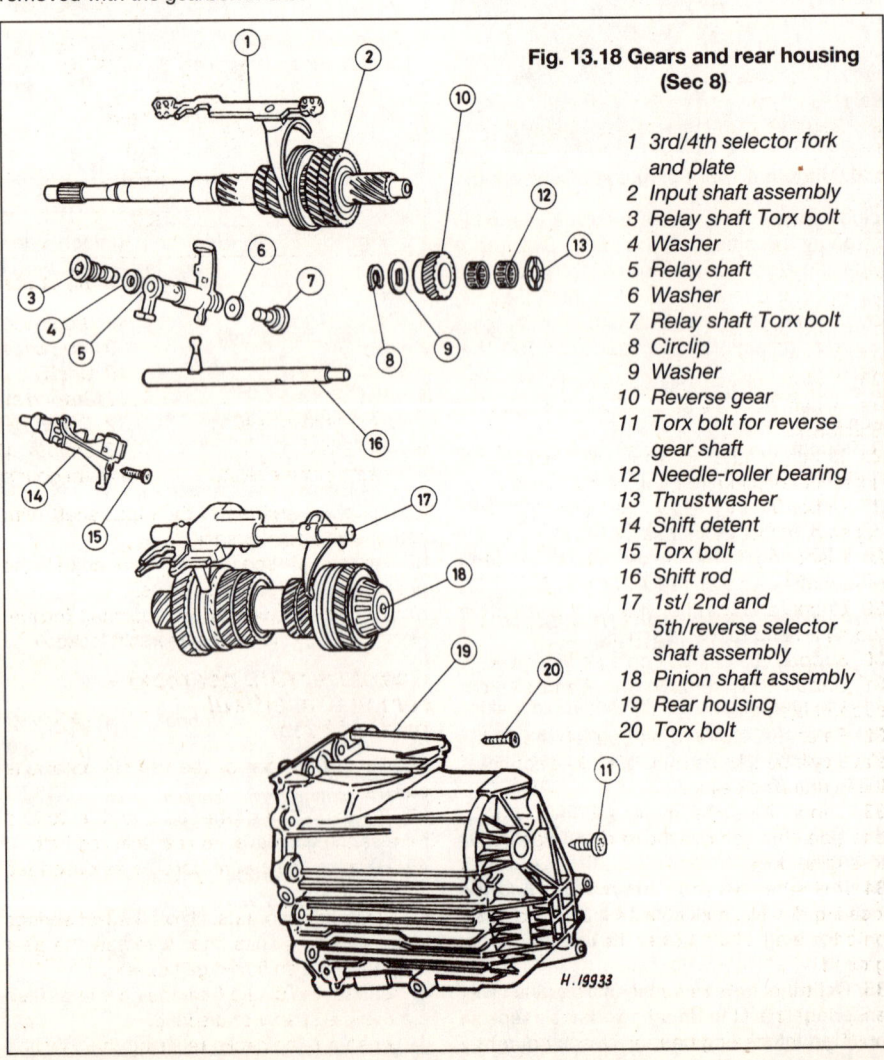

Fig. 13.18 Gears and rear housing (Sec 8)

1 3rd/4th selector fork and plate
2 Input shaft assembly
3 Relay shaft Torx bolt
4 Washer
5 Relay shaft
6 Washer
7 Relay shaft Torx bolt
8 Circlip
9 Washer
10 Reverse gear
11 Torx bolt for reverse gear shaft
12 Needle-roller bearing
13 Thrustwasher
14 Shift detent
15 Torx bolt
16 Shift rod
17 1st/ 2nd and 5th/reverse selector shaft assembly
18 Pinion shaft assembly
19 Rear housing
20 Torx bolt

Supplement: Revisions and information on later models 13•15

12 Refit in reverse, connecting the front shift rod to the gear lever first, then connect it to the rear shift rod.
13 On completion, adjust the shift linkage as described in Chapter 6.

Procon-ten safety system
14 Refer to Section 13 for details.

Manual gearbox (012) – general description
15 The general comments given in Section 1 of Chapter 6 apply. The 012 gearbox is a five-speed plus reverse unit, with synchromesh on all gears. Unlike conventional gearboxes, the reverse gears and idler are in constant mesh.
16 The gearbox and final drive share a common oil supply and are 'fitted for life'. Oil changing is therefore not specified.

Manual gearbox (012) – removal and refitting
17 Raise the front of the vehicle onto axle stands or ramps.
18 Disconnect the battery negative terminal.
19 Remove the upper gearbox-to-engine bolts, accessible from on top.
20 Disconnect the electronic speedometer by squeezing the spring clips of the connector together. Where fitted, also disconnect the multi-function switch connector (photos).
21 Remove the engine splash panel where fitted.
22 Using a jack with a padded head, take the weight of the engine.
23 Disconnect the exhaust downpipe from the exhaust manifold. Lower the exhaust and recover the gasket.
24 Detach the downpipe from the gearbox, separate the exhaust in front of the catalyst and remove the exhaust downpipe.
25 If fitted, release the cables for the Procon-ten system from the gearbox with reference to Section 13.
26 Unscrew the lockbolt and slide the gearshift coupling from the gearshift rod.
27 Unbolt and withdraw the inner right-hand constant velocity joint heat shield.
28 Disconnect the inner ends of both driveshafts as described in Chapter 8.
29 Unbolt and withdraw the heat shield from the right-hand rubber mounting.
30 Support the gearbox on a padded jack.
31 Unbolt and remove the gearbox rear support brackets.
32 Refer to Chapter 5 and unbolt the clutch slave cylinder. There is no need to disconnect the hydraulic pipeline.
33 Unbolt the starter motor and hang it up to one side, then remove the remaining gearbox-to-engine bolts.
34 Pull the gearbox rearwards off the locating dowels, making sure it does not drop onto the input shaft. Lower the gearbox to the ground.
35 Refitting is a reversal of removal, first ensuring that the locating dowels are in position in the engine rear web, and lightly

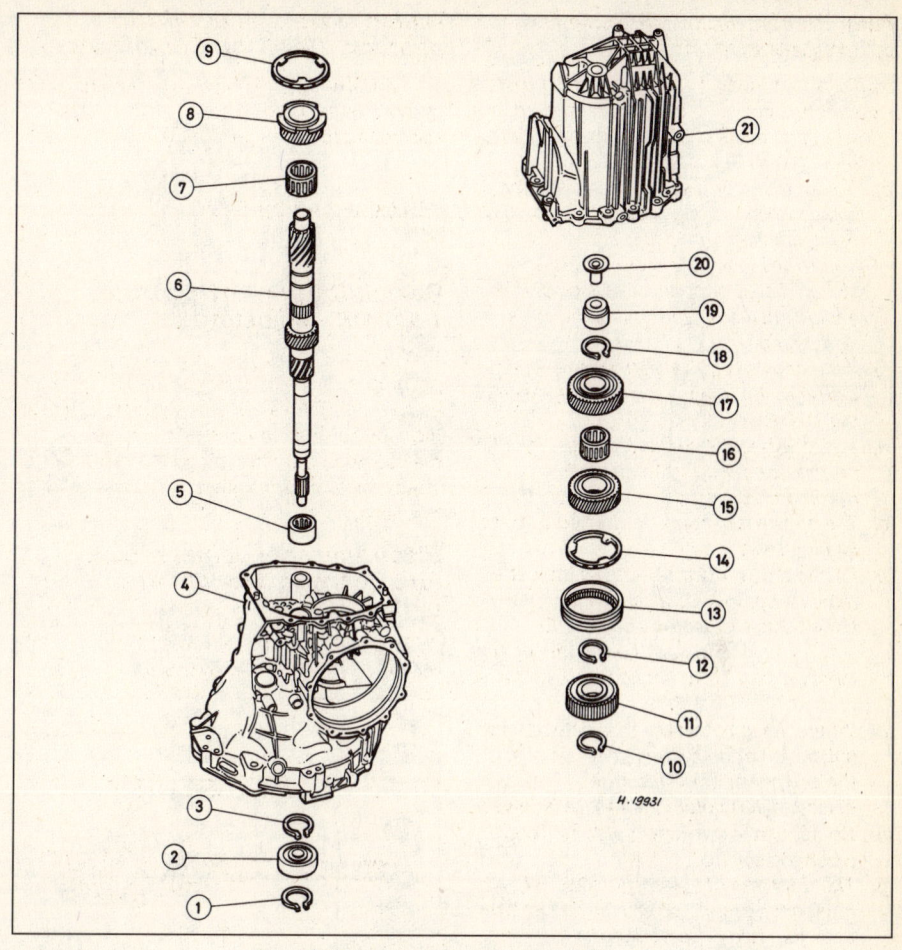

Fig. 13.19 Input shaft components (Sec 8)

1 Circlip (outer)
2 Bearing
3 Circlip (inner)
4 Main housing
5 Needle-roller bearing
6 Input shaft
7 Needle-roller bearing
8 3rd speed gear
9 3rd gear synchro-ring
10 Circlip
11 3rd/4th synchro-hub
12 Circlip
13 3rd/4th synchro-sleeve
14 4th gear synchro-ring
15 4th speed gear
16 Needle-roller bearing
17 5th speed gear
18 Circlip
19 Needle-roller bearing
20 Plastic sleeve
21 Rear housing

lubricate the splines of the input shaft with high melting point grease.
36 On completion, check and adjust the gearbox and engine mountings.
37 Tighten all bolts to the specified torque, using locking fluid on the gearshift lockbolt.

Gear lever (012 gearbox) – removal, overhaul and refitting
38 Raise the front of the vehicle onto axle stands.
39 Pull back the rubber boot and undo and remove the gear lever-to-rear shift rod bolt.
40 Remove the centre console as described in Section 13.
41 Undo the two nuts, lift off the leaf springs and connecting links, then withdraw the gear lever from the shift linkage housing.
42 Extract the circlip from the gear lever then remove the spacer and spring.
43 Prise out the circlip retaining the ball stop to the ball housing, then remove the ball stop and withdraw the gear lever from the housing.
44 Clean all the components then examine them for wear and damage. Renew as necessary.
45 Reassembly and refitting are a reversal of removal, noting the following points.
46 Apply a small amount of general purpose grease to all moving contact parts.
47 The bush and spring are located on the right-hand side of the ball stop, and the rounded end of the bush faces the gear lever.
48 The gear lever can only be inserted one way round.
49 Always renew the gear lever-to-lever shift rod bolt.
50 The ball stop circlip rounded side faces the bearing, and the reverse detent points to the left.
51 On completion of refitting, adjust the shift linkage as described later.

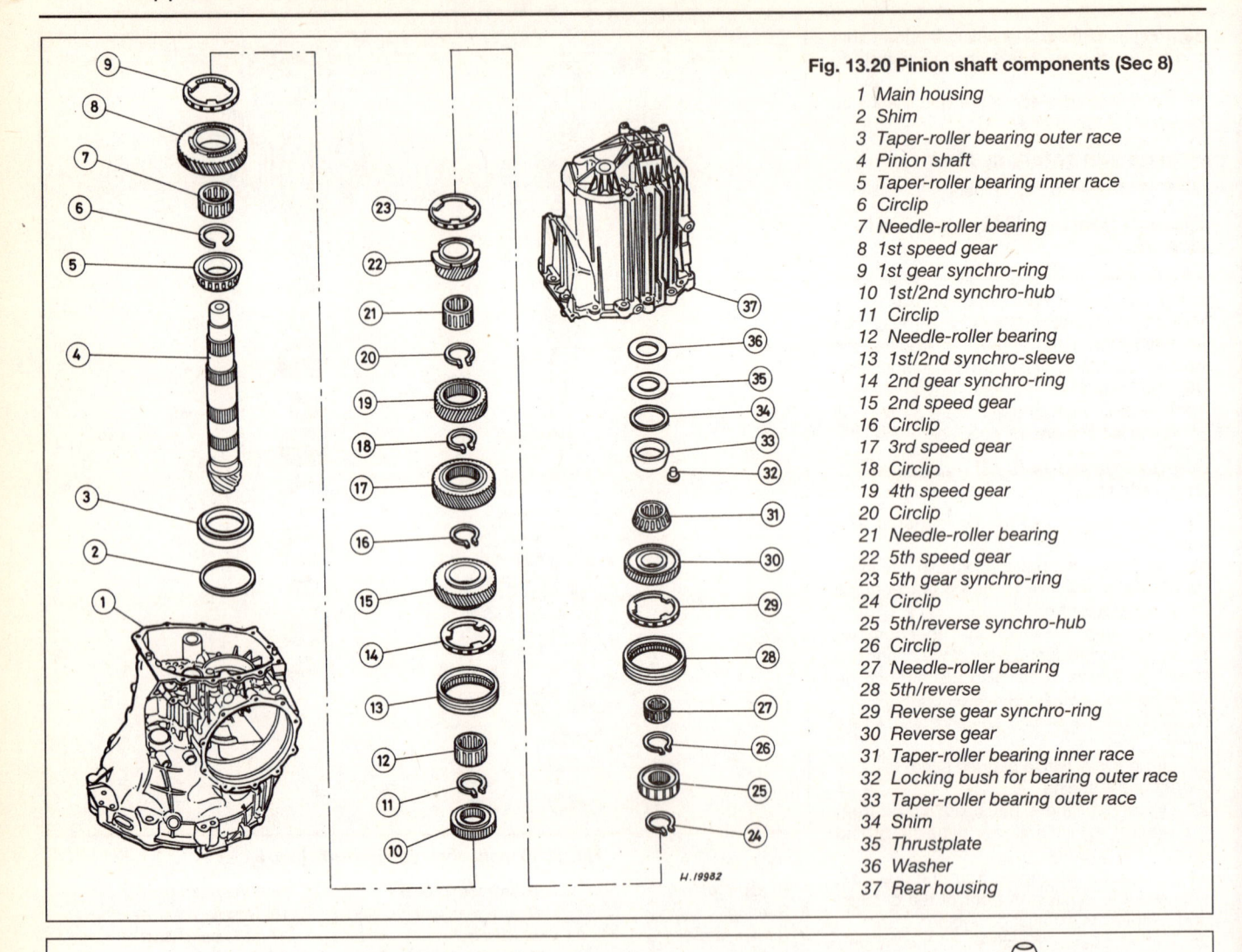

13•16 Supplement: Revisions and information on later models

Fig. 13.20 Pinion shaft components (Sec 8)

1. Main housing
2. Shim
3. Taper-roller bearing outer race
4. Pinion shaft
5. Taper-roller bearing inner race
6. Circlip
7. Needle-roller bearing
8. 1st speed gear
9. 1st gear synchro-ring
10. 1st/2nd synchro-hub
11. Circlip
12. Needle-roller bearing
13. 1st/2nd synchro-sleeve
14. 2nd gear synchro-ring
15. 2nd speed gear
16. Circlip
17. 3rd speed gear
18. Circlip
19. 4th speed gear
20. Circlip
21. Needle-roller bearing
22. 5th speed gear
23. 5th gear synchro-ring
24. Circlip
25. 5th/reverse synchro-hub
26. Circlip
27. Needle-roller bearing
28. 5th/reverse
29. Reverse gear synchro-ring
30. Reverse gear
31. Taper-roller bearing inner race
32. Locking bush for bearing outer race
33. Taper-roller bearing outer race
34. Shim
35. Thrustplate
36. Washer
37. Rear housing

Fig. 13.21 Gear lever components (vehicles with 012 gearbox) (Sec 8)

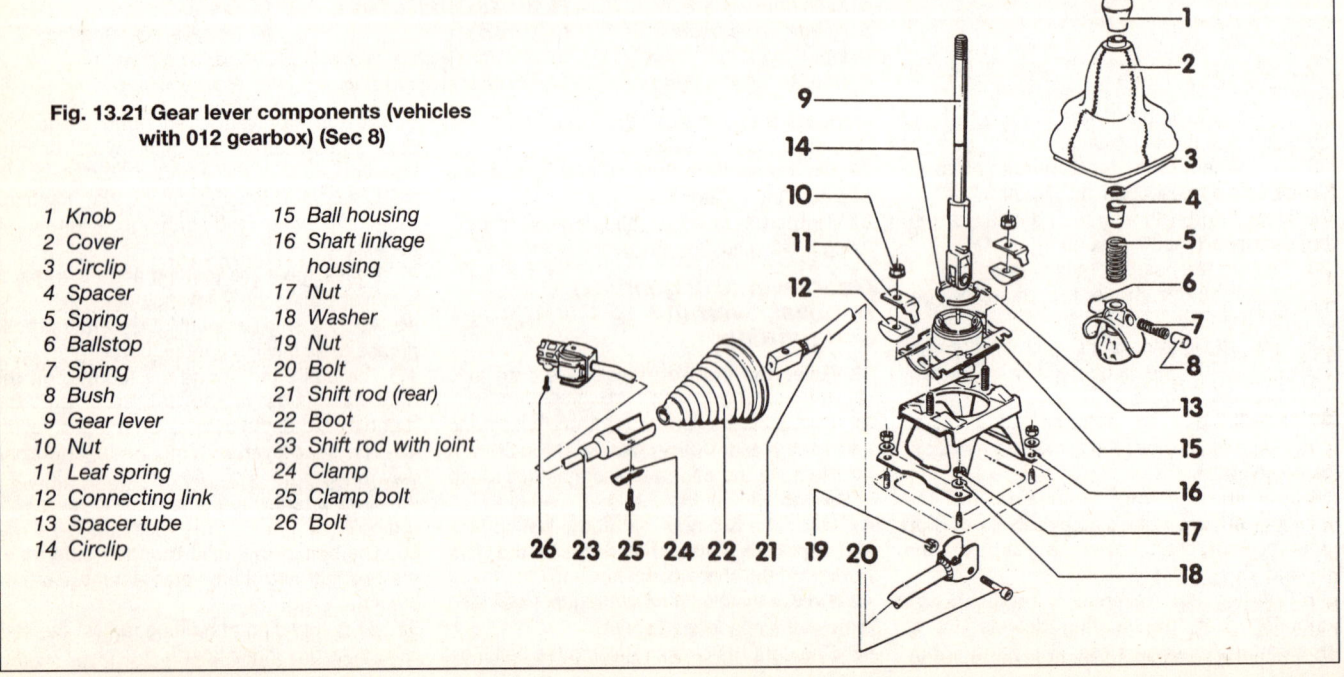

1. Knob
2. Cover
3. Circlip
4. Spacer
5. Spring
6. Ballstop
7. Spring
8. Bush
9. Gear lever
10. Nut
11. Leaf spring
12. Connecting link
13. Spacer tube
14. Circlip
15. Ball housing
16. Shaft linkage housing
17. Nut
18. Washer
19. Nut
20. Bolt
21. Shift rod (rear)
22. Boot
23. Shift rod with joint
24. Clamp
25. Clamp bolt
26. Bolt

Supplement: Revisions and information on later models 13•17

Gear shift linkage (012 gearbox) – adjustment

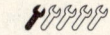

52 Place the gear lever in neutral.
53 Loosen the shift rod clamp bolt.
54 Position the gear lever vertically.
55 Check that the distance from the ball stop lugs to the housing is equal on both sides. If not, loosen the mounting nuts and move the mounting to obtain the correct clearance.
56 Tighten the shift rod clamp bolt without disturbing the setting of the gear lever, then recheck the ball stop lug clearance.
57 Check that all gears can be selected freely and that the reverse safety stop is effective. If necessary, loosen the ball housing mounting nuts and turn the ball housing slightly. Tighten the nuts.
58 In neutral, the gear lever should be in the 3rd/4th gear plane.
59 Refit the centre console and remove the vehicle from axle stands.

9 Automatic transmission

Selector modification (1987 models)

1 During 1987 the selector mechanism was modified so that it is impossible to shift out of 'P' unless the footbrake is depressed. The modification can be made to earlier vehicles.
2 The components used to make the modification are shown in Fig. 13.22. The solenoid is energised via the brake light switch.
3 If the system malfunctions, remove the centre console (Chapter 11, Section 24). With the ignition on, the footbrake depressed and the selector lever in 'P', the solenoid should retract the latch to the position shown in Fig. 13.23. With the brake pedal released, the solenoid must extend so that the latch locks the threaded pin (Fig. 13.24). Adjust if necessary within the limits of the solenoid mounting bracket.

Selector modification, August 1988 on – adjustment

4 From August 1988-on, a new selector mechanism on which it is impossible to select a drive gear when the lever is in 'P' or 'N' unless the footbrake is depressed, is fitted. Adjustment procedures follow.

Solenoid

5 Remove the centre console as described in Section 13.
6 Select 'R'.
7 Unbolt the selector lever gate housing and lift the gate off.
8 Loosen the solenoid bolts.
9 Position a 1.0 mm (0.04 in) feeler blade between the solenoid and the selector lever.
10 Push the solenoid against the feeler blade

Fig. 13.22 Automatic transmission selector interlock components (Sec 9)

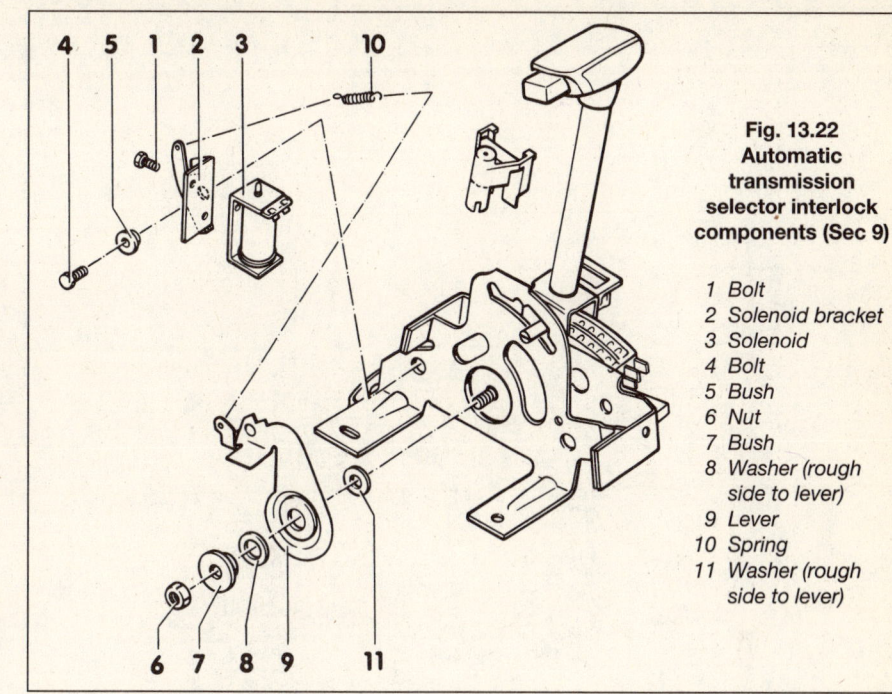

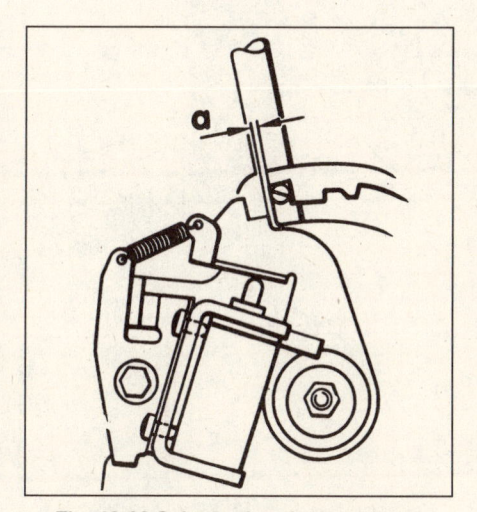

1 Bolt
2 Solenoid bracket
3 Solenoid
4 Bolt
5 Bush
6 Nut
7 Bush
8 Washer (rough side to lever)
9 Lever
10 Spring
11 Washer (rough side to lever)

Fig. 13.23 Selector interlock released (Sec 9)
a = 0 to 1.0 mm (0 to 0.04 in)

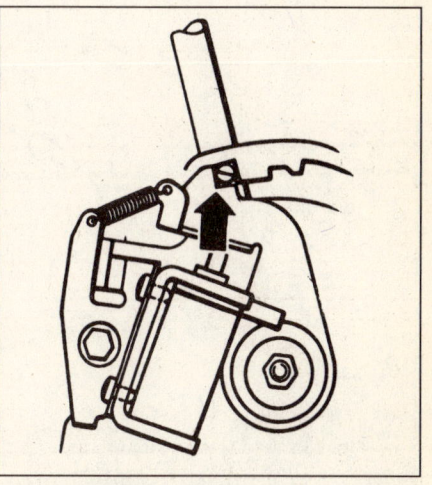

Fig. 13.24 With brake pedal released, latch moves to lock threaded pin (arrowed) (Sec 9)

and selector lever, and tighten the solenoid bolts.
11 Refit and adjust the selector lever gate housing as follows.

Selector lever gate housing

12 Before fitting the gate, position the clevis on the selector lever centrally so that, with the solenoid energised, the solenoid pin locks the clevis.
13 Fit the selector lever gate so that the lever is in 'N'.
14 The travel of the selector lever between 'N' to 'R' and 'N' to 'D' should be equal. Tighten the selector lever gate retaining bolts.

Selector lever switch

15 Push a 4.0 mm drill through the switch housing and into the hole in the switch lever.
16 Select 'N'.
17 Fit the selector lever switch so that the drive dog engages with the lever shaft.
18 Tighten the switch bolts and remove the drill.

Functional check

19 After installing the complete selector lever gate housing, carry out the following functional check.
20 Check that it is only possible to start the engine in 'N' or 'P'.
21 Select 'R' and check that the reversing lights illuminate.
22 If the selector lever positions are not synchronised, turn the selector lever switch

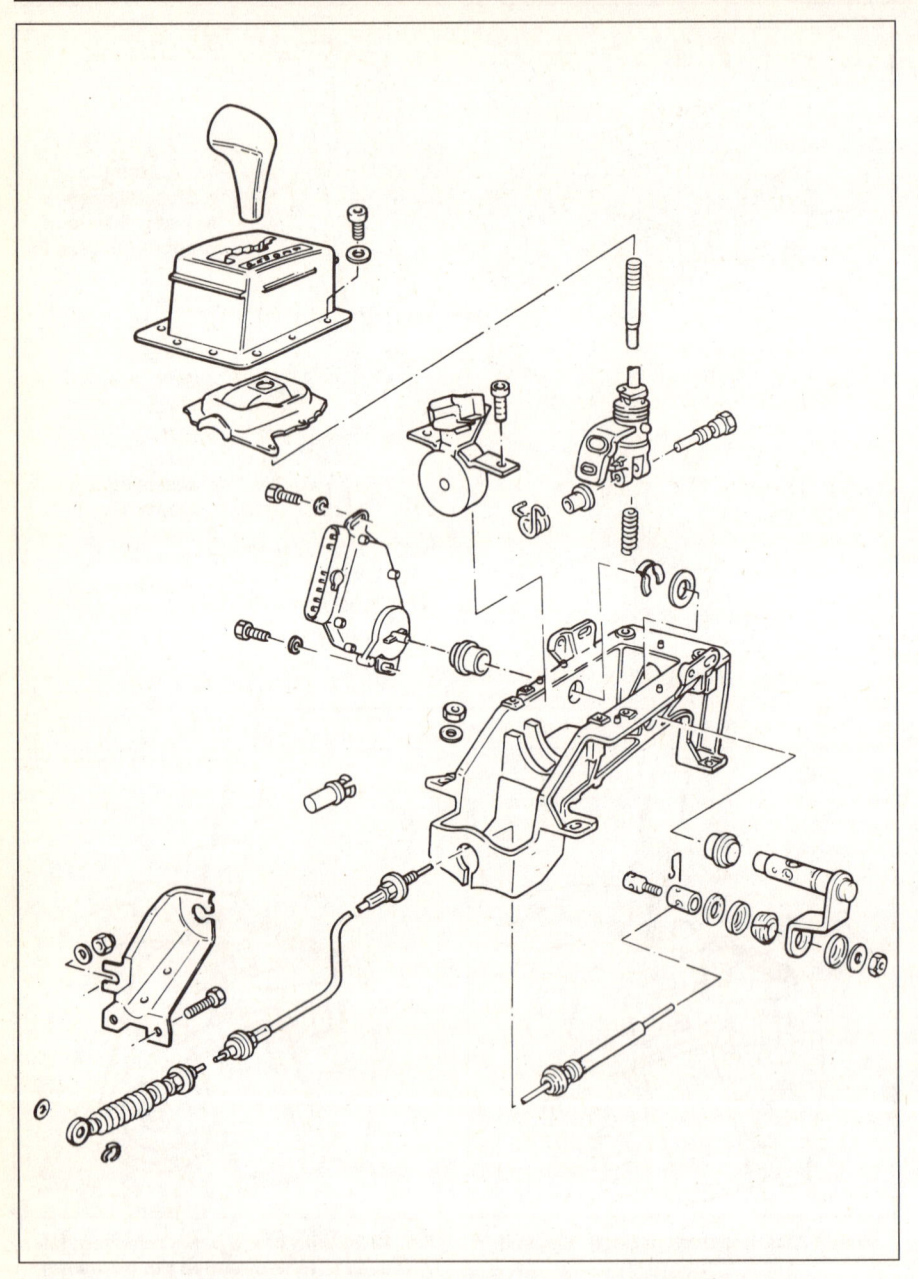

13•18 Supplement: Revisions and information on later models

Fig. 13.25 Exploded view of the 1988-on selector mechanism (Sec 9)

9.23 Selector lever illumination bulb location (1988-on) (arrowed)

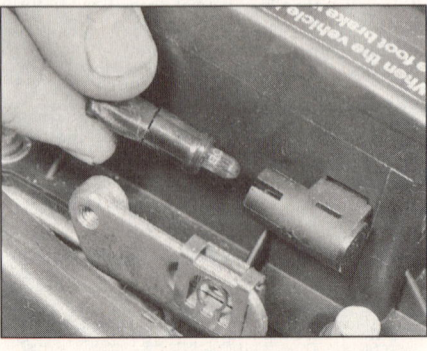

9.24 Pulling the bulb holder from the bulb housing

slightly in the slotted holes and repeat the functional check.

Selector lever illumination bulb (1988-on) – renewal

23 The bulb is housed on the side of the selector lever assembly (photo). To gain access to the bulb the centre console must be removed as described in Section 13.
24 Pull the bulb holder from the bulb housing (photo). The bulb is a push fit in the holder.
25 Refit in reverse order.

10 Driveshafts

Driveshafts (engine code NF with automatic transmission, 1989-on) – removal, refitting and overhaul

1 From 1989-on the driveshafts on vehicles with the new four-speed automatic transmission and 100 kW (130 bhp) engine (code NF) are fitted with modified driveshafts.
2 The removal and refitting procedures remain as described in Chapter 8.
3 However, the inner and outer joints cannot be overhauled, although the outer joint can be renewed separately.
4 The inner joint is only supplied complete with a new driveshaft.
5 If re-greasing of the joints is necessary, the inner joint must be filled with 250 g (8.75 oz) of grease part number G 000 604, with additional grease being applied to the boot as necessary. The outer joint must be filled with 90 g (3.15 oz) of grease part number G 6. The CV joint should be filled with 40 g (1.4 oz) of grease and the driveshaft boot should have 50 g (1.75 oz) spread into it.

11 Braking system

Twin piston front disc brake calipers general

1 From the beginning of 1986, certain models are fitted with twin piston front disc calipers. Removal, refitting and overhaul procedures are similar to those described in Chapter 9 for the Girling caliper.

Brake pad renewal (models with twin piston front disc brakes)

2 Proceed as in Chapter 9, Section 3. Note also that if two of the new pads have retainer springs (Fig. 13.27), these must be fitted in the outboard positions.

Rear disc caliper (1989-on) – overhaul

3 The procedure is basically as described in Chapter 9, Section 12, but note that the piston

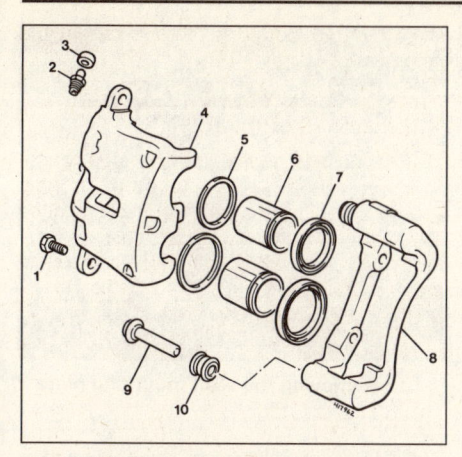

Supplement: Revisions and information on later models 13•19

Fig. 13.26 Twin piston front brake caliper (Sec 11)

1 Guide pin bolt
2 Bleed screw
3 Dust cap
4 Caliper body
5 Piston seal
6 Piston
7 Dust cap
8 Carrier bracket
9 Guide pin
10 Dust boot

now has a slotted end in place of the Allen key recess for screwing the piston in or out of the caliper.

4 A special tool is used by Audi dealers for this purpose, or a suitable piece of square section bar can be used.

Rear brake caliper (all models with rear disc brakes) – refitting

5 It is recommended that the caliper be primed with brake fluid before refitting. Position the caliper with the piston facing downward and introduce fresh brake fluid via the bleed screw until it emerges from the brake hose aperture. Temporarily plug the aperture and tighten the bleed screw.

6 New calipers are supplied already primed with fluid.

Vacuum servo unit – pushrod adjustment

7 Later vacuum servo units have an adjustable clevis. Before fitting such a unit, screw the clevis up or down the pushrod to achieve the specified dimension (Fig. 13.28).

Anti-lock braking system relays – general

8 Besides the two relays on the hydraulic modulator (Chapter 9, Section 29) there are other relays associated with the system. These are as follows.

9 On models up to 1984, an ABS step relay in position 7 or 8 on the additional relay carrier controls the on and off switching of the system. A voltage protection relay, in position 11 or 7, protects the electronic control unit from voltage fluctuations.

10 On 1985 and later models, a combination relay in position 5 on the additional relay carrier fulfils both the above functions.

11 Switch off the ignition before removing or refitting any of these relays.

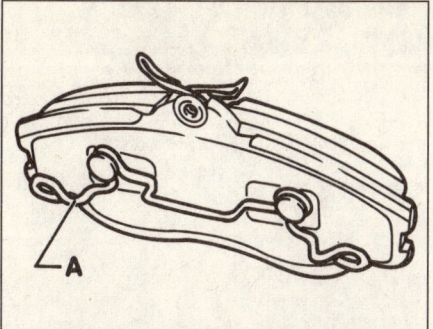

Fig. 13.27 Retainer springs (A) fitted to outboard brake pads (Sec 11)

Brake light switch (all models) – removal and refitting

12 Remove the parcel shelf on the driver's side.

13 Disconnect the wiring plug from the brake light switch (photo).

14 Unscrew the brake light switch from the securing clip and remove it.

15 When refitting, screw the switch in until the plunger is depressed by contact with the brake pedal.

16 Reconnect the wiring plug and check the switch for correct operation. Adjust as necessary by screwing the switch in or out. On completion, refit the parcel shelf.

12 Suspension and steering

Front suspension strut top mounting modification

1 On Audi 100 models from chassis number 44 DA 140 640 (Saloon)) and 44 EA 011 838 (Avant) the strut top mounting components have been modified. When renewing top mounting components on earlier models, the complete set of modified parts (Fig. 13.29) must be fitted. It is permissible for one strut to be modified and not the other.

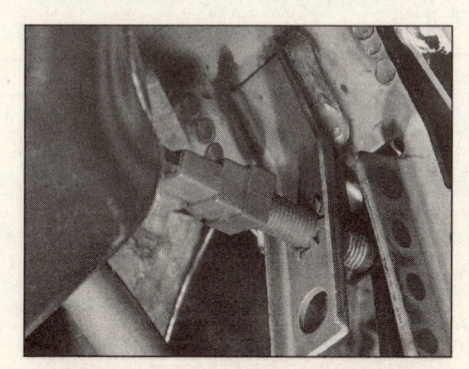

11.13 Brake light switch with wiring plug connected

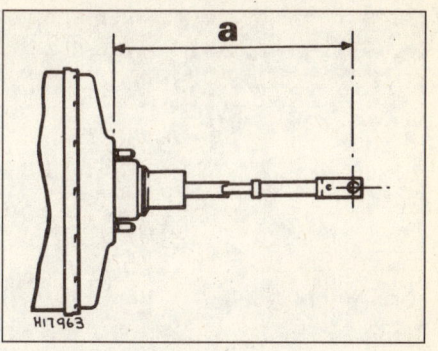

Fig. 13.28 Vacuum servo pushrod adjustment (Sec 11)

a = 249.0 mm (9.80 in)

2 Always have the camber checked after renewing front strut components.

Front shock absorber (all models) – removal and refitting

3 The front shock absorbers can be removed either in the course of dismantling the suspension (Chapter 10, Section 4) or independently as described here. In either case, tool VAG 2069 (or equivalent) will be required. This tool is needed for undoing and

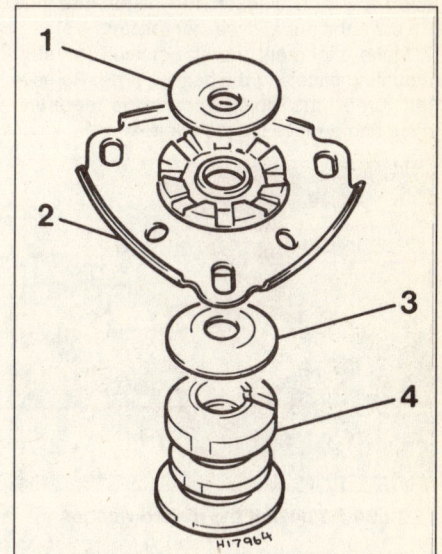

Fig. 13.29 Suspension strut mounting – modified components (Sec 12)

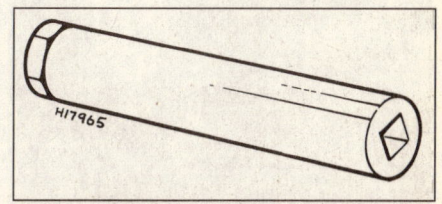

Fig. 13.30 Special tool 2069 for use on the shock absorber screwcap. Hexagon is approximately 34.0 mm (1.34 in) across flats (Sec 12)

12.5 Removing the strut top mounting cover

12.6 Slackening the piston rod nut

12.7 Removing the strut mounting plate

tightening the screw cap which secures the shock absorber in the strut. The screw cap is very tight and the tool must be a good fit; attempts to improvise using box spanners and flattened tubes were not successful in the workshop.

4 To remove a shock absorber without dismantling or removing the strut, proceed as follows.

5 With the weight of the vehicle on its wheels, remove the cover from the strut top mounting (photo).

6 Counterhold the piston rod with a 7.0 mm Allen key and slacken the piston rod nut. Remove the nut and washer (photo).

7 Make alignment marks between the strut mounting plate and the bearing plate. Remove the three nuts which secure the mounting plate and remove the plate (photo).

12.9A Removing the dished washer...

12.9B ...followed by the bump stop

8 Turn the steering wheel to align the piston rod in the centre of the spring retainer.

9 Remove the dished washer and the bump stop from the piston rod (photos).

10 Wedge the spring against the wheel arch with a block of wood to stop it moving in subsequent operations.

11 Using VAG tool 2069 (or equivalent), undo the screw cap which secures the shock absorber in the strut (photo).

12 Lift out the shock absorber.

13 Commence refitting by inserting the shock absorber into the strut.

14 Fit the screw cap and cover. Tighten the screw cap to the specified torque (Chapter 10 Specifications). Remove the wooden block.

15 Fit the bump stop. Working through the spring coils adjust the position of the boot so that it covers the threaded cap.

16 Refit the dished washer and the strut mounting plate. Secure the plate with three new nuts tightened to the specified torque (Chapter 10). Observe the alignment marks made during dismantling or the camber will be incorrect.

17 Fit the washer and a new piston rod nut. Counterhold the piston rod and tighten the nut to the specified torque (Chapter 10).

18 Refit the strut top mounting cover.

Rear anti-roll bar – general

19 A rear anti-roll bar is fitted to cars with self-levelling rear suspension, and to all 200 models.

12.11 The screw cap (arrowed) must now be undone with the special tool

20 No fitting details or tightening torques were available at the time of writing.

Power steering fluid (models with self-levelling suspension) – level checking

21 When self-levelling rear suspension is fitted, the fluid level in the reservoir will vary according to vehicle load. For this reason two sets of level marks are provided.

22 Use the upper set of marks when the vehicle is unladen, and the lower set when it is fully laden.

Air bag safety system – general description

23 Models fitted with the air bag safety system have the lettering 'AIRBAG' on the steering wheel padded cover and also on a sticker inside the glove compartment.

24 The air bag system works in conjunction with the Procon-ten safety system to give the driver additional protection in even of a severe frontal impact, provided the seat belt is being worn.

25 The system consists of an inflatable bag with a gas generator incorporated in the steering wheel, and an electronic control and monitoring unit with warning lamp.

26 The design of the system is such that it is triggered in event of severe front impact only where the direction of impaction is within 30° of either side of the straight ahead position. It

Fig. 13.31 Power steering fluid reservoir carries two sets of level marks when self-levelling suspension is fitted (Sec 12)

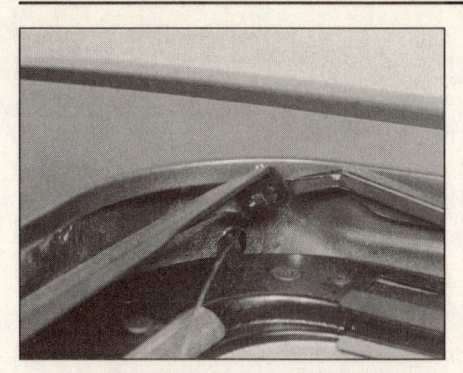

Supplement: Revisions and information on later models 13•21

13.2 Probing a sunroof drain hole

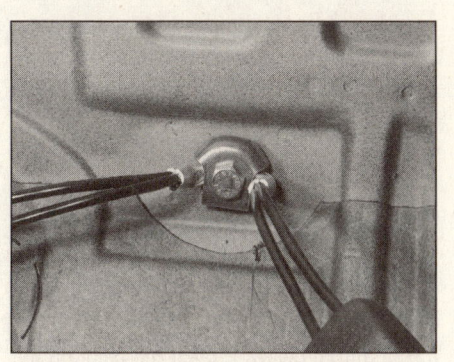

13.7A A front inertia reel (B-pillar trim removed)

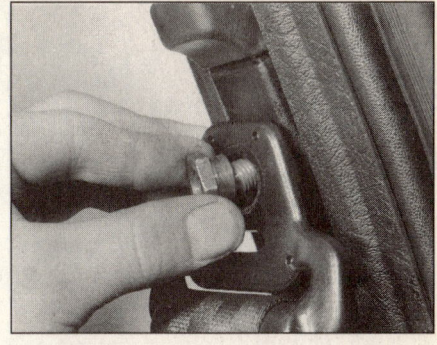

13.7B Removing a front seat belt upper mounting

13.7C Rear seat belt buckle anchor point under the seat cushion

is not triggered in minor frontal, side on or rear end collisions, nor in roll-over or other accidents where no significant forces are placed on the front of the vehicle.

Air bag safety system – testing

27 The air bag warning lamp should illuminate for about 10 seconds every time the ignition is switched on.
28 If the lamp does not come on when the ignition is switched on, or does not switch off after approximately 10 seconds, or comes on or flickers during driving there is a fault in the system which must be investigated by a VAG dealer immediately.
29 On no account must any part of the system be worked on by anyone other than authorised VAG personnel as injury to self or damage to vehicle may result.

Air bag safety system – precautions

(a) Do not stick anything on the hub of the steering wheel or obstruct or modify the system in any way
(b) Use only a dry cloth and plain water to clean the steering wheel
(c) The air bag and components must be renewed ten years after manufacture. The renewal date is written on a sticker inside the glove compartment lid
(d) Any work on the system; or removal and installation of system components for other repair work must only be carried out

by a VAG dealer. This includes the removal of the steering wheel
(e) The system is capable of operating once only and must be renewed if triggered
(f) Disposal of the system's components involves special regulations and the advice of a VAG dealer must be sought before discarding any components

13 Bodywork and fittings

Sunroof drain hoses (all models)

1 When fitted, the sunroof has four drain hoses, one at each corner. The front hoses run down inside the A-pillars and end above the front door lower hinges the rear hoses run down inside the C-pillars (Saloon) or D-pillars (Avant), and into the rear wheel arches.
2 Keep the drain hoses clear by probing them periodically with a length of wire (photo). If the hoses become blocked, water may leak into the interior of the vehicle.

Seat belts (all models) – general care and maintenance

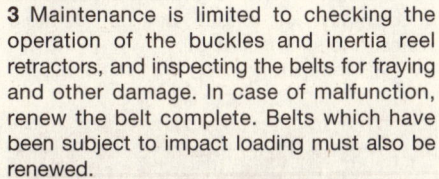

3 Maintenance is limited to checking the operation of the buckles and inertia reel retractors, and inspecting the belts for fraying and other damage. In case of malfunction, renew the belt complete. Belts which have been subject to impact loading must also be renewed.
4 Do not dye or bleach the belts, nor attempt to clean them with solvents or strong detergent. Clean the belts periodically with mild soap and water. After cleaning, keep the belts extended until they are dry.

Seat belts (all models) – removal and refitting

5 Details will vary according to trim and equipment, but the following guidelines apply in all cases.
6 Remove seats or interior trim as necessary for access to the belt and reel mountings.
7 Remove the mounting nuts or bolts, noting

carefully the fitted positions of all spacers and washers (photos).
8 Refit in reverse order, tightening the mounting bolts to the specified torque.
9 An exploded view of the height adjustable types used on later models appear in Figs. 13.32 and 13.33.

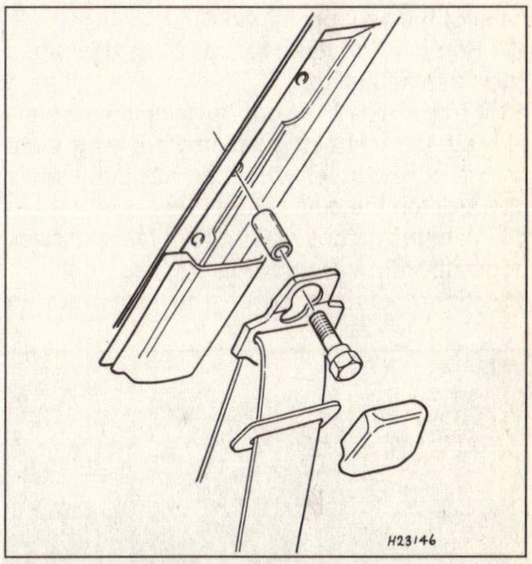

Fig. 13.32 Exploded view of adjustable height front seat belt upper attachment to 'B' pillar (early type) (Sec 13)

Fig. 13.33 Exploded view of adjustable height front seat belt upper attachment to 'B' pillar (later type) (Sec 13)

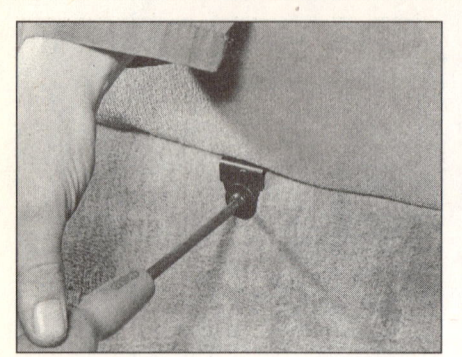

13•22 Supplement: Revisions and information on later models

13.10 Removing a rear seat cushion screw

13.11 Straightening a seat back securing clip

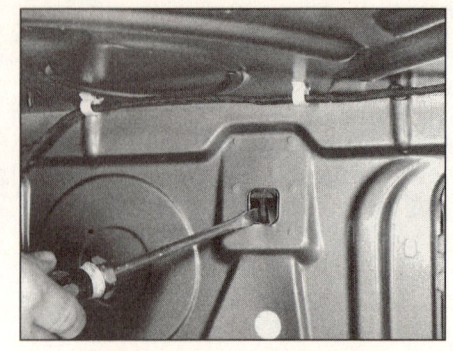

13.13 Releasing a head restraint guide tongue from inside the boot

Rear seat (Saloon with head restraints) – removal and refitting

10 Remove the two screws which secure the seat cushion (photo). Lift the cushion and pull it forwards to remove it.
11 Lever up the two clips which secure the base of the seat back (photo).
12 Remove the head restraints as described later in this Section.
13 From inside the boot, release the tongues of the head restraint guides by pressing them with a screwdriver whilst an assistant pulls upwards on the guides (photo).
14 With the guides released, lift the seat back and withdraw it. Remove the guides.
15 When refitting, place the seat back in position, insert the guides and press them home (photo).
16 Bend over the two clips at the base of the seat back by tapping them with a hammer. Make sure that the seat belt buckles are not trapped behind the seat back.
17 Refit the seat cushion and head restraints.

Head restraints (all models) – removal and refitting

18 Remove the hairpin clip from each head restraint guide using a small screwdriver to prise them free (photo).
19 Lift the head restraint out of the guides to remove it.
20 Refit by inserting the head restraint into the guides. Insert the hairpin clips and push them home.

Interior mirror (all models) – removal and refitting

21 Remove the grub screw (when fitted) from beside the mirror balljoint.
22 Pull the mirror off the mounting (photo).
23 The mirror mounting is bonded to the windscreen glass with special adhesive; do not attempt to remove it. If the mounting is accidentally detached, use a suitable adhesive to stick it back on.
24 Refit the mirror by applying a little silicone lubricant to the balljoint, then placing the mirror over the balljoint and thumping it home with a plastic or hide mallet.
25 Refit and tighten the grubscrew where applicable.

Door mirror glass (all models) – renewal

Manually adjusted type

26 Carefully lever the glass out of the mirror housing, using a wooden or plastic wedge inserted from below. Protect the paint on the mirror housing with a piece of tape or rag.
27 When the glass has been freed from the balljoint, unhook the adjuster linkage and spring from the inboard end. Remove the glass.
28 Refit by engaging the adjuster linkage and spring. Position the glass on the balljoint and press it firmly in the centre until it snaps home. Wear substantial gloves during this operation to prevent injury should the glass break.

Electrically adjusted type

29 The glass is retained by a bayonet type fixing. A rotating ring on the back of the glass engages with the mirror internal components (photo).
30 The glass is released from the mirror by inserting a small screwdriver through the hole

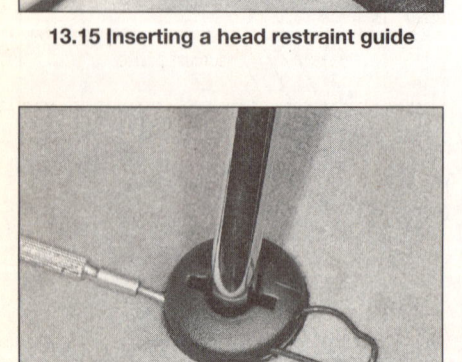

13.15 Inserting a head restraint guide

13.18 Removing a head restraint hairpin clip

13.22 Removing the interior mirror. The mirror shown has no grub screw beside the balljoint

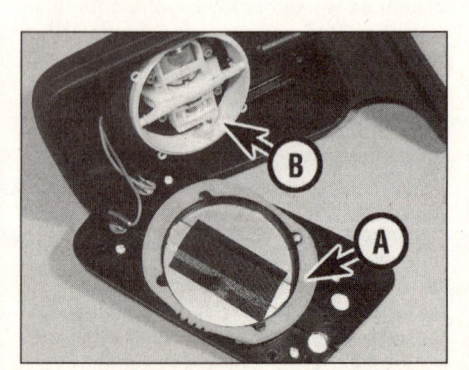

13.29 Mirror with glass removed. Rotating ring (A) engages with internal components (B)

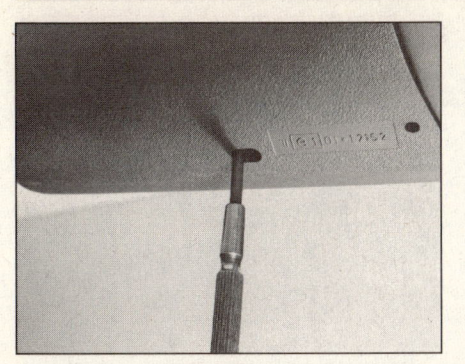

Supplement: Revisions and information on later models 13•23

13.30 Using a small screwdriver to rotate the securing ring

13.33A Lug on rear of glass (A)...

13.33B ...must engage with recess (B)

in the underside of the mirror and rotating the securing ring (photo). The ring has teeth to facilitate this operation.

31 If the glass has a heating element, disconnect the wiring connectors, noting their locations.

32 To fit the mirror glass, first connect the heater element connectors (of applicable).

33 When fitting the glass to the mirror body it is important that the lugs on the rear of the glass all engage with the recesses in the internal components (photos). It is impossible to check correct engagement by angling the mirror back to peer inside.

34 Secure the glass by rotating the ring, using a small screwdriver pushed through the hole in the underside of the mirror.

Door mirror (manually adjusted type) – removal and refitting

35 Prise the plastic cover from the control knob. Undo the screw and pull off the knob (photos).

36 Remove the trim plate to expose the mirror securing screws (photo). The trim plate itself may be secured by a screw, or it may simply unclip.

37 Support the mirror and remove the three securing screws. Withdraw the mirror, peeling the rubber boot off the door. Be careful not to lose the screws or washers in the door cavity (photo).

38 Refit by reversing the removal operations.

Use liquid soap or hand cleaner on the edges of the rubber boot to aid fitment to the door.

Door mirror (electrically adjusted type) – removal and refitting

39 Remove the trim plate securing screw(s) and take off the trim plate (photo).

40 Undo the cross-headed screws which secure the mirror.

41 Lower the door window and pull the mirror from the door, being careful not to damage the rubber mounting gaiter.

42 Support the disconnected mirror assembly.

43 Raise the window.

44 Disconnect the battery negative terminal.

13.35A Prise out the plastic cover...

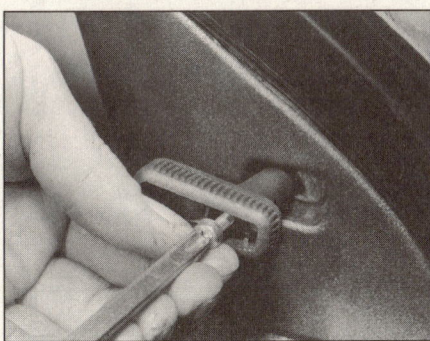

13.35B ...and undo the securing screw

13.36 Mirror securing screws exposed by removing the trim plate

13.37 Removing the door mirror

13.39 Removing the trim plate (electric mirror)

13.48 Driver's door mirror multi-plug in the footwell

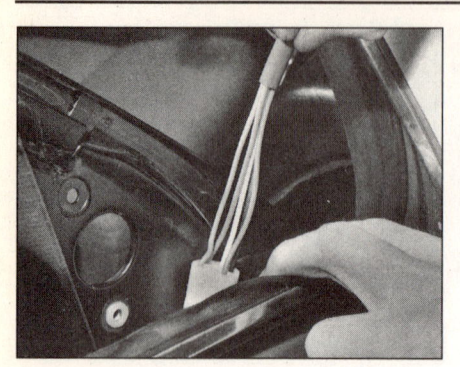

13•24 Supplement: Revisions and information on later models

13.50 Withdrawing the multi-plug from the door

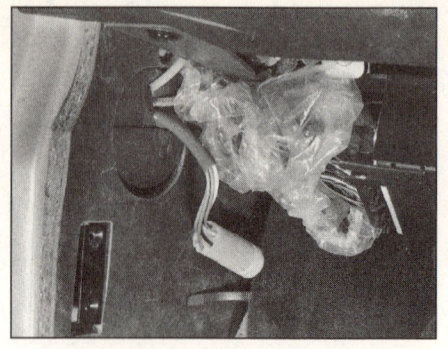

13.52 Passenger door mirror multi-plug

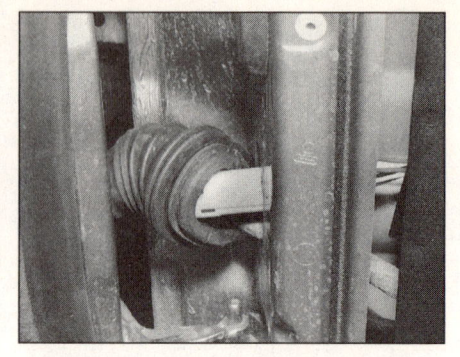

13.53 Door gaiter pulled back to facilitate passage of the multi-plug and cable

45 Remove the door inner trim panel as described later in this Section. Disconnect the wiring multi-plugs as necessary.

Driver's door mirror

46 Remove the parcel shelf and lower facia panel. Disconnect wiring multi-plugs as necessary.
47 Remove the screws securing the bonnet release lever and footwell trim panel, and remove the panel.
48 The mirror wiring multi-plug is now accessible in the upper corner of the footwell (photo).
49 Disconnect the multi-plug and feed it through the bodywork-to-door gaiter and the door, removing all cable clips.
50 Pull free the door exterior embellisher trim and pull the multi-plug through the enlarged aperture (photo). The mirror is now fully disconnected.

Passenger door mirror

51 The procedure is the same as given for the driver's door mirror, but note the following difference.
52 To gain access to the wiring multi-plug, it is only necessary to remove the footwell trim panel and lift the ignition control unit out of its bracket (photo).

Either mirror

53 Refitting is a reversal of removal. Be sure to use cable clips to retain the cable within the door. Passing the multi-plug and cable through the bodywork-to-door gaiter will be easier if one end of the gaiter is pulled from its panel (photo).
54 Temporarily reconnect the battery and check that the mirror is working properly before refitting the footwell and door trim panels.

Air conditioning – further precautions and maintenance

55 The following points are additional to those given in Chapter 11, Section 31.
56 Run the air conditioning for at least five minutes each month, even in cold weather. This will ensure the continued distribution of lubricant throughout the system and prevent seals from drying out.

57 Do not operate the system if a refrigerant leak is evident, or the system has discharged. Remove the compressor drivebelt to prevent damage in such a case.
58 Have the refrigerant charge checked periodically and replenished as necessary. Some leakage will occur over long periods, even in normal use.

Fully automatic air conditioning – general

59 Later models may be equipped with fully automatic air conditioning. With this system, once a given cabin temperature has been selected, the air conditioning programmer operates the temperature control flap and varies the blower motor speed automatically to maintain the set temperature. Manual override control is also possible.
60 If the system malfunctions, check that the cable from the programmer to the temperature control flap is not kinked or binding. Also check the flap for free operation.
61 Further investigation should be carried out by a VAG dealer. Various modifications have been made to the system components on later models.

Procon-ten safety system – general description

62 The Procon-ten (Programmed Contraction and Tension) safety system is a series of cables connected to both front seat belt inertia reels and to the steering column. The

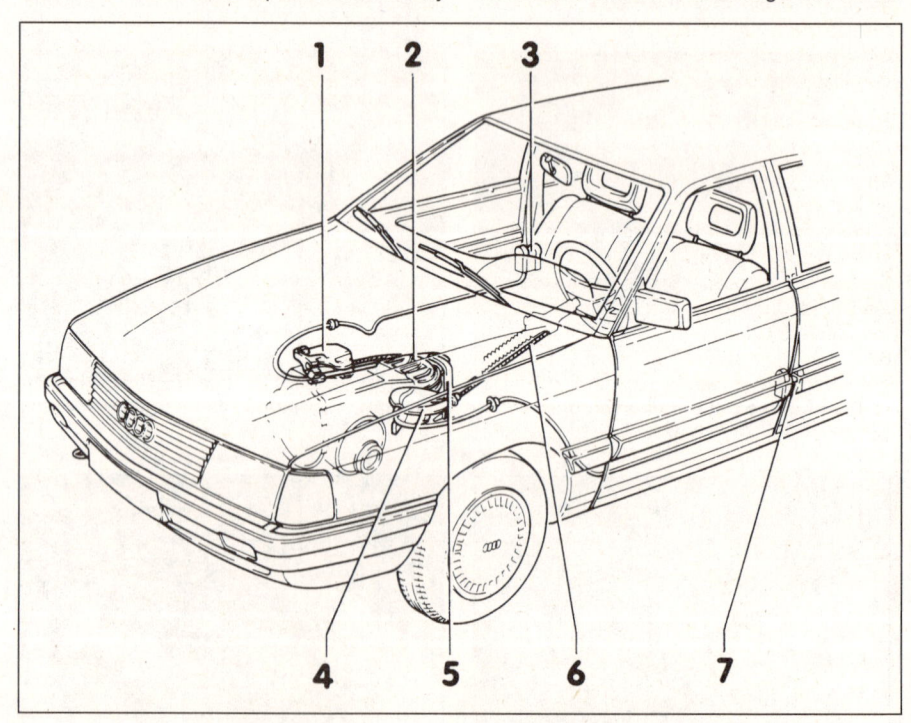

Fig. 13.34 Procon-ten safety system (Sec 13)

1 Anchor bracket
2 Cable tensioner
3 Inertia reel seat belt and cable
4 Guide bracket
5 Cable retainer
6 Steering column cable
7 Inertia reel seat belt and cable

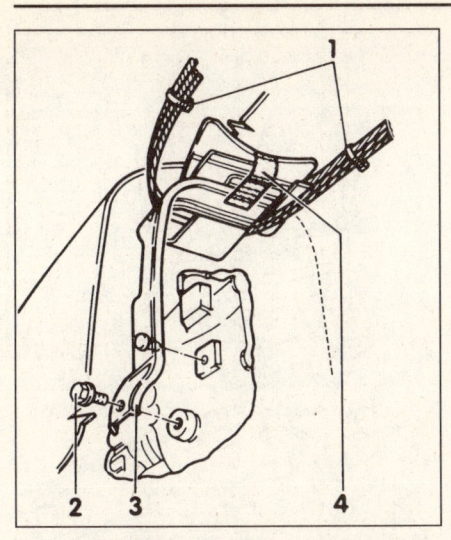

Fig. 13.35 Cable retainer on 016 gearbox (Sec 13)

1 Cable ties
2 Bolt
3 Cable retainer
4 Adhesive tape

cables are routed around the anchor bracket on the right-hand chassis member, a guide bracket on the left-hand chassis member, and a tensioner bracket on the gearbox housing.
63 In event of a frontal collision where the engine/transmission unit is pushed rearwards, the cables will automatically be tensioned by the movement of the engine/transmission unit and the steering column will be collapsed and the seat belts retracted.
64 The Procon-ten system is available as an optional extra on vehicles sold in the UK.

Procon-ten safety system – inspection

65 If any one part of the Procon-ten system is activated in an accident, the complete system must be renewed, including the steering column tube. It should be noted that the inertia reel seat belt and tensioner cable are joined together as one unit and cannot be renewed individually.
66 If slight movement occurs at the dovetail guide on the steering column tube, the steering column contraction system is then activated. A coloured spot of sealing paint is applied to the column tube to help detect any movement and the paint seal is broken if any movement occurs.
67 If either of the seat belts cannot be pulled out, or a belt will not retract by itself, then the seat belt tensioning system has activated.
68 If any one individual component of the Procon-ten system becomes defective in service for reasons other than accident impact, then that component can be renewed individually.

Procon-ten system components – removal and refitting

Steering column cable

69 On vehicles with manual transmission unbolt the cable retainer from the gearbox.
70 Cut through the plastic cable ties securing the cables together.
71 Remove the adhesive tape from the cable retainer (there is no need to renew the tape, it is only used to keep the retainer in position during assembly).
72 On vehicles with automatic transmission prise open the retaining clips on the cable tensioner and detach the cable clamps on the transmission tunnel.
73 On all vehicles, pull the retaining clips from the anchor bracket on the right-hand side of the vehicle and from the guide bracket on the left-hand side.

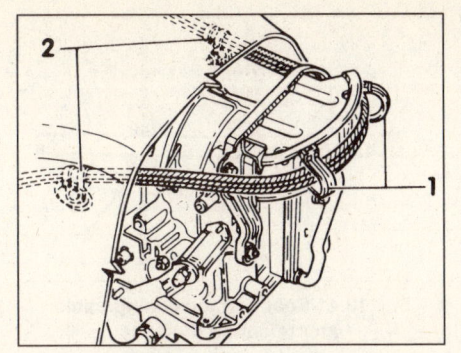

Fig. 13.36 Cable retainer on automatic transmission housing (Sec 13)

1 Retaining clips
2 Cable clips on transmission tunnel

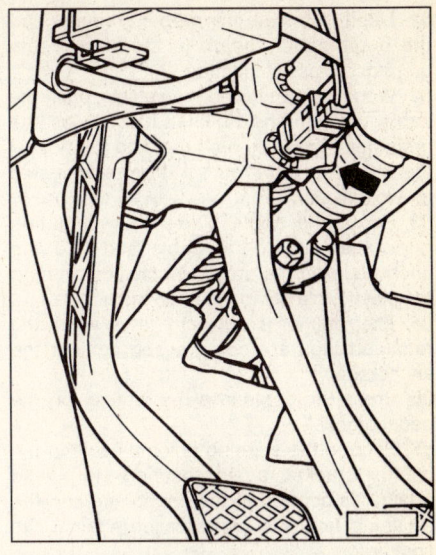

Fig. 13.37 steering column cable retainer (arrowed) (Sec 13)

74 Disengage the steering column cable from the anchor bracket. Use a punch if it is tight. It is not necessary to disengage the seat belt tensioning cables.
75 Remove the parcel shelf and inner cover from the driver's side as described in Chapter 11, Section 23.
76 Prise the rubber grommet from the bulkhead where the cable passes through. Prise the grommet into the interior of the vehicle.
77 Press the steering column cable from the retainer, release it from the steering column attachment and pull the cable through into the interior of the vehicle.
78 Before commencing refitting, obtain and fit a new plastic retainer to the end of the cable, and new retaining clips on the anchor bracket and guide bracket.
79 If a new cable is being fitted ensure the correct cable for the gearbox type is obtained, as the cables differ according to gearbox type.
80 Keep the ends of the cable and inside surfaces of the plastic retainers and cable anchorages clean and free from grease and oil. Do not use any lubricant on them.

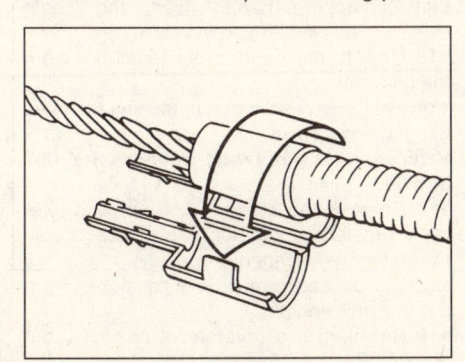

Fig. 13.38 Plastic retainer on bowden cable (Sec 13)

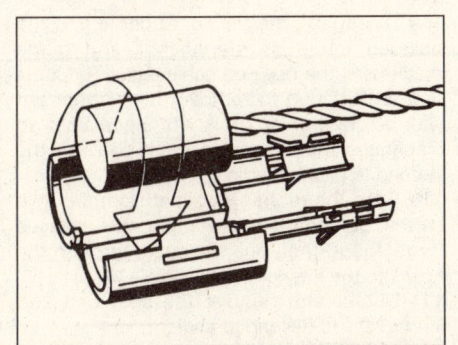

Fig. 13.39 Plastic retainer on inner cable (Sec 13)

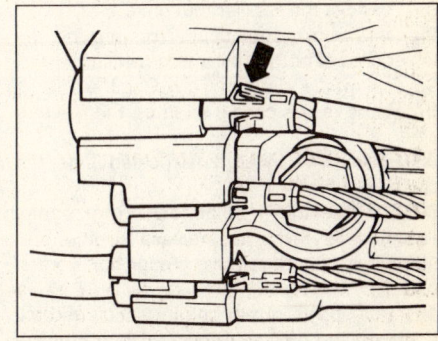

Fig. 13.40 Cables correctly inserted in brackets (Sec 13)

81 Lightly lubricate the rubber grommet and the outer cable sheath in the area of the grommet to assist in fitting.
82 Working from inside the vehicle, push the cable through the bulkhead as far as the grommet. Press the grommet into the hole in the bulkhead and ensure it is properly seated to avoid leaks.
83 Route the cable below the ventilation duct, then insert the cable end into the anchorage on the steering column, centring the plastic retainer in the anchorage.
84 The retainer is correctly fitted when the retaining lugs are compressed against the anchorage.
85 Press the cable into the retainer on the pedal bracket.
86 Engage the steering column cable in the anchor bracket, again ensuring the plastic retainer is centred in the anchorage and the retaining lugs are compressed against the anchorage.
87 Route the cable around the cable tensioner on the gearbox and the guide bracket on the left-hand side.
88 Make sure the cable is correctly routed, it should be the uppermost cable throughout its route, then fit the new retaining clips onto the anchor and guide brackets.

Caution: the Procon-ten system may not function correctly if the retaining clips are omitted or incorrectly fitted.

89 On manual transmission vehicles, push the cable retainer forward over all three cables as far as it will go on the cable tensioner.
90 Fit the retainer over its locating lug on the gearbox and fit the tighten the securing bolt to the specified torque.
91 Using new plastic cable ties, tie all three cables together halfway between the cable tensioner on the gearbox and the guide bracket on the one side and the anchor bracket on the other.

Seat belt tensioning cable

92 Access is made easier if both front seats are first removed as described in Chapter 11.
93 Detach the front and rear door seals from around the area of the B-pillar trim panels.
94 Remove the B-pillar trim panels.
95 Detach the door seals from around the lower area of both A-pillar trim panels.
96 Pull off the trim panel covering the sills.
97 Remove the parcel shelf on the driver's side.
98 Remove the inner panel located under the parcel shelf.
99 Remove the A-pillar lower trim panel, together with the bonnet release lever.
100 Where fitted, remove the ignition control unit.
101 Pull up the carpet and insulation and roll it toward the centre of the vehicle out of the way.
102 Cut through the lower cable tie securing

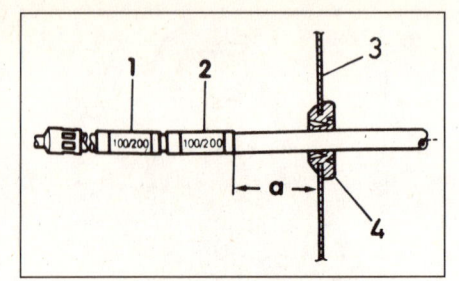

Fig. 13.41 Seat belt tensioning cable identification (Sec 13)

1 Label – only on right-hand drive vehicles
2 Label – on all vehicles (labels are lettered left or right)
3 Bulkhead
4 Grommet
Dimension a = 60 to 70 mm (2.4 to 2.8 in)
Label colour:
White . . . .012 gearbox
Brown . . .016 manual gearbox
Green . . .087/089 automatic transmission

the seat belt cable and wiring loom together, then unclip the remainder of the cable from the sill.
103 On the passenger side, remove the A-pillar lower trim panel, and where fitted, remove the fuel injection control unit.
104 Remove the two panels from under the facia.
105 Cut through the cable ties securing the cable and the wiring loom together, then unclip the remainder of the cable from the sill.
106 On vehicles with a manual gearbox, unbolt the cable retainer from the gearbox and cut through the cable ties securing the three cables together. Remove the adhesive tape from the cable retainer. There is no need to replace the tape, it is only used during factory assembly.
107 On vehicles with automatic transmission, bend back the cable retaining clips on the cable tensioner and remove the clamps on the transmission tunnel.
108 On all types, pull the retaining clips off the anchor bracket on the right-hand side, and from the guide bracket on the left-hand side.
109 Disengage the tensioner cable and the bowden cable at the anchor and guide brackets. if the bowden cable sheath or cable end are difficult to remove, drive them out with a pin punch. It is not necessary to disengage the steering column cable or the second tensioner cable.
110 Prise the rubber grommet from the hole in the bulkhead where the cable passes through and then pull the cable through the hole into the interior of the vehicle.
111 Unbolt and remove the seat belt and inertia reel as described earlier.
112 Before refitting the cable, renew the plastic retainers on the end of the cable cores, the plastic retainers, and anchorages for the

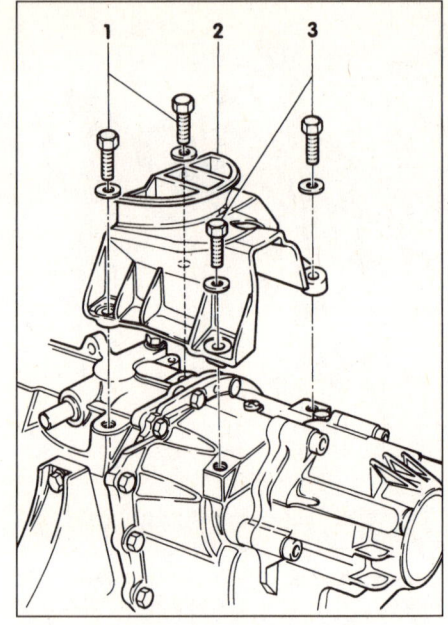

Fig. 13.42 Cable tensioner on 016 manual gearbox (Sec 13)

1 Front belts 2 Tensioner 3 Rear bolts

cable ends on the anchor guide brackets are kept clean and free from oil or grease. Do not lubricate these components.
113 The distance between the label on the bowden cable outer sheath and the bulkhead (not the grommet) should be as shown in Fig. 13.41. Note also the cable identification.
Important: after refitting any of the cables or the cable tensioner, there must be a clearance of 20 to 30 mm between all three cables and the cable tensioner on the gearbox. measured in the centre position. If this clearance is incorrect, check that the plastic retainers are correctly fitted in the anchorages, and that the correct cables are fitted.

Cable tensioner

Note: on vehicles with the 012 gearbox. the cable tensioner is part of the gearbox housing and cannot be removed from the gearbox.
Vehicles with manual gearbox 016
114 Release the steering column and seat belt tensioning cables from the cable tensioner as described previously.
115 Unbolt and remove the tensioner from the gearbox.
116 Refit in reverse order, tightening the bolts to specified torque.
Vehicles with automatic transmission 087 and 089
117 Release the steering column and seat belt tensioning cables from the cable tensioner as described previously.
118 Unbolt and remove the tensioner from the transmission unit.
119 Refitting is a reversal of removal, but always renew the cable retaining clips on the tensioner and tighten the tensioner retaining bolts to the specified torque.

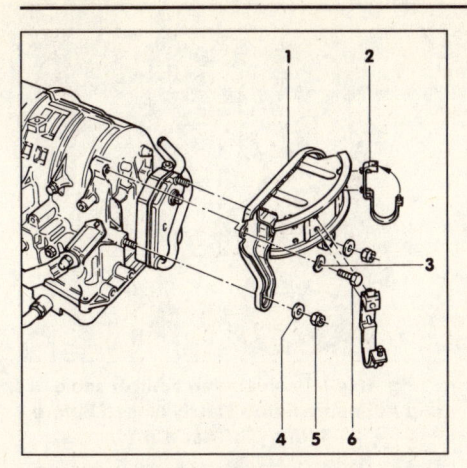

Supplement: Revisions and information on later models

Fig. 13.43 Cable tensioner on automatic transmission (Sec 13)

1 Tensioner 3 Spring washer 5 Nut
2 Retaining clip 4 Flat washer 6 Bolt

Guide bracket

120 Release the steering column and seat belt tensioning cables from the guide bracket as described previously.
121 Unbolt and remove the guide bracket from the chassis member.
122 Refit in reverse order, tightening the securing bolts to the specified torque.

Anchor bracket

123 Release the steering column and seat belt tensioning cables from the anchor bracket.
124 Unbolt and remove the bracket from the chassis member.

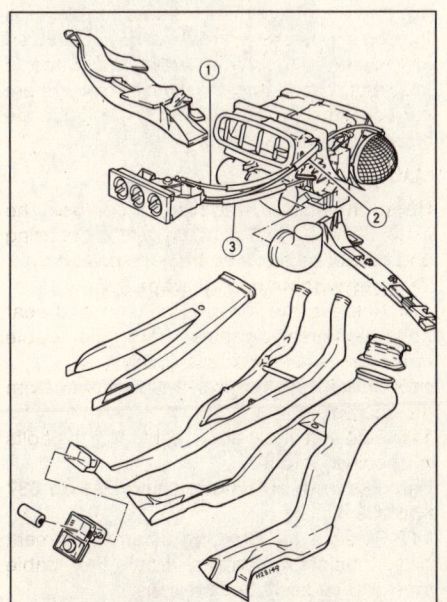

Fig. 13.46 Exploded view of heater assembly with rotary controls (Sec 13)

1 Temperature regulator control cable
2 Fresh air flap control cable
3 Distribution flap control cable

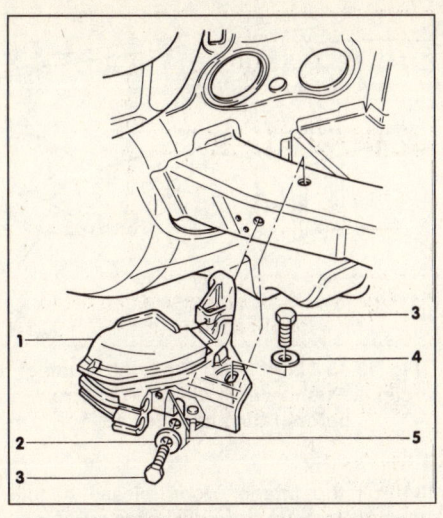

Fig. 13.44 Guide bracket on transmission member (Sec 13)

1 Guide bracket
2 Washer (only fitted to vehicles with automatic transmission not fitted with air conditioning or self-levelling suspension
3 Bolt
4 Washer
5 Bracket (only fitted to vehicles with manual gearboxes and to vehicles with automatic transmission fitted with air conditioning

125 Refit in reverse order, tightening the securing bolts to the specified torque.

Heater controls (rotary, 1988-on) – removal and refitting

126 The procedure is covered under centre console removal.

Heater control assembly and cables (rotary, 1988-on) removal and refitting

127 Remove the heater controls and release the control assembly from the centre console as described previously. Depending on the degree of work to be carried out, it may be possible to leave the centre console in position and operate through the centre console side panel apertures with these removed.

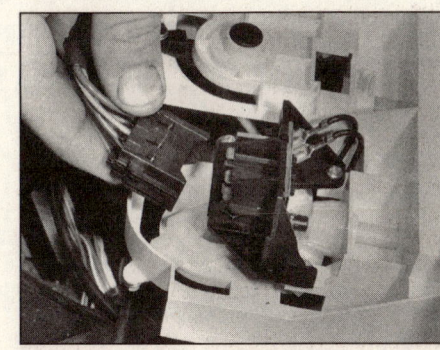

13.128 Disconnect the multi-plug from the rear of the unit

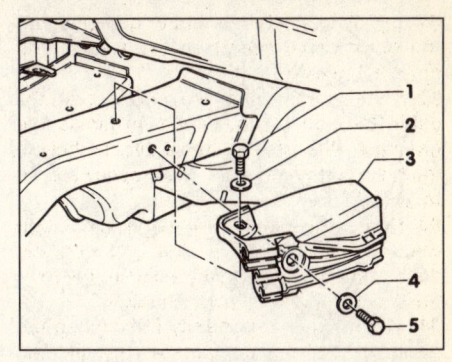

Fig. 13.45 Anchor bracket on transmission member (Sec 13)

1 Bolt 4 Washer
2 Washer 5 Bolt
3 Anchor bracket

128 Disconnect the multi-plug from the rear of the unit (photo).
129 Unclip the control cables from the unit and then unhook their ends from the controls (photo).
130 The heater ends of the cables are unclipped in a similar manner, noting that the temperature regulating cable end and fresh air cable end are accessible from the plenum chamber in the engine compartment.
131 When refitting the cables, the controls and flaps must be set as follows before fitting the securing clips:

Temperature control cable – temperature control knob to hot, control flap lever pushed in toward engine bulkhead.
Distribution flap – distribution control knob to 'instrument panel air outlet', distribution control flap pulled fully away from engine bulkhead.
Fresh air control cable – blower control to 'O', shut-off flap closed.

132 The remaining refitting procedure is a reversal of removal.

Interior door trim panel (1988-on) – removal and refitting

Front door

133 On later types, remove the cover from the door mirror base.

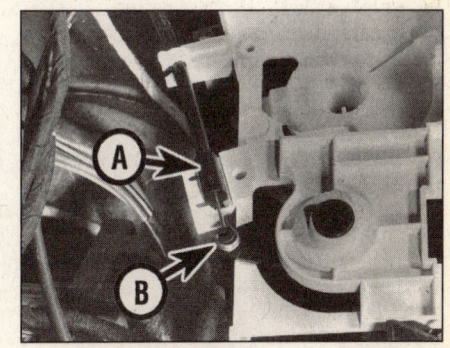

13.129 Control cable clip (A) and attachment to lever (B)

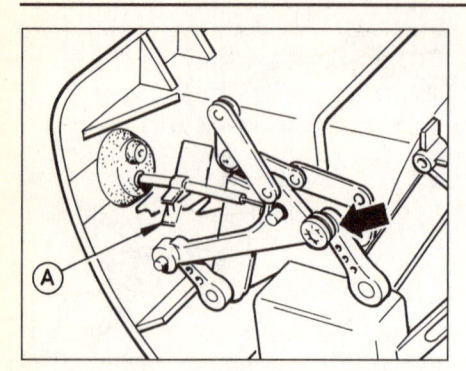

Fig. 13.47 Temperature regulator flap control cable clip A. Push lever in direction of arrow before fitting clip (Sec 13)

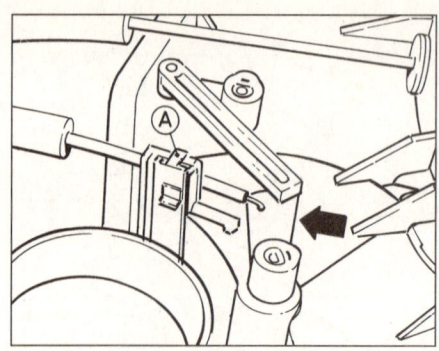

Fig. 13.48 Distribution flap control cable clip A. Push lever in direction of arrow before fitting clip (Sec 13)

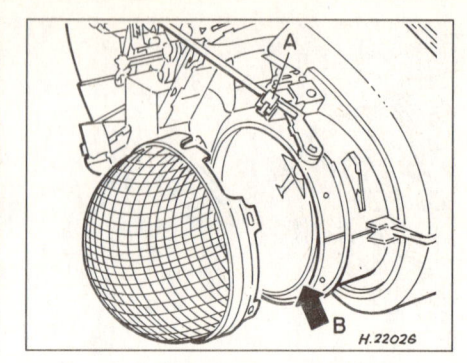

Fig. 13.49 Fresh air flap control cable clip A. Ensure flap B is fully closed before fitting clip (Sec 13)

134 Pull the interior door release handle outward, remove the now revealed screw, then push the assembly forwards to release it from the trim panel (photo).
135 Unhook the assembly from the control cable, first releasing the spring clip (photo).
136 Remove the screw from under the release handle (photo).
137 Unscrew the screws securing the armrest and detach the armrest (photo).
138 Where fitted, pull out the switch plate from the armrest and disconnect the multi-plug (photos).
139 Remove the screw from the top of each panel (photo).

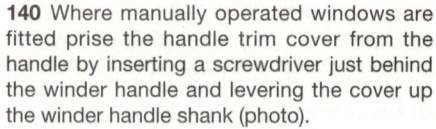

140 Where manually operated windows are fitted prise the handle trim cover from the handle by inserting a screwdriver just behind the winder handle and levering the cover up the winder handle shank (photo).
141 Remove the winder handle securing screw and withdraw the handle (photo).
142 Where fitted, prise out the door courtesy lamp and disconnect the wires.
143 Carefully prise the trim panel from the door using a flat bladed fork. This is done by inserting the forked tool underneath the plastic location clips so that the blades of the tool are positioned at either side of the clips. The clips can now be carefully prised from their housing. Following this procedure,

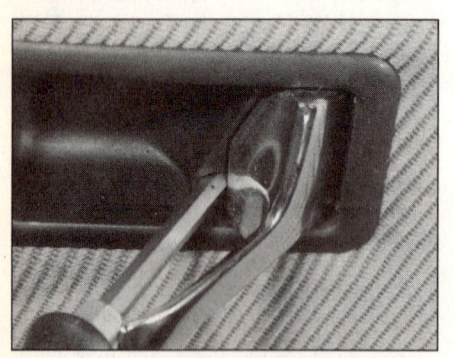

13.134 Removing the screw from the interior release handle

13.135 Release the spring clip and unhook the control cable

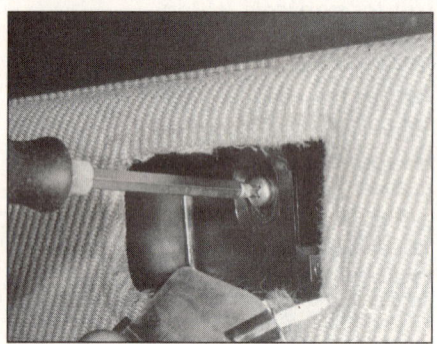

13.136 Remove the screw from under the release handle

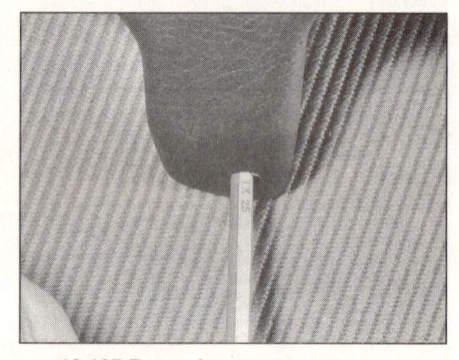

13.137 Removing an armrest screw

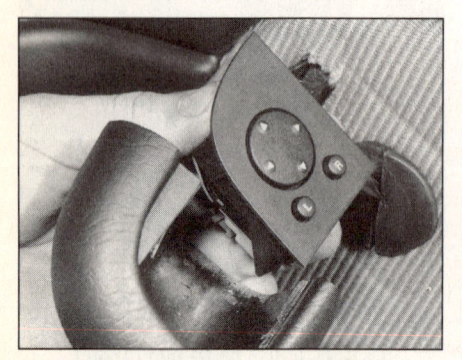

13.138A Pull out the switch plate. . .

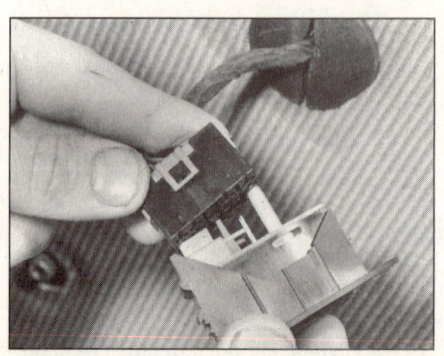

13.138B . . .and disconnect the multi-plug

13.139 Trim panel top end securing screw

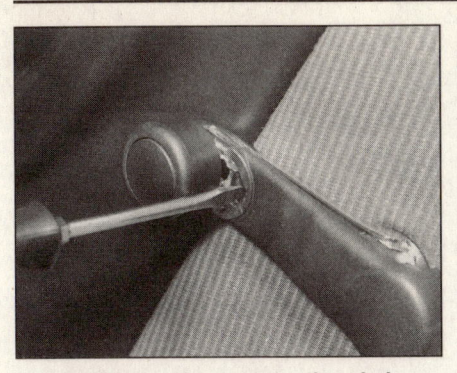

Supplement: Revisions and information on later models 13•29

13.140 Lever the cover up the winder handle shank

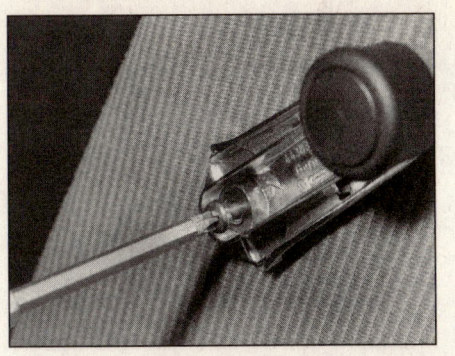

13.141 Remove the winder handle securing screw

should ensure that all the clips and the door panel remain undamaged.

Rear door

144 The procedure is similar to that described for the front door, but the armrest is slightly different. On Avant models, the rear speaker must be disconnected or removed as necessary.

Boot lid lock (1988-on) – general

145 From 1988-on the boot lid lock has been repositioned to the rear panel beside the rear lamp cluster, but the general arrangement of the lock and latch is similar to earlier models.

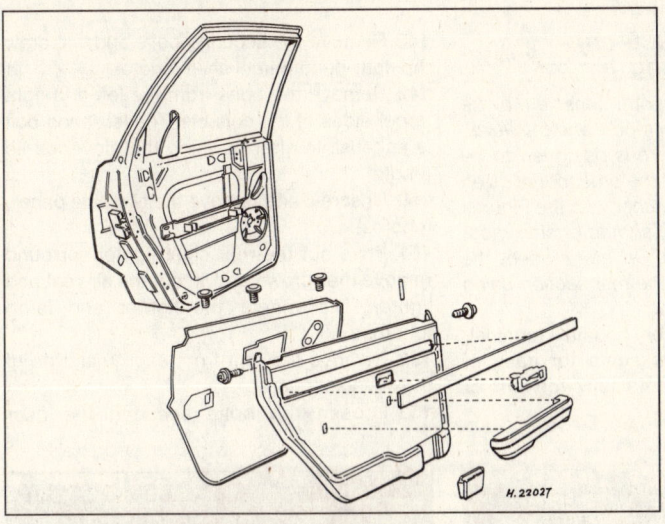

Fig. 13.50 Exploded view of 1988-on rear door trim panel and fittings (Sec 13)

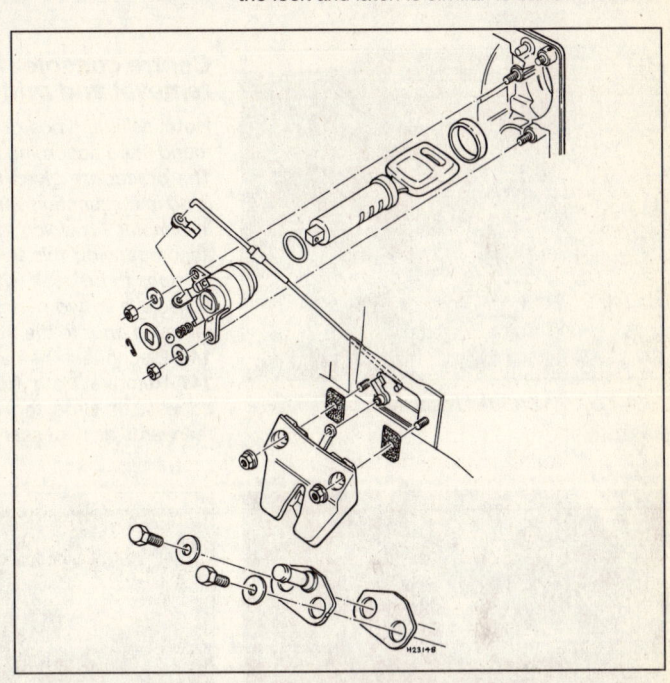

Fig. 13.51 Exploded view of 1988-on boot lid lock and latch assembly (Sec 13)

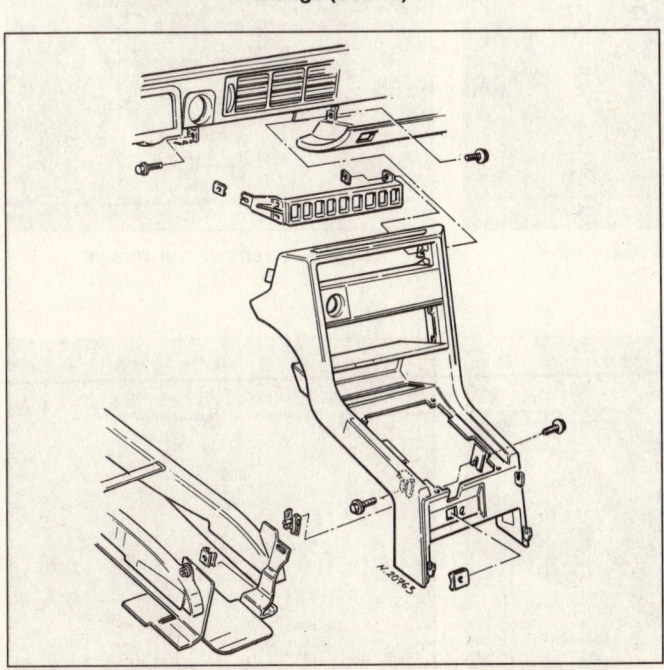

Fig. 13.52 Exploded view of front section of split type centre console (1988-on) (Sec 13)

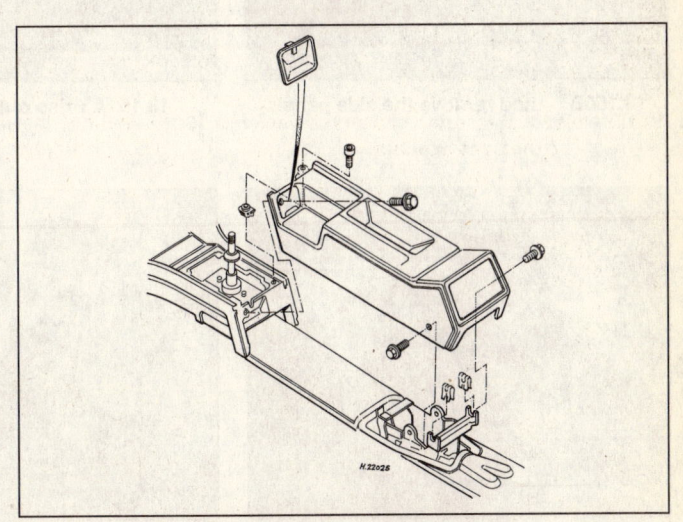

Fig. 13.53 Exploded view of rear section of split type centre console (1988-on) (Sec 13)

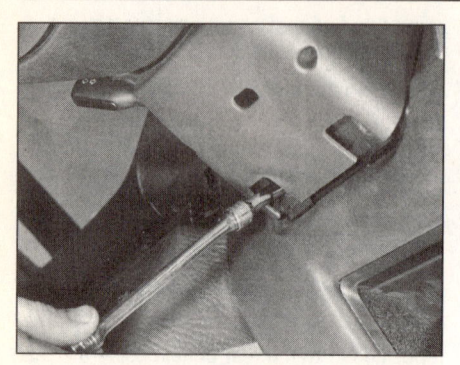

13•30 Supplement: Revisions and information on later models

13.148A Removing the bolts securing the right-hand parcel shelf...

13.148B ...and pulling out the shelf

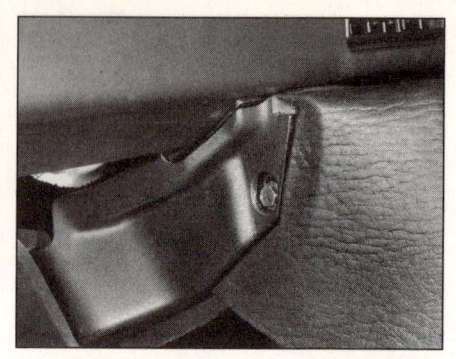

13.149 Upper left-hand side console securing bolt viewed with glovebox lid open

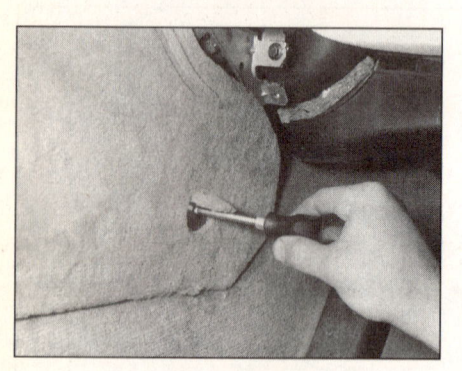

13.150A Unscrew...

Centre console (1988-on) – removal and refitting

Note: *several types of centre console may be found fitted according to model and trim level. The procedure given here is designed to be used in conjunction with the procedures given in Chapter 11, which together with the Figures accompanying this text, should enable most versions to be dealt with. On later models, the console is in two parts, the rear section being removed prior to the front.*

146 Disconnect the battery negative terminal.
147 Remove both front seats for ease of access, or slide the seats fully forward or rearwards as necessary.
148 Remove the securing bolts and withdraw the right-hand parcel shelf (photos).
149 Remove the bolts from the left and right upper sides of the console. The left-hand bolt is accessible after opening the glovebox lid (photo).
150 Unscrew and remove the two side panels (photos).
151 Prise out the rear cigar lighter surround remove the screws and lift out the air vent and lighter. Disconnect the lighter and lamp (photos).
152 Remove the bolt from each rear side of the console (photo).
153 Loosen the bolts securing the gear

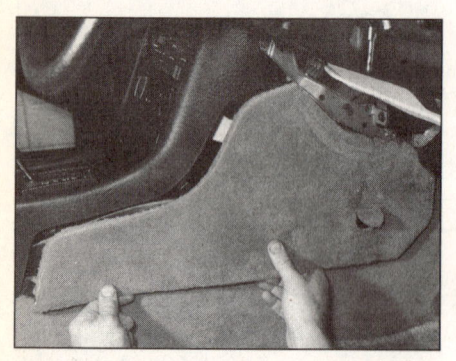

13.150B ...and remove the side panels

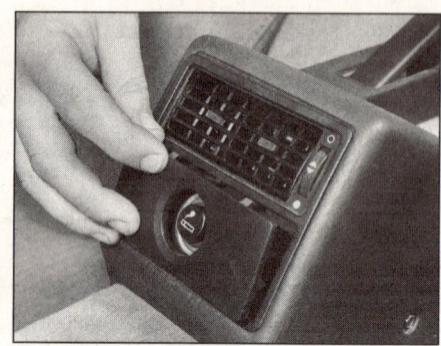

13.151A Prise out the surround...

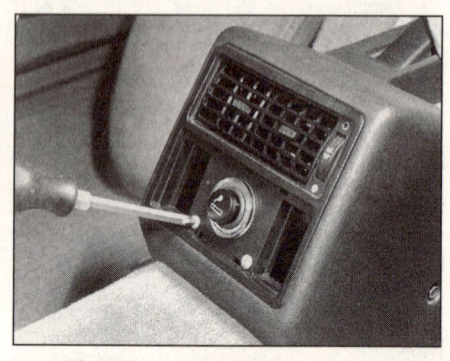

13.151B ...remove the screws...

13.151C ...lift out the air vent and lighter...

13.151D ...and disconnect the lighter and lamp

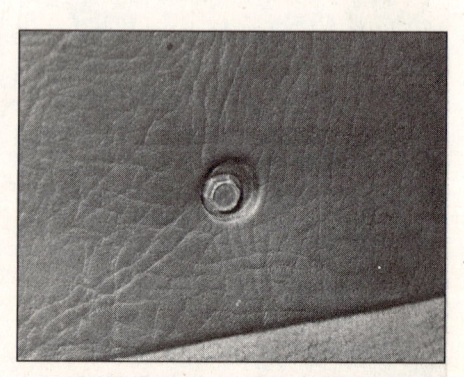

13.152 Console rear securing bolt

13.153A Loosen the bolts...

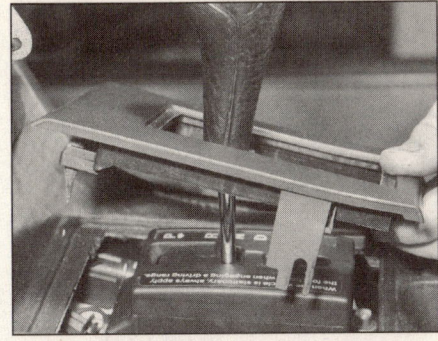

13.153B ...and lift out the surround

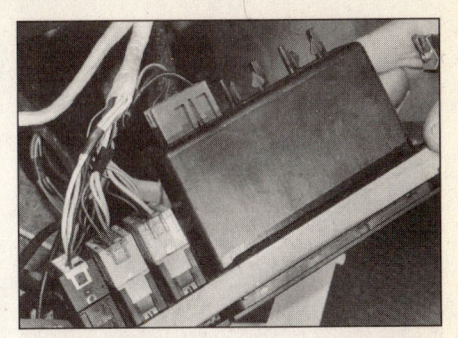

13.155 Multi-plugs on rear of switch housing

lever/selector lever surround and lift out the surround (photos). It may be necessary to unscrew the lever knob to remove the surround.
154 Remove the radio as described in Section 14.
155 Push the upper switch housing rearwards out of the centre console. If the housing or switches are to be removed disconnect the switches and digital clock (photo).
156 Pull off the heater control knobs (photo).
157 Remove the screws from the heater panel surround and lift off the surround (photos).
158 Unscrew the heater control unit from the console (photo).
159 Pull out the front ashtray and disconnect the ashtray illumination bulb (photos).
160 Reach behind the console and disconnect the front cigar lighter.
161 Pull the handbrake lever fully up and release the plastic handle grip by depressing the lug on the underside. Slide the grip from the lever (photos).
162 Manoeuvre the console over the handbrake lever and out of the vehicle (photo).
163 Refitting is a reversal of removal.

13.156 Pull off the heater control knobs

13.157A Remove the screws...

13.157B ...and lift off the surround

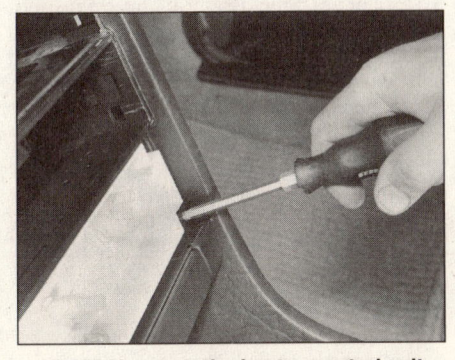

13.158 Unscrew the heater control unit

13.159A Pull out the ashtray...

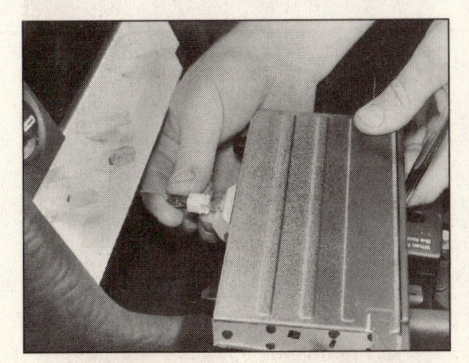

13.159B ...and disconnect the bulb

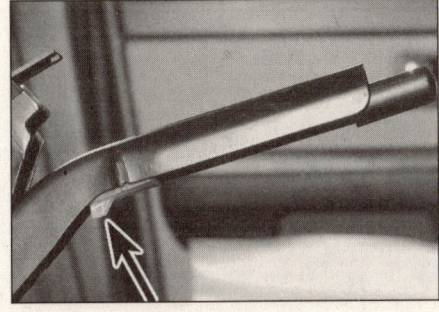

13.161A Depress the lug (arrowed) (handle removed for clarity)...

13.161B ...and slide off the grip

13•32 Supplement: Revisions and information on later models

13.162 Manoeuvre the console over the handbrake lever and out of the vehicle

Fig. 13.54 Ambient air temperature multi-plug and temperature indicator securing screws (arrowed) (Sec 14)

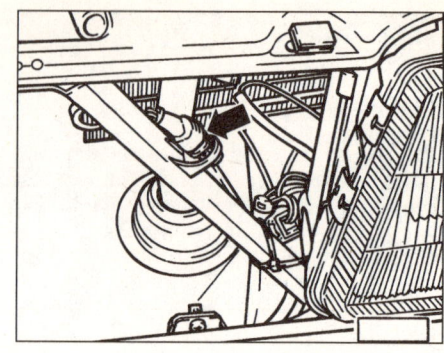

Fig. 13.55 Ambient air temperature sensor plug (arrowed) (Sec 14)

14 Electrical system

Starter motor (1.1 kW with reversing gear) – overhaul

1 The 1.1 kW starter motor has no field windings, but uses permanent magnets instead. These magnets are fragile. Do not drop or strike the starter motor, nor clamp the magnet housing in a vice.

Bulb failure warning system – general

2 The exterior lights on many models have a bulb failure warning system. Failure is detected by monitoring the current drawn by pairs of bulbs, the imbalance resulting from the failure of one bulb triggering the warning.
3 It will be realised that if both bulbs fail at once, no warning will result. Fitting replacement bulbs of different wattage, or sometimes even of different make, can cause false warnings.
4 If it is wished to install a towbar, consult a VAG dealer or other specialist concerning the fitting of the trailer socket. Extra current drawn by the trailer lights could damage the bulb failure warning unit if allowed to flow through it.

Dim-dip lighting system – description

5 From 1987 model year the lights are wired such that it is not possible to drive on parking lights (sidelights) alone. If the parking lights and the ignition are both switched on, the headlight dipped beams are automatically illuminated at reduced intensity hence the name 'dim-dip'.
6 The main components of the system are a relay and a resistor. A wiring diagram appears at the end of this Supplement.

Ambient air temperature indicator – removal and refitting

7 Remove the instrument panel as described in Chapter 12, Section 17.
8 Disconnect the multi-plug from the temperature indicator.
9 Remove the screws securing the connector and temperature indicator to the instrument panel and withdraw the assembly.
10 Refitting is the reverse sequence to removal.

Ambient air temperature sensor – removal and refitting

11 Remove the radiator grille as described in Chapter 11, Section 22.
12 Disconnect the sensor plug mounted near the left-hand headlamp unit.
13 Unclip and withdraw the temperature sensor from the front panel.
14 Refitting is the reverse sequence to removal.

Alternator drivebelt tension (engine code DR and DS) adjustment

15 When adjusting the tension of the alternator drivebelt on engine code DR or DS with the later type toothed adjustment arm/nut assembly. tighten the nut ('B' in Fig. 12.4) to the specified torque using a torque wrench.

Side repeater lamp – bulb renewal

16 Carefully, so as not to damage the paintwork, prise up the rear of the lamp unit, then pull it rearwards to disengage the front securing lug (photo).
17 Pull the bulb holder from the lens unit (photo).
18 The bulb is a push fix in the bulb holder.
19 Refitting is the reverse sequence to removal.

Heater control unit illumination bulb (1988-on models) – renewal

20 Remove the rotary controls and trim panel as described in Section 13.
21 The bulb, which is now accessible is a push fit in its holder (photo).
22 Refit the trim panel and controls.

14.16 Prise up the rear of the lamp unit

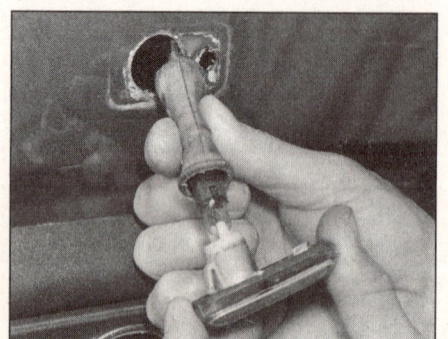

14.17 Pull the bulb holder from the lens unit

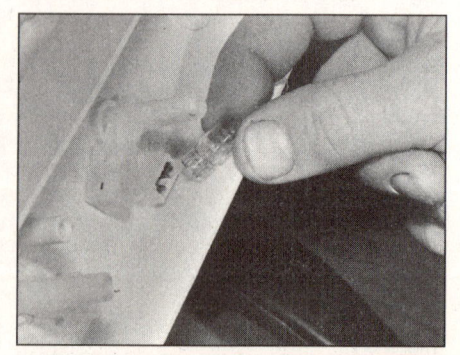

14.21 Removing heater control panel illumination bulb

Headlamp beam adjustment (mechanical) – general

23 On certain models, the headlamp beam height can be adjusted to compensate for different load levels.
24 Mechanical adjustment is carried out by raising or lowering the button above each headlamp unit, accessible with the bonnet open. See photo 20.8A in Chapter 12.
25 The buttons should be raised with the vehicle normally loaded, and depressed for heavy loads. Remember that incorrectly set beam height can cause annoyance and be dangerous by causing dazzle to oncoming road users.

Headlamp beam adjustment (electric) – general

26 Certain models from mid-1989 are fitted with electrical headlamp beam height adjustment as standard.
27 The adjustment can only be operated with the headlamps on dipped beam.
28 Whenever headlamp beam adjustment is being carried out (Chapter 12, Section 21), the electric adjuster control must be in the zero position.
29 Rear paragraph 28 above.

Headlamp beam adjustment (electric) – servicing

Adjuster control

30 The adjuster control is mounted in the centre console. To remove the control, prise it carefully from the console and disconnect the wires. Refit in reverse.

Servo motor

31 On both 100 and 200 models, remove the relevant headlamp as described in Chapter 12, Section 20, but also disconnect the servo motor.
32 On 100 models, release the servo motor from the headlamp housing by turning the servo clockwise on the right-hand headlamp and anti-clockwise on the left-hand headlamp.
33 Raise the motor slightly and insert a small screwdriver through the opening in order to release the retaining catch by pushing the catch toward the operating shaft, at the same time pulling the servo motor rearwards.
34 On 200 models, the procedure is the same as for 100 models, but there is no retaining catch to release.
35 To refit the motor, on 100 models remove the cover from the headlamp bulb.
36 Press the motor into the retainer catch so that it engages fully, holding the reflector steady through the bulb aperture (do not touch the reflector with bare fingers). Lock the motor in position by turning it back to its original position.
37 The refitting procedure is the same on 200 models, but again there is no retaining catch.
38 On both 100 and 200 models, refit the headlamp units.

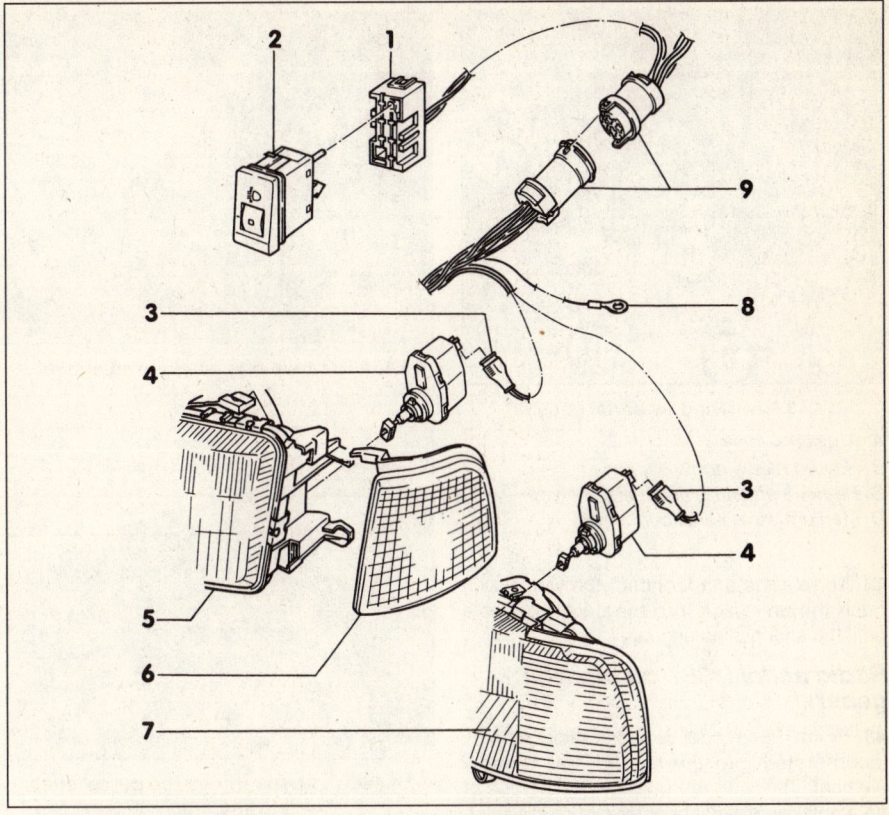

Fig. 13.56 Components of the headlamp beam electrical adjustment system (Sec 14)

1 Plug (in instrument panel loom)
2 Adjustment switch (in facia)
3 Servo motor connector
4 Servo motor
5 Headlamp (Audi 100)
6 Direction indicator lamp
7 Headlamp (Audi 200)
8 Earthing point (under left side of instrument panel)
9 Connector (in loom behind instrument panel)

Radio/cassette player (DIN fitting) – removal and refitting

39 Later models are fitted with a radio/cassette player secured in the centre console by standard DIN fittings. To remove the unit, two DIN fitting extraction tools will be needed. These are supplied with the radio, but if they have been lost, can be obtained from in-car entertainment specialists (ICE).
40 Insert the prongs of the tools into the holes at each side of the unit until they are heard to 'click' home. Pull them apart and outward to withdraw the unit. Depending on how the wiring is secured, it may be necessary to remove the centre console side panels to release the wiring before the unit can be withdrawn completely. Disconnect the wiring from the back of the unit (photos).
41 Release the extraction tools from the unit by depressing the spring clips with a screwdriver.

14.40A Radio/cassette player partially withdrawn showing use of DIN fitting tools

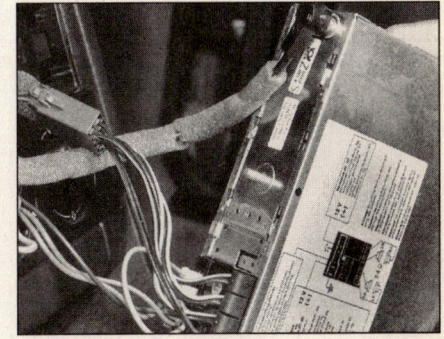

14.40B Wiring connections on rear of unit

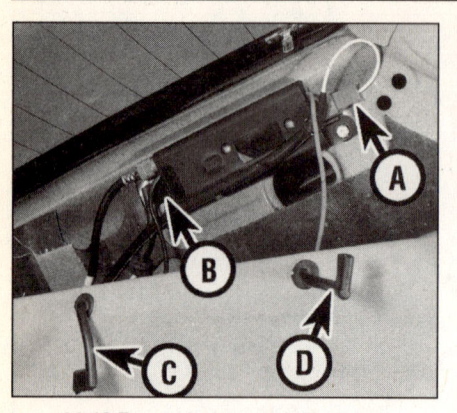

14.43 Rear window aerial booster

A Booster supply
B Heated rear window supply
C Heater element/VHF aerial connector
D Medium wave aerial connector

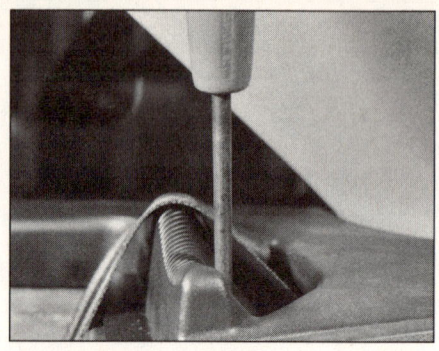

14.46A Remove one screw from above...

14.46B ...and one screw from in front...

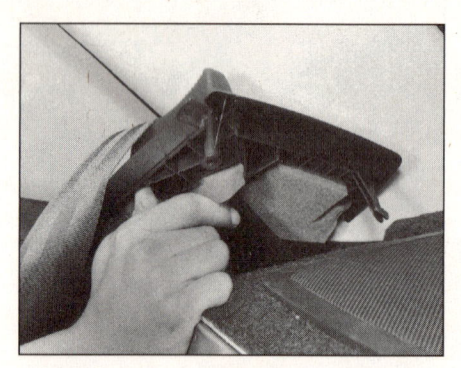

14.46C ...then remove the parcel shelf trim panel

14.49 Unclipping the rear audio control block

42 To refit the unit, connect the wiring with push the unit back into the centre console until the spring clips engage.

Radio aerial (1987-on models) – general

43 From 1987 model year, the radio aerial is incorporated into the heated rear window element. This is made possible by the use of an amplifier, or aerial booster mounted behind the left-hand D-pillar trim (photo).

44 If the aerial malfunctions, check that all connections are tight and that fuse number 16 is intact. Check also that battery voltage is present at the booster supply terminal when the radio is switched on, and at the heated rear window supply terminal, when this is switched on (ignition on).

45 Further checking should be left to an Audi dealer or other specialist.

Rear loudspeaker and audio controls (Saloon) – removal and refitting

46 Remove the rear seat (Section 13), then remove the trim panels at each end of the rear parcel shelf. These panels are each secured by two screws (photos).

47 Lift out the parcel shelf, at the same time disconnecting the multi-plug from the audio control block.

48 The loudspeakers may be removed from the parcel shelf after undoing the securing screws or clips, and disconnecting the wiring accessible from inside the boot.

49 To remove the audio control block, unclip it from the parcel shelf (photo).

50 Refitting is a reversal of removal.

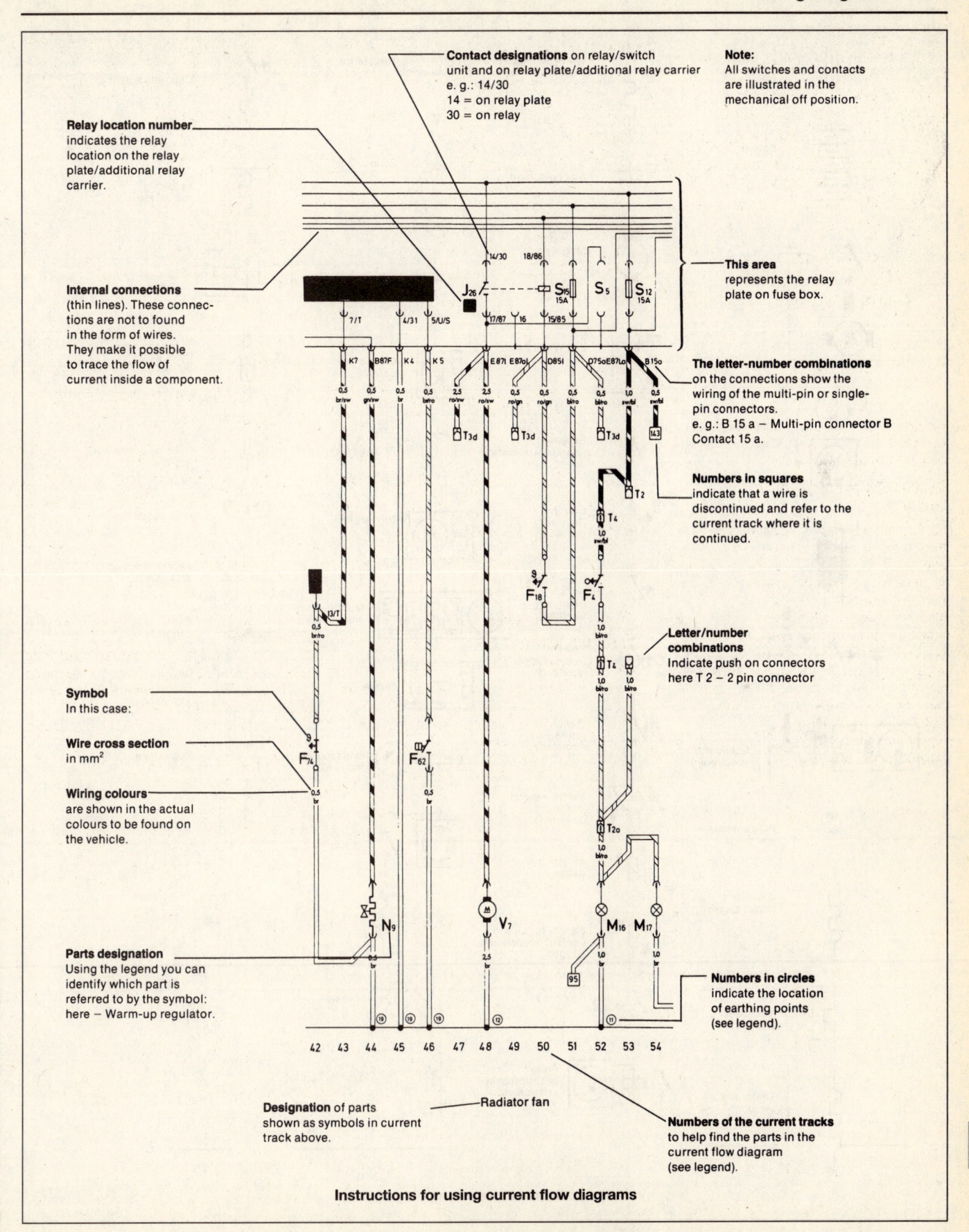

Wiring diagrams 14•1

Relay location number indicates the relay location on the relay plate/additional relay carrier.

Contact designations on relay/switch unit and on relay plate/additional relay carrier
e. g.: 14/30
14 = on relay plate
30 = on relay

Note: All switches and contacts are illustrated in the mechanical off position.

Internal connections (thin lines). These connections are not to be found in the form of wires. They make it possible to trace the flow of current inside a component.

This area represents the relay plate on fuse box.

The letter-number combinations on the connections show the wiring of the multi-pin or single-pin connectors.
e. g.: B 15 a – Multi-pin connector B Contact 15 a.

Numbers in squares indicate that a wire is discontinued and refer to the current track where it is continued.

Letter/number combinations Indicate push on connectors here T 2 – 2 pin connector

Symbol In this case:

Wire cross section in mm²

Wiring colours are shown in the actual colours to be found on the vehicle.

Parts designation Using the legend you can identify which part is referred to by the symbol: here – Warm-up regulator.

Numbers in circles indicate the location of earthing points (see legend).

Designation of parts shown as symbols in current track above.

Radiator fan

Numbers of the current tracks to help find the parts in the current flow diagram (see legend).

Instructions for using current flow diagrams

14•2 Wiring diagrams

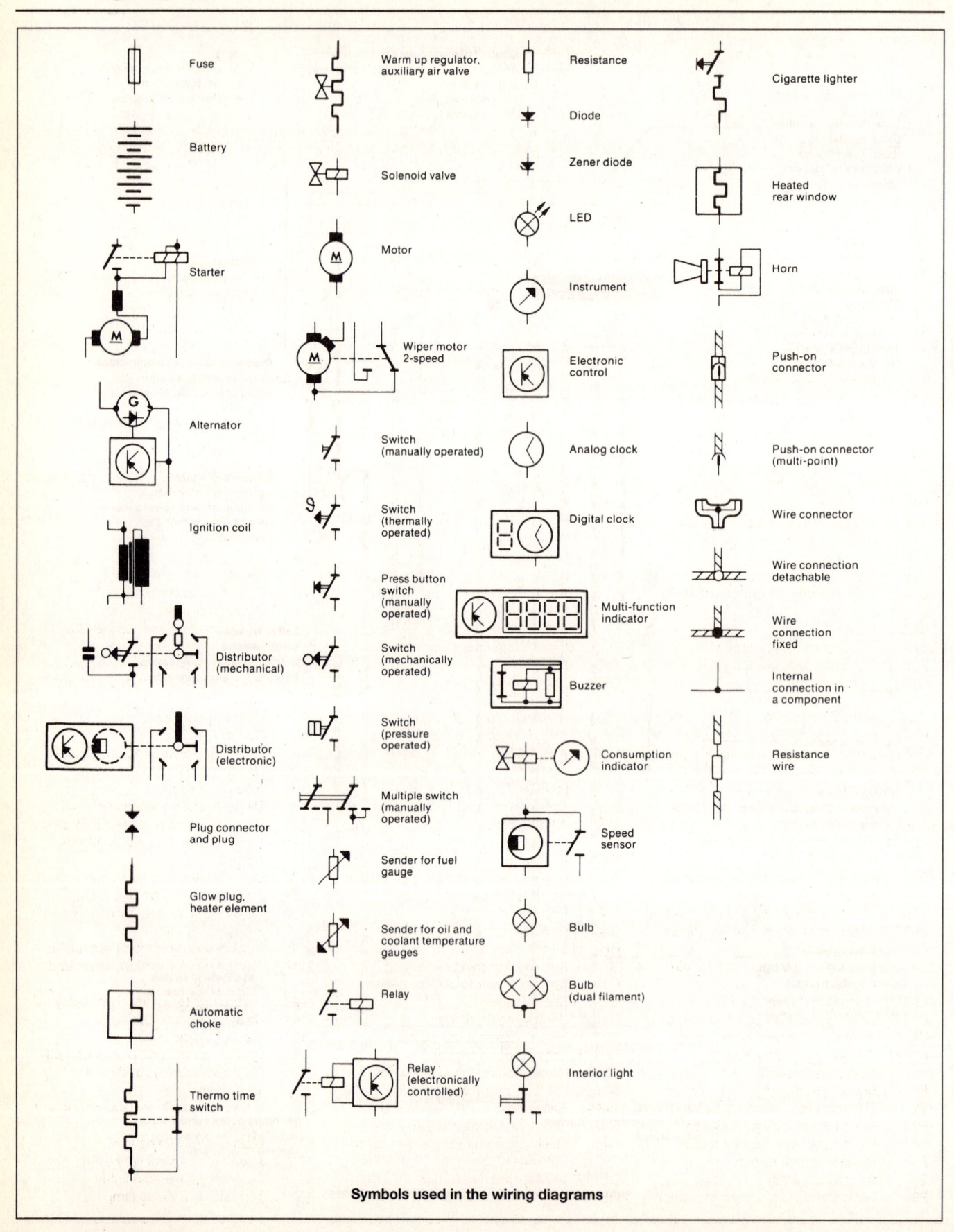

Symbol	Description
	Fuse
	Battery
	Starter
	Alternator
	Ignition coil
	Distributor (mechanical)
	Distributor (electronic)
	Plug connector and plug
	Glow plug, heater element
	Automatic choke
	Thermo time switch
	Warm up regulator, auxiliary air valve
	Solenoid valve
	Motor
	Wiper motor 2-speed
	Switch (manually operated)
	Switch (thermally operated)
	Press button switch (manually operated)
	Switch (mechanically operated)
	Switch (pressure operated)
	Multiple switch (manually operated)
	Sender for fuel gauge
	Sender for oil and coolant temperature gauges
	Relay
	Relay (electronically controlled)
	Resistance
	Diode
	Zener diode
	LED
	Instrument
	Electronic control
	Analog clock
	Digital clock
	Multi-function indicator
	Buzzer
	Consumption indicator
	Speed sensor
	Bulb
	Bulb (dual filament)
	Interior light
	Cigarette lighter
	Heated rear window
	Horn
	Push-on connector
	Push-on connector (multi-point)
	Wire connector
	Wire connection detachable
	Wire connection fixed
	Internal connection in a component
	Resistance wire

Symbols used in the wiring diagrams

Wiring diagrams

Key for all wiring diagrams

The wiring diagrams are of the current flow type where each wire is shown in the simplest line form without crossing over other wires.

The fuse/relay panel is at the top of the diagram and the combined letter/figure numbers appearing on the panel terminals refer to the multi-plug connector in letter form and the terminal in figure form.

Internal connections through electrical components are shown by a single line.

The encircled numbers along the bottom of the diagram indicate the earthing connecting points as given in the key.

Space limitations mean that only a representative range of diagrams can be included.

Not all items are fitted to all models

No	Description
A	Battery
B	Starter
C	Alternator
C1	Voltage regulator
D	Ignition/starter switch
E1	Lighting switch
E2	Indicator switch
E3	Hazard warning light switch
E4	Headlight dimmer/flasher switch
E7	Foglight switch
E8	Switch for sliding roof
E9	Fresh air blower switch
E13	Fresh air blower switch (lower lever) or Heating switch
E15	Heated rear window switch
E17	Starter inhibitor switch and reversing light switch
E18	Rear foglight switch
E19	Parking light switch
E20	Instrumen/dash panel lighting control
E22	Intermittent wiper switch
E23	Foglight and rear foglight switch
E26	Glovebox light switch
E39	Electric window switch
E40	Window lifter switch, left
E41	Window lifter switch, right
E45	Automatic cruise control switch
E46	Switch unit for cruise control
E52	Rear left window lifter switch (in door)
E53	Rear left window lifter switch (in console)
E54	Rear right window lifter switch (in door)
E55	Rear right window lifter switch (in console)
E56	Sliding roof cut-out switch (closed)
E57	Sliding roof cut-out switch (open)
E83	ABS switch
E87	Controls and display unit for air conditioning
E93	Button for autocheck system
E99	Lighting regulator, dash controls
E103	Switch for heated seats, stage
E107	Switch for window lifter (in passenger's door)
F	Brake light switch
F1	Oil pressure switch (1.8 bar)
F2	Front left door contact switch
F3	Front right door contact switch
F4	Reversing light switch
F5	Boot light switch
F9	Handbrake warning system switch

No	Description
F10	Rear left door contact switch
F11	Rear right door contact switch
F14	Coolant temperature warning switch (overheating)
F15	Gearbox switch (1st gear on 5 speed box)
F18	Radiator fan thermoswitch
F21	Hydraulic servo unit warning switch
F22	Oil pressure switch (0.3 bar)
F26	Thermotime switch
F34	Brake fluid level warning contact
F36	Cruise control clutch pedal switch
F47	Automatic cruise control brake pedal switch
F51	Overheating fuse (in resistance carrier)
F52	Coolant temperature warning switch (overheating)
F54	Radiator fan thermoswitch
F59	Central locking system switch
F60	Idle switch
F61	Thermo switch for V
F62	Gearshift indicator vacuum switch
F66	Low coolant level switch
F68	Gear switch for gearshift indicator
F74	Idle stabilization thermo-switch
F75	Hydraulic fluid warning contact
F76	Electronic thermoswitch
F77	Windscreen washer fluid warning contact
F81	Full-throttle switch
F87	Thermoswitch for fan run-on
F96	Altitude sensor
G	Fuel gauge sender
G1	Fuel gauge
G2	Coolant temperature gauge sender
G3	Coolant temperature gauge
G4	Firing point sender
G5	Rev counter
G6	Electric fuel pump
G17	Ambient temperature sensor
G19	Potentiometer for airflow meter
G21	Speedometer
G22	Speedometer sender
G27	Engine temperature sensor
G28	Engine speed sender
G38	Cruise control induction sender
G39	Lambda probe with heater
G40	Hall sender
G42	Intake air temperature sender
G43	Flashing sender for warning lamp K28 and K33
G51	Consumption indicator
G58	Sender for consumption indicator

No	Description
G61	Knock sensor
G62	Coolant temperature sender unit
H	Horn control
H1	Horn
H2	High and low tone horn
J2	Indicator flasher relay
J4	Horn relay
J5	Foglight relay
J6	Voltage stabiliser
J17	Fuel pump relay
J21	Electronic fuel injection control unit
J26	Radiator fan relay
J31	Intermittent wash/wipe relay
J31	Intermittent wash/wipe relay
J39	Headlight washer system relay
J43	K-Jetronic relay (diode)
J51	Window lifter relay
J52	Glow plug relay
J59	Relief relay (for X-contact)
J60	Automatic gearbox relay
J72	Sliding roof relay
J81	Intake manifold preheating relay (1)
J85	Alarm system control unit
J87	DIS (Idling stabilization) switch unit
J88	Electronic ignition system control unit
J95	Cold start valve cycle relay
J97	Relay for V
J98	Gearshift indicator control unit (3)
J101	Radiator fan 2nd stage relay
J104	ABS control unit
J114	Oil pressure monitor switch unit
J118	Relay for brake pad wear indicator
J122	Main control unit for auto check system
J123	Bulb monitoring device, front
J124	Bulb monitoring device, rear
J136	Control unit for seat adjustment with memory
J138	Control unit for radiator fan run-on
J139	Switch unit for window lifters and sliding roof
J140	Switch unit for interior light delay
J141	Relay for switch lighting
J152	Sidelight/radio buzzer
J154	Ignition control unit (knock control)
J190	Changeover relay for dim-dip lighting unit
J222	Main control unit for Autocheck system
K1	Main beam warning light
K2	Alternator warning light
K3	Oil pressure warning light
K5	Turn signal warning lamp

Key to all wiring diagrams (continued)

No	Description
K6	Emergency light system warning lamp
K10	Heated rear window warning lamp
K13	Rear foglight warning lamp
K14	Handbrake warning lamp
K16	Fuel reserve warning light
K20	Warning lamp for closed doors
K28	Coolant temperature warning light
K32	Brake pad wear warning lamp
K33	Brake fluid level warning lamp
K34	Brake light warning light
K35	Tail light warning light
K37	Windscreen washer fluid level warning light
K43	Coolant temp warning lamp (too cold)
K47	ABS warning lamp
K48	Gearshift indicator warning lamp
K49	Warning light for 'red triangle' symbol
K50	Warning light for 'OK' symbol
K52	Warning light for battery charge condition warning light
K64	Emergency light and right turn signal warning lamp
K65	Left turn signal warning lamp
K65	Left turn signal warning lamp
K66	Warning lamp for all-electronic ignition
L1	Twin filament headlight bulb, left
L2	Twin filament headlight bulb, right
L8	Clock light bulb
L10	Instrument panel insert light bulbs
L13	Main beam headlight bulb, left
L14	Main beam headlight bulb, right
L15	Ashtray light bulb
L16	Fresh air controls light bulb
L19	Gearshift scale light
L20	Rear foglight bulb
L21	Heater controls light bulb
L22	Foglight bulb, left
L23	Foglight bulb, right
L28	Engine compartment light bulb or cigarette lighter light bulb
L29	Engine compartment light bulb
L32	Rear cigarette lighter light bulb
L40	Front and rear foglight switch bulb
L46	Rear foglight bulb left
L47	Rear foglight bulb right
L48	Ashtray lighting bulb rear left
L49	Ashtray lighting bulb rear right
M1	Sidelight bulb, left
M2	Tail light bulb, right
M3	Sidelight bulb, right
M4	Tail light bulb, left
M5	Indicator bulb, front left
M6	Indicator bulb, rear left
M7	Indicator bulb, front right
M8	Indicator bulb, rear right
M9	Brake light and tail light bulb, left
M10	Brake light and tail light bulb, right
M16	Reversing light left
M17	Reversing light right

No	Description
N	Ignition coil
N1	Automatic choke
N9	Warm-up valve
N12	Brake pad wear indicator, right
N13	Brake pad wear indicator, left
N16	Two-way valve for increased idling speed
N17	Brake pad wear indicator, right or Cold start valve
N18	EGR valve
N23	Series resistance for fresh air blower
N24	Series resistance for fresh air blower with overheating fuse
N41	TCI control unit
N51	Heat resistance for intake manifold preheating
N52	Heat resistance (part throttle channel heating/carburetor)
N54	Two-way valve for full throttle enrichment
N55	ABS hydraulic modulator
N60	Solenoid valve for consumption indicator
N62	Idling speed – acceleration valve
N65	Solenoid valve for deceleration cut-off
N70	Coil with final output stage
N71	Control valve for idle stabilisation
N73	Differential pressure regulator
N74	Resistance wire
N80	Solenoid valve, activated charcoal filter
O	Distributor
P	Spark plug connector
Q	Spark plug
R	Radio connection
R1	Aerial connection
S1 to S22	Fuses in relay plate/fusebox
S24	Fuse for sliding roof (auxiliary fuse holder)
S26	Separate fuse for instrument cluster
S27	Separate fuse for knock control unit
S28	Separate fuse for KE III-Jetronic control unit
S43	Thermo cut-out
T1	Single connector, various locations
T1a	Single connector, various locations
T1b	Single connector, various locations
T1c	Single connector, behind dashboard, slip ring connection
T1d	Single connector, behind dashboard
T1e	Single connector, behind dash
T1f	Single connector, behind dashboard
T1g	Single connector, behind dash
T1h	Single connector, behind dash
T1j	Single connector, behind dash
T2	2-pin connector, various locations
T2a	2-pin connector, various locations or 4-pin connector, engine compartment right
T2b	2-pin connector, behind dashboard
T2c	2-pin connector, engine compartment, left

No	Description
T2d	2-pin connector, engine compartment
T2e	2-pin connector, various locations
T2f	2-pin connector, various locations
T2g	2-pin connector, engine compartment, right
T2h	2-pin connector, various locations
T2i	2-pin connector, right suspension strut
T2j	2-pin connector, behind dashboard, fader connection
T2k	2-pin connector, rear door, left
T2l	2-pin connector, rear door, right
T2m	2-pin connector, behind dashboard, power aerial connection
T2u	2-pin connector, behind console, electric aerial
T2x	2-pin connector, behind dash panel
T2y	2-pin connector, behind dash panel, diagnosis plug
T3	3-pin connector, various locations
T3a	3-pin connector, various locations
T3b	3-pin connector, various locations
T3c	3-pin connector, various locations
T3d	3-pin connector, various locations
T3e	3-pin connector, behind dashboard
T3f	3-pin connector, behind dashboard, connection for beam height adjustment
T3g	3-pin connector, behind dashboard
T3h	3-pin connector, behind dash
T3r	3-pin connector, behind dash
T4	4-pin connector, various locations
T4a	4-pin connector, various locations
T4b	4-pin connector, various locations
T4c	4-pin connector, various locations
T4d	4-pin connector, dash panel insert
T4e	4-pin connector, behind dashboard
T5	5-pin connector, behind dash
T5a	5-pin connector, behind dash
T5j	5-pin connector, behind console
T6	6-pin connector, behind dash
T6a	6-pin connector, behind dash
T6b	6-pin connector, behind dashboard
T6c	6-pin connector, behind dash
T6d	6-pin connector, behind dashboard
T6g	6-pin connector, behind dash
T6h	6-pin connector, behind dash
T6k	6-pin connector, behind dash
T8	8-pin connector, behind dash
T8a	8-pin connector, behind dash, coding plug
T9	9-pin connector, behind dashboard
T9a	9-pin connector, behind dashboard
T10	10-pin connector, behind dash
T10a	10-pin connector, behind dash
T10b	10-pin connector, behind dash
T10d	10-pin connector, behind dash
T10f	10-pin connector, behind dash
T12	12-pin connector, dash panel insert
T14	14-pin connector, dash panel insert
T14a/	14-pin connector, instrument cluster
T26	26-pin connector, on dash insert

Wiring diagrams

Key to all wiring diagrams (continued)

No	Description
T26a	26-pin connector, on dash insert
T35	Connector for terminal 15
T36	Connector for terminal 30
T37	Connector for terminal 58
U1	Cigarette lighter
U10	Trailer socket
U9	Cigarette lighter, rear
V	Windscreen wiper motor
V1	Sliding roof motor
V2	Fresh air blower
V5	Windscreen washer pump
V7	Radiator fan
V11	Headlight washer pump
V14	Window lifter motor, left
V15	Window lifter motor, right
V18	Control unit for automatic cruise control
V26	Window lifter motor, rear left
V27	Window lifter motor, rear right
V34	Aux washer pump motor
V37	Central locking motor, Bi-pressure pump
V38	Injector cooling blower motor
W	Interior light
W3	Boot light
W6	Glovebox light
W11	Reading lamp, rear left
W12	Reading lamp, rear right
X	Number plate light
Y2	Digital clock
Z	Heated rear window
Z1	Heated rear window
*	Certain models only
**	Certain models only
***	Certain models only
****	Certain models only
*****	Certain models only

Colour code

BK	Black
bl	Blue
BL	Blue
br	Brown
BR	Brown
G	Green
ge	Yellow
gn	Green
gr	Grey
GY	Grey
li	Violet
R	Red
ro	Red
V	Violet
W	White
ws	White
Y	Yellow

Earthing points

No	Description
1	Battery earth strap
6	Alternator earth strap
7	Alternator – engine
8	Behind dashboard
9	Engine compartment, left
9	Engine compartment, left
11	Luggage compartment
12	In front left harness
13	In dashboard harness
14	Near handbrake
15	Below parcel shelf
16	Under rear seat or near handbrake
17	On inlet manifold
18	Behind headliner
23	In harness for all electronic ignition
25	Intake manifold
32	Behind dash

No	Description
41	Under rear shelf
44	A-pillar left, bottom
50	Left of boot
81	Instrument loom
82	Front left loom
83	Front right loom
84	Engine block, front right loom
86	Rear loom
87	Rear loom
89	Electric window wiring loom
99	Console wiring loom
124	Engine compartment wiring loom, right
144	Dash panel insert for Motronic wiring loom
A2	Positive (+) connection in instrument loom
A19	Dash panel wiring loom, 58d
A20	Dash panel wiring loom, 15a
A23	Dash panel wiring loom
C4	In front left loom
C5	Connection 1, brake pad wear monitor
C6	Connection 2, brake pad wear monitor
C7	Connection 3, brake pad wear monitor
C8	Connection 4, brake pad wear monitor

Relay sockets

No	Description
1	Switch unit for window lifters and and sliding roof, auxiliary relay plate 1
13	Window lifter relay, auxiliary relay plate 1
16	Thermo cut-out, auxiliary relay plate 1

14•6 Wiring diagrams

Wiring diagram for 1983 1.9 litre Audi 100

Wiring diagrams 14•7

Wiring diagram for 1983 1.9 litre Audi 100 (continued)

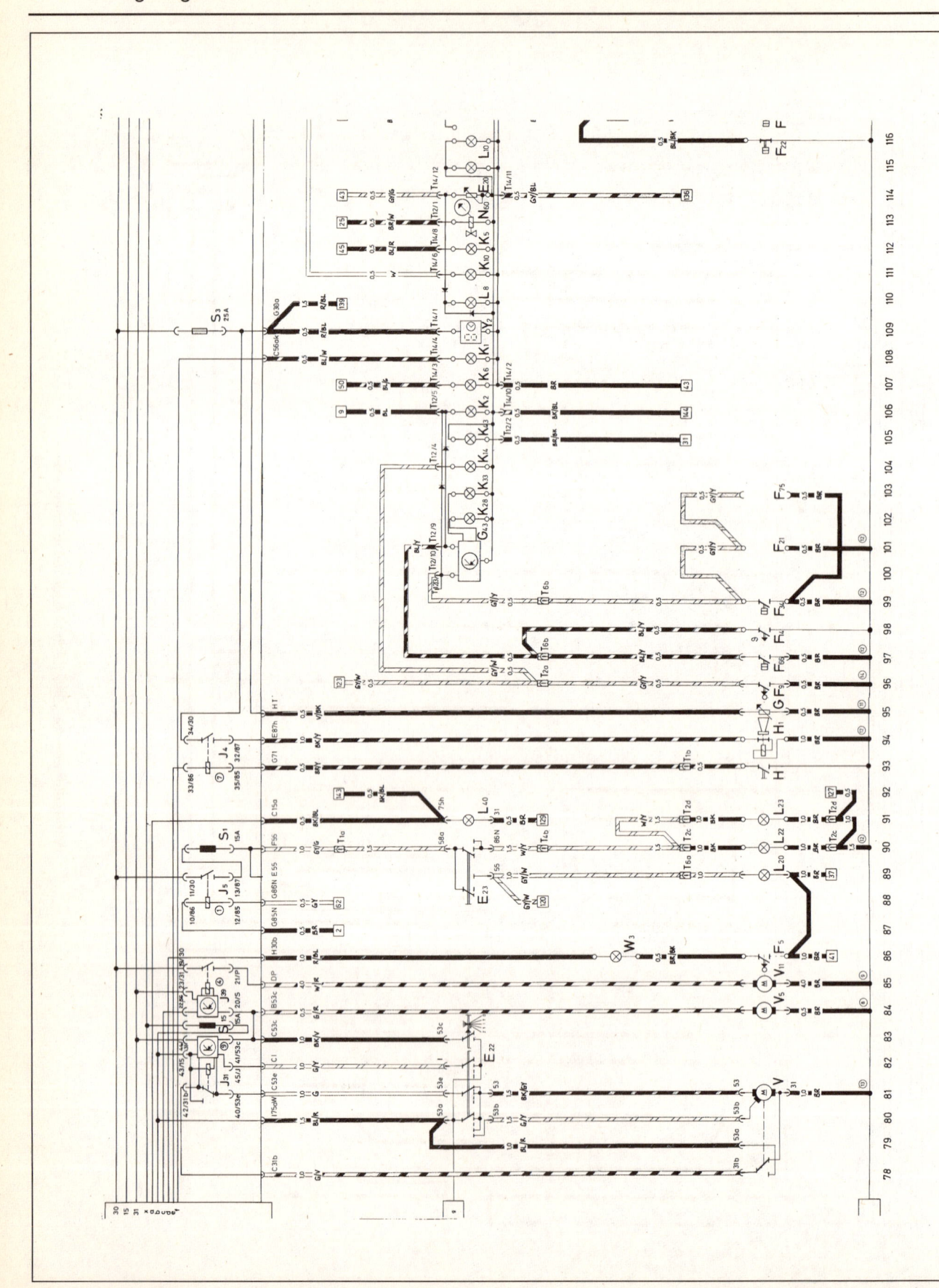

14•8 Wiring diagrams

Wiring diagram for 1983 1.9 litre Audi 100 (continued)

Wiring diagrams 14•9

Wiring diagram for 1983 1.9 litre Audi 100 (continued)

14•10 Wiring diagrams

Wiring diagram for automatic transmission

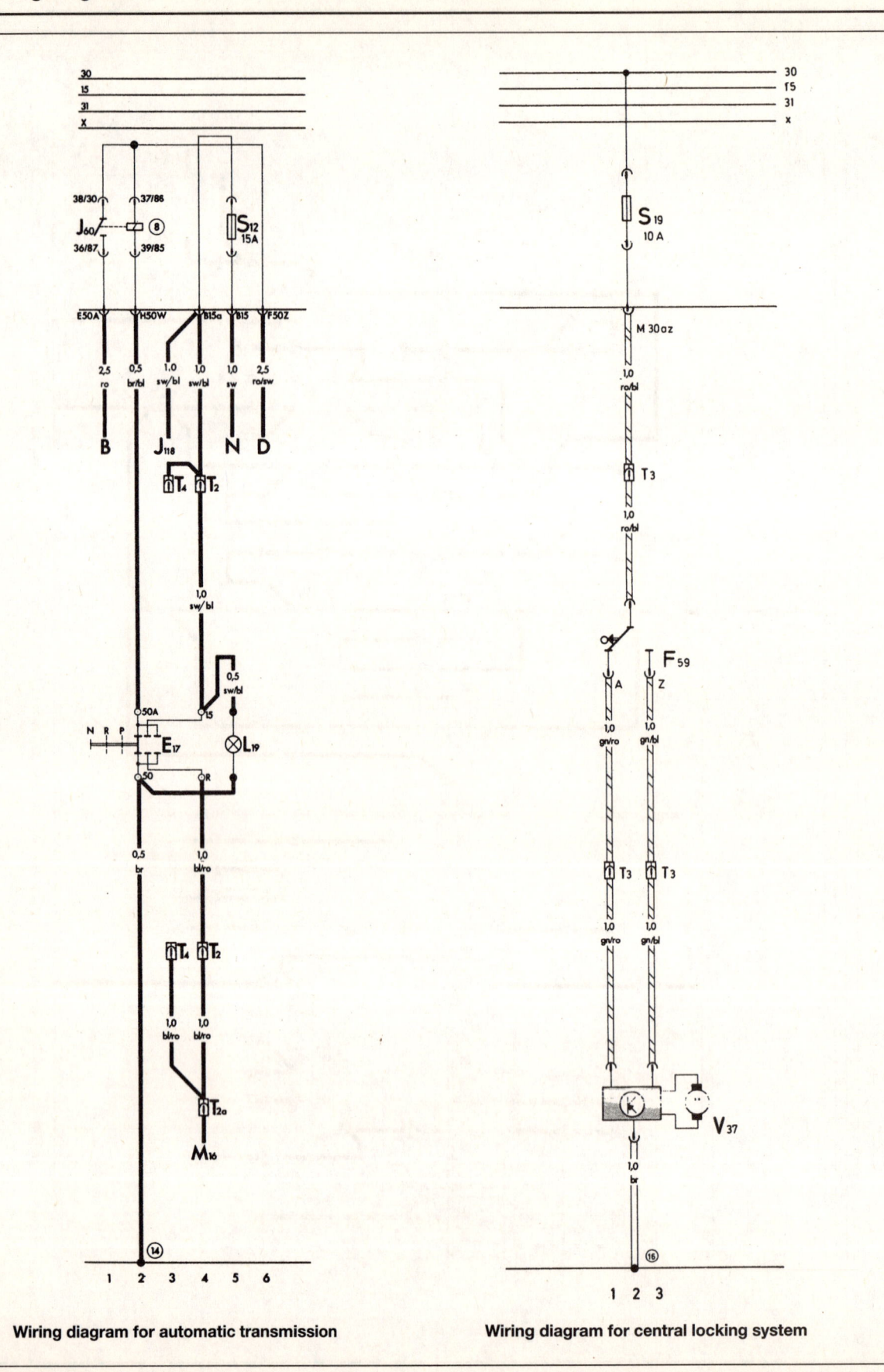

Wiring diagram for central locking system

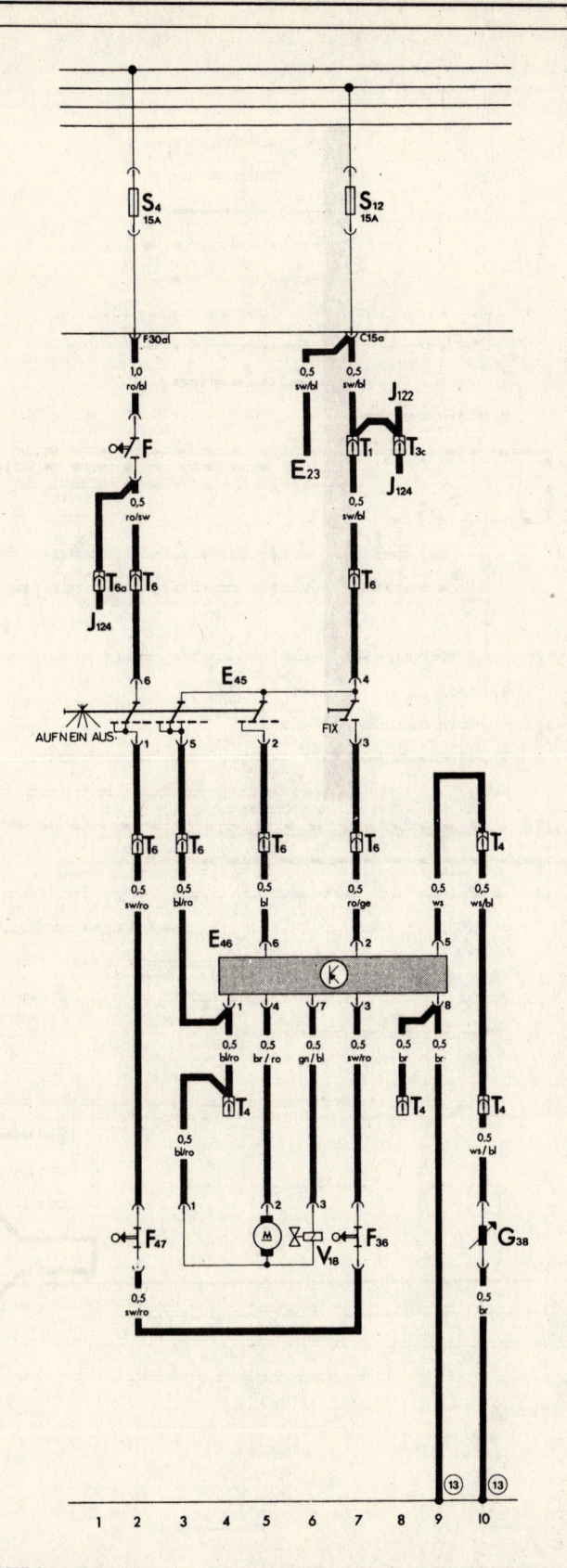

Wiring diagrams 14•11

Wiring diagram for cruise control on manual gearbox models

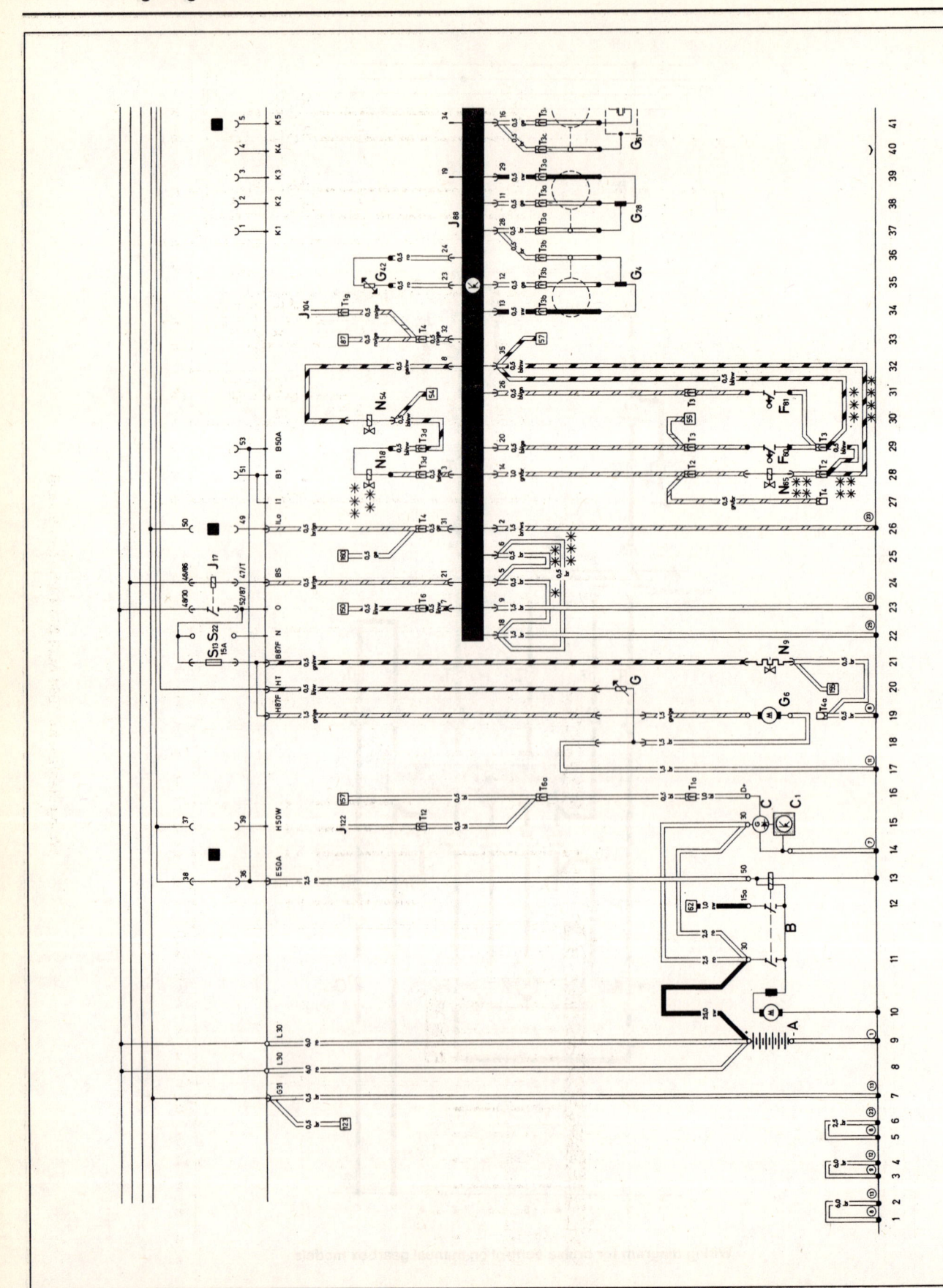

Wiring diagram for 1984 Audi 200 Turbo

Wiring diagrams 14•13

Wiring diagram for 1984 Audi 200 Turbo (continued)

14•14 Wiring diagrams

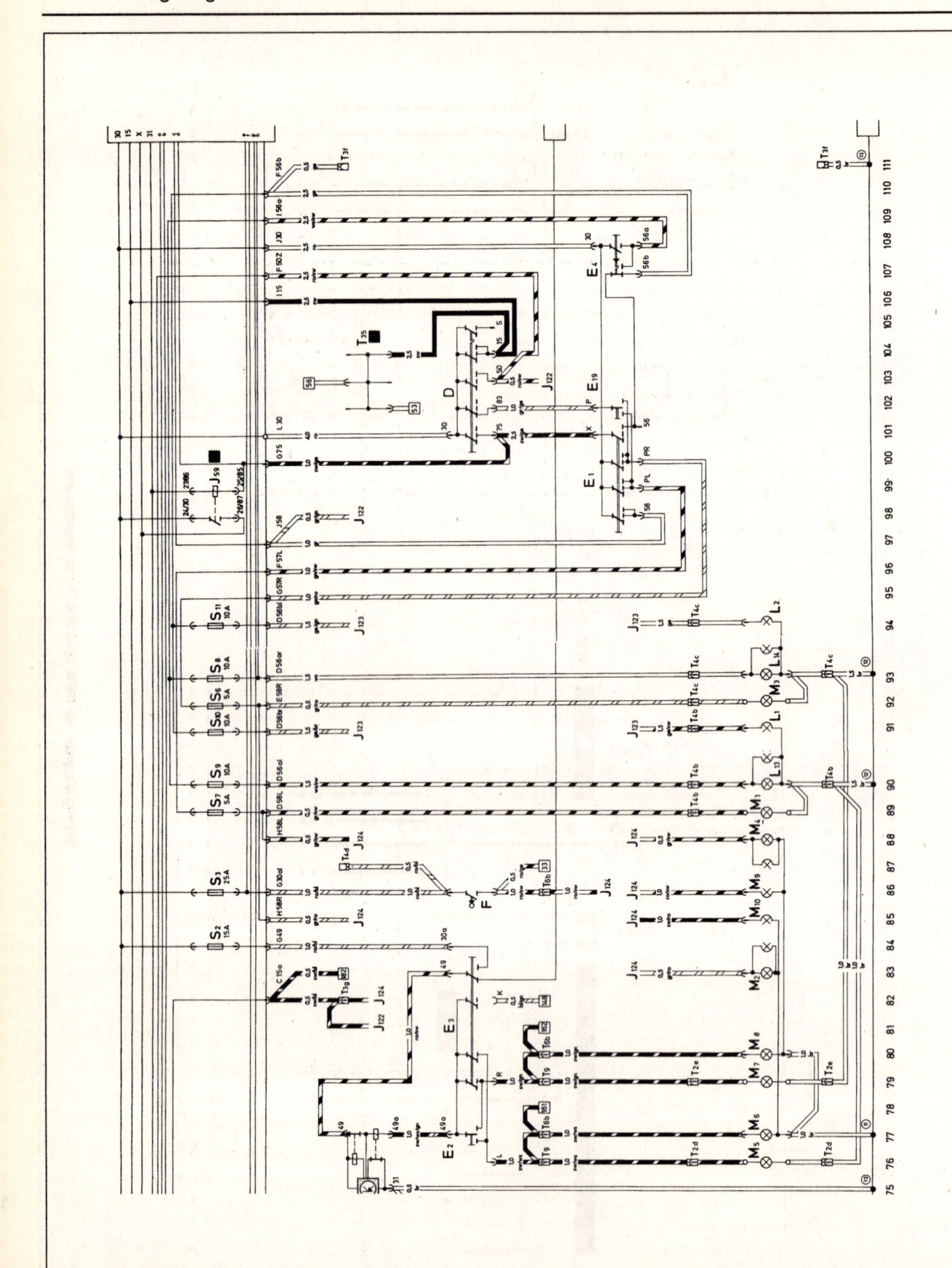

Wiring diagram for 1984 Audi 200 Turbo (continued)

Wiring diagrams 14•15

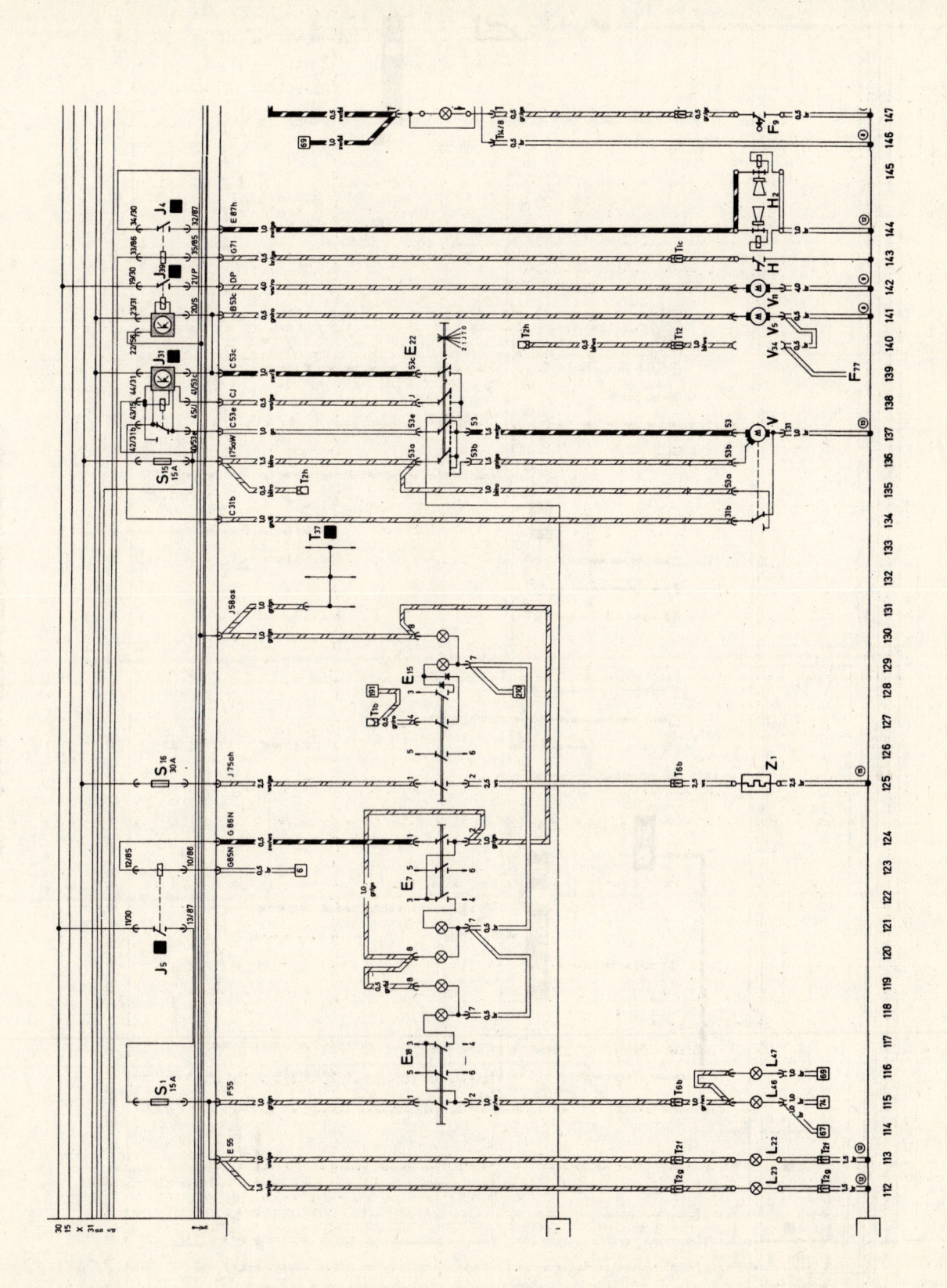

Wiring diagram for 1984 Audi 200 Turbo (continued)

14•16 Wiring diagrams

Wiring diagram for 1984 Audi 200 Turbo (continued)

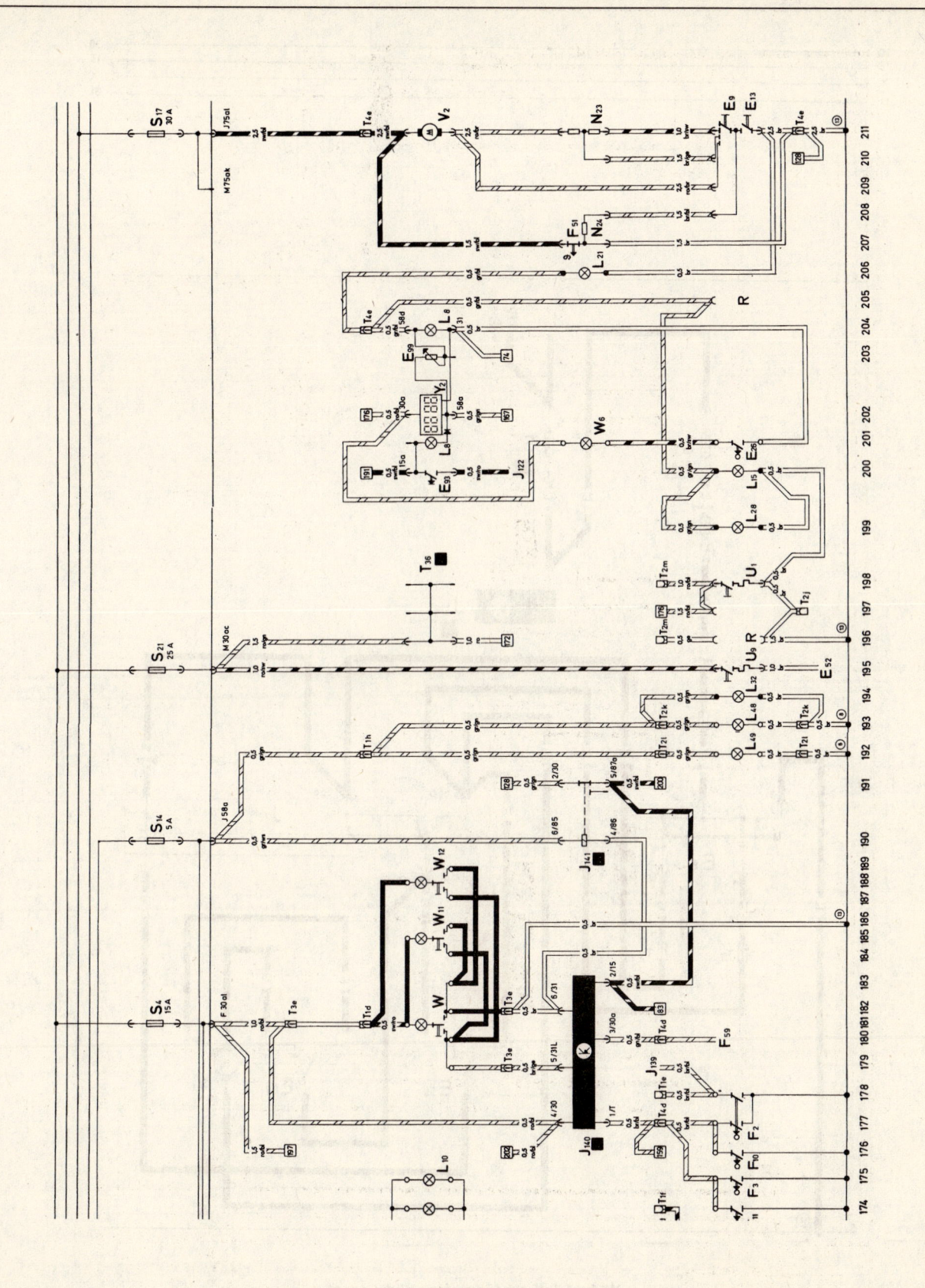

Wiring diagram for 1984 Audi 200 Turbo (continued)

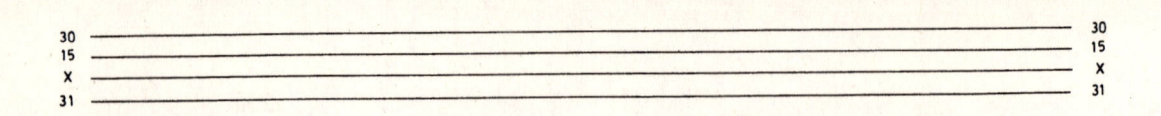

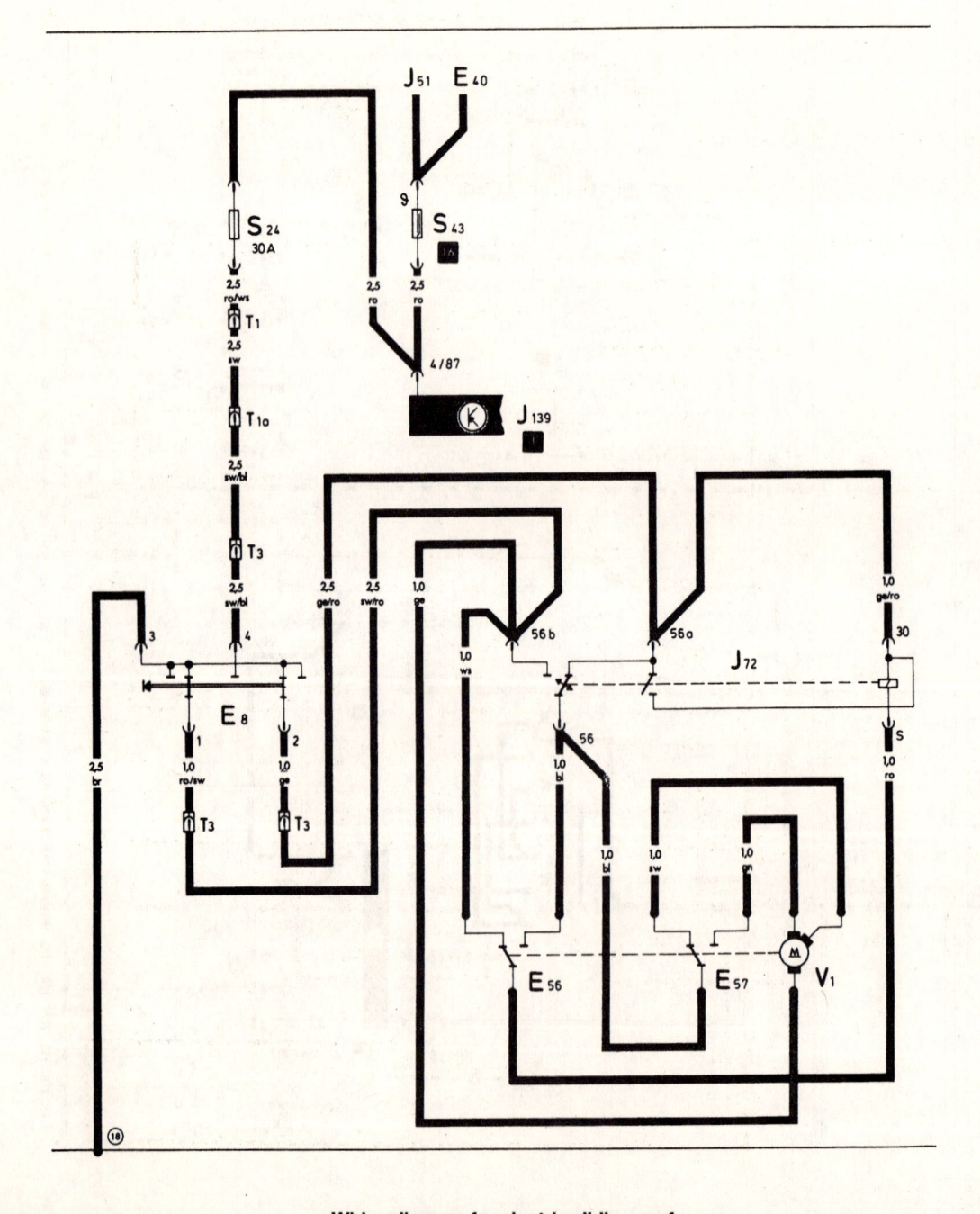

Wiring diagram for electric sliding roof

Wiring diagrams 14•19

Wiring diagram for electric windows

14•20 Wiring diagrams

Wiring diagram for auto check system

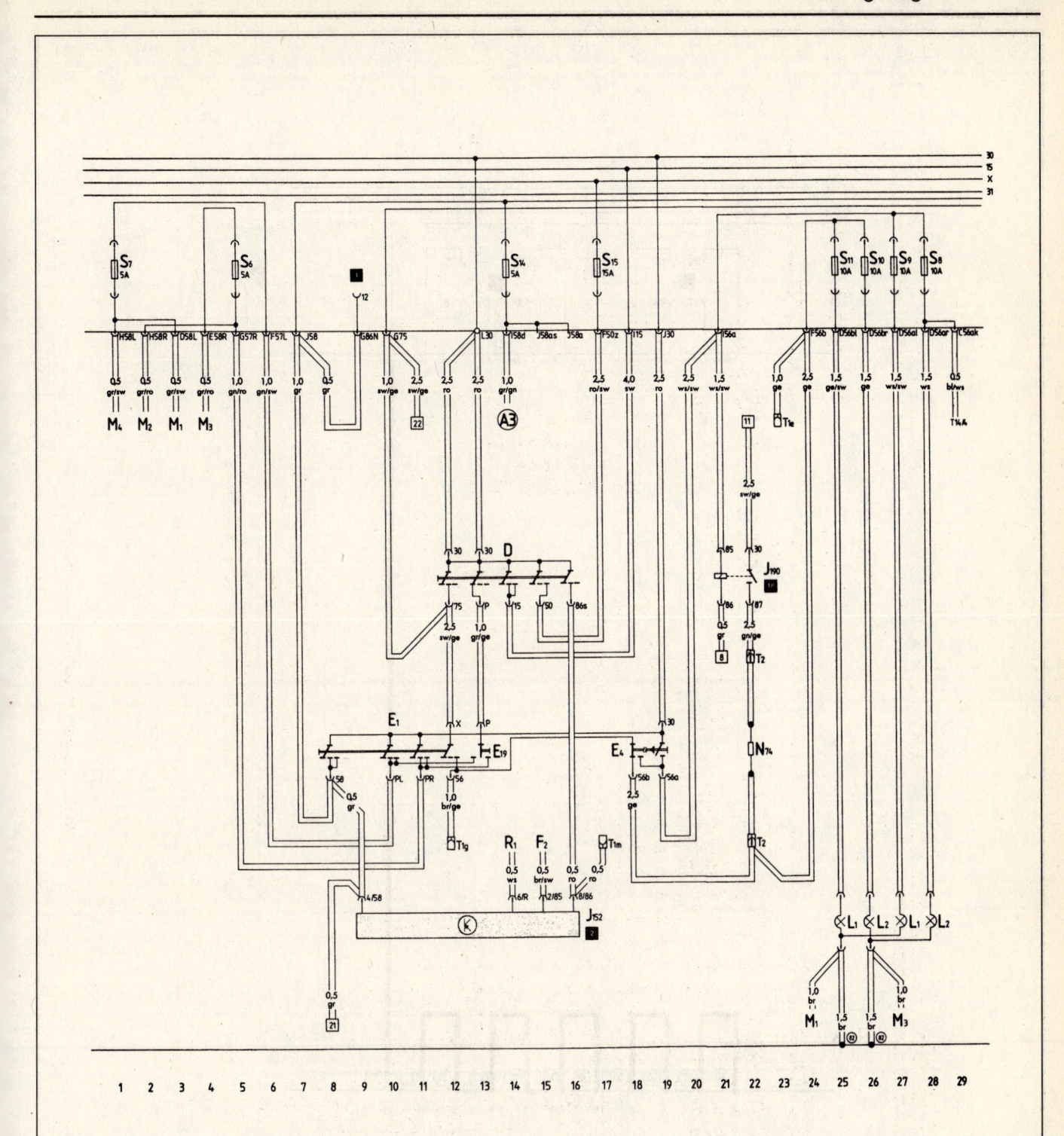

Wiring diagram for dim-dip lighting

14•22 Wiring diagrams

Wiring diagram for earth connections - 2.3 litre NF engine

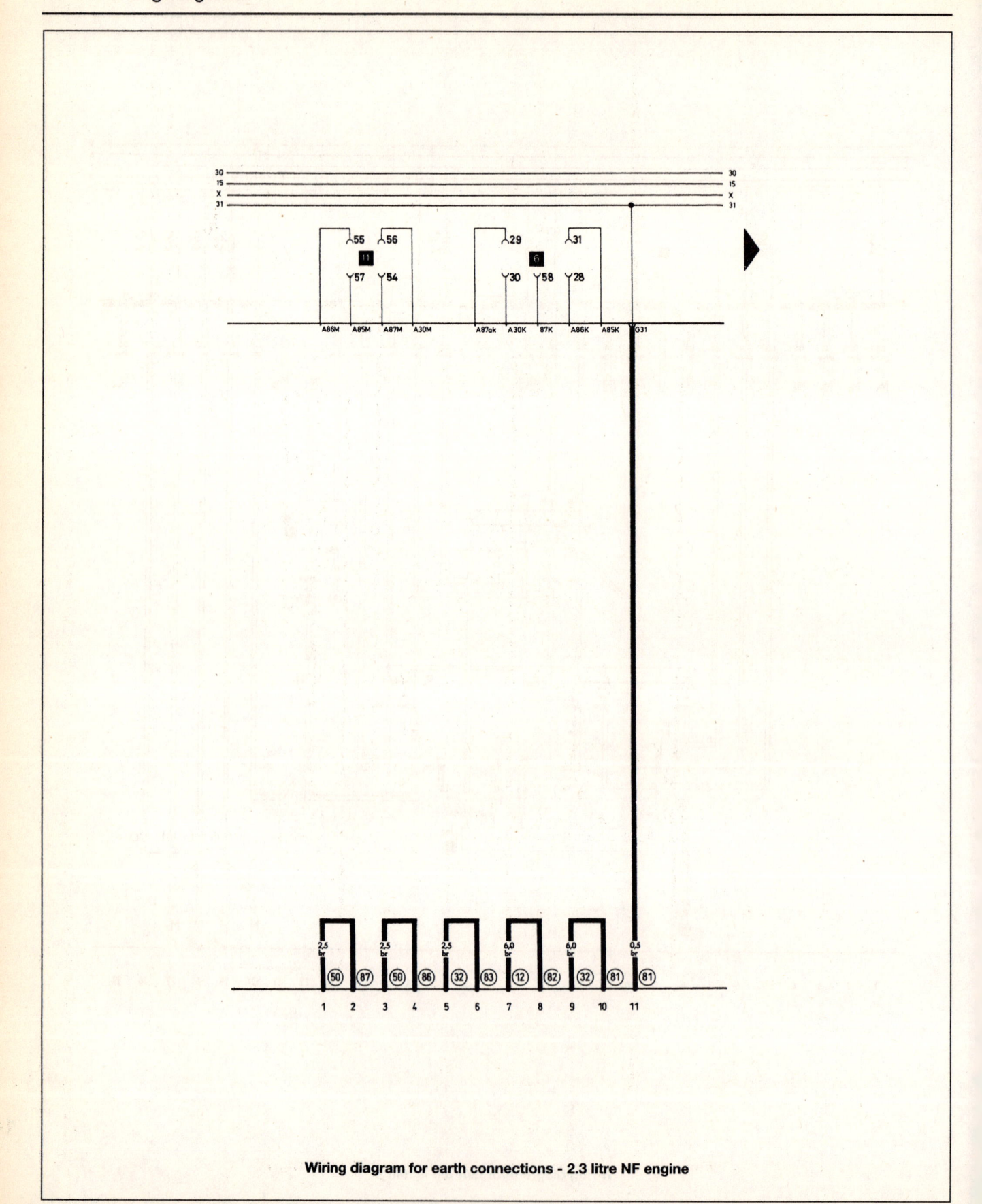

Wiring diagrams 14•23

Wiring diagram for battery, starter and alternator - 2.3 litre NF engine

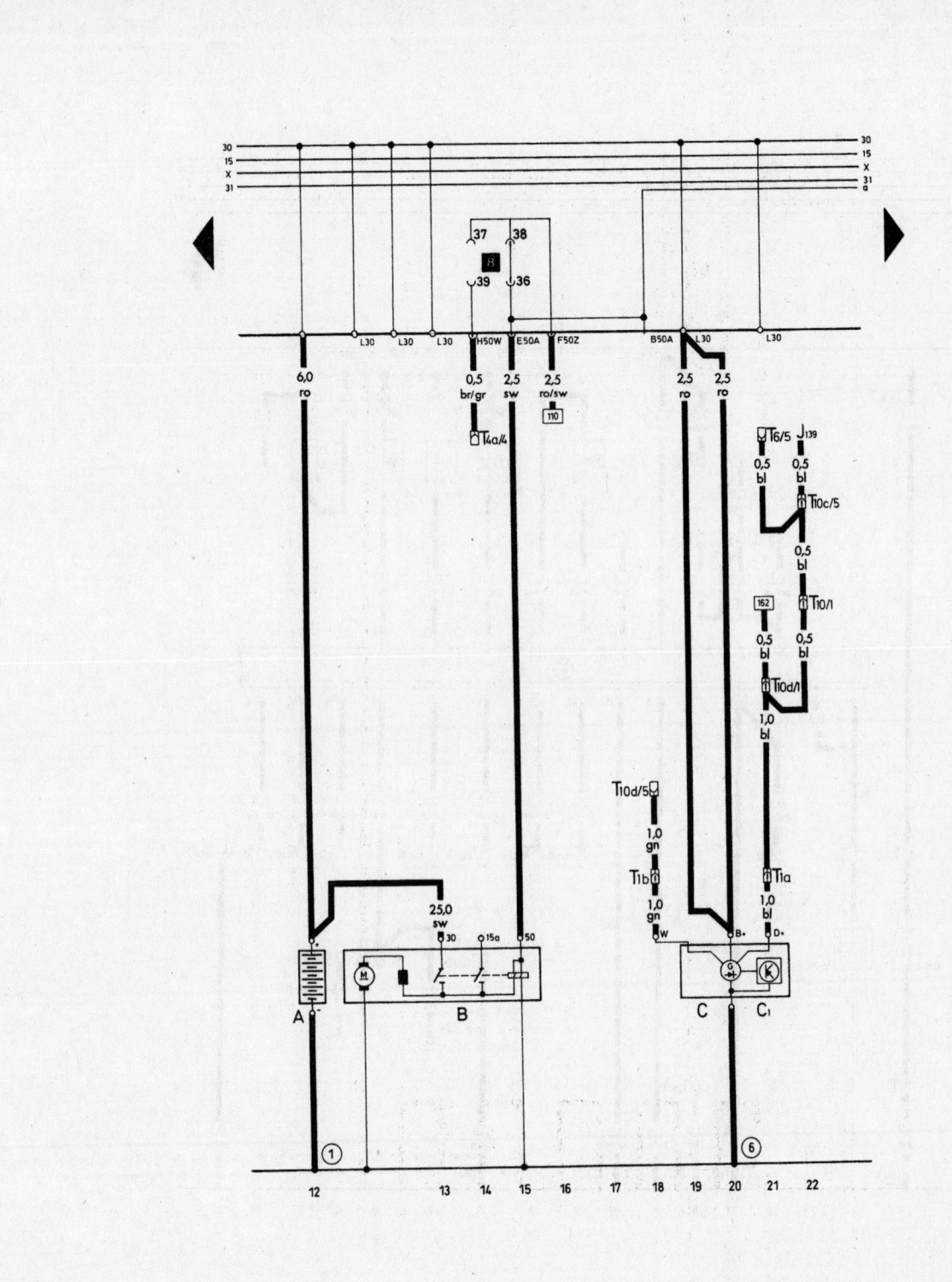

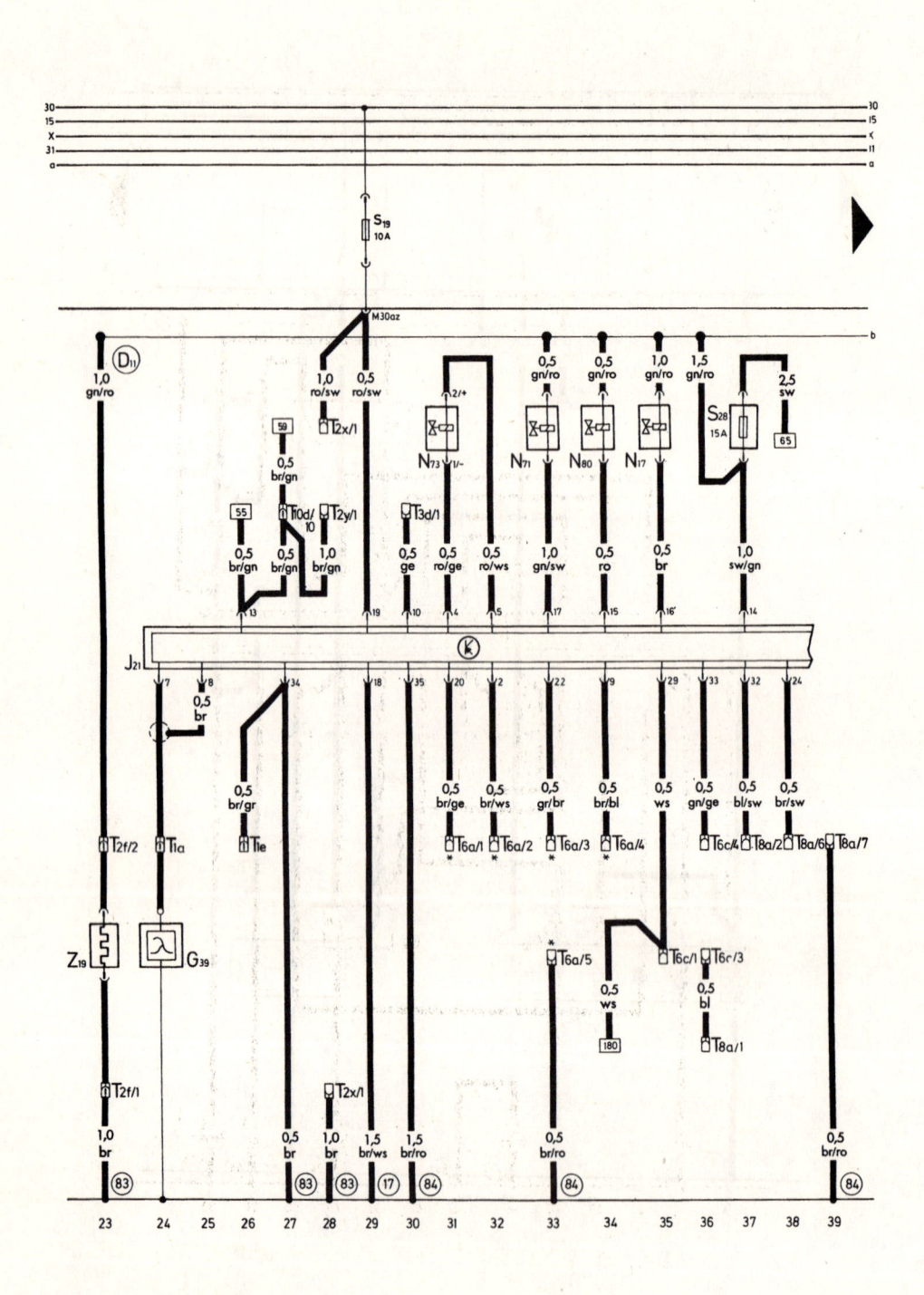

Wiring diagram for KE-Jetronic control unit, heated Lambda probe, diagnosis probe plug and coding plug - 2.3 litre NF engine

Wiring diagrams 14•25

Wiring diagram for KE-Jetronic control unit, electronic ignition control unit with knock control, and throttle switch - 2.3 litre NF engine

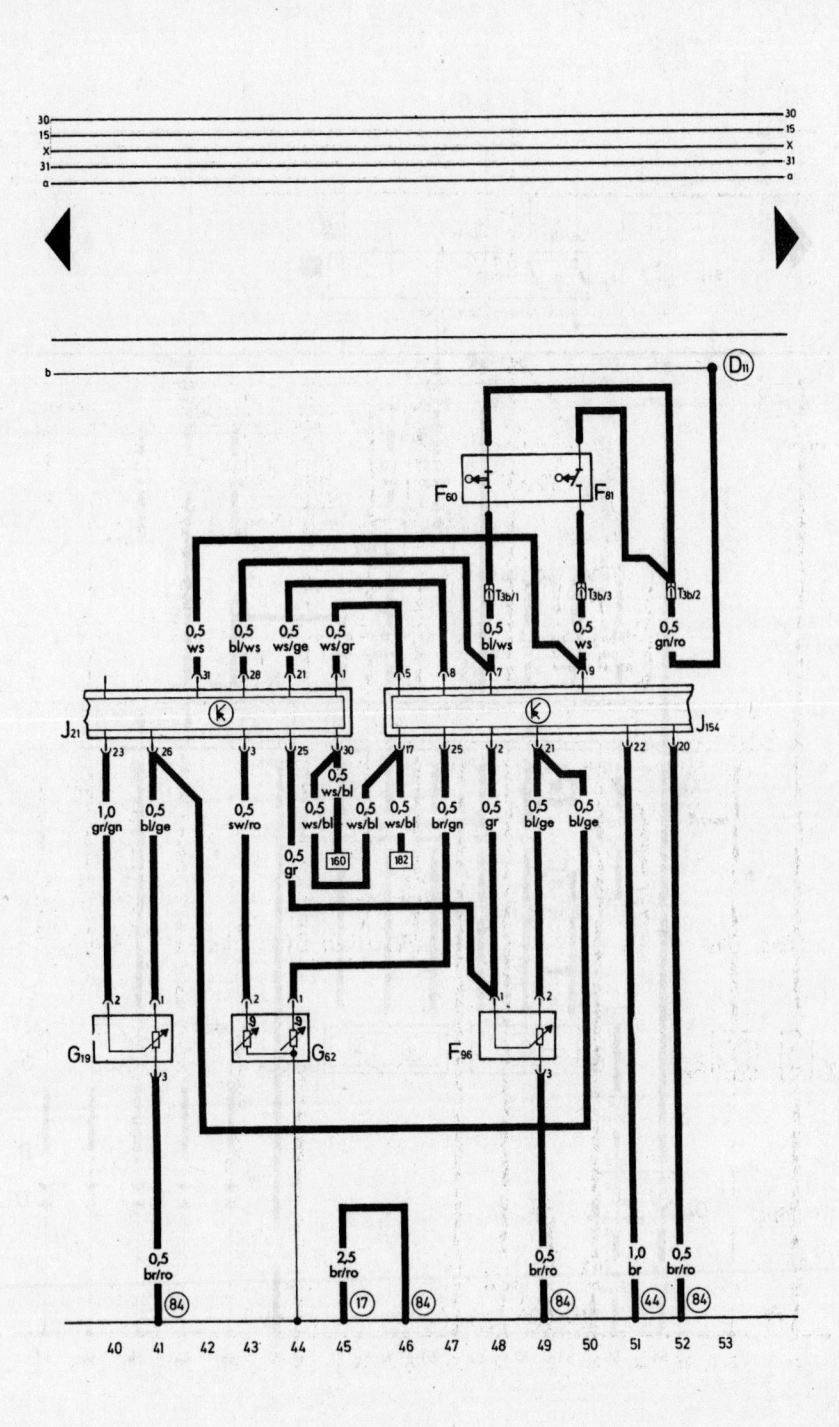

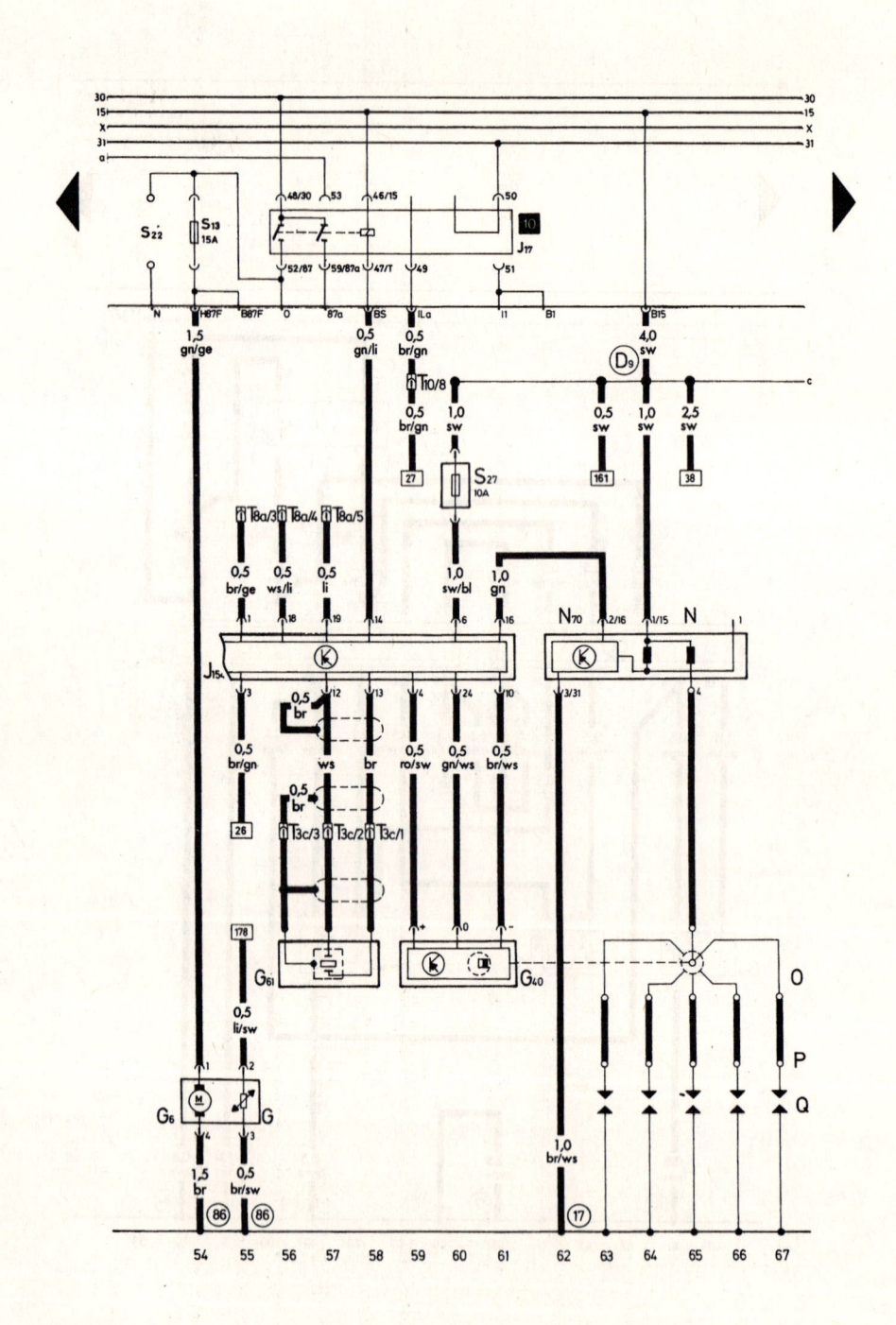

Wiring diagram for electronic ignition control unit with knock control, fuel pump relay, knock sensor, and ignition coil - 2.3 litre NF engine

Wiring diagrams 14•27

Wiring diagram for radiator fan run-on – 2.3 litre NF engine

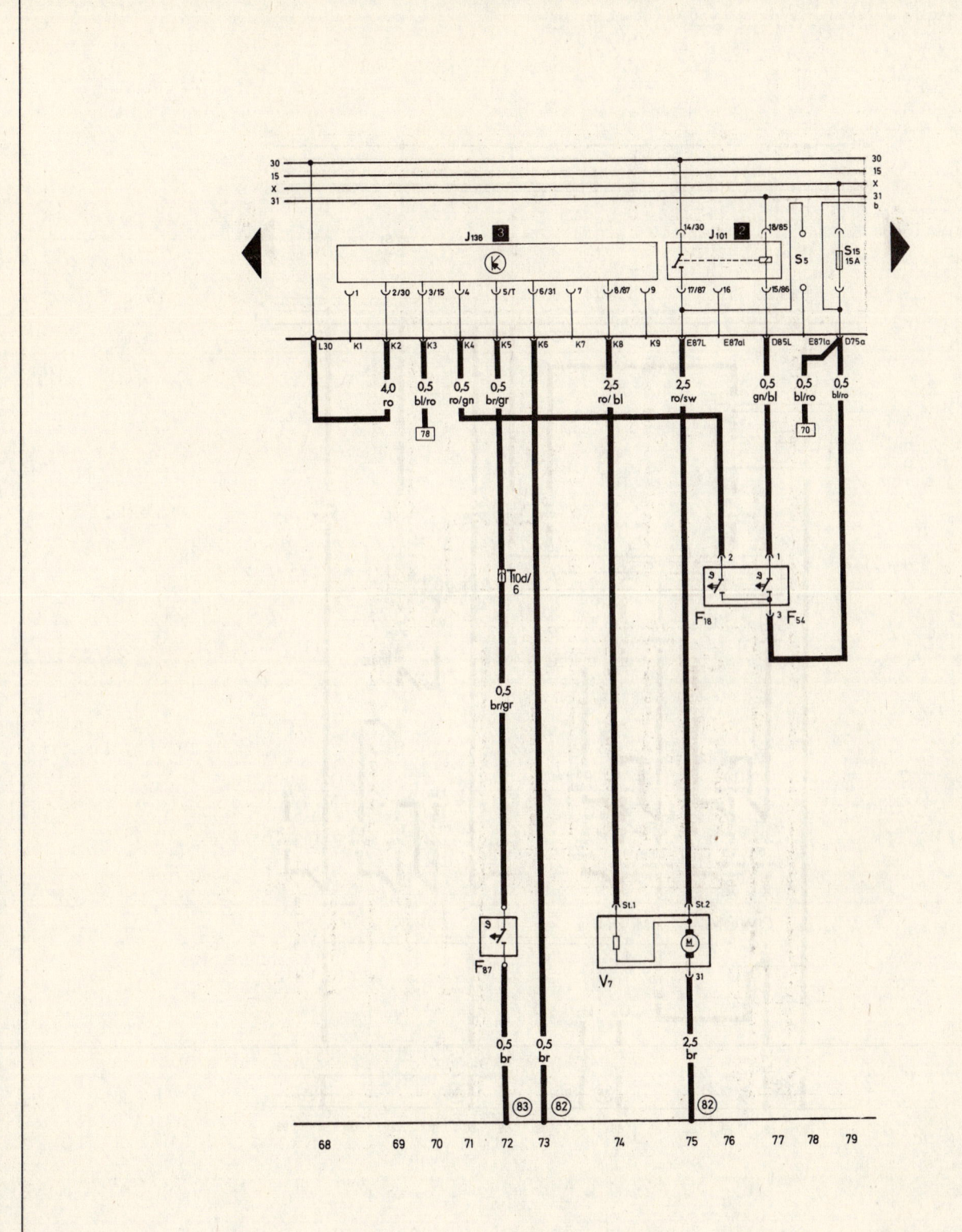

Wiring diagram for indicators and hazard lights, rear lights and brake lights - 2.3 litre NF engine

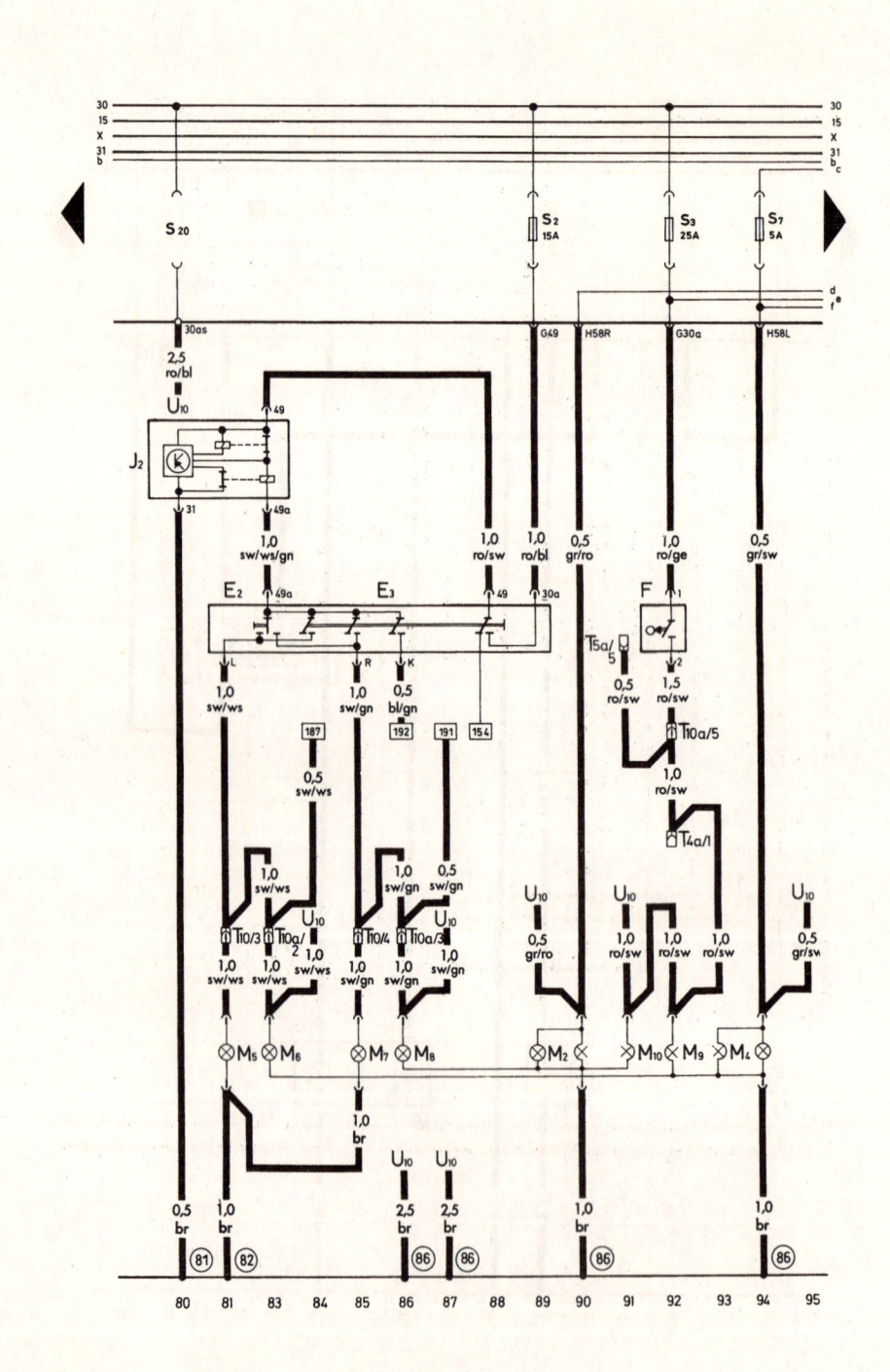

Wiring diagrams 14•29

Wiring diagram for ignition switch, lighting switch, buzzer for side-lights and radio, and side lights - 2.3 litre NF engine

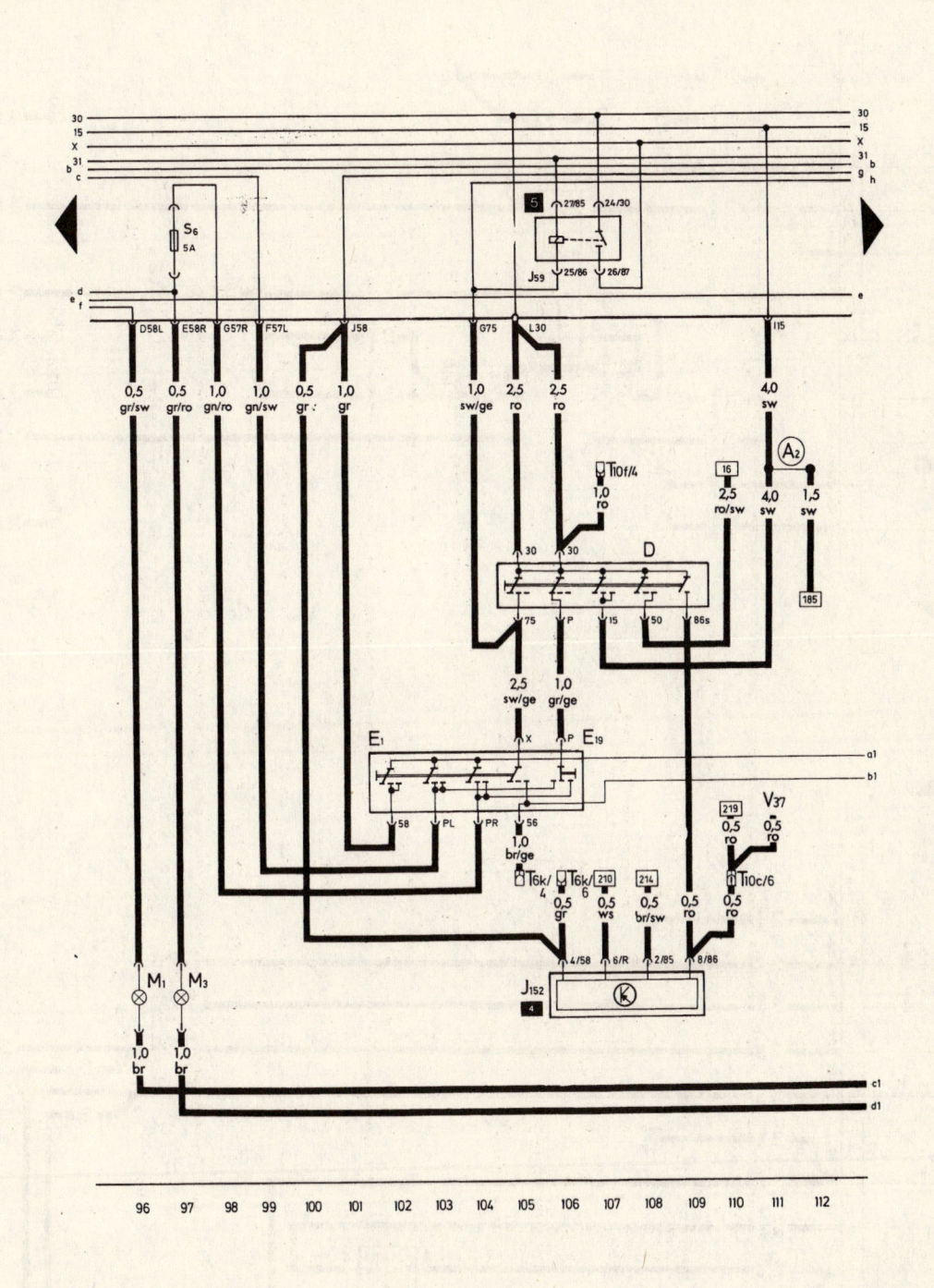

14•30 Wiring diagrams

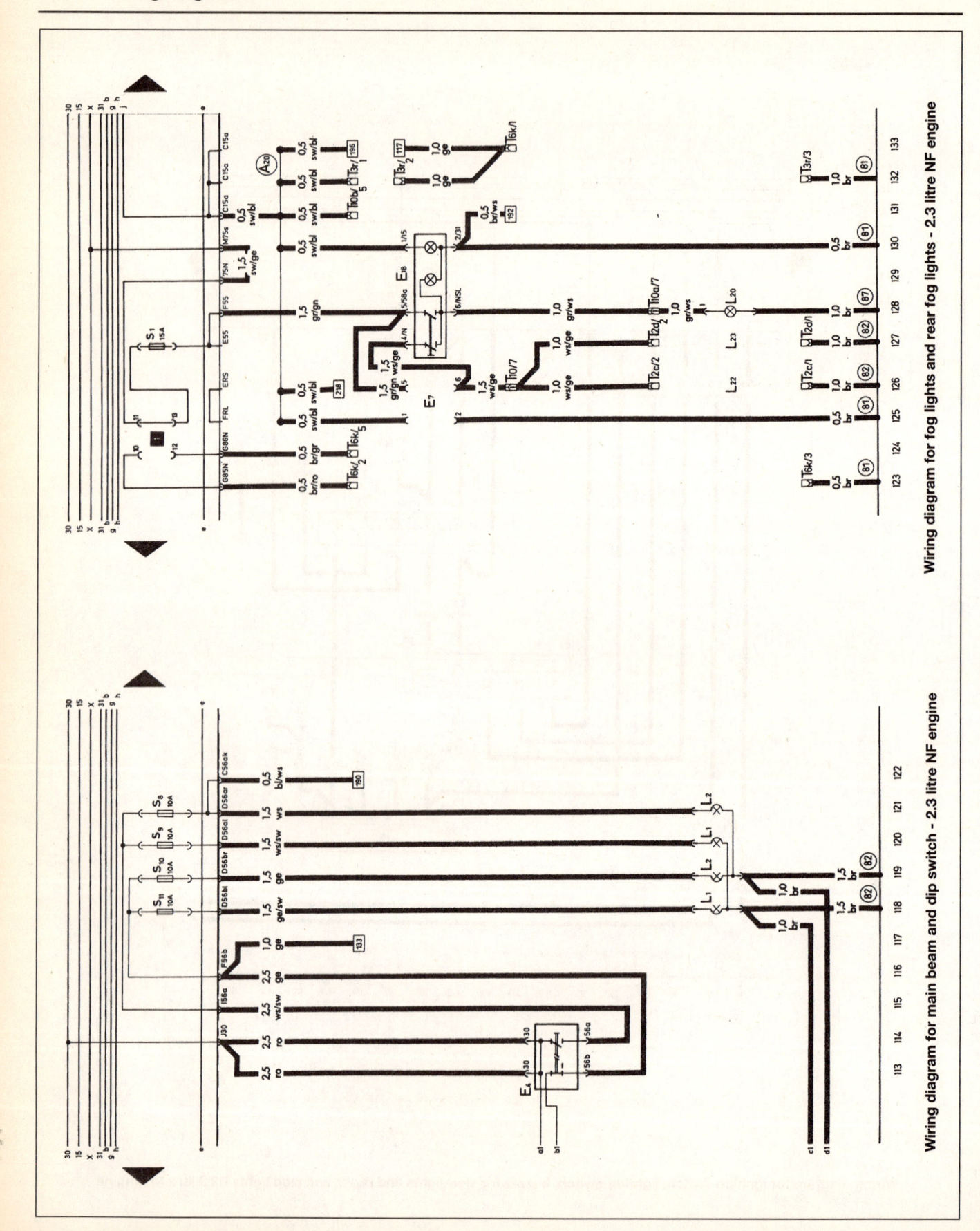

Wiring diagram for fog lights and rear fog lights - 2.3 litre NF engine

Wiring diagram for main beam and dip switch - 2.3 litre NF engine

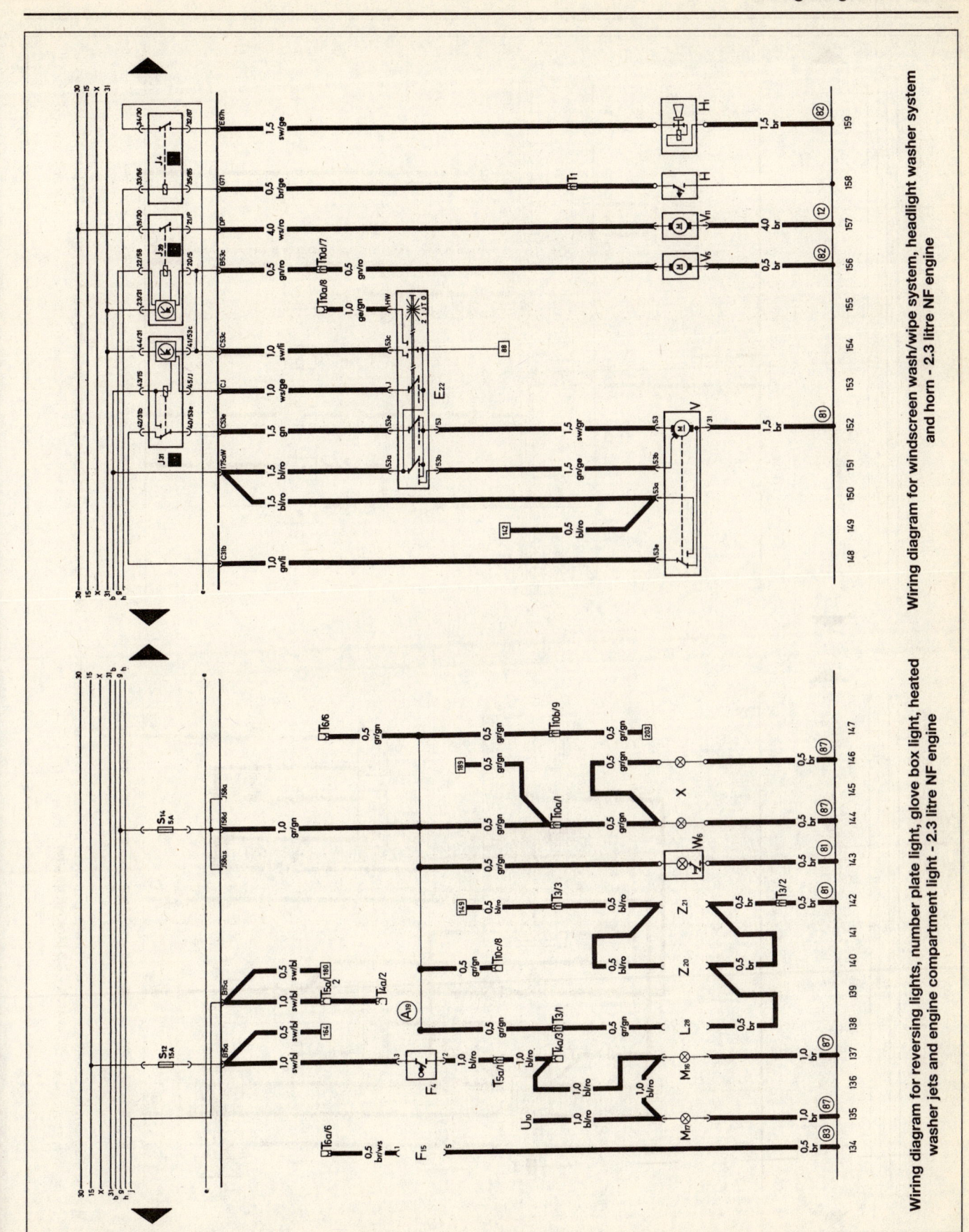

Wiring diagram for windscreen wash/wipe system, headlight washer system and horn - 2.3 litre NF engine

Wiring diagram for reversing lights, number plate light, glove box light, heated washer jets and engine compartment light - 2.3 litre NF engine

14•32 Wiring diagrams

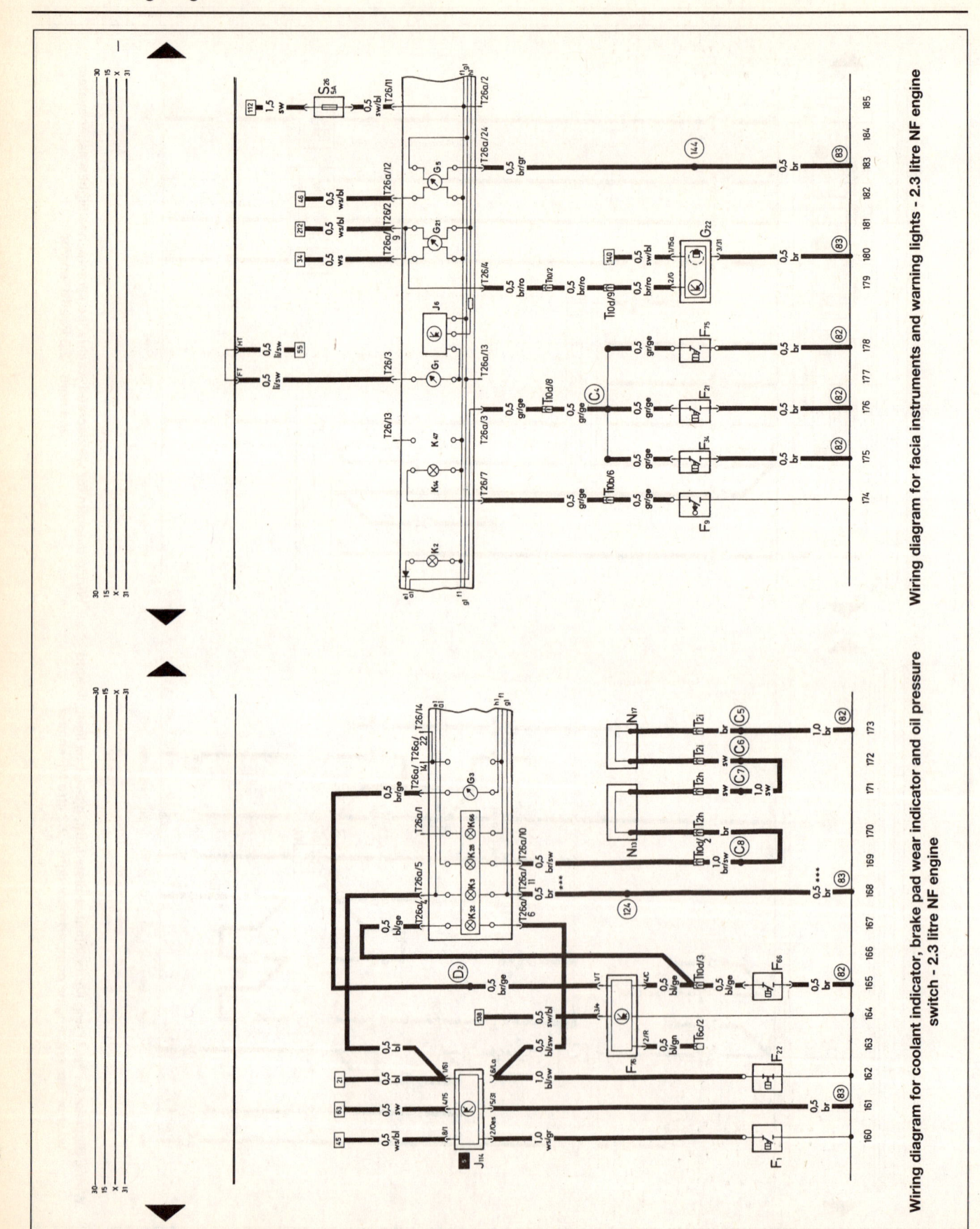

Wiring diagram for facia instruments and warning lights - 2.3 litre NF engine

Wiring diagram for coolant indicator, brake pad wear indicator and oil pressure switch - 2.3 litre NF engine

Wiring diagrams 14•33

Wiring diagram for heated rear window and interior fan - 2.3 litre NF engine

Wiring diagram for dashboard lighting and warning lights - 2.3 litre NF engine

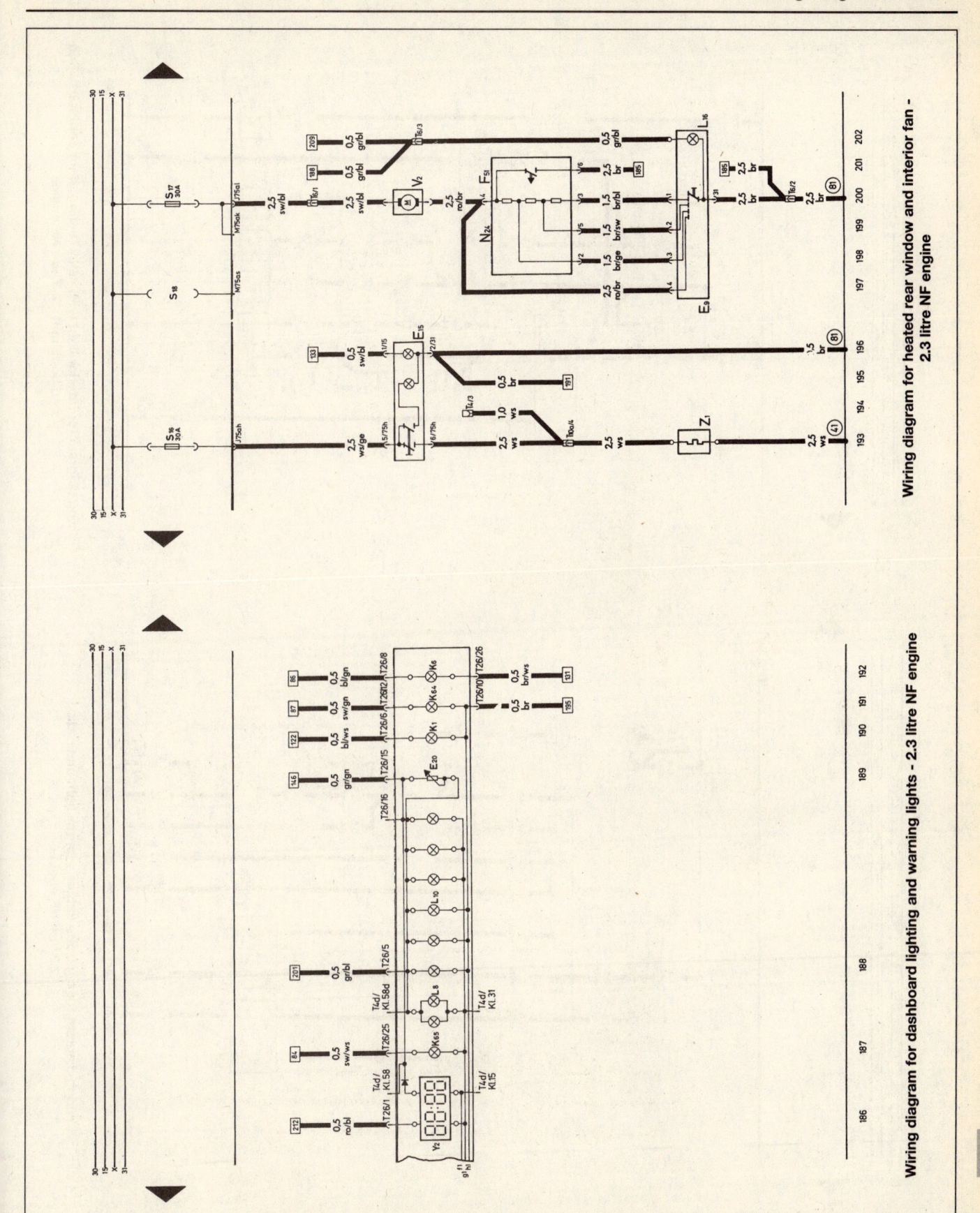

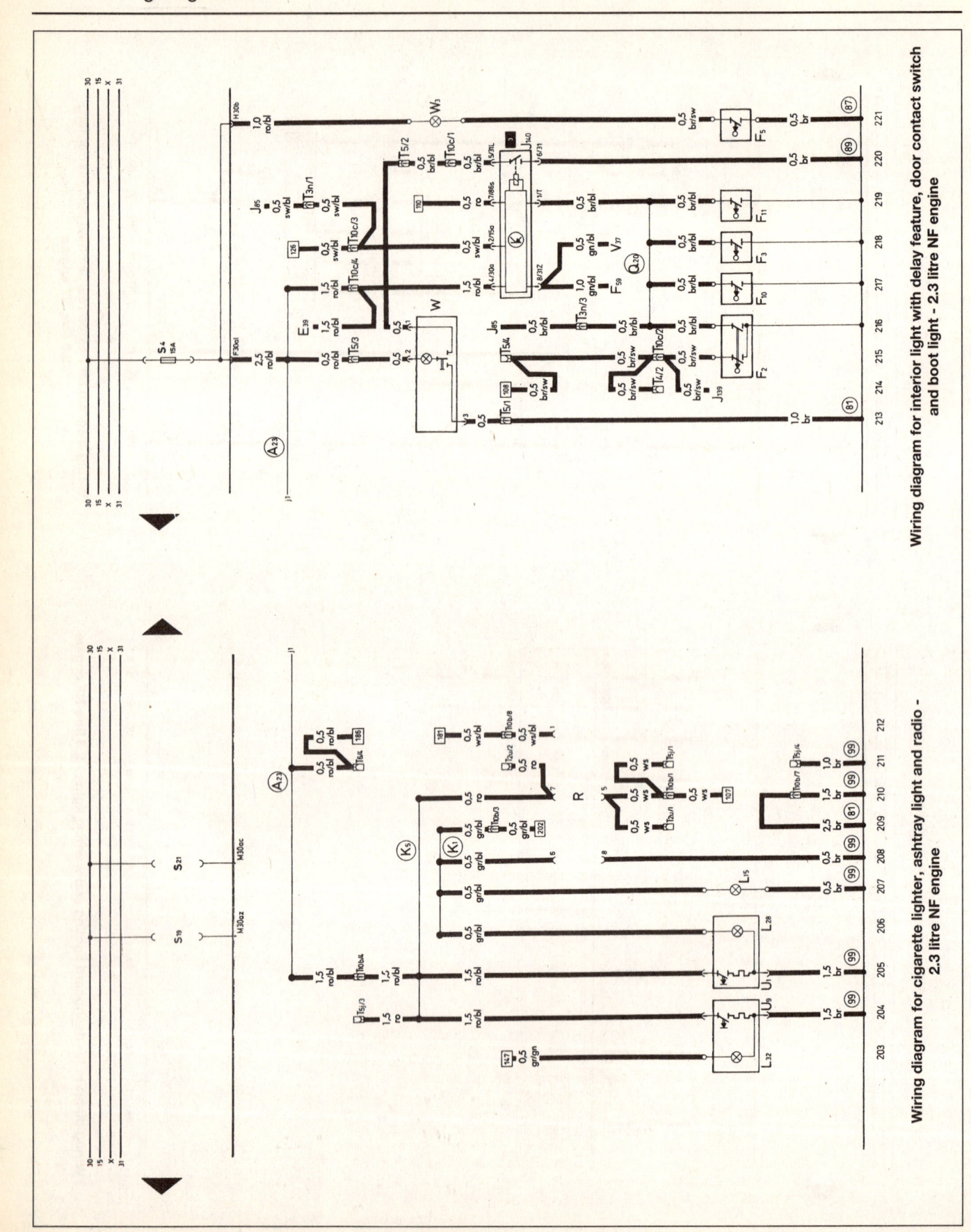

Wiring diagram for interior light with delay feature, door contact switch and boot light - 2.3 litre NF engine

Wiring diagram for cigarette lighter, ashtray light and radio - 2.3 litre NF engine

MOT Test Checks REF•1

This is a guide to getting your vehicle through the MOT test. Obviously it will not be possible to examine the vehicle to the same standard as the professional MOT tester. However, working through the following checks will enable you to identify any problem areas before submitting the vehicle for the test.

Where a testable component is in borderline condition, the tester has discretion in deciding whether to pass or fail it. The basis of such discretion is whether the tester would be happy for a close relative or friend to use the vehicle with the component in that condition. If the vehicle presented is clean and evidently well cared for, the tester may be more inclined to pass a borderline component than if the vehicle is scruffy and apparently neglected.

It has only been possible to summarise the test requirements here, based on the regulations in force at the time of printing. Test standards are becoming increasingly stringent, although there are some exemptions for older vehicles. For full details obtain a copy of the Haynes publication Pass the MOT! (available from stockists of Haynes manuals).

An assistant will be needed to help carry out some of these checks.

The checks have been sub-divided into four categories, as follows:

1 Checks carried out **FROM THE DRIVER'S SEAT**

2 Checks carried out **WITH THE VEHICLE ON THE GROUND**

3 Checks carried out **WITH THE VEHICLE RAISED AND THE WHEELS FREE TO TURN**

4 Checks carried out on **YOUR VEHICLE'S EXHAUST EMISSION SYSTEM**

---

1 Checks carried out **FROM THE DRIVER'S SEAT**

Handbrake

☐ Test the operation of the handbrake. Excessive travel (too many clicks) indicates incorrect brake or cable adjustment.

☐ Check that the handbrake cannot be released by tapping the lever sideways. Check the security of the lever mountings.

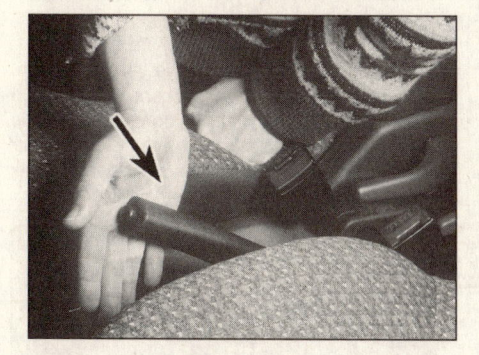

Footbrake

☐ Depress the brake pedal and check that it does not creep down to the floor, indicating a master cylinder fault. Release the pedal, wait a few seconds, then depress it again. If the pedal travels nearly to the floor before firm resistance is felt, brake adjustment or repair is necessary. If the pedal feels spongy, there is air in the hydraulic system which must be removed by bleeding.

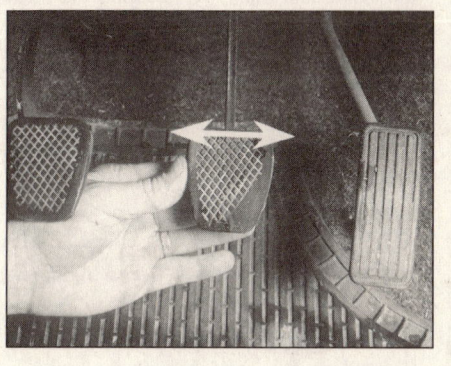

☐ Check that the brake pedal is secure and in good condition. Check also for signs of fluid leaks on the pedal, floor or carpets, which would indicate failed seals in the brake master cylinder.

☐ Check the servo unit (when applicable) by operating the brake pedal several times, then keeping the pedal depressed and starting the engine. As the engine starts, the pedal will move down slightly. If not, the vacuum hose or the servo itself may be faulty.

Steering wheel and column

☐ Examine the steering wheel for fractures or looseness of the hub, spokes or rim.

☐ Move the steering wheel from side to side and then up and down. Check that the steering wheel is not loose on the column, indicating wear or a loose retaining nut. Continue moving the steering wheel as before, but also turn it slightly from left to right.

☐ Check that the steering wheel is not loose on the column, and that there is no abnormal movement of the steering wheel, indicating wear in the column support bearings or couplings.

Windscreen and mirrors

☐ The windscreen must be free of cracks or other significant damage within the driver's field of view. (Small stone chips are acceptable.) Rear view mirrors must be secure, intact, and capable of being adjusted.

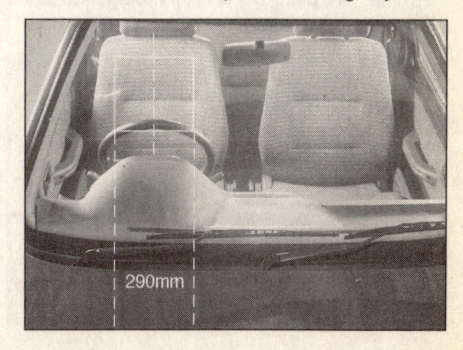

REF•2 MOT Test Checks

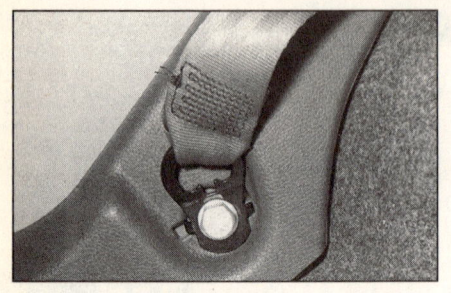

Seat belts and seats

Note: *The following checks are applicable to all seat belts, front and rear.*

☐ Examine the webbing of all the belts (including rear belts if fitted) for cuts, serious fraying or deterioration. Fasten and unfasten each belt to check the buckles. If applicable, check the retracting mechanism. Check the security of all seat belt mountings accessible from inside the vehicle.

☐ The front seats themselves must be securely attached and the backrests must lock in the upright position.

Doors

☐ Both front doors must be able to be opened and closed from outside and inside, and must latch securely when closed.

2 Checks carried out WITH THE VEHICLE ON THE GROUND

Vehicle identification

☐ Number plates must be in good condition, secure and legible, with letters and numbers correctly spaced – spacing at (A) should be twice that at (B).

☐ The VIN plate (A) and homologation plate (B) must be legible.

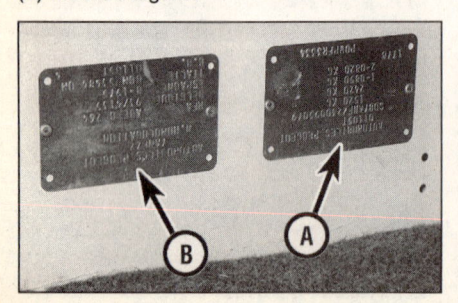

Electrical equipment

☐ Switch on the ignition and check the operation of the horn.

☐ Check the windscreen washers and wipers, examining the wiper blades; renew damaged or perished blades. Also check the operation of the stop-lights.

☐ Check the operation of the sidelights and number plate lights. The lenses and reflectors must be secure, clean and undamaged.

☐ Check the operation and alignment of the headlights. The headlight reflectors must not be tarnished and the lenses must be undamaged.

☐ Switch on the ignition and check the operation of the direction indicators (including the instrument panel tell-tale) and the hazard warning lights. Operation of the sidelights and stop-lights must not affect the indicators - if it does, the cause is usually a bad earth at the rear light cluster.

☐ Check the operation of the rear foglight(s), including the warning light on the instrument panel or in the switch.

Footbrake

☐ Examine the master cylinder, brake pipes and servo unit for leaks, loose mountings, corrosion or other damage.

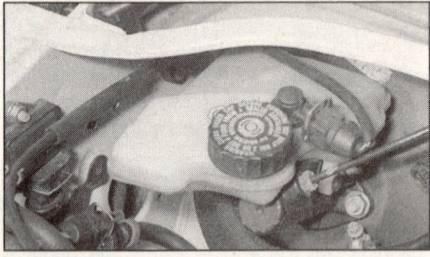

☐ The fluid reservoir must be secure and the fluid level must be between the upper (A) and lower (B) markings.

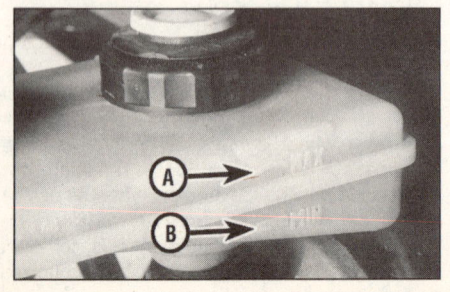

☐ Inspect both front brake flexible hoses for cracks or deterioration of the rubber. Turn the steering from lock to lock, and ensure that the hoses do not contact the wheel, tyre, or any part of the steering or suspension mechanism. With the brake pedal firmly depressed, check the hoses for bulges or leaks under pressure.

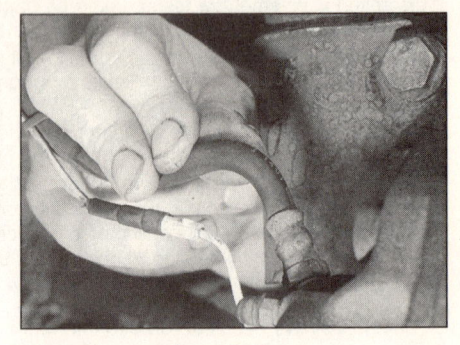

Steering and suspension

☐ Have your assistant turn the steering wheel from side to side slightly, up to the point where the steering gear just begins to transmit this movement to the roadwheels. Check for excessive free play between the steering wheel and the steering gear, indicating wear or insecurity of the steering column joints, the column-to-steering gear coupling, or the steering gear itself.

☐ Have your assistant turn the steering wheel more vigorously in each direction, so that the roadwheels just begin to turn. As this is done, examine all the steering joints, linkages, fittings and attachments. Renew any component that shows signs of wear or damage. On vehicles with power steering, check the security and condition of the steering pump, drivebelt and hoses.

☐ Check that the vehicle is standing level, and at approximately the correct ride height.

Shock absorbers

☐ Depress each corner of the vehicle in turn, then release it. The vehicle should rise and then settle in its normal position. If the vehicle continues to rise and fall, the shock absorber is defective. A shock absorber which has seized will also cause the vehicle to fail.

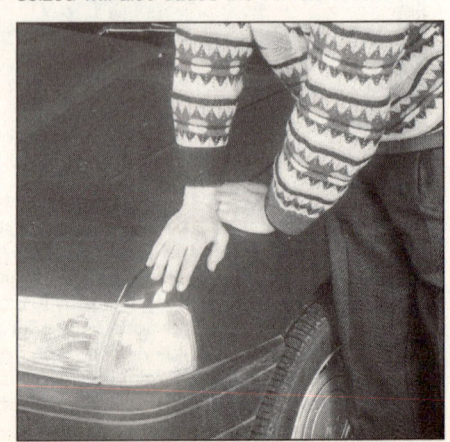

MOT Test Checks REF•3

Exhaust system

☐ Start the engine. With your assistant holding a rag over the tailpipe, check the entire system for leaks. Repair or renew leaking sections.

3 Checks carried out WITH THE VEHICLE RAISED AND THE WHEELS FREE TO TURN

Jack up the front and rear of the vehicle, and securely support it on axle stands. Position the stands clear of the suspension assemblies. Ensure that the wheels are clear of the ground and that the steering can be turned from lock to lock.

Steering mechanism

☐ Have your assistant turn the steering from lock to lock. Check that the steering turns smoothly, and that no part of the steering mechanism, including a wheel or tyre, fouls any brake hose or pipe or any part of the body structure.
☐ Examine the steering rack rubber gaiters for damage or insecurity of the retaining clips. If power steering is fitted, check for signs of damage or leakage of the fluid hoses, pipes or connections. Also check for excessive stiffness or binding of the steering, a missing split pin or locking device, or severe corrosion of the body structure within 30 cm of any steering component attachment point.

Front and rear suspension and wheel bearings

☐ Starting at the front right-hand side, grasp the roadwheel at the 3 o'clock and 9 o'clock positions and shake it vigorously. Check for free play or insecurity at the wheel bearings, suspension balljoints, or suspension mountings, pivots and attachments.
☐ Now grasp the wheel at the 12 o'clock and 6 o'clock positions and repeat the previous inspection. Spin the wheel, and check for roughness or tightness of the front wheel bearing.

☐ If excess free play is suspected at a component pivot point, this can be confirmed by using a large screwdriver or similar tool and levering between the mounting and the component attachment. This will confirm whether the wear is in the pivot bush, its retaining bolt, or in the mounting itself (the bolt holes can often become elongated).

☐ Carry out all the above checks at the other front wheel, and then at both rear wheels.

Springs and shock absorbers

☐ Examine the suspension struts (when applicable) for serious fluid leakage, corrosion, or damage to the casing. Also check the security of the mounting points.
☐ If coil springs are fitted, check that the spring ends locate in their seats, and that the spring is not corroded, cracked or broken.
☐ If leaf springs are fitted, check that all leaves are intact, that the axle is securely attached to each spring, and that there is no deterioration of the spring eye mountings, bushes, and shackles.

☐ The same general checks apply to vehicles fitted with other suspension types, such as torsion bars, hydraulic displacer units, etc. Ensure that all mountings and attachments are secure, that there are no signs of excessive wear, corrosion or damage, and (on hydraulic types) that there are no fluid leaks or damaged pipes.
☐ Inspect the shock absorbers for signs of serious fluid leakage. Check for wear of the mounting bushes or attachments, or damage to the body of the unit.

Driveshafts (fwd vehicles only)

☐ Rotate each front wheel in turn and inspect the constant velocity joint gaiters for splits or damage. Also check that each driveshaft is straight and undamaged.

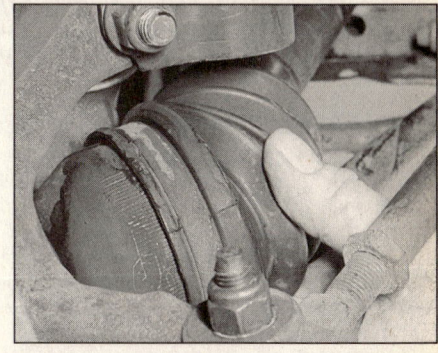

Braking system

☐ If possible without dismantling, check brake pad wear and disc condition. Ensure that the friction lining material has not worn excessively, (A) and that the discs are not fractured, pitted, scored or badly worn (B).

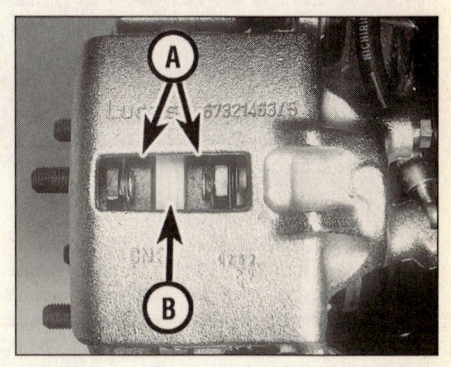

☐ Examine all the rigid brake pipes underneath the vehicle, and the flexible hose(s) at the rear. Look for corrosion, chafing or insecurity of the pipes, and for signs of bulging under pressure, chafing, splits or deterioration of the flexible hoses.
☐ Look for signs of fluid leaks at the brake calipers or on the brake backplates. Repair or renew leaking components.
☐ Slowly spin each wheel, while your assistant depresses and releases the footbrake. Ensure that each brake is operating and does not bind when the pedal is released.

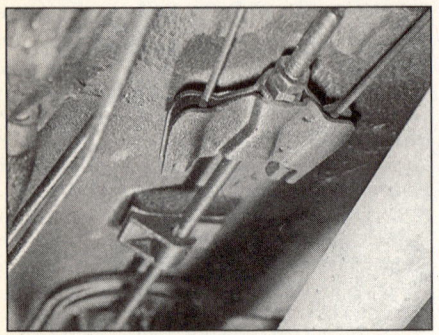

REF•4 MOT Test Checks

☐ Examine the handbrake mechanism, checking for frayed or broken cables, excessive corrosion, or wear or insecurity of the linkage. Check that the mechanism works on each relevant wheel, and releases fully, without binding.

☐ It is not possible to test brake efficiency without special equipment, but a road test can be carried out later to check that the vehicle pulls up in a straight line.

Fuel and exhaust systems

☐ Inspect the fuel tank (including the filler cap), fuel pipes, hoses and unions. All components must be secure and free from leaks.

☐ Examine the exhaust system over its entire length, checking for any damaged, broken or missing mountings, security of the retaining clamps and rust or corrosion.

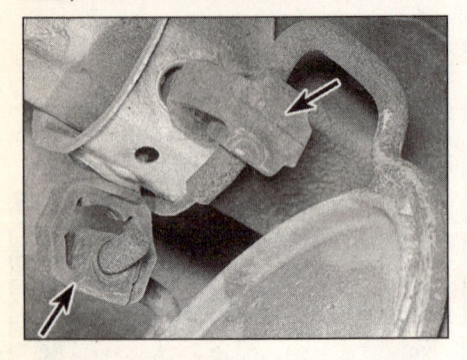

Wheels and tyres

☐ Examine the sidewalls and tread area of each tyre in turn. Check for cuts, tears, lumps, bulges, separation of the tread, and exposure of the ply or cord due to wear or damage. Check that the tyre bead is correctly seated on the wheel rim, that the valve is sound and properly seated, and that the wheel is not distorted or damaged.

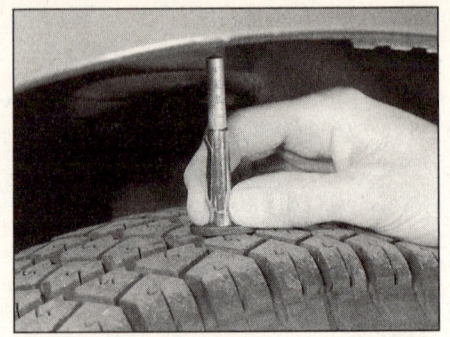

☐ Check that the tyres are of the correct size for the vehicle, that they are of the same size and type on each axle, and that the pressures are correct.

☐ Check the tyre tread depth. The legal minimum at the time of writing is 1.6 mm over at least three-quarters of the tread width. Abnormal tread wear may indicate incorrect front wheel alignment.

Body corrosion

☐ Check the condition of the entire vehicle structure for signs of corrosion in load-bearing areas. (These include chassis box sections, side sills, cross-members, pillars, and all suspension, steering, braking system and seat belt mountings and anchorages.) Any corrosion which has seriously reduced the thickness of a load-bearing area is likely to cause the vehicle to fail. In this case professional repairs are likely to be needed.

☐ Damage or corrosion which causes sharp or otherwise dangerous edges to be exposed will also cause the vehicle to fail.

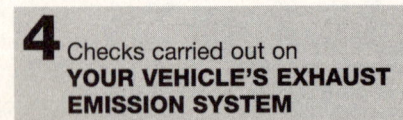

4 Checks carried out on YOUR VEHICLE'S EXHAUST EMISSION SYSTEM

Petrol models

☐ Have the engine at normal operating temperature, and make sure that it is in good tune (ignition system in good order, air filter element clean, etc).

☐ Before any measurements are carried out, raise the engine speed to around 2500 rpm, and hold it at this speed for 20 seconds. Allow the engine speed to return to idle, and watch for smoke emissions from the exhaust tailpipe. If the idle speed is obviously much too high, or if dense blue or clearly-visible black smoke comes from the tailpipe for more than 5 seconds, the vehicle will fail. As a rule of thumb, blue smoke signifies oil being burnt (engine wear) while black smoke signifies unburnt fuel (dirty air cleaner element, or other carburettor or fuel system fault).

☐ An exhaust gas analyser capable of measuring carbon monoxide (CO) and hydrocarbons (HC) is now needed. If such an instrument cannot be hired or borrowed, a local garage may agree to perform the check for a small fee.

CO emissions (mixture)

☐ At the time or writing, the maximum CO level at idle is 3.5% for vehicles first used after August 1986 and 4.5% for older vehicles. From January 1996 a much tighter limit (around 0.5%) applies to catalyst-equipped vehicles first used from August 1992. If the CO level cannot be reduced far enough to pass the test (and the fuel and ignition systems are otherwise in good condition) then the carburettor is badly worn, or there is some problem in the fuel injection system or catalytic converter (as applicable).

HC emissions

☐ With the CO emissions within limits, HC emissions must be no more than 1200 ppm (parts per million). If the vehicle fails this test at idle, it can be re-tested at around 2000 rpm; if the HC level is then 1200 ppm or less, this counts as a pass.

☐ Excessive HC emissions can be caused by oil being burnt, but they are more likely to be due to unburnt fuel.

Diesel models

☐ The only emission test applicable to Diesel engines is the measuring of exhaust smoke density. The test involves accelerating the engine several times to its maximum unloaded speed.

Note: *It is of the utmost importance that the engine timing belt is in good condition before the test is carried out.*

☐ Excessive smoke can be caused by a dirty air cleaner element. Otherwise, professional advice may be needed to find the cause.

Tools and Working Facilities

Introduction

A selection of good tools is a fundamental requirement for anyone contemplating the maintenance and repair of a motor vehicle. For the owner who does not possess any, their purchase will prove a considerable expense, offsetting some of the savings made by doing-it-yourself. However, provided that the tools purchased meet the relevant national safety standards and are of good quality, they will last for many years and prove an extremely worthwhile investment.

To help the average owner to decide which tools are needed to carry out the various tasks detailed in this manual, we have compiled three lists of tools under the following headings: *Maintenance and minor repair*, *Repair and overhaul*, and *Special*. Newcomers to practical mechanics should start off with the *Maintenance and minor repair* tool kit, and confine themselves to the simpler jobs around the vehicle. Then, as confidence and experience grow, more difficult tasks can be undertaken, with extra tools being purchased as, and when, they are needed. In this way, a *Maintenance and minor repair* tool kit can be built up into a *Repair and overhaul* tool kit over a considerable period of time, without any major cash outlays. The experienced do-it-yourselfer will have a tool kit good enough for most repair and overhaul procedures, and will add tools from the *Special* category when it is felt that the expense is justified by the amount of use to which these tools will be put.

Maintenance and minor repair tool kit

The tools given in this list should be considered as a minimum requirement if routine maintenance, servicing and minor repair operations are to be undertaken. We recommend the purchase of combination spanners (ring one end, open-ended the other); although more expensive than open-ended ones, they do give the advantages of both types of spanner.

☐ Combination spanners:
  Metric - 8, 9, 10, 11, 12, 13, 14, 15, 16, 17, 19, 21, 22, 24 & 26 mm
☐ Adjustable spanner - 35 mm jaw (approx)
☐ Set of feeler gauges
☐ Spark plug spanner (with rubber insert)
☐ Spark plug gap adjustment tool
☐ Brake bleed nipple spanner
☐ Screwdrivers:
  Flat blade - approx 100 mm long x 6 mm dia
  Cross blade - approx 100 mm long x 6 mm dia
☐ Combination pliers
☐ Hacksaw (junior)
☐ Tyre pump
☐ Tyre pressure gauge
☐ Oil can
☐ Oil filter removal tool
☐ Fine emery cloth
☐ Wire brush (small)
☐ Funnel (medium size)

Repair and overhaul tool kit

These tools are virtually essential for anyone undertaking any major repairs to a motor vehicle, and are additional to those given in the *Maintenance and minor repair* list. Included in this list is a comprehensive set of sockets. Although these are expensive, they will be found invaluable as they are so versatile - particularly if various drives are included in the set. We recommend the half-inch square-drive type, as this can be used with most proprietary torque wrenches. If you cannot afford a socket set, even bought piecemeal, then inexpensive tubular box spanners are a useful alternative.

The tools in this list will occasionally need to be supplemented by tools from the *Special* list:

☐ Sockets (or box spanners) to cover range in previous list
☐ Reversible ratchet drive (for use with sockets) **(see illustration)**
☐ Extension piece, 250 mm (for use with sockets)
☐ Universal joint (for use with sockets)
☐ Torque wrench (for use with sockets)
☐ Self-locking grips
☐ Ball pein hammer
☐ Soft-faced mallet (plastic/aluminium or rubber)
☐ Screwdrivers:
  Flat blade - long & sturdy, short (chubby), and narrow (electrician's) types
  Cross blade - Long & sturdy, and short (chubby) types
☐ Pliers:
  Long-nosed
  Side cutters (electrician's)
  Circlip (internal and external)
☐ Cold chisel - 25 mm
☐ Scriber
☐ Scraper
☐ Centre-punch
☐ Pin punch
☐ Hacksaw
☐ Brake hose clamp
☐ Brake bleeding kit
☐ Selection of twist drills
☐ Steel rule/straight-edge
☐ Allen keys (inc. splined/Torx type) **(see illustrations)**
☐ Selection of files
☐ Wire brush
☐ Axle stands
☐ Jack (strong trolley or hydraulic type)
☐ Light with extension lead

Special tools

The tools in this list are those which are not used regularly, are expensive to buy, or which need to be used in accordance with their manufacturers' instructions. Unless relatively difficult mechanical jobs are undertaken frequently, it will not be economic to buy many of these tools. Where this is the case, you could consider clubbing together with friends (or joining a motorists' club) to make a joint purchase, or borrowing the tools against a deposit from a local garage or tool hire specialist. It is worth noting that many of the larger DIY superstores now carry a large range of special tools for hire at modest rates.

The following list contains only those tools and instruments freely available to the public, and not those special tools produced by the vehicle manufacturer specifically for its dealer network. You will find occasional references to these manufacturers' special tools in the text of this manual. Generally, an alternative method of doing the job without the vehicle manufacturers' special tool is given. However, sometimes there is no alternative to using them. Where this is the case and the relevant tool cannot be bought or borrowed, you will have to entrust the work to a franchised garage.

☐ Valve spring compressor **(see illustration)**
☐ Valve grinding tool
☐ Piston ring compressor **(see illustration)**
☐ Piston ring removal/installation tool **(see illustration)**
☐ Cylinder bore hone **(see illustration)**
☐ Balljoint separator
☐ Coil spring compressors (where applicable)
☐ Two/three-legged hub and bearing puller **(see illustration)**

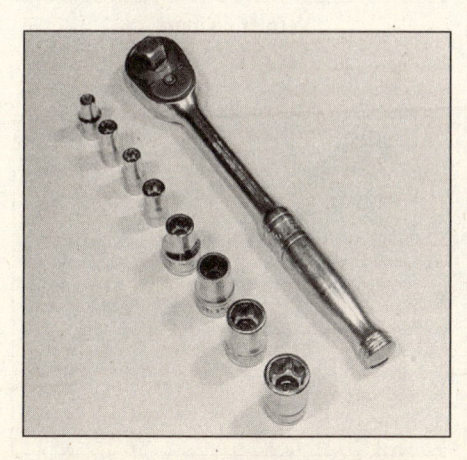

Sockets and reversible ratchet drive

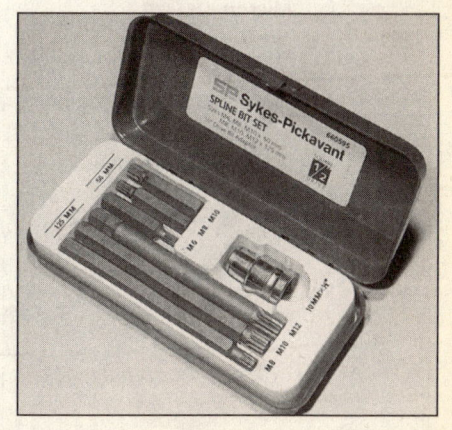

Spline bit set

Tools and Working Facilities

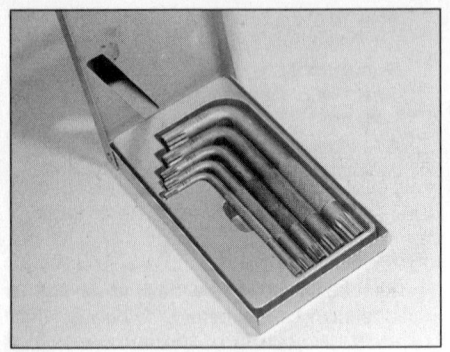

REF•6

Spline key set

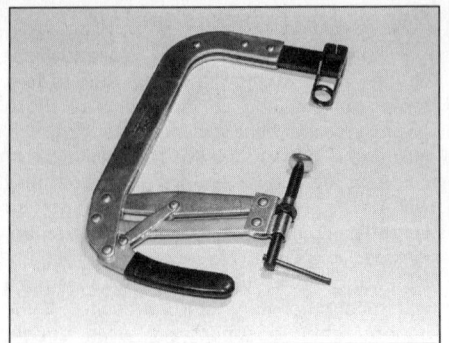

Valve spring compressor

Piston ring compressor

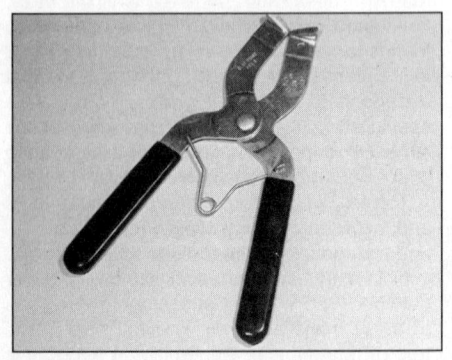

Piston ring removal/installation tool

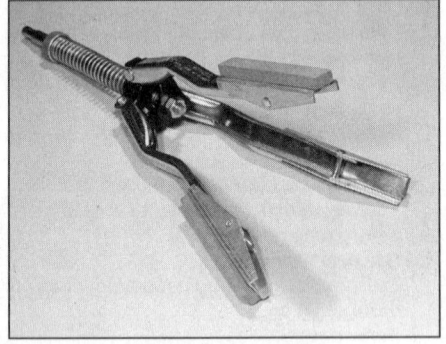

Cylinder bore hone

Three-legged hub and bearing puller

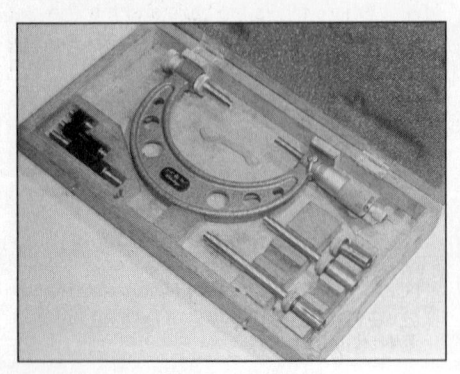

Micrometer set

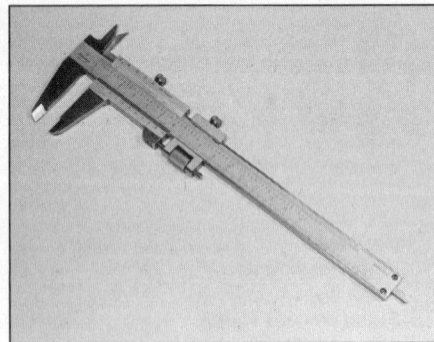

Vernier calipers

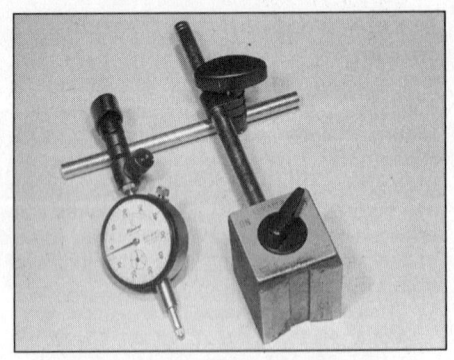

Dial test indicator and magnetic stand

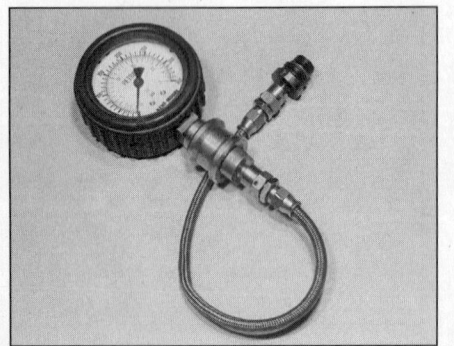

Compression testing gauge

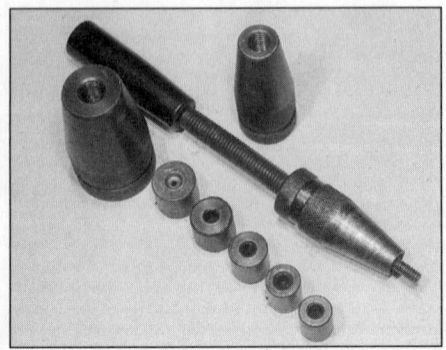

Clutch plate alignment set

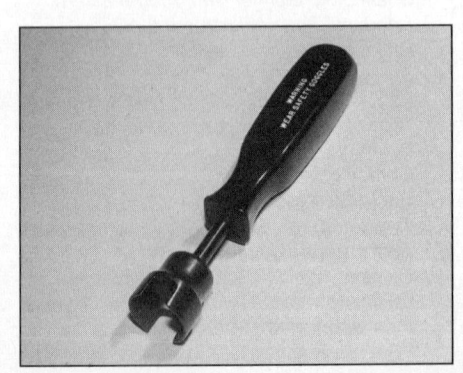

Brake shoe steady spring cup removal tool

Tools and Working Facilities

- ☐ Impact screwdriver
- ☐ Micrometer and/or vernier calipers *(see illustrations)*
- ☐ Dial gauge *(see illustration)*
- ☐ Universal electrical multi-meter
- ☐ Cylinder compression gauge *(see illustration)*
- ☐ Clutch plate alignment set *(see illustration)*
- ☐ Brake shoe steady spring cup removal tool *(see illustration)*
- ☐ Bush and bearing removal/installation set *(see illustration)*
- ☐ Stud extractors *(see illustration)*
- ☐ Tap and die set *(see illustration)*
- ☐ Lifting tackle
- ☐ Trolley jack

Buying tools

For practically all tools, a tool factor is the best source, since he will have a very comprehensive range compared with the average garage or accessory shop. Having said that, accessory shops often offer excellent quality tools at discount prices, so it pays to shop around.

Remember, you don't have to buy the most expensive items on the shelf, but it is always advisable to steer clear of the very cheap tools. There are plenty of good tools around at reasonable prices, but always aim to purchase items which meet the relevant national safety standards. If in doubt, ask the proprietor or manager of the shop for advice before making a purchase.

Care and maintenance of tools

Having purchased a reasonable tool kit, it is necessary to keep the tools in a clean and serviceable condition. After use, always wipe off any dirt, grease and metal particles using a clean, dry cloth, before putting the tools away. Never leave them lying around after they have been used. A simple tool rack on the garage or workshop wall for items such as screwdrivers and pliers is a good idea. Store all normal spanners and sockets in a metal box. Any measuring instruments, gauges, meters, etc, must be carefully stored where they cannot be damaged or become rusty.

Take a little care when tools are used. Hammer heads inevitably become marked, and screwdrivers lose the keen edge on their blades from time to time. A little timely attention with emery cloth or a file will soon restore items like this to a good serviceable finish.

Working facilities

Not to be forgotten when discussing tools is the workshop itself. If anything more than routine maintenance is to be carried out, some form of suitable working area becomes essential.

It is appreciated that many an owner-mechanic is forced by circumstances to remove an engine or similar item without the benefit of a garage or workshop. Having done this, any repairs should always be done under the cover of a roof.

Wherever possible, any dismantling should be done on a clean, flat workbench or table at a suitable working height.

Any workbench needs a vice; one with a jaw opening of 100 mm is suitable for most jobs. As mentioned previously, some clean dry storage space is also required for tools, as well as for any lubricants, cleaning fluids, touch-up paints and so on, which become necessary.

Another item which may be required, and which has a much more general usage, is an electric drill with a chuck capacity of at least 8 mm. This, together with a good range of twist drills, is virtually essential for fitting accessories.

Last, but not least, always keep a supply of old newspapers and clean, lint-free rags available, and try to keep any working area as clean as possible.

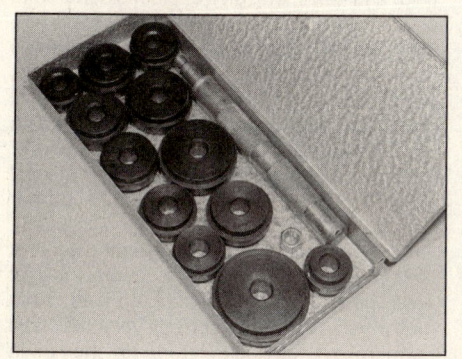

Bush and bearing removal/installation set

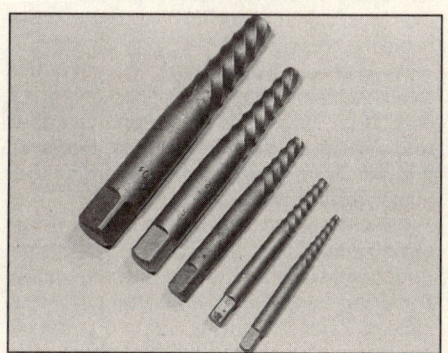

Stud extractor set

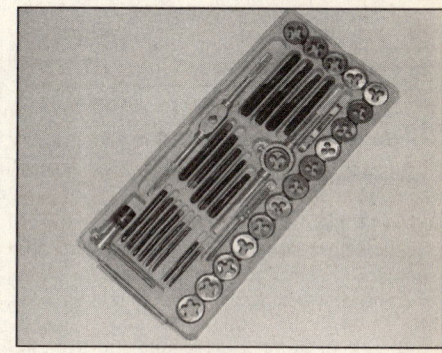

Tap and die set

General Repair Procedures

Whenever servicing, repair or overhaul work is carried out on the car or its components, it is necessary to observe the following procedures and instructions. This will assist in carrying out the operation efficiently and to a professional standard of workmanship.

Joint mating faces and gaskets

When separating components at their mating faces, never insert screwdrivers or similar implements into the joint between the faces in order to prise them apart. This can cause severe damage which results in oil leaks, coolant leaks, etc upon reassembly. Separation is usually achieved by tapping along the joint with a soft-faced hammer in order to break the seal. However, note that this method may not be suitable where dowels are used for component location.

Where a gasket is used between the mating faces of two components, ensure that it is renewed on reassembly, and fit it dry unless otherwise stated in the repair procedure. Make sure that the mating faces are clean and dry, with all traces of old gasket removed. When cleaning a joint face, use a tool which is not likely to score or damage the face, and remove any burrs or nicks with an oilstone or fine file.

Make sure that tapped holes are cleaned with a pipe cleaner, and keep them free of jointing compound, if this is being used, unless specifically instructed otherwise.

Ensure that all orifices, channels or pipes are clear, and blow through them, preferably using compressed air.

Oil seals

Oil seals can be removed by levering them out with a wide flat-bladed screwdriver or similar implement. Alternatively, a number of self-tapping screws may be screwed into the seal, and these used as a purchase for pliers or some similar device in order to pull the seal free.

Whenever an oil seal is removed from its working location, either individually or as part of an assembly, it should be renewed.

The very fine sealing lip of the seal is easily damaged, and will not seal if the surface it contacts is not completely clean and free from scratches, nicks or grooves.

Protect the lips of the seal from any surface which may damage them in the course of fitting. Use tape or a conical sleeve where possible. Lubricate the seal lips with oil before fitting and, on dual-lipped seals, fill the space between the lips with grease.

Unless otherwise stated, oil seals must be fitted with their sealing lips toward the lubricant to be sealed.

Use a tubular drift or block of wood of the appropriate size to install the seal and, if the seal housing is shouldered, drive the seal down to the shoulder. If the seal housing is unshouldered, the seal should be fitted with its face flush with the housing top face (unless otherwise instructed).

Screw threads and fastenings

Seized nuts, bolts and screws are quite a common occurrence where corrosion has set in, and the use of penetrating oil or releasing fluid will often overcome this problem if the offending item is soaked for a while before attempting to release it. The use of an impact driver may also provide a means of releasing such stubborn fastening devices, when used in conjunction with the appropriate screwdriver bit or socket. If none of these methods works, it may be necessary to resort to the careful application of heat, or the use of a hacksaw or nut splitter device.

Studs are usually removed by locking two nuts together on the threaded part, and then using a spanner on the lower nut to unscrew the stud. Studs or bolts which have broken off below the surface of the component in which they are mounted can sometimes be removed using a proprietary stud extractor. Always ensure that a blind tapped hole is completely free from oil, grease, water or other fluid before installing the bolt or stud. Failure to do this could cause the housing to crack due to the hydraulic action of the bolt or stud as it is screwed in.

When tightening a castellated nut to accept a split pin, tighten the nut to the specified torque, where applicable, and then tighten further to the next split pin hole. Never slacken the nut to align the split pin hole, unless stated in the repair procedure.

When checking or retightening a nut or bolt to a specified torque setting, slacken the nut or bolt by a quarter of a turn, and then retighten to the specified setting. However, this should not be attempted where angular tightening has been used.

For some screw fastenings, notably cylinder head bolts or nuts, torque wrench settings are no longer specified for the latter stages of tightening, "angle-tightening" being called up instead. Typically, a fairly low torque wrench setting will be applied to the bolts/nuts in the correct sequence, followed by one or more stages of tightening through specified angles.

Locknuts, locktabs and washers

Any fastening which will rotate against a component or housing in the course of tightening should always have a washer between it and the relevant component or housing.

Spring or split washers should always be renewed when they are used to lock a critical component such as a big-end bearing retaining bolt or nut. Locktabs which are folded over to retain a nut or bolt should always be renewed.

Self-locking nuts can be re-used in non-critical areas, providing resistance can be felt when the locking portion passes over the bolt or stud thread. However, it should be noted that self-locking stiffnuts tend to lose their effectiveness after long periods of use, and in such cases should be renewed as a matter of course.

Split pins must always be replaced with new ones of the correct size for the hole.

When thread-locking compound is found on the threads of a fastener which is to be re-used, it should be cleaned off with a wire brush and solvent, and fresh compound applied on reassembly.

Special tools

Some repair procedures in this manual entail the use of special tools such as a press, two or three-legged pullers, spring compressors, etc. Wherever possible, suitable readily-available alternatives to the manufacturer's special tools are described, and are shown in use. Unless you are highly-skilled and have a thorough understanding of the procedures described, never attempt to bypass the use of any special tool when the procedure described specifies its use. Not only is there a very great risk of personal injury, but expensive damage could be caused to the components involved.

Environmental considerations

When disposing of used engine oil, brake fluid, antifreeze, etc, give due consideration to any detrimental environmental effects. Do not, for instance, pour any of the above liquids down drains into the general sewage system, or onto the ground to soak away. Many local council refuse tips provide a facility for waste oil disposal, as do some garages. If none of these facilities are available, consult your local Environmental Health Department for further advice.

With the universal tightening-up of legislation regarding the emission of environmentally-harmful substances from motor vehicles, most current vehicles have tamperproof devices fitted to the main adjustment points of the fuel system. These devices are primarily designed to prevent unqualified persons from adjusting the fuel/air mixture, with the chance of a consequent increase in toxic emissions. If such devices are encountered during servicing or overhaul, they should, wherever possible, be renewed or refitted in accordance with the vehicle manufacturer's requirements or current legislation.

OIL CARE
FOLLOW THE CODE
OIL BANK LINE
0800 66 33 66

Note: It is antisocial and illegal to dump oil down the drain. To find the location of your local oil recycling bank, call this number free.

Fault Finding

Introduction

The vehicle owner who does his or her own maintenance according to the recommended schedules should not have to use this section of the manual very often. Modern component reliability is such that, provided those items subject to wear or deterioration are inspected or renewed at the specified intervals, sudden failure is comparatively rare. Faults do not usually just happen as a result of sudden failure, but develop over a period of time. Major mechanical failures in particular are usually preceded by characteristic symptoms over hundreds or even thousands of miles. Those components which do occasionally fail without warning are often small and easily carried in the vehicle.

With any fault finding, the first step is to decide where to begin investigations. Sometimes this is obvious, but on other occasions a little detective work will be necessary. The owner who makes half a dozen haphazard adjustments or replacements may be successful in curing a fault (or its symptoms), but he will be none the wiser if the fault recurs and he may well have spent more time and money than was necessary. A calm and logical approach will be found to be more satisfactory in the long run. Always take into account any warning signs or abnormalities that may have been noticed in the period preceding the fault – power loss, high or low gauge readings, unusual noises or smells, etc – and remember that failure of components such as fuses or spark plugs may only be pointers to some underlying fault.

The pages which follow here are intended to help in cases of failure to start or breakdown on the road. There is also a Fault Diagnosis Section at the end of each Chapter which should be consulted if the preliminary checks prove unfruitful. Whatever the fault, certain basic principles apply. These are as follows:

Verify the fault. This is simply a matter of being sure that you know what the symptoms are before starting work. This is particularly important if you are investigating a fault for someone else who may not have described it very accurately.

Don't overlook the obvious. For example, if the vehicle won't start, is there petrol in the tank? (Don't take anyone else's word on this particular point, and don't trust the fuel gauge either!) If an electrical fault is indicated, look for loose or broken wires before digging out the test gear.

Cure the disease, not the symptom. Substituting a flat battery with a fully charged one will get you off the hard shoulder, but if the underlying cause is not attended to, the new battery will go the same way. Similarly, changing oil-fouled spark plugs for a new set will get you moving again, but remember that the reason for the fouling (if it wasn't simply an incorrect grade of plug) will have to be established and corrected.

Don't take anything for granted. Particularly, don't forget that a 'new' component may itself be defective (especially if it's been rattling round in the boot for months), and don't leave components out of a fault diagnosis sequence just because they are new or recently fitted. When you do finally diagnose a difficult fault, you'll probably realise that all the evidence was there from the start.

Electrical faults

Electrical faults can be more puzzling than straightforward mechanical failures, but they are no less susceptible to logical analysis if the basic principles of operation are understood. Vehicle electrical wiring exists in extremely unfavourable conditions – heat, vibration and chemical attack and the first things to look for are loose or corroded connections and broken or chafed wires, especially where the wires pass through holes in the bodywork or are subject to vibration.

All metal-bodied vehicles in current production have one pole of the battery 'earthed', ie connected to the vehicle bodywork, and in nearly all modern vehicles it is the negative (–) terminal. The various electrical components – motors, bulb holders, etc – are also connected to earth, either by means of a lead or directly by their mountings. Electric current flows through the component and then back to the battery via the bodywork. If the component mounting is loose or corroded, or if a good path back to the battery is not available, the circuit will be incomplete and malfunction will result. The engine and/or gearbox are also earthed by means of flexible metal straps to the body or subframe; if these straps are loose or missing, starter motor, generator and ignition trouble may result.

Assuming the earth return to be satisfactory, electrical faults will be due either to component malfunction or to defects in the current supply. Individual components are dealt with in Chapter 12. If supply wires are broken or cracked internally this results in an open-circuit, and the easiest way to check for this is to bypass the suspect wire temporarily with a length of wire having a crocodile clip or suitable connector at each end. Alternatively, a 12V test lamp can be used to verify the presence of supply voltage at various points along the wire and the break can be thus isolated.

If a bare portion of a live wire touches the bodywork or other earthed metal part, the electricity will take the low-resistance path thus formed back to the battery: this is known as a short-circuit. Hopefully a short-circuit will blow a fuse, but otherwise it may cause burning of the insulation (and possibly further short-circuits) or even a fire. This is why it is inadvisable to bypass persistently blowing fuses with silver foil or wire.

Fault Finding

Spares and tool kit

Most vehicles are supplied only with sufficient tools for wheel changing; the *Maintenance and minor repair* tool kit detailed in *Tools and working facilities*, with the addition of a hammer, is probably sufficient for those repairs that most motorists would consider attempting at the roadside. In addition a few items which can be fitted without too much trouble in the event of a breakdown should be carried. Experience and available space will modify the list below, but the following may save having to call on professional assistance:

- [ ] Spark plugs, clean and correctly gapped
- [ ] HT lead and plug cap – long enough to reach the plug furthest from the distributor
- [ ] Distributor rotor
- [ ] Drivebelt(s) — emergency type may suffice
- [ ] Spare fuses
- [ ] Set of principal light bulbs
- [ ] Tin of radiator sealer and hose bandage
- [ ] Exhaust bandage
- [ ] Roll of insulating tape
- [ ] Length of soft iron wire
- [ ] Length of electrical flex
- [ ] Torch or inspection lamp (can double as test lamp)
- [ ] Battery jump leads
- [ ] Tow-rope
- [ ] Ignition waterproofing aerosol
- [ ] Litre of engine oil
- [ ] Sealed can of hydraulic fluid
- [ ] Emergency windscreen
- [ ] Wormdrive clips
- [ ] Tube of filler paste

If spare fuel is carried, a can designed for the purpose should be used to minimise risks of leakage and collision damage. A first aid kit and a warning triangle, whilst not at present compulsory in the UK, are obviously sensible items to carry in addition to the above. When touring abroad it may be advisable to carry additional spares which, even if you cannot fit them yourself, could save having to wait while parts are obtained. The items below may be worth considering:

- [ ] Clutch and throttle cables
- [ ] Cylinder head gasket
- [ ] Alternator brushes
- [ ] Tyre valve core

One of the motoring organisations will be able to advise on availability of fuel, etc, in foreign countries.

Engine will not start

Engine fails to turn when starter operated

- [ ] Flat battery (recharge use jump leads or push start)
- [ ] Battery terminals loose or corroded
- [ ] Battery earth to body defective
- [ ] Engine earth strap loose or broken
- [ ] Starter motor (or solenoid) wiring loose or broken
- [ ] Automatic transmission selector in wrong position, or inhibitor switch faulty
- [ ] Ignition/starter switch faulty
- [ ] Major mechanical failure (seizure)
- [ ] Starter or solenoid internal fault (see Chapter 12)

Starter motor turns engine slowly

- [ ] Partially discharged battery (recharge, use jump leads, or push start)
- [ ] Battery terminals loose or corroded
- [ ] Battery earth to body defective
- [ ] Engine earth strap loose
- [ ] Starter motor (or solenoid) wiring loose
- [ ] Starter motor internal fault (see Chapter 12)

Starter motor spins without turning engine

- [ ] Flywheel gear teeth damaged or worn
- [ ] Starter motor mounting bolts loose

Engine turns normally but fails to start

- [ ] Damp or dirty HT leads and distributor cap (crank engine and check for spark)
- [ ] No fuel in tank (check for delivery at carburettor)
- [ ] Automatic choke faulty (carburettor engine)
- [ ] Fouled or incorrectly gapped spark plugs (remove, clean and regap)
- [ ] Other ignition system fault (see Chapter 4)
- [ ] Other fuel system fault (see Chapter 3)
- [ ] Poor compression (see Chapter 1)
- [ ] Major mechanical failure (eg camshaft drive)

Engine fires but will not run

- [ ] Automatic choke faulty (carburettor engine)
- [ ] Air leaks at carburettor or inlet manifold
- [ ] Fuel starvation (see Chapter 3)
- [ ] Ballast resistor defective, or other ignition fault (see Chapter 4)

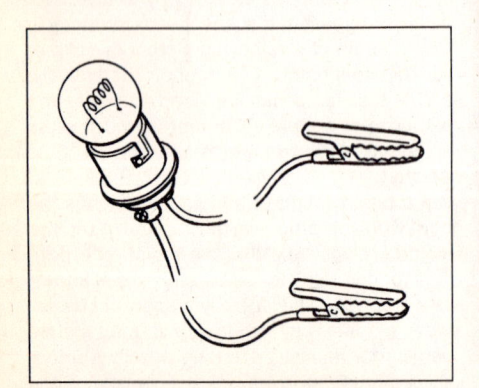

A simple test lamp is useful for checking electrical faults

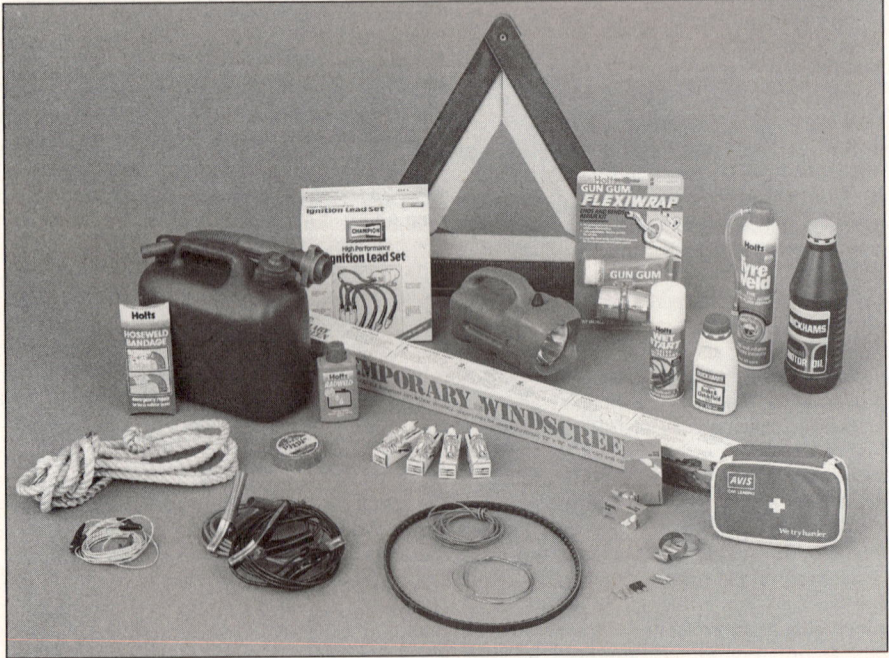

Carrying a few spares may save you a long walk!

Fault Finding REF•11

Engine cuts out and will not restart

Engine cuts out suddenly – ignition fault
- ☐ Loose or disconnected LT wires
- ☐ Wet HT leads or distributor cap (after traversing water splash)
- ☐ Coil failure (check for spark)
- ☐ Other ignition fault (see Chapter 4)

Engine misfires before cutting out – fuel fault
- ☐ Fuel tank empty
- ☐ Fuel pump defective or filter blocked (check for delivery)
- ☐ Fuel tank filler vent blocked (suction will be evident on releasing cap)
- ☐ Carburettor needle valve sticking
- ☐ Carburettor jets blocked (fuel contaminated)
- ☐ Other fuel system fault (see Chapter 3)

Engine cuts out – other causes
- ☐ Serious overheating
- ☐ Major mechanical failure (eg camshaft drive)

Crank engine and check for a spark. Note use of insulated tool

Engine overheats

Ignition (no-charge) warning light illuminated
- ☐ Slack or broken drivebelt — retension or renew (Chapter 2)

Ignition warning light not illuminated
- ☐ Coolant loss due to internal or external leakage (see Chapter 2)
- ☐ Thermostat defective
- ☐ Low oil level
- ☐ Brakes binding
- ☐ Radiator clogged externally or internally
- ☐ Electric cooling fan not operating correctly
- ☐ Engine waterways clogged
- ☐ Ignition timing incorrect or automatic advance malfunctioning
- ☐ Mixture too weak

Note: *Do not add cold water to an overheated engine or damage may result*

Low engine oil pressure

Note: *Low oil pressure in a high-mileage engine at tickover is not necessarily a cause for concern. Sudden pressure loss at speed is far more significant. In any event check the gauge or warning light sender before condemning the engine.*

Gauge reads low or warning light illuminated with engine running
- ☐ Oil level low or incorrect grade
- ☐ Defective gauge or sender unit
- ☐ Wire to sender unit earthed
- ☐ Engine overheating
- ☐ Oil filter clogged or bypass valve defective
- ☐ Oil pressure relief valve defective
- ☐ Oil pick-up strainer clogged
- ☐ Oil pump worn or mountings loose
- ☐ Worn main or big-end bearings

Engine noises

Pre-ignition (pinking) on acceleration
- ☐ Incorrect grade of fuel
- ☐ Ignition timing incorrect
- ☐ Distributor faulty or worn
- ☐ Worn or maladjusted carburettor
- ☐ Excessive carbon build-up in engine

Whistling or wheezing noises
- ☐ Leaking vacuum hose
- ☐ Leaking carburettor or manifold gasket
- ☐ Blowing head gasket

Tapping or rattling
- ☐ Incorrect valve clearances (where applicable)
- ☐ Worn valve gear
- ☐ Worn timing chain or belt
- ☐ Broken piston ring (ticking noise)

Knocking or thumping
- ☐ Unintentional mechanical contact (eg fan blades)
- ☐ Worn drivebelt
- ☐ Peripheral component fault (generator, water pump, etc)
- ☐ Worn big-end bearings (regular heavy knocking, perhaps less under load)
- ☐ Worn main bearings (rumbling and knocking, perhaps worsening under load)
- ☐ Piston slap (most noticeable when cold)

Buying spare parts/vehicle identification numbers

Buying spare parts

Spare parts are available from many sources. Audi have many dealers throughout the country and other dealers, accessory stores and motor factors will also stock Audi spare parts. Our advice regarding spare parts sources is as follows:

Officially appointed vehicle main dealers: This is the best source of parts which are peculiar to your vehicle and are otherwise not generally available (eg. complete cylinder heads, internal transmission components, badges, interior trim, etc). It is also the only place at which you should buy parts if your vehicle is still under warranty. To be sure of obtaining the correct parts it will always be necessary to give the storeman your vehicle's engine and chassis number, and if possible to take the 'old' part along for positive identification. Remember that many parts are available on a factory exchange scheme – any parts returned should always be clean! It obviously makes good sense to go straight to the specialists on your vehicle for this type of part for they are best equipped to supply you.

Other dealers and auto accessory shops – These are often very good places to buy materials and components needed for the maintenance of your car (eg, oil filters, spark plugs, bulbs, fan belts, oils and greases, touch-up paint, filler paste, etc). They also sell general accessories, usually have convenient opening hours, charge lower prices and can often be found not far from home.

Motor factors – Good factors will stock all of the more important components which wear out relatively quickly (eg, clutch components, pistons, valves, exhaust systems, brake cylinders/pipes/hoses/seals/shoes and pads, etc). Motor factors will often provide new or reconditioned components on a part exchange basis – this can save a considerable amount of money.

Vehicle identification numbers

Modifications are a continuing and unpublicised process in vehicle manufacture. Spare parts manuals and lists are compiled on a numerical basis, the individual vehicle numbers being essential for correct identification of the component required.

The vehicle identification plate is located on the right-hand side of the engine compartment front panel on UK models, or on the inside of the luggage compartment lid on North American models. The vehicle identification number is also located on the bottom left-hand side of the windscreen on North American models and is visible from the outside.

The engine number is stamped on the left-hand side of the cylinder block.

The manual gearbox number is stamped on the right-hand side of the gearbox, above the drive flange.

The automatic transmission number is stamped inside the torque converter housing, but the transmission type number is on the top of the gear casing.

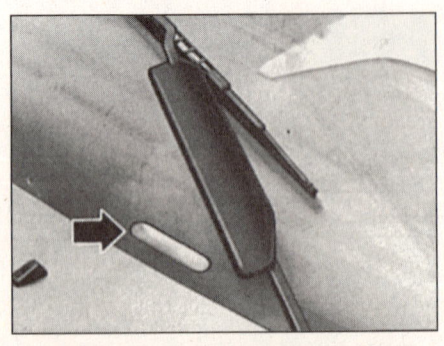

Vehicle identification plate on UK models

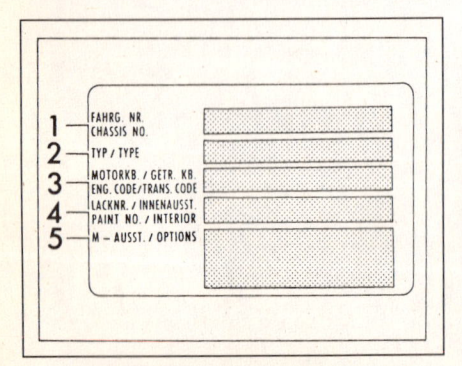

Vehicle identification label on North American models

Vehicle identification number on North American models, viewed through the windscreen

The engine number

Conversion Factors REF•13

Length (distance)
Inches (in)	x 25.4	= Millimetres (mm)	x 0.0394	=	Inches (in)
Feet (ft)	x 0.305	= Metres (m)	x 3.281	=	Feet (ft)
Miles	x 1.609	= Kilometres (km)	x 0.621	=	Miles

Volume (capacity)
Cubic inches (cu in; in^3)	x 16.387	= Cubic centimetres (cc; cm^3)	x 0.061	=	Cubic inches (cu in; in^3)
Imperial pints (Imp pt)	x 0.568	= Litres (l)	x 1.76	=	Imperial pints (Imp pt)
Imperial quarts (Imp qt)	x 1.137	= Litres (l)	x 0.88	=	Imperial quarts (Imp qt)
Imperial quarts (Imp qt)	x 1.201	= US quarts (US qt)	x 0.833	=	Imperial quarts (Imp qt)
US quarts (US qt)	x 0.946	= Litres (l)	x 1.057	=	US quarts (US qt)
Imperial gallons (Imp gal)	x 4.546	= Litres (l)	x 0.22	=	Imperial gallons (Imp gal)
Imperial gallons (Imp gal)	x 1.201	= US gallons (US gal)	x 0.833	=	Imperial gallons (Imp gal)
US gallons (US gal)	x 3.785	= Litres (l)	x 0.264	=	US gallons (US gal)

Mass (weight)
Ounces (oz)	x 28.35	= Grams (g)	x 0.035	=	Ounces (oz)
Pounds (lb)	x 0.454	= Kilograms (kg)	x 2.205	=	Pounds (lb)

Force
Ounces-force (ozf; oz)	x 0.278	= Newtons (N)	x 3.6	=	Ounces-force (ozf; oz)
Pounds-force (lbf; lb)	x 4.448	= Newtons (N)	x 0.225	=	Pounds-force (lbf; lb)
Newtons (N)	x 0.1	= Kilograms-force (kgf; kg)	x 9.81	=	Newtons (N)

Pressure
Pounds-force per square inch (psi; lbf/in^2; lb/in^2)	x 0.070	= Kilograms-force per square centimetre (kgf/cm^2; kg/cm^2)	x 14.223	=	Pounds-force per square inch (psi; lbf/in^2; lb/in^2)
Pounds-force per square inch (psi; lbf/in^2; lb/in^2)	x 0.068	= Atmospheres (atm)	x 14.696	=	Pounds-force per square inch (psi; lbf/in^2; lb/in^2)
Pounds-force per square inch (psi; lbf/in^2; lb/in^2)	x 0.069	= Bars	x 14.5	=	Pounds-force per square inch (psi; lbf/in^2; lb/in^2)
Pounds-force per square inch (psi; lbf/in^2; lb/in^2)	x 6.895	= Kilopascals (kPa)	x 0.145	=	Pounds-force per square inch (psi; lbf/in^2; lb/in^2)
Kilopascals (kPa)	x 0.01	= Kilograms-force per square centimetre (kgf/cm^2; kg/cm^2)	x 98.1	=	Kilopascals (kPa)
Millibar (mbar)	x 100	= Pascals (Pa)	x 0.01	=	Millibar (mbar)
Millibar (mbar)	x 0.0145	= Pounds-force per square inch (psi; lbf/in^2; lb/in^2)	x 68.947	=	Millibar (mbar)
Millibar (mbar)	x 0.75	= Millimetres of mercury (mmHg)	x 1.333	=	Millibar (mbar)
Millibar (mbar)	x 0.401	= Inches of water (inH$_2$O)	x 2.491	=	Millibar (mbar)
Millimetres of mercury (mmHg)	x 0.535	= Inches of water (inH$_2$O)	x 1.868	=	Millimetres of mercury (mmHg)
Inches of water (inH$_2$O)	x 0.036	= Pounds-force per square inch (psi; lbf/in^2; lb/in^2)	x 27.68	=	Inches of water (inH$_2$O)

Torque (moment of force)
Pounds-force inches (lbf in; lb in)	x 1.152	= Kilograms-force centimetre (kgf cm; kg cm)	x 0.868	=	Pounds-force inches (lbf in; lb in)
Pounds-force inches (lbf in; lb in)	x 0.113	= Newton metres (Nm)	x 8.85	=	Pounds-force inches (lbf in; lb in)
Pounds-force inches (lbf in; lb in)	x 0.083	= Pounds-force feet (lbf ft; lb ft)	x 12	=	Pounds-force inches (lbf in; lb in)
Pounds-force feet (lbf ft; lb ft)	x 0.138	= Kilograms-force metres (kgf m; kg m)	x 7.233	=	Pounds-force feet (lbf ft; lb ft)
Pounds-force feet (lbf ft; lb ft)	x 1.356	= Newton metres (Nm)	x 0.738	=	Pounds-force feet (lbf ft; lb ft)
Newton metres (Nm)	x 0.102	= Kilograms-force metres (kgf m; kg m)	x 9.804	=	Newton metres (Nm)

Power
Horsepower (hp)	x 745.7	= Watts (W)	x 0.0013	=	Horsepower (hp)

Velocity (speed)
Miles per hour (miles/hr; mph)	x 1.609	= Kilometres per hour (km/hr; kph)	x 0.621	=	Miles per hour (miles/hr; mph)

Fuel consumption*
Miles per gallon (mpg)	x 0.354	= Kilometres per litre (km/l)	x 2.825	=	Miles per gallon (mpg)

Temperature
Degrees Fahrenheit = (°C x 1.8) + 32   Degrees Celsius (Degrees Centigrade; °C) = (°F - 32) x 0.56

* It is common practice to convert from miles per gallon (mpg) to litres/100 kilometres (l/100km), where mpg x l/100 km = 282

Glossary of Technical Terms

A

ABS (Anti-lock brake system) A system, usually electronically controlled, that senses incipient wheel lockup during braking and relieves hydraulic pressure at wheels that are about to skid.

Air bag An inflatable bag hidden in the steering wheel (driver's side) or the dash or glovebox (passenger side). In a head-on collision, the bags inflate, preventing the driver and front passenger from being thrown forward into the steering wheel or windscreen.

Air cleaner A metal or plastic housing, containing a filter element, which removes dust and dirt from the air being drawn into the engine.

Air filter element The actual filter in an air cleaner system, usually manufactured from pleated paper and requiring renewal at regular intervals.

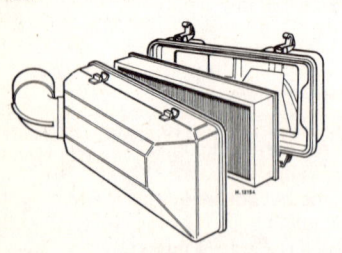

Air filter

Allen key A hexagonal wrench which fits into a recessed hexagonal hole.

Alligator clip A long-nosed spring-loaded metal clip with meshing teeth. Used to make temporary electrical connections.

Alternator A component in the electrical system which converts mechanical energy from a drivebelt into electrical energy to charge the battery and to operate the starting system, ignition system and electrical accessories.

Alternator (exploded view)

Ampere (amp) A unit of measurement for the flow of electric current. One amp is the amount of current produced by one volt acting through a resistance of one ohm.

Anaerobic sealer A substance used to prevent bolts and screws from loosening. Anaerobic means that it does not require oxygen for activation. The Loctite brand is widely used.

Antifreeze A substance (usually ethylene glycol) mixed with water, and added to a vehicle's cooling system, to prevent freezing of the coolant in winter. Antifreeze also contains chemicals to inhibit corrosion and the formation of rust and other deposits that would tend to clog the radiator and coolant passages and reduce cooling efficiency.

Anti-seize compound A coating that reduces the risk of seizing on fasteners that are subjected to high temperatures, such as exhaust manifold bolts and nuts.

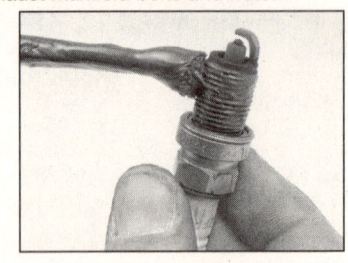

Anti-seize compound

Asbestos A natural fibrous mineral with great heat resistance, commonly used in the composition of brake friction materials. Asbestos is a health hazard and the dust created by brake systems should never be inhaled or ingested.

Axle A shaft on which a wheel revolves, or which revolves with a wheel. Also, a solid beam that connects the two wheels at one end of the vehicle. An axle which also transmits power to the wheels is known as a live axle.

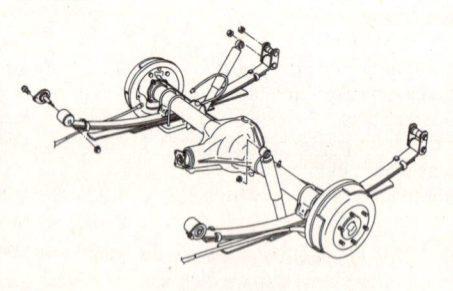

Axle assembly

Axleshaft A single rotating shaft, on either side of the differential, which delivers power from the final drive assembly to the drive wheels. Also called a driveshaft or a halfshaft.

B

Ball bearing An anti-friction bearing consisting of a hardened inner and outer race with hardened steel balls between two races.

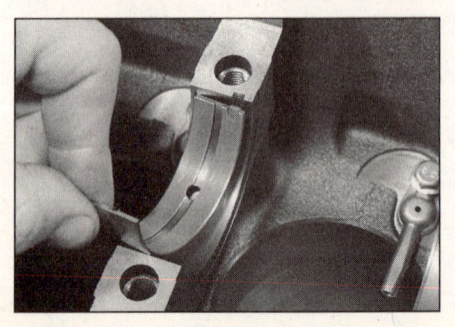

Bearing

Bearing The curved surface on a shaft or in a bore, or the part assembled into either, that permits relative motion between them with minimum wear and friction.

Big-end bearing The bearing in the end of the connecting rod that's attached to the crankshaft.

Bleed nipple A valve on a brake wheel cylinder, caliper or other hydraulic component that is opened to purge the hydraulic system of air. Also called a bleed screw.

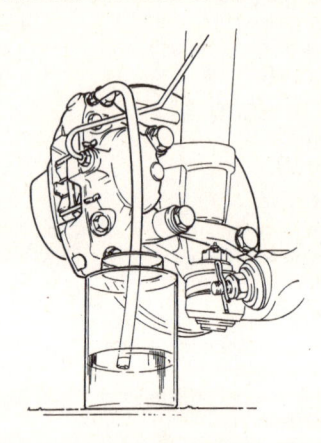

Brake bleeding

Brake bleeding Procedure for removing air from lines of a hydraulic brake system.

Brake disc The component of a disc brake that rotates with the wheels.

Brake drum The component of a drum brake that rotates with the wheels.

Brake linings The friction material which contacts the brake disc or drum to retard the vehicle's speed. The linings are bonded or riveted to the brake pads or shoes.

Brake pads The replaceable friction pads that pinch the brake disc when the brakes are applied. Brake pads consist of a friction material bonded or riveted to a rigid backing plate.

Brake shoe The crescent-shaped carrier to which the brake linings are mounted and which forces the lining against the rotating drum during braking.

Braking systems For more information on braking systems, consult the *Haynes Automotive Brake Manual*.

Breaker bar A long socket wrench handle providing greater leverage.

Bulkhead The insulated partition between the engine and the passenger compartment.

C

Caliper The non-rotating part of a disc-brake assembly that straddles the disc and carries the brake pads. The caliper also contains the hydraulic components that cause the pads to pinch the disc when the brakes are applied. A caliper is also a measuring tool that can be set to measure inside or outside dimensions of an object.

Glossary of Technical Terms REF•15

Camshaft A rotating shaft on which a series of cam lobes operate the valve mechanisms. The camshaft may be driven by gears, by sprockets and chain or by sprockets and a belt.

Canister A container in an evaporative emission control system; contains activated charcoal granules to trap vapours from the fuel system.

Canister

Carburettor A device which mixes fuel with air in the proper proportions to provide a desired power output from a spark ignition internal combustion engine.

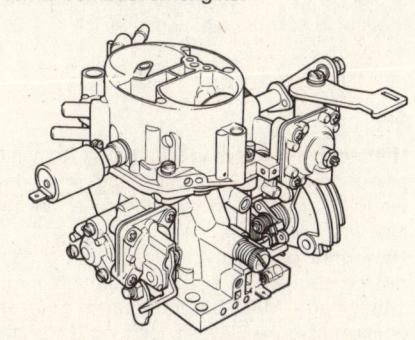

Carburettor

Castellated Resembling the parapets along the top of a castle wall. For example, a castellated balljoint stud nut.

Castellated nut

Castor In wheel alignment, the backward or forward tilt of the steering axis. Castor is positive when the steering axis is inclined rearward at the top.

Catalytic converter A silencer-like device in the exhaust system which converts certain pollutants in the exhaust gases into less harmful substances.

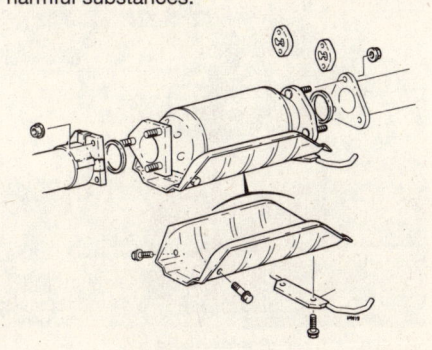

Catalytic converter

Circlip A ring-shaped clip used to prevent endwise movement of cylindrical parts and shafts. An internal circlip is installed in a groove in a housing; an external circlip fits into a groove on the outside of a cylindrical piece such as a shaft.

Clearance The amount of space between two parts. For example, between a piston and a cylinder, between a bearing and a journal, etc.

Coil spring A spiral of elastic steel found in various sizes throughout a vehicle, for example as a springing medium in the suspension and in the valve train.

Compression Reduction in volume, and increase in pressure and temperature, of a gas, caused by squeezing it into a smaller space.

Compression ratio The relationship between cylinder volume when the piston is at top dead centre and cylinder volume when the piston is at bottom dead centre.

Constant velocity (CV) joint A type of universal joint that cancels out vibrations caused by driving power being transmitted through an angle.

Core plug A disc or cup-shaped metal device inserted in a hole in a casting through which core was removed when the casting was formed. Also known as a freeze plug or expansion plug.

Crankcase The lower part of the engine block in which the crankshaft rotates.

Crankshaft The main rotating member, or shaft, running the length of the crankcase, with offset "throws" to which the connecting rods are attached.

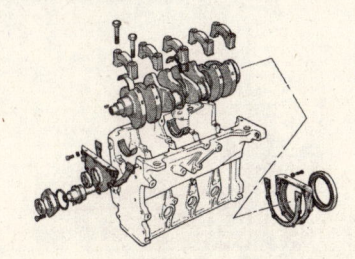

Crankshaft assembly

Crocodile clip See Alligator clip

D

Diagnostic code Code numbers obtained by accessing the diagnostic mode of an engine management computer. This code can be used to determine the area in the system where a malfunction may be located.

Disc brake A brake design incorporating a rotating disc onto which brake pads are squeezed. The resulting friction converts the energy of a moving vehicle into heat.

Double-overhead cam (DOHC) An engine that uses two overhead camshafts, usually one for the intake valves and one for the exhaust valves.

Drivebelt(s) The belt(s) used to drive accessories such as the alternator, water pump, power steering pump, air conditioning compressor, etc. off the crankshaft pulley.

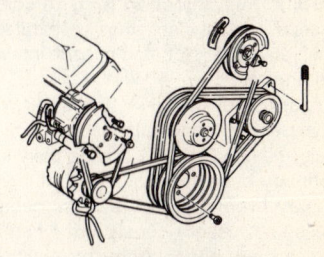

Accessory drivebelts

Driveshaft Any shaft used to transmit motion. Commonly used when referring to the axleshafts on a front wheel drive vehicle.

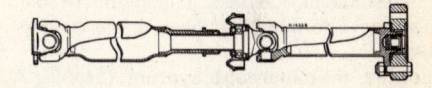

Driveshaft

Drum brake A type of brake using a drum-shaped metal cylinder attached to the inner surface of the wheel. When the brake pedal is pressed, curved brake shoes with friction linings press against the inside of the drum to slow or stop the vehicle.

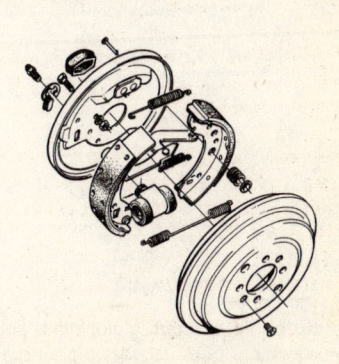

Drum brake assembly

Glossary of Technical Terms

E

EGR valve A valve used to introduce exhaust gases into the intake air stream.

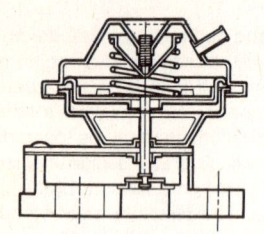

EGR valve

Electronic control unit (ECU) A computer which controls (for instance) ignition and fuel injection systems, or an anti-lock braking system. For more information refer to the *Haynes Automotive Electrical and Electronic Systems Manual*.

Electronic Fuel Injection (EFI) A computer controlled fuel system that distributes fuel through an injector located in each intake port of the engine.

Emergency brake A braking system, independent of the main hydraulic system, that can be used to slow or stop the vehicle if the primary brakes fail, or to hold the vehicle stationary even though the brake pedal isn't depressed. It usually consists of a hand lever that actuates either front or rear brakes mechanically through a series of cables and linkages. Also known as a handbrake or parking brake.

Endfloat The amount of lengthwise movement between two parts. As applied to a crankshaft, the distance that the crankshaft can move forward and back in the cylinder block.

Engine management system (EMS) A computer controlled system which manages the fuel injection and the ignition systems in an integrated fashion.

Exhaust manifold A part with several passages through which exhaust gases leave the engine combustion chambers and enter the exhaust pipe.

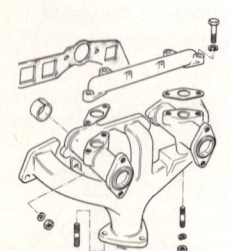

Exhaust manifold

F

Fan clutch A viscous (fluid) drive coupling device which permits variable engine fan speeds in relation to engine speeds.

Feeler blade A thin strip or blade of hardened steel, ground to an exact thickness, used to check or measure clearances between parts.

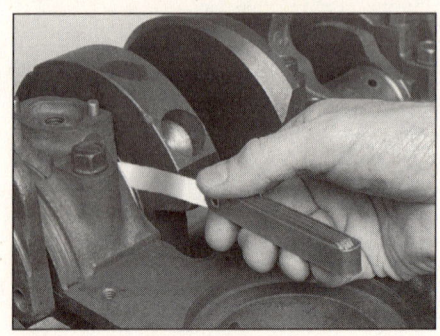

Feeler blade

Firing order The order in which the engine cylinders fire, or deliver their power strokes, beginning with the number one cylinder.

Flywheel A heavy spinning wheel in which energy is absorbed and stored by means of momentum. On cars, the flywheel is attached to the crankshaft to smooth out firing impulses.

Free play The amount of travel before any action takes place. The "looseness" in a linkage, or an assembly of parts, between the initial application of force and actual movement. For example, the distance the brake pedal moves before the pistons in the master cylinder are actuated.

Fuse An electrical device which protects a circuit against accidental overload. The typical fuse contains a soft piece of metal which is calibrated to melt at a predetermined current flow (expressed as amps) and break the circuit.

Fusible link A circuit protection device consisting of a conductor surrounded by heat-resistant insulation. The conductor is smaller than the wire it protects, so it acts as the weakest link in the circuit. Unlike a blown fuse, a failed fusible link must frequently be cut from the wire for replacement.

G

Gap The distance the spark must travel in jumping from the centre electrode to the side electrode in a spark plug. Also refers to the spacing between the points in a contact breaker assembly in a conventional points-type ignition, or to the distance between the reluctor or rotor and the pickup coil in an electronic ignition.

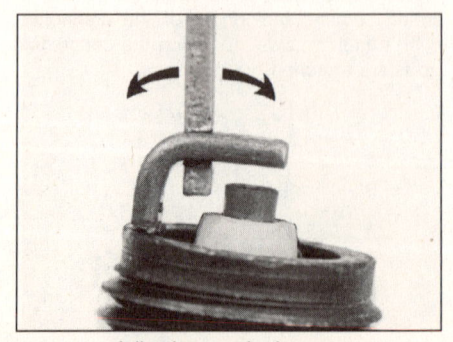

Adjusting spark plug gap

Gasket Any thin, soft material - usually cork, cardboard, asbestos or soft metal - installed between two metal surfaces to ensure a good seal. For instance, the cylinder head gasket seals the joint between the block and the cylinder head.

Gasket

Gauge An instrument panel display used to monitor engine conditions. A gauge with a movable pointer on a dial or a fixed scale is an analogue gauge. A gauge with a numerical readout is called a digital gauge.

H

Halfshaft A rotating shaft that transmits power from the final drive unit to a drive wheel, usually when referring to a live rear axle.

Harmonic balancer A device designed to reduce torsion or twisting vibration in the crankshaft. May be incorporated in the crankshaft pulley. Also known as a vibration damper.

Hone An abrasive tool for correcting small irregularities or differences in diameter in an engine cylinder, brake cylinder, etc.

Hydraulic tappet A tappet that utilises hydraulic pressure from the engine's lubrication system to maintain zero clearance (constant contact with both camshaft and valve stem). Automatically adjusts to variation in valve stem length. Hydraulic tappets also reduce valve noise.

I

Ignition timing The moment at which the spark plug fires, usually expressed in the number of crankshaft degrees before the piston reaches the top of its stroke.

Inlet manifold A tube or housing with passages through which flows the air-fuel mixture (carburettor vehicles and vehicles with throttle body injection) or air only (port fuel-injected vehicles) to the port openings in the cylinder head.

Glossary of Technical Terms

J

Jump start Starting the engine of a vehicle with a discharged or weak battery by attaching jump leads from the weak battery to a charged or helper battery.

L

Load Sensing Proportioning Valve (LSPV) A brake hydraulic system control valve that works like a proportioning valve, but also takes into consideration the amount of weight carried by the rear axle.

Locknut A nut used to lock an adjustment nut, or other threaded component, in place. For example, a locknut is employed to keep the adjusting nut on the rocker arm in position.

Lockwasher A form of washer designed to prevent an attaching nut from working loose.

M

MacPherson strut A type of front suspension system devised by Earle MacPherson at Ford of England. In its original form, a simple lateral link with the anti-roll bar creates the lower control arm. A long strut - an integral coil spring and shock absorber - is mounted between the body and the steering knuckle. Many modern so-called MacPherson strut systems use a conventional lower A-arm and don't rely on the anti-roll bar for location.

Multimeter An electrical test instrument with the capability to measure voltage, current and resistance.

N

NOx Oxides of Nitrogen. A common toxic pollutant emitted by petrol and diesel engines at higher temperatures.

O

Ohm The unit of electrical resistance. One volt applied to a resistance of one ohm will produce a current of one amp.

Ohmmeter An instrument for measuring electrical resistance.

O-ring A type of sealing ring made of a special rubber-like material; in use, the O-ring is compressed into a groove to provide the sealing action.

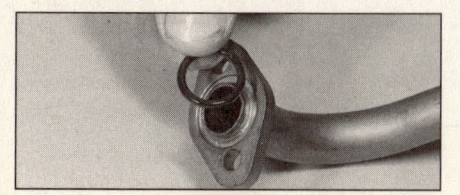

O-ring

Overhead cam (ohc) engine An engine with the camshaft(s) located on top of the cylinder head(s).

Overhead valve (ohv) engine An engine with the valves located in the cylinder head, but with the camshaft located in the engine block.

Oxygen sensor A device installed in the engine exhaust manifold, which senses the oxygen content in the exhaust and converts this information into an electric current. Also called a Lambda sensor.

P

Phillips screw A type of screw head having a cross instead of a slot for a corresponding type of screwdriver.

Plastigage A thin strip of plastic thread, available in different sizes, used for measuring clearances. For example, a strip of Plastigage is laid across a bearing journal. The parts are assembled and dismantled; the width of the crushed strip indicates the clearance between journal and bearing.

Plastigage

Propeller shaft The long hollow tube with universal joints at both ends that carries power from the transmission to the differential on front-engined rear wheel drive vehicles.

Proportioning valve A hydraulic control valve which limits the amount of pressure to the rear brakes during panic stops to prevent wheel lock-up.

R

Rack-and-pinion steering A steering system with a pinion gear on the end of the steering shaft that mates with a rack (think of a geared wheel opened up and laid flat). When the steering wheel is turned, the pinion turns, moving the rack to the left or right. This movement is transmitted through the track rods to the steering arms at the wheels.

Radiator A liquid-to-air heat transfer device designed to reduce the temperature of the coolant in an internal combustion engine cooling system.

Refrigerant Any substance used as a heat transfer agent in an air-conditioning system. R-12 has been the principle refrigerant for many years; recently, however, manufacturers have begun using R-134a, a non-CFC substance that is considered less harmful to the ozone in the upper atmosphere.

Rocker arm A lever arm that rocks on a shaft or pivots on a stud. In an overhead valve engine, the rocker arm converts the upward movement of the pushrod into a downward movement to open a valve.

Rotor In a distributor, the rotating device inside the cap that connects the centre electrode and the outer terminals as it turns, distributing the high voltage from the coil secondary winding to the proper spark plug. Also, that part of an alternator which rotates inside the stator. Also, the rotating assembly of a turbocharger, including the compressor wheel, shaft and turbine wheel.

Runout The amount of wobble (in-and-out movement) of a gear or wheel as it's rotated. The amount a shaft rotates "out-of-true." The out-of-round condition of a rotating part.

S

Sealant A liquid or paste used to prevent leakage at a joint. Sometimes used in conjunction with a gasket.

Sealed beam lamp An older headlight design which integrates the reflector, lens and filaments into a hermetically-sealed one-piece unit. When a filament burns out or the lens cracks, the entire unit is simply replaced.

Serpentine drivebelt A single, long, wide accessory drivebelt that's used on some newer vehicles to drive all the accessories, instead of a series of smaller, shorter belts. Serpentine drivebelts are usually tensioned by an automatic tensioner.

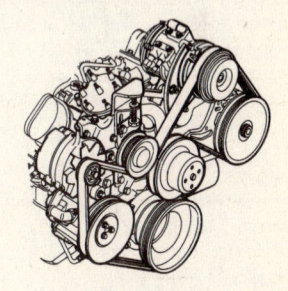

Serpentine drivebelt

Shim Thin spacer, commonly used to adjust the clearance or relative positions between two parts. For example, shims inserted into or under bucket tappets control valve clearances. Clearance is adjusted by changing the thickness of the shim.

Slide hammer A special puller that screws into or hooks onto a component such as a shaft or bearing; a heavy sliding handle on the shaft bottoms against the end of the shaft to knock the component free.

Sprocket A tooth or projection on the periphery of a wheel, shaped to engage with a chain or drivebelt. Commonly used to refer to the sprocket wheel itself.

Starter inhibitor switch On vehicles with an

Glossary of Technical Terms

automatic transmission, a switch that prevents starting if the vehicle is not in Neutral or Park.
Strut See MacPherson strut.

T

Tappet A cylindrical component which transmits motion from the cam to the valve stem, either directly or via a pushrod and rocker arm. Also called a cam follower.
Thermostat A heat-controlled valve that regulates the flow of coolant between the cylinder block and the radiator, so maintaining optimum engine operating temperature. A thermostat is also used in some air cleaners in which the temperature is regulated.
Thrust bearing The bearing in the clutch assembly that is moved in to the release levers by clutch pedal action to disengage the clutch. Also referred to as a release bearing.
Timing belt A toothed belt which drives the camshaft. Serious engine damage may result if it breaks in service.
Timing chain A chain which drives the camshaft.
Toe-in The amount the front wheels are closer together at the front than at the rear. On rear wheel drive vehicles, a slight amount of toe-in is usually specified to keep the front wheels running parallel on the road by offsetting other forces that tend to spread the wheels apart.
Toe-out The amount the front wheels are closer together at the rear than at the front. On front wheel drive vehicles, a slight amount of toe-out is usually specified.
Tools For full information on choosing and using tools, refer to the *Haynes Automotive Tools Manual*.
Tracer A stripe of a second colour applied to a wire insulator to distinguish that wire from another one with the same colour insulator.
Tune-up A process of accurate and careful adjustments and parts replacement to obtain the best possible engine performance.
Turbocharger A centrifugal device, driven by exhaust gases, that pressurises the intake air. Normally used to increase the power output from a given engine displacement, but can also be used primarily to reduce exhaust emissions (as on VW's "Umwelt" Diesel engine).

U

Universal joint or U-joint A double-pivoted connection for transmitting power from a driving to a driven shaft through an angle. A U-joint consists of two Y-shaped yokes and a cross-shaped member called the spider.

V

Valve A device through which the flow of liquid, gas, vacuum, or loose material in bulk may be started, stopped, or regulated by a movable part that opens, shuts, or partially obstructs one or more ports or passageways. A valve is also the movable part of such a device.
Valve clearance The clearance between the valve tip (the end of the valve stem) and the rocker arm or tappet. The valve clearance is measured when the valve is closed.
Vernier caliper A precision measuring instrument that measures inside and outside dimensions. Not quite as accurate as a micrometer, but more convenient.
Viscosity The thickness of a liquid or its resistance to flow.
Volt A unit for expressing electrical "pressure" in a circuit. One volt that will produce a current of one ampere through a resistance of one ohm.

W

Welding Various processes used to join metal items by heating the areas to be joined to a molten state and fusing them together. For more information refer to the *Haynes Automotive Welding Manual*.
Wiring diagram A drawing portraying the components and wires in a vehicle's electrical system, using standardised symbols. For more information refer to the *Haynes Automotive Electrical and Electronic Systems Manual*.

Index

Note: *References throughout this index relate to Chapter•page number*

A

ABS - 9•17, 9•18, 13•19
Accelerator cable - 3•7, 3•19, 13•7
Accelerator pedal and linkage - 7•4
Accelerator pump - 3•13, 3•15, 3•16
Acknowledgements - 0•4
Aerial - 13•34
Air bag safety system - 0•5, 13•20, 13•21
Air cleaner - 3•3, 3•18
Air conditioning - 11•16, 13•24
Air intake temperature sender - 4•10
Air temperature control - 3•4, 3•18
Airflow meter - 3•19, 3•22
Airflow sensor lever and control plunger - 3•23
Alternator - 12•3, 12•4, 13•32
Altitude sensor - 13•11
Ambient air temperature indicator - 13•32
Anti-lock braking system - 9•17, 9•18, 13•19
Anti-roll bar - 10•5, 13•20
Antifreeze - 0•16, 2•1, 2•4
Asbestos - 0•5
ATF - 0•16, 7•2
Audio controls - 13•34
Auto-check system - 12•20
Automatic choke - 3•14
Automatic transmission - 7•1 *et seq*, 13•17
Automatic transmission fault finding - 7•6
Automatic transmission fluid - 0•16, 7•2
Axle - 10•6

B

Backfire - 1•36, 3•28
Battery - 0•5, 12•3
Battery fault - 12•22
Big-end bearing caps - 13•7
Bleeding brakes - 9•13
Bleeding clutch - 5•7
Bleeding power-assisted steering - 10•14
Body corrosion - REF•4
Bodywork - 11•1 *et seq*, 13•21
Bonnet - 11•7, 11•8
Boot lid - 11•8, 13•29

Boot lid lights - 12•15
Boot lid lock - 11•8
Brake fluid - 0•16, 9•2
Brake light switch - 13•19
Brake pipes and hoses - 9•13
Brake pressure regulator - 9•12
Braking system - 9•1 *et seq*, 12•19, 13•18, 13•18, REF•1, REF•2, REF•3
Braking system fault finding - 9•20
Bulb failure warning system - 13•32
Bulbs - 12•13
Bumpers - 11•9
Burning - 0•5

C

Cable tensioner - 13•26
Cables - 3•7, 3•19, 5•2, 7•6, 9•15, 11•8, 12•12, 13•7, 13•25, 13•27
Calipers - 9•4, 9•5, 9•10, 13•18, 13•19
Camshaft - 1•8, 1•10, 1•11, 1•12, 1•25, 1•30, 1•31, 13•6
Capacities - 0•7
Carburettor - 3•7, 3•8, 3•12
Cassette player - 12•18, 13•33
Catalytic converter - 3•26, 13•12
Central door locking system - 11•14
Centre console - 11•13, 12•10, 13•30
Charcoal filter - 13•11
Choke pull-down system - 3•13, 3•15, 3•16
Choke valve gap - 3•13, 3•14, 3•16
Clutch - 5•1 *et seq*, 12•19, 13•14
Clutch fault finding - 5•8
Clutch fluid - 0•16, 5•1
CO adjustment - 13•10
CO emissions (mixture) - REF•4
Cold start valve - 3•21, 3•22, 13•9, 13•11
Compensation units - 3•21
Computer - 12•20
Connecting rods - 1•18, 1•19, 1•35
Console - 11•13, 12•10, 13•30
Constant velocity joint grease - 8•1
Contents - 0•2
Control switch - 12•19
Control unit - 12•7, 12•8, 12•19, 13•11
Conversion factors - REF•13

Coolant - 13•7
Coolant renewal - 2•7
Coolant temperature sender - 2•7, 4•10
Cooling fan - 2•7
Cooling system - 2•1 *et seq*, 13•7
Cooling system fault finding - 2•7
Courtesy light - 12•10, 12•16
Crankcase ventilation system - 3•26
Crankshaft - 1•17, 1•19, 1•33, 1•35, 13•6, 13•7
Cruise control system - 12•18
Crushing - 0•5
Cylinder bores - 1•18, 1•35
Cylinder head - 1•8, 1•11, 1•12, 1•27, 1•30, 13•6, 13•7

D

Dents in bodywork - 11•2
Diaphragm pressure switch - 13•9
Dim-dip lighting system - 13•32
Dimensions - 0•6
Direction indicators - 12•13, 13•32
Discs - 9•6, 9•12
Distributor - 4•3, 4•5, 4•8
Diveplate - 1•16
Door striker - 11•7
Doors - 11•3, 11•4, 11•5, 11•6, 13•27, 13•29, REF•2
Drivebelts - 10•15, 11•16, 12•4, 13•32
Driveplate - 1•33, 13•7
Driveshafts - 8•1 *et seq*, 13•18, REF•3
Driveshafts fault finding - 8•5
Driving lamps - 12•14
Drums - 9•8

E

Electric bypass air heating element - 3•13
Electric shock - 0•5
Electrical equipment -
Electrical faults - REF•9
Electrical system - 12•1 *et seq*, 13•32, REF•2
Electrical system fault finding - 12•22
Electronic control unit - braking system - 9•19

Index

Emission control system - 3•26, 3•27, 13•12
Engine - 1•1 et seq, 13•6
Engine fault finding - 1•36, 3•28, 4•13, REF•10, REF•11
Engine oil - 0•16, 1•2, 1•5, 13•6
Engine oil pressure - REF•11
Environmental considerations - REF•8
Evaporative fuel control - 3•26
Exhaust emission checks - REF•4
Exhaust gas recirculation (EGR) - 3•26
Exhaust manifold - 3•16, 3•27, 13•12
Exhaust system - 3•16, 3•28, REF•3

F

Facia - 11•10, 12•10
Fan - 2•7
Fast idling speed - 3•13, 3•14, 3•15
Fault finding - REF•9 et seq
Fault finding – automatic transmission - 7•6
Fault finding - braking system - 9•20
Fault finding - clutch - 5•8
Fault finding - cooling system - 2•7
Fault finding - driveshafts - 8•5
Fault finding - electrical system - 12•22
Fault finding - engine - 1•36
Fault finding - fuel system (carburettor models) - 3•28
Fault finding - fuel system (fuel injection models) - 3•28
Fault finding - ignition system - 4•13
Fault finding - manual gearbox - 6•14
Fault finding - suspension and steering - 10•18
Filling - 11•2
Fire - 0•5
Flywheel - 1•16, 1•33, 13•7
Foglamp - 12•14
Fuel accumulator - 3•24
Fuel consumption high - 3•28
Fuel cut-off two-way valve - 3•15
Fuel distributor - 3•21
Fuel gauge fault - 12•22
Fuel gauge sender unit - 3•7, 3•18, 13•8
Fuel injection system - 3•19, 3•21
Fuel injectors - 3•24, 13•9, 13•11
Fuel metering distributor - 3•22
Fuel pump - 3•6, 3•23, 13•8
Fuel tank - 3•6, 3•18, 13•7
Fuel, exhaust and emission control systems - 3•1 et seq, 13•7, REF•4
Fuel, exhaust and emission control systems fault finding - 3•28
Full throttle switch - 4•10
Fully Electronic Ignition system - 13•13, 13•14
Fume or gas intoxication - 0•5
Fuses - 12•7

G

Gaiter - 10•14
Gashes in bodywork - 11•2
Gaskets - REF•8
Gear lever - 13•15

Gearbox - See *Manual gearbox*
Gearbox oil - 0•16, 6•2
Gearshift lever and linkage - 6•11, 6•12, 13•14, 13•17
Glossary of technical terms - REF•14
Glovebox lamp - 12•16
Grille - 11•10

H

Handbrake - 9•14, 9•15, REF•1
Handles - 11•5
HC emissions - REF•4
Head restraints - 13•22
Headlamp - 12•12, 12•13, 12•18, 13•33
Heater - 11•14, 13•27, 13•32
Horn - 12•18
HT leads - 4•13
Hub bearings - 10•5, 10•9
Hydraulic brake pipes and hoses - 9•13
Hydraulic fluid - 0•16, 5•1, 9•2
Hydraulic modulator - 9•18
Hydraulic servo unit - 9•15, 9•16
Hydraulic tappets - 13•6
Hydrofluoric acid - 0•5

I

Idle speed - 3•12, 3•14, 3•15, 3•21, 13•10
Idle speed stabilisation valve - 13•11
Idle stabilisation - 3•21
Idle switch - 4•10
Idle/overrun control valve - 3•16
Ignition (no-charge) warning light fault - REF•11
Ignition coil - 4•6, 4•8
Ignition control unit - 4•11
Ignition fault - 12•22
Ignition light fault - 12•22
Ignition switch - 12•8
Ignition system - 4•1 et seq, 13•12
Ignition system fault finding - 4•13
Ignition timing - 4•5, 4•8, 13•14
Ignition timing sender - 4•9, 4•12
Indicator - 12•13, 13•32
Injectors - 3•24
Inlet manifold - 3•16, 3•24, 13•11
Inlet manifold preheater - 3•14, 3•15
Instrument fault - 12•22
Instrument panel - 12•10, 12•16
Intercooler - 3•26
Interior light - 12•10, 12•16
Interior reading light - 12•16
Intermediate shaft - 1•16
Introduction to the Audi 100 and 200 - 0•4

J

Jacking - 0•8
Joint mating faces - REF•8
Jump starting - 0•11

K

K and KE-Jetronic fuel injection systems - 13•9
KE III-Jetronic fuel injection system - 13•10, 13•11

L

Lambda closed loop system - 13•9
Lambda sensor - 13•11
Leaks - 0•9
Lights inoperative - 12•22
Locknuts, locktabs and washers - REF•8
Locks - 11•1, 11•8, 11•9, 12•8, 13•29
Loudspeaker - 13•34
Lubricants and fluids - 0•16
Luggage compartment light - 12•16

M

Manifolds - 3•16, 3•24, 3•27, 13•11
Manual gearbox - 6•1 et seq, 13•14, 13•15
Manual gearbox fault finding - 6•14
Manual gearbox oil - 0•16, 6•2
Master cylinder - 5•3, 9•12
Mirrors - 13•22, 13•23, 13•24, REF•1
Misfire - 1•36, 3•28, 4•13, REF•11
Mixture - 3•21, 13•10
MOT test checks - REF•1 et seq
Mountings - 1•21, 1•35

N

Number plate light - 12•15

O

Oil - engine - 0•16, 1•2, 1•5, 13•6
Oil - gearbox - 0•16, 6•2
Oil consumption high - 1•36
Oil pressure - REF•11
Oil pump - 1•17, 1•33
Oil seals - 1•17, 1•33, REF•8
Overheating - 2•7, REF•11
Overrun cut-off - 3•21
Oxygen sensor system - 3•27

P

Pads - 9•3, 9•8
Panhard rod - 10•8
Parking lights - 12•13
Pedals - 5•2, 7•4, 9•14, 12•19, 13•14
Pinking - REF•11
Piston ring end gap - 13•6
Pistons - 1•18, 1•19, 1•35, 13•6
Plastic components - 11•3
Poisonous or irritant substances - 0•5
Power operated windows - 11•14
Power steering fluid - 0•16, 10•2, 13•20
Power steering gear - 10•15, 10•16
Pre-ignition - REF•11
Pressure accumulator - 9•16
Pressure regulator - 9•12
Pressure relief valve - 3•22
Procon-ten safety system - 13•15, 13•24, 13•25

Index

R

Radiator - 2•4
Radiator grille - 11•10
Radio - 12•18, 13•33
Rear axle - 10•6
Rear lamp cluster - 12•15
Rear window - 11•9
Relays - 12•7, 12•8, 13•19
Release bearing and mechanism - 5•5
Repair procedures - REF•8
Respraying - 11•2
Routine maintenance - 0•12 et seq
Routine maintenance - automatic transmission - 7•2
Routine maintenance - bodywork and underframe - 11•1
Routine maintenance - braking system - 9•2
Routine maintenance - clutch - 5•2
Routine maintenance - cooling system - 2•3
Routine maintenance - driveshafts - 8•1
Routine maintenance - electrical system - 12•2
Routine maintenance - engine - 1•6, 1•22
Routine maintenance - fuel, exhaust and emission control systems - 3•3, 3•17
Routine maintenance - ignition system - 4•3, 4•8
Routine maintenance - manual gearbox - 6•2
Routine maintenance - seat belts - 13•21
Routine maintenance - suspension and steering - 10•2
Routine maintenance - upholstery and carpets - 11•2
RPM sender - 4•9, 4•12
Rust holes in bodywork - 11•2

S

Safety first! - 0•5
Scalding - 0•5
Scratches in bodywork - 11•2
Screw threads and fastenings - REF•8
Seat belt tensioning cable - 13•26
Seat belts - 13•21, REF•2
Seats - 11•14, 12•20, 13•22, REF•2
Selector lever - 7•6, 13•17, 13•18
Self-levelling suspension - 10•9, 10•10, 10•11
Self-levelling suspension fluid - 0•16
Servo motor - 13•33
Servo unit - 9•15, 9•16, 12•20, 13•19
Shock absorbers - 10•3, 10•7, 13•19, REF•2, REF•3
Shoes - 9•6
Side marker lights - 12•13
Side repeater lamps - 13•32
Sidelights - 12•13
Slave cylinder - 5•4, 13•14
Solenoid - 13•17
Spare parts - REF•10, REF•12
Spark plugs - 4•6, 4•13, 13•12
Speakers - 12•18
Speed sensor - 9•19
Speedometer - 12•12, 13•14
Springs - REF•3
Starter inhibitor switch - 7•6
Starter motor - 12•5, 12•6, 13•32
Starter motor fault - 12•22, REF•10
Starting fast idle and overrun fuel cut-off two-way valve - 3•15
Starting fault - 13•9
Steering - 10•2
Steering angles - 10•17
Steering column - 10•12, 13•25, REF•1
Steering column lock - 12•8
Steering damper - 10•14
Steering fault - 10•18
Steering gear - 10•14, REF•3
Steering wheel - 10•11, REF•1
Stop light switch - 13•19
Strut - 10•3, 10•4, 10•7, 13•19
Sump - 1•17, 1•33
Sunroof - 11•9, 13•21
Supplement: Revisions and information and later models - 13•1 et seq
Suspension and steering - 10•1 et seq, 13•19, REF•2, REF•3
Suspension and steering fault finding - 10•18
Switches - 2•7, 3•22, 4•10, 7•6, 12•8, 12•9, 12•10, 13•9, 13•17, 13•19

T

Tailgate - 11•9, 12•15, 12•17
Tappets - 1•10, 1•12, 1•25, 1•31
Temperature gauge fault - 12•22
Temperature sender unit - 2•7
Temperature time valve - 3•16
Thermo-pneumatic valve - 3•15
Thermostat - 2•5
Thermotime switch - 3•22, 13•9
Throttle setting - 3•15
Throttle valve gap adjustment - 3•13, 3•14
Tie-rod - 10•12
Timing - 4•5, 4•8
Timing belt - 1•14, 1•31
Tools - REF•5, REF•7, REF•8, REF•10
Torque converter - 7•3
Towing - 0•8
Track control arm - 10•6
Transmission - See *Manual gearbox* or *Automatic transmission*
Trim panel - 11•3, 13•27
Turbocharger - 3•24, 3•25, 3•26
Tyre wear - 10•18
Tyres - 0•10, 10•3, 10•17, REF•4

U

Unleaded fuel - 13•7

V

Vacuum pump - 12•20
Vacuum servo unit - 9•15, 12•20, 13•19
Valve clearances - 1•13, 1•31
Valve cover - 13•7
Valves - 1•10, 1•12, 1•30
Vehicle identification - REF•2, REF•12
Ventilation grille - 11•10

W

Warm-up regulator - 3•21, 3•22
Washer system - 12•17, 12•18
Water pump - 2•6
Weights - 0•6
Wheel alignment - 10•17
Wheel bearings - REF•3
Wheel cylinder - 9•7
Wheels - 10•3, 10•17, REF•4
Window glass - 11•9
Windscreen - 11•9, 12•16, 12•17, REF•1
Wiper arms - 12•16, 12•17
Wiper blades - 12•16, 12•17
Wiper motor - 12•17
Working facilities - REF•7

Haynes Manuals – The Complete List

Title	Book No.
ALFA ROMEO	
Alfa Romeo Alfasud/Sprint (74 - 88)	0292
Alfa Romeo Alfetta (73 - 87)	0531
AUDI	
Audi 80 (72 - Feb 79)	0207
Audi 80, 90 (79 - Oct 86) & Coupe (81 - Nov 88)	0605
Audi 80, 90 (Oct 86 - 90) & Coupe (Nov 88 - 90)	1491
Audi 100 (69 - Sept 76)	0162
Audi 100 (Oct 76 - Oct 82)	0428
Audi 100 (Oct 82 - 90) & 200 (Feb 84 - Oct 89)	0907
AUSTIN	
Austin Allegro 1100, 1300, 1.0, 1.1 & 1.3 (73 - 82)	0164
Austin Ambassador (82 - 84)	0871
Austin/MG Maestro 1.3 & 1.6 (petrol)(83 - 95)	0922
Austin Maxi (69 - 81)	0052
Austin/MG Metro (80 - May 90)	0718
Austin Montego 1.3 & 1.6 (84 - 94)	1066
Austin/MG Montego 2.0 (petrol)(84 - 95)	1067
Mini (59 - 69)	0527
Mini (69 - 95)	0646
Austin/Rover Diesel Engine 2.0 litre (86 - 93)	1857
BEDFORD	
Bedford CF (petrol)(69 - 87)	0163
Bedford HA Van (64 - 83)	0607
Bedford Rascal (86 - Oct 94)	3015
BL	
BL Princess & BLMC 18-22 (75 - 82)	0286
BMW	
BMW 316, 320 & 320i (4-cyl)(75 - Feb 83)	0276
BMW 320, 320i, 323i & 325i (6-cyl) (Oct 77 - Sept 87)	0815
BMW 520i & 525e (Oct 81 - June 88)	1560
BMW 525, 528 & 528i (73 - Sept 81)	0632
BMW 3 Series (sohc, petrol)(81 - 93)	1948
BMW 5 Series (sohc, petrol)(81 - 93)	1948
BMW 1500, 1502, 1600, 1602 & 2000 (59 - 77)	0240
CITROEN	
Citroën 2CV, Ami & Dyane (67 - 90)	0196
Citroën AX (petrol & diesel)(87 - 94)	3014
Citroën BX (83 - 94)	0908
Citroën CX (75 - 88)	0528
Citroën GS & GSA (71 - 85)	0290
Citroën Visa (79 - 88)	0620
Citroën Xantia (petrol & diesel)(93 - Oct 95)	3082
Citroën ZX (diesel)(91 - 93)	1922
Citroën ZX (petrol)(91 - 94)	1881
Citroën Diesel Engines 1.7 & 1.9 litres (84 - 94)	1379
COLT	
Colt 1200, 1250 & 1400 (79 - May 84)	0600
Colt Galant (74 - 78) & Celeste (76 - 81)	0236
Colt Lancer (74 - 77)	0419
DAIMLER	
Daimler Sovereign (68 - Oct 86)	0242
Daimler Double Six (72 - 88)	0478

Title	Book No.
DATSUN (see also Nissan)	
Datsun 120Y (73 - Aug 78)	0228
Datsun 1300, 1400 & 1600 (69 - Aug 72)	0123
Datsun Cherry (71 - 76)	0195
Datsun Cherry (79 - Sept 82)	0679
Datsun Pick-up (75 - 78)	0277
Datsun Sunny (Aug 78 - May 82)	0525
Datsun Violet (78 - 82)	0430
FIAT	
Fiat 124 (66 - 75)	0080
Fiat 126 (73 - 87)	0305
Fiat 127 (71 - 83)	0193
Fiat 500 (57 - 73)	0090
Fiat 850 (64 - 81)	0038
Fiat Panda (81 - 95)	0793
Fiat Regata (84 - 88)	1167
Fiat Strada (79 - 88)	0479
Fiat Tipo (88 - 91)	1625
Fiat Uno (82 - 93)	0923
Fiat X1/9 (74 - 89)	0273
FORD	
Ford Capri II & III 1.6 & 2.0 (74 - 87)	0283
Ford Capri II & III 2.8 & 3.0 (74 - 87)	1309
Ford Cortina Mk III 1300 & 1600 (70 - 76)	0070
Ford Cortina Mk III 1600 & 2000 (70 - 76)	0295
Ford Cortina Mk IV & V 1.6 & 2.0 (76 - 83)	0343
Ford Cortina Mk IV & V 2.3 V6 (77 - 83)	0426
Ford Escort (75 - Aug 80)	0280
Ford Escort Mk II Mexico, RS 1600 & RS 2000 (75 - 80)	0735
Ford Escort fwd (Sept 80 - Sept 90)	0686
Ford Escort (Sept 90 - Feb 95)	1737
Ford Fiesta (inc. XR2)(76 - Aug 83)	0334
Ford Fiesta (inc. XR2)(Aug 83 - Feb 89)	1030
Ford Fiesta (Feb 89 - 93)	1595
Ford Granada (Sept 77 - Feb 85)	0481
Ford Granada (Mar 85 - 94)	1245
Ford Mondeo (93 - 95)	1923
Ford Orion (83 - Sept 90)	1009
Ford Orion (Sept 90 - Feb 95)	1737
Ford Sierra 1.3, 1.6, 1.8 & 2.0 (82 - 93)	0903
Ford Sierra 2.3, 2.8 & 2.9 (82 - 91)	0904
Ford Scorpio (Mar 85 - 94)	1245
Ford Transit Mk 1 (diesel)(65 - Feb 78)	0418
Ford Transit Mk 1 (petrol)(65 - Feb 78)	0377
Ford Transit Mk 2 (petrol)(78 - Jan 86)	0719
Ford Transit Mk 3 (petrol)(Feb 86 - 89)	1468
Ford Transit (diesel)(Feb 86 - 95)	3019
Ford Diesel Engines 1.6 & 1.8 litre (fwd)(84 - 95)	1172
Ford Diesel Engines 2.1, 2.3 & 2.5 litres (77 - 90)	1606
Ford Vehicle Carburettors	1783
FREIGHT ROVER	
Sherpa (74 - 87)	0463
HILLMAN	
Hillman Avenger (70 - 82)	0037
Hillman Minx & Husky (56 - 75)	0009
HONDA	
Honda Accord (76 - Feb 84)	0351
Honda Accord (Feb 84 - Oct 85)	1177

Title	Book No.
Honda Civic 1200 (73 - 79)	0160
Honda Civic (Feb 84 - Oct 87)	1226
JAGUAR	
Jaguar E Type (61 - 72)	0140
Jaguar MkI & II, 240 & 340 (55 - 69)	0098
Jaguar XJ6, XJ & Sovereign (68 - Oct 86)	0242
Jaguar XJ12, XJS & Sovereign (72 - 88)	0478
LADA	
Lada 1200, 1300, 1500 & 1600 (74 - 91)	0413
Lada Samara (87 - 91)	1610
LANCIA	
Lancia Beta (73 - 80)	0533
LAND ROVER	
Land Rover Series II, IIA & III (petrol)(58 - 85)	0314
Land Rover Series IIA & III (diesel)(58 - 85)	0529
Land Rover 90, 110 & Defender (diesel)(83 - 95)	3017
Land Rover Discovery (diesel)(89 - 95)	3016
MAZDA	
Mazda 323 rwd (77 - Apr 86)	0370
Mazda 323 fwd (Mar 81 - Oct 89)	1608
Mazda 626 fwd (May 83 - Sept 87)	0929
Mazda B-1600, B-1800 & B-2000 Pick-up (72 - 88)	0267
Mazda RX-7 (79 - 85)	0460
MERCEDES-BENZ	
Mercedes-Benz 190 & 190E (83 - 87)	0928
Mercedes-Benz 200, 240, 300 (diesel) (Oct 76 - 85)	1114
Mercedes-Benz 250 & 280 (68 - 72)	0346
Mercedes-Benz 250 & 280 (123 Series) (Oct 76 - 84)	0677
MG	
MG Maestro 1.3 & 1.6 (83 - 95)	0922
MG Metro (80 - May 90)	0718
MG Montego 2.0 (84 - 95)	1067
MG Midget & AH Sprite (58 - 80)	0265
MGB (62 - 80)	0111
MITSUBISHI	
Mitsubishi Shogun & L200 Pick-Ups (83 - 94)	1944
Mitsubishi 1200, 1250 & 1400 (79 - May 84)	0600
MORRIS	
Morris Ital 1.3 (80 - 84)	0705
Morris Marina 1700 (78 - 80)	0526
Morris Marina 1.8 (71 - 78)	0074
Morris Minor 1000 (56 - 71)	0024
NISSAN (See also Datsun)	
Nissan Bluebird 160B & 180B (rwd) (May 80 - May 84)	0957
Nissan Bluebird fwd (May 84 - Mar 86)	1223
Nissan Bluebird T12 & T72 (Mar 86 - 90)	1473
Nissan Cherry N12 (Sept 82 - 86)	1031
Nissan Micra K10 (83 - Jan 93)	0931
Nissan Primera (90 - 95)	1851
Nissan Stanza (82 - 86)	0824
Nissan Sunny B11 (May 82 - Oct 86)	0895
Nissan Sunny (Oct 86 - Mar 91)	1378
OPEL	
Opel Ascona & Manta B Series (Sept 75 - 88)	0316

Title	Book No.
Opel Kadett C Series (Nov 73 - Nov 79)	0395
Opel Kadett D Series (fwd)(Nov 79 - Oct 84)	0634
PEUGEOT	
Peugeot 106 (petrol & diesel)(91 - 94)	1882
Peugeot 205 (83 - 95)	0932
Peugeot 305 (78 - 89)	0538
Peugeot 306 (petrol & diesel)(93 - 95)	3073
Peugeot 309 (86 - 93)	1266
Peugeot 405 (88 - 95)	1559
Peugeot 405 (diesel)(88 - 96)	3198
Peugeot 504 (68 - 82)	0161
Peugeot 504 (diesel)(74 - 82)	0663
Peugeot 505 (79 - 89)	0762
Peugeot Diesel Engines 1.7 & 1.9 litres (82 - 94)	0950
Peugeot Diesel Engines 2.0, 2.1, 2.3 & 2.5 litres (74 - 90)	1607
PORSCHE	
Porsche 911 (65 - 85)	0264
Porsche 924 & 924 Turbo (76 - 85)	0397
RANGE ROVER	
Range Rover V8 (70 - Oct 92)	0606
RELIANT	
Reliant Robin & Kitten (73 - 83)	0436
RENAULT	
Renault 4 (61 - 86)	0072
Renault 5 (72 - Feb 85)	0141
Renault 5 (Feb 85 - 95)	1219
Renault 6 (68 - 79)	0092
Renault 9 & 11 (82 - 89)	0822
Renault 12 (70 - 80)	0097
Renault 14 (77 - 83)	0362
Renault 15 & 17 (72 - 79)	0763
Renault 16 (65 - 79)	0081
Renault 18 (79 - 86)	0598
Renault 19 (petrol)(89 - 94)	1646
Renault 19 (diesel)(89 - 95)	1946
Renault 21 (86 - 94)	1397
Renault 25 (84 - 86)	1228
Renault Clio (petrol)(91 - 93)	1853
Renault Clio (diesel)(91 - 95)	3031
Renault Fuego (80 - 86)	0764
ROVER	
Rover 213 & 216 (84 - 89)	1116
Rover 214 & 414 (Oct 89 - 92)	1689
Rover 216 & 416 (Oct 89 - 92)	1830
Rover 820, 825 & 827 (petrol)(86 - 95)	1380
Rover 2000, 2300 & 2600 (77 - 87)	0468
Rover 3500 (76 - 87)	0365
Rover Metro (May 90 - 91)	1711
Rover Diesel Engine 2.0 litre (86 - 93)	1857
SAAB	
Saab 95 & 96 (66 - 76)	0198
Saab 99 (69 - 79)	0247
Saab 90, 99 & 900 (79 - Sept 93)	0765
Saab 9000 (4-cyl)(85 - 95)	1686
SEAT	
Seat Ibiza & Malaga (85 - 92)	1609
SIMCA	
Simca 1100 & 1204 (67 - 79)	0088
Simca 1301 & 1501 (63 - 76)	0199
SKODA	
Skoda 1000 & 1100 (64 - 78)	0303

Title	Book No.
Skoda Estelle 105, 120, 130 & 136 (77 - 89)	0604
Skoda Favorit (89 - 92)	1801
SUBARU	
Subaru 1600 (77 - Oct 79)	0237
Subaru 1600 & 1800 (Nov 79 - 90)	0995
SUZUKI	
Suzuki SJ Series, Samurai & Vitara (82 - 94)	1942
Suzuki Supercarry (86 - Oct 94)	3015
TALBOT	
Talbot Alpine, Solara, Minx & Rapier (75 - 86)	0337
Talbot Horizon (78 - 86)	0473
Talbot Samba (82 - 86)	0823
Talbot Sunbeam (77 - 82)	0435
TOYOTA	
Toyota 2000 (75 - 77)	0360
Toyota Celica (78 - Jan 82)	0437
Toyota Celica (Feb 82 - Sept 85)	1135
Toyota Corolla (rwd)(80 - 85)	0683
Toyota Corolla (fwd)(Sept 83 - Sept 87)	1024
Toyota Corolla (Sept 87 - 92)	1683
Toyota Hi-Ace & Hi-Lux (69 - Oct 83)	0304
Toyota Starlet (78 - Jan 85)	0462
TRIUMPH	
Triumph Acclaim (81 - 84)	0792
Triumph GT6 (62 - 74)	0112
Triumph Herald (59 - 71)	0010
Triumph Spitfire (62 - 81)	0113
Triumph Stag (70 - 78)	0441
Triumph TR2, 3, 3A, 4 & 4A (52 - 67)	0028
Triumph TR7 (75 - 82)	0322
Triumph Vitesse (62 - 74)	0112
VAUXHALL	
Vauxhall Astra (80 - Oct 84)	0635
Vauxhall Astra & Belmont (Oct 84 - Oct 91)	1136
Vauxhall Astra (Oct 91 - Oct 92)	1832
Vauxhall Carlton (Oct 78 - Oct 86)	0480
Vauxhall Carlton (Nov 86 - 93).	1469
Vauxhall Cavalier 1300 (77 - July 81)	0461
Vauxhall Cavalier 1600, 1900 & 2000 (75 - July 81)	0315
Vauxhall Cavalier (fwd)(81 - Oct 88)	0812
Vauxhall Cavalier (Oct 88 - 94)	1570
Vauxhall Chevette (75 - 84)	0285
Vauxhall Corsa (Mar 93 - 94)	1985
Vauxhall Magnum (73 - 77)	0294
Vauxhall Nova (83 - 93)	0909
Vauxhall Rascal (86 - Oct 94)	3015
Vauxhall Victor & VX4/90 FD Series (67 - 72)	0053
Vauxhall Viva HC (70 - 79)	0047
Vauxhall Diesel Engines 1.6 & 1.7 litres (82 - 94)	1222
VOLKSWAGEN	
VW Beetle 1200 (54 - 77)	0036
VW Beetle 1300 & 1500 (65 - 75)	0039
VW Beetle 1302 & 1302S (70 - 72)	0110
VW Beetle 1303, 1303S & GT (72 - 75)	0159
VW Golf 'Mk 1' 1.1 & 1.3 (74 - June 84)	0716
VW Golf 'Mk 1' 1.5, 1.6 & 1.8 (74 - 85)	0726
VW Golf 'Mk 1' (diesel)(78 - June 84)	0451
VW Golf 'Mk 2' (Mar 84 - 92)	1081
VW Golf 'Mk 3' (petrol & diesel)(Feb 92 - 95)	3097

Title	Book No.
VW Jetta 'Mk 1' 1.1 & 1.3 (74 - June 84)	0716
VW Jetta 'Mk 1' 1.5, 1.6 & 1.8 (74 - 85)	0726
VW Jetta 'Mk 1' (diesel)(78 - June 84)	0451
VW Jetta 'Mk 2' (Mar 84 - 92)	1081
VW LT vans & light trucks (76 - 87)	0637
VW Passat (73 - Sept 81)	0238
VW Passat (Sept 81 - May 88)	0814
VW Passat (May 88 - 91)	1647
VW Polo & Derby (76 - Jan 82)	0335
VW Polo (82 - Oct 90)	0813
VW Santana (Sept 81 - May 88)	0814
VW Scirocco 'Mk 1' 1.5, 1.6 & 1.8 (74 - 85)	0726
VW Scirocco (82 - 90)	1224
VW Transporter 1600 (68 - 79)	0082
VW Transporter 1700, 1800 & 2000 (72 - 79)	0226
VW Transporter with air-cooled engine (79 - 82)	0638
VW Type 3 (63 - 73)	0084
VW Vento (petrol & diesel)(Feb 92 - 95)	3097
VOLVO	
Volvo 66 & 343, Daf 55 & 66 (68 - 79)	0293
Volvo 142, 144 & 145 (66 - 74)	0129
Volvo 240 Series (74 - 93)(2nd Edition)	0270
Volvo 262, 264 & 260/265 (75 - 85)	0400
Volvo 340, 343, 345 & 360 (76 - 91)	0715
Volvo 440, 460 & 480 (87 - 92)	1691
Volvo 740 & 760 (petrol)(82 - 91)	1258
YUGO/ZASTAVA	
Yugo/Zastava (81 - 90)	1453

NEW TECH BOOKS	
Automotive Brake Manual	3050
Automotive Electrical & Electronic Systems	3049
Automotive Tools Manual	3052
Automotive Welding Manual	3053

SPECIAL INTEREST AUTOMOTIVE BOOKS	
Automotive Fuel Injection Systems	9755
Car Bodywork Repair Manual	9864
Caravan Manual	9894
Dishwasher Manual (New Edition)	9866
Ford Vehicle Carburettors	1783
Haynes Technical Data Book ('87 to '96)	1996
How To Keep Your Car Alive	9868
In-Car Entertainment Manual (2nd Edition)	9862
Japanese Vehicle Carburettors	1786
Kitcar Builder's Manual (2nd Edition)	H898
Pass the MOT!	9861
Small Engine Repair Manual	1755
Solex & Pierburg Carburettors	1785
SU Carburettors	0299
Weber Carburettors (to '79)	0393
Weber Carburettors ('79 to '91)	1784

All the manuals featured on these pages are available through good motor accessory shops and book stores. In case of difficulty, contact **Haynes Publishing** on 01963 440635

Preserving Our Motoring Heritage

The Model J Duesenberg Derham Tourster. Only eight of these magnificent cars were ever built – this is the only example to be found outside the United States of America

Almost every car you've ever loved, loathed or desired is gathered under one roof at the Haynes Motor Museum. Over 300 immaculately presented cars and motorbikes represent every aspect of our motoring heritage, from elegant reminders of bygone days, such as the superb Model J Duesenberg to curiosities like the bug-eyed BMW Isetta. There are also many old friends and flames. Perhaps you remember the 1959 Ford Popular that you did your courting in? The magnificent 'Red Collection' is a spectacle of classic sports cars including AC, Alfa Romeo, Austin Healey, Ferrari, Lamborghini, Maserati, MG, Riley, Porsche and Triumph.

A Perfect Day Out

Each and every vehicle at the Haynes Motor Museum has played its part in the history and culture of Motoring. Today, they make a wonderful spectacle and a great day out for all the family. Bring the kids, bring Mum and Dad, but above all bring your camera to capture those golden memories for ever. You will also find an impressive array of motoring memorabilia, a comfortable 70 seat video cinema and one of the most extensive transport book shops in Britain. The Pit Stop Cafe serves everything from a cup of tea to wholesome, home-made meals or, if you prefer, you can enjoy the large picnic area nestled in the beautiful rural surroundings of Somerset.

John Haynes O.B.E., Founder and Chairman of the museum at the wheel of a Haynes Light 12.

Graham Hill's Lola Cosworth Formula 1 car next to a 1934 Riley Sports.

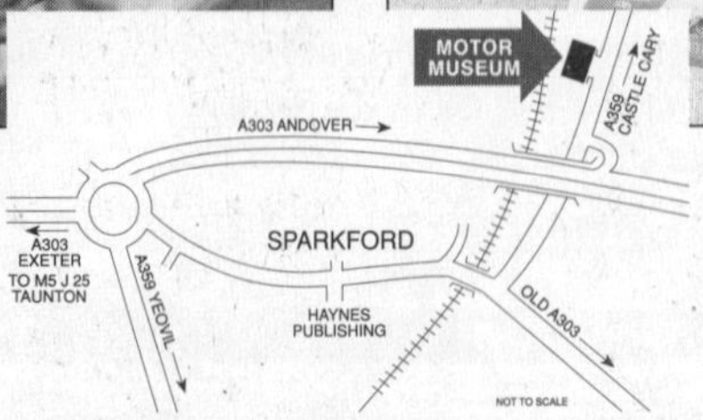

The Museum is situated on the A359 Yeovil to Frome road at Sparkford, just off the A303 in Somerset. It is about 40 miles south of Bristol, and 25 minutes drive from the M5 intersection at Taunton.
Open 9.30am - 5.30pm (10.00am - 4.00pm Winter) 7 days a week, *except Christmas Day, Boxing Day and New Years Day*
Special rates available for schools, coach parties and outings Charitable Trust No. 292048